Scott Donaldson

FITZGERALD & HEMINGWAY

{WORKS AND DAYS}

COLUMBIA UNIVERSITY PRESS

NEW YORK

Columbia University Press

Publishers Since 1893

New York   Chichester, West Sussex

Copyright © 2009 Scott Donaldson

Library of Congress Cataloging-in-Publication Data

Donaldson, Scott, 1928–

Fitzgerald and Hemingway : works and days / Scott Donaldson.

p.   cm.

Includes bibliographical references and index.

ISBN 978-0-231-14816-0 (cloth) : alk. paper) — ISBN 978-0-231-51978-6 (e-book)

1. Fitzgerald, F. Scott (Francis Scott), 1896–1940—Criticism and interpretation.

2. Hemingway, Ernest, 1899–1961—Criticism and interpretation. I. Title.

PS3511.I9Z589   2009

924'/63—dc22

2008049122

Columbia University Press books are printed on permanent and durable acid-free paper.

This book is printed on paper with recycled content.

Printed in the United States of America

c 10 9 8 7 6 5 4 3 2 1

CONTENTS

Ernest Hemingway

FITZGERALD AND HEMINGWAY

INTRODUCTION

I HAVE BEEN uncommonly lucky in the academic world. Armed with a doctorate in American studies from the University of Minnesota, I started teaching at the College of William and Mary in Virginia in September 1966. I shared an office on the third floor of the Wren Building, one of the oldest and handsomest college buildings in the United States. For nearly a month the rain coursed down through the huge trees outside my window— William and Mary is a great campus for dendrophiles—before the sun came out to brighten the late autumn days. Aside from the precipitation, I had very little to complain about.

As a beginning assistant professor of English, I was assigned two sessions of freshman composition, one of them meeting at eight A.M. Saturday. This was the scut work of the department and involved grading fifty papers a week and trying 1) to avoid placing sarcastic notations such as "native speaker of English?" in my marginal comments, and 2) to cajole students into writing in their own voice, instead of the wooden formal tones they'd been encouraged to adopt by well-meaning if clueless secondary school instructors. There were always a few in each class of twenty-five students (in later years reduced to fifteen) who caught on at once, to our mutual delight. Besides, in my other two courses, I could talk about stories and novels and poems and plays and get paid for it. It seemed wrong somehow.

In the mid-1960s, William and Mary was converting itself from a sleepy Southern college to a vibrant small university. Many of my new colleagues came there with degrees from the Ivy League and the best state universities. We bonded as the advance guard, eager to speed the transformation. And by and large the students we had the privilege of teaching were excellent. W&M is a state university (a fact not many people are aware of) and hence more affordable than almost any private college, and it was the first state institution on the East Coast to become coeducational. The legislators of Virginia wisely decided to limit the college's size and to admit a number of students from out-of-state. In practical terms, this meant that many bright young people from Virginia and the eastern states competed for a limited number of spots in each freshman class.

In the uproar of the late 1960s, tensions sprang up at William and Mary as on most of the nation's campuses. The students were more liberal than their parents, who more or less expected the college to look after their young as if at an extended summer camp. The new recruits to the faculty were more liberal than the students and often found themselves at odds with a conservative administration happy to operate in loco parentis. It made for lively times.

Unlike most of my colleagues, I had already spent a decade in the real world, earning my way as a newspaper reporter and editor. This meant that I was equipped to write about the authors whose work interested me in language most readers could understand and accustomed as a professional to getting those words down on paper. This gave me a leg up the ladder, and my fascination with a few important American writers gave me plenty to write about. I spent twenty-eight years at William and Mary, minus time off here and there for senior Fulbrights and visiting fellowships, as well as research grants from the National Endowment for the Humanities and the college itself. During most of that time I was allowed to teach the work of F. Scott Fitzgerald and Ernest Hemingway, both in survey courses and, more intensively, in upper-division and M.A.-level seminars. So I deepened my understanding of these authors as part of my regular teaching duties, and one can hardly overestimate what you can learn from intelligent and interested students. And I was fortunate, too, that journals and quarterlies and collections were willing to publish what I had to say. When I left the newspaper business, allotting three years to obtain a Ph.D., it was with the hope that in due course I might write things that would not be used to wrap the fish in, next day or next week. That worked out splendidly.

Looking through my c.v., I discover that over the past four decades I have published three biographies, edited (and contributed pieces to) three volumes of criticism, and written forty-two articles on Fitzgerald and Hemingway. The biographies are *By Force of Will: The Life and*

Art of Ernest Hemingway (1977); *Fool for Love, F. Scott Fitzgerald* (1983); and *Hemingway vs. Fitzgerald: The Rise and Fall of a Literary Frinedship* (1999). The edited volumes are *Critical Essays on F. Scott Fitzgerald's "The Great Gatsby"* (1984); *New Essays on "A Farewell to Arms"* (1990); and the *Cambridge Companion to Hemingway* (1996). The articles, like the books, are spread out evenly over the forty-year period, about half appearing in the 1970s and 1980s, and half in the 1990s and 2000s.

I am not through writing about these writers and their stories and novels. But in my eightieth year and with the encouragement of many colleagues, it is time to collect the best of what I've so far set down on paper about them. *Fitzgerald and Hemingway: Works and Days* presents the twenty-four most important pieces—eleven on Fitzgerald, thirteen on Hemingway. Almost all of these are drawn from the forty-two published articles. Two—one each on *The Sun Also Rises* and *A Farewell to Arms*—are adapted from *By Force of Will*. One, written in 2006, appears here for the first time. The earliest article, "Hemingway's Morality of Compensation," was originally published in *American Literature* in 1971, later embedded in *By Force of Will*, and subsequently reprinted twice in studies of that novel. The most recent is the long 2006 essay on "The Last Great Cause: Hemingway's Spanish Civil War Writing" that I've withheld for publication in this book. In addition to the "Morality of Compensation" article, eight other essays included here have been reprinted in collections, some of them more than once: a testimony to their value both to students and teachers and the wider reading public. *Fitzgerald and Hemingway: Works and Days* makes available in one place significant insights into the life and work of two great American writers— insights that otherwise would have to be tracked down in separate places.

I undertook the project of collecting these essays with the innocent notion that they might simply speak for themselves. But others, notably Jackson Bryer, pointed out the virtue of shaping them into a new book, and of course they were right. So, to begin with, over a six-month period I substantially revised everything. Some of this was mechanical enough. The articles had to be converted into a single scholarly form, for example. Pieces written for literary quarterlies like the *Sewanee Review*, and those in scholarly journals like *American Literature*, and those written on invitation for books like *Writing the American Classics*—all following different approaches toward acknowledgment of sources—were reconfigured into a standard style, with parenthetical citations in the text and a bibliography section at the end. I solved the problem of footnotes by doing away with them (there weren't many), either through outright omission or including them in the body of the article.

Going over the essays, I discovered—and in revision have tried to repair—more than a few stylistic imperfections. My tendency has been to write too long, so these essays were cut, some of them substantially. I excised wholesale chunks of copy from the essay on Fitzgerald's political development, for instance, where too often I put in everything instead of letting a few telling examples make a point. I used fewer adjectives and adverbs throughout, worked toward more direct subject-verb-object sentences in place of ones beginning with dependent clauses—a practice first urged upon me by Malcolm Cowley three decades ago—and eliminated superfluous connective tissue: "and later" (when else?) and "in that story" (where else?).

Then there was the problem of repetition. Certain favorite passages found their way into different articles. Recalling Zelda Sayre's reluctance to marry an impecunious suitor like himself, Fitzgerald comments in *The Crack-Up* that thereafter he "cherish[ed] an abiding distrust, an animosity, toward the leisure class—not the conviction of the revolutionist but the smoldering hatred of a peasant" and was unable "to stop thinking that at one time a sort of *droit du seigneur* might have been exercised to give one of them [his] girl." That quotation cropped up in three different essays. Similarly, the beginning of Fitzgerald's "General Plan" for *Tender Is the Night* appeared in two. I deleted these duplications and others, and think I caught them all.

As a biographer (seven biographies of twentieth-century American writers) I have always been drawn to making connections between an author's life and work. Not exact parallels, of course. Hemingway's early Nick Adams stories depict his father, Dr. Adams, as an ineffectual fellow dominated by his wife, and we know that Ernest felt that way about his own parents. But that does not mean that his father, Dr. Hemingway, was humiliated in precisely the same way as Dr. Adams in "The Doctor and the Doctor's Wife." Fiction, as John Cheever insisted, is not "crypto-autobiography." Hemingway and Fitzgerald used their imaginative genius to create fiction *out of* their experience, instead of merely *about* it. But the emotional impetus, the psychological drive to tell their particular stories came from the life. The more we know about them as people, the better we will be able to understand their work. These essays are unified, then, by an awareness of the interconnectedness between biography and criticism.

They are also linked, somewhat paradoxically, by a commitment to the benefits of close reading. I was educated during the late stages of the New Criticism, an approach to literature that preached reliance on the text itself to the exclusion of biographical or historical data. I rejected the second part of that approach, refusing to consider of no account the life of the writer and the times, but enthusiastically adopted the emphasis on reading one word after another. I. A. Richards's great *Practical Criticism* showed how to read a poem: with entire attention, more than once, and without falling prey to personal irrelevancies. Following that path, with novels as artful as *The Great Gatsby* and *A Farewell to Arms*, led to fresh insights with each rereading.

Then, too, in order to present one's interpretations with authority, you have to dig into the resources that these authors left behind. In my case that meant immersion in the Fitzgerald holdings at Princeton's Firestone library and the Hemingway collection at the John F. Kennedy Library in Boston. I spent a semester as a visiting fellow at Princeton, where every day I had the pleasure—as I told friends—of "reading Fitzgerald's mail." In fact, his incoming correspondence did provide invaluable information for several essays, most particularly the one on *The Crack-Up*. But there was much to be gleaned as well from his notes and scrapbooks, drafts and false starts.

I first did time with the Hemingway documents at the Kennedy in the 1970s, when the collection was housed in a modest Waltham warehouse, and I returned on many occasions since, most recently in the spring of 2007. Originally established as a gift from Mary Hemingway, Ernest's widow, the archive constitutes an invaluable resource. Hemingway did not throw things away, and the collection's curators have done a splendid job over the years of organizing and cataloguing thousands of documents. Critics and biographers and enthusiasts—anyone interested in the writer and his work—can learn a great deal there.

One major theme of this book is that Fitzgerald and Hemingway occupied common ground as compulsive revisers of their work. This will not surprise anyone about Hemingway, whose stature as an artist—especially in his fiction of the 1920s and early 1930s—has been firmly established. But it might surprise those who have tended to regard Fitzgerald along the lines he himself laid down at the beginning of his career as a somewhat carefree fellow afflicted with genius, who casually tossed off his stories and novels. That image comes crashing down through consideration of the drafts of *This Side of Paradise*, the crucial alterations that transformed *Trimalchio* (his penultimate version) into *The Great Gatsby*, and the long, tortured accumulation of history and ideas and personal experience that led to *Tender Is the Night*: all of these matters are discussed in these essays.

As the Hemingway section on "The Craftsman at Work" illustrates, he ordinarily put a story-in-progress through three or more drafts before publication. In a famous comment on the process of composition, he said that he tried to write on the principle of the iceberg. Seven-eighths of it lay under water, and as a writer you could eliminate anything you knew and it would only strengthen your iceberg. The emphasis fell on leaving things out, and in the case of *A Farewell to Arms* he did make several cuts that notably affect the characterization. Yet with the stories, his drafts reveal, the important changes were as likely to take the form of additions as deletions. It was the same with Fitzgerald. From *Trimalchio*, he *excised* Daisy's proposal to Gatsby that they run away together (a solution to their dilemma often advocated by undergraduates). Gatsby would have none of it; he wanted to go back and be respectably married in her house in Louisville, fixing in time and place the moment when they fell in love. And neither, in the end, would Fitzgerald, who must have seen that it was out of character for Daisy to suggest a course of action that would compromise the security of her social position. Yet to soften Daisy's portrait, he *added* to *Trimalchio* the single most evocative celebration of her remarkable voice, when at the end of Gatsby's last party she sings in a contralto that tips "her warm human magic" into the night.

❖ ❖ ❖

One reason we turn to serious literature is to help make sense of our lives. I don't mean the homilies of didactic texts, spelled out in block letters by pasteboard figures. Nor is it a matter of simply identifying with virtuous characters or recoiling from evil ones, as in pop culture. In great stories, the people are too complicated for that. There's something of Iago in most of us, but that does not make us villains: it makes us part of the same complex human community.

In revisiting and reassembling what I've written about Fitzgerald and Hemingway over the years, I was struck by how much of it fell into recognizable patterns. Initially, I planned to organize the essays according to chronology—to look at *Gatsby* before *Tender*, unpack *The Sun Also Rises* before *For Whom the Bell Tolls*. And for the most part I've followed that sensible procedure, but with exceptions to accommodate essays that clearly should be grouped according to theme. Not until I had revised and reshaped and reconsidered them did these categories present themselves, and more insistently with Fitzgerald than with Hemingway.

The Fitzgerald section begins with "The Search for Home," focusing first on St. Paul and then on Maryland. Fitzgerald was born in St. Paul, the home of his mother's family, and spent his formative early teens there. He was sent to the best country day school and took dancing lessons with the children of the city's leading families. He felt himself an outsider nonetheless. And when he and Zelda came back for the birth of their daughter he felt that way still. His mother was not fashionable, his father had failed in business, they were Irish Catholics, and, perhaps most important of all, the Fitzgeralds never owned a home in St. Paul. The city left him with a sense of himself as someone who could never quite gain acceptance in a social universe he yearned to inhabit, nose pressed to the window to see the carnival of the elite within. St. Paul and its social structure gave him the wound he needed to become a great writer

He never situated a novel there, but St. Paul figures significantly in some of Fitzgerald's best stories, notably "The Ice Palace" and "Winter Dreams," as well as in several of the patently autobiographical Basil Duke Lee stories he wrote in the late 1920s. Like many of the essays here, and more than most, "St. Paul Boy" combines biographical detail with analysis of the fiction to establish what the place meant to him—and why he could never feel at home there.

"Fitzgerald's Romance with the South," written much earlier, jumps ahead from the young lad in St. Paul to the troubled writer as he approached forty, and yet both essays speak to the situation of the author as outcast in search of somewhere he belongs. Like his father before him, Scott Fitzgerald never owned a house of his own. He and Zelda traveled restlessly, stopping in a series of rented homes or apartments or hotel rooms. It made for an expensive style of life, with costs beyond the simply monetary. When she was institutionalized for her mental illness, Zelda wrote her husband touching letters in which she imagined them living in a cottage with daughter Scottie gamboling in a garden full of flowers. It was not to be. Still, in the mid 1930s, her need for treatment led the family to temporary quarters in and around Baltimore. This brought Scott close to Montgomery County, Maryland, where his father had spent his youth—and to Washington, D.C., where Edward and Mollie Fitzgerald moved for their last years. During that period, Scott came to accept his father for the first time and to identify with the part of the world where the family roots stretched back to colonial times. Maryland never really became Fitzgerald's home (no place did), but he felt comfortable enough there to choose it as his final resting place.

That as many as five different essays can be logically subsumed under a category called "Love, Money, and Class" testifies to the importance of this theme in his life and work. Fitzgerald declared that like most authors, he had but a few different stories to tell, reconfigured in each retelling. He also said that the most basic story of all was that of the poor boy in love with the rich girl. The Fitzgeralds were never really poor. Scott was raised in reasonably prosperous upper-middle-class surroundings. Nonetheless, he fancied himself among the underprivileged as he courted girls—Ginevra King, most importantly—who occupied a social stratum he could never ascend to. In story after story he rang minor variations on that pattern. Ambitious boy pursues uncapturable rich girl, and despite making a fortune is defeated. It is the story of Dexter Green and Judy Jones in "Winter Dreams," and of Gatsby and Daisy Fay in *The Great Gatsby*, with the difference that at the end of the story Dexter feels devastated by the loss of the illusions that in their magical glory once gave color to his world while at the end of the novel Gatsby clings to these illusions unto death.

One lesson of Fitzgerald's fiction about love and marriage—a topic as vital to his work as to that of Jane Austen a century and more earlier—is that simply making money will not win the golden girl. In *This Side of Paradise* (1920) that seemed to be the case, for Rosalind Connage rejects Amory Blaine to marry the richest among her suitors. Five years later, Fitzgerald knew better. An idealist about love if not about the material world, Jay Gatsby makes his fortune but cannot compete with the combination of wealth and social position that Tom Buchanan is born to. It is also clear in that great novel, as in "The Rich Boy" and the Josephine Perry stories and, above all, in *Tender Is the Night*, that those who profit from the lucky lottery of birth end up emotionally crippled as a consequence. Devereux Warren commits incest. Baby Warren settles for onanistic love of self. Nicole Warren, inheriting the white crook's eyes of her grandfather, casts Dr. Diver aside once he has served his purpose.

There is more than that to the essays grouped under this heading. The essay on *Paradise*, for instance, touches on the author's drafts of the novel over a two-year period. The long one on *Tender* goes much deeper into the process of composition over the nine agonizing years it took to complete the novel, exploring the many shocks of that period from 1925 through 1934: Zelda's collapse; the death of the fathers; boom turning to bust; and his reading in Lawrence, Freud, Jung, and popular Marxist thought.

"A Short History of *Tender Is the Night*" hence serves as a bridge to the extended examination of Fitzgerald's own articles and essays in part 3, "Fitzgerald and His Times." "Fitzgerald's Nonfiction" illustrates the sharp division between the youthful author at the beginning of his career and the veteran professional fifteen years later. Fitzgerald contributed to the success of his earliest fiction by adopting the stance of the carefree amateur. He and Zelda—an extraordinarily handsome couple—misbehaved in liquor-fueled escapades that were eagerly reported in the press: riding on the tops of taxicabs and jumping fully clothed into the Plaza fountain, for example. They became celebrities, in other words, and Fitzgerald contributed to his own image as a larky lighthearted chronicler of the Jazz Age in a series of forgettable features for the magazines.

These earned him money but also earned him a reputation that was difficult to shake off. He tried to hard to do so, though, in the serious and interesting essays of the 1930s. In "Early Success," "My Lost City," and the three "Crack-Up" articles, Fitzgerald shifted 180 degrees away from the foolishness of pieces like "Why Blame It on the Poor Kiss If the Girl Veteran of Many Petting Parties Is Prone to Affairs After Marriage?" and "What Kind of Husbands Do 'Jimmies' Make?" "The Crack-Up" portrayed a writer in extremity, one who had lost energy and enthusiasm for life and who no longer had much tolerance for other people or for himself. These 1936 essays brought him a good deal of censure from other writers, and in them Fitzgerald was not entirely forthcoming about the role that drinking played in his deterioration. But to set them down at all showed a courage and a maturity he would not have been capable of a decade earlier. So, too, Fitzgerald's political development—a not at all casual matter—belied his public image as a literary playboy. Or it would have done so during his lifetime but for the persistent stereotyping of celebrity, a problem that was to beset Hemingway as well.

In the end, of course, Fitzgerald has outlasted his celebrity to achieve his proper standing as one of the nation's great writers. "A Death in Hollywood," written for the Fitzgerald centenary observances in 1996, reconstructs the poignant details of his passing and pays modest tribute to his accomplishment. Like the preceding one on politics, this essay relies on interviews with that short list of survivors who knew him in his lifetime, as well as on conversations and correspondence with a number of contemporary writers—Joan Didion, Tobias Wolff, Allan Gurganus, Amy Clampitt—who were glad to express their admiration for Fitzgerald and acknowledge what they owed to him.

❖ ❖ ❖

Like many professional writers, Ernest Hemingway got his start in the newspaper business. "Hemingway of the *Star*" traces his apprentice years with the *Toronto Star*, which sent him to Europe in his early twenties and more or less gave him his head. He learned a lot on the job, both about writing for a wide audience and about the ways of the world. During his brief stint with the *Kansas City Star* when he was only eighteen, Hemingway absorbed the useful lessons of its style sheet—use short sentences, go light on adjectives, etc.—lessons that were to form an important part of the new American prose style he fashioned for his short stories and novels of the middle and late 1920s. Traipsing around the European continent, he discovered the failings of ordinary people and famous statesmen and so added a dash of cynicism to his otherwise spare dispatches.

This opening essay resurrects in brief two Hemingway articles that the Toronto newspapers were unable or unwilling to print: an excellent profile of the French prime minister, Georges Clemenceau, and a fascinating and possibly libelous sketch of a consummate Canadian con man. In addition, it reveals Hemingway's own slightly unethical practice of receiving expenses from as many as three separate organizations while presumably representing only the *Toronto Star*. And it concludes as it must, with his escape from the fourth estate into fiction. He knew intuitively that he had to get away from newspapers as a regular occupation: he'd seen too many would-be novelists wasting away in city rooms. Gertrude Stein gave him a useful shove in that direction as well. Quit reporting and stick to stories, she advised him.

And so he did, beginning in 1923 and continuing until his last years. He never entirely abandoned the profession, though. He used the competence he'd acquired working for the *Star* to turn out articles for *Esquire* in the mid-1930s and to send dispatches from the front as a war correspondent during the Spanish Civil War and World War II. You had to be there, his newspaper days taught Hemingway, and he wrote with as much authority about the people and places in his fiction as about those he'd interviewed or seen as a journalist.

To write stories instead of news accounts, he set himself the task of mastering a craft that could not be encompassed in a style book. Part 6, "The Craftsman at Work," examines the drafts of two short and highly autobiographical stories to demonstrate the skill with which he transformed personal experience into something that would last. This section also includes a wide-ranging study of his stories about men and women in and out of love. It has always seemed to me that Hemingway was at his very best in this kind of story. Only in the last few years, however, did I begin to notice how often the principals in these stories avoided eye contact as an indication of things going wrong. "The Averted Gaze in Hemingway's Fiction" documents this particular form of subtext as it is used in place of conventional overt commentary by the narrator. One of the pleasures of literary study involves finding out techniques and themes in the text, without signposts to guide the reader.

"Hemingway's Morality of Compensation" provides another instance of this kind of discovery. In 1970 and 1971 I was a senior Fulbright lecturer in

Finland, teaching *The Sun Also Rises* to students at Åbo Akademi. I'd read the novel several times before, but on this occasion was astonished by the sheer number of monetary transactions in the novel, spelled out in meticulous detail. There were too many of these to be accidental, and it became apparent that they were included to underline the novel's essential ethical point. Hemingway's book about the untidy lives of expatriates was, he insisted, a very moral one. The moral is that you have to earn your way in the world, although on the surface this is not immediately apparent. It is possible to enjoy the company of the dissolute, who may be attractive like Brett and amusing like Mike, but that does not mean we should embrace their sloughing off of obligations.

Mike Campbell is a minor character, Bill Gorton another, and Hemingway uses their different kinds of humor to emphasize the morality of the novel. The two of them are very funny together, but each has a style all his own. Bill's joking either depends on nonsensical repetition, as in the stuffed-dog conversation, or on topical satire, as in his bantering with Jake at Burguete. Mike uses self-deprecation, an initially winning posture that loses its charm over time. He makes fun of his own financial unreliability in a series of witty remarks and anecdotes, but in the end, that cannot excuse his continuing irresponsibility. Bill likes Mike, or wants to like him, but his face "sort of changed" when he discovers—late in the novel—that Mike can't pay a gambling debt. Both of these articles on *The Sun Also Rises* address the ethical foundations of the novel.

The two essays on *A Farewell to Arms* are even more closely linked through their exploration of the character of Frederic Henry, first as a lover and then as a warrior. "Frederic Henry, Selfish Lover" appeared in *By Force of Will* (1977), and "Frederic Henry's Pose of Passivity" six years later. During the interim, I had an opportunity to read the drafts of *A Farewell to Arms* at the Kennedy Library. The most important changes Hemingway made, I found, altered dialogue and deleted passages of philosophical reflection designed to render Frederic a more sympathetic character. This fact confirmed a conviction that Hemingway meant to create an antihero in Frederic, a narrator who in telling his own story is less than forthcoming about himself. In preparing *Fitzgerald and Hemingway: Works and Days*, I shifted copy around and otherwise revised to shape both articles into one coherent essay arguing that conclusion.

In his effort to portray life as he found it, rather than a smoothed-over version, Hemingway did not shy away from writing dialogue and exploring behavior that official arbiters of taste found offensive. Almost all of his books were censored at one time or another, and the section on censorship investigates two such incidents. The first involved suppression of the *Scribner's* magazine serialization of *A Farewell to Arms* by the Boston police chief. Through the publicity it generated, this action did not harm magazine circulation and undoubtedly stimulated eventual sales of the novel. Yet it also had an unfortunate effect on the book as it appeared. Worried by the Boston restriction and fearful that a more wide-reaching censorship by the United States mails might follow, Hemingway capitulated to his publishers and eliminated much of the novel's realistic barracks language.

Actually, what most bothered the Boston authorities was not the dialogue in *A Farewell to Arms* but its unjudgmental depiction of a love affair out of wedlock. The Boston police chief found that "salacious," although Hemingway did not describe Catherine and Frederic's lovemaking in any detail. Fifteen years later, a U.S. Army general also invoked the word "salacious" to condemn an edition of Hemingway stories that was being circulated to servicemen during World War II. Determined to guide the troops under his command on the path to righteous reading, the general commandeered copies of the book and was prepared to destroy them until—in an interesting conflict between fellow officers—another general intervened to prevent a further assault on the First Amendment. Hemingway probably knew nothing about this incident. Gertrude Stein apparently did, for documents pertaining to it turned up among her papers at Yale's Beinecke Library.

The long essay on "The Last Great Cause: Hemingway's Spanish Civil War Writing," published here for the first time, demonstrates how the single great political commitment of the author's life led him first to idealize and then to make fictional capital out of the Republican cause. Hemingway wrote about the war in almost every way possible: in war correspondence dispatched under siege and in battle, in a propaganda film, in a play, in short stories, in contributions to various left-wing magazines and newspapers, and most successfully in *For Whom the Bell Tolls* (1940). Reporting and fiction and outright propaganda intersect in those various and uneven writings, as he attempted to show how it was in Spain, where—he was convinced—World War II might have been averted. The story is told through examination of that writing and through the introduction of several people who were instrumental in solidifying Hemingway's leanings. His four trips to the war during 1937 and 1938 brought him close to the communist filmmaker Joris Ivens; to the writer Martha Gellhorn, who was his lover and later his wife; and to *New York Times* correspondent Herbert Matthews. They were under fire together in Spain and acquired through that experience a lifelong devotion to the antifascist Loyalist cause.

That it was to be a lost cause may have added to Hemingway's dedication, somewhat as the romance of the lost Confederate cause had its appeal for Fitzgerald. That the two writers shared other difficulties emerges in the part 10, "Last Things," on Hemingway's suicide and his dealings with celebrity. Both writers had to adapt themselves to failed fathers, for example. In Hemingway's case the process was converted into a crisis when his father killed himself in 1929. Suicide, he knew, set a terrible example for one's offspring—he addressed the theme directly in *For Whom the Bell Tolls*—yet in the end depression had its way.

Hemingway died the most famous writer of his time, and (we can confidently say now) the most famous writer of the twentieth century. Fitzgerald died almost forgotten and far too young at forty-four. They both suffered from the culture of celebrity that was developing during their lifetimes. Fitzgerald early adopted a public pose as a charming and casual amateur in the arts, and that image stayed with him throughout his career and for some time after he died. Hemingway, on the other hand, developed his public persona over an extended period. There can be little doubt that he chose the image of the rugged warrior-sportsman as a shield against invasion of his own extraordinarily complicated personality—in particular his emotional vulnerability—by outsiders. Once these stereotypes took hold, they proved hard to get rid of and undoubtedly damaged the reputations of both writers before and beyond the grave. At the very least, the public images clouded the picture of Fitzgerald and Hemingway as they should be remembered: as writers only. Fortunately for the rest of us, their books have been great enough to withstand the handicap of celebrity. In rewriting these pieces I came to better know and understand Fitzgerald, Hemingway, and their work. I hope that will be true for those who read them as well.

{ F. Scott Fitzgerald }

PART I

◈ THE SEARCH FOR HOME ◈

{ 1 }

ST. PAUL BOY

It needs a complex social machinery to set a writer in motion.

—HENRY JAMES, *HAWTHORNE*

I

A good deal has been made of F. Scott Fitzgerald's hometown by commentators on his work, but the fact is that he spent precious little time there. He was born in St. Paul in September 1896 and left eighteen months later. The next decade was spent in Buffalo and in Syracuse. The Fitzgeralds did not return to St. Paul until the summer of 1908, shortly before Scott's twelfth birthday. From 1908 to 1911 the family lived in St. Paul, and Scott attended St. Paul Academy. Then he was sent east, first to the Newman School in Hackensack, New Jersey, and afterward to Princeton. During this period (1911 through 1917) Fitzgerald ordinarily spent his summers and Christmas vacations in St. Paul. This was followed by a two-year absence during his service in the U.S. Army and his brief career in the advertising business in New York. Fitzgerald did not come back to St. Paul until the summer of 1919, when he rewrote *This Side of Paradise* (1920) in a burst of activity and so won the hand of Zelda Sayre. He and Zelda stayed in the East after they were married in New York in the spring of 1920, but when their child was to be born, they "played safe and went home to St. Paul." Scott and Zelda arrived in August 1921. Scottie was born in October. A year later they left the city permanently.

After infancy, then, Scott Fitzgerald lived in St. Paul for three years during prep school, half a dozen summers thereafter, nine months in 1916 and

1917 when he was sent home from Princeton for academic reasons, nine months in 1919 and 1920, and fourteen months in 1921 and 1922: about ten years, altogether. In one sense, of course, the amount of time is immaterial. Scott Fitzgerald's mother's family was based in St. Paul; his father moved there to seek his fortune; he himself was born there. Stay away as he assuredly did for the last half of his life, St. Paul was always the place he came from. But there is more to it than that. The city itself, his family's position within its particular social structure, and his interaction with others there played an essential role in shaping his life and career.

St. Paul had its unprepossessing start in 1837, when the Canadian Pierre ("Pigs Eye") Parrant built the first birch-roofed cabin, uncorked his jug, and began to sell whiskey to the Indians. The town grew rapidly, in good part because of its location at the head of navigation on the Mississippi River. By the late nineteenth century St. Paul had become a thriving community that inspired the admiration of famous visitors.

In *Life on the Mississippi* (1883), Mark Twain declared it to be a "wonderful town" constructed in "solid blocks of honest brick and stone" and having "the air of intending to stay." The Mississippi and the railroads made it an ideal site for commerce, and like most outsiders Twain was struck by the physical beauty of the place, its high bluffs offering a wide view of the river and the lowlands. Twain also celebrated the growth of the bustling twin city of Minneapolis on the western side of the Mississippi, which though developed later than St. Paul had already surpassed it in population. And he called special attention to White Bear Lake, which was to play an important role in Fitzgerald's early life. White Bear had "a lovely sheet of water, and is being utilized as a summer resort by the wealth and fashion of the state," Twain observed. There were several summer resorts around St. Paul and Minneapolis, he went on, but White Bear Lake was "*the* resort" (486–93).

Twain's contemporary Charles Dudley Warner—they were coauthors of *The Gilded Age* (1873)—also singled out St. Paul for praise. St. Paul and Minneapolis were both fast-growing cities inhabited by handsome, vigorous, and active people, he reported in a March 1887 article for *Harper's Magazine*, but he preferred St. Paul because of its picturesque location on the bluffs. Warner was especially impressed by Summit Avenue, another setting that was to play a significant role in Scott Fitzgerald's life. Located high above the city and offering splendid views of the winding river below, Summit was "almost literally a street of palaces" (qtd. in Castle, *History of St. Paul*, 126–28).

It may be that Edward Fitzgerald, who was born in Maryland and descended from some of its oldest colonial families, read these or other encomiums about St. Paul and so decided to move there. At any rate, he journeyed west to join the flood of newcomers that tripled the population between 1880 and 1895. He married St. Paul's Mary (Mollie) McQuillan in 1890. Mollie was the eldest child of Philip Francis (P. F.) and Louisa McQuillan. An immigrant from Ireland, P. F. came upriver to St. Paul from Galena, Illinois, in 1857 and launched a successful wholesale grocery business. When he died twenty years later, at forty-three, he left behind a fortune of more than $250,000.

Mollie was twenty-nine and Edward thirty-seven at the time of their marriage. They had two little girls in the first few years, but both of them died in an 1896 epidemic even while Mollie was pregnant with her only son. Francis Scott Key Fitzgerald, named for a distant relative on his father's side of the family, was born September 24, 1896, and assumed the burdens of the replacement child. Much was expected of him. He was, in effect, to make up for the loss of his dead older sisters (Martin, "Biography and Humanity," 53–54). Scott's mother overprotected her baby boy and became "half insane with pathological, nervous worry" at the least hint of illness. Even after Scott was joined by his sister Annabel in 1901, she continued to pamper and spoil her clever and handsome son.

Mollie "just missed being beautiful," her husband once said, but that was Southern gallantry. In photographs she faces the camera with a forbiddingly dark gaze and looks somewhat dowdy. She seemed to one of Scott's contemporaries to have "worn the same dress all her life." Sometimes her shoes did not match. When she walked to daily mass, she invariably carried an umbrella and wore a gloomy countenance. Aside from church-related functions, she and her husband had little involvement in the social life of the community. In his first novel Fitzgerald invented a mother for his autobiographical hero who in her elegance and charm stood sharply in opposition to his own mother. But at least he usually provided his fictional characters with mothers. Often they are given no fathers at all.

Along with good looks and good manners, Edward Fitzgerald bequeathed to his son a taste for romantic poetry and lost causes. Born near Rockville, Maryland, in 1855, he glorified the Confederacy in stories he told about the Civil War. Scott, who delighted in these yarns, admired his father's graceful ways. But Edward lacked the drive required to achieve success and, apparently, was an alcoholic. In St. Paul he started a business manufacturing wicker furniture, the American Rattan and Willow Works, a venture that failed in the wake of the panic of 1897. Edward then took a position with Procter and Gamble that moved the family to Buffalo and Syracuse. He lost his job in the spring of 1908, traumatizing young Scott.

"Please don't let us go to the poor-house," he prayed (Turnbull, *Fitzgerald*, 17), but there was no danger of that. Instead the Fitzgeralds limped back to St. Paul to live on the largesse of the McQuillans. His father was given a desk and a title in the family business but nothing much to do. At fifty-five, Edward Fitzgerald was a defeated man.

Scott Fitzgerald was thus burdened with a father who had twice failed in business and an eccentric mother who, despite her inheritance, did not move comfortably in the social circles she yearned for her children to occupy. In an often-quoted letter to John O'Hara in 1933, Fitzgerald summed up his situation: "I am half black Irish and half old American stock with the usual exaggerated ancestral pretensions. The black Irish half of the family had the money and looked down upon the Maryland side of the family who had, and really had, that certain series of reticences and obligations that go under the poor old shattered word 'breeding.'" As a result, he "developed a two-cylinder inferiority complex." If he became king of Scotland tomorrow, Fitzgerald insisted, he "would still be a parvenu" (*Letters*, 503).

In *F. Scott Fitzgerald and the Art of Social Fiction*, Brian Way links Fitzgerald with Henry James and Edith Wharton as keenly observant "historians of manners" who wrote "social fiction" (vii–viii). That social class matters is a dirty little secret many Americans are inclined to deny. Motivated by democratic sentiments and the myth that in this nation more than anywhere else on earth it is not only possible but nearly obligatory to make one's way from rags to riches—hence realizing the American dream—we tell one another that there are no significant barriers between the classes. Fitzgerald knew better, for unlike the wellborn Wharton and James and some of the English novelists who created the novel of manners, he had looked around him, seen the social barriers, and tried to surmount them.

Some interpreters of Fitzgerald's life and work maintain that "the McQuillan family and their grandson [Scott] Fitzgerald were very much insiders, a part of St. Paul society." By way of evidence they cite the McQuillans' generous contributions to the Catholic Church and the fact that Mollie's younger sister was maid of honor at the wedding of the daughter of railroad tycoon James J. Hill. P. F McQuillan was indeed a substantial benefactor of the Catholic Church. He participated in the group that brought the Sisters of the Visitation from St. Louis to St. Paul. Mollie and her sisters attended the school these nuns founded, and so did Scott's sister Annabel. Later Mollie showed off her son at the Convent of the Visitation, bringing him along to recite poetry and sing songs for the nuns. So extensive was the family's support that when Scott and Zelda went to Europe in the spring of 1921, Archbishop Dowling of St. Paul tried to arrange an audience with the pope. "None have merited more of the Church in this city" than the McQuillans, he wrote (Hackl, *"Still Home to Me,"* 14–15, 62–63).

This evidence seems impressive but depends entirely on the prominence of the McQuillans among the city's lace-curtain Irish families. Scott himself was hardly impressed. He described his mother's family as "straight 1850 potato famine Irish" (qtd. in Mizener, *Far Side of Paradise,* 4) and therefore at a significant remove from the top of St. Paul's social hierarchy. Few Irish Catholics were among Scott's boyhood companions. Some of his friends believed that Catholics were plotting to overthrow the government. Scott and other boys who lived atop the bluffs fought mock battles with the "micks" from Lower Town, descendants of the Irish immigrants.

In *The Far Side of Paradise* (1951), the first biography of Fitzgerald, Arthur Mizener discoursed upon the makeup of St. Paul in the early years of the twentieth century. The city at that time, he wrote, had both "a great deal of the simple and quite unselfconscious democracy of the old middle-western cities" and "its wealth and its inherited New England sense of order. The best people in St. Paul are admirable and attractive people, but they are, in their quiet way, clearly the best people. They do not forget their Maine or Connecticut 'connection': they send their children to Hotchkiss or Hill or Westover, to Yale or Princeton, to be educated; they are, without ostentation or affectation, cosmopolitan" (16). Mizener's comments may grate against democratic sensibilities; the remark about "the best people," in particular, sounds offensively snobbish. But that does not mean that he was wrong about St. Paul.

In several observations of his own, Fitzgerald described in detail that "sense of order" Mizener observed. St. Paul felt "a little superior" to such other Midwestern cities as Minneapolis, Kansas City, and Milwaukee, Fitzgerald wrote in reviewing Grace Flandrau's novel *Being Respectable* (1923). The other cities were but two generations old, while St. Paul was a "three generation" town: more settled, more conservative, more "complacent" (Flandrau's word) than the brash and bustling younger cities. It also was significantly more eastern in its outlook. In the 1850s, Fitzgerald points out, the climate of St. Paul was reputed to be exceptionally healthy, and consequently "there arrived an element from the East who had both money and fashionable education. These Easterners mingled with the rising German and Irish stock, whose second generation left the cobbler's last, forgot the steerage, and became passionately 'swell' on its own account. But the pace was set by the tubercular Easterners" (qtd. in *Miscellany,* 141).

Five years later Fitzgerald elaborated on the social structure established by these settlers:

> There were the two or three nationally known families—outside of them
> rather than below them the hierarchy began. At the top came those whose
> grandparents had brought something with them from the East, a vestige of
> money and culture; then came the families of the big self-made merchants,
> the "old settlers" of the sixties and seventies, American-English-Scotch, or
> German or Irish, looking down upon each other somewhat in the order
> named. . . . After this came certain well-to-do "new people"—mysterious,
> out of a cloudy past, possibly unsound.

Like so many structures, Fitzgerald concludes, "this one did not survive
the cataract of money that came tumbling down upon it with the war."
But it *was* the hierarchy in place during his prep school and college years
when he sought to climb his way up the ladder. Fitzgerald understood
precisely where he belonged: on his mother's side among the respectable
Irish "old settlers" who were generally looked down upon both by the cul-
tured Easterners and by the Scotch-English and the Germans, and, on his
father's side, at best among the "possibly unsound" newcomers (qtd. in
Donaldson, *Fool for Love*, 10–11).

The Fitzgeralds' position in this hierarchy was nicely symbolized by
their places of residence. Scott was born in an apartment at the San Mateo
Flats, 481 Laurel Avenue, a short walk from Summit Avenue. The next
year, his grandmother Louisa McQuillan built a substantial (if not particularly imposing) home on Summit, but she sold it two years later. When
the Fitzgeralds returned to the city from Buffalo in 1908, Scott and his
sister Annabel moved in with their grandmother at 294 Laurel. During the
succeeding decade, the family occupied at least five different domiciles,
the first three of them on Holly Avenue, like Laurel close to "the Summit
Avenue area," or "the Summit Avenue section," or "the Summit Avenue
neighborhood," as biographers have termed it. But not on Summit itself.

As the St. Paul historian John J. Koblas observes, these various homes—
all of them within a twelve-square-block area near Summit—offered young
Scott "the relative stability of residing within a single definable community
and having a secure circle of friends." But at the same time the boy could not
help being conscious of his family's precarious position as renters rather than
owners of homes, living on the fringes of St. Paul's best street. His multiple
residences differentiated him from that circle of friends who grew up, like
Nick Carraway in *The Great Gatsby*, in a community "where dwellings are still
called through decades by a family's name" (*Fitzgerald in Minnesota*, 184).

According to one architectural historian, "St. Paul's Summit Avenue
stands as the best-preserved American example of the Victorian monu-

mental residential boulevard." Blight and economic downturns have diminished its luster, but Summit remains the city's "high street": characteristically a street rising above the rest of the community, both in physical location and in social stature (Donaldson, *Fool for Love*, 12–13). Electric trolleys and a tunnel made the elevated setting available for building in the 1880s, when the empire builder James J. Hill (greatly admired by Jay Gatsby's father and by Rudolph Miller's father in the story "Absolution") built his mansion near the eastern end of the avenue. Other leading families followed suit (Hackl, *"Still Home to Me,"* 50–51). By the time Fitzgerald was born, Summit Avenue ruled.

A character in *Being Respectable* takes a Sunday-afternoon walk along the most fashionable stretch of Summit, strolling unhurriedly up one side "past the opulent houses he knew so well" and down the other side "past more opulent houses he knew equally well." Between the houses on the south side, "sudden dreamy prospects" of the gray, winding river came into his view, "composed" by the walls of the houses and the trees. In the little park at Summit and Western, he sat and looked for a long time at the river and the green pastures and groves of trees beyond. Then it grew dark and the lights came out: "sparkling yellow stars in the gray," moving lights on the river, and the bridges like "necklaces, glittering tenderly." Thus did the novelist Grace Flandrau, Fitzgerald's friend and also a native of St. Paul, celebrate her city's most elegant street (18–19). There is no closely comparable passage in Fitzgerald's writing, although in "Winter Dreams" his character Dexter Green waxes rhapsodic about Judy Jones's home one summer night (the street, given no name, is undoubtedly Summit Avenue): "The dark street lightened, the dwellings of the rich loomed up around them, he stopped his coupe in front of the great white bulk of the Mortimer Joneses house, somnolent, gorgeous, drenched with the splendor of the damp moonlight. Its solidity startled him" (*Short Stories*, 232).

The mansion's solidity, Dexter explains, presented a striking contrast to Judy's young beauty, its sturdiness accentuating her slightness and, perhaps, the fragility of the dream he has invested in her. The Jones house, like Nick Carraway's, was a dwelling as assuredly permanent as the Fitzgeralds' serial domiciles were shakily temporary. Edward and Mollie Fitzgerald finally did achieve an address on Summit Avenue, first moving into a brownstone-front row house at 593 Summit in 1915, and then to 599 Summit in 1918, the house where Scott rewrote *This Side of Paradise*. The house at 599 Summit has been officially designated a National Historical Landmark, though as landmarks go, this one has singularly little to do with the famous figure associated with it. He lived there less than a year. Moreover, it was a rented house—neither Scott nor his father ever owned a home of his own—and a row house rather than one of the sprawling free-standing houses that dominated the avenue. When he wrote Alida Bigelow the news that Scribner's had accepted his novel for publication, he headed the letter

> (599 Summit Avenue)
>> In a house below the average
>>> Of a street above the average
>>>> In a room below the roof.

(QTD. IN DONALDSON, FOOL FOR LOVE, 13)

That there was never to be a "Fitzgerald house" in St. Paul set Scott and Annabel apart from their companions. So did his family's lack of a summer place at White Bear Lake. By the 1880s St. Paul's wealthiest citizens were building summer cottages at the lake, and in his youth Scott rode the streetcar out to spend evenings or weekends in those cottages, but it was hardly the same as going to a place of one's own or, once there, sailing in a boat of one's own (Irish, "The Myth of Success," 180). Sensitive as he was to social gradations, Fitzgerald knew he faced considerable handicaps when he came back from Buffalo and tried to establish himself as a boy who *belonged*.

Mollie Fitzgerald did what she could to advance her son's campaign to conquer St. Paul. "Her great hope was her son, whom she loved extravagantly as a woman will when her husband has in some way disappointed her," as the biographer Andrew Turnbull observed (*Fitzgerald*, 27). She could not eradicate her husband's failure, but she could and did use the McQuillan resources to enroll Scott in St. Paul Academy, the community's leading private preparatory school, and to send him to dancing school with the children of the city's most prominent families. The three years Scott spent in St. Paul, beginning in the summer of 1908 after his father's dismissal by Procter and Gamble and ending with his departure for the Newman School in the fall of 1911, constituted the longest period he was to live in the city of his birth. They were supremely important years in shaping the way he looked at the world around him.

II

Scott Fitzgerald was a precocious lad in many ways. He was extremely good-looking, after the model of his father. He had a quick and retentive mind. He liked participating in neighborhood games and took a leading role in organizing them. He learned how to attract girls and took an uncommon interest in how he stood vis-à-vis other boys in their affections. His mother cosseted him, dressed him up, and showed him off but rarely imposed any discipline. Hence she encouraged what he called "my first childish love of myself," an egotism that led him to repudiate his unsatisfactory parents and imagine himself a foundling, the son of "a king who ruled the whole world" (Turnbull, *Fitzgerald*, 28). He had rejected this fantastic notion by the time he came back to St. Paul in 1908 but continued to regret the progenitors. "My father is a moron and my mother is a neurotic," he wrote his editor, Maxwell Perkins, in 1926. "Between them they haven't . . . the brains of Calvin Coolidge" (*Dear Scott/Dear Max*, 134–35).

At St. Paul Academy (S.P.A.), where the city's elite sent their sons to be prepared for college, it is safe to say that Scott Fitzgerald was the only boy whose father had twice failed in business and had no occupation. And probably the only boy without a substantial family home. And one of the very few Irish Catholics.

Saddled with these handicaps, he made matters worse by letting his ego run unchecked: bragging, showing off in class, asking too many questions about money and class to his bewildered and annoyed schoolmates. *Now and Then*, the school newspaper, offers conclusive testimony that he struck his fellow students as insufferably cocky. By and large the paper described events at the school, and participants in them, in highly favorable terms. The watchword was much the same as that at Blake, S.P.A.'s rival school in Minneapolis: Boost, Don't Knock. Nonetheless, *Now and Then* printed several gibes directed at Fitzgerald during his first year at S.P.A. "Young Scotty is always bubbling over with suppressed knowledge" was the initial barb, followed by the accusation that he was the author of a book called *How to Run the School*. The severest criticism of all came in Sam Kennedy's "Personals" item for the Easter 1909 issue: "If anybody can poison Scotty to stop his mouth in some way, the school at large and myself will be obliged" (S.P.A. Fitzgerald Archive). Fitzgerald at twelve obviously talked too much and knew (or pretended to know) too much to satisfy his schoolmates. He wanted desperately to be popular but managed to alienate those he most desired to please. The root of the problem was the overweening sense of self-importance his mother had instilled in him. As he was to write his daughter when she was about to enter prep school, "I didn't know till 15 that there was anyone in the world except me" (*Letters*, 5).

The high road to success at St. Paul Academy led through athletics, especially football. When the school was founded in 1900, coprincipal C. N. B. Wheeler, himself a college athlete at Harvard, established the tradition (borrowed from Groton) that every boy, whatever his size or age, was required to play football. Fitzgerald tried gamely to make himself into a football player but was ill equipped to excel at the sport. Although quite fast, he was rather slight and not particularly well coordinated. Nor did he earn good grades, for he lacked disciplined study habits. In class, his mind was often occupied with stories rather than with his daily lessons. In the back of notebooks he scrawled plot summaries and tried out characters' names. Wheeler, who taught English and history, recognized his inventive bent and encouraged him to write these juvenile adventures.

Now and Then printed four of Fitzgerald's apprentice stories. One of these celebrated the triumph of "Reade, Substitute Right Half," an improbable tale of a "light-haired stripling" who comes off the bench to make a saving tackle and intercept a pass for the winning touchdown. At which point the crowd cheers, "Reade! Reade! Reade!"—the final words of the story. For young Fitzgerald, eager to prove his worth, victory counted for little without recognition.

This football story was the second that Scott published in the school newspaper. The first was called "The Mystery of the Raymond Mortgage," despite the fact that the thirteen-year-old author neglected to mention the mortgage in his story. When it appeared in the September 1909 *Now and Then*, the fledgling author read his story "at least six times" and hung around the school corridors to ask other boys, as casually as he could, if they chanced to have read it.

Fitzgerald's other two stories in *Now and Then* both dealt with the Civil War. In "A Debt of Honor," a Confederate soldier falls asleep on guard duty but later redeems himself by fighting bravely in combat. In "The Room with the Green Blinds," Fitzgerald rewrote history by imagining John Wilkes Booth's escape after assassinating Lincoln. Booth is eventually captured and killed in this revisionary account. Murdering the president may have been going too far, but Scott was enough the son of his father to inherit his Southern sympathies. During his first public debate at S.P.A., he and two other lads upheld the negative on "Resolved: that the South was not justified in seceding," and their team was awarded the decision (S.P.A. Fitzgerald Archive).

Fitzgerald's boyhood stories established that he was different but didn't earn him popularity. The popular success he achieved during his formative years in St. Paul came through the games and clubs he organized among the neighborhood children and through his youthful encounters with girls. Scott was forever forming secret clubs. He was secretary of the White Handkerchief Club, chief scout of the Boys' Secret Service of St. Paul, and founder and president of the Cruelty to Animals Society, the Gooserah Club, and the Scandal Detectives. Among the boys who joined these clubs were Cecil Read, Paul Dallion, Bob Clark, and Mac Seymour, all of whom attended Central High School, not S.P.A. Fitzgerald recalled the initiation rites for one of these short-lived organizations. "Paul and I subjected [Cecil] to . . . eat[ing] raw eggs and . . . operat[ed] on him with saw, cold ice, and needle" (Turnbull, *Fitzgerald*, 24; S.P.A. Fitzgerald Archive).

Read, one of Scott's closest friends (note the similarity of his name to the fictional halfback Reade), later looked back on these shenanigans without animosity. Scott was "a great leader and organizer," he reported for the NBC *Biography in Sound* broadcast about Fitzgerald (S.P.A. Fitzgerald Archive). During the summers he often invited Scott to visit him at his family's place on White Bear Lake. His mother would put half a dozen cots on the sleeping porch, where Scott, Cecil, and other boys lay awake and talked about their future plans. On one of those nights, Read recalled, Fitzgerald told him that he wanted to go to Princeton, he wanted to join University Cottage Club, and he wanted to write a play for the Triangle Club. He also revealed that he hoped to write a great Catholic novel. Fitzgerald accomplished his college goals, but the novel went unwritten.

A fine reminiscence of Fitzgerald during this period comes in a 1970 letter that his lifelong friend Alida Bigelow Butler wrote in response to an inquiry from students at St. Paul Academy. Soon after his return to St. Paul in 1908, Scott, "quite short, blond, sharp nose, eager darting blue eyes," developed a crush on Alida. In good weather he would come over in his knickerbockers to sit on her porch and talk. "Scott must have asked questions because that was his habit. He wanted people's reactions in those days, reactions about other people. There was a 'character' book phase . . . Scott engineered the project, which was for each one of us— boys and girls—to make headings in the notebook [for] favorite girl and boy (choices 1, 2, 3), favorite sport, book, game, blond or brunette [preference]. Then more personal: what boy would I like to kiss, etc.? When we had once written in the notebook and had by any method tried to read the other persons' notebooks, the fun died down. The fun was in the organization of the project, not the project itself." And Scott was invariably the organizer (S.P.A. Fitzgerald Archive).

When they were twelve and thirteen, Alida and Scott and the other children in the neighborhood went to dancing school together. On Saturday afternoons twenty boys and twenty girls strolled down Grand Avenue to Ramaley Hall, the girls carrying their slippers and the boys their patent leather shoes. "Professor" William H. Baker, a sometime bartender at White Bear

Yacht Club, conducted the dancing lessons. An apple-shaped man with a bald head, Baker was impeccably dressed in tails and white kid gloves as he guided his young charges through the waltz and two-step. Until the music began, the girls sat on one side of the room and the boys on the other. The orchestra consisted of "a tinkling piano, played by a not very young lady."

At dancing school, Alida observed, Scott demonstrated no particular feeling for music and not much grace of movement. In her recollection, he was awkward physically and knew it. Invited to summer outings at the Bigelow home on Manitou Island (in White Bear Lake), he participated in childhood games but was regularly beaten in high-jump contests by Eleanor Alair and didn't even try to play tennis. Still, "all the girls wanted to dance with Scott because he was Scott the instigator, the ringleader, the boy who asked questions, the boy who was handsome" (S.P.A. Fitzgerald Archive).

As was to be the case throughout his life, Fitzgerald was far more successful in attracting females than in making friends with males. "When he had been in St. Paul only a month, five girls confessed that he was their favorite boy," Turnbull wrote. His favorite girl that summer was Violet Stockton, a visitor from Atlanta. In his "Thoughtbook," fourteen pages of notebook paper he kept locked beneath his bed, he described the girls he had crushes on and how he ranked in their affections. Violet, for example, was a year older than Scott, "very pretty with dark brown hair and eyes big and soft" and a Southern accent he found entrancing. The "Thoughtbook" describes in some detail their juvenile lovers' quarrel and the conversation in which they ironed out the misunderstanding and made up. As a piece of dialogue, very much to the life, it surpasses anything in Fitzgerald's S.P.A. stories.

> "Violet," I began, "Did you call me a brat?"
>
> "No."
>
> "Did you say that you wanted your ring and your pictures and your hair back?"
>
> "No."
>
> "Did you say you hated me?"
>
> "Of course not, is that what you went home for?"
>
> "No, but Archie Mudge told me those things yesterday evening."
>
> "He's a little scamp," said Violet indignantly.
>
> (TURNBULL, *FITZGERALD*, 19–20)

The reference to wanting "your hair back" probably refers to Scott's habit of collecting samples of girls' hair, which he carefully wound around toothpicks and pinned for safekeeping. At Alida Bigelow's he would produce his collection of hair swatches and ask those assembled to identify the girls they had come from.

In the pages of his "Thoughtbook," Fitzgerald was beginning to be a writer, someone caught up in the emotions awakened by experience yet capable of describing them in objective detail. The repeated references to his ranking with girls—was he first, or second, or third in the affections of the girl of the moment?—reflected his obsessive concern with gradations in status. At the same time, each particular girl was becoming more than a name on a list. "For the first time in his life," like his fictional counterpart Basil Duke Lee, he was beginning to realize "a girl as something opposite and complementary to him, and he was subject to a warm chill of mingled pleasure and pain" (Turnbull, *Fitzgerald*, 30).

"It is not necessary to send a boy away to school in order to have him properly prepared for college," proclaimed an S.P.A. advertisement in the 1910 Twin City Bluebook. "Our graduates are just as well prepared as those of any school in the country." In the ten years since the school was founded, the ad pointed out, the school had placed "sixty boys at Yale, Harvard, Princeton, University of Minnesota and other colleges." Despite such assurances, many boys transferred to eastern prep schools during this period. The lower forms at S.P.A. customarily enrolled about sixteen boys, but the graduating classes averaged only five or six (S.P.A. Fitzgerald Archive). Fitzgerald joined the eastward-bound students in the fall of 1911 when his parents, with financial aid from his devout aunt, Annabel McQuillan, decided to send him to Newman, a Catholic school in Hackensack, New Jersey, for his junior and senior years.

Pleased to start fresh at an eastern prep school, Fitzgerald unfortunately repeated the mistakes he'd made at St. Paul Academy, with the difference that without a second universe of home and neighborhood to escape to, his unpopularity mattered more. "All one can know," he once observed, "is that somewhere between thirteen, boyhood's majority, and seventeen, when one is a sort of counterfeit young man, there is a time when youth fluctuates hourly between one world and another—pushed ceaselessly forward into unprecedented experiences and vainly trying to struggle back to the days when nothing had to be paid for" (qtd. in Mizener, *The Far Side of Paradise*, 27). At Newman he paid.

Evaluating himself at fifteen with remarkable candor, Fitzgerald admitted to a dominating philosophy of "aristocratic egotism." He thought himself "a fortunate youth," capable because of his "facility and superior mentality" of doing a great deal of good or evil. *Physically*, he marked himself "handsome, of great athletic *possibilities*, and an extremely good dancer."

Socially, he was convinced that he had "charm, magnetism, poise," so that he could dominate others and exert "a subtle fascination over women." *Mentally*, he was vain of his quick mind and ingenuity. On the other hand, he thought himself "worse than most boys" *morally* because of a "latent unscrupulousness and the desire to influence people in some way, even for evil." In addition, he was selfish, lacked a sense of honor, and could be cold to others. *Psychologically*, he had "a curious cross section of weakness" in his character and could easily be thrown off his "poise into a timid stupidity." He knew he was "fresh" and not popular with older boys. *Generally*, and worst of all, he "lacked the essentials" and "had no real courage, perseverance or self-respect."

In this account a solipsistic Fitzgerald takes as much delight in his faults as in his virtues. "There seemed to have been a conspiracy to spoil me and all my inordinate vanity was absorbed from that," he wrote. His self-love was fragile; it could "be toppled over at one blow by an unpleasant remark or a missed tackle," and yet "underneath the whole thing lay a sense of infinite possibilities that was always with me whether vanity or shame was my mood" (qtd. in Turnbull, *Fitzgerald*, 34–35).

Thinking so much of and about himself, Fitzgerald was a prime candidate to fail in the adolescent competition for acceptance at Newman. Once again he showed off his "rather extraordinary fund of general information in class" and pointed out others' mistakes. On the football field he annoyed his companions by telling them what to do, then in an attempt to make things right offered a boastful untruth: "Excuse me for bossing everyone around, but I'm used to being captain of the teams in St. Paul."

As at S.P.A., football counted for a great deal at Newman, and during a game against Newark Academy, Scott disgraced himself by avoiding a head-on tackle. "Do that again," quarterback Charles (Sap) Donahoe warned, "and I'll beat you up myself." He tackled bravely thereafter, Fitzgerald claimed, because he was more frightened of Donahoe than of any opposing ballcarrier. In due course Donahoe became his good friend, but during his first months at Newman he made no real friends at all (Turnbull, *Fitzgerald*, 35; Mizener, *The Far Side of Paradise*, 28–29).

The only bright moments of that desolate year came when he was allowed off campus to see Broadway shows. "When I was fifteen," he later recalled, "I went into the city from school to see Ina Claire in *The Quaker Girl* and Gertrude Bryan in *Little Boy Blue*." Together they blended into "one lovely entity, the girl" (Bruccoli, *Some Sort of Epic Grandeur*, 33). Then during Christmas vacation he saw a production of *Alias Jimmy Valentine*, which, together with his reading of Arsene Lupin stories, prompted him to write a play called *The Captured Shadow*. It was performed in St. Paul in August 1912 by the Elizabethan Dramatic Club, a group of young people recruited by Fitzgerald and directed by Elizabeth Magoffin (hence the "Elizabethan" club). An audience of more than two hundred turned out for the play, which raised sixty dollars for the Baby Welfare Association and generated favorable notices in the local newspapers. "Much comment was elicited by the young author's cleverness," a reviewer noted. "ENTER SUCCESS!" Scott wrote in his scrapbook next to the clippings. At last, he was beginning to receive the recognition he coveted.

From early boyhood on Fitzgerald demonstrated a theatrical bent. When he was ten, he was making up shows about the American Revolution, in which he wore a red sash in the role of Paul Revere. In Buffalo he and his friend Hamilton Wende regularly took in Saturday stage matinees. Afterward they would reenact scenes, in which Fitzgerald showed a remarkable capacity to repeat long sections of dialogue. Back in St. Paul, he went to the vaudeville shows at the Orpheum Theater, then rushed home to reenact what he had seen. He organized and put on plays at the homes of his companions: in Teddy Ames's living room, Alida Bigelow's basement, Cecil Read's attic. At thirteen he perfected a routine to entertain and shock streetcar passengers, in which he reeled around, pretending to be drunk. "I imagined he would become an actor of the variety type," S.P.A.'s Wheeler remarked.

The Captured Shadow involves a gentleman burglar (one of Fitzgerald's youthful preoccupations) who is so much the gentleman that he returns everything he steals. The drama borrows heavily from its sources and tries for humor throughout, introducing a well-bred alcoholic who falls out of chairs and a number of gags lifted directly from joke books. Yet "[for] all its grotesqueries," Fitzgerald said, "the result was actually interesting—it was a play."

In his senior year in prep school (1912–13) Scott improved as a football player, wrote three separate stories for the *Newman News*, and became less desperately unpopular than during the previous year. But his greatest public success came during the summer with another play for the Elizabethan Dramatic Club. *Coward*, a Civil War melodrama, is built around the slowly awakening resolve of a young Southerner to join the Confederate Army in order to protect his home and loved ones. *Coward* outdrew *The Captured Shadow* and made more money for charity. It was presented first at the St. Paul YWCA and then, on demand for an encore, at White Bear Yacht Club. Fitzgerald not only wrote and acted in the play but also served as stage manager. "THE GREAT EVENT," he noted in his scrap-book. The following summer brought another great event with his play called *Assorted Spirits*, a farcical exploration of the ghost world that was his last production for the Elizabethan Club. "Scott Fitzgerald, the 17-year-old playwright . . . turned out a roaring farce and is clever throughout," one reviewer commented (Fitzgerald, *St. Paul Plays*, 3–10).

The plays he wrote and acted in and stage-managed during the summers brought him the attention and applause he was never able to earn at St. Paul Academy. For his subsequent career, of course, the theater proved a false start, for after his prep school and college days, Fitzgerald went back to fiction almost entirely. When he next returned to St. Paul for an extended stay, it was to rewrite *This Side of Paradise*.

Like his father before him, Scott staggered home in the summer of 1919 an apparently defeated man, with the difference that at twenty-two Fitzgerald had plenty of time to recover. Still, the prospects for success did not seem promising. Because of ill health and poor grades, he had not graduated from Princeton with the class of 1917. In the army he completed a draft of his first novel and, when stationed near Montgomery, Alabama, met the beautiful and headstrong Zelda Sayre, the girl he was to marry. Fitzgerald's novel was turned down by Scribner's, although Perkins encouraged him to make some changes and try again. After the war he secured a job as an advertising copywriter in New York, work that he neither liked nor devoted himself to wholeheartedly. His heart remained in Alabama, where Zelda was taking her time making up her mind. In June 1919 she broke off their engagement: Scott simply did not qualify as good husband material. In reaction he quit his job and took the train to St. Paul in order to reshape his novel. If he had a publishing contract, he felt sure, Zelda and her parents would be ready to accept him.

He worked hard over the summer of 1919, writing in an attic room at 599 Summit every day and of an evening talking with Father Joe Barron, the writer Donald Ogden Stewart, and his boyhood friend Richard (Tubby) Washington. In September he shipped his manuscript off to Scribner's and waited. Then the postman rang with Maxwell Perkins's special-delivery letter accepting his novel, and a joyful Fitzgerald celebrated by announcing the news to everyone he knew. He "was in a sort of trance all day," he told Perkins (Mizener, *The Far Side of Paradise*, 95).

Scott and Zelda were married in New York a few days after *This Side of Paradise* was published. The book made an immediate success, attracting readers with its depiction of a young hero in revolt against the received values of the time. The Fitzgeralds themselves became public figures for their partying and outrageous behavior in and around New York. They returned to St. Paul in August 1921, seeking a setting where Zelda could have her child and Scott could write free of their hectic existence. Neither childbirth nor geography changed their ways, however. During the fourteen months Scott and Zelda spent in St. Paul, from August 1921 to October 1922, they succeeded in scandalizing the community. As a boy Fitzgerald tried to impress St. Paul with his considerable talent. In young manhood, his career as a writer well underway, he (and Zelda) seemed determined to shock his home town instead. It was as if he was thumbing his nose at a place that was loath to accept him.

The Fitzgeralds were twice evicted from dwellings during their brief sojourn in St. Paul. On arrival they rented a cottage in Dellwood, the most exclusive section around White Bear Lake. Unlike most of the neighboring homes, the cottage was equipped for winter use, and Scott and Zelda signed a lease for a year's stay. Less than two months later, they were asked to leave. During an all-night party the furnace went out, and the Fitzgeralds—not noticing—let the water pipes freeze and burst. So, in early October, Scott and Zelda packed up and moved to the Hotel Commodore, an apartment hotel. They were living there when, on October 26, their daughter Scottie was born.

Their friend Xandra Kalman next found the young family an in-town residence at 626 Goodrich Avenue. "New Address/Permanent!" Scott scribbled to Max Perkins. The house provided the Fitzgeralds with their most comfortable and sensible living arrangement in St. Paul. Scott rented a small office downtown where he revised the page proofs of his second novel, *The Beautiful and Damned* (1922), and wrote his story "The Popular Girl." But neither Scott nor Zelda was prepared to settle down to a conventional domestic life. They continued to offend the proprieties, and almost always drinking was involved (Koblas, *Fitzgerald in Minnesota*, 35–41).

On December 1, Fitzgerald gave a talk at the Women's City Club of St. Paul. His friend Tom Boyd wrote an account for the *St. Paul Daily News* that captured the spirit(s) of the occasion. "Just before my first novel came out," Boyd reported Fitzgerald as saying, "Mr. Perkins . . . told me that he thought it would be a very nice thing if I spoke. . . . It was quite a remarkable speech. Several children were carried out screaming." In other remarks, Fitzgerald denied knowing anything about flappers. "The flapper is interested in shocking people. None of my heroines ever cared enough about people to know whether they were shocking them or not." He did provide a few items of information about himself. "I am 25. Married, white, and I have never been in jail—voluntarily. I have no political opinions. I don't know how to play the piano and I can't hammer brass." The tone of the talk, it seems safe to speculate, ran counter to that of most speeches delivered at the Women's City Club (Wycherly, "F the Lecturer").

Scott and Zelda combined talents to compose a mock front page of the "St. Paul Daily Dirge" for the "Bad Luck Ball" held at the University Club on Friday the thirteenth of January. In this satirical piece the Fitzgeralds thumbed their noses at St. Paul. "Cotillion Is Sad Failure" read the headline, followed by the subhead "Frightful Orgy at University Club." In the stories, the community's leading lights were castigated, by their real names, for supposed misbehavior. Two of them, for example, are described as engaging in a "sordid fist fight" at the ball, exactly the sort of thing that might be expected of St. Paul's "vain frivolous peacocks" (Mizener, *The Far Side of Paradise*, 149).

By June 1922 Zelda had grown restless at their Goodrich Avenue home, and the Fitzgeralds moved to the White Bear Yacht Club for sunshine, relaxation, and a change of pace. Summer parties naturally gravitated to the club, and the Fitzgeralds joined in the merriment. They were alike in believing that "if you were good enough you not only could live according to the hedonistic code of the twenties but would probably turn out better for doing so" (*The Far Side of Paradise*, 163). The club disagreed. For the second time in a year the Fitzgeralds were asked to leave their place of residence. At the end of August they went back to the Commodore. In the middle of October they headed east to rent a house in Great Neck, Long Island. Fitzgerald never lived in St. Paul again, but as a setting it was to figure prominently in his fiction.

III

In "The Ice Palace" (1920), a story written before he and Zelda were married, Scott Fitzgerald drew sharp lines of demarcation between the climate, the culture, and the people of Montgomery, Alabama, and those of St. Paul, Minnesota, communities disguised as "Tarleton, Georgia" and a "Northern city." "The Ice Palace" had its origin in two separate incidents of late 1919. In November Scott was in St. Paul, coming home from a motion-picture show, when "a scattering of confetti-like snow blew along the street" and he thought of the long bleak winters he had spent there. A few weeks later he was visiting Zelda in Montgomery, where everything seemed warm and comfortable. She took him to a graveyard and told him he would never understand how she felt about the Confederate graves. He responded that he understood so well that he could put it down on paper. The next day, riding the train north, it came to him "that it was all one story" (Hackl, *"Still Home to Me,"* 53). He wrote the graveyard into "The Ice Palace," and the snow as well.

The story opens on a languid September day in Tarleton, with Sally Carrol Happer resting "her nineteen-year-old chin [exactly Zelda's age] on a fifty-two-year-old" windowsill. Sally Carrol raises herself upright "with profound inertia" in order to go swimming with her friend Clark Darrow, who has been "dozing round the lazy streets" of his home town since graduating from Georgia Tech. On their drive to the swimming hole, everything and everybody they pass looks drugged. Downtown, "the population *idled casually* across the streets and a drove of low-moaning oxen were being urged along in front of a *placid* street-car; even the shops seemed only *yawning* their doors and *blinking* their windows in the sunshine before retiring into a state of utter and finite *coma*." Out in the country they encounter "a *drowsy* picturesqueness" as the heat flows down, "never hostile, only comforting, like a *great warm nourishing bosom for the infant earth*" (*Short Stories*, 48–52, italics mine). Sally Carrol is sound asleep by the time they reach the swimming hole.

Acculturated though she is to sleepy Southern ways, Sally Carrol wants "to go places and see people," wants her mind to grow, wants to live where things happen on a big scale. So she becomes engaged to Harry Bellamy, who is tall, broad, brisk, energetic, and very much a Yankee. Reenacting Scott and Zelda's experience, Sally Carrol takes Harry to the graveyard, where she romanticizes the lost cause of the Confederate soldiers. There were "streaks of strange courtliness and chivalry in some of these boys," she maintains, and they "died for the most beautiful thing in the world— the dead South." He understands, Harry says. And in mid-January when she comes to his city (of St. Paul), he promises to show her the enchantments of a different landscape. "There's a winter carnival on, and if you've never really seen snow it'll be like fairy-land to you."

"Will I be cold?" she asks, and he reassures her. She may freeze her nose but won't be shivery cold. "It's hard and dry, you know" (54). Sally Carrol has her doubts, for she doesn't like cold in any form, and as it turns out St. Paul in winter proves to be anything but fairyland. During her train ride north, it is very cold in the Pullman, and the porter has no extra blanket to give her. In the morning, the snow has filtered into the vestibules between cars as she stumbles her way to the dining car. "Sometimes a solitary farmhouse would fly by" outside the window, "ugly and bleak and lone on *the white waste*; and with each one she had an instant of *chill compassion* for the souls shut in there waiting for spring" (55, italics mine).

It's too cold in St. Paul even for kissing, Sally Carrol finds. Harry encourages her to "feel the pep in the air," but she feels instead the frozen ambience of the place. Unlike her home, this Northern city has no real past to celebrate. The library in the Bellamy house is full of rows upon rows of books and is furnished "with a lot of fairly expensive things" that look "about fifteen years old." She cannot help contrasting it with "the battered old library at home," with its huge medical books and oil paintings of her great-uncles and an old but still luxurious couch that showed the scars of its mending forty-five years ago (56). Northerners make no concessions to her Southern ways. Harry's mother insists on calling her "Sally" instead of "Sally Carrol" and disapproves of her smoking. His Scandinavian sister-in-law seems incredibly listless, and it remains for a college professor—a newcomer from Philadelphia—to explain why. The people of St. Paul are "freezing up," he thinks, gradually becoming gloomy and melancholy like Swedes (59–60). In a climactic scene Sally Carrol nearly freezes to death in the maze of the winter carnival's ice palace. Harry rescues her, but now she is determined to go back home to the golden sunlight with its "quite enervating yet oddly comforting heat" (69). The story comes full circle at the end, with Sally Carrol resting her chin on the windowsill and Clark Darrow stopping by in his ancient Ford to take her swimming.

The ice palace Sally Carrol got lost in resembled the actual ones erected for St. Paul's winter carnival. The largest of these, built in 1886, rose "three stories in the air, with battlements and embrasures and narrow icicled windows," and with a maze, just as in the story (Koblas, *Fitzgerald in Minnesota*, 54). Fitzgerald may have seen photographs of that ice palace, and he certainly knew about the one erected in 1916, when the city's winter carnival resumed after some years of inactivity. "The Ice Palace" was faithful to the past in this sense and proved uncannily accurate as a prediction of the future.

Zelda Sayre did not come to St. Paul before she and Scott were married in the spring of 1920. When she arrived there a year and a half later, her response to the weather precisely followed the lines her husband sketched out in the story. Zelda stuck it out through one St. Paul winter, but she and Scott were gone before the first snows of the next one.

To judge by his various writings on the subject, Fitzgerald himself was of two minds about the wintry weather of his home town. In "Winter Dreams," his protagonist, Dexter Green, skis across the Sherry Island golf course at Black Bear Lake "when the days became crisp and gray, and the long Minnesota winter shut down like the white lid of a box." At such times the country made Dexter feel a "profound melancholy. . . . When he crossed the hills, the wind blew cold as misery, and if the sun was out he tramped with his eyes squinted up against the hard dimensionless glare" (*Short Stories*, 217). During the long fallow winter Dexter dreams of the things he aims one day to possess. But the most glittering prize of all, the wealthy and beautiful Judy Jones, remains beyond his grasp.

In this story Fitzgerald surely had in mind his own rejection by Ginevra King, a girl every bit as desirable as Judy Jones, and just as inaccessible. Ginevra came from Lake Forest, the exclusive enclave north of Chicago, and Scott met her during a Christmas party at St. Paul's Town and Country Club when she was visiting her school friend Marie Hersey. Scott fell deeply in love with Ginevra and courted her throughout his college years. Losing her was one of the great disappointments of his life. Although married and a new father at the time he wrote "Winter Dreams" at the White Bear Yacht Club during the summer of 1922, the story poignantly evoked the pain of that loss.

But some of Fitzgerald's memories of winter contradicted the bleak views presented in "The Ice Palace" and "Winter Dreams." He fondly remembered the sleigh rides of his youth, for example. "It would be three when we set out in thick coats and sweaters, the girls flushed and consciously athletic, the boys slightly embarrassed but rakish in jumping off and on with complete abandon, to a chorus of little shrieks of simulated anxiety. At a dusky five o'clock we'd reach our destination, usually a club, and have hot chocolate and chicken sandwiches and a dance or two by the gramophone" (qtd. in Koblas, *Fitzgerald in Minnesota*, 41–42).

In *The Great Gatsby*, Fitzgerald's narrator recalls taking the train home from prep school and college at Christmastime. When it pulled out of Chicago's Union Station into the winter night heading northwest to the Twin Cities, "and the real snow, our snow, began to stretch out beside us and twinkle against the windows, and the dim lights of small Wisconsin stations moved by, a sharp wild brace came suddenly into the air. We drew in deep breaths of it as we walked back from dinner through the cold vestibules, unutterably aware of our identity with this country for one strange hour, before we melted indistinguishably into it again."

"That's my Middle West," he continues in celebration, "the thrilling, returning trains of my youth, and the street lamps and sleigh bells in the frosty dark and the shadows of holly wreaths thrown by lighted windows on the snow" (137). Unlike Sally Carrol Happer, Nick Carraway takes in deep drafts of the frigid air and finds them bracing rather than chilling. The cold, like the snow ("our snow"), was part of him. Eventually, though, Fitzgerald renounced those "damn Minnesota winters" (Fitzgerald, *Life in Letters*, 271) while continuing to look back on certain events with nostalgia.

The adventures of Basil Duke Lee, written in 1928 and 1929 and collected in *The Basil and Josephine Stories*, closely track Fitzgerald's youth in St. Paul and at the Newman School. The stories present recognizable people and places from his boyhood and can be traced to their origins in the yearly ledger he kept. Two ledger entries of his fourteenth year, for example, directly link to his story called "The Scandal Detectives." March 1911: "—the founding of 'The Scandal Detectives.'" April 1911: "—the Scandal detectives go after Reuben." Similarly, the September 1911 entry—"Attended state fair and took chicken on roller coaster"—helped form the basis of "A Night at the Fair." Yet another story, "The Captured Shadow," borrows its title from Scott's second boyhood play. It is the perspective Fitzgerald adopts in these stories that takes them beyond a mere recounting of the triumphs and humiliations of his young protagonist.

Writing in his early thirties, Fitzgerald looked back at himself in the guise of the teenager Basil Duke Lee (a name whose exact rhythm and aristocratic overtones are reminiscent of Francis Scott Key). The Basil stories admirably display the "double vision" that Malcolm Cowley noted in Fitzgerald's writing. The calamitous things that happen to Basil are so moving that a sensitive reader cannot help empathizing with him. Yet these disasters are at the same time depicted with ironic detachment. The author occupies a position both within and without the action, as if he were simultaneously the emotionally involved participant and the philosophical observer (Bryer and Kuehl, introduction, xxii–xxiv). Occasionally Fitzgerald seems to regard his autobiographical protagonist as if he were another person entirely. After depicting Basil's disastrous first year at St. Regis, for example, the authorial voice reflects on his hero's present situation and future prospects. "[Basil] believed that everything was a matter of effort . . . and his fantastic ambition was continually leading him to expect too much. He wanted to be a great athlete, popular, brilliant, and always happy. During this year at school, where he had been punished for his 'freshness,' for fifteen years of thorough spoiling at home, he had grown uselessly introspective, and this interfered with that observation of others which is the beginning of wisdom" (78).

Basil struggles to succeed despite his undue egotism and his precarious position as "one of the poorest boys in a rich boys' school" (59). Unreasonable expectations lead him to a succession of embarrassing defeats. Yet he sloughs off these setbacks and slogs along through adolescence, for he possesses that essential *vitality* whose loss Fitzgerald was to lament in the essays of *The Crack-Up* (1936). At the end of "He Thinks He's Wonderful," Basil realizes that he has lost his chance to travel west with the enchanting Minnie Bibble by bragging about himself too eagerly and too long. "He lay on his bed, baffled, mistaken, miserable but not beaten. Time after time, the same vitality that had led his spirit to a scourging made him able to shake off the blood like water" and to go on, wounded, "to new disasters and new atonements" (97–98).

In the earliest Basil Duke Lee stories, the protagonist exhibits this vitality by functioning as neighborhood organizer and inventor, just as Fitzgerald had. The characters in the stories are modeled on Fitzgerald's St. Paul companions. Margaret Armstrong becomes Imogene Bissel; Marie Hersey is Margaret Torrence; Cecil Read is Riply Buckner; Reuben Warner is Hubert Blair; the Ameses' yard with its tree house becomes the Whartons' yard; and the youthful Basil, blessed with imagination, is of course Scott Fitzgerald: "a shining-eyed, brown-haired boy of fourteen, rather small as yet, and bright and lazy at school" (17).

His imagination led Basil/Scott to create "THE BOOK OF SCANDAL," containing dubious revelations about a neighbor's supposed criminal past and a local lad's attendance at the burlesque show. As a scandal detective Basil attempts to emulate the suave example of Arsene Lupin, the gentleman burglar in the Maurice Leblanc stories Fitzgerald had been reading. Lupin segues into "that elusive gentleman, Basil Lee, better known as the Shadow" (55). By whatever name, this greatly admired character is a *gentleman* burglar" (43), a romanticized figure who moves smoothly in the highest social circles and by his bravado manages to control and dominate them.

The theme of sexual competition pervades the Basil Duke Lee stories. Basil/Scott is persistently confronted by a rival in the person of Hubert Blair/Reuben Warner, an acrobatically graceful lad who "possessed the exact tone that all girls of fourteen, and a somewhat cruder type of grown women, find irresistible" (50). This description owed its jaundiced tone to various boyhood defeats Scott suffered at Reuben's hands. "It was at a Saturday night party in [Ben Griggs's] house in 1911," according to Koblas, "that Scott lost his childhood sweetheart Margaret Armstrong to his old friend and nemesis Reuben Warner" (*Fitzgerald in Minnesota*, 22).

Even in fiction, Basil/Scott cannot defeat his rival. In "A Night at the Fair," a story that takes place at the Minnesota State Fair, Hubert Blair seems to have lost the game when he strolls by the assembled crowd in the company of a "chicken" (a "common girl," Fitzgerald explains) he has just picked up. The Van Schellingers, in their box, are properly horrified and invite Basil who, luckily, has just abandoned his "chicken," to sit in their box as they watch a reenactment of the Battle of Gettysburg. (These reenactments were regularly presented at Minnesota State Fairs of the time.) Later, he rides home with the desirable Gladys Van Schellinger.

There is a tender touching of hands, and Gladys, who like Basil is going east to school, urges him to come see her the next day. Then she turns to him, her breath warm against his cheek. "Basil—Basil, when you come tomorrow, will you bring that Hubert Blair?" (*Basil*, 57).

This putdown in "A Night at the Fair" is one of several that Fitzgerald's hero suffers in the nine Basil Duke Lee stories. Usually Basil deserves the blows for letting his outsize ego run out of control. "Hubert Blair is the nicest boy in town and you're the most conceited," Margaret Torrence tells him "with deep conviction" (25). When he goes east to school, Basil hopes to shake off his unpopularity in a new environment that he romanticizes: "Beyond the dreary railroad stations of Chicago and the night fires of Pittsburgh, back in the old states, something went on that made his heart beat fast with excitement" (147). But Basil has not yet grown up enough to recognize that other people exist. He continually boasts about himself, offers unasked-for advice, and achieves at St. Regis (Newman) the same sorry status he'd earned at Country Day (S.P.A.): that of "the freshest boy in school." The headmaster, who has seen many students come and go, is bewildered by Basil's immediate and extraordinary unpopularity among schoolmates and teachers alike. "It was most probably one of those intangible questions of personality," he concludes (60).

After an unhappy year at St. Regis, Basil comes home for the summer, having learned "that others had wills as strong as his, and more power" (92). He affects a posture of consideration for others, and for a time it looks as if he will finally conquer St. Paul after all. During a game of Truth on Imogene Bissel's veranda, Gladys Van Schellinger (the only young person present who arrived in a limousine) confesses that Basil is her favorite boy in St. Paul, if not in the East, and Imogene declares Basil her favorite boy, period. But these public victories turn Basil's head, and soon he is waxing expansive as he instructs Joe Gorman. He himself had been unpopular at school for a while, Basil admits, "because I was fresh, I guess. But the thing must be that some boys are popular with boys and some are popular with girls." Joe should be more polite to older people, Basil advises him. He should stop wearing white ties, for nobody who went east to school wore them. It would be even better if Joe himself went east to school. On and on Basil goes, as if to transform Joe Gorman from "little more than a Midwestern bumpkin to an Easterner bursting with *savoir-faire* and [like himself] irresistible to girls" (83–85). Joe, of course, does not appreciate hearing about his shortcomings and converts Basil's ramblings into one brief damning sentence: "Joe said you told him that all the girls thought you were wonderful." "I never said anything like that," Basil indignantly protests, but the damage has been done (90). Once again he has talked too much and must suffer the consequences.

Although Basil brings most of his humiliations upon himself, Fitzgerald makes it clear that his young hero operates at a disadvantage. The issue of social class runs through the stories, quietly revealing Basil's unsteady position on the edge of the city's aristocracy. Basil, like Scott, is stigmatized, for example, for having a father not worth talking about. Mr. Lee's name is pointedly omitted in several places. The Van Schellingers introduce Basil as "Alice Riley's boy" (51), with no mention of his father. Basil happily reflects that "this summer he and his mother and sister were going to the lakes and next fall he was starting away to school" (21). At St. Regis he gets a letter from his mother with the news that "Grandfather is going abroad to take the waters and he wants you and me to come too" (69). It is as if Basil's father did not exist.

Like his creator, Basil is fully aware of his economic dependence on his mother's family. "Where would we be," Mollie Fitzgerald used to remark at the dinner table, "if it wasn't for Grandfather McQuillan?" (Donaldson, *Fool for Love*, 6). In response to a letter from Basil's mother, the St. Regis headmaster calls him on the carpet for poor grades. "I believe you have been sent here at a certain amount of—ah—sacrifice" (*Basil*, 59), he harrumphs, as Basil writhes in shame. His family's financial circumstances are forcefully brought home to him in "Forging Ahead," when his mother loses a great deal of money in the stock market and tells Basil that she cannot afford to send him to Yale, the college he's long dreamed of attending.

In the early 1910s, driving an automobile represented a way of establishing one's standing among the rich. Fitzgerald's ledger for July 1912 contains two possibly related entries: "Began to feel lack of automobile" and "growing unpopular." Both of these apply to the adventures of Basil Duke Lee. In "A Night at the Fair," Basil is too young to drive but not too young to recognize the connection between possession of an automobile and sexual power. At the fair, he and his friend Riply are transfixed by the sight of a Blatz Wildcat (Stutz Bearcat), small, red, low-slung, and "for the next five years . . . the ambition of several million American boys." A blonde, baby-faced girl reclines on the sloping seat of the car, which is driven by a pink-faced, pink-haired young man in a yellow suit. This is Speed Paxton, son of a local brewer. Speed is "dimly terrible," and his fancy automobile will not win him access to St. Paul's coming-out parties. But Basil and Riply envy him for the chariot he drives and the provocative girl at his side (38). The next day, having decided he will not go to the fair (his new long pants have not arrived), Basil thinks of the girls he will not meet as a result: the most desirable girls imaginable, riding off in Blatz Wildcats without his having kissed them (47).

The next year Basil, now old enough to drive, feels increasingly frustrated by the lack of a family car. He rides the train back from the East with Margaret Torrence, who announces that "we're going to get an automobile . . . and I'm going to learn to drive." "That's fine," Basil lamely replies, while wondering if his grandfather (again, there is no father in sight) might let him drive his electric (79). The lack of an automobile figures most prominently in "He Thinks He's Wonderful," a story set during the summer of 1912. "An element of vast importance had made its appearance with the summer; suddenly the great thing in Basil's crowd was to own an automobile. Fun no longer seemed available save at great distances, at suburban lakes or remote country clubs. Walking downtown ceased to be a legitimate pastime. On the contrary, a single block from one youth's house to another's must be navigated in a car. Dependent groups formed around owners who began to wield what was, to Basil at least, a disconcerting power" (86). The extent of that power is brought home when Basil must more or less beg a ride to a Saturday-night dance at the lake.

In this story, Basil's fortunes swing wildly between the poles of joy and despair. In separate incidents his unfortunate habit of boasting brings him down from the heights. Imogene Bissel is attracted to him at the dance, but when she leads him to a private spot at the end of the pier he cannot stop talking about himself long enough to seize his opportunity. Conspicuously uninvited to a party Joe Gorman has organized, he is lucky enough to meet the visiting Minnie Bibble instead. They get along wonderfully until he bores her father by talking about himself. That mistake is forgotten, though, in a rather contrived happy ending. It so happens that his grandfather will let him use the electric in the afternoons if he keeps the batteries charged and washes the car once a week. And it so happens that Imogene Bissel has not gone to Joe Gorman's house party after all and would love to go riding in the electric with him. As the story concludes, they are cruising down Crest Avenue at a heady fifteen miles an hour, Basil triumphantly at the wheel, the girl of the moment at his side.

His grandfather's electric hardly stacks up against a Blatz Wildcat, but Basil makes it serve in his ongoing entanglements with girls. Minnie Bibble comes back into the picture in "Forging Ahead," during a period when Basil is working to help pay his way to Yale. They meet during a dance at the "Lake Club." Minnie, from New Orleans, will be staying three weeks and is eager to renew their romantic liaison. He could come out to the lake in the evenings to see her, she suggests. "It's only half an hour in a car." When he points out that he doesn't have a car, she is undeterred: "I mean you can get your family's car." But "it's an electric," he says, meaning only an electric and slower than a gasoline-driven car (156).

Then Minnie boldly takes the initiative, presenting herself at Basil's house one afternoon as he comes home from work. She has only an hour before she must rejoin her family in town. They could take a ride in her car, she suggests, but the chauffeur might get in the way. "He listens," she explains. So the electric is made to serve after all. The chauffeur drops them off at "grampa's house," and Basil steers the electric to a secluded spot on the bluffs. "Suddenly she was whispering in his arms, 'You're first, Basil—nobody but you'" (158). Fade-out to bliss.

The Basil Duke Lee stories constitute Fitzgerald's closest fictional representation of his teenage years in St. Paul. At times he considered looking much further back into his origins. In June 1922 he wrote Perkins from White Bear that he was thinking about launching a third novel. "Its locale will be the middle west and New York at 1885 I think. It will concern less superlative beauties than I run to usually and will be centered on a smaller period of time. It will have a catholic element" (*Dear Scott/Dear Max*, 61). The third novel turned out to be *The Great Gatsby* (1925), Fitzgerald's masterpiece. *Gatsby* bears little resemblance to the historical novel with "a catholic element" that he proposed, except for its contrast between the East, as the locus of opportunity, and the Middle West, as the locus of morality. And although not so identified, Nick Carraway's home town is clearly St. Paul. Fitzgerald wrote a good deal less about St. Paul, Minnesota, than Faulkner did about Oxford, Mississippi, and a good deal more about it than Hemingway did about Oak Park, Illinois. None of them could shake off the heritage of the places they came from.

IV

A number of St. Paul people who knew Fitzgerald or whose parents and grandparents knew him deprecate any assertion that he had reason to feel insecure about his social position. The St. Paul where Roger Kennedy, historian and former director of the Smithsonian Institution, grew up (a generation later than Fitzgerald) was not at all hierarchical. "Scott was a part of us," insisted Norris Jackson, who married Betty Ames and moved into the house that Fitzgerald commemorated for its spacious backyard in the Basil stories (Hackl, *"Still Home to Me,"* 12). Kennedy and Jackson, like most others who share their conviction, felt quite comfortable and secure about their own social standing in the community. They accepted Fitzgerald without so much as thinking about it. If he was beset by worries about his status, it must have been because he let his overactive imagination transform reality.

To a certain degree these St. Paulites are right. Fitzgerald, like his fellow Irishman John O'Hara, can fairly be called the master of the imagined slight. He repeatedly embarrassed and abased himself before those he considered his betters, Gerald and Sara Murphy, for example. In order to remember—and perhaps to cultivate—such incidents, he kept lists of where and by whom he had been snubbed. Undoubtedly Fitzgerald exaggerated the slights he suffered throughout his life and, in particular, during his youth in St. Paul. But his home town was complicit to a degree in inspiring those feelings. Scott did not invent the social structure of St. Paul that he described in his nonfiction and dramatized in several stories and novels. In a very real sense, the city contributed to the sense of inferiority his parents bequeathed to Scott Fitzgerald.

A dream he had in the spring of 1931, shortly after his father's funeral, plumbs the depths of Fitzgerald's insecurity. In the dream he is living with his clumsy old mother in an upstairs apartment. On another floor there is a group of rich and handsome young men he would like to know better. He talks with one of them, who seems amiable but does not encourage the acquaintance—"whether because he considers me poor, unimportant, ill bred or of ill renown I don't know, or rather don't think about—only I scent the polite indifference *and even understand it*" (italics mine). Next he discovers there is a dance downstairs to which he has not been invited. He feels that if "they" knew how important he was, he would have been asked to attend.

The dream circles back to his mother. They have been quarreling, possibly, Fitzgerald proposes, because of his "ill-humour at being neglected by the people downstairs." He mistakenly wanders into the party and stammers "something absurd" to one of the fashionable young men. As he escapes, his mother calls out "in a too audible voice from an upper story." He reflects: "I don't know whether I am angry with her for clinging to me, or because I am ashamed of her for not being young and chic, or for disgracing my conventional sense by calling out, or because she might guess I'd been hurt and pity me, which would have been unendurable, or all those things. Anyway I call back at her some terse and furious reproach."

Further gaffes by his mother follow. She complains that she is not being served an adequate portion of food, but those serving her decline to remedy the situation. Mother and son go home together, where she locates a book for Scott and pathetically asks him if it isn't a book he'd loved and lost in his childhood. It resembles that book but is not quite the right one. Later in the dream she calls out to him once more, and he again answers angrily (Donaldson, *Fool for Love*, 13–15).

This dream suggests how closely Fitzgerald's sense of social insecurity related to his feelings about his mother. If only she had been richer, smarter, better bred, more attractive, then the young men would presumably have welcomed Scott into their company and seen to it that he was invited to the dance. The dream itself he recorded for Margaret Egloff, a psychiatrist and intimate friend he met in Switzerland during the time that Zelda was institutionalized. After extended conversations with Fitzgerald, Egloff concluded that he yearned to identify with, and become one with, "the rich, powerful, and chic of the world. . . . The fact that he was not born into that society galled him, and he hated himself for his own and everyone else's snobbery" (*Fool for Love*, 15). He despised his mother for her social aspirations and hated himself for adopting them. He understood how foolish it was to care so desperately about the good opinion of people he did not, at bottom, even respect, but he could not stop himself.

Fitzgerald had a hard time making up his mind about his home town, and his home town reciprocated the feeling. "I no longer regard St. Paul as my home any more than the eastern seaboard or the Riviera," Scott wrote Marie Hersey in 1934. After all, he pointed out, his father was an easterner, and he himself had gone east to college and never returned after the fourteen-month stay in 1921 and 1922. Near the end of his life he embraced the Maryland roots of his father's family, reaching back to early colonial times. He chose to be buried in Rockville, beside the graves of his parents. Yet in another mood he wrote Xandra Kalman in the late 1930s that St. Paul was "still home to me" and told her that he planned to bring his daughter, Scottie, to St. Paul for the summer, so she could see where he'd been brought up—a plan that did not materialize (S.P.A. Fitzgerald Archive).

Writers are rarely honored in their lifetimes by the places where they grew up. Like Fitzgerald, they are usually too bold in unmasking pretensions and challenging conventional mores to please genteel society. And often, like Fitzgerald, they rebel against their roots by one or another kind of overt misbehavior. Clifton Read remembers sailing at White Bear one summer when Fitzgerald was just beginning to publish stories and overhearing a prim young wife remark about him, "Well, he may have talent, but he's too racy for me" (S.P.A. Fitzgerald Archive). Not even the revival of interest in Fitzgerald's work during the 1950s and 1960s reconciled St. Paul to its wayward native son. Not, in fact, until a hundred years after his birth, and fifty-six years after his death in Hollywood did his home town unbend to honor Fitzgerald as one of its most eminent citizens.

Garrison Keillor had much to do with this recognition. First, he saw to it that the World Theater in downtown St. Paul, from which the *Prai-*

rie Home Companion radio show usually broadcasts, was renamed the Fitzgerald Theater. For the centenary itself in 1996, he brought some of the nation's greatest writers together to pay homage to Fitzgerald and his work. Leading citizens in the community joined in the observances, commissioning a handsome statue of Fitzgerald in Rice Park, downtown.

At the end of his essay "Early Success" (1937), Fitzgerald looks back on the days when he was beginning his career and dreaming of success. Sometimes, he says, he can make his way back "into the mind of that young man with cardboard soles" in his shoes, "creep up on him, surprise him on an autumn morning in New York or a spring night in Carolina when it is so quiet that you can hear a dog barking in the next county" (*Crack-Up*, 90). As aftercomers we may catch a glimpse of the author in St. Paul when he was even younger, still a boy too full of himself, insecure about his social status, unpopular in his overeagerness to please, consumed by dreams of mastery, and wonderfully imaginative in conceiving dramatic situations that would remove him, for a time, from cold harsh reality.

To catch that glimpse, let us walk with Scott past the handsome homes of Summit Avenue, the street where he did not quite belong. It is Saturday afternoon, August 24, 1912, the day after the successful performance of his play *The Captured Shadow*. During our walk, we pause at the bluff to gaze at the winding Mississippi and the bustle of the city below. The boy at our side has every right to be proud of himself, and for a time he goes on expansively about the play and the old man who told him, "You'll be heard from one day," after the curtain came down, and the newspaper reporter who asked him if he was really only fifteen (*Basil*, 119). Then a mood of melancholy steals over him, mirroring the hint of fall in the late summer air. Part of that feeling comes from the hollowness like fear that comes after completing a work: his play was over, done and gone. A greater part derives from the boy's beginning to understand that, no matter what he does, it will not alter the way most people in his home town regard him. A few weeks earlier, in an incident he would never forget, he had been conspicuously left out of a party that was organized right before his eyes.

We should not wish it otherwise. Lacking the heritage of disappointment and embarrassment and defeat that St. Paul bestowed on him, Fitzgerald might not have written the great stories or *The Great Gatsby* or *Tender Is the Night*. More than anywhere else he lived, and he lived in many places, it was his home town—the Midwestern yet eastern-leaning city of St. Paul—that made Fitzgerald the great writer he became: ever sensitive to social mortification, ever yearning after the uncapturable.

{ 2 }

FITZGERALD'S ROMANCE WITH
THE SOUTH

I

I suppose that poetry is a Northern man's dream of the South.

—FITZGERALD, *SHORT STORIES*

Settling into a house in the San Fernando Valley in 1938, Scott Fitzgerald thought the place rather drab, but when Buff Cobb came for a visit, admired the garden, and remarked that its fence pickets looked "like little gravestones in a Confederate graveyard," Fitzgerald ran inside to tell Sheilah Graham that Buff had "made the place livable! We've got romance in the house" (Graham and Frank, *Infidel*, 266–67).

F. Scott Fitzgerald's attitudes toward the American South were shaped by two important relationships: with his wife, Zelda Sayre of Alabama, and with his father, Edward Fitzgerald of Maryland. Born and bred in the North, Fitzgerald developed an early tug toward the country of his father's youth, sympathizing with the lost cause of the Confederacy and admiring the impeccable manners of the Old South. This tendency to glamorize the South, inherited from his father, he never lost.

It was different with the reckless young girl who caught him on the rebound at a 1918 dance in Montgomery. Zelda materialized before his eyes in her fluffy organdy beneath a wide-brimmed hat as "the very incarnation of a Southern belle" (Turnbull, *Fitzgerald*, 86–87). Perhaps Fitzgerald fell in love with the image as much as with the girl; she brought glitteringly alive to him his own ties to the South. Together they took flower-scented walks where the wall "was clamp and mossy . . . [and] the wisteria along the fence was green and the shade was cool and life was old" (Turnbull, *Fitzgerald*, 275, 101–2). To celebrate their engagement, they strolled past the headstones of the Confederate dead, and Zelda told him he would never understand how she felt about those graves, but he insisted that he did—and proved it in "The Ice Palace."

To Fitzgerald their marriage seemed symbolic, "the mating of the age" between the golden beauty of the South and the brilliant success of the North (Milford, *Zelda*, 306). But Zelda, like any mere mortal, was inadequate to the ideal; their marriage fractured even before her beauty faded and her mind fissured. As early as 1922, the honeymoon barely over, he wrote Edmund Wilson of "the complete, fine and full-hearted selfishness and chill-mindedness of Zelda" (*Letters*, 331). That disillusionment, suggested by his novels, is spun out in half a dozen stories Fitzgerald wrote during the 1920s about the confrontation of a young man from the North with the woman he loves from the South: stories that could hardly have been more autobiographical.

This theme occupies center stage in "The Ice Palace" (1920), which contrasts the Southern—Sally Carrol Happer, indolence, heat, and a sense of the past peculiar to Tarleton, Georgia—with the Northern—her fiancé Harry Bellamy, vigor, cold, and the three-generation newness of St. Paul, Minnesota. Fitzgerald told his friend Alexander McKaig that Zelda's ideas were "entirely responsible" for "The Ice Palace" (Turnbull, *Fitzgerald*, 115).

But it is her story in another, more significant way as well, for the action is filtered through the consciousness of her fictional double, Sally Carrol. The sympathies of the reader are enlisted on Sally Carrol's side and on the side of the South in the clash of cultures. She is frightened and lost in the frozen North: we tremble for her. But she is also lovely and intelligent, and despite her comic lassitude she retains a certain dignity: we are charmed by her.

The romantic appeal of the South was mingled in Fitzgerald's mind with the golden girl. For Southern young men he had only scorn: in his fiction they are weak, indolent, and not especially bright. It is the Southern girl in whom Fitzgerald invests his romantic illusions—and it is by the Southern girl, too, that these illusions are shattered.

In two stories of 1924, "Gretchen's Forty Winks" and "'The Sensible Thing,'" he sketches out the sources of this disillusionment. Gretchen, married to young advertising man Roger Halsey, "was a Southern girl, and any question that had to do with getting ahead in the world always tended to give her a headache" (Fitzgerald, *Short Stories*, 168). Totally selfish, she insists on entertaining herself with another man while her husband struggles through six weeks of day-and-night work to establish himself in the advertising business. "I'll go out with him all I want," she tells Roger when he objects. "Do you think it's any fun living here with you?" (177). In a slick magazine ending (the story ran in the *Saturday Evening Post*), Roger succeeds and Gretchen spurns the other man, who suffers a nervous breakdown, but her "complete, fine, and full-hearted selfishness" has stretched the bonds of matrimony to the breaking point. And "'The Sensible Thing'"—"about Zelda and me, all true," Scott assured Maxwell Perkins—reflects Fitzgerald's abiding resentment at Zelda for stringing him along and torturing him with other beaus during their courtship.

Fitzgerald's ultimate rejection of the Southern belle, however, did not come until 1929 with "The Last of the Belles." The setting is Tarleton during World War I, and the young lady is Ailie Calhoun,

> the Southern type in all its purity. . . . She had the adroitness sugar-coated with sweet, voluble simplicity, the suggested background of devoted fathers, brothers and admirers stretching back into the South's heroic age, the unfailing coolness acquired in the endless struggle with the heat. There were notes in her voice that ordered slaves around, that withered up Yankee captains, and then soft, wheedling notes that mingled in unfamiliar loveliness with the night.
>
> (450)

She is, in short, all artifice (Fitzgerald knew what he was doing with that "adroitness sugar-coated" and her "soft, wheedling notes"), and she holds in thrall several young pilots who are training nearby.

A heartless coquette, Ailie is as easily reconciled to the death by suicide of one of her rejected admirers (once she is assured that no one will know he has died for her) as she is willing to add to her string the most prized beau of a close friend. The hapless narrator Andy returns after the war to confess his love for Ailie, but she demands not merely love but worship. Dejectedly, he tours the now deserted site of the wartime camp, looking for his youth "in a clapboard or a strip of roofing or a rusty tomato can." But it is no good: his youth like the camp has been dismantled, and "in another month Ailie would be gone, and the South would be empty for [him] forever" (462–63).

Like Basil in "Basil and Cleopatra," another story of 1929, Andy has con-fused place and person, so that "wherever she was, became a beautiful and enchanted place. . . . He thought the fascination was inherent in the locality, and long afterwards a commonplace street or the mere name of a city would exude a peculiar glow, a sustained sound, that struck his soul alert with delight" (165). Basil decides not to pursue his beloved Minnie Bibble (Fitzgerald would not have used that name for a Southern heroine in 1920), and Andy, although he may cherish his memory of Ailie and the South he associates with her, knows both that the dream is over and that she was, after all, unworthy of the dream.

The Southern belle that Scott Fitzgerald bodied forth with the charm-ing and vulnerable Sally Carrol in 1920 was transformed by 1929 into the vicious and calculating Ailie Calhoun. The girls come from the same town, they shop at the same drug store, but there is a world of difference between them. The fictional approach mirrors the distortion of the dream: Sally Carrol tells her own story, but Andy narrates "The Last of the Belles." Despite his incurable love, he possesses the insight to dissect the unlovely personality of Ailie Calhoun. Originally Andy came to the wartime camp as if "on a magic carpet that had landed on the Southern countryside," and he parked on dates "under the broken shadow of a mill where there was the sound of running water and restive squawky birds and over everything a brightness that tried to filter in anywhere—into the lost nigger cabins, the automobile, the fastnesses of the heart. The South sang to us—" (458). But the carpet whisked him back to his home in the North, the brightness faded, and the song turned to dissonance.

As the decade wore on, the fascination that Zelda and the South held for Scott Fitzgerald wore off, and he reached the conclusion that he was locked with his wife in a struggle for survival. In "Two Wrongs" (1930), Fitzgerald suggests one way the struggle might have ended. Bill McChesney, Irish, a drunken producer down on his luck, is married to Emmy Pinkard, dancer, of Delaney, South Carolina. She succeeds in her career, while his health cracks.

In fact, of course, it was Zelda who cracked, and Fitzgerald, left in charge of their daughter Scottie's upbringing, made certain that she avoided those Southern influences that he thought had incapacitated Zelda. He sent her to Miss Walker's and then to Vassar in the Northeast, though not without misgivings. Scottie must not, he warned, let the at-mosphere of wealth and social snobbery at such schools turn her head. When Scottie proposed inviting ninety guests to a party in Baltimore, her father cut the list to sixty (counting on ten or twelve refusals) and chastised her for putting on airs. "If I thought that the Ethel Walker School was going to give you a peculiar idea of what your financial resources are, it would have been far, far better to send you to a modest school here in the Carolina mountains" (*Letters*, 13).

This was an empty threat, really, for Fitzgerald was unalterably opposed to sending Scottie to a Southern school. Still more frightening dangers lurked there than in the East. Though the American South was "tropical and early maturing," it had not, he believed, learned the lessons of other warm climates: "it has never been part of the wisdom of France and Spain to let young girls go unchaperoned at sixteen and seventeen." When Scottie visited her aunt Cecilia Taylor in Norfolk, Fitzgerald cautioned Mrs. Taylor twice in the same letter against letting his daughter consort with any "sixteen-year-old boys who have managed to amass a charred keg and an automobile license as their Start-in-Life. . . . I mean that, about any unreliable Virginia boys taking my pet around. I will never forget it was a Norfolk number . . . who gave me my first drink of whiskey" (*Letters*, 417–18).

Southern boys were not to be trusted, and an air of moral carelessness and intellectual laziness lay over the whole region. Fitzgerald referred to several of Scoittie's friends as "feebs of the Confederacy." When it was proposed that Scottie should spend the summer after graduating from Miss Walker's on visits to her aunt in Norfolk and her mother in Montgomery, Fitzgerald sent her to a summer session at Harvard instead. "You remember," he reminded Zelda in June 1940, "your old idea that people ought to be born on the shores of the North Sea and only in later life drift south toward the Mediterranean in softness? . . . I want Scottie to be hardy and keen and able to fight her own battles and Virginia didn't seem to be the right note—however charming" (*Letters*, 80, 118–19).

The strain of environmental determinism apparent in this letter dictated that Scottie should avoid the insidious appeal of warmer softer climes in order to grow up tough and strong. "Scottie at her best is as she is now with a sense of responsibility and determination. She is at her absolute worst when she lies on her back and waves her feet in the air," Scott wrote Zelda in August 1939. "I am not particularly sorry for a youngster who is thrown on his own at 14 or so and has to make his way through school and college, the old sink or swim spirit—I suppose, *au fond*, the difference of attitude between the North and the old South" (*Letters*, 108).

II

When Zelda cuttingly referred to his father as an Irish policeman, Fitzgerald
retaliated by slapping Zelda hard across the face.

—MILFORD, *ZELDA*

You could call Scott Fitzgerald's father a failure; you could say that he
lacked the drive required of the successful businessman. His son said these
things about Edward Fitzgerald more than once. But not even Zelda, who
knew where to plant the barb, could with impunity reduce her husband's
father to the demeaning status of the Irish cop on the beat.

Fitzgerald regretted Edward Fitzgerald's lack of achievement, but his father remained for him a figure deserving of respect for his style, his manners, and his breeding. If the stock was tired, it was also very old American stock, and Scott was proud of his paternal ancestry. Forever analyzing
himself and his origins, Fitzgerald tended to regard his mother and his
father as almost polar opposites. His well turned-out father came from a
good family but failed in business; his inelegant mother was the daughter
of a successful wholesale grocer. Fitzgerald valued the roots more than the
money. As John Kuehl observed, given Fitzgerald's tendency to "identify
autobiographical and historical events," it seems probable "that his financially inept but 'Old American stock' father came to symbolize pre–Civil
War southern aristocracy while his mother's financially successful but
'black Irish' relatives came to represent post–Civil War northern *nou-
veaux riches*" (Fitzgerald, *Apprentice*, 35).

Edward Fitzgerald qualified as the product of pre-Revolutionary, not
merely pre–Civil War, breeding. Through his mother he was related to
"the Scotts, the Keys, the Dorseys, the Ridgeleys, the Tildens and the
Warfields," all of whom—save for the Keys—"had been in Maryland since
the first half of the sixteen hundreds" (Turnbull, *Fitzgerald*, 337). It was the
connection with Francis Scott Key that Fitzgerald, like his mother, most
coveted. She named her son after him and used to advise his boyhood
companions of the relationship, stressing that Scott "was second to none
in honor of his birth." Fitzgerald himself, inheriting her social insecurity,
claimed the famous Key as his great-grandfather or great-uncle. The connection was not that close; Scott's father's great-great-grandfather was the
brother of Francis Scott Key (*Fitzgerald*, 12, 114, 6–7).

Fitzgerald inherited more than an early-American bloodline from his
father. In a reminiscnce written after Edward Fitzgerald died in 1931, Scott

observed that "always deep in my subconscious I have referred judgments back to him, what he would have thought, or done. . . . He loved me—and felt a deep responsibility for me. I was born several months after the sudden death of my two elder sisters—he felt what the effect of this would be on my mother, that he would be my only moral guide. He became that to the best of his ability" (qtd. in Mizener, *The Far Side of Paradise*, 11). Only slightly altered, the same words are used to characterize Dick Diver's father in *Tender Is the Night* (203).

The morality Edward Fitzgerald taught Scott depended upon a code of honor, an awareness of the existence and rights of others that sometimes worked against his mother's tendency to spoil their son, and the highly developed "sense of the fundamental decencies" that—Nick Carraway observes on the first page of *The Great Gatsby*—he inherited from *his* father. But it was the way this moral standard found expression, the manners that derived from the code, that Scott Fitzgerald most admired in his father. "Southern manners *are* better," he wrote Scottie in June 1940, and added, "especially the rather punctilious deference to older people" (*Letters*, 76). Fitzgerald was cautioning his daughter against any youthful inclination to condescend to her elders. It was a lesson he had well learned from his own father. "Once when I went in a room as a young man," so Edward Fitzgerald told his son, "I was confused so I went up to the oldest woman there and introduced myself and afterwards the people of that town always thought I had good manners." Recalling that incident in "The Death of My Father," Fitzgerald concluded that his father had acted not merely from a desire to please but "from a good heart that came from another America—he was much too sure of what he was . . . to doubt for a moment that his own instincts were good" ("Death," 187–89).

The same incident is also recorded in "The Romantic Egotist," Fitzgerald's first draft for *This Side of Paradise*, where the young protagonist reflects on the difference between himself and his father. "Father had a distinct class sense—I suppose because he was a Southerner. He used to tell me things as precepts of the 'School of Gentlemen' and I'd use them as social tricks with no sense of courtesy whatever" (qtd. in Sklar, *Fitzgerald*, 27). Though he could hardly become a Southern gentleman himself, Fitzgerald felt an affectionate nostalgia for his father's native state. Maryland, he wrote in 1924, was the "loveliest of states, the white-fenced rolling land. This was the state of Charles Carroll of Carrollton, of colonial Annapolis in its flowered brocades. Even now every field seemed to be the lawn of a manor. . . . Here my great-grandfather's great-grandfather was born—and my father too on a farm near Rockville called Glenmary" (Fitzgerald, "Cruise," 62–63).

Maryland became for him an idyllic place, and he resisted any disturbing manifestations of reality. Jason, the protagonist of "Lo, the Poor Peacock," drives the seventy miles from Baltimore to his grandfather's farm in a haze of pleasure, passing "villages he had never wanted to ask the names of, so much did he cherish the image of them in his heart" (*Stories*, 156).

For most of the four years from 1932 to 1936, the Fitzgeralds lived in three separate locations in and around Baltimore, while Zelda underwent treatment at the Phipps Clinic and Sheppard-Pratt Hospital. During this period it became clear that Zelda would require more or less permanent institutional care, and Scott suffered his own "Crack-Up." Despite these woes, however, Fitzgerald felt more at home in Maryland than anywhere else on earth. "Baltimore is warm and pleasant," he wrote in September 1935. "I love it more than I thought—it is so rich with memories—it is nice to look up the street and see the statue of my great uncle [Key] and to know Poe is buried here and that many ancestors of mine have walked in the old town by the bay. I belong here, where everything is civilized and gay and rotted and polite." And the thought of being buried there, resting alongside Zelda in "some old graveyard," he added, was really a happy one, "not melancholy at all" (*Letters*, 531). The next year, after moving to North Carolina, he wrote Baltimore friends that though he "was never a part of Baltimore" he loved the place and would have been content there, were he not such a wanderer (qtd. in Nason, "Afternoon," 10–12).

If Fitzgerald the wanderer had a spiritual home, it was located neither in Zelda's Alabama nor in the hills of Carolina and Virginia, where he periodically retreated to dry out or refresh himself, nor in his native Minnesota but in the flatlands of his father's Maryland. In his foreword to a book of etchings showing *Colonial and Historic Homes of Maryland* (1939), Fitzgerald acknowledged that "there must be hundreds and hundreds of families in such an old state whose ancestral memories are richer and fuller than mine" but he nonetheless considered himself "a native of the Maryland Free State through ancestry and adoption." After citing names of such distinguished relatives as "Caleb Godwin of Hockley-inye-Hole, or Philip Key of Tudor Hall, or Pleasance Ridgeley," he unabashedly signed himself "Francis Scott Key Fitzgerald" (foreword, unpaginated).

When he was a little boy, Edward Fitzgerald stood on the fence outside his Maryland home "watching the butternut battalions of Early stream by on their surprise attempt at Washington, the last great threat of the Confederacy." This story was one he told his son, along with other Civil War yarns. Much of his early childhood in Minnesota, Scott recalled, was spent in asking his father such questions as:

"—and how long did it take Early's column to pass Glenmary that day? (That was a farm in Montgomery County.)"

And:

"tell me again how you used to ride through the woods with a spy up behind you on the horse."

Or:

"Why wouldn't they let Francis Scott Key off the British frigate?"

(FOREWORD)

Edward Fitzgerald's sympathies, and Scott's, rested with the Confederacy; son like father was imbued with the romance of the lost Southern cause. American history fascinated Edward Fitzgerald, and he so transmitted his enthusiasm that his son "remembered from his sixth year books about the Revolution and the Civil War" and before his twelfth year began to write his own history of the United States. This interest in the American past, together with "certain ineradicable" tastes in poetry (which included Poe and Byron), Edward Fitzgerald bequeathed to his son (Fitzgerald, *Crack-Up*, 174).

Above all, the Civil War stories imprinted themselves in Scott's mind, so that much of his juvenile writing took the Civil War as its setting (and some of his late fiction as well, since an incident about a spy hung by his thumbs appears in "The End of Hate," the last serious story published in Fitzgerald's lifetime). Two stories written at St. Paul Academy, when Scott was fourteen and fifteen years old, spin improbable tales of Southern gallantry.

One of them, "A Debt of Honor," introduces a theme Fitzgerald would often explore. Private Jack Sanderson, a Virginia soldier, falls asleep on sentry duty and is pardoned from death for his dereliction by the intervention of Gen. Robert E. Lee, on the grounds that that the boy was "awfully young and of good family too." Given another chance, Jack fights heroically at Chancellorsville, putting Union troops to flight. No matter that Sanderson died in his bravery: "he had paid his debt" (*Apprentice*, 36–38). This 1910 story, like Fitzgerald's 1913 Civil War play *Coward*, takes as its hero a Southern lad who first fails, then gloriously succeeds for the cause.

Failure and success, and the thin line between them, permeate the mature Fitzgerald's depiction of such protagonists as Jay Gatsby and Dick

Diver. It is not improbable that this theme first presented itself to young Fitzgerald in the person of his father, a failure by conventional standards whom his son could not repudiate, yet always "a Southern gentleman" whose well-bred display of "reticences and obligations" gave his son a model of behavior he could only hope to emulate. His father had not succeeded in the eyes of the world, but unlike Zelda and the contemporary deep South she'd grown up in, he lived up to Fitzgerald's image of him as an aristocratic and admirable representative of the Old South.

Scott came back from Europe to attend his father's memorial service in 1931 and saw him laid to rest in the cemetery of St. Mary's Church in Rockville, Maryland. It seemed very friendly, he thought, to leave him there among all his relations. A few years later, his mother was laid to rest in the same place, and Fitzgerald thought it would be fitting to join them there in due course.

Scott died in December 1940, and his body was duly brought back to Maryland. But because he was not a practicing Catholic and had received neither extreme unction before he died nor conditional absolution immediately afterward, the church authorities did not permit him to be buried alongside his parents. Instead he was buried in Rockville Union Cemetery, two miles away. Zelda's remains were laid at his side in 1948 after she died in a fire at Highlands hospital in Asheville, North Carolina.

That might have been that but for the persistent campaign of the Fitzgeralds' daughter, Scottie, to move her parents to St. Mary's where they belonged. With the aid of the Rockville Woman's Club and a young priest "who couldn't have cared less about the doctrine of the thing," Scott and Zelda's remains were transferred there in 1975. It took thirty-five years to happen, and St. Mary's is surrounded by highways and high-rises, but "at least," Scottie wrote, "he's there with his parents and grandparents and other relatives from the Maryland he loved."

PART II

◈ LOVE, MONEY, AND CLASS ◈

[3]

THIS SIDE OF PARADISE

FITZGERALD'S COMING OF AGE NOVEL

F SCOTT FITZGERALD started writing *This Side of Paradise* when he was still a Princeton undergraduate and published it when he was only twenty-three. The book launched Fitzgerald's career as one of the nation's greatest novelists; it also established him as a spokesman for and chronicler of the life and times of his generation. His story of Amory Blaine's passage through adolescence and youth toward maturity has a universal appeal, yet it's very much a young person's novel, speaking most eloquently to readers between fifteen and thirty.

Publishing *This Side of Paradise* was of crucial importance to Fitzgerald's private and professional life, and it did not come easily. He began writing in November 1917, while waiting for his army commission to come through. World War I was raging in Europe, and Fitzgerald was determined to make his mark before facing combat and possibly death. Dispatched to Fort Leavenworth, Kansas, he continued to work on the book. "Every evening, concealing my pad behind Small Problems for Infantry, I wrote paragraph after paragraph on a somewhat edited history of me and my imagination" (qtd. in West, *The Making*, 10). When his military duties for the week ended at one o'clock Saturday afternoon, he hurried to the officers' club to turn out "smeary pencil pages" in a room full of smoke and conversation and rattling newspapers. At the end of three months Fitzgerald produced a draft of 120,000 words, twenty-three chapters in prose and verse. He put in almost everything, including poems and stories and plays written while in college, and he did no revising. There wasn't time for it.

The resulting manuscript—*The Romantic Egotist*, with a protagonist named Stephen Palms—was sent to Scribner's in May 1918. Only Maxwell Perkins, then a junior editor at the conservative publishing house, liked the book, but he managed to persuade his doubting colleagues to give Fitzgerald another chance. On August 19, Scribner's mailed Fitzgerald one of the most hopeful rejection letters ever written. He was then stationed at Camp Sheridan, Alabama, where he had met and fallen in love with Zelda Sayre of Montgomery. To win her hand in marriage, he would have to prove his ability to make money in the risky and often unrewarding profession of letters. So when Scribner's suggested that he make some changes and resubmit his novel, Fitzgerald responded rapidly: too rapidly, for he failed to revise along the lines the publisher had recommended. In October 1918 the manuscript came back again, rejected for the second time.

Scribner's isolated two particular problems with *The Romantic Egotist*. First, it contained too much irrelevant detail. Second, and more important, it didn't "work up to a conclusion." Stephen Palms went to school and to college and to war but did not seem to "arrive" anywhere, or "find himself" in the process. "In short . . . the story does not culminate in anything as it must to justify the reader's interest as he follows it" (qtd. in West, *The Making*, 17). This was the problem that confronted Fitzgerald when he embarked on a second and full-scale revision in the summer of 1919. By that time, he had been discharged from the army, and in a futile attempt to establish himself as a breadwinner, he worked in an advertising agency in New York for some months. When Zelda broke off their engagement, he quit his job, went on a monumental binge, and retreated to his parents' house in St. Paul to rewrite his novel. His hero was now called Amory Blaine, and the book was retitled *The Education of a Personage*, first, and then *This Side of Paradise*.

Through the hot months of the summer, Fitzgerald labored long hours in his third floor room at 599 Summit Avenue, scrapping superfluous material, revising almost every scene from *The Romantic Egotist*, and adding a number of new ones designed to demonstrate Amory's growth. He stayed on the wagon throughout, permitting himself only cigarettes and Coca-Cola. Literary success was at stake, and the love of the girl in Alabama. In early September, the rewritten novel reached Scribner's, and two weeks later, on September 16, Maxwell Perkins wrote Fitzgerald to accept the book for publication.

Overjoyed, the young writer ran up and down Summit Avenue telling friends and acquaintances the good news. Borne along by "that first wild wind of success," everything broke right for him. "That week the postman rang and rang," he recalled, "and I paid off my terrible small debts, bought a suit, and woke up every morning with a world of ineffable toploftiness and promise" (*My Lost City*, 186). *Scribner's Magazine*, which had been regularly rejecting his stories, bought two of them. *The Smart Set* took a story and a one-act play. When Fitzgerald agreed to terms with Perkins, he pushed for early publication of the book. "I have so many things dependent on its success—including, of course, a girl" (*Dear Scott/Dear Max*, 21). In November, he traveled to Montgomery and renewed his engagement with Zelda Sayre. *This Side of Paradise* clinched matters. "It's so nice to know that you really *can* do things—*anything*," Zelda wrote him (*Dear Scott, Dearest Zelda*, 38).

On March 20, 1919, her parents, who had discouraged the match, officially announced the engagement. On March 26, *This Side of Paradise* was published. On April 3, Scott and Zelda were married in the rectory of St. Patrick's Cathedral in New York.

A bumpy road lay ahead, for Fitzgerald was never able to reconcile himself entirely to having to demonstrate his financial prospects as a condition of marriage. As he recorded his feelings fifteen years later, "The man with the jingle of money in his pocket who married the girl . . . would always cherish an abiding distrust, an animosity, toward the leisure class—not the conviction of a revolutionist, but the smouldering hatred of a peasant" (*My Lost City*, 147). It seemed wrong to him, as it did to Amory Blaine, that the richest man should get the most beautiful girl.

Though acknowledging that *This Side of Paradise* abounded "in energy and life," Perkins cautioned Fitzgerald against expecting too much by way of sales. The book was so different that it was hard to predict how it would sell, he pointed out (*Dear Scott/Dear Max*, 21), and first novels rarely commanded a large audience. Privately, Scribner's would have been happy with selling five thousand copies, while Fitzgerald brashly announced that he expected to sell twenty thousand in the first year. Both guessed low. *This Side of Paradise* sold forty thousand copies in the year after publication, and though it has not become a classroom standard like *The Great Gatsby* and *Tender Is the Night*, the book has attracted a wide readership ever since.

In the critical arena, however, Fitzgerald's first novel has been largely undervalued. This was not the consequence of the initial reviews, which for the most part ranged from very good to sensational. H. L. Mencken congratulated Fitzgerald for offering "a truly amazing first novel—original in structure, extremely sophisticated in manner, and adorned with a brilliancy" rare in American writing (Mencken, "Books," 28). Robert Benchley commented that he wasn't sure if *This Side of Paradise* was a great book, but he was sure that the novel represented something *new* and he was inclined to hail its creator as a genius (Benchley, "Books," 14).

What was particularly new was Fitzgerald's candid attempt to capture the behavior and thoughts of young people. As a picture of the daily existence of college men, the *New York Times Review of Books* observed, the book was nearly perfect ("With College Men," 240). No one else, another reviewer noted, "has given us so real and intimate a study of college life, of the relationship at that age between boys and girls, of the juvenile struggles for recognition, power, and leadership and the intrigues incidental to it, of the things young men in college think about and do." If the novel showed signs of immaturity, well and good. Only a young writer could have written it at all ("With College Men," 21).

By and large, then, *This Side of Paradise* got off to a good start both from reviewers and readers. The subsequent critical neglect of the book derived principally from two other sources: its abundant textual errors, especially in spelling, and the cold hand that Edmund Wilson, Fitzgerald's fellow Princetonian, passed over the novel.

So numerous and obvious were the mistakes that literary gossip dubbed Fitzgerald "the Princeton Daisy Ashford," a slurring reference to *The Young Visitors*, a 1919 novel that had supposedly been written by a nine-year-old girl named Daisy Ashford. As James L. W. West III observed in *The Making of "This Side of Paradise,"* for the number of careless errors the text of this novel probably had no equal in American literature (104–5). Fitzgerald was a notoriously poor speller, especially of proper names, and he did not always choose the right word. This was unfortunate but by no means fatal. Such technical problems were customarily smoothed out during the publishing process. But Perkins was a poor copy editor, and in the end no one at Scribner's checked the text for accuracy. As a result, Fitzgerald was lampooned as a muddleheaded and immature author. In his "Conning Tower" column for the *New York Tribune*, F.P.A. (Franklin P. Adams) presented examples of the book's more egregious errors. Fitzgerald, naturally troubled, sent three separate lists of corrections to Scribner's during the months after publication, but the publishers did little, then or later, to make changes. To this day, any close reader will discover dozens of correctible errors in *This Side of Paradise*. Only a fraction of the blame rests with Fitzgerald himself. As he wrote in exasperation years after publication, "My God—did they expect me to spell? If I was such a hot shot couldn't the proof-readers do the spelling?" (qtd. in West, *The Making*, 119).

Mechanical errors aside, Edmund Wilson's commentary probably did the most damage to the critical reception of Fitzgerald's first novel. At Princeton, Fitzgerald formed friendships with Wilson and John Peale Bishop, fellow students with far greater literary sophistication than himself who tended to look down on him as talented but naive. Both Wilson, class of 1916, and Bishop, class of 1917, served as editors of the *Nassau Literary Magazine*, where Fitzgerald published some of his earliest stories and poems. And both turn up as characters in *This Side of Paradise*, Bishop as Thomas Parke D'Invilliers and Wilson in a cameo appearance as Tanaduke Wylie. Bishop was generally supportive of his classmate during the composition of his novel. After reading a draft of *The Romantic Egotist* in January 1918, Bishop made two useful suggestions for revision. First, he advised Fitzgerald not to be so hard on his protagonist, for readers might be too easily prejudiced against him. Second, he warned against including everything in Fitzgerald's experience. "Retain only significant events and ride them hard," he counseled (Fitzgerald, *Correspondence*, 27–28).

This was not easy for Fitzgerald to do, for he was then under the influence of H. G. Wells, who had been embroiled in a famous dispute with Henry James about the proper form of the novel. Wells advocated the novel of saturation—putting in everything; James, the novel of selection—concentrating on a few important scenes. Fitzgerald came down squarely on Wells's side; it seemed truer to life, for one thing. He was also under the spell of the British novelist Compton Mackenzie and his "quest novel," *Sinister Street*, which ran to more than a thousand pages. Much of that book's material could profitably have been eliminated, but the capacity for selection eluded Mackenzie. That was the danger Bishop—and Wilson, more bluntly—were warning Fitzgerald against.

When he read *This Side of Paradise* in advance of publication, Wilson responded with a withering critique of the book's immaturity and of its models. "I have just read your novel with more delight than I can well tell you. It ought to be a classic in a class with *The Young Visitors* [the Daisy Ashford book]. . . . Your hero is an unreal imitation of Michael Fane of *Sinister Street* who was himself unreal. . . . As an intellectual Amory is a fake of the first water and I read his views on art, politics, religion and society with more riotous mirth than I should care to have you know. . . . Cultivate a universal irony and do read something other than contemporary British novelists" (*Letters*, 45–46).

Wilson's public assessment of Fitzgerald and his first two novels, which appeared in the March 1922 *Bookman*, established a path for subsequent commentators to follow. The essay began with the poet Edna St. Vincent Millay's observation that Fitzgerald reminded her of a "stupid old woman" who was given a valuable diamond. There was "symbolic truth" in that characterization, Wilson agreed, for Fitzgerald like the ignorant woman had been granted "imagination without intellectual control of it . . . the desire for beauty without an aesthetic ideal; and . . . a gift for expression without very many ideas to express" ("The Literary Spotlight," 20). Having thus deflated Fitzgerald in general, Wilson directed his fire against *This Side of Paradise* in particular.

"It has almost every fault and deficiency that a novel can possibly have," he asserted. It was "highly imitative" of Mackenzie's *Sinister Street*. Like that model, the book was "really not *about* anything" and amounted to little more than "a gesture of indefinite revolt." The story itself was immaturely imagined and "always just verging on the ludicrous." Finally, *This Side of Paradise* ranked as "one of the most illiterate books of any merit ever published. . . . Not only is it ornamented with bogus ideas and faked literary references, but it is full of literary words tossed about with the most reckless inaccuracy." At this point, Wilson shifted from diatribe to faint praise. Fitzgerald's novel committed almost every possible sin, but not "the unpardonable sin: it [did] not fail to live. The whole preposterous farrago [was] animated with life." And though Fitzgerald mishandled words throughout—Wilson provided several examples—and played "the language entirely by ear," it was also true that he had "an instinct for graceful and vivid prose" ("The Literary Spotlight," 22).

After Fitzgerald's death in 1940, Wilson played a significant role in restoring his posthumous reception. He edited both *The Last Tycoon* and *The Crack-Up*, for example. Yet even then Wilson could not resist looking down on his immensely gifted college friend as his intellectual inferior. In an essay of 1944 he once again touched on the shortcomings of Fitzgerald's misguided literary enthusiasms: "I want to be one of the greatest writers who have ever lived, don't you?" Fitzgerald said to him shortly after college. "I had not myself really quite entertained that fantasy," Wilson sardonically pointed out, "because I had been reading Plato and Dante. Scott had been reading Booth Tarkington, Comptom Mackenzie, H. G. Wells and Swinburne." He respected Fitzgerald for the "intoxicated ardor" of his ambition, Wilson added, but he had done his homework and resented his friend's success (qtd. in Mizener, *The Far Side of Paradise*, 35).

Given Wilson's eminence as a critic and his friendship with Fitzgerald, it was to be expected that others might follow his lead in stressing the novel's shallowness and aesthetic flaws while praising its animation and life. And Fitzgerald himself, motivated by his lifelong admiration for Wilson's intellectual powers, came to accept Wilson's patronizing viewpoint and to belittle his own work. He disparaged his novel as a "romance and a reading list" (*Crack-Up*, 176) and said of Amory's affair with Eleanor—perhaps the weakest part of the book—that it was so funny he could hardly bear to read it. But he did not finally repudiate *This Side of Paradise*. The book was riddled with mistakes and rife with intellectual pretension, he acknowledged, but it was true to life emotionally. He'd put a lot of himself into it.

One of *This Side of Paradise*'s greatest virtues was that it was written with so sure a sense of the times. Fitzgerald not only got all the songs and dances right, he also functioned as an insightful social historian. Sometime early in the twentieth century, the United States crossed a line of demarcation from a stable society based on solid Victorian values to an unstable one adrift in moral and cultural confusion. Most commentators fix the 1920s as the time of that change, yet as Henry F. May argued in *The End of American Innocence*, "many different kinds of people [were] cheerfully laying dynamite in the hidden cracks" of the massive nineteenth-century walls during the previous decade (x–xi). Through faithful rendering of the adventures of Amory Blaine and his friends, Fitzgerald depicted some of these acts of sabotage.

The most drastic change involved the relations between the sexes. Fitzgerald obviously meant to shock his readers when he wrote that "none of the Victorian mothers—and most of the mothers were Victorian—had any idea how casually their daughters were accustomed to be kissed." This popular daughter, or P.D., as she is called, indulged in three-A.M. after-dance suppers and talked of "every side of life . . . with furtive excitement." A spy from inside his generation, Amory recorded the progress of this girl from "belle" to "flirt" to "baby vamp." And from his own experience, he demonstrated how the game of courtship played out with several different girls.

In Amory's encounters with Myra St. Claire, Isabelle Borgé, and Rosalind Connage, the winner is not the one who refuses a first kiss—no one does—but the one who decides when the kissing will stop. Amory is pleased that Myra will kiss him but is immediately repelled by the act. When he declines her command to "kiss me again," her vanity is wounded and he carries the day (21).

At the party where he meets Isabelle, an accomplished flirt, he gains the upper hand by means of his "line"—"I've got an adjective that just fits you" (67), but others interrupt them before they can actually kiss. Months later, at the Princeton prom, these two attractive antagonists do finally come together in what is for Amory a moment of victory. "As in the story books, she ran into [his arms], and on that half-minute, as their lips first touched, rested the high point of vanity, the crest of his young egotism" (88). The triumph is short-lived, however, for Amory's shirt stud leaves a small blue spot on Isabelle's neck, and when he is not properly sympathetic, she will not let him kiss her again. Amory realizes that he "had not an ounce of real affection for Isabelle," but he is disturbed at her refusal. "It wasn't dignified to come off second best, pleading with a doughty warrior like Isabelle" (90).

The love game escalates into full-scale combat with Rosalind, for Amory *does* care for her, terribly, and cannot persuade her to marry him. Fitzgerald presents their love affair in the form of a drama, complete with dialogue and stage directions, and does so with remarkable skill and feeling. In Rosalind Connage, he combines the two golden girls of his own experience: the beautiful and wealthy Ginevra King of Lake Forest, Illinois, whom he had courted for two years and lost, and the flirtatious and daring Zelda Sayre, whom he met on the rebound. In both cases Fitzgerald, like Amory, faced rejection for lack of money. On first meeting, Amory and Rosalind kiss more than once, and she makes it clear that she understands her role in the battle of the sexes. She is a commodity if not a corporation: "'Rosalind, Unlimited.' Fifty-one shares, name, good-will, and everything goes at $25,000 a year," she unashamedly introduces herself (163). Then she asserts her dominance by deciding she has had enough of kissing for the moment.

Rosalind is beautiful, selfish, physically courageous, and very much in charge. There used to be two kinds of kisses, she instructs a repudiated suitor. "First when girls were kissed and deserted; second, when they were engaged. Now there's a third kind, where the man is kissed and deserted. . . . Given a decent start any girl can beat a man nowadays" (170). Amory is swept away by her, despite the calculation that leads her to break off their relationship. "You've already wasted two months on a theoretical genius who hasn't a penny to his name," her mother chides her, "but *go* ahead, waste your life on him." Rosalind objects to her mother's sarcasm, yet when she next sees Amory, she tells him she has decided to marry a millionaire rival. "Come over here and kiss me," he says, but her answer is "no" (181). It's not that she doesn't love him, she explains, but "I can't be shut away from the trees and flowers, cooped up in a little flat, waiting for you. You'd hate me in a narrow atmosphere. I'd make you hate me" (182). The emotional impact of this scene came from life; when Fitzgerald composed it, Zelda was sending him much the same message in her letters. "All the material things are nothing," she wrote him, but "I'd just hate to live a sordid, colorless existence, because you'd soon love me less—and less" (*Dear Scott/Dearest Zelda*, 15).

❖ ❖ ❖

Like many first novels, then, *This Side of Paradise* is highly autobiographical. What happens to Amory Blaine, particularly his emotional reactions, closely parallels what happened to young Scott Fitzgerald. In one respect, the author allows his hero a more glamorous background than his own. His mother, Mollie McQuillan Fitzgerald, was a rather dowdy daughter of a successful merchant, a far cry from the beautiful, fabulously wealthy Beatrice Blaine, whose social connections included cardinals and queens. Beatrice has her weaknesses—a fondness for drink, a tendency to hypochondria, and relapses in faith that summon fawning doctors and priests to her side—but she also has style. In *This Side of Paradise* Fitzgerald gave Amory Blaine the kind of mother he himself would have liked to have. Amory's father, on the other hand, remains a pallid character fashioned along the lines of Edward Fitzgerald, the author's sire. Stephen Blaine appears on the first page, "an unassertive figure" (11) who does not understand his wife, and he dies quietly and inconspicuously a hundred pages later, without otherwise figuring in the novel.

Given the substantially autobiographical nature of his book, Fitzgerald faced a difficult task in arriving at an ending. How was he, at twenty-three, supposed to bring the story of his hero of the same age to a convincing conclusion? Or as he himself described the dilemma, how could he "intrigue the hero into a 'philosophy of life' when [his] own ideas were in much the state of Alice's after the hatter's tea-party"? His solution was to bring Amory back to Princeton for the final scene, where he stretches out his arms to a "crystalline, radiant sky" and cries, "I know myself, but that is all." In the manuscript, as West notes, there was no period at the end of the sentence, but instead a dash that laid emphasis on the open-ended future. It is not known when or why or by whom the dash was converted to a period (*The Making*, 74).

Whether Amory has succeeded in meeting the Socratic maxim of "know thyself" may be in doubt. Such hard-to-achieve knowledge usually comes only at the end of a long lifetime. But he *has* learned a great deal about himself and the society he lives in and in the process has grown in character and maturity. The Amory Blaine of the last pages, who has suffered a withering defeat in the battle of the sexes, is a far more sympathetic and attractive figure than the callow and conceited schoolboy we meet at the beginning. He has, in effect, grown up.

Much of Amory's development takes place through a process of trying and discarding various roles. Like Dick Diver in *Tender Is the Night*, Amory is something of an actor, and it is entirely natural for him to play a part. Not to pose, Monsignor Darcy tells him, might be for him the greatest pose of all. In his youthful vanity, Amory conceives of himself as a boy marked for glory, and he dreams of becoming a great halfback or the world's youngest general or a Broadway habitué in evening dress. Such fantasies do little harm, and he does achieve at least one moment of glory by scoring the game's only touchdown for St. Regis against Groton.

Early in the novel Amory prepares an inventory of his traits, just as Fitzgerald had when he was sent east to Newman school at fifteen. Amory declares himself "exceedingly handsome," socially charming, with a gift for fascinating women, mentally superior, but morally weak, susceptible to selfishness and vanity and lacking courage, perseverance, and self-respect (25).

The trouble is that he revels just as much in his weaknesses as his strengths. Amory associates goodness with stupidity, and intelligence like his own with a capacity for evil. It is left to the sagacious Clara, a woman too good for any man, to explode this pose for Amory. "The reason you have so little self-confidence, even though you gravely announce to the occasional philistine that you think you're a genius, is that you've attributed all sorts of atrocious faults to yourself and are trying to live up to them" (135).

To Amory, Clara seems a modern saint, with an aura of golden radiance about her. But his principal religious mentor is Darcy, a character modeled on Monsignor Sigourney Fay, the Catholic priest who took a deep interest in Fitzgerald during his prep school and college days—and to whom *This Side of Paradise* was dedicated. Worldly and cultivated, Darcy first appears clad in full purple regalia and resembling a Turner sunset. He has written two novels, we learn, one of them—just before his conversion to the faith—violently anti-Catholic. With a touch of irony, Fitzgerald calls Darcy's present commitment into some doubt as well: "He was intensely ritualistic, startlingly dramatic, loved the idea of God enough to be a celibate, and rather liked his neighbor" (30).

Darcy virtually adopts young Amory as a son, serving as a rich, clever, and exotic replacement for his drab father. He encourages Amory to talk and brings out the best in him, but for both of them the Catholic religion is mostly a matter of appearances. For a time at Princeton, Amory affects a sort of inspiration he does not really feel, pretending, for example, to fall into a mystic daze while reading the life of Saint Teresa.

Amory chose to attend Princeton instead of Yale or Harvard because he thought of it as "lazy and good-looking and aristocratic" (31). Besides, Princeton had a reputation as "the pleasantest country club in America." Once enrolled, Amory at once becomes embroiled in the social politics of the institution. More then anything, he wants to be admired. Amory's college career shadows that of Fitzgerald. He doesn't really mind the "glittering caste system" of the place, he tells another freshman. "I like having a bunch of hot cats on top, but gosh . . . I've got to be one of them" (50). For the next two years he pursues the success that had eluded him at St. Regis. He makes his mark on the *Princetonian* and the Triangle Club, and—like his creator—is elected to Cottage, one of the most prestigious eating clubs, in the spring of his sophomore year. He is ready to take his proper place among the leaders of his class, except that he flunks a makeup math exam and becomes ineligible.

The vision of Princeton presented in book 1 of *This Side of Paradise* did not sit well with alumni and naturally annoyed President John Grier Hibben, who wrote Fitzgerald a letter of remonstrance. In descriptive passages, Hibben acknowledged, Fitzgerald had effectively invoked the beauty of Princeton's Gothic campus. But, he protested, "I cannot bear to think that our young men are merely living for four years in a country club and spending their lives wholly in a spirit of calculation and snobbishness." Perhaps he had overstressed "the country club atmosphere," Fitzgerald admitted (qtd. in Bruccoli, *Some Sort of Epic Grandeur*, 128–29), but at the time he was writing the book he was still embittered by what his own scholastic ineligibility had cost him on that March afternoon when it became clear that there were to be no badges of pride, no medals, after all. As he later described it: "A year of terrible disappointment and the end of all college dreams. Everything bad in it was any own fault" (Fitzgerald, *Ledger*, unpaginated).

In the wake of this disappointment, Amory is introduced to a new way to confront experience. Monsignor Darcy outlines the difference between a *personality*, which is "a physical matter almost entirely," and a *personage*, who is never thought of apart from what he has done. A personality gets by on charm. A personage accomplishes. Amory had thought of himself as a personality, one who tries out various roles for himself to please his fellows. Darcy insists that he must stop performing and act in the real world, that both of them are personages who must "do the next thing" (100–102).

Amory meets a real personage in Burne Holiday, a radical student embarked on a campaign to do away with the snobbish club system at Princeton, a system that Woodrow Wilson—simply "Woodrow" in the novel—opposed during his tenure as president of the university. Burne is an idealist who does the next thing in trying to produce constructive change. His campaign fails in the end, but meanwhile Amory has found a new idol on whom to pattern himself. Fitzgerald contrasts Amory's admiration for Burne Holiday with his earlier enthusiasm for Dick Humbird. Humbird qualifies as a personality: an undergraduate with charisma but little depth of character who dies in a drunken automobile accident. Amory initially yearns to achieve Humbird's social ease and personal magnetism. Eventually, though, he comes to value Holiday—every inch a personage—for his "intense earnestness," a quality that in his previous arrogance he associated with dullness. "Burne stood vaguely for a land Amory hoped he was drifting toward—and it was almost time that land was in sight" (117).

The single incident that best illustrates Amory's moral progress is the sacrifice he makes for his friend Alec Connage, Rosalind's brother. Significantly, this occurs *after* he has been jilted by Rosalind. Alec takes his girlfriend Jill to an Atlantic City hotel for drinking and illicit sex. When the house detective breaks in, Amory intervenes to take the blame. In so doing, he puts himself and his reputation at risk, but he makes the sacrifice anyway. Amory, who still has difficulty thinking well of himself, characterizes his deed as "supercilious" (225) or prideful, and he cannot resist putting on a show of bravado for the house detective. But this is not just another self-indulgent pose: Amory's sacrifice is a genuine act of altruism.

Oddly, the presence of the Devil, or at least his aura, has much to do with determining Amory's change of attitude. In his mind, female beauty and sex are inextricably linked with evil. In two incidents where a casual sexual tryst impends, Amory is horrified to sense the Devil in the room. The first occurs in the New York apartment of a chorus girl. Amory is about to succumb to a night of pleasure when he has a vision of a horrible pale man across the room, whose feet are encased in pointed moccasins. He realizes that this is the Devil, and flees in panic. The second encounter with the Devil takes place in Atlantic City, again where the sin of fornication impends. This time, Amory stands his ground, makes a selfless sacrifice, and drives Satan away.

In *This Side of Paradise*, Fitzgerald carries his principal character through a series of failures and disappointments to a measure of maturity. Amory loses his chance for eminence at Princeton and loses the girl he loves. Yet in the process he also rids himself of his self-absorbed vanity and begins to emerge as a personage rather than a personality. His political debate with Jesse Ferrenby's father in the final pages may seem like little more than just another pose. As Amory admits, he has never really argued the case for socialism before that auto trip. But he is a different person than he was as a college boy, one who has been hurt along the way and now wants to be of service to others—a resolve that comes to him at Monsignor Darcy's funeral—and not merely to himself. He has most of his life ahead of him, and Fitzgerald has given him a good start on that long road.

{ 4 }

POSSESSIONS IN *THE GREAT GATSBY*

READING *GATSBY* CLOSELY

THE ENVELOPE OF CIRCUMSTANCES

Two hundred and eighty pages into *The Portrait of a Lady*, Madame Merle carries on an instructive conversation with Isabel Archer about marriage prospects. Madame Merle, very much a woman of the world, feels sure that there is an "inevitable young man" (287) with a mustache in Isabel's past, but knows that he doesn't really count, whether he has a castle in the Apennines or an ugly brick house on Fortieth Street.

"I don't care anything about his house," Isabel responds, eliciting from Madame Merle a lecture born of experience.

"When you have lived as long as I, you will see that every human being has his shell, and that you must take the shell into account. By the shell I mean the whole envelope of circumstances. There is no such thing as an isolated man or woman; we are each of us made up of a cluster of appurtenances." Then Madame Merle shifts from these generalizations to the contents of her own closet. "I know that a large part of myself is in the dresses I choose to wear. I have a great respect for *things*! One's self for other people is one's expression of one's self; and one's house, one's clothes, the book one reads, the company one keeps—these things are all expressive."

Isabel will have none of it. She is determined to be independent, not enclosed by any shell or envelope. She feels sure that no mere object can express her inmost self. "Nothing that belongs to me is any measure of me;

on the contrary, it's a limit, a barrier, and a perfectly arbitrary one," Isabel insists. "My clothes may express the dressmaker, but they don't express me" (287–88).

Isabel is wrong, of course. And it is because of her headstrong pursuit of absolute freedom that Madame Merle is able to trap her into confinement in the worst possible marriage.

When T. S. Eliot wrote F. Scott Fitzgerald that *The Great Gatsby* seemed to him "the first step that American fiction has taken since Henry James" (qtd. in Fitzgerald, *Crack-Up*, 310), he linked the two writers as *social* novelists in whose work the issue is joined between innocence and experience, between those who repudiate artificial limitations and those who recognize and respect the envelope of circumstances, between the individual yearning for independence and the society forever reining him in. Fitzgerald, like James, understood that the pursuit of independence was doomed from the start. Try though they might, Fitzgerald's characters find it impossible to throw off "the cluster of appurtenances" and invent themselves anew. That is the lesson, or one of the lessons, of *The Great Gatsby*.

One's house, one's clothes: they do express one's self, and for no one more than for Jay Gatsby. It is in good part because of the clothes he wears that Tom Buchanan is able to undermine him as a competitor for Daisy. "'An Oxford man!' [Tom] was incredulous. 'Like hell he is! He wears a pink suit'" (95). Yes, and for tea a white flannel suit with silver shirt and gold tie (66). And drives a monstrously long cream-colored car, a veritable "circus wagon," in Tom's damning phrase (94). And inhabits a huge mansion where he throws drunken parties "for the world and its mistress" (49). Gatsby's clothes, his car, his house, his parties all brand him as newly rich, unschooled in the social graces and sense of superiority ingrained not only in Tom Buchanan but also in Nick Carraway.

With women, the right clothes and accessories matter even more. In *Tender Is the Night*, for example, the elegant Nicole Diver is fixed in the reader's mind as the woman who wears a "string of creamy pearls" even on the beach. Nicole's wealth and what it can buy are evoked when she goes shopping in Paris with the young actress Rosemary Hoyt.

> With Nicole's help Rosemary bought two dresses and two hats and four pairs of shoes with her money. Nicole bought from a great list that ran two pages, and bought the things in the windows besides. Everything she liked that she couldn't possibly use herself, she bought as a present for a friend. She bought colored beads, folding beach cushions, artificial flowers, honey, a guest bed, bags, scarfs, love birds, miniatures for a doll's house,

and three yards of some new cloth the color of prawns. She bought a dozen bathing suits, a rubber alligator, a travelling chess set of gold and ivory, big linen handkerchiefs for Abe, two chamois leather jackets of kingfisher blue and burning bush from Hermes—bought all these things not a bit like a high-class courtesan buying underwear and jewels, which were after all professional equipment and insurance, but with an entirely different point of view. Nicole was the product of much ingenuity and toil. For her sake trains began their run at Chicago and traversed the round belly of the continent to California; chicle factories fumed and link belts grew link by link in factories; men mixed toothpaste in vats and drew mouthwash out of copper hogsheads; girls canned tomatoes quickly in August or worked rudely at the Five-and-Tens on Christmas Eve; half-breed Indians toiled on Brazilian coffee plantations and dreamers were muscled out of patent rights in new tractors—these were some of the people who gave a tithe to Nicole and, as the whole system swayed and thundered onward, it lent a feverish bloom to such processes of hers as wholesale buying, like the flush of a fireman's face holding his post before a spreading blaze. She illustrated very simple principles, containing in herself her own doom, but illustrated them so accurately that there was grace in the procedure, and presently Rosemary would try to imitate it.

(54–55)

Brilliant though it is, this is not Fitzgerald's most famous list. That comes at the beginning of chapter 4 of *Gatsby*, when Nick reconstructs from his jottings on the margins of a July 1922 railroad timetable a roster of those who attended Gatsby's parties. Many of them seem to have been transplanted from their natural habitats in the animal and vegetable kingdoms to Gatsby's blue lawn, where they misbehave among the whisperings and the champagne and the stars. From the menagerie, for example, emerged the Leeches and Dr. Webster Civet, who drowned up in Maine, and a whole clan named Blackbuck as well as Cecil Roebuck and Edgar Beaver, whose hair turned cotton-white one winter afternoon, and James B. ("Rot-Gut") Ferret and Francis Bull. Up from the sea swam the Fishguards and S. B. Whitebait and the Hammerheads and Beluga, the tobacco importer, and Beluga's girls. Another set of girls bearing the melodious names of flowers sprouted there, as did Newton Orchid, who controlled a movie studio, and Clarence Endive, who came only once and got into a fight, and Henry L. Palmetto, who killed himself by jumping in front of a subway train, and Ernest Lilly and George Duckweed. "All these people came to Gatsby's house in the summer," Nick dryly concludes (49–51).

This makes for wonderful entertainment and does not bear too much analysis, but Nicole's shopping list is another matter. For one thing, it was created nearly a decade after the publication of *Gatsby*, at a time when Fitzgerald's political convictions had moved sharply and programmatically to the left. In his "General Plan" for *Tender*, he couched the downfall of his principal character in terms of Marxian class struggle:

> The novel should do this. Show a man who is a natural idealist, a spoiled priest, giving in for various causes to the ideas of the haute bourgeoisie, and in his rise to the top of the social world losing his idealism, his talent and turning to drink and dissipation. Background one in which the leisure class is at their truly most brilliant & glamorous such as Murphys.

Fitzgerald posits this version of Dr. Diver as a man "like myself brought up in a family sunk from haute bourgeoisie to petit bourgeoisie, yet expensively educated." This protagonist in the "General Plan," which Fitzgerald probably set down in the summer of 1932, is "in fact a communist liberal-idealist" who goes so far as to send his son to Soviet Russia to educate him (qtd. in Bruccoli, *Some Sort of Epic Grandeur*, 335–36).

By the time he took Nicole and Rosemary shopping in Paris, Fitzgerald was persuaded that capitalism was a corrupt and dying economic system. Thus it is that his list is divided into two: the first describing what Nicole bought and the second picturing those who toiled and slaved so she could make her purchases.

The most extraordinary thing about Nicole's shopping is that she buys indiscriminately. True, she brings a long list with her and undoubtedly buys a number of things jotted down there, like the handkerchiefs for Abe North and the miniatures for the dollhouse, probably, but we have no way of knowing exactly which ones, for Fitzgerald does not reproduce the list. Instead he emphasizes the variety of her purchases, ranging from the trivial impulse buy of the rubber alligator to such a solid and usable item as the guest bed. Nicole buys not only items on her list but "the things in the windows besides," buys not only for herself but for her friends. She also buys in quantity: a dozen bathing suits, two chamois leather jackets. She buys whatever strikes her fancy. Money is not an issue.

The second half of the passage switches from the items purchased to the various workers who "gave a tithe to Nicole," as if she were a goddess commanding 10 percent of their earnings. In the process, as David Lodge puts it, Nicole becomes transformed from "the consumer and collector of commodities, objects, things . . . [into] herself a kind of commodity—the final, exquisite, disproportionately expensive and extravagantly wasteful product of industrial capitalism" (*The Art of Fiction*, 64). For her sake, Fitzgerald insists with metaphorical eroticism, trains "traversed the round belly of the continent." For her sake, too, shopgirls worked on Christmas Eve and "dreamers"—idealists, Fitzgerald called them in his "General Plan"—"were muscled out" of their inventions by ruthless robber barons like Nicole's grandfather.

As Fitzgerald saw it in 1934, not only was capitalism breathing its last, but so were the children and grandchildren of those who accumulated wealth by exploiting others. Nicole's wholesale buying might lend "a feverish bloom" to the system, but the blaze that would destroy it was spreading out of control. To underscore her recklessness, Fitzgerald differentiates Nicole's spending from both that of the "high-class courtesan" and that of the young actress Rosemary. The courtesan might seem extravagant in her expenditures for underwear and jewelry, but these after all represent "professional equipment and insurance," in that order. Nicole's wealth, on the other hand, is so vast that she need indulge in no such pragmatic considerations, a point of contrast made still more vividly with reference to Rosemary.

Like Fitzgerald himself, Rosemary cannot help admiring the "grace" with which Nicole exchanged minuscule segments of her fortune for miscellaneous wares in the stores. She even tries to follow Nicole's example, but the effort is beyond her. In order to spend so heedlessly, you had to grow up rich, and Fitzgerald portrays Rosemary as a child of the middle class, spending her own hard-earned money. "With Nicole's help" she buys two dresses, two hats, and four pairs of shoes: something of a splurge for her, but money spent carefully for clothing she will put to use.

Forty pages later the women go shopping again. On this occasion, as on the first, Nicole buys both artificial flowers and colored beads, and she further demonstrates her profligacy by expending more than a thousand francs on toy soldiers for her son. Rosemary's buying is more purposeful and practical: a diamond for her mother, scarves and cigarette cases for "business associates in California." Fitzgerald describes the pleasure that such shopping afforded Nicole and Rosemary. "It was fun spending money in the sunlight of the foreign city, with healthy bodies under them that sent streams of color up to their faces; with arms and hands, legs and ankles that they stretched out . . . with the confidence of women lovely to men" (97). The two women are similar in loveliness and enjoyment of the day, quite different in their attitude toward money.

LOVE OUT OF CLASS

Myrtle Wilson's purchases in *The Great Gatsby* make an even more striking contrast to those of Nicole Diver. Married to the pallid proprietor of a gas station in the ash-heaps, Myrtle must cross a vast social divide to reach the territory of the upper class. Her sensuality enables her to attract Tom Buchanan, and in the small apartment that Tom rents as a place of assignation, she pitifully attempts to put on airs. But what Myrtle buys and plans to buy during the Sunday party in chapter 2 tellingly reveals her status. She aims for extravagance but has had no experience with it.

When Myrtle and Tom and Nick Carraway, who has been commandeered by Tom to "meet his girl," reach Grand Central Station, she buys a copy of the gossip magazine *Town Tattle* at the newsstand and "some cold cream and a small flask of perfume" from the drugstore's cosmetics counter. Next she exercises her discrimination by letting several taxicabs go by before selecting a lavender-colored one—not quite a circus wagon, perhaps, but unseemly in its showy color. Then she stops the cab in order to "get one of those dogs" for the apartment from a sidewalk salesman. This man resembles John D. Rockefeller and is, like him, less than straightforward in his business dealings. He claims that the puppy he fetches from his basket is a male Airedale, and he demands ten dollars for it. In fact the dog is a mongrel bitch, and in a gesture Myrtle must have found wonderfully cavalier, Tom pays the inflated price with a characteristic insult. "Here's your money. Go and buy ten more dogs with it" (23–24).

Myrtle becomes emboldened in her pretensions amid the surroundings of their hideously overcrowded apartment. Under the inspiration of whiskey, a private interlude with Tom, and her third costume change of the day—this time into "an elaborate afternoon dress of cream-colored chiffon" that rustles as she sweeps across the room—she assumes an "impressive hauteur." Complimented on the dress, Myrtle cocks an eyebrow disdainfully. The dress, she announces, is just a crazy old thing she slips on when she doesn't care how she looks. The eyebrows go up again when the elevator boy is slow in bringing ice. "These people!" she declares. "You have to keep after them all the time" (26–27).

Waxing ever more expansive, Myrtle promises to give Mrs. McKee the dress off her back. She's "got to get another one tomorrow" anyway, as but one item on a shopping list that includes a "massage and a wave and a collar for the dog and one of those cute little ashtrays where you touch a spring, and a wreath with a black silk bow" for her mother's grave. "I got to write down a list so I won't forget all the things I got to do," she announces, the "I got" idiom betraying her humble origins. The list itself, with its emphasis on ashes and dust, foreshadows her eventual demise (31).

Such reminders of Myrtle's unfortunate position as Tom's mistress and victim are required to prevent her from becoming a merely comic figure. As it is, Fitzgerald skewers her affectations with obvious relish. On arrival at the apartment house, he writes, Myrtle casts "a regal homecoming glance around the neighborhood" (25). Once inside, she flounces around the place, her voice transformed into "a high mincing shout" and her laughter becoming progressively more artificial (27). Tom brings her crashing to earth when Mr. McKee, the photographer, comments that he'd "like to do more work" for the wealthy residents of Long Island. With a shout of laughter, Tom proposes that McKee secure a letter of introduction from Myrtle to her husband so that McKee could take photographs of him: "George B. Wilson at the Gasoline Pump," perhaps (28). Neither Chester McKee nor Myrtle Wilson, it is clear, will gain access to the privileged precincts of East Egg. When Myrtle makes so bold as to repeat Daisy's name, Tom breaks her nose with a slap of his open hand.

Among Myrtle's purchases, the dog of indeterminate breeding best symbolizes her own situation. She is, for Tom, a possession to be played with, fondled, and in due course ignored. "Tom's got some woman in New York," Jordan says by way of breaking the news to Nick, who is bewildered by the locution. "Got some woman?" he repeats blankly (15). In her politically and grammatically incorrect manner, Mrs. McKee understands the concept perfectly. If Chester hadn't come along at the right time, she tells Myrtle, the "little kyke" who'd been after her for years would "of got [her] sure" (29). In the same fashion, Myrtle wants to "get" a dog for the apartment. "They're nice to have—a dog" (24).

The connection between Myrtle and the dog as creatures to be kept under restraint is underlined by the collar she plans to buy and by the expensive leather-and-silver leash her husband discovers on her bureau, arousing his suspicions (123). During Nick's final meeting with Tom, Fitzgerald twice evokes the dog comparison. According to Tom, who does not know Daisy was driving at the time, Gatsby deserved to die, for he "ran over Myrtle like you'd run over a dog and never even stopped his car." And Tom himself cried like a baby, he bathetically insists, when he went to give up the flat and saw "the box of dog biscuits sitting there on the sideboard" (139). For the times, Tom was hardly unusual in regarding women as objects to be possessed, either temporarily, as in the case of Myrtle, or permanently, if like Daisy Fay they warrant such maintenance through their beauty and background and way of presenting themselves.

The disparity between Nicole's extensive two-page guide to the day's shopping and Myrtle's sorry little list—dog collar, ashtray, wreath—nicely measures the social distinction between them. Nicole spends with the abandon of third-generation wealth, whereas Myrtle's planned expenditures, like her manner of speaking, betray her position somewhere in the lower middle class. Her inferior status makes her a convenient conquest for Tom. Traditionally, the patrician male slides down the social scale to carry on his affairs, for such relationships require no long-term commitment and can easily be broken off. Tom does not dismiss Myrtle in the course of the novel—indeed he seems to be trying to continue the affair—but there is no question that she would eventually be discarded, like the Santa Barbara chambermaid he was discovered with shortly after his marriage to Daisy or the woman that caused the trouble in Chicago or, for that matter, the office girl Nick relinquishes.

Jay Gatsby, son of Henry Gatz before he reimagines himself into a son of God, has risen from much the same stratum as Myrtle Wilson. The limitations of this background finally make it impossible for him to win the enduring love of Daisy Fay Buchanan. And, like Myrtle, he is guilty of a crucial error in judgment. They are alike unwilling or unable to comprehend that it is not money alone that matters, but money combined with secure social position. In the attempt to transcend their status through a show of possessions, they are undone by the lack of cultivation that drives them to buy the wrong things. At that point they fall victim to what Ronald Berman calls "the iron laws of social distinction" (*Gatsby and Modern Times*, 71).

The sheer exhibitionism of Myrtle's three-dress afternoon prefigures what we are soon to see in Gatsby's clothes closet. Still more than him, she is under the sway of appearances. On successive pages, she describes first how disillusioned she was to discover that her husband had married her in a borrowed suit, and second how thrilled she was to encounter Tom Buchanan on the commuter train in his "dress suit and patent leather shoes." When his white shirt front presses against her arm, she is erotically overcome (30–31).

In depicting the unhappy end of Myrtle Wilson and Jay Gatsby, Fitzgerald was painting a broad-brush portrait of his own experience. Near the novel's close, Nick condemns Tom and Daisy as careless people who "smashed up things and creatures and then retreated back into their money or their vast carelessness or whatever it was that kept them together" (139). In this bitter passage, Fitzgerald was writing about himself as well as the characters. "The whole idea of Gatsby," as he put it, "is the unfairness of a poor young man not being able to marry a girl with money. The theme comes up again and again because I lived it" (qtd. in Turnbull, *Fitzgerald*, 150)—lived it with Ginevra King, who serves as the principal model for Daisy, and very nearly again with Zelda Sayre.

In rejecting Scott as a suitor, Ginevra made it painfully clear that there were boundaries he could not cross. Two quotations from Fitzgerald's ledger, recorded after visits to Ginevra's home in Lake Forest, document his disappointment in love. The better known of these, "Poor boys shouldn't think of marrying rich girls," probably came from Ginevra's father. Fitzgerald took the remark to heart, as directed at him. But the second quotation—a rival's offhand "I'm going to take Ginevra home in my electric"—may have hurt just as much, for Scott had no car at all with which to compete for her company. She came from a more exalted social universe, one he could visit but not belong to. In an interview about their relationship more than half a century later, Ginevra maintained that she never regarded young Fitzgerald as marriageable material, never "singled him out as anything special" (Donaldson, *Hemingway vs. Fitzgerald*, 33–36).

On the most banal level, *The Great Gatsby* documents the truism that money can't buy you love, or at least not the tainted money Gatsby acquires in his campaign to take Daisy away from her husband. It would have been difficult for him to compete with Tom's resources, in any event. Nick describes the Buchanans as "enormously wealthy," and Tom himself as a notorious spendthrift. When he and Daisy moved from Lake Forest (the location is significant) to East Egg, for example, he brought along a string of polo ponies. "It was hard to realize that a man in my own generation was wealthy enough to do that," Nick observes (8).

Part of Gatsby's dream is to turn back the clock and marry Daisy in a conventional wedding, but there, too, he would have been hard put to equal Tom's extravagance. When Tom married Daisy in June 1919, he brought a hundred guests in four private railway cars. It took an entire floor of the hotel to put them up. As a wedding gift he presented Daisy with "a string of pearls valued at three hundred and fifty thousand dollars" (60)—a tremendously impressive sum in 1919 (or any other time), but nonetheless marked down from "seven hundred and fifty thousand dollars" in *Trimalchio*, the early version of the novel Fitzgerald sent Maxwell Perkins in the fall of 1924. He must have decided that the higher figure was beyond belief (*Trimalchio*, 62).

In tying up the threads, Nick offers a final glimpse of Tom outside a jewelry store on Fifth Avenue. As they part, Tom goes into the store "to buy a pearl necklace" for Daisy or some other conquest, "or perhaps only a pair of cuff buttons" (139–40), a suggestion that there is something as unsavory about Tom as about Meyer Wolfshiem, the man who fixed the World Series.

Even discounting how much there is of it, Tom's "old money" has a power beyond any that Gatsby can command. Tom's wealth and background win the battle for Daisy despite his habitual infidelities: an outcome that seems not only grossly unfair but morally wrong, for another point Fitzgerald is making is that if you have enough money and position you can purchase immunity from punishment. Actions have consequences, we remind our children, but some people can evade those consequences. Gatsby probably avoids prosecution for bootlegging and bond rigging by distributing his resources on a quid pro quo basis, and he rather callously applies that principle to his personal life as well. Once he did the police commissioner a favor; now he can break the speed limit. Nick arranges a meeting with Daisy; Gatsby offers him a business connection.

Gatsby's evasions, however, are nothing compared to those of the Buchanans. Daisy commits vehicular manslaughter, then compounds the felony by letting others think Gatsby was driving. In directing Wilson to West Egg, Tom escapes the wrath he knows should be directed at him and becomes an accessory to murder. In a magazine article published the year prior to *Gatsby*, Fitzgerald inveighed against children of privilege who drive automobiles recklessly, knowing that Dad will bribe the authorities should they happen to run over anyone when drunk ("What Kind of Husbands," 187). And in "The Rich Boy," published the year after the novel, his protagonist nonchalantly drives lovers to suicide without feeling the slightest stab of guilt. The message in all these cases would seem to be that if you have the right background, you can get away with murder. In *Gatsby* itself, the two characters who fall in love above their station pay with their lives for their presumption, while Tom and Daisy assuage any discomfort they may feel over cold chicken and ale. Get mixed up with the Buchanans, and you end up dead.

PEASANT AND PLUTOCRAT

In "The Crack-Up," written in 1936, Fitzgerald ruefully recounted the reluctance of Zelda Sayre to marry him just after World War I, when his prospects as a husband and provider looked mighty bleak. To win her over, he rewrote *This Side of Paradise* and had it accepted, but the experience left him "with an abiding distrust . . . toward the leisure class—not the conviction of the revolutionist but the smoldering hatred of the peasant. In the years since then," he reflected, "I have never been able to stop wondering where my friends' money came from, nor to stop thinking that at one time a sort of *droit du seigneur* might have been exercised to give one of them my girl" (*My Lost City*, 147). Marx made much the same point in a famous passage. "I am ugly, but I can buy the most beautiful woman for myself. Consequently I am not ugly, for the effect of my ugliness, its power to repel, is annulled by money. . . . Does not my money, therefore, transform all my incapacities into their opposites?" (Marx, *Early Writings*, 191).

Commentators often stress Fitzgerald's ambivalence toward the moneyed classes, distrusting the rich yet envying them and working to obtain enough money to emulate the grace that some of them managed to bring into their lives. Over the course of his career, though, Fitzgerald's admiration for the rich faded, and his criticism of their way of life intensified. What began as a merely personal complaint assumed a more general political importance, leading to the attack on capitalism dramatized in *Tender Is the Night*.

John Dos Passos, who was creating his own fictional indictment of capitalism in *U.S.A.*, hailed Fitzgerald for the "whole conception" of *Tender*. The novel, he wrote Fitzgerald, revealed "the collapse of one of the great afterthewar imperial illusions. The way you first lay in the pretty picture and then start digging under the surface is immense—and gives you a kind of junction of your two types of writing that ought to be damned useful in the future: the SatEvePost wishfulfillment stuff as a top layer and the real investigation of living organism underneath." That double vision gave *Tender* an "enormous" power, Dos Passos felt.

The Great Gatsby is not as overtly left-wing as *Tender Is the Night*. It is highly unlikely that Fitzgerald had read any Marx when he wrote *Gatsby*, but he was fully aware of contemporary political thinking. As many have noted, one of Fitzgerald's strengths is that he kept so keenly in touch with the social and cultural milieu of his time. Too often, however, these observers have concentrated on his awareness of popular music, say, or automobiles or football players, and he certainly was au courant with all of these. The tendency has been to regard Fitzgerald as an intellectual lightweight, a stereotype that does not take sufficient account of his sensitivity to and fascination with the ideas coursing through the culture. He was hardly a practicing intellectual—few great novelists are—but he was listening and reading and thinking about the wider world, and increasingly so as he matured from a callow undergraduate to "a writer only" at the end of "The Crack-Up." To sum up, there is a good deal more than romantic wonder in his fiction. It is hardly surprising that in his great novel of 1925, Fitzgerald intuitively grasped and illustrated basic Marxian precepts.

In a perceptive essay, Ross Posnock has shown "how deeply Marx's cri tique of capitalism is assimilated into [*Gatsby's*] imaginative life" ("A New World,'" 201). In particular, Posnock focuses on two ideas that are pervasive in the novel: the overall process of *reification*, and its consequent expression in *commodity fetishism*. In effect, Fitzgerald went one step beyond Henry James in *The Portrait of a Lady*. James believed we were necessarily defined by the things we surround ourselves with. A generation later, Fitzgerald understood that we were at risk of becoming commodities ourselves.

Reification, as Marx's disciple Georg Lukács explained it, "requires that a society learn to satisfy all its needs in terms of commodity exchange." But commodities take on a mystical life of their own as they are converted from mere "products of men's hands" into "independent beings endowed with life." This is what Marx meant by commodity fetishism. But he went further: the worker himself became a thing to be bought and used, like the objects produced by his labor. And further yet: under capitalism not only the worker but everything and everybody was "transformed into a commercial commodity." People became objects to be bought and sold (qtd. in Posnock, "A New World,'" 202–3).

In *Gatsby*, Daisy represents the most desirable object of all. She is invariably associated with the things that surround her, her car and her house and, most of all, her voice. Fitzgerald's evocation of that voice constitutes a tour de force. Everyone remembers Gatsby's remark that her voice is "full of money," but that judgment comes only after several brilliant descriptions and demonstrations of its power. When we first meet Daisy at the Buchanans' dinner party, Nick speaks of her "low, thrilling voice" and its promise that "she had done gay, exciting things just a while since and that there were gay, exciting things hovering in the next hour" (11). Men found her voice hard to forget. Daisy rarely "says" things. She "murmurs" or "whispers" instead, compelling the listener forward for her breathless message. Often, she speaks flirtatiously. When she comes to tea at Nick's, she asks him, "Is this absolutely where you live, my dearest one?" with an "exhilarating ripple" in her voice, and then "low" in his ear, "Are you in love with me? . . . Or why did I have to come alone?" (67). After Gatsby appears, Daisy says something "low" in his ear too and he turns toward her with a rush of emotion. That voice, Nick decides, couldn't be overdreamed. With "its fluctuating, feverish warmth," it sang "a deathless song" (75).

On her next appearance, at one of Gatsby's parties, Daisy's voice plays "murmurous tricks in her throat" (81). If Nick wants to kiss her anytime during the evening, she whispers, she'll be glad to arrange it. At the end of the party Daisy begins to sing with the music. This passage, which Fitzgerald added in revising the galley proofs of *Trimalchio*, is the most poetic evocation of all. Daisy's "husky, rhythmic whisper," he writes, brought out "a meaning in each word that it had never had before and would never have again. When the melody rose her voice broke up sweetly, following it, in a way contralto voices have, and each change tipped out a little of her warm human magic upon the air" (84).

Only after these extensive preliminaries does Fitzgerald introduce Gatsby's revelation about Daisy's voice. It's "an indiscreet voice," Nick comments. "It's full of . . ." He hesitates, enabling Gatsby to fill in the blank with, "her voice is full of money." Nick immediately sees that Gatsby is right and leaps from the now totally commodified voice—for Marx, money was the most magical commodity of all—to the physical origins that made it possible: "High in a white palace the king's daughter, the golden girl . . ." (93–94).

Daisy's voice can arouse real emotion in others even when what she has to say is calculated or artificial. She herself is most deeply moved by Gatsby's spectacular display of his many expensive shirts. From the cabinets in his bedroom, Gatsby tosses them onto the table: "shirts of sheer linen and thick silk and fine flannel . . . shirts with stripes and scrolls and plaids in coral and apple green and lavender and faint orange with monograms of Indian blue." This near orgy of commodity celebration is too much for Daisy, who sobs into the folds of his beautiful shirts (72–73, Posnock, " 'A New World,' " 208).

"In an age of violent emotions, objects become as expressive as the people who live among them," the novelist Charles Baxter has commented, with this scene in mind. "There is a subtle anthropomorphism on almost every page of *The Great Gatsby*, as befits a novel about idolatry and consumerism" (*Burning Down the House*, 92–93). In the world of the novel, it works both ways: as inanimate objects take on human characteristics, people are reduced to commodities.

The culture of consumption on exhibit in *The Great Gatsby* was made possible by the growth of a leisure class in early-twentieth-century America. As the novel demonstrates, this development subverted the foundations of the Protestant ethic, replacing the values of hard work and thrifty abstinence with a show of luxury and idleness (Spindler, *American Literature*, 150). The principal interpreter of the phenomenon was Fitzgerald's fellow Midwesterner, the perceptive and satirical Thorstein Veblen. Born in Wisconsin to Norwegian immigrant parents, Veblen pursued a rather undistinguished career in academia—his Stanford students didn't cotton to his dryly ironic style—before finding his niche at New York's New School for Social Research in 1919. There his career prospered. Radical journals disseminated his ideas; Veblen clubs sprang up around the nation; and he achieved widespread fame as a prophet and savant (Hobson and Veblen, *Veblen and the Theory*, 17–20).

Fitzgerald may not have read Veblen, but he was certainly aware of him. For his review of H. L. Mencken's *Prejudices: Second Series* in 1921, Fitzgerald commented that he was overwhelmed by the honor of commenting on the Sage of Baltimore's work. "It seems cruel," he wrote, "that the privilege could not have gone to Thorstein Veblen" (*Correspondence*, 75).

The best known of Veblen's three major works is *The Theory of the Leisure Class* (1899). That groundbreaking book provided an overview of the emergence of a leisure class but gained much of its popularity by virtue of the author's snide commentary on that class. Veblen advanced three basic ideas under the chapter headings of "Pecuniary Emulation," "Conspicuous Leisure," and (in a phrase that quickly became part of the language) "Conspicuous Consumption." All three are vividly illustrated in the pages of *The Great Gatsby*.

In an industrial society, Veblen pointed out, accumulated property replaced the "trophies of predatory exploit" as a sign of potency. In order to establish one's worth and earn the esteem of others, one had to achieve economic success—and show it. The competition to rival the very rich required acquisition of material goods in order to create "an invidious comparison" between oneself and those less successful. Veblen called this process "pecuniary emulation," and judged it to have become the primary motive for the accumulation of wealth. In every modern industrial economy, wealth and its display played a part in determining social status. But the part was larger in the United States, where affluence could more easily surmount traditional barriers of birth and class. As Veblen summarized the point, "the outcome of modern industrial development has been to intensify emulation and the jealousy that goes with emulation, and to focus the emulation and the jealousy on the possession and enjoyment of material goods" (Hobson and Veblen, *Veblen and the Theory*, 28 34, 54–55).

According to this theory, one might suppose that Jay Gatsby could capture his dream through his extraordinary success in gaining wealth and putting it on display. But Veblen added an important caveat, that inherited wealth was "even more honorific" than wealth acquired through one's own efforts. Only those who inherited money could live a life of leisure naturally and comfortably, for they inherited gentility along with their wealth, and "with the inheritance of gentility goes the inheritance of obligatory leisure." If you were born into this new leisure class, you were obliged to abstain "from productive work" as evidence of your status, for, in Veblen's words, "esteem is awarded only on evidence." Nick comes from a genteel background, but the family money has evaporated and he must find a socially approved occupation—the bond business—to support himself. Gatsby has all the money he could possibly need, and ostentatiously presents it for public view, but has not acquired the manners and social stature that come with inherited wealth. Only Tom qualifies as a fully validated member of the new leisure class (Hobson and Veblen, *Veblen and the Theory*, 36, 48–49, 76).

The contrast between the three men is tellingly disclosed during the scene when Tom stops by Gatsby's house on an afternoon horseback ride with a man named Sloane and a female companion who may or may not be Mrs. Sloane. The riders are invited in for a drink (Nick is also on hand), and after a couple of highballs the lady accompanying Mr. Sloane becomes quite expansive. Gatsby must come to dinner with them, she insists (and Nick too, she adds), but Mr. Sloane does not join in the invitation and tries to hurry their departure. Nick intuits the situation at once and politely declines. Gatsby, however, "wanted to go and he didn't see that Mr. Sloane had determined he shouldn't." Nor does Gatsby really belong in this company, if only because he doesn't have a horse of his own. He'd learned to ride in the army, had not been brought up with horses in the style of the honorifically idle rich. Significantly, though, the obtuse Tom has failed to acquire the social sensitivity expected of one in his genteel circumstances. Like Gatsby, he is blind to what is going on between Sloane and his companion. "Doesn't [Gatsby] know she doesn't want him?" he demands of Nick (80–81).

The lower and middle classes were naturally involved in the quest for pecuniary emulation. But in the conventional social and economic structure at the turn of the century, the husband of the family was usually compelled to work, so it fell to his wife to indulge in vicarious consumption on his behalf. According to Veblen, "unproductive consumption of goods" was "a mark of prowess and a perquisite of human dignity," and this was especially true of consumption of "the more desirable things." Unemployed members of the leisure class were expected to develop discriminating tastes, whether for apparel or architecture, games or narcotics. Cultivation of this aesthetic faculty was not easy. It demanded a "more or less arduous application to the business of learning how to live a life of ostensible leisure in a becoming way."

Inasmuch as "conspicuous consumption of valuable goods" represented "a means of reputability to the gentleman of leisure," he might be forgiven occasional overconsumption in sex or liquor. Drunkenness even tended to become a mark of the superior status of those able to afford such a costly vice. Thus in "The Rich Boy," written immediately after *Gatsby*, Fitzgerald created a protagonist who becomes shamefully intoxicated but in apologizing is able to excuse himself and affect a certain "moral superiority" (*Short Stories*, 322–24), much as Tom dismisses his extramarital adventures as basically unimportant.

It was obviously wasteful, Veblen acknowledged, to pursue a life of conspicuous consumption. Yet he held that "in order to be reputable," one's consumption had to be wasteful: a waste of time and effort and a waste of goods. Veblen slyly insisted that he used the term "waste" in a purely scientific sense, just as he used the word "invidious" in speaking of invidious distinctions. In neither case, he maintained, did he intend any "undertone of depreciation." It is easy to imagine how this kind of irony, reasonably effective on the page, might have sailed past the college students Veblen was lecturing to. Fitzgerald plays no such rhetorical games. He makes perfectly clear his feelings about the Buchanans, the careless, murderous couple who represent the full flowering of Veblen's leisure class (Hobson and Veblen, *Veblen and the Theory*, 68–69, 70–71, 74–75, 84–85, 96–97).

THE INESSENTIAL HOUSES

In a culture where pecuniary emulation predominates, the single most important object by which to declare one's status is the house. In *The Great Gatsby*, Fitzgerald masterfully discriminates between Tom Buchanan and Jay Gatsby, the rivals for Daisy's love, on the basis of the very different homes they occupy on Long Island. And houses serve to define other characters as well, in particular Nick and Daisy.

Though he lacks the Buchanans' financial resources, Nick shares their privileged background. At Yale, he belonged to the same senior society as Tom, and few organizations are more selective than Yale senior societies. During the course of the novel, to be sure, Nick lives for eighty dollars a month in a weather-beaten cardboard bungalow "squeezed between two huge places [one of them belonging to Gatsby] that rented for twelve or fifteen thousand a season," at least fifty times as much as Nick was paying. But after the disastrous summer of 1922 limps to its end, Nick can return to the "Carraway house" in the Midwestern city where his "well-to-do, prominent" family has lived for three generations (7–8, 137).

In Louisville, similarly, Daisy grew up in the Fay house. Gatsby meets her there in 1917, when red, white, and blue banners patriotically whipped in the summer wind. "The largest of the banners and the largest of the lawns belonged to Daisy Fay's house" (59). The home entirely enchants the poor young officer from the shores of Lake Superior, who has never seen such a beautiful house before. He invests the place with "a ripe mystery," and senses "a hint of bedrooms upstairs more beautiful and cool than other bedrooms . . . of romances that were not musty and laid away already in lavender but fresh and breathing and redolent of this year's shining motor cars" (116). The magic for Gatsby, in this commodified universe, is inevitably linked to expensive objects, just as Daisy herself, the gleaming golden girl, is repeatedly depicted as dressed in white, driving her white roadster, living in a white palace.

As Fitzgerald re-creates the romance, Gatsby did not fall in love with Daisy until two days after he seduced her. They are sitting on her porch, which is mysteriously "bright with the bought luxury of starshine": mysteriously because in the everyday world star shine is not for sale. The wicker settee takes on anthropomorphic qualities, "squeak[ing] fashionably as [Daisy] turned toward him and he kissed her lovely and curious mouth." (That squeaking settee may have derived from memories of Edward Fitzgerald's failed career in the wicker-furniture business.) When Daisy speaks, her amazing voice rendered "huskier and more charming" than ever by the cold she's caught, Gatsby makes his eternal commitment to her, and to "the youth and mystery that wealth imprisons and preserves" (117).

After the war, after Daisy has married and gone away, Gatsby spends the last of his mustering-out pay on a pilgrimage to Louisville, staying a week to revisit the streets they walked, the out-of-the-way places they drove to in her white car, and the house that "always seemed to him more mysterious and gay than other houses" (119). Later, he makes it an impossible condition of his impossible dream of recovering the past that they go back to Louisville to be married from her wonderful house.

In Gatsby's imagination, Daisy and her house are inseparable, while she comfortably changes location from the house in Louisville to an elegant home in Lake Forest and finally to the mansion Tom buys for her among the "white palaces of fashionable East Egg." In fact, the Buchanans' place is a *red* and white Georgian Colonial overlooking the bay. Whatever its color, it is a magical place, where nature is harnessed for the pleasure of its inhabitants.

Even the lawn has superhuman qualities. On its course up from the beach, it runs for a quarter-mile, jumps over sundials and brick walls, drifts up the outside wall, and even seems to grow a little way into the house itself. A breeze blows through a rosy-colored room from French windows ajar at either end, and there on an enormous couch repose Daisy Buchanan and Jordan Baker in their white dresses. The two young women are "buoyed up" on the couch "as though upon an anchored balloon." Their dresses ripple in the breeze, as if they have just returned from a short flight around the house. Then Tom comes in, shuts the rear windows, cutting off the wind, and the skirts balloon slowly to the floor (9–10). Fitzgerald liked the antigravity effect so much that he reprised it for the Divers' dinner party in *Tender Is the Night*. There, bewitched by Dick's charm, the table seemed to rise "a little toward the sky like a mechanical dancing platform" (34).

The most memorable adornment of the Buchanans' home—the green light at the end of their dock that Gatsby can see from across the bay—also assumes supernatural importance. Before he and Daisy are reunited, the light radiates an aura of enchantment for Gatsby, representing a lost love just beyond his grasp. Once he sees and touches the actual rather than the idealized Daisy, the beacon begins to lose its "colossal significance" for him (73).

When Nick comes to Tom and Daisy's for dinner, the decorum of the evening is shattered by Myrtle's phone calls, and in an effort to change the subject, Tom proposes taking Nick to see the stables, in which he takes particular pride. The subject of the stables comes up again on Nick's next visit to the Buchanans', during the climactic and stiflingly hot Sunday afternoon. On this occasion Daisy and Jordan are once more dressed in white and lying on an enormous couch, but in the heat of the day the awnings are drawn, the room is darkened, and they are weighted down like "silver idols" (90).

Despite the oppressive weather, Tom proclaims his legerdemain. A few pages earlier, Gatsby had his famous conversation with Nick about the passage of time. "Can't repeat the past?" he says. "Why of course you can" (86). Gatsby will discover that he cannot repeat the past, but Tom does, in his way, manage to turn back the calendar. "I've heard of making a garage out of a stable," he tells Gatsby, "but I'm the first man who ever made a stable out of a garage" (92). After this, as if to demonstrate the anachronism of the trick Tom has played on time and progress, they all pile into cars for the drive to Manhattan.

As Tom and Nick and Jordan return from the city later that day, the Buchanans' magical home contravenes the law of gravity, "float[ing] suddenly toward them through the dark, rustling trees," with two windows on the second floor abloom with light (111). Against such violations of natural law, Gatsby can hardly compete. His gigantic house remains sadly earthbound throughout.

When opposed to Nick's modest summer quarters, or even the Buchanan mansion that once was owned by "Demaine, the oil man," Gatsby's huge "imitation of some Hôtel de Ville in Normandy" (8) looms large. It is a house that declares itself, that looks like the World's Fair when all the lights are turned on.

As Nick comments during Gatsby's first party, in his experience "young men didn't . . . drift coolly out of nowhere and buy a palace on Long Island Sound" (41). Rumors circulate about Gatsby's past: he killed a man; he was a German spy during the war. He spreads some of them himself, as in his recital for Nick's benefit of an impossibly romantic past involving tigers and rubies. "I didn't want you to think I was just some nobody," he explains (54). This phrase finds an echo, in a novel rife with echoes, during the confrontation scene at the Plaza, when Tom remarks that he doesn't intend to "sit back and let Mr. Nobody from Nowhere make love to [his] wife" (101). In a sense, Tom is right to characterize Gatsby in this way. The outsized house, together with the lavish parties and the garish clothing, the automobiles and the aquaplane, represent his attempt to establish himself as Somebody, or at least not Nobody.

The trouble is that these possessions, which Gatsby shows off like a peacock his plumage, proclaim him as an arriviste. Nick describes Gatsby's mansion as "a colossal affair by any standard," and it is no accident that he borrows the adjective from the promotional language of motion-picture advertisements. On the exterior, the house features a tower (for what conceivable purpose?) that looks "spanking new under a thin beard of raw ivy"(8). The thin beard, the only anthropomorphizing quality cited, makes the place seem less rather than more attractive, despite its marble swimming pool and forty acres of meticulously tended lawn and garden. And, significantly, Gatsby's place is situated in downscale West Egg, not socially impeccable East Egg.

The enormous house, it turns out, has something of a history. A brewer built it a decade earlier and tried to bribe his neighbors into having their roofs thatched with straw. But this ridiculous endeavor to recover the past collapsed when the neighbors obstinately refused to play their assigned role as peasants to the brewer's lord of the manor.

Gatsby bought the mansion not to lord it over the neighbors but solely because it was situated across the bay from Daisy. Despite the undoubted impressiveness of the place, however, he lacks the confident assurance about it that Tom displays when showing his mansion to visitors. "I've got a nice place here" (10), Tom *tells* Nick, brooking no dissent. "My house looks well, doesn't it?" Gatsby *asks* Nick, seeking validation. "See how the whole front of it catches the light," he remarks, and then Daisy appears, the brass buttons on her dress gleaming in the sunlight (70–71).

Gatsby takes Nick and Daisy on a tour of his Hôtel de Ville. As they walk up from the big postern, Daisy admires everything about the huge place—the feudal silhouette, the gardens with the mingled odors of jonquil and hawthorn and plum blossom and kiss-me-at-the-gate. Inside, Gatsby leads them through an architecturally eclectic mishmash. The house contains a little something from every period: Restoration salons and Marie Antoinette music rooms, period bedrooms and an Adam study. Gatsby gives them a glass of chartreuse from a cupboard in the study, opens two "hulking" cabinets in the bedroom to display the suits and shirts made by his man in England, and calls on Klipspringer, his "boarder," to play two tellingly inappropriate tunes—"The Love Nest" and "Ain't We Got Fun?" Daisy professes to love everything, and before leaving she proposes the kind of experiment in transforming nature that seems possible only to the Buchanans of the world. She and Gatsby stand at the window gazing at the pink and golden clouds over the sea. "I'd like just to get one of those clouds," she whispers, "and put you in it and push you around" (74).

The most significant room in the house is its facsimile of the Merton College library at Oxford. (Fitzgerald knew this room well, not from Oxford but from its reproduction at Princeton's University Cottage Club.) So much about the house was calculated for show, as part of a performance, that the owl-eyed man at Gatsby's party is astounded to discover that the books are real, though uncut and unread. He's "a regular Belasco," Owl Eyes remarks, associating Gatsby with the well-known Broadway producer (38).

Gatsby's house is for show, certainly, and so are his parties. When Daisy wonders how he can live there alone, Gatsby says he keeps the place "always full of interesting people . . . who do interesting things. Celebrated people" (71). Finally Daisy and Tom are prevailed upon to come across the bay to one of the parties. The evening does not go well. Gatsby "certainly must have strained himself to get this menagerie together," Tom comments, and with some accuracy, considering the names of the guests. Daisy defends the assembled crowd, and by extension Gatsby himself, but without conviction. She is less than amused when a drunken girl asks to be put under a cold shower. And although she professes to like the movie star who is striking attitudes for the benefit of partygoers, in *Trimalchio* she balks at Gatsby's suggestion that she supply the star with the name of her hairdresser. She is appalled by West Egg in general, this place of raw emotions that "Broadway had begotten upon a Long Island fishing village" (82–84; *Trimalchio*, 85–86).

The party marks the beginning of the end for Daisy and Gatsby. Daisy didn't have a good time, a discouraged Gatsby tells Nick afterward, sensing that their romance has gone sour. At this stage in *Trimalchio*, Daisy frantically proposes that they run away together. Gatsby rejects the idea, and in telling Nick about it, he stares at his house. "She even wants to leave that," he said bitterly. "I've gotten these things for her, and now she wants to run away" (*Trimalchio*, 89). In an earlier passage from the novel as published, Fitzgerald underlined the proliferation of Gatsby's things. *His* guests came to *his* blue gardens, dived from *his* raft, and sunned on *his* beach while *his* two motorboats slit the waters of the Sound, *his* Rolls-Royce brought groups out from the city, and *his* station wagon met every train. But what good were all those possessions if Daisy was not pleased?

Thereupon Gatsby ends the parties, fires the servants, lets the place deteriorate. It is dusty and in disarray when Nick comes early in the morning after the disastrous day at the Plaza and the fatal accident on the road. In its emptiness the house seems even more enormous than usual. Together Gatsby and Nick throw open the windows, and Gatsby tells him the real story of what he learned from Dan Cody and how he fell in love with Daisy Fay. After breakfast together, Nick unburdens himself to Gatsby that he's worth more than all the East Egg crowd, and, fearing the worst, reluctantly takes the train into town. He is still there when George Wilson finds his way to Gatsby's house and pool, sometime between two and four in the afternoon.

Taking responsibility for the funeral arrangements, Nick keeps vigil at the house until Gatsby's father arrives. Henry C. Gatz brings two mementoes of his son that he produces for Nick's inspection. One is a boyhood schedule and list of general resolves written on the flyleaf of a Hopalong Cassidy book. This document sets forth an ambitious program for personal improvement reminiscent of the recommendations in Benjamin Franklin's autobiography: "Study needed inventions"; "Practice elocution, poise and how to attain it"; "No more smokeing or chewing." "It just shows you," Mr. Gatz declares, in a surge of pride for his son's not quite successful attempt to reinvent himself.

Mr. Gatz's other treasure is a photograph of Gatsby's house, "cracked in the corners and dirty with many hands," which he fishes out of his wallet to show Nick. "Look there," he says, and again, "Look there." He and Nick are standing in the hall of the house, but as far as Mr. Gatz is concerned they might be anywhere. What matters is the soiled photograph in his hands, which is more real to him than the house itself. "It's a very pretty picture. It shows up well," Mr. Gatz observes (134–35). It is appropriate that he should be fixated on a photographic image that seems to freeze time (Dessner, "Photography," 176). Father and son alike prefer the imagined to the real, the irrecoverable romantic past to the inescapable material present.

On the night before returning to the Midwest, Nick pays a final visit to the "huge incoherent failure of a house" that in its effrontery mirrored Gatsby's own ostentation. Concerned as always with propriety, Nick erases an obscene word some boy has scrawled on the front steps. Then he strolls down to the beach, sprawls on the sand, lets his mind wander in search of a moral: "As the moon rose higher the inessential houses began to melt away"—inessential because inescapably concrete, solid, and substantial, and thus unworthy of the wonder the Dutch sailors felt upon beholding for the first time the "fresh, green breast of the new world" (140), or of Gatsby's wonder when he first spied the green light at the end of Daisy's dock and stretched his arms toward a dream that would forever elude his grasp.

This makes for a moving, even uplifting conclusion. But *The Great Gatsby* conveys another message as well. It tells a cautionary tale about the debilitating effects of money and social class on American society and those who seek fulfillment within its confines. Fitzgerald wrote in a world full of clocks and calendars, Malcolm Cowley once observed, thinking of the author's immersion in the culture of his time. But as Cowley also famously remarked, in his fiction Fitzgerald regarded that culture both from within, as someone typical of and essentially involved in it, and from without, as a more or less disinterested and hardheaded observer. Fitzgerald's masterpiece remains an brilliant example of social history even as it uncovers the cracks in the glittering surface, the poison eating its way underneath. It is this double vision that makes *The Great Gatsby* great.

{ 5 }

THE TROUBLE WITH NICK

READING *GATSBY* CLOSELY

NICK CARRAWAY is a snob. He dislikes people in general and deni-
grates them in particular. He dodges emotional commitments.
Neither his ethical code nor his behavior is exemplary: propriety
rather than morality guides him. He is not entirely honest about himself and frequently misunderstands others. Do these shortcomings mean
that Nick is an unreliable narrator? At times and in part, yes. But they
also mean that he is the perfect narrator for *The Great Gatsby* and that
Fitzgerald's greatest technical achievement in the novel was to invent this
narrative voice at once "within and without" the action.

The first clue to Nick's makeup comes on the first page of the book,
where he totally misunderstands his father's advice. "Whenever you feel
like criticizing any one," his father had told him in his "younger and more
vulnerable years," he was to remember that not everyone had enjoyed the
advantages he has had. Clearly Nick's father is advising tolerance here, and
it seems likely that he had detected in his son a somewhat disturbing pro-
pensity to find fault. Nick, however, interprets the remark as a judgment
on others, who lack what he calls that "sense of the fundamental decencies . . . unequally parcelled out at birth" (5) and consequently misbehave.
This interpretation, Nick acknowledges, is an extraordinarily judgmental
one, the interpretation of a snob who admits to the charge as if to say
that there are far worse things than snobbery in the world: bad manners,
for example. Nick's undoubted "advantages," which include good schools,

social position, family background, and even an exclusive senior society at Yale, may eventuate in an awareness of the "fundamental decencies" if one construes the phrase narrowly as conforming to conventional standards of propriety, but they hardly guarantee any moral acumen. So it is with Nick Carraway. Above all he disapproves of those who do *not know how to act*. That is why it takes him so long to ascertain that Jay Gatsby, a walking compendium of social gaucheries, is nonetheless worth any number of Buchanans.

Nick's misunderstanding of his father should also put us on guard against his claim that he's "inclined to reserve all judgments," especially when in the next breath he speaks of the "veteran bores" and "wild, unknown men" who have made him privy to "intimate revelations . . . usually plagiaristic and marred by obvious suppressions." Had they suppressed less, Nick might have been more interested. "Reserving judgments is a matter of infinite hope," he observes, and he is not the character in the novel possessed by infinite hope. He listens to confessions since he is "a little afraid of missing something" (5) otherwise: a vicarious sense of having drunk his cup to the lees. But he does not suspend judgment. Nick judges, and condemns, practically everyone he meets in the course of the novel.

Collectively he speaks of closing off his interest in the "abortive sorrows and short-winded elations of men" (6). Introducing individual specimens of this sorry genus, he delineates more specific physical deficiencies. Tom Buchanan has straw hair, a hard mouth, a supercilious manner, and a cruel body with which he pushes people around. There had been men at Yale who hated his guts, and if Nick is not among them, it's not because he can't see why. His wife Daisy, Nick's second cousin once removed, speaks in a thrilling voice, but she murmurs so low that people must bend toward her to hear. Her insincere remark about having "been everywhere and seen everything and done everything" (17) strikes Nick as "a trick of some sort" to exact an emotional commitment from him.

With the lower orders Nick is still less charitable. Myrtle Wilson, smoldering with vitality, carries her "excess flesh sensuously" (23) and comically takes on airs in the West 158th St. apartment Tom has secured for their rendezvous. Meyer Wolfshiem is presented as a small Jew with tiny eyes, a flat nose in whose nostrils "fine growths of hair" luxuriate, and cuff buttons made of "finest specimens of human molars" (55, 57). Sentence is passed rapidly on minor characters. Myrtle's sister Catherine—"a slender, worldly girl of thirty" with a sticky bob of red hair, rakishly painted eyebrows, and eternally jangling bracelets—is disposed of in a paragraph (26).

In the catalog of those who attend Gatsby's parties, people are labeled and found wanting by name alone. "The Dancies came, too, and S. B. Whitebait, who was well over sixty, and Maurice A. Flink, and the Hammerheads, and Beluga the tobacco importer, and Beluga's girls": something is fishy here (50).

Nick's basic contempt for mankind emerges in what he says and thinks as well as in descriptions of others. His particular way of telling the story has been variously characterized in the critical literature on *The Great Gatsby*, but surely a dominant characteristic of that voice is its irony. This sometimes leads to light-hearted bantering in conversation, as with Daisy. Is she missed in Chicago, she asks? "All the cars have the left rear wheel painted black as a mourning wreath," he answers, "and there's a persistent wail all night along the north shore" (11), a wittily casual remark that takes on resonance as the novel's motif of careless driving develops. Would Nick like to hear about the butler's nose, she inquires? "That's why I came over to-night," he responds (14). His unspoken thoughts, however, tend toward the more hostile levity of sarcasm.

In his mind Nick constantly puts others down. After listening to Tom Buchanan maunder on about impending racial struggles and the increasing (or is it declining?) heat of the sun, Nick devastates the man he has helped to cuckold when, with his eyes finally opened to the affair between Daisy and Gatsby, Tom begins to expound on the scientific proof for his "second sight" and then stops, the "immediate contingency" having "pulled him back from the edge of the theoretical abyss" (94–95). Soon after, Nick characterizes Tom's hypocritical defense of family solidarity as "impassioned gibberish" (101). Buchanan deserves such scornful treatment, but what of poor Henry Gatz, who proudly shows Nick his dead son's schedule for self-improvement, written in his copy of *Hopalong Cassidy*? "He was reluctant to close the book, reading each item aloud and then looking eagerly at me. I think he rather expected me to copy down the list for my own use," Nick sniffily observes (135). Then there is the "persistent undergraduate" who brings Jordan Baker to one of Gatsby's parties under the impression that sooner or later she will "yield him up her person" (37). When that prospect fails to develop, the undergraduate becomes engaged in "an obstetrical conversation with two chorus girls" and "implore[s]" Nick to join him (42). As Wolfshiem remarks in another sense, the undergraduate has "a wrong man" (56). Nick is not interested in making improper connections. He's not interested in making any *lasting* connections at all.

Nick Carraway carefully avoids emotional entanglements. He writes letters signed "Love, Nick" to a girl back home, but one reason he's come to New York is to avoid "being rumored into marriage" with her (19). Unable to stop thinking how "a faint mustache of perspiration" develops on her upper lip when she plays tennis (48), he finally severs the relationship. In the East he has "a short affair with a girl who lived in Jersey City and worked in the accounting department," but he lets it "blow quietly away" when her brother begins "throwing mean looks" in his direction (46). Jordan, his social peer, poses a more serious threat to his bachelor status. He is attracted to her hard, jaunty body and superior chin-in-air attitude, even though he knows she will lie to avoid responsibility and cheat to win at golf. But in the end she seems too much of a piece with Tom and Daisy, so he breaks off with her, too, before returning to the Middle West. It is not surprising that Nick has reached thirty without being married or engaged: he does not reserve judgment, he reserves himself. Prufrock-like, he contemplates his future: "a decade of loneliness, a thinning list of single men to know, a thinning briefcase of enthusiasm, thinning hair" (106).

In the light of this pattern, one regards with suspicion Nick's claim that releasing himself from a "vague understanding" with the girl back home before pursuing another with Jordan makes him "one of the few honest people" he's ever known (48). In an early draft, Fitzgerald wrote "one of the few decent people," later altering it to "honest." Apparently thinking that he had made Nick too unreliable as a narrator, in revision he also "added material which stressed Nick's belief in his own honesty and deleted passages which might undercut [his] integrity," such as offering Gatsby and Daisy the keys to his house (Parr, "Individual Responsibility," 678). Still, where honesty is concerned, it is undeniable that Nick regards telling the truth as less important than avoiding the unseemly. A case in point is his remark that Catherine had shown "a surprising amount of character" at Myrtle's inquest by falsely swearing that her sister "had been into no mischief whatever" (127), a lie designed to avert a public scandal.

Social decorum ranks high on Nick's scale of values, certainly higher than honesty, and it guides his attitude toward sexual morality. Adultery abounds in The Great Gatsby. It is rather the expected thing among the idle rich. As Jordan says, Daisy "ought to have something in her life" (63). Only those who contract liaisons with lovers of higher social standing (Myrtle and Gatsby), though, are punished for their sin or for their presumptuousness. What most concerns Nick about this extramarital coupling is the manner in which the affair is conducted. Daisy, he thinks, should "rush out of the house, child in arms" upon discovering Tom's infidelity. Nor can he approve of the way Tom orchestrates the affair, taking his mistress to popular restaurants to show her off and then abandoning her to chat with acquaintances. Tom further concocts the falsehood that Daisy is Catholic to explain to Myrtle why he cannot be divorced. As voyeur Nick is curious to see Tom's girl; as snob he has no desire to know her. When they do meet, Myrtle proves a veritable model of social pretentiousness. In clothes, in gestures, in conversation, Nick presents her as simply ridiculous. Not until Tom breaks her nose does she merit any sympathy whatever.

Nick himself appears rather ridiculous when, in his obsession with propriety, he twice insists on having actually been invited to Gatsby's first party, unlike most of the gate crashers. Moreover, although all around him people are conducting themselves "according to the rules of behavior associated with amusement parks" (34), he repeatedly tries to meet and thank his host, as at a formal gathering. This proves difficult, and meanwhile Jordan turns up, relieving him of the danger of addressing "cordial remarks to passers-by" (35). When be finally does encounter Gatsby late in the evening, Nick is caught off guard: he'd been expecting "a florid and corpulent person in his middle years" (40). For a long time Gatsby continues to confound Nick's expectations. Unlike almost everyone else in Nick's world, he resists classification.

It's not merely that Nick is curious about Gatsby: *everyone* is curious about him. But while others merely speculate about Gatsby's relationship with von Hindenburg or his career as a killer, Nick is exposed through two rather remarkable coincidences—moving in next door and knowing Daisy—to more intimate revelations from the figure of mystery himself. Gatsby's first preposterous account (wealthy parents from the western city of San Francisco, war hero educated at Oxford who subsequently "lived like a young rajah in all the capitals of Europe . . . collecting jewels, chiefly rubies, hunting big game, painting a little . . . and trying to forget something very sad") tends to confirm Nick in his view of his neighbor as pretentious arriviste, inventing a background to replace the one he lacks. Even though Gatsby produces the medal from Montenegro and the cricket photograph, Nick is not persuaded: "Then it was all true," he proclaims in ironic overstatement. "I saw the skins of tigers flaming in his palace on the Grand Canal; I saw him opening a chest of rubies to ease, with their crimson-lighted depths, the gnawings of his broken heart" (52–53). Nick's cynicism is further underlined in two subsequent incidents. Stopped for speeding, Gatsby flashes the policeman a white card which purchases instant immunity. "What was that?" Nick asks. "The picture of Oxford?" (54). Later, during the tour of the mansion and after the lavish display of shirts, Nick has a characteristically sardonic thought: "I was going to ask to see the rubies when the phone rang . . ." (73).

Under the circumstances Nick hardly expects *any* section of Gatsby's fabulous story to be true, yet when Gatsby modifies his tale to explain why and for how long he'd actually gone to Oxford, Nick is willing to put all the young rajah balderdash out of mind: "I had one of those renewals of complete faith in him that I'd experienced before" (101). Part of Nick wants to believe in Gatsby, just as another part holds him up for ridicule.

The snob in Nick Carraway finds Gatsby contemptible. He makes the point both on the second page of the novel ("Gatsby . . . represented everything for which I have an unaffected scorn") and on page 120 ("I disapproved of him from beginning to end"). Significantly, this second statement immediately follows Nick's "You're worth the whole damn bunch put together" speech. He can simultaneously praise Gatsby, in other words, and still disapprove of the "gorgeous pink rag of a suit" he's wearing, scorn his "old sport" affectation, disapprove of his ostentatious Hôtel de Ville and extravagant parties, scorn his shady business "gonnegtions"—above all, disapprove of his social incompetence.

Gatsby obviously lacks that "sense of the fundamental decencies" that comes with the right background. He seems to think that his awful parties are socially respectable gatherings. Yet Nick facilitates Gatsby and Daisy's affair by inviting the two of them for tea ("Don't bring Tom," he warns her), and he encourages their continuing relationship by "remaining watchfully in the garden" while they talk on the steps of his house for half an hour (66, 82). The question is why. Jordan asked him to arrange the tea, for one thing, and Nick dislikes Tom and knows of his unfaithfulness and brutality. But he would not have so willingly played the role of go-between had he not felt a curious kinship with the "elegant young roughneck" (40) in the mansion next door.

The fact is that Nick, like Gatsby, has romantic inclinations. But while Gatsby guides his life by his dream, Nick carefully separates romance from reality. What he most admires in Gatsby is the "extraordinary gift for hope," the "romantic readiness" he has found in no one else (6). Nick's first glimpse of his neighbor comes after the dinner party at the Buchanans, when he returns home to catch sight of someone on the lawn next door. He is about to call out (having concluded, in his obsessive concern with etiquette, that Jordan's mentioning Gatsby "would do for an introduction") when the solitary figure stretches "out his arms across the water" as if to reach the green light at the end of Daisy's dock. Far away though Nick is, he could swear that the man is trembling (20). Gatsby trembles elsewhere and so do Tom, Daisy, and Mr. Gatz. Nick does not, himself, tremble, but it is a physical reaction he can understand and identify with. It appeals to the side of his nature that conjures up "sumptuous and romantic apartments" concealed above Wilson's garage (!) in the valley of ashes (22), the side that imagines entering the lives of "romantic women" on Fifth Avenue, so long as "no one would ever know or disapprove." But as that last thought suggests, Nick is too proper, too emotionally cautious, to bring his fantasies about strangers to life: who would introduce them? He contents himself with vicarious experience instead. Walking alone through the theater district, Nick watches and dreams: "Forms leaned together in the taxis as they waited, and voices sang, and there was laughter from unheard jokes, and lighted cigarettes outlined unintelligible gestures inside. Imagining that I, too, was hurrying toward gayety and sharing their intimate excitement, I wished them well" (46–47). In something of the same spirit, he wishes Gatsby and Daisy well, too.

Nick imagines glamorous encounters but reads about banking after dinner in the Yale Club. Gatsby makes his fortune and sets out to capture the rest of his dream. Because of Gatsby's remarkable commitment to that dream—exactly the sort of commitment Nick declines to make—Nick can almost forgive Gatsby his presumption in courting Daisy under cover of a uniform that let "her believe he was a person from much the same strata as herself." Because of it he can very nearly pardon Gatsby's taking Daisy "one still October night," taking her "because he had no real right to touch her hand" (116). Because of it, too, he can temporarily efface from memory Gatsby's tactless offer of a chance to "pick up a nice bit of money" in return for arranging the meeting with Daisy (65). On the evidence, it's clear that Gatsby as parvenu will manage to do or say the wrong thing if given an opportunity to do so. Yet Nick finally puts aside his offended sense of propriety and decides to stick it out with Gatsby. After his death, in fact, "it grew upon me [Nick] that I was responsible, because no one else was interested—interested, I mean, with that intense personal interest to which every one has some vague right at the end" (127–28). So, for the only time in his life, Nick makes a commitment himself. And it is because this decision is so difficult for him, a man who invariably observes the social amenities and keeps his emotional distance, that it seems inevitable for the rest of us. That is why he is the right narrator for *The Great Gatsby*.

Fitzgerald enhances his accomplishment in point of view by not letting the change in Nick go beyond the bounds of credibility. Thus even while taking his "intense personal interest" in Gatsby, he behaves very much like the old Nick, trying to arrange a proper funeral with a respectable company of mourners and without sightseers. Moreover, he goes through the ritual of shaking hands with Tom *despite* finding out that Tom had directed the murderous Wilson to Gatsby's house. "I shook hands with him; it seemed silly not to, for I felt suddenly as though I were talking to a child" (140). But Tom and Daisy are not children who damage toys that can be replaced or scrawl dirty words Nick himself can erase. The Buchanans destroy *people*. Myrtle Wilson, George Wilson, and Jay Gatsby are dead because of them, and they do not even feel remorse. Even at the end, then, Nick lets the social forms obscure his moral judgment.

Nor is Nick converted into a practicing romantic by Gatsby's example. The logic of Fitzgerald's technique demands that only the narrator go inside Gatsby's head. When Nick does so in a series of reflections on Gatsby's ecstatic commitment to Daisy, he repeatedly imposes his own reserve on Gatsby's thoughts. On the day of the tea, for example, Nick notes an expression of bewilderment on Gatsby's face and decides that there "must have been moments even that afternoon when Daisy tumbled short of his dreams—not through her own fault, but because of the colossal vitality of his illusion" (75). Similarly, on the day of Gatsby's death, Nick has an idea that Gatsby didn't believe Daisy would telephone "and perhaps he no longer cared. If that was true he must have felt that he had lost the old warm world, paid a high price for living too long with a single dream" (126). Nothing that Gatsby says or does warrants either of these conclusions. Nick is unable to conceive of the depth of Gatsby's dream.

Throughout the novel Gatsby is associated with the night, and more particularly with the moon. In four of the nine chapters the action ends with Gatsby alone in the night, and twice—near the end of chapter 3, when a "wafer of a moon" shines over Gatsby's house as he gestures farewell to his guests (46) and again at the very end of chapter 7, where Nick leaves Gatsby "standing there in the moonlight—watching over nothing" (114), the moon seems to symbolize Gatsby's capacity for reverie. Hence it is deeply significant that on the last pages of the novel Nick Carraway, alone in the dark, wanders over to Gatsby's house in the moonlight, sprawls on the sand, and thinks of Gatsby's wonder when he saw the green light at the end of Daisy's dock (181–82). For a moment, perhaps, Nick felt a sense of identity with the moon person who had lived and died next door. But only for a moment, and then the rational Nick takes over to provide the novel with its coda about the Dutch sailors and the corruption of the American dream.

Nick Carraway and Jimmy Gatz come from the same part of the country, but they belong to vastly different worlds. At the Buchanans, Nick plays the naif by asking Daisy, "Can't you talk about crops or something?" But this comes from a man who is simultaneously evaluating the "corky but rather impressive claret" (14). Nick is no farmer from the country. He graduated from Yale, and so did his father. He knows about El Greco and Kant and Petronius. He has a sense of history. At college he wrote editorials, which hardly makes him "literary" (as he claims) but does suggest a breadth of knowledge and a judgmental nature. Moreover, unlike Gatsby, Nick has a place where he's known and accepted to go back to in St. Paul.

He has learned a good deal during the summer of 1922 about the power of the unrealizable dream and about the recklessness and selfishness of the very rich. Yet aside from a diminished curiosity that desires "no more riotous excursions with privileged glimpses into the human heart" (5), Nick's basic way of life seems unlikely to change. What has happened to Gatsby can hardly cure his misanthropy or open the floodgates of his emotional reserve. But if Nick is not much altered, many others have been. *The Great Gatsby* is a novel that has made a difference in the lives of many who have or will read it. One does not have to like Nick Carraway to discover something about oneself in the tale he tells.

{ 6 }

MONEY AND MARRIAGE IN
FITZGERALD'S STORIES

I write about Love and Money; what else is there to write about?

—JANE AUSTEN

I

Most authors constantly repeat themselves, Scott Fitzgerald observed in 1933. "We have two or three great and moving experiences in our lives," he continued, and on the basis of these experiences "we tell our two or three stories—each time in a new disguise—maybe ten times, maybe a hundred, as long as people will listen" (*My Lost City*, 86–87). One of the stories Fitzgerald told over and over again was about the struggle of the poor young man to win the hand of the rich girl. That had "always" been his situation, he remarked. He grew up "a poor boy in a rich town; a poor boy in a rich boy's school; a poor boy in a rich man's club at Princeton" (qtd. in Turnbull, *Fitzgerald*, 150).

He exaggerated his poverty. The Fitzgeralds were not badly off except in relation to the fabulously wealthy. But they did have less money than most families whose sons and daughters went to dancing school or college with Scott, and so he grew up thinking of himself as at a disadvantage in courting rich girls. Love and money became almost inextricably entangled in his mind and in his fiction. Almost everyone who has written about Fitzgerald has commented on his obsession with this topic, but usually they have concentrated on the novels, not the stories that reveal his changing attitudes toward money and marriage.

Rudolph Miller in "Absolution" (1924) suffers a "furious" attack of shame when he has no money for the church collection box, since Jeanne Brady, in the pew behind him, might notice (*Short Stories*, 268). In "Rags Martin-Jones and the Pr-nce of W-les" (1924), an imaginary merchant offers to sell the rich and beautiful Rags "some perfectly be-*oo*-tiful love," and he'll gladly send for a fresh supply since there's "so much money to spend" (*Short Stories*, 277). But if you don't have anything for the collection box, the girl will notice. And if you don't have enough to spend, the merchant will not bother. No money, no love. "If you haven't got money," Philip Dean instructs the hapless Gordon Sterrett in "May Day" (1920), "you've got to work and stay away from women" (*Short Stories*, 102).

Sterrett is a weakling who commits suicide when he wakes from a sodden drinking bout to find himself rejected by the society girl who used to love him and married to a "Jewel" of the lower classes. In this as in many other stories the poor young man engages in unequal combat with a wealthy competitor. "Remember," a precociously cynical Fitzgerald wrote at nineteen, "in all society nine girls out of ten marry for money and nine men out of ten are fools" (*Apprentice*, 126). He often felt discriminated against in such an environment. Occasionally he treated his predicament humorously:

Those wealthy goats
In raccoon coats
  can wolf you away from me

he complained in "Oh, Sister, Can You Spare Your Heart," a jingle in his notebooks (*Notebooks*, 135). But such levity was rare, for he had been badly hurt.

Fitzgerald rang variations on the theme in his two best novels and in dozens of short stories. These were based—sometimes loosely, sometimes with almost photographic fidelity to the facts—on his love for two girls, Ginevra King and Zelda Sayre. Fitzgerald wooed Ginevra King of Chicago throughout 1915 and 1916, but she remained unwilling to commit herself to him. In August 1916, he went to visit her at her summer home in Lake Forest. "Once I thought that Lake Forest was the most glamorous place in the world," he wrote two decades later. "Maybe it was" (*Letters*, 84). As Ginevra's visiting beau, he escorted her to parties, dinners, and dances. But he also spent a "bad day at the McCormicks," endured a "Disappointment," and heard someone declare, "Poor boys shouldn't think of marrying rich girls" (*Ledger*, unpaginated). A few months later he and

Ginevra broke up conclusively, but Fitzgerald did not soon stop caring about her.

Still, he fell in love with Zelda Sayre of Montgomery, Alabama, in September 1918, the month of Ginevra's wedding to William Mitchell ("beautiful Billy Mitchell," Fitzgerald had noted in his *Ledger* entry for August 1916). Zelda was widely known in Montgomery for her daring. Fitzgerald thought that "by temperament she was the most reckless" of all the women he ever knew. Nonetheless, Zelda "was cagey about throwing in her lot" with him before he had proved himself as a moneymaker. So at war's end Fitzgerald went off to New York, "the land of ambition and success," to make his fortune. When the fortune failed to develop, Zelda's devotion flagged; and after a desperate trip back to Montgomery, Fitzgerald boarded a Pullman car for her benefit and then sneaked back into the daycoach when the train got underway. In the summer of 1919 he gave up his job in New York, went west to St. Paul to rewrite *This Side of Paradise*, and in September learned that Scribner's would bring out his novel in the spring. In the meantime, he cranked out short stories and wired to the South such materialistic messages of love as "I HAVE SOLD THE MOVIE RIGHTS OF HEAD AND SHOULDERS TO THE METRO COMPANY FOR TWENTY-FIVE HUNDRED DOLLARS I LOVE YOU DEAREST GIRL" (Mizener, *The Far Side of Paradise*, 79–104).

"Essentially," Fitzgerald knew, "I got my public with stories of young love" (*Letters*, 128). And in the stories he began selling to the *Saturday Evening Post* in 1919 and 1920 it was almost always young love in high society. As early as New Year's Eve of 1920, he was complaining to Maxwell Perkins that he'd "go mad if I have to do another debutante, which is what they want" (*Letters*, 145). Readers started a Fitzgerald story not always sure of a happy ending, but with confidence that he would provide a glimpse of a glamorous social world few of them had ever inhabited. So stereotyped was this social setting that his illustrators usually presented the characters as handsome creatures in full evening dress. The men wore tuxedos or tails, the women gowns, though there might be no reason whatever on the basis of the story for them to be so attired. In "The Bowl" (1928), for example, the male protagonist is described as customarily wearing tan or soft gray suits with black ties. Yet in the illustrations he appears in formal evening clothes.

Fitzgerald's novels of love and money usually attack the rich. The Buchanans treat Jay Gatsby brutally, then escape while his dream and life blood ebb away. The Warrens retain Doctor Diver until they've used up his vitality, then dismiss him. The stories are less consistent in their attitude toward the wealthy, yet most of them can be classified as falling within one of two strains. One group of stories depicts the success, or seeming success, of the poor young man in wooing the rich girl. In the other, more effective group, the young man is rejected in his quest or if successful is subsequently disappointed.

The usual trouble with stories of the first kind is that they are not persuasive. At least subconsciously, Fitzgerald must have realized this, for he often tricked out such tales with fantasy or with outrageous challenges to reader disbelief. "The Offshore Pirate" (1920) provides a case in point. As the first sentence declares, it tells the "unlikely story" of the winning of Ardita Farnam, a yellow-haired embodiment of the golden girl. Ardita is bored by the predictable round of her social life, and eager, so she says, to cast her lot with anyone who will show some imagination. That someone turns out to be Toby Moreland, a rich boy playing at poverty. He attracts her interest by pretending to be a musician who has risen to wealth first by way of his talent, then by stealing the jewels of society matrons. He commandeers Ardita's yacht but though fascinated, she withholds her hand:

> "We can get married in Callao."
> "What sort of life can you offer me? I don't mean that unkindly, but seriously, what would become of me if the people who want that twenty-thousand-dollar reward ever catch up with you?"
>
> (SHORT STORIES, 90)

It would be different if she were "a little, poor girl dreaming over a fence in a warm cow country" and he, newly rich with ill-gotten gains, had come along to astonish her with his munificence. Then she'd stare into the windows of the jewelry store and want the "big oblong watch that's platinum and has diamonds all round the edge" but would decide "it was too expensive and choose one of white gold for a hundred dollars." And he'd say, "Expensive? I should say not!" and "pretty soon the platinum one would be gleaming" on her wrist (*Short Stories*, 90). She wishes it were that way, but it isn't, so Ardita turns her suitor down until, at the end, she finds to her relief that he is both imaginative *and* extremely wealthy. A rich boy may charm his girl by pretending to have been poor, like Toby Moreland and like George Van Tyne in "The Unspeakable Egg" (1924), who wins his Fifi by playing the role of a bearded, disheveled roustabout (*The Price Was High*, 126–42). But of course it does not work the other way around.

A good many Fitzgerald stories hinge upon an actual rather than imaginary reversal of fortune. In these tales, he posits an America where the ambitious, hard-working lad rises to receive the romantic reward due him. Generally, stories that conform to this "boy makes money, gets girl" pattern are among the worst Fitzgerald ever wrote. They tend to be overplotted to the point where manipulation of character and circumstance becomes obvious. They lack verisimilitude and conviction. Commenting on two such stories—"Presumption" and "The Adolescent Marriage"—written in the fall and winter of 1925 and 1926, Robert Sklar observes that the author of *The Great Gatsby* had "put his matured art and intellectual perception into the requirements of slick magazine stories . . . as if he were an adolescent boy forced to wear short pants" (Sklar, *Fitzgerald*, 215–16).

In "Presumption," the more interesting of the two, Juan Chandler pursues a rich debutante, Noel Garneau. Juan comes from middle-class circumstances in Akron and swims beyond his depth in the social waters of Culpepper Bay. "You're not in any position to think anything serious about Noel Garneau" (*The Price Was High*, 187), his cousin Cora reminds him, and Noel does in fact reject him at first, though only partly because of his relative poverty. Juan really loses his chance when he foolishly tries to make her jealous. He can contemplate only one way to remedy the situation: by making a proper fortune. "I haven't any money and I'm in love with a girl who has," he confesses to a golfing partner who turns out, by the sort of coincidence that makes these stories embarrassing, to be Noel's father. Mr. Garneau advises Juan to stick it out.

> "Does the girl care about you?" he inquired.
> "Yes."
> "Well, go after her, young man. All the money in the world hasn't been made by a long shot"
>
> (*THE PRICE WAS HIGH*, 189).

Driven by these words of encouragement, Juan drops out of college to get wealthy, and eighteen months later he presents himself to Noel as a rich young man. Though she is now engaged, he follows her from Boston to New York, where he presents his case to her aunt, the soignée Mrs. Poindexter:

> "I've been called presumptuous in this matter, and perhaps to some extent I am. Perhaps all poor boys who are in love with wealthy girls are

presumptuous. But it happens that I am no longer a poor boy, and I have good reason to believe that Noel cares for me."

(THE PRICE WAS HIGH, 200)

Here, as Sklar points out, Fitzgerald reworks the *Gatsby* plot, and when Juan reads the note Noel has left directing her aunt to dismiss the "intolerable bore" who is pursuing her with his "presumptuous whining," he assumes all is lost. Juan then realized, Fitzgerald writes, "that fundamentally they were all akin—Cousin Cora, Noel, her father, this cold, lovely woman here [her mother]—affirming the prerogative of the rich to marry always within their caste, to erect artificial barriers and standards against those who could presume upon a summer's philandering" (*The Price Was High*, 201). The words could hardly ring truer. But wait! It's a case of mistaken identity, and the bore Noel speaks of is Mr. *Templeton*, the man she'd been engaged to, and she'll be delighted to see and fall in love with and marry the newly rich Mr. *Chandler*.

"Presumption" ran as the lead story in the January 9, 1926, *Saturday Evening Post*. Like all of Fitzgerald's work, it has its moments. But along with "The Adolescent Marriage" (1926) and such later *Post* publications as "The Rubber Check" (1932), "More Than Just a House" (1933), and "The Family Bus" (1933), it fails for lack of emotional conviction. John O'Hara wrote Fitzgerald admiring his portrait of Lew Lowrie, the "climber" in "More Than Just a House." He always did the "climber" well, O'Hara told him, and rightly so, for Fitzgerald the author felt a natural sympathy for the poor young man on the make. But as he grew older, he could no longer care passionately whether his young man won the golden girl. Although the magazines wanted him to continue turning out commercial love stories, by the early 1930s he was losing interest in such "inessential and specious matters" and could no longer write them convincingly (Turnbull, *Fitzgerald*, 300).

Occasionally Fitzgerald shifted the sexes as a variation on his basic theme. Thus in such early stories as "Myra Meets His Family" (1920) and "The Popular Girl" (1922), a poor girl sets her cap for a rich boy. The author's sympathy switches to the woman in this situation; Fitzgerald will not or cannot identify with the rich young man. At twenty-one, Myra Harper "can still get any man she wants," and she wants Knowleton Whitney: "You know what a wiz he is on looks, and his father's worth a fortune, they say. . . . He's smart as a whip, and shy—rather sweetly shy—and they say his family has the best-looking place in Westchester County" (*The Price Was High*, 13–14). Warned about Myra's reputation as a gold digger, Whitney invites her to the mansion where he tests her devotion by introducing her to awful people (actors hired for the occasion) masquerading as his parents. He soon confesses his plot, but Myra still exacts her revenge by staging a phony wedding and leaving him cold immediately afterward. The rich boy is bested, albeit rather cruelly. In "The Popular Girl," Fitzgerald settles for a more conventional happy ending. Yanci Bowman pretends to a wealth and social position that will, she thinks, impress her rich beau. But he loves her, not her background, and once she has spent her last dime they blissfully ride into Manhattan—and the future—together.

II

Fitzgerald's tales of rejection and disappointment are far more effective than those where true love unpersuasively conquers all. They are more deeply felt, more true to the life. The stories of rejection also serve to demonstrate the author's growing maturity of outlook, his disturbing sense that pursuit and capture of the golden girl was not really worth all the trouble and heartache. He felt anything but philosophical about the matter when he wrote *This Side of Paradise*, however. The section of that novel called "The Debutante"—really a short story in the form of a playlet, with dialogue and stage directions—painfully relives Fitzgerald's rejection by Ginevra King.

Initially Rosalind Connage, the debutante, agrees to marry Amory Blaine when he's "ready" for her, despite the fact that he's making a paltry thirty-five dollars a week. But soon she changes her mind, choosing a rich suitor instead. "I don't want to think about pots and kitchens and brooms. I want to worry whether my legs will get slick and brown in the summer" (183), she explains. Her selfishness is appalling, but Fitzgerald will not condemn her. In a concluding stage direction, he assigns Rosalind a capacity for feeling like his own: "*(And deep under the aching sadness that will pass in time, Rosalind feels that she has lost something, she knows not what, she knows not why)*" (184).

A decade later Fitzgerald reworked the same material in "A Snobbish Story" (1930), showing much less sympathy for the rich girl involved. In this story as in four others of 1930 and 1931, she is Josephine Perry, Lake Forest debutante. Josephine becomes attracted to John Bailey, a *Chicago Tribune* reporter and aspiring playwright, but Bailey comes from Bohemia, not the upper-class suburbs, and has a wife who lives apart from him. He casts Josephine as the lead in his play, called *Race Riot*, and comes to the Perrys' home to interest her father in backing the production. While he's there, a policeman appears with the disturbing news that Bailey's wife has tried to take her life. Bailey thereupon disappears, while Mr. and Mrs. Perry chastise their daughter about consorting with "people like that" who had no business upsetting the decorum of Lake Forest.

Josephine accepts their criticism and determines that she will no longer involve herself with potential trouble. She decides that "any value she might have was in the immediate, shimmering present—and thus thinking, she threw in her lot with the rich and powerful of the world forever" (*Basil* 269). Thereafter she falls victim to what Fitzgerald, in the title of another of his stories about her, calls "Emotional Bankruptcy." While Rosalind Connage had supposedly been tenderhearted, though hardheaded on the question of marriage, Josephine Perry becomes equally tough of heart and head. The difference lies not in the girl who sat for both portraits but in Fitzgerald's perception of that girl and the nature of the struggle to win her hand. In his better stories of the 1920s, he gradually deromanticized the girl and deemphasized the glory of the quest.

The rich girl is still vibrant as Judy Jones in the great "Winter Dreams" (1922). Dexter Green, the poor young man in the story, commits himself to pursuing her with an abundant supply of ambition and energy. He feels driven to possess not only Judy but everything she represents: "He wanted not association with glittering things and glittering people—he wanted the glittering things themselves. Often he reached out for the best without knowing why he wanted it—and sometimes he ran up against the mysterious denials and prohibitions in which life indulges" (*Short Stories*, 220–21). To get Judy's attention, he manages to make a success of himself, and, as he had hoped, his ability to earn money dramatically transforms their relationship. On their first dinner date, she confesses that she's had "a terrible afternoon. There was a man I cared about, and this afternoon he told me out of a clear sky that he was poor as a church-mouse." Her interest in him, she confesses, had not been strong enough to stand the shock. Then this dialogue ensues:

> "Let's start right," she interrupted herself suddenly. "Who are you, anyhow?"
> For a moment Dexter hesitated. Then:
> "I'm nobody," he announced. "My career is largely a matter of futures."
> "Are you poor?"
> "No," he said frankly. "I'm probably making more money than any man my age in the Northwest. I know that's an obnoxious remark, but you advised me to start right."

There was a pause. Then she smiled and the corners of her mouth drooped and an almost imperceptible sway brought her closer to him, looking up into his eyes.

And then they kiss, her kisses "like charity, creating want by holding back nothing at all" (*Short Stories*, 226). But Dexter does not win the girl after all, and at the end of the story he is shocked and disillusioned to hear Judy spoken of as "faded" and "a little too old" for her husband in Detroit (234).

The loss of romantic illusions forms a central motif in stories of this type. Jonquil Cary in "'The Sensible Thing'" (1924) fends off the proposal of George O'Kelly until he is "ready" for her. This code word, also used by Rosalind to Amory and by Zelda to Scott, meant that the suitor must first establish himself financially. Until he did so, she would remain "nervous" (another code word used by both the fictional Jonquil and the real Zelda) about the prospect of marriage. Heeding the message, the ambitious O'Kelly strikes out for South America, makes his pile, and returns to claim his girl. But some of the magic has gone: "as he kissed her he knew that though he search through eternity he could never recapture those lost April hours. . . . There are all kinds of love in the world, but never the same love twice" (*Short Stories*, 301).

A still bitterer disillusionment awaited some of those who—like George O'Kelly—eventually win the girl. Then they are liable to find, as in "Gretchen's Forty Winks" (1924) and "The Adjuster" (1925), that they have married creatures of exquisite irresponsibility and selfishness. What's more, Fitzgerald implies that the possession of money and the idle hours that come with it encourage adultery. Luella Hemper in "The Adjuster" is bored. She "honestly wanted something to do. If she had a little more money and a little less love, she could have gone in for horses or for vagarious amour. Or if they had a little less money, her surplus energy would have been absorbed by hope and even by effort" (*Six Tales*, 142). But she falls in between and concentrates instead on making her husband's life miserable.

Money also confers a license for misbehavior on Anson Hunter in Fitzgerald's brilliant "The Rich Boy" (1926). Anson feels no more compunction about breaking hearts than about getting drunk. When caught in a compromising situation he simply refuses to apologize. But Anson pays deeply for his privileges, since he is unable to commit himself to any one woman, even to the one he thought he loved. His financial capacity is balanced by an emotional incapacity. The rich boy cannot give, only receive. Fitzgerald bids him adieu with this reflection:

I don't think he was ever happy unless some one was in love with him, responding to him like filings to a magnet, helping him to explain himself, promising him something. What it was I do not know. Perhaps they promised that there would always be women who would spend their brightest, freshest, rarest hours to nurse and protect that superiority he cherished in his heart.

(*SHORT STORIES*, 349)

Fitzgerald's mature view of the relationship between love and money is that too much money militates against true love. Such wealth is destructive because "those who have it lose the capacity to feel for others" (Kennedy, "Are Our Novelists Hostile," 33). This is true of the Buchanans and the Warrens of his novels, the Anson Hunters and Josephine Perrys of his stories. In this respect, the young man on the rise holds an emotional advantage over both his rich competitors and the golden girl he is pursuing.

The story that best illustrates Fitzgerald's altered perception of this relationship is "The Bridal Party," published in the *Saturday Evening Post* on August 9, 1930. On the surface this appears to be yet another tale about the poor boy losing the girl to another, much better-off young man. Michael Curly comes to Paris where he runs across Caroline Dandy and her fiancé, Hamilton Rutherford. As Michael remembers,

He had met Caroline Dandy when she was seventeen, possessed her young heart all through her first season in New York, and then lost her, slowly, tragically, uselessly, because he had no money and could make no money; because, with all the energy and good will in the world, he could not find himself; because, loving him still, Caroline had lost faith and begun to see him as something pathetic, futile and shabby, outside the great, shining stream of life toward which she was inevitably drawn.

(*SHORT STORIES*, 561–62)

Her "entire clan," Michael believes, had aligned themselves against him: "What a little counter he was in this game of families and money!" (563).

In Paris, though, Michael unexpectedly comes into an inheritance and resolves to take up his courtship once again. And again he fails, though not for lack of resources. Caroline prefers Rutherford for his solidity and decisiveness, she tells Michael. "It was that more than the question of . . . money" (566). She proves the point by sticking with Rutherford when he discovers, on the night of his stag party, that he has lost every cent he's made and must start over.

Michael goes to their wedding expecting to feel sorrow. But his own financial windfall combines with champagne and the "ceremonial function" to obliterate the pain. "All the bitterness melted out of him suddenly and the world reconstituted itself out of the youth and happiness that was all around him, profligate as the spring sunshine." Yet though "cured" of his sorrow, Michael may also be "cured," the last sentence suggests, of ever feeling so deeply again. "He was trying to remember which one of the bridesmaids he had made a date to dine with tonight as he walked forward to bid Hamilton and Caroline Rutherford good-by" (576).

Through its ironic view of the narrator-protagonist, "The Bridal Party" repudiates the belief, often implied and sometimes articulated in Fitzgerald's early fiction, that money could purchase almost anything or anybody one wanted to buy. To young Dalyrimple, returning from World War I, it seemed that "happiness was what he wanted—a slowly rising scale of gratifications of the normal appetites—and he had a strong conviction that the materials, if not the inspiration of happiness, could be bought with money" (*Flappers*, 166). Fitzgerald wrote "Dalyrimple Goes Wrong" in 1920. A decade later, in such stories as "The Bridal Party," "The Swimmers" (1929), and "Babylon Revisited" (1931), he demonstrated the relative impotence of money.

Henry Marston of "The Swimmers" is deceived by his French wife, Choupette, and seeks to keep custody of their children while divorcing her. His wife's lover, an aggressive American businessman named Wiese, tells Marston that he has no chance, that Wiese's money will insure that the children remain with Choupette. "Money is power,'" Wiese insists. "Money made this country, built its great and glorious cities, created its industries, covered it with an iron network of railroads. It's money that harnesses the forces of Nature, creates the machine and makes it go when money says go, and stop when money says stop" (*Short Stories*, 508). As if to illustrate how wrong he is, the motorboat in which Wiese delivers this speech sputters to a halt, and they are drifting out to sea, apparently at the mercy of the Atlantic, when Marston, the only swimmer of the three, agrees to swim for help in return for custody of the children. Skill and knowledge carry the day. For Marston as for Fitzgerald, it was not money but "a willingness of the heart" (512) that defined America.

"Babylon Revisited," one of Fitzgerald's best stories, also focuses on the issue of child custody. During the boom of the 1920s, Charlie Wales got rich and then wasted his time in drinking and lost his wife to illness. Charlie was so badly off when his wife died that her sister and brother-in-law assumed care of Honoria, the Waleses' daughter. When the boom turned to bust, a reformed Charlie comes to Paris to try to get Honoria back. At the end he finds he cannot yet gain custody of her and reflects with bitter irony on the days and nights when it seemed that one could purchase forgetfulness, when a man could lock his wife out in the snow (as he had done) "because the snow of twenty-nine wasn't real snow. If you didn't want it to be snow, you just paid some money" (*Short Stories*, 633). Charlie's money seems to him to have been as much a handicap as a blessing, however. His wife's sister still resents the profligate way Charlie threw his money around after making a killing in the stock market of the 1920s. Now that he has lost that fortune and started to build another anew, he alienates her again by announcing how well he's doing. Nor can he, yet, entirely shake free of the drunken companions his money had enabled him to dissipate away his life with a few years before. So he must wait still longer for Honoria, the only girl left for him. In the meantime he can only "send her a lot of things," though, he thinks in anger, that "was just money—he had given so many people money" (633).

In the mid-1920s, Jacob Booth, the hero of "Jacob's Ladder" (1927), made $800,000 in real estate. Then "he had tried—tried hard—for a year and a half to marry one of the richest women in America" (*Short Stories*, 353). If he had loved her, he could have had her. But Jacob did not love her; he pursued her because of the glitter of wealth that surrounded her. A similar halo hovered in the vicinity of many of the rich girls Fitzgerald's young men were forever pursuing in his stories of the 1920s. But during his last years as a writer, he rarely sent his male characters out in quest of the golden girl. He had learned by then that the halo was slightly tarnished and the glitter not always gold. He had also discovered that there were other things as powerful as money and that having excessive wealth rarely worked to the benefit of those who possessed it. Besides, by then he had told his recurring story of money and marriage—sometimes in pedestrian fashion, sometimes superlatively well—often enough.

[7]

A SHORT HISTORY OF
TENDER IS THE NIGHT

I

As F. Scott Fitzgerald said of himself, the man who started *Tender Is the Night* was not the one who finished it (qtd. in Bruccoli, *Some Sort of Epic Grandeur*, 369). It could hardly have been otherwise, for the years from 1925 to 1934 saw the author's private universe fall apart while the world outside descended into decadence and depression. Fitzgerald had an affair—or said he did—with the young actress Lois Moran, to balance the affair Zelda had—or said she did—with the French aviator Edouard Jozan. During drinking bouts Scott alienated friends, got into fights with strangers, and landed in jail several times. Zelda suffered through spells of ill health and at least one abortion. Living in a series of rented apartments and houses, the Fitzgeralds became estranged. Zelda threw herself into the dance with a fervency bordering on madness, then slipped over the line in the most severe of her recurrent mental breakdowns. The stock market collapsed. Scott's father died. Zelda's father died. All the fathers died, and with them went the assurance and the solidity of the era between the wars.

Anyone could see that Spengler was right, that Yeats was right: the West was in decline, the center could not hold, the old values did not obtain. It even began to seem that Marx was right. Certainly he spoke to the troubled times, as did Freud and Jung. *Tender Is the Night* reflected all those changes, even as it told the story of one talented and charming man dwindling from early promise into middle-aged oblivion. Like almost everything Fitzgerald wrote, the novel makes a deeply personal statement. It also stands as his testimony to modernism.

The book did not start out so ambitiously. As he originally conceived the idea for his novel during the cold rainy months of the fall and winter of 1924 and 1925, Fitzgerald had no more than a glimmer of such a sweeping scheme in mind. On 1 May 1925, to be sure, he wrote Maxwell Perkins that his next novel would be "something really NEW in form, idea, structure—the model for the age that Joyce and Stein are searching for, that Conrad didn't find" (*Letters*, 182). But that amazing (and never-defined) envelope was to contain a rather unpromising plot.

The protagonist of Fitzgerald's earliest draft toward *Tender Is the Night* is a twenty-one-year-old Southerner named Francis Melarky who was kicked out of West Point and then worked as a technician in Hollywood, where he became emotionally involved with a young actress. Francis, a hot-tempered youth, is now traveling in Europe with his domineering mother. On the Riviera they meet a group of charming American expatriates, including Seth and Dinah Roreback (or Rorebeck, or Piper), and Abe Herkimer (or Grant, or North), an alcoholic composer. Abe and Francis serve as seconds in a duel between Gabriel Brugerol (later Tommy Barban) and Albert McKisco, a writer who retains his name and integrity as a character throughout. Francis goes to Paris with the Rorebacks, where he falls in love with Dinah. Fitzgerald's narrative broke off here, but he planned to follow Francis through a process of degeneration. Eventually, he was to murder his mother in a drunken rage (Bruccoli, *Composition*, 26–27). Fitzgerald worked on this basic version, stage one in the three-stage, twelve-draft history of the book's composition, from 1925 until 1929. He called it variously *Our Type*, *The World's Fair*, *The Melarky Case*, and *The Boy Who Killed His Mother* (Bruccoli, *Composition*, 23) and got about a fourth of it down on paper.

Fitzgerald projected this new novel—and exaggerated its progress toward completion—in the wake of the financial disappointment of *The Great Gatsby*. He had hoped that *Gatsby* would sell 75,000 or 80,000 copies, enough to wipe out his debt to Scribner's and stake him to a block of time for the new book. He had written and revised *Gatsby* under firm, self-imposed discipline and felt that he had earned a respite from his labors. But *Gatsby* sold only 20,000 copies, and he was forced to turn out stories for the *Saturday Evening Post* (at $2,000 a crack, as of late 1924) to make ends meet. Resenting this necessity, he denigrated the results. As soon as he was far enough ahead on "trash," he wrote Perkins, he would devote full time to his next novel. If that one did not sell, he might as well give up and go to Hollywood (Fitzgerald, *Dear Scott/Dear Max*, 102).

So it was a discouraged writer who set down the first drafts of *Our Type*: professionally discouraged and personally humiliated. Zelda's affair with Jozan in the summer of 1924, at the very time when he was tearing along on the last stretches of *Gatsby*, hit Fitzgerald hard. He felt shattered, as Andrew Turnbull put it, because "he really believed in love, and in what two people [could] build against the world's cheap skepticism" (*Fitzgerald*, 145). And the apparent sexual success of the dark, strong naval aviator with his wife called his very manhood into question. There followed a disastrous stay in Rome. Late in October 1924 Fitzgerald mailed the typescript of *The Great Gatsby* to Perkins. Two weeks later he and Zelda and Scottie journeyed to Italy for five months in Rome and Capri that left him with an abiding hatred of the Italians and a nagging memory of "just about the rottenest thing that ever happened in my life" (qtd. by Cowley, note, 354).

They went to Rome for no better reason than that Zelda had been reading Henry James's *Roderick Hudson*. They knew no one, and for social companionship briefly attached themselves to the cast of *Ben Hur*, then being filmed in "papier-mâché arenas" grander than the real ones. Aside from this diversion, Fitzgerald disliked everything he encountered. The weather was execrable. He was drinking far too much and was often angry. He was furious when he was displaced from a restaurant table in favor of an Italian who possessed or pretended to a title. After one evening of revelry, he started a brawl in a nightclub. After another, he got into an altercation with a cabdriver who insisted on overcharging him. Blows were struck, and Fitzgerald was summarily taken to jail. These incidents precipitated a magazine article, "The High Cost of Macaroni," that was never published, and Fitzgerald then rewrote the fight with the cabdriver as the first chapter of the Melarky version of his novel. This fight was later relocated to the seventh chapter of the Melarky version and finally to the end of book 2 of *Tender Is the Night*, by which time Dick Diver had replaced the young Hollywood technician as the novel's protagonist.

Fitzgerald could hardly have known in 1925 how appropriate the setting would be to the decline and fall of Dick Diver, a character he had not yet invented. In "The High Cost of Macaroni" he characterized Italy as "a dead land where everything that could be done or said was done long ago, for whoever is deceived by the pseudo activity under Mussolini is deceived by the spasmodic last jerk of a corpse" (qtd. in Turnbull, *Fitzgerald*,

148). The language was extravagant, but in fact Rome offered "a perfect microcosm" of what had once been great and had now become debased in Western civilization. It was the one city in the world where Diver might most appropriately suffer through his own process of abasement and degradation. In this way, what might otherwise have seemed merely his private downfall was linked to a more general malaise (Roulston, "Dick Diver's Plunge").

The cabdriver-fight scene in Rome, written originally for stage one, the Melarky version, was eventually transplanted to stage three, and that was true of almost everything he wrote from 1926 through 1929. Different though it may have been in initial conception, Fitzgerald was able to lift characters and scenes from this version, polish them up, move them around, and use them to his purpose in the novel he published in 1934. Though he was to circulate the myth that he wrote and threw away hundreds of thousands of words, the fact is—as Matthew Bruccoli has shown in his invaluable book on the novel's composition—that very little Fitzgerald wrote, even during stage one, had to be wholly discarded.

II

Fitzgerald's correspondence with the agent Harold Ober and the editor Maxwell Perkins from 1925 to 1934 tells a repetitive tale of promises made and promises broken. Again and again Fitzgerald assured both men that he would soon complete his novel in progress. Yet he refused, despite their urging, to settle on a title or even to reveal much of what he had in mind. He would say only that his novel was to be based in part on the famous Leopold and Loeb murder case of 1924, on the January 1925 murder of her mother by a sixteen-year-old San Francisco girl named Dorothy Ellingson, and on "Zelda & me & the hysteria of last May & June in Paris. (Confidential)" (*Dear Scott/Dear Max*, 117–20; Bruccoli, *Composition*, 18). On the strength of no more information than that, in June 1926 Ober sold serial rights to *Liberty* magazine for $35,000 (*As Ever*, 89–92; *Dear Scott/Dear Max*, 144). Here was a bonanza well within reach. All Fitzgerald needed to do was to finish the novel and put it in the mail. He could not bring it off.

The initial deadline Fitzgerald set himself was fall 1926, gradually extended to the end of the year, to March 1927, to June 1927, and so on. In the beginning he projected a book of about 75,000 words, slightly longer than *Gatsby* though only half the length of the eventual *Tender*. In letters to Ober and Perkins, he radiated confidence that he could finish the novel at or close to his original deadline. So *Liberty* advertised the serial in its December 11, 1926, issue, and Scribner's made plans for book publication soon after the last magazine installment.

From the start in mid-1925, Fitzgerald had been celebrating the quality of his work in progress to Perkins (he did not do so to Ober). The book was "going to be great," he insisted. It was "wonderful." It would establish him as "the best American novelist." In February 1926, after reporting T. S. Eliot's praise of *Gatsby* as "the first step forward American fiction had taken since Henry James," Fitzgerald added in exultation, "Wait till they see the new novel!" (*Dear Scott/Dear Max*, 121, 125, 128, 134). Naturally Perkins was eager to publish the book. When nothing was forthcoming from Fitzgerald during the early months of 1927, Perkins twice attempted to spur him into action.

The World's Fair sounded like a fine title, Perkins wrote on January 20, 1927. Why didn't they announce it now? That would give Fitzgerald "a sort of proprietorship" over the title and generate interest in the novel. At that time Fitzgerald was in Hollywood, where he spent six weeks working on a Constance Talmadge movie called *Lipstick* (his script was not used). He also became seriously interested in the young actress Lois Moran, the model for Rosemary Hoyt. Don't give out the title yet, he wired Perkins from California; he'd deliver the novel to *Liberty* in June. In early April, after the Fitzgeralds moved to a rented mansion called Ellerslie outside Wilmington, Delaware, Perkins tried again. If Fitzgerald would send the title, and some text, and "enough of an idea to make an effective wrap," Scribner's could put out a dummy. But, Perkins added, the important thing was to finish the novel, after all, and he certainly didn't mean to harass his author (*Dear Scott/Dear Max*, 146–47; Bruccoli, *Composition*, 50).

Neither of these overtures stimulated progress on the novel. Fitzgerald's private life was in such disorder as to prevent him from doing any sustained work. What energy he could summon up went into short stories, for these could produce income rapidly and did not demand the extended concentration a novel required. As Fitzgerald later described the problem in a letter of March 11, 1935, to Perkins, you could write a short story on a bottle, but not a novel. A novel required organizational skill, fine judgment, and mental speed—all of which deserted him under the influence of alcohol. "If I had one more crack at [*Tender Is the Night*] cold sober I believe it might have made a great difference" (*Dear Scott/Dear Max*, 218–19).

According to Bruccoli, Fitzgerald made "no progress at all" on the book during 1927, 1928, and half of 1929. That was not what he told Perkins, however. As the new year of 1928 came around the corner, he pleaded for "patience yet a little while" from his publisher. Scribner's investment, he said, was not at risk. In reply, Perkins assured him that the firm felt "no anxiety whatever" about the book. But the editor did confess, in his letter of January 3, 1928, that he worried about all the time elapsing between *Gatsby* and the new novel. Perkins still anticipated no extended delay. "We can count on your novel for the fall, can't we?" he asked Fitzgerald on January 24, 1928. "It must be very nearly finished now" (*Dear Scott/Dear Max*, 149–50). These well-meaning comments from an eager and supportive editor must have rankled in Fitzgerald's breast as the days and weeks and months slid away.

Liquor eased the passage of time, or seemed to, as is manifest in Edmund Wilson's account of "A Weekend at Ellerslie" from late February 1928. Thornton Wilder attended the Fitzgeralds' house party, as did Gilbert and Amanda Seldes, John and Anna Biggs, Esther Strachey (Gerald Murphy's sister), and the cast of Zoe Akins's *The Furies*, then playing Wilmington. When the carousing turned frantic Wilson decided to escape a day early. Before he left, Fitzgerald read him and Seldes one of the Riviera chapters from his novel in progress. It was impressive work, but Wilson knew better than to ask when the book would be completed. Any inquiry along that line, he had learned, was liable to produce "a sharp retort" ("A Weekend," 375). Wilson understood that it was Fitzgerald's conscience that lashed out at him, but that did not make the situation any less uncomfortable.

Another subject much on Fitzgerald's mind during that Delaware weekend was World War I. In inviting Wilson to the party, he referred to the "slaughter of Paschendale" and to the troops "shivering in the lagoons at Ypres" ("A Weekend," 373). On the wall of his study at Ellerslie he hung the trench helmet he had been issued but never wore in action. He seemed fascinated with an album of photographs showing mutilated soldiers. Wilson did not know what to make of this until *Tender Is the Night* emerged, with its characterization of the war as a watershed in Western history and as a parallel to hostilities between the sexes.

Throughout 1928 Fitzgerald continued to promise delivery of the Melarky-matricide version he had in fact virtually abandoned. "ALL COMPLETED AUGUST," he wired Ober's office in June, by way of asking for a deposit to his bank account. "Done sure in September," he wrote Perkins late in July (*As Ever*, 113; *Dear Scott/Dear Max*, 152). Finally, on November 28, he sent Perkins "the first fourth of the book (2 chapters, 18,000 words)." In addition he wrote that he was patching up chapters 3 and 4 and would deliver those soon. But he sailed for Europe in March 1929 without delivering any more of the manuscript, even though—in stage one, fourth draft—he had in fact finished four chapters. "I hate to leave without seeing you," he wrote Perkins, "and I hate to leave without the ability to put the finished ms in your hands" (qtd. in Bruccoli, *Composition*, 56–58). The two chapters he mailed that November were the only ones that either Perkins or Ober would see until another five years had elapsed.

By the middle of 1929, Fitzgerald decided at last that the Melarky version was not going to work out. For one thing, matricide was a subject, as Wilson remarked, that "might well have taxed Dostoevsky" ("A Weekend," 375). Secondly, Fitzgerald must have sensed that his protagonist was not sufficiently interesting or attractive to command the attention of readers. Even his name was all wrong, for while Francis echoed Fitzgerald's given name, Melarky smacked of slang.

A new approach was called for, and Fitzgerald began to uncover it during his March 1929 journey across the Atlantic. In his story called "The Rough Crossing," written shortly after the boat docked in France, cracks begin to develop in the marriage of Adrian and Eva Smith. Adrian, a thirtyish playwright who has lately become a celebrity, pairs off during their Atlantic crossing with a lovely young girl named Betsy D'Amido. Betsy's very youth seems to transfer itself to him in a kind of romantic ecstasy. Here (as once earlier, in a 1927 story called "Jacob's Ladder") he was transmuting his feeling for Lois Moran into fiction, and laying the groundwork for the Dick Diver–Rosemary Hoyt affair.

"One Trip Abroad," a story published in 1930, went still further into the dissolving-marriage theme. Nicole and Nelson Kelly inherit some money and go to Europe, where they succumb to the dissipation of expatriate society. Like the Smiths, the Kellys drink too much and quarrel with each other. They also are unfaithful to each other. Wherever they travel in Europe, they meet another couple, still younger than they, who are obviously going through a process of steady deterioration. At the end, Nicole comes to understand that the other couple serve as their doubles. "They're us! They're us!" she tells her husband. "Don't you see?" (*Short Stories*, 597).

Both of these stories functioned as trial runs for stage two of *Tender Is the Night*, "the Kelly-shipboard version" in Bruccoli's terminology. "I am working night & day on novel from new angle that I think will solve previous difficulties," Fitzgerald wrote Perkins in mid-summer 1929 (*Dear Scott/Dear Max*, 156). The "new angle," the surviving drafts reveal, involved the transatlantic voyage of Lew and Nicole Kelly, a successful young film director and his wife. During the trip Lew is attracted to an aspiring young actress named Rosemary, who sneaks into first class in order to meet and make an impression on him. Later, presumably, the film director was to undergo much the same pattern of degeneration as Francis Melarky. Fitzgerald finished only two chapters of this version; it did not solve his "previous difficulties." But stage two wove another major theme into the thickening tapestry of his novel in progress.

Armed with the Kelly-shipboard material, Fitzgerald once again projected an early completion of his book. "SENDING THREE FOURTH OF NOVEL SEPT 30TH STARTING NEW STORY NEXT WEEK CAN YOU DEPOSIT THREEFIFTY," he cabled his agent on 29 August 1929. All he needed, he thought, was a little free time, a clear month here, a couple of months there, but it was the middle of November before, as he wrote both Perkins and Ober, he could contemplate "two uninterrupted months" ahead for the novel. Meanwhile, Ober was importuning him to mail half the manuscript, or even a smaller portion, to keep *Liberty* interested. He asked in October 1929, in December 1929, and, rather plaintively, in March 1930, "Couldn't you send over a few chapters of the novel. . . . Otherwise it means 1931." This last request inspired Fitzgerald to a rationalization. It would be "ruinous" to let *Liberty* start serializing an uncompleted novel, he pointed out. Besides, what if they didn't like the first part? The ever-patient Ober replied that he had talked to *Liberty*, that they wouldn't think of beginning serial publication until they had the complete manuscript, and that there was "not the least likelihood" of their turning it down.

After that, the subject of the novel faded out of the Fitzgerald-Ober correspondence until May 19, 1931, when the agent sent a message designed to boost the author's ego and, with luck, produce results. "I believe," Ober began, "and others, who are much more competent judges than I, believe that you ought to go further than any American writer and I think now is the time for you to get down to hard work and finish the novel" (*As Ever*, 144, 153–54, 158, 162, 165, 167–68, 177).

Though subjected to repeated delays and disappointments, neither Ober nor Perkins was ready to give up on Fitzgerald or his book. Such patience is not invariably rewarded, but in this case it eventually was. The novel could not possibly have achieved the power of its final form without the passage of nine years between inception and completion. Fitzgerald began in 1925 with no more than a melodramatic plot, a devotion to the apocalyptic ideas of Oswald Spengler, and an admiration for Gerald and Sara Murphy.

An extraordinary couple, the Murphys moved easily among the expatriate rich and formed lasting friendships with the great artists of the day:

Picasso and Leger, Dos Passos and Hemingway among them. Fitzgerald envied the Murphys their social ease with both groups and often behaved badly in their company, particularly during the liquid summer of 1925. In stage one of his novel the characters of Seth and Dinah Piper were fashioned after the Murphys. Like their originals, the Pipers knew how to make the world brighter for everyone around them. In other words, they had charm. He had spent almost five years, Fitzgerald commented in September 1929, on a novel dealing with "the insoluble problems of personal charm" (*Letters*, 495). The figure of Seth Piper–Gerald Murphy personified that quality. Dick Diver in the early Cap d'Antibes scenes of *Tender Is the Night*, raking the sand, supervising the revels, and giving too much of himself to others, closely resembles Piper-Murphy of stage one. Later in the published novel, however, the Divers were to become composite characters, modeled more closely on the Fitzgeralds than the Murphys.

III

At every stage of composition, *Tender Is the Night* depicted the decline of its principal character. And in each version Fitzgerald located this personal tragedy within the context of a wider cultural malaise. Underlying this pattern was the influence of Oswald Spengler's *Decline of the West*. Fitzgerald read Spengler during the summer he spent writing *Gatsby* (1924), he later maintained in a letter to Perkins. That seems improbable, as Spengler's magnum opus was not translated into English until 1926. In any event, by 1927 Fitzgerald had become a disciple of the German philosopher. "He and Marx are the only modern philosophers that still manage to make sense in this horrible mess," he wrote Perkins. He was especially impressed by Spengler's "dominant supercessive idea" that the West was in the throes of a fatal malady. In the final deterioration of the West, Spengler believed, money would replace aristocracy, and "monied thugs" and "new Caesars" would take control. Fitzgerald imposed this concept on the framework of his novel: Spengler provided him with an intellectual rationale for his own conviction that something was terribly wrong at the very heart of Western civilization (Lehan, *Fitzgerald and the Craft*, 30–35).

In *Tender Is the Night* sexual degeneration serves as a metaphor for this cancerous decline. Devereux Warren's incestuous relationship with his daughter Nicole exemplifies this moral corruption, but is only the most obvious of a number of examples in Fitzgerald's novel. In addition to echoes of incest in the Dick Diver–Rosemary Hoyt relationship and elsewhere, other forms of sexual deviance penetrate every corner of the book's expatriate society. Campion, Dumphry, and the Chilean youth Francisco are overtly homosexual. Mary North Minghetti and Lady Caroline Sibly-Biers are almost certainly lesbians, as are the cobra-headed women at the party on the rue Monsieur.

Moreover, Fitzgerald cut still other passages portraying what he regarded as sexual perversion, presumably to avoid offending public taste. One example is the "Wanda Breasted" episode, which Malcolm Cowley printed as an appendix to his 1951 revised edition of the novel. This scene conveys the disgust of Francis Melarky (and the author) at discovering that Wanda, a girl he has desired, was "a hysterical Lesbian." "God damn these women!" he thinks (*Tender* [1951], 344–45).

Fitzgerald might have written a first-rate novel by weaving his rhetorical and storytelling magic around such materials as the Jozan–Lois Moran adulteries, his relationship with the Murphys, and Spengler's notion of a dying culture. But he could not have written the novel that became *Tender Is the Night* without living through Zelda's breakdown on April 23, 1930, and her subsequent unsuccessful attempts to regain her health. Her collapse fit perfectly into his Spenglerian outlook: the world had proved too much for her or, more specifically, the postwar world that invited women to compete against men.

Here Fitzgerald grafted onto Spengler the basic argument of D. H. Lawrence's *Fantasia of the Unconscious*: that modern men and women were engaged in a struggle for dominance and that women were winning. Lawrence's book, which Fitzgerald read in the spring of 1930, inveighed against a reversal of sex roles in contemporary society. As Lawrence saw it, contemporary man was losing sight of his principal objective in life—a "disinterested craving . . . to make something wonderful out of his own head and his own self"—as a consequence of his sexual desires. Trying to please the female, Lawrence felt, led to male weakness, and women naturally proceeded to fill the vacuum of leadership. The generic modern woman, he wrote, "becomes the fearless inwardly relentless, determined positive party. . . . She is now a queen of the earth, and inwardly a fearsome tyrant." These ideas appealed to Fitzgerald, and logically so, because they so nearly reflected his own. "I believe," he wrote Mrs. Bayard Turnbull as stage three of *Tender* was taking shape in September 1932, "that if one is interested in the world into which willy-nilly one's children will grow up the most accurate data can be found in the European leaders, such as Lawrence, Jung, and Spengler" (qtd. in Sklar, *Fitzgerald*, 260–63; also see Wexelblatt, "Fitzgerald and Lawrence").

Fitzgerald wrote Lawrence into *Tender* in his account of the visit to the battlefield at Amiens. A less obvious borrowing involved Dick Diver, who is defeated by the sexual as well as the monetary power of his wife. He would not have abandoned his profession, his drive to build "something wonderful" out of himself, but for the exigencies of his passion for Nicole. And Zelda's collapse is also interpreted in Lawrencian terms. The character most closely modeled on Zelda in the novel is not Nicole but the nameless desperately ill woman artist, tortured by eczema, whom Dick Diver attempts to cure. Though he cannot save her, in a long discussion doctor and patient explore the crucial theme of the war between the sexes. She has been driven to her plight, Diver tells the dying woman, because she has insisted on doing battle against men in a deadly competition. Unlike Nicole Diver and Mary North and Rosemary Hoyt, she has been unwilling to feign conceding dominance to men while turning that apparent concession to her advantage.

In almost everything he wrote Fitzgerald focused on the competition between the sexes. In his early fiction the contest is more a game than a battle: Amory Blaine and the girls he courts only play at love. But soon the competition takes on mortal consequences, as for Myrtle Wilson and Jay Gatsby. In *Tender Is the Night* the sexes battle in open warfare, and except for Diver's unfortunate female patient the women win the battle, while the men either die, like Abe North and the Englishman Maria Wallis shoots in the Gare St. Lazare, or fade away like Diver himself. There can be little doubt that the author regarded his marriage with Zelda Sayre Fitzgerald as just such a struggle for survival. In *Tender Is the Night* he imagines how it might have been were he, like Diver, to lose while Zelda-Nicole emerged from the field triumphant. And the battleground on which they fight it out, in a novel that is full of references to warfare, is that of psychiatry.

Opinions vary as to the accuracy and validity of Fitzgerald's understanding of psychology. He did a considerable amount of reading and research on the subject and profited from extended conversations with Zelda's Jungian doctors and with Margaret Egloff, a young divorcée studying with Jung in Switzerland. Nonetheless, Henry Dan Piper was probably right that the author "really did not know enough about psychiatry to treat it authoritatively" (*Fitzgerald*, 222–23). Fitzgerald's central character, for example, seems too much an amalgam of charm and vulnerability, of Murphy and himself, to be convincing as a scientist and doctor. And his method of treatment consists of little more than telling his patients to control themselves.

Moreover, Fitzgerald converted Freud's concept of transference from a stage in the psychoanalytic process to a vampiresque exchange of energy in which the patient gains strength by draining the vitality of the healer. This interpretation of "transference" manifestly had more to do with Fitzgerald's own situation than with the psychoanalytical model. He saw himself as undergoing "emotional bankruptcy," with much of his diminishing resources having evaporated in the course of his marriage. But *Tender Is the Night* is a novel, not a scientific treatise, and should be assessed on those grounds. Fitzgerald was interested in showing how men and women in postwar times had become locked in mortal combat. On that basis, as the *Journal of Nervous and Mental Disease* commented in 1935, the novel succeeds splendidly. "For the psychiatrist and psycho-analyst," the review observed, "the book is of special value as a probing story of some of the major dynamic interlockings in marriage" (qtd. in Berman, "*Tender Is the Night*," 35).

By the fall of 1931 Zelda was thought to be well enough to leave institutional care, and the Fitzgeralds returned to the United States. Zelda stayed in Montgomery while Scott went to Hollywood in search of funds to finance an extended period of work on the novel. Now, at last, he was very nearly ready to launch into stage three, rescuing what was usable from the first two stages—about 35,000 words—and adding another 115,000 words to the script that became *Tender Is the Night*. There remained but to add a Marxist plank to the intellectual substructure provided by Spengler, Lawrence, and Jung. On arrival in Alabama, Fitzgerald told a newspaper interviewer that he was "somewhat of a Communist in ideals." He not only read *New Russia's Primer*, a simplified account of the Five Year Plan circulated by the Book-of-the-Month Club, but was enough impressed by it to insist that Zelda read it also and discuss it with Scottie. Anticipating the drumbeat of revolution, he suggested she take their money out of the bank in Montgomery, in advance of an economic collapse. When he formulated his "General Plan" for stage three early in 1932, he couched much of it in Marxist terms. The protagonist was to have been "brought up in a family sunk from haute bourgeoisie to petit bourgeoisie." Though Diver was to be "a communist-liberal-idealist, a moralist in revolt," he was to suffer his decline as a consequence of "living under patronage ect. & among the burgeoise." In the end, having cured his homicidal wife, he is but a shell of his former self (Donaldson, "Political Development"; Bruccoli, *Composition*, 76–82; Fitzgerald's spelling).

Obviously Fitzgerald did not follow much of this plan, for Dr. Diver has no discernible political position. Yet *Tender Is the Night* does contain a strong political component. In the opening section, for example, the White Russians who once frequented the hotels of the Riviera are glimpsed driving taxicabs. At the Divers' party, McKisco's socialism meets its match in Barban's anarchic strength; later the soldier of fortune Barban is employed to rescue Russian aristocrats. In a large measure, though, the novel makes its statement not through any overt commentary but by depicting the corruption and callousness of the haute bourgeoisie, with Baby Warren as the prime example, and by delineating the downfall of an older, better time. As John Dos Passos was to remark, "the whole conception of the book is enormous—and so carefully understated that—so far as I know—not a single reviewer discovered it." *Tender Is the Night*, he told Fitzgerald, demonstrated "the collapse of one of the great after-war imperial delusions. . . . The way you first lay in the pretty picture and then start digging under the surface is immense" (Fitzgerald, *Correspondence*, 358).

IV

In January 1932 Zelda Fitzgerald, who had begun working on a novel of her own, suffered a relapse and was taken to Baltimore for treatment. At about the same time her husband set down his extensive "General Plan" for stage three of his novel. In addition to its political-economic comments, the plan included a plot outline and descriptive details about major characters such as Dick, Nicole, "the actress" (Rosemary Hoyt), and "The Friend" (Tommy Barban). Fitzgerald's model for this plan came from Emile Zola's notes for *L'Assommoir*, as recorded in Matthew Josephson's *Zola and His Time*. He acknowledged the indebtedness in a note to Josephson and recommended a similar working procedure to John O'Hara (Bruccoli, *Composition*, 86; Fitzgerald, *Letters*, 539).

With this preliminary task accomplished, Fitzgerald was confident as never before. Characteristically, though, he underestimated the difficulty and duration of the job ahead. On January 15, 1932, he wrote Perkins that he was $6,000 ahead and was going to spend "five consecutive months on the novel. . . . Am replanning it to include what's good in what I have, adding 41,000 new words & publishing" (*Dear Scott/Dear Max*, 173). But it would require another two years and more than 100,000 "new words" before *Tender Is the Night* was ready for publication.

The most immediate roadblocks to progress came from Zelda's illness and the threat posed by *her* novel. Despite being institutionalized at Phipps Clinic and limited to two hours a day of concentrated work, over a six-week period she finished the novel she had begun in Alabama. Then, not altogether disingenuously, she sent the typescript to Max Perkins first and to her husband second. When Fitzgerald read this draft of *Save Me the Waltz*, he was outraged. "PLEASE DO NOT JUDGE OR IF NOT ALREADY DONE EVEN CONSIDER ZELDAS BOOK UNTIL YOU GET REVISED VERSION," he wired Perkins on March 16. The same day, he wrote an angry letter to Dr. Mildred Squires, the psychiatrist who had been treating his wife (and to whom her novel was dedicated). Therein he spelled out his two major objections to her book. In the first place, Zelda had used the name "Amory Blaine" for her male protagonist, "a somewhat anemic portrait painter." And of course Amory Blaine was the name of the autobiographical hero in Fitzgerald's *This Side of Paradise*. He did not like the borrowing, and he did not like being made a fool of. Second, he thought that Zelda was preempting his turf and appropriating his subject matter. Then, too, he must have felt a measure of shame that Zelda had completed a novel in a few short months, despite a severe breakdown, while his had been seven years in preparation, so far. Worst of all, he considered himself betrayed. Zelda had written her book, he maintained, "under a greenhouse which is my money, my name, and my love." Yet she felt no responsibility toward the greenhouse, knocking glass out of the roof whenever she chose (Mayfield, *Exiles*, 181–87; Bruccoli, *Some Sort of Epic Grandeur*, 322–25).

In explaining why she delayed sending him the script, Zelda wrote Scott that she wanted to avoid the kind of "scathing criticism" he'd recently given her stories. And, she confessed, "I was also afraid we might have touched on the same material." Basically her letter was one of apology, placing her husband in control of the family literary productions. From that time on he took over, guiding Zelda's revisions, keeping Perkins informed, and even telling the editor how much (and how little) to praise his wife's work. By the middle of May he sent the rewritten *Save Me the Waltz* to Scribner's with his evaluation that the novel was now a good one, perhaps very good. The book was published on October 7, 1932, and sold about 1,400 copies. The reviews were indifferent (Bruccoli, *Some Sort of Epic Grandeur*, 326–29).

It is easy to understand how Zelda Fitzgerald's prose, full of improbable metaphors, linking apparently inappropriate nouns and adjectives, might have blinded reviewers to her novel's merits. Like *This Side of Paradise*, her husband's first novel, *Save Me the Waltz* commits any number of sins against literary art, yet it does not fail to live. Alabama Beggs and her sisters come vividly to life in the opening sections, as does her sexual attraction to the Frenchman Jacques Chevre-Feuille and her frantic pursuit of excellence in ballet. Her husband, the successful painter David Knight, is a much less successfully realized character and verges on villainy in his casual willingness to be seduced by the actress Gabriele Gibbs in Paris. The novel draws substantially on the Fitzgeralds' recent experience for its subject matter, more so than does *Tender Is the Night*. But there are also striking similarities between the two novels.

A number of episodes in *Save Me the Waltz* prefigure similar ones in *Tender Is the Night*. In Zelda's novel Alabama Beggs Knight is forced to give up employment as a ballet dancer in Naples to return to the bedside of her dying father. In *Tender* Dick Diver is called back to the United States by the death of his father. The Knights' child Bonnie is given a bath in dirty water, much like the one the Divers' children take at the Minghettis'. David Knight is cursed with the same sort of compulsion to please others that helps to undermine Dick Diver; both of them muse on the matter in precisely the same language: "So easy to be loved—so hard to love" (*Save Me the Waltz*, 204). Alabama assumes a Nicole-like toughness in reflecting on her attraction to Jacques: "You took what you wanted from life, if you could get it, and you did without the rest" (98). *Waltz*'s Dickie Axton shoots her lover in the Gare de l'Est; *Tender*'s Maria Wallis shoots hers in the Gare St. Lazare.

The Fitzgeralds' novels also share a number of common themes. One is the importance of work and the way it can be compromised by possession of wealth. Dick Diver succumbs to the lure of leisure that his wife's money provides; Nicole occupies much of her time in fabulous spending sprees. Spending money "played a big part" in Alabama's life as well, until she lost, through her work in the ballet, "the necessity for material possessions." Both Zelda and Scott deplored the illusions that American children are brought up on through fairy tales and the blandishments of commercial advertising; lumbered with such Pollyannaish expectations, they are ill equipped to confront harsh reality. And *Waltz*, like *Tender*, included at least one section in which socialism is regarded with some sympathy (*Save Me the Waltz*, 190–98, 177–78, 35, 204, 98, 104, 210, 138–39, 206, 86).

None of these resemblances troubled Fitzgerald unduly. *Save Me the Waltz* remained, after all, the story of Zelda Sayre—the narrative of an attractive and willful Southern belle who marries a successful Northern artist, sees her marriage collapse through infidelity during a long period of expatriation in France, and recovers her dignity through immersion in the ballet. The novel told almost all of Zelda's story, omitting only the crucial fact of her mental illness. This was a subject her doctors warned her against writing about, but she turned to it nonetheless after the disappointment of *Save Me the Waltz*'s reception. In the spring of 1933 Scott found out about it and immediately tried to stop her. His novel in progress was going to deal with Nicole Diver's schizophrenia. To have Zelda exploring the same subject in her writing seemed intolerable, and it was on this specific issue that the famous literary battle between them was joined. Fitzgerald took the position that whatever happened to either of them belonged to him to use in his fiction, as he was the professional writer whose work paid the bills. On these grounds he sometimes signed stories and articles (or signed them jointly, as "by F. Scott and Zelda Fitzgerald") that were substantially written by his wife. On the same grounds, he took excerpts from Zelda's mentally troubled letters and reassigned them to Nicole.

In a long and exceedingly bitter confrontation witnessed by Dr. Thomas Rennie on May 28, 1933, the Fitzgeralds debated this issue. "What is the matter with Scott," she said by way of retaliation to his claims of professional privilege, "is that he has not written that book and if he will ever get it written, why, he won't feel so miserable and suspicious and mean towards everybody else." Zelda reluctantly agreed not to write about insanity until Scott finally finished his novel. After that, she said, she would insist on her artistic independence, even if it meant divorce (Bruccoli, *Some Sort of Epic Grandeur*, 348–55).

V

Throughout the summer and early fall of 1933 Fitzgerald worked hard to ready stage three for the presses. "The novel has gone ahead faster than I thought," he wrote Perkins on September 25. In about a month he would "appear in person" in his publisher's office, "carrying the manuscript and wearing a spiked helmet. . . . *Please do not have a band as I do not care for music*" (*Dear Scott/Dear Max*, 181–83).

By this time it had been decided to serialize the book in *Scribner's* magazine. *Scribner's* paid $10,000 for the rights, with $6,000 of that applied to his debt at the book publishers. It is hard to say exactly what motivated this decision; the original *Liberty* contract, secured by a healthy advance, was for several times that sum. It may be that Fitzgerald opted for *Scribner's* largely out of loyalty to Perkins, who had been supportive throughout the long hiatus between novels. It may be that he regarded *Scribner's*, a respected monthly, as a more fitting medium for a serious novel than either *Liberty*, a weekly that had (in Perkins's phrase) recently become "horribly cheap" or the monthly *Cosmopolitan*. In addition, as

Ober pointed out, a weekly like *Liberty* would be hard put to find space for a novel as long as Fitzgerald's. In any event, serial publication would be a good thing, Fitzgerald felt, because he had written "a book that only gives its full effect on second reading" (*As Ever*, 199–201; *Dear Scott/Dear Max*, 183–85, 188–89). He was right about his novel—*Tender* does profit from second (or third, or many) readings—if somewhat naive to expect that critics or the general public would actually read both the magazine serial and the book.

Scribner's printed the novel in four installments, beginning in January 1934. Fitzgerald delivered his manuscript late in October 1933, but he was by no means finished with it at that stage. He was an inveterate reviser of his own prose, making changes up to the last possible moment. In this instance he did extensive rewriting on the serial galleys before magazine publication, and then again on the book galleys that were set from the *Scribner's* serial. In the end he ran out of time to revise because book publication was scheduled for April 12, 1934, only a few weeks after the appearance of the final magazine installment. As long as he could, Fitzgerald retouched for felicity of expression, but neither he nor Perkins gave the book the kind of scrupulous editorial attention it deserved. As a result, *Tender Is the Night* has never appeared in a well-edited text. The book is full of misspellings, particularly of foreign words, and is further flawed by errors in chronology.

Once he had his general plan for this novel firmly in mind, Fitzgerald completed it in little more than a year. Rather remarkably, he was able to salvage most of stage one by reassigning much of the material about Francis Melarky either to Rosemary Hoyt or to Dick Diver. It was not a matter of merely lifting copy from one draft and plunking it down in another. Fitzgerald substantially reworked the old Melarky material and added new dialogue and action to flesh out his portraits, especially that of his protagonist. Then, of course, he had the tale of Nicole's violation and madness, and of the ruin of the Divers' marriage, to tell afresh.

Stage three of the novel went through several titles, each of them focused clearly on Dick Diver. The first draft was called *The Drunkard's Holiday*, the second draft *Doctor Diver's Holiday*, and as late as October 29, 1933, he wrote editor Alfred Dashiell of *Scribner's* magazine that his title would be, simply, *Richard Diver* (*Correspondence*, 318). The final change to *Tender Is the Night*, made over Perkins's objections, seems in retrospect a masterstroke, for its echo of Keats's romantic and melancholy "Ode to a Nightingale" admirably captured the spirit of the novel. Keats's famous ode, Fitzgerald said, was a poem he read often, and always with tears in his eyes. In addition, he thought of the phrase in connection with love, and with love as a battle. The word *night* "does a great deal for the title," he told Archibald MacLeish. "Women are different by day and by night and night has its own particular relationship to love. . . . There is a difference in depth of a woman's face when she's defending herself in full light and in the dark, when she's not defending herself" (Bruccoli, *Composition*, 174–75, 180; MacLeish, *Reflections*, 90).

Having fixed on a title, Fitzgerald labored over the serial galleys, altering word order here, making changes for the ear there. Besides these stylistic distinctions he made significant deletions and additions in moving from magazine to book copy. Some of these were dictated by standards of taste at the time: he could treat the subject of incest far more openly for Scribner's the book publishers than for *Scribner's* magazine, for example. Yet he cut more material than he added in revising. He omitted six scenes from the serial, totaling about thirty pages, and added only a few new pages. Two of the deleted scenes describe Abe North's adventures in the Ritz Hotel bar. One has to do with a rather messy affair between Dick Diver and a governess in Innsbruck. Three take place on shipboard during Diver's return from his father's funeral (Bruccoli, *Composition*, xxi, 191, 198–99, 202).

In one of these shipboard scenes the now-successful novelist Albert McKisco brings his typewriter on deck each day to work in public, hence becoming "the most noticeable figure on the ship." McKisco is annoyed when a female novelist, also on board, sets up her typewriter on deck to compete with him. This scene obviously denigrated McKisco and hence detracted from the effect of his function as an opposite to Diver. Abe North's alcoholism and failure foreshadow what will happen to Fitzgerald's protagonist, as many readers have noticed. But the reversal between McKisco and Diver—McKisco's rise nicely contrasts with Diver's decline—has largely escaped critical notice (Terry, "Albert McKisco's Role").

Among the additions, perhaps the most significant is a conversation between Dick and Rosemary as they part in Rome. "I guess I'm the Black Death," Diver tells her. "I don't seem to bring people happiness any more." And, in fact, after Rome he is seen only once more in his former role as one who bestows "carnivals of affection" on others.

This happens at the jail in Antibes, where Diver talks the chief of police into releasing Mary Minghetti and Lady Caroline after their transvestite adventure. Though Diver is not proud of himself for fixing "this thing he didn't give a damn about," the incident shows him as capable of helping others even after Nicole decides she no longer requires his services.

An editorial problem arose at *Scribner's* magazine in connection with the jail scene. The final installment of the novel ran overlong, and Perkins wired Fitzgerald asking him to cut the episode from 1,250 words to 800. In response, the author pointed out that the rescue was absolutely necessary: "OTHERWISE DICKS CHARACTER WEAKENS... IT IS NEEDED AND WAS WRITTEN TO BOLSTER HIM UP IN INEVITABLY UNDIGNIFIED CUCKOLD SITUATION." In this case, instead of cutting, Fitzgerald actually lengthened the scene to 1,400 words in final serial galleys. "It is legitimate to ruin Dick," he pointed out, "but it is by no means legitimate to make him ineffectual" (*Correspondence*, 329; *Dear Scott/Dear Max*, 191).

Manifestly, Fitzgerald wanted to preserve some trace of the "dignified and responsible" protagonist he had depicted in the first part of the book. This determination probably accounted for the extremely important deletion he made in the semifinal draft for the serial. In both the *Drunkard's Holiday* and the *Doctor Diver's Holiday* drafts, the book ends with Diver drunk. In the one version he falls on his face after making the sign of the cross; in the other he is helped away by a waiter Baby Warren sends to his aid. In the actual ending Fitzgerald softened this motif. Even here, admittedly, Diver takes "a big drink" of brandy after bidding his children good-bye and drinks anisette with Mary Minghetti on Gausse's terrace. It is still morning, but he is "already well in advance of the day . . . where a man should be at the end of a good dinner." The liquor, probably, facilitates Diver's making Mary feel that he cares about her. When that charade is over and he stands up to bless the beach, he sways a little but does not need assistance (Bruccoli, *Composition*, 173; Cowley, note, 356; Fitzgerald, *Tender* [1934], 310). It would have been too great an indignity, Fitzgerald must have decided, to let Diver exit staggering.

From the beginning of his career Fitzgerald thought of himself as something of an advertising expert. (He had worked briefly in a New York advertising agency in 1919.) So he was liberal with advice to Perkins about the proper way to introduce *Tender Is the Night*. The novel had been a long time in progress, but that should be played down, he said. "No exclamatory 'At last, the long awaited,'" he advised, for people would only say, "Oh yeah" to that. Above all he wanted to avoid any suggestion of frivolity. This was "a horse of a different color" from his *Saturday Evening Post* stories. "Please do not use the phrase 'Riviera' or 'gay resorts,'" he cautioned Perkins. It might even be appropriate to include a suggestion that "after a romantic start, a serious story unfolds." He was also "absolutely dead" on any kind of ballyhoo or personal publicity. "The reputation of a book must grow from within upward, must be a natural growth," he insisted. (*Dear Scott/Dear Max*, 186–87, 192–94). *Tender Is the Night* was to illustrate his point precisely. It was a novel undervalued in its own time, one whose reputation has developed over the decades.

VI

When at last *Tender Is the Night* was published, Fitzgerald had high hopes for it. "It's good, good, good," he told another writer (Cowley, introduction, x), as he confidently awaited confirmation of that from the book-buying public, from the critics, and from his literary colleagues. Financially, the novel's sales may have been hurt by its serialization in *Scribner's*, and book sales generally were poor in that rock-bottom Depression year. Under the circumstances *Tender* sold well, though not nearly so well as Fitzgerald had anticipated. There were three printings totaling about 15,000 copies during the spring of 1934. In April and May the book ranked tenth on the *Publisher's Weekly* best-seller lists. The Literary Guild made it an alternate selection and apparently considered it for a more prominent place in its offerings. (It had been a mistake "to refuse the Literary Guild subsidy," Fitzgerald wrote Perkins a year after publication.) In all, sales earned him royalties of about $5,000, less than what he needed to pay his debts (Bruccoli, *Some Sort of Epic Grandeur*, 367).

The reviews varied widely. Gilbert Seldes, who knew both Fitzgerald and the Riviera well, chose to demolish a cliché of the book-reviewing trade in praising *Tender*. It was not a book he could not put down, Seldes said. It was a book he *had* to put down because it evoked life with such intensity that he had "to stop, to think and to feel." At the opposite end of the range of opinion were those who tarred the author with the brush of the Jazz Age writer; no matter what he wrote, some reviewers were unwilling to give him thoughtful attention. The most typical attitude, perhaps, was struck by Fanny Butcher in the *Chicago Tribune*, who relied upon yet another catch phrase in classifying the novel. It was, she concluded, "a brilliant failure" (Seldes, "True to Type," 292–93; Butcher, "New Fitzgerald Book," 298–99).

To the extent that the reviews were unfavorable, it was not so much a consequence of the subject matter as Fitzgerald had feared and subsequent literary historians have assumed. *Tender* was published, after all, in the trough of the Depression, and it might have been anticipated that his depiction of rich expatriates on the Riviera would rub politically sensitive readers the wrong way. At least one such left-wing critic, Philip Rahv in the *Daily Worker*, criticized the author for writing about such characters at all. Rahv recognized that the novel portrayed the imminent collapse of the leisure class, "dying in hospitals for the mentally diseased, in swanky Paris hotels and on the Riviera beaches." But, he maintained, Fitzgerald discerned "a certain grace" in the last contortions of this class, and this apparent sympathy drove Rahv to a patently wrong-headed diatribe in the *Daily Worker* headlined "Dear Mr. Fitzgerald, You Can't Duck a Hurricane Under a Beach Umbrella." This reaction, however, was the exception and not the rule. Most of the adverse criticism of *Tender* focused not on political issues but on literary technique.

A number of reviewers thought the book poorly structured because beginning with Rosemary's adoring point of view on the Riviera aroused a "categorical expectancy" that was violated as she faded out of the book and it concentrated instead on Dick Diver's downfall. Fitzgerald was enough disturbed about this charge to recommend to novelist Joseph Hergesheimer that he open the book in the middle and read on from there. Hergesheimer had earlier told Fitzgerald that it was "almost impossible to write a book about an actress," and he was not the only one—Fitzgerald's letter pointed out—to be repelled by the apparent triviality of the opening (Chamberlain, "Books of the Times," [April 1934], 294–96; Fitzgerald, *Letters*, 532–33).

A still more frequent objection, one that cropped up often in the early reviews, maintained that Diver's disintegration was insufficiently prepared for. Even Fitzgerald's former mentor at Princeton, Dean Christian Gauss, paused at the end of a laudatory letter to remind the author that he had had the feeling, while reading part 3 of the magazine serial, "that Dick went haywire too fast." Part of the difficulty, he believed, stemmed from that romantic beginning, in which Diver was bodied forth in such glowing terms. Many readers, then and now, did not *want* to see him suffer and decline. Others, rather simplistically, objected that there was no one reason to account for his degeneration, as if so complex a matter as the breakup of a personality could be reduced to a single cause or to one traumatic event. Diver's crack-up, as Bruccoli observed, "is deeply rooted in his character—in his desire to please, in his egotism, and in his romantic view of life" (Bruccoli, *Composition*, 109, 198). Or he sacrifices himself to restore his wife's health. Or he is victimized by her wealth and the casual brutality of the rich, and by the moral corruption festering around him. If Fitzgerald learned anything from Zelda's illness, it was that human beings could not be stereotyped and labeled. So Diver is not Charm, any more than Macbeth is Ambition.

Unlike the reviewers, most of Fitzgerald's fellow authors immediately saw the virtues of the novel. "It's so tightly knit together that it can't be read in pieces," John Dos Passos remarked. He had been "enormously thrown off by the beginning" but later realized how well it worked. *Tender Is the Night* surpassed *The Great Gatsby*, John Peale Bishop wrote Fitzgerald. It established him as "a true, a beautiful and a tragic novelist." It was "one of the great books of the world," John O'Hara decided at once (*Correspondence*, 358–59; O'Hara, *Selected Letters*, 90). And there were further encomiums from James Branch Cabell, Archibald MacLeish, and others. But one important colleague remained to be heard from during the first weeks after publication.

"Do you like the book?" Fitzgerald wrote Hemingway on May 10, 1934. "For God's sake drop me a line and tell me one way or another." Ernest could not hurt his feelings either way, Scott assured him. Hemingway took Fitzgerald at his word and replied with his "old charming frankness." He found fault with the composite characters in the novel (Murphy-Fitzgerald-Diver, for instance), a subject that led to further correspondence between the two writers. In addition, he lectured Fitzgerald severely. *Tender Is the Night* proved that Fitzgerald could think, he conceded. Yet aside from that it was flawed because "a long time ago you stopped listening except to the answers to your own questions," and not listening had a way of drying writers up.

Most of all, Hemingway disapproved of Fitzgerald's exploring his own troubles in fiction. "Forget your personal tragedy," Hemingway instructed him. "We are all bitched from the start and you especially have to be hurt like hell before you can write seriously. But when you get the damned hurt use it—don't cheat with it. . . . You see, Bo, you're not a tragic character. Neither am I. All we are is writers and what we should do is write." It was too bad that he'd married someone who "wants to compete with you and ruins you" and also too bad also that he was "a rummy," though no more a rummy than James Joyce or most good writers. After so much by way of faultfinding, Hemingway ended with encouragement for the future. "You can write twice as well now as you ever could. All you need to do is write truly and not care about what the fate of it is" (*Letters*, 307–8; Hemingway, qtd. in Bruccoli, *Some Sort of Epic Grandeur*, 375–76).

In effect, Hemingway's letter had less to do with the novel than with what he regarded as Fitzgerald's waste of his talent. Within a year he amended his judgment in favor of *Tender*. "A strange thing," he wrote Perkins on April 15, 1935, "is that in retrospect his *Tender is the Night* gets better and better. I wish you would tell him I said so" (qtd. in *Dear Scott/Dear*

Max, 219). Fitzgerald was happy to get the news, for he was preoccupied with exactly what Hemingway had warned him against: worrying about the fate of his book.

The appearance of *Tender Is the Night* found Fitzgerald in the same rocky financial position he had occupied after *Gatsby* emerged nine years earlier. In debt, he could not afford even a brief period of "filling up" before returning to work on *Saturday Evening Post* stories. At least he now had a property that might be sold to Hollywood or Broadway, he assumed. *Gatsby* had brought in $15,000 for screen rights, and the play based on the novel earned him another $18,000; naturally, he hoped for a similar return from *Tender*. Even before publication, Harold Ober was negotiating with the studios for screen rights. RKO showed the most interest, he wrote Fitzgerald on March 8, 1934, and both of them speculated about possible casting. Fitzgerald proposed the actress Ann Harding for Nicole, but RKO and Ober thought Katharine Hepburn might be better. All agreed that Fredric March would make an effective Dick Diver. This remained idle speculation, however, for RKO's nibble did not become a bite. Nonetheless, in April and May Fitzgerald and his young Baltimore protégé, Charles Marquis (Bill) Warren, turned out a treatment for the films. Fitzgerald sent Warren to Hollywood to peddle their adulterated version: in an incredible upbeat ending, Dick operates to save Nicole's life (*As Ever*, 203–4, 209; Bruccoli, *Composition*, 25; Bruccoli, *Some Sort of Epic Grandeur*, 380–81).

Warren had no luck, but by January 1935 United Artists was considering another treatment of the novel for its star Miriam Hopkins. United Artists was unlikely to buy the book outright, Ober reported, but producer Samuel Goldwyn might want to take an option on the rights and then pay Fitzgerald to work on the screenplay. In response Fitzgerald said he hated Hollywood "like poison'" but might be persuaded to spend six weeks there at a guaranteed $2,000 a week (*As Ever*, 215–17). Nothing came of that lead, either. *Tender Is the Night* was not made into a film until 1961.

Fitzgerald pursued Broadway much as he had Hollywood. By December 1934 he had lined up another young author, Robert Spafford, to fashion a play based on the novel. Ober was not enthusiastic about this arrangement, as Spafford was so inexperienced. Far more promising were the options that the producer Sam H. Grisman took in 1935 and 1936, with veteran theater hands Jack Kirkland and Austin Parker to write the dramatization. Neither Spafford nor the Grisman-Kirkland-Parker team came up with anything saleable, however. So it was with some desperation that

Fitzgerald welcomed an overture from the dramatists Cora Jarrett and Kate Oglebay in October 1937: "Something must be done within the next two years to keep the book alive," he wrote Ober. By January 1938 a contract was signed with Jarrett and Oglebay, with the dramatists and the novelist to split royalties and receipts down the middle. Within a few weeks Jarrett produced a script that Fitzgerald thought was excellent, if almost too faithful to the original. In a surge of optimism he once again speculated about possible casting. Margaret Rawlings seemed a very good choice for Nicole; Beulah Bondi did not. Robert Montgomery had spoken to him about playing Dick Diver. But the Jarrett-Oglebay team could not secure backing for their script, and no one else has since (*As Ever*, 211–12, 218–19, 225, 227, 228, 230–31, 256–57, 341, 345–54; *Letters*, 570). *Tender Is the Night* has yet to be seen in a major theatrical production.

In addition to angling for a film or play based on *Tender*, Fitzgerald sought to keep his book alive through republication. The original Scribner's edition seemed to have run its course by May 1936, when the author wired Donald Klopfer and Bennett Cerf proposing that *Tender* be published in the inexpensive and popular Modern Library format. *Gatsby* had come out in the Modern Library in 1934, and Fitzgerald thought it would be beneficial both to the publishers and to himself to have two of his books represented in the series. Despite some initial encouragement and discussions by mail over several months, Klopfer and Cerf—especially Cerf—decided against a Modern Library edition (*Dear Scott/Dear Max*, 230, 277; *Letters*, 536–37).

Another two years passed without any action on *Tender*. Then, in March 1938 Perkins revealed his "secret hope that we could some day—after a big success with a new novel—make an omnibus book of 'This Side of Paradise,' 'The Great Gatsby,' and 'Tender Is the Night.'" But, he added, "we must forget that plan for the moment." Ignoring Perkins's comment about the need for a new novel, Fitzgerald leaped at the suggestion. He was in Hollywood for an extended stay, and an omnibus volume would be a way of keeping his name before the reading public. "How remote is that idea," he asked, "and why must we forget it[?]" The economy provided one reason, Perkins responded. The Depression was bottoming out again, and Scribner's was selling only about a third as many copies as during prosperous times. Besides, he doubted that *Tender* had yet taken on the patina of "romantic glamour" that books from the past sometimes acquired (*Dear Scott/Dear Max*, 242–47).

Though neither the Modern Library edition nor the omnibus volume came to pass, Fitzgerald continued to plot for the future of his novel. *Ten-*

der was, he felt confident, a book that people would not forget if only they had a chance to read it. And despite its brief appearance on the best-seller charts in 1934, he thought it had not really had its chance. Hard times had militated against sales, but perhaps the fault had been his as well. What if he were to do some rearranging?

As early as his correspondence with the Modern Library in mid-1936, Fitzgerald contemplated making alterations in *Tender*. His initial telegram to Cerf broached the subject thus: "IF I MADE CERTAIN CHANGES TO-WARD THE END WHICH I SEE NOW ARE ESSENTIAL COMMA IT WOULD MAKE ALL THE DIFFERENCE IN THE SPLIT UP OF THE TWO PRINCIPAL CHARACTERS." Three months later, now mindful that the inexpensiveness of the Modern Library volumes depended on printing from the original plates, he reassured Cerf that any revisions would take the form of *inserted* pages with "terse and graceful" headings as a guide to the reader, or at worst minor rewritings that conformed to "equivalent line lengths," in order to avoid expensive typesetting and printing costs. "DO YOU THINK THAT ONCE PUBLISHED A BOOK IS FOREVER CRYS-TALIZED [?]" Fitzgerald inquired (*Correspondence*, 432; *Letters*, 540–41).

VII

By December 24, 1938, Fitzgerald had become convinced that *Tender* needed restructuring. "Its great fault is that the *true* beginning—the young psychiatrist in Switzerland—is tucked away in the middle of the book." Reshaping to begin with Diver in his young manhood would, he estimated, "require changes in half a dozen other pages" (*Dear Scott/Dear Max*, 250–51). Soon thereafter, he set about making such an alteration in his personal copy of the novel, cutting pages loose from the binding and reassembling them to conform to this scheme:

ANALYSIS OF TENDER:

I Case History 151–212 61 pps (change moon) p. 212
II Rosemary's Angle 3–104 101 pps. p. 3
III Casualties 104–148, 213–224 55 pps. (-2) (120 & 121)
IV Escape 225–306 82 pps.
V The Way Home 306–408 103 pps. (-8) (332–341)

In his private copy, located in the Firestone Library at Princeton, he followed almost all of this plan, which besides rearranging the text involved eliminating the two-page and eight-page sections noted in parentheses: the first appearance of the materialistic newspaper vendor (120–21) and the visit to the Minghettis (332–41). On the inside front cover of this copy he wrote in pencil: "This is the *final* version of the book as I would like it."

"Final version" he may have called it, yet there are indications that Fitzgerald intended to do more than rearrange the narrative and delete a few scenes. He also planned to go through the entire novel one last time, revising as he went along. He did just that in the first two chapters of the copy at Princeton, where he made a number of brief but important revisions: cutting some phrases entirely, improving others, catching some spelling errors, changing punctuation. Then, next to a penciled asterisk near the end of chapter 2, he wrote, "This is my mark to say that I have made final corrections up to this point" (Cowley, introduction, xii–xiii). Evidently, Fitzgerald had still more alterations in mind. As he wrote in his notebooks, "Tender is less interesting toward the climax because of the absence of conversation. The eye flies for it and skips essential stuff for they don't want their characters resolved in desiccation and analysis but like me in action that results from the previous. All the more reason for *emotional* planning" (Bruccoli, *"The Last of the Novelists,"* 155). This note, with its insight into reader psychology (the eye "flies" for conversation amid gray pages and wants characterization acted out), suggests that Fitzgerald might have worked for more dialogue toward the end of the novel, and for more scene and picture, in Jamesian terms, had he been able to complete his "final corrections."

Though Fitzgerald did not complete fine-tuning his novel, his notes planning the revision and his chopped-up copy of the book warranted the publication in 1951 of what its editor, Malcolm Cowley, called "the author's final version." For a few years Scribner's circulated both versions of the novel, before reverting to the original. The publishers elected to use the 1934 text in their Scribner Library paperback, published in 1960, and that is the version of the novel read in most college classes. Yet an error by an employee of the publishers in the early 1970s resulted in a large paperback run of the 1951 text, and students of that period are likely to have read that version.

Which version is better continues to stimulate debate. Basically, Cowley argued in his introduction, the 1951 version represented an improvement over the 1934 one because it focused on Dick Diver from the very start and traced his downfall chronologically, avoiding the flashback necessitated by beginning with Rosemary's point of view on the Riviera. (Cowley also corrected some of the novel's errors.) But any clarity that might have been gained in this way, critics objected, could hardly make up for the elements of mystery and suspense that were sacrificed. "It seemed to take the magic out" of the novel, Hemingway commented. Besides, it was more realistic to introduce Diver in midcareer. That was, after all, the way that we became acquainted with most people in real life, Ford Madox Ford maintained. We meet them, become interested in them, and subsequently find out what we can about them. In fiction also, it made more sense to "get [one's protagonist] in with a strong impression, and then work backwards and forwards over his past" (Cowley, note, xiv–xvi; Hemingway, *Selected Letters*, 743; Bruccoli, *Composition*, 10–11, 15).

The most thorough and effective argument against the 1951 version was made by Brian Higgins and Hershel Parker in a long essay. Of their many points, two carry the greatest weight. First, Higgins and Parker maintained that by not starting with Rosemary's admiring picture of Diver, the novel failed to provide him with the stature that could render his ultimate defeat truly significant. We can hardly feel tragic about Diver's collapse, they observed, "because we have scarcely been allowed to think well of him."

Their second, and more telling, objection had to do with the way the novel was written. Complicated as the nine-year composition of *Tender* certainly was, it seems clear that Fitzgerald wrote his novel in the order it originally came to him, starting with the Riviera material, shifting back to Diver's early career, and then coming forward into the future. It follows that the author, as he sat down to work on book 2, must have had what he had written in book 1 more or less in mind, and so on through the book. As John Dewey asserted, "the artist is controlled in the process of his work by his grasp of the connection between what he has already done and what he is to do next." The order of composition matters a great deal, and artists are apt to underestimate the damage they may do, in retroactive attempts at revision, by restructuring their fiction (Higgins and Parker, "Sober Second Thoughts"; H. Parker, *Flawed Texts*, 72–79, 219).

The Cowley version has its defenders as well as its detractors. These include Wayne Booth, in his *Rhetoric of Fiction*, and Milton R. Stern in his fine introduction to *Critical Essays on "Tender Is the Night."* In this essay Stern takes up (and attempts to dispose of) the various grounds for objection and ends by calling for well-edited printing of *both* versions. That may be too much to hope for, with the 1934 version clearly in the ascendancy. Yet most would surely agree with Stern that "a carefully edited fair edition" of *Tender Is the Night* is badly needed (Booth, *Rhetoric of Fiction*, 190–95; Stern, "Introduction," 25–30).

In arriving at an ultimate assessment of the merits of *Tender*, few have been unable to resist comparing it to Fitzgerald's other great novel. In several ways it stands at the opposite end of the spectrum from *Gatsby*. Fitzgerald himself drew the lines of distinction in a letter to John Peale Bishop on April 7, 1934, a few days before the novel was published. His intention was "entirely different" this time, he explained. "The dramatic novel has canons quite different from the philosophical, now called psychological, novel. One is a kind of *tour de force* and the other a confession of faith. It would be like comparing a sonnet sequence with an epic" (*Letters*, 363). *Gatsby* was his dramatic novel and *Tender* his psychological one; *Gatsby* his sonnet sequence, brief, emotionally charged, and tightly knit, *Tender* his epic, large if not sprawling in theme and scope.

The contrast between the two books is underlined by their endings. *Gatsby* in effect ends with Jay Gatsby floating mortally wounded on a pneumatic mattress in the pool of his grotesque mansion. Nick Carraway tells us about the funeral, about his chance meeting with Tom Buchanan in New York, about the carelessness of the rich, above all about the wonder of Gatsby's capacity to dream. But the novel is, as Fitzgerald said, a dramatic one and reaches its climax when George Wilson shoots Gatsby dead. It is much more difficult to fix on one particular scene as the climax of *Tender*.

As Alan Trachtenberg has pointed out, the novel is best regarded as one of "process," whose "movements are more elaborately and calculatedly subtle and complex" than was true of *Gatsby*. To grasp the implications of *Tender* one must allow "feelings and hints to accumulate" episode by episode ("The Journey Back," 138–43, 152). So it is appropriate to end with a "dying fall," Diver's fading out of Cap d'Antibes sunshine into a lackluster future in upstate New York. No authorial voice, no Carraway standing in for Fitzgerald, is allowed around to point the moral and generalize. At the end of an epic there is too much to take in, too much to think and feel about, to be encapsulated by any narrator.

PART III

◈ FITZGERALD AND HIS TIMES ◈

[8]

FITZGERALD'S NONFICTION

THE EARLY MAGAZINE ARTICLES

F. Scott Fitzgerald will be remembered primarily for his novels and stories, but during his twenty years as a professional writer, he also produced an important and revealing body of work in the form of articles and essays and correspondence. The very best of these—the autobiographical pieces written in the 1930s—command the lyrical magic and emotional power of his most lasting fiction. And even at their least meritorious, in the advertisements for himself Fitzgerald composed as a beginning author, these articles reveal a great deal about the way he wanted to present himself to his readers. Read chronologically, they trace the rise and fall of his career from the publication *This Side of Paradise* in March 1920 to his final years in Hollywood.

In accepting *This Side of Paradise* for publication, the editor Maxwell Perkins at Scribner's asked Fitzgerald for a photograph and some publicity material. "You have been in the advertising game long enough to know the sort of thing," Perkins added (Fitzgerald, *Dear Scott/Dear Max*, 21). In fact, Fitzgerald had worked only four months for the Barron Collier agency in New York, from March to July 1919, but he did understand how promotion could help sell books and was eager to cooperate in the enterprise. In a letter presented at the American Booksellers' Convention and included on a leaf added to several hundred copies of the novel, he began to establish a public personality designed to shock and attract his audience.

Fitzgerald had been struggling to complete *This Side of Paradise* for two years—longer, if one considers how much of the book is borrowed from his undergraduate writing at Princeton—and it had gone through two substantial revisions before Scribner's accepted it. But to the booksellers, Fitzgerald acknowledged none of these difficulties: "to write it . . . took three months; to conceive it, three minutes; to collect all the data in it, all my life." The idea for the novel had first come to him the previous July, he lied, and he regarded the process of composition as "a substitute form of dissipation." As an author, he was writing "for the youth of his own generation, the critics of the next, and the schoolmasters of ever afterward." In signing off, Fitzgerald reverted to the dissipation motif. "So, gentlemen, consider all the cocktails mentioned in this book drunk by me as a toast to the Booksellers' Convention" (*Letters*, 477–78).

Fitzgerald was so pleased with this letter that he retailed its best lines to the wider audience of the *New York Tribune* on May 7, 1920, in a feature article demonstrating that he did indeed know his way around in the world of publicity. The supposed occasion for the article was an interview with Fitzgerald conducted by Carleton R. Davies. But Davies was fictitious: both questions and answers were written by Fitzgerald himself. The idea for this mock interview came from him as well, in a proposal to the advertising manager at Scribner's (Bruccoli and Bryer, eds., *Fitzgerald in His Own Time*, 162).

The image that emerges from Fitzgerald's flippant remarks to the booksellers is that of a brash young genius who has tossed off a novel as cavalierly as the characters in his novel toss back a drink. His appeal is to a youthful audience who will presumably be delighted to join him in repudiating the outmoded mores of the past. Read the book, he seems to be saying, for our mutual profit. At the same time, the author wants more than immediate reward. One eye is cocked on the sales figures, the other looks for approval from the critics and even from posterity.

By any standard, the sales of *This Side of Paradise* were remarkable. Its portrayal of the younger generation, and particularly of the flapper and her liberated ways, made the twenty-three-year-old author famous overnight. Buoyed on the first wave of success, he reviewed his brief career in "Who's Who—and Why," in the *Saturday Evening Post* for September 18, 1920. "The history of my life," Fitzgerald began, "is the history of the struggle between an overwhelming urge to write and a combination of circumstances bent on keeping me from it." The essay reviewed the various literary ventures of the author in the making, from musical comedy and poetry to short stories and a novel. The tone throughout is lighthearted and confident, even when Fitzgerald is making fun of himself. According to his account, for instance, he produced the first draft of his novel while in infantry training at Fort Leavenworth, hurrying to the officers' club every Saturday afternoon to work at breakneck speed through Sunday evening. Over the weekends of three months, Fitzgerald maintains, he set down a novel of 120,000 words. Only then could he allow himself to concentrate on his military training: "I went to my regiment happy. I had written a novel. The war could go on" (Fitzgerald, *Afternoon*, 84–85).

As in the letter to the booksellers and the mock interview, Fitzgerald characterized himself as a youth blessed with talent far beyond his years. The pose exasperated some commentators, who thought it hopelessly sophomoric, while others were merely amused by the author's presentation of himself as a youth afflicted with genius. His friend Ring Lardner effectively reduced the image to absurdity: "Mr. Fitzgerald sprang into fame with his novel *This Side of Paradise* when only three years old and wrote the entire book with only one hand" (qtd. in Woodward, *Fitzgerald: The Artist*, 15).

In the early years of his career, handsome Scott Fitzgerald and his beautiful wife, Zelda, cooperated fully with the media effort to portray them as exemplars of flaming youth. During much of the time from 1920 to 1924 they lived in Connecticut and Long Island, suburban extensions of New York City, the publicity capital of the nation. For both of them, as Fitzgerald wrote in "My Lost City," Manhattan "was inevitably linked up with Bacchic diversions, mild or fantastic" (*My Lost City*, 111). Newspaper columnists eagerly recorded these diversions, from a table-side interview at a night club to their midnight dive into the Pulitzer fountain: accounts well documented in Jeffrey Harris Woodward's splendid book *F. Scott Fitzgerald: The Artist as Public Figure* (53).

Even to his literary friends, Fitzgerald was dwindling into a celebrity instead of a writer and, as Robert Sklar put it, "not a celebrity to whom particular deference need be paid" (Sklar, *Fitzgerald*, 121). In the public mind, he was indelibly associated with a younger generation determined to defy its elders. It did not help that he titled his first two collections of short stories *Flappers and Philosophers* (1920) and, over the objections of Perkins, *Tales of the Jazz Age* (1922). Flappers and sheiks drawn by John Held Jr. danced frantically on the jacket of the second volume, and Fitzgerald contributed jaunty vignettes to introduce each of the stories. " 'The Camel's Back,' " he revealed, "was written during one day in the city of New Orleans, with the express purpose of buying a platinum and diamond wrist watch which cost six hundred dollars. I began it at seven in the morning and finished it at two o'clock the same night." Published originally in the *Saturday Evening Post*, this amusing yarn about a drunken evening at a Midwestern party was chosen as an O'Henry Prize story for 1920. Despite this honor, Fitzgerald said he "liked it least" (*Tales*, 5) of all the stories in *Tales of the Jazz Age*.

These comments, and those that introduced other stories in the book, dramatized the author as someone who could turn out fiction with disarming ease and gain expensive rewards therefrom. Writing, for him, seemed a casual occupation that in no way inhibited the pursuit of a pleasurable and carefree existence (Woodward, *Fitzgerald: The Artist*, 65). But if he refused to take himself seriously as an artist, he could hardly expect others to do so: a problem that came to the fore with the reception of his second novel, *The Beautiful and Damned*, published in March 1922.

Written under the influence of H. L. Mencken, *The Beautiful and Damned* is a dark and serious novel that portrays the decline and fall of Anthony and Gloria Patch, a hedonistic young couple obviously modeled on the Fitzgeralds themselves. A number of critics, expecting less weighty fare, chose to ignore its pessimistic message. "With what gusto, what exuberance of youth, what vitality Fitzgerald writes," one commented. "He has romance and imagination and gaiety," observed another. "Perhaps when he is a little older he will be less larky and unsteady" (qtd. in Woodward, *Fitzgerald: The Artist*, 90). Fitzgerald encouraged this larky, unsteady view of himself in a lighthearted piece on "How I Would Sell My Book If I Were a Bookseller" (January 1923). In a defensive opening, Fitzgerald claimed that he had not known *This Side of Paradise* was "a flapper book" until George Jean Nathan told him it was. His heroines were complicated and individual women, he insisted, not stereotypical and rather dull flappers. But, getting down to business, he admitted that the best way to sell *The Beautiful and Damned* would be to cash in on the public perception of his work. "This is a novel by Fitzgerald," booksellers might say to customers, "the fella that started all that business about flappers. I understand that his new one is terribly sensational (the word 'damn' is in the title). Let me put you down for one" (Bruccoli and Bryer, eds., *Fitzgerald in His Own Time*, 167–68).

In "What I Think and Feel at Twenty Five" (September 1922), Fitzgerald obliquely addressed the issue of his reputation. The article opens with an old family friend objecting to the gloominess of Fitzgerald's new novel. The author was young and healthy and successful and happily married: why did he have to write such unpleasant books? Next a newspaper interviewer comes to call. Was the rumor true that he and Mrs. Fitzgerald were going to commit suicide at thirty because they dreaded middle age? And would their suicide be "largely on account of past petting-parties?" Fitzgerald's answer to them both was that as he grew older he did indeed feel more vulnerable. Once only *he* could be hurt, he pointed out, but now—at twenty-five—he could be wounded through his family. "Attack him through his wife!" "Kidnap his child!" "Tie a tin can to his dog's tail!" Fitzgerald wrote in humorous fashion, but the basic point was serious enough. In another article written eighteen months later, he noted "that ghastly moment once a week when you realize that it all depends on you—wife, babies, house, servant, yard and dog. That if it wasn't for you, it'd all fall to pieces" (Bruccoli and Bryer, eds., *Fitzgerald in His Own Time*, 213–16, 184–86).

Fitzgerald was no longer so careless of consequences as he had been two years before. His image as a representative of the unbridled younger generation was proving difficult to get rid of. Sometimes it seemed that as a legendary figure associated with that generation he was to be held responsible for any and all of its excesses. In May 1922, for example, Burton Rascoe reported in his *New York Tribune* column that Fitzgerald, in the course of a conversation with Robert Bridges, the editor of *Scribner's Magazine*, had leaned over and plucked six gray hairs from Bridges's beard. The anecdote was entirely apocryphal, and Fitzgerald was obliged to write a letter of protest to Rascoe and one of apology to Bridges. It was time to shake off the role of the playboy genius and assume the responsibilities of the dedicated artist.

One unfortunate component of Fitzgerald's public persona was his reputation as a spendthrift, and in this case the reputation was well earned. Fitzgerald careened around New York with large bills protruding from his pockets. He lectured his mother to the effect that all great men spent freely. He and Zelda certainly did so, whether they could afford to or not. Edmund Wilson focused on Scott's precarious financial condition in a *New Republic* essay couched as an imaginary dialogue between a blithe Fitzgerald, as representative of the younger generation of writers, and the dignified and distinguished literary historian Van Wyck Brooks, speaking for his elders. In conversation, Fitzgerald laments that he cannot live at Great Neck (Long Island) for less than thirty-six thousand a year, and that to support himself he has "to write a lot of rotten stuff that bores me and makes me depressed." Brooks gently chides the young author. His heavy expenses laid him open to exploitation by the popular magazines, and Fitzgerald himself seemed to have descended to the language of advertising in expressing himself and to have fallen into the trap of regarding his writing more as a commercial than an artistic endeavor (Wilson, "Imaginary Conversations," 253–54).

Here Wilson was obviously hectoring his Princeton friend Fitzgerald, whom he considered his intellectual and moral inferior. The $36,000 figure was drawn directly from "How to Live on $36,000 a Year," Fitzgerald's piece for the *Saturday Evening Post* of April 5, 1924. In this article, Fitzgerald details his financial results for 1923. He and his wife had begun the year determined to save some money. Family living expenses they estimated at about $1,500 a month, and income from writing at $2,000: presto, an annual saving of $6,000. But expenses ran higher and income lower than anticipated, especially after Fitzgerald's play *The Vegetable* bombed in out-of-town tryouts. As the year neared its end, he found that they had spent $36,000, or twice as much as they had budgeted, and were $5,000 in debt. There was only one solution.

"Over our garage," he wrote, "is a large bare room whither I now retired with pencil, paper, and the oil stove, emerging the next afternoon at five o'clock with a 7,000-word story." That averted the immediate crisis, but "it took twelve hours a day for five weeks to rise from abject poverty back into the middle class" (*My Lost City*, 35). This was not an exaggeration, or not much of one. Between November 1923 and April 1924 Fitzgerald produced eleven short stories and several magazine articles, and he earned nearly $20,000. Such a lavish expenditure of energy could not go on indefinitely, Fitzgerald realized, and he was curious about where all the money had gone. To find out, he and Zelda assembled their account books and household records, and worked out the figures. With everything they could think of accounted for, their monthly expenditures came to only $2,000, or $1,000 less than they had actually spent. A thousand dollars had vanished each month, it seemed, without buying anything at all.

Fitzgerald's bewilderment at this discovery had its comic side: "Good heavens! . . . We've just lost $12,000" (*My Lost City*, 37). He worked this same vein in "How to Live on Practically Nothing a Year," a sequel to the "$36,000" article that related the Fitzgeralds' decision to escape "from extravagance and clamor" and "to find a new rhythm" for their lives in the Old World. In the spring of 1924, they set out for the Riviera, armed with capital of $7,000 and a determination to live for the summer on "practically nothing" while Scott was writing *The Great Gatsby*. But the change of location did not solve their financial problems. The Riviera was supposed to be a winter resort, and much cheaper in the summer, but the French saw them coming and immediately jacked up their prices. At the end of the summer, the $7,000 was gone. And in the south of France, as on Long Island, the Fitzgeralds were unable to figure out exactly *where* it had gone, except that they were sure that they had been victimized by the real estate agent, the maid and the cook, the butcher, and the grocer.

The humor in these articles depended on reader willingness to identify with the plight of the Fitzgeralds as a young newly rich bourgeois family unable to cope with their circumstances. In other articles of this period, like "The Cruise of the Rolling Junk" (February–March–April 1924) and "My Old New England House on the Erie" (August 1925), Fitzgerald again played the role of the bumbling incompetent, easily hoodwinked by those who knew far more than he about houses and automobiles.

In actuality, of course, there was nothing particularly funny about Fitzgerald's lifelong inability to make ends meet. No matter how much money he made, at every stage of his career he was in debt to his publisher and agent. His letters to Perkins and to Ober vividly tell the unhappy story. "I hoped that at last [!] being square with Scribners I could remain so," he wrote Perkins in some desperation on December 31, 1920, with his career barely begun. But he was at his wits' end, and so worried that he was "utterly unable to write." Couldn't Perkins send him the $1,600 he needed as an advance on his next novel, or as a loan at the same interest it cost them to borrow, or as a month's loan with his "next ten books as security?" (*Life in Letters*, 44).

Perkins responded to this appeal, as he responded to almost all such appeals for the next decade and a half. The pattern was the same with Ober, who during the three months between September and December 1927 was bombarded by no fewer than nine telegraphed requests from Fitzgerald for funds as an advance on a "two-part sophisticated football story" aimed at the *Saturday Evening Post*. "Can you deposit five hundred?" Fitzgerald's first wire inquired, and the succeeding ones asked for 500, 500 more, 300, 100, 100, 400, 200, and 250, with repeated promises that the story was almost completed or that he would be coming in to deliver it no later than "tomorrow morning" (*Life in Letters*, 150–53). Things were going so badly in the mid-1930s that Fitzgerald signed over part of his life insurance to secure his debts to Perkins and Ober. He was forever struggling to live within his income.

Nonfiction articles provided one way of supporting himself, one that proved relatively important, especially during the mid-1920s. The initial self-promoting pieces brought in nothing at all, but in 1922, when his highest story price was $1,000, he was paid $800 for his reflections on what he thought and felt at twenty-five. In 1924, his two essays on how to live on a great deal of money and how to live on not much sold for $1,000 and $1,200 (*Ledger*, unpaginated). In most of the articles from this period, Fitzgerald—and on occasion his wife—held forth as experts on such matters as courtship and marriage, childrearing, the rich, and the war between the sexes. The magazines and newspaper syndicates that commissioned these pieces wanted the Fitzgerald byline, for he had been firmly established in the public mind as a spokesman for the younger generation. Who else knew more about what was happening to these rebellious young people? The very celebrity that undercut his artistic reputation made it possible for him to earn easy money as a putative expert, and he was no more able to resist this opportunity than he was to stop churning out formulaic stories for the popular magazines.

In an April 1922 example of his expertise on the younger generation, Fitzgerald was depicted as a debonair professor lecturing with the aid of a map of the United States. He was described as the "young St. Paul authority on the flapper," and the subject under discussion was the difference between the girls of the South, the East, and the Midwest. In this competition, the Midwestern flapper—"unattractive, selfish, snobbish, egotistical, utterly graceless"—finished a distant third. Next came the rather sophisticated Eastern girl, with the Southern girl a clear winner for, among other things, "retain[ing] and develop[ing] her ability to entertain men." Of course, Fitzgerald admitted, he was somewhat prejudiced on the subject, having married a Southern girl (Woodward, *Fitzgerald: The Artist*, 59–61).

Three separate articles in the spring of 1924 dealt with the difficulties young couples faced after marriage. The most interesting of these, "Why Blame It on the Poor Kiss If the Girl Veteran of Many Petting Parties Is Prone to Affairs After Marriage?" was syndicated by Metropolitan Newspaper Service to its subscribing papers under the alternate title of "Making Monogamy Work." Making it work was not easy, for in Fitzgerald's view monogamy was "not (not yet at least) the simple natural way of human life." On balance he regarded marriage favorably, for it kept people out of messes and required less time and money than supporting a chorus girl. But opportunities to stray abounded and were becoming more pervasive. As an example he cited the case of Harry and Georgianna (hypothetical clones of Scott and Zelda), "two highly strung and extremely attractive young people" who had married with the understanding that when the first flush was over, they were to be "free to ramble." Four years later, living in the highly permissive atmosphere of New York City, they began to seek illicit companions and straightaway drove each other mad with jealousy.

The only sensible course, they decided, "was to remain always together. Harry never goes to see a woman alone nor does Georgianna ever receive a man when Harry is not there. As a result, theirs was one of the extremely rare, truly happy marriages."

What of the girl who engaged in so many premarital petting parties? If anything, Fitzgerald suggests, those parties "tend[ed] to lessen a roving tendency." A girl who discovered before she married that there was more than one man in the world was, he reasoned, "less liable to cruise" later on. In conclusion, Fitzgerald acknowledged that he could provide no sure formula for making monogamy work. On the constructive side, though, he believed in "early marriage, easy divorce and several children" (Woodward, *Fitzgerald: The Artist*, 128–29; Bruccoli and Bryer, eds., *Fitzgerald in His Own Time*, 179–84).

As it happened, he and Zelda were destined to have no more than one child: their daughter, Scottie, born in October 1921. Despite his limited experience as a father, Fitzgerald wrote two articles for women's magazines on how to bring up children. "Imagination and a Few Mothers" (June 1923, *Ladies Home Journal*) presents two very different women. Mrs. Judkins is a hopeless worrier whose every moment is tortured by fears that her joyously blooming daughter is on the verge of a nervous breakdown and that her vigorously active son is not getting enough rest. As a result, she overprotects her children and denies them the right to full self-realization. In contrast with Mrs. Judkins (who bears a family resemblance to Fitzgerald's mother), he invents the enlightened Mrs. Paxton. Because she understands that "the inevitable growth of a healthy child is a drifting away from the home" (*My Lost City*, 61), Mrs. Paxton stays out of her children's way and lets them grow up on their own. Generalizing on the grounds of these manufactured cases, Fitzgerald deplores those mothers who control and monitor their children. Where influence on the child is the issue, a "woman happy with her husband is worth a dozen child-worshippers" (*My Lost City*, 65).

"Wait Till You Have Children of Your Own!" for the July 1924 *Woman's Home Companion* elaborates on this doctrine of permissiveness. The article is noteworthy for the initial appearance in print of Zelda's (and Daisy Buchanan's) childbirth remark that she hopes her baby daughter will be "a beautiful little fool." But this is hardly the message Fitzgerald wants to convey. The previous generation, in his judgment a dull and worthless one, had attempted to guide its young according to outmoded values. This was a mistake, and he will force no standards on his children, Fitzgerald insists, for nothing that they are told will be of any value compared to what they find out for themselves. In a closing peroration, he advances his ideal chil-drearing program. "We shall give" our children "a free start, not loading them up with our own ideas and experiences. . . . We will not even inflict our cynicism on them as the sentimentality of our fathers was inflicted on us. . . . We shall not ask much of them—love if it comes freely, a little polite-ness, that is all. They are free, they are little people already, and who are we to stand in their light?" (*My Lost City*, 75–76).

According to Fitzgerald, rich boys were especially likely to grow up with-out developing self-reliance. In "What Kind of Husbands Do 'Jimmies' Make?" (March 1924) Fitzgerald deprecates "that peerless aristocrat, that fine flower of American civilization, young Mr. Jimmy Worthington." Jimmy learns early that his father's money will pay for his sins, that "if he has the bad luck to run over someone when he's drunk, his father will buy off the family and keep him out of jail." Nor is Jimmy encouraged like the young English aristocrat to pursue a life of service by going into politics and running the government. Instead, he joins the American leisure class—"the most shal-low, most hollow, most pernicious leisure class in the world"—and lives a life of privilege without ever grasping the idea that privilege implies respon-sibility. In the United States, Fitzgerald maintains, the greatest Americans have "almost invariably come from the very poor class—Lincoln, Edison, Whitman, Ford, Mark Twain." These men formed their character in the forge of experience, while the young rich boys of the 1920s were shaped into complete parasites: healthy, good-looking, and perfectly useless (Bruccoli and Bryer, eds., *Fitzgerald in His Own Time*, 186–87, 191).

Oddly enough, this dissection of the rich came from a writer who was unable to get along on the princely income of $36,000 a year. In this ar-ticle, as in much of his fiction, Fitzgerald situated himself both within and without the world of the wealthy. It was as if while dancing among the favored few inside the ballroom, he simultaneously stood outside gazing through the window at the brilliant party within. This was very much the position of Nick Carraway in *The Great Gatsby* and of the narrator in "The Rich Boy," two stunning accomplishments that put his reaction to the rich—which seems basically pedestrian in his magazine articles—into lasting form.

The same point could be made about Fitzgerald's changing attitudes toward women. The spate of essays that he produced in 1924 to help pay off debts subsided, not to be resumed until the country slid into the 1930s and he was inspired to trace his own rise and fall against the background of the nation's economic debacle. In one final venture into the genre of the expert, however, Fitzgerald announced the arrival of the independent woman. As the title "Girls Believe in Girls" (February 1930) suggested, this woman no longer believed that she had anything to learn from men. The flapper had vanished in favor of "the contemporary girl," who possessed beauty, charm, and courage and radiated poise and self-confidence. She had also, in a somewhat frightening development, become sexually liberated: "The identification of virtue with chastity no longer exists among girls over twenty," Fitzgerald wrote, although his readers were welcome to pretend that it did if it gave them any comfort. He expected wonders from this independent girl. It was "the poor young man" he was worried about (Bruccoli and Bryer, eds., *Fitzgerald in His Own Time*, 210–11). Just as his mundane pronouncements about the rich were reinvigorated in fiction, so the confident New Woman of this article was to engage the young man he worried about in a dramatic fictional struggle between the sexes—and to emerge victorious, like Nicole Diver at the end of *Tender is the Night*.

AFTER THE JAZZ AGE

The Fitzgeralds' own history, as Scott was well aware, paralleled that of the nation. As the boom began in 1920, he had his private triumph with the publication of *This Side of Paradise* and his marriage to Zelda. A decade later, the stock market crash of October 29, 1929, mirrored their declining fortunes and was closely followed by Zelda's mental collapse in April 1930. The passing of the decade marked a watershed for the Fitzgeralds, and for his writing career. In his essays thereafter he dropped the pose of the expert and was moved to consider the not entirely golden past.

Drinking lay at the heart of Fitzgerald's problems, as close readers of his fiction might have intuited. Yet however compulsively his characters may have consumed liquor, Fitzgerald was not ready, in assessing his own life, to draw the connection between excessive drinking and physical or emotional breakdown. He treats the issue with levity in "A Short Autobiography," which appeared in the May 25, 1929, *New Yorker*. This fragmentary piece purports to tell the story of the author's life in the form of diary entries about his liquor intake through the years. It begins with "1913: The four defiant Canadian Club whiskeys at the Susquehanna in Hackensack" and concludes, unapologetically, with "1929: A feeling that all liquor has been drunk and all it can do for one has been experienced, and yet—*Garçon, un Chablis-Mouton 1902, et pour commencer, une petite carafe de vin rosé. C'est ça—merci*" (*My Lost City*, 97–99).

In "My Lost City" (July 1932), Fitzgerald writes that in the latter years of the boom, "many people who were not alcoholics were lit up four days out of seven . . . and the hangover became a part of the day as well allowed-for as the Spanish siesta." Then he immediately distances himself from this pattern. "Most of my friends drank too much—the more they were in tune to the times the more they drank." Only when he came to New York City to visit those friends, as in 1927, for example, was he caught up in a frenzy that "deposited" him a few days later "in a somewhat exhausted state on the train to Delaware." In his view, liquor was a symptom of what had gone wrong, not a cause. More at fault were those who had made fortunes overnight and did not bother with manners. In the speakeasies, "there was nothing left of joviality but only a brutishness that corrupted the new day." Everywhere, morals were looser (*My Lost City*, 112–13).

In his articles about marriage and childrearing of the mid-1920s, Fitzgerald consistently criticized the social conventions of the time for limiting the experiences available to the young and thereby stunting their growth. By the 1930s, however, he looked back on a decade of recklessness and waste and decided that *too much* freedom was at fault. If anything, he observed in a September 1933 *New York Times* interview, the older generation had failed to pass along a proper sense of the "eternally necessary human values." As a result, his contemporaries lacked "religious and moral convictions" and were rendered "incompetent to train their children" (Woodward, *Fitzgerald: The Artist*, 254–55, 264). In his notebooks, also, Fitzgerald regarded the permissive policies he had once advocated with a jaundiced eye.

Fitzgerald proclaimed the death of the era in his November 1931 "Echoes of the Jazz Age," an essay of reminiscence more about the times than himself. The age, he wrote, had lasted only ten years. It had been born about the time of the May Day riots in 1919 and had "leaped to a spectacular death in October, 1929," much as one of his classmates tumbled "accidentally" from a skyscraper in Philadelphia and another purposely from a skyscraper in New York (*My Lost City*, 130, 136). The word "jazz" itself had progressed toward respectability: originally it meant sex, then dancing, then music. But the generation it spawned was the wildest ever—"a whole race going hedonistic, deciding on pleasure" (132). The most hedonistic migrated to the winter resorts at Palm Beach and Deauville, or alternatively to the summer Riviera where you "could get away with more" (135). Fitzgerald was ambivalent about those wasted years. Like Charlie Wales in "Babylon Revisited" (February 1931), the boom years had taught him the true meaning of the word *dissipate*: "to dissipate into thin air; to make nothing out of something" (*Short Stories*, 620). But also like Wales, he could not entirely forget how "rosy and romantic" (*My Lost City*, 138) it had all seemed when he was young and could still feel everything with great intensity.

In fact, the greatest loss Fitzgerald had suffered, it became clear in his several autobiographical essays of the mid-1930s, was the capacity to feel as deeply as he once had. He had succumbed to "emotional bankruptcy" (in the phrase he used to title a story of August 1931) and so had very nearly lost all capacity to write. In "One Hundred False Starts" (March 1933) he directly confronted this dilemma. His output as a professional writer was slacking off, for he could find so little that he really cared about to convert to fiction. There was no shortage of serviceable plots; he could find a thousand of them in criminal law libraries and the personal revelations of friends and acquaintances. But these would not work. As a professional writer, he had to start out with an emotion—one that was close to him and that he could understand (*My Lost City*, 87).

This essential part of his creed he underlined in a rather harsh commentary on a story that young Frances Turnbull sent him in November 1938. She had not invested enough of her own emotional capital in the story, Fitzgerald told her. He was afraid that "the price for doing professional work" was a good deal higher than she was prepared to pay. "You've got to sell your heart, your strongest reactions, not the little minor things that only touch you lightly," he told her. The only thing writers had to sell—especially young writers—was their emotions. This was as true of Dickens in *Oliver Twist*, he pointed out, as it was of Hemingway in *In Our Time* or of himself in *This Side of Paradise*, when he was writing about a love affair "still bleeding as fresh as the skin wound on a haemophile" (*Life in Letters*, 368).

The discouragement of many false starts, Fitzgerald observed in his essay, had made him almost ready to quit. In his troubled state he went to an old Alabama Negro for advice.

"Uncle Bob, when things get so bad that there isn't any way out, what do you do then?"

"Mr. Fitzgerald," he said, "when things get that-away I wuks."

That was good advice, he decided, for work "was almost everything" (*Afternoon*, 135). He insisted on the point time and again in letters from Hollywood to Scottie at Vassar. The strongest statement came in a July 7, 1938, letter that he implored Scottie to read twice, bitter though it might seem. The basic message was that Scottie's mother had ruined her life because she was brought up spoiled. Zelda "realized too late that work was dignity, and the only dignity, and tried to atone for it by working herself, but it was too late and she broke and is broken forever" (*Letters*, 46–47). Never again, he added, did he want to see women raised to be idlers. This interpretation undoubtedly laid too much emphasis on Zelda's highly permissive upbringing—she was the baby of the family—as the cause of her mental breakdown. Fitzgerald obviously wanted to frighten Scottie into working hard at college. But he was also expressing his own convictions. When he called work "the only dignity," he meant it.

In "Ring" (October 1933), a memorial essay on Ring Lardner, Fitzgerald wrote about a friend and fellow writer who had failed to pour enough of himself into his craft. Lardner had been the most amiable of drinking companions during Fitzgerald's time in Great Neck. "Many the night," he reports, "we talked over a case of Canadian ale until bright dawn" (*My Lost City*, 91), yet no link is suggested between Lardner's drinking and the "impenetrable despair" that dogged him for a dozen years before his death.

The saddest part of the story, as Fitzgerald related it, was that Ring had not lived up to his promise as an artist. The causes were several. Lardner spent too much time helping others. He did not aim high enough. He adopted a cynical attitude toward his work. And, above all, he did not express his innermost thoughts and feelings. Once Fitzgerald suggested to him that he should write something "deeply personal," but Lardner refused: by his lights, "telling all" simply wasn't done. "So one is haunted," Fitzgerald observes in his elegy, "not only by a sense of personal loss but by a conviction that Ring got less percentage of himself on paper than any other American of the first flight" (*My Lost City*, 94).

Fitzgerald's memorial essay on Ring Lardner reads very much like a cautionary tale directed at himself. Confession was good for art as well as the soul, and Lardner's mistake warned against concealing the contents of his own mind and heart. At the time, Fitzgerald was profoundly concerned with his own literary reputation. In the month of Lardner's passing, he wrote Perkins suggesting an fresh "advertising approach" for *Tender is the Night*. Scribner's, he suggested, should put out a statement along these lines:

> For several years the impression has prevailed that Scott Fitzgerald had abandoned the writing of novels and in the future would continue to write only popular short stories. His publishers knew different and they are very glad now to be able to present a book which is in line with his three other highly successful and highly esteemed novels, thus demonstrating that Scott Fitzgerald is anything but through as a serious novelist.

In retrospect, this copy seems almost pathetic. Its mixture of verb tenses, shaky grammar ("knew different") and unfortunate repetitions ("highly successful and highly esteemed") make it sound as if Fitzgerald were trying to reassure *himself* that he was "anything but through" (*Life in Letters*, 241). The nine-year lapse between his two greatest novels shook his confidence, and he never stopped excoriating himself for letting it happen. As he wrote Scottie in June 1940, "I wish now I'd *never* relaxed or looked back—but said at the end of *The Great Gatsby*: 'I've found my line—from now on this comes first'" (*Life in Letters*, 451).

Fitzgerald's "Sleeping and Waking" (December 1934) further revealed a man seriously at unease with himself. A victim of insomnia, he lay awake in the early hours beset by thoughts of "Horror and waste—Waste and horror—what I might have been and done that is lost, spent, gone, dissipated, unrecapturable" (*My Lost City*, 167). He could neither relive the past nor summon the emotional intensity that had once brought his fiction to life. Desperately searching for material, he tried a series about a father and daughter, the Gwen stories, and another about the medieval Count of Darkness, but these rank among the worst of his stories. His well was running dry. As he observed in his notebooks, there seemed less weather than in his youth, and "practically no men and women at all" (*Crack-Up*, 128).

"THE CRACK-UP" AND BEYOND

So in November 1935 he tried something different. He holed up in the mountains of western North Carolina, at the Skylands Hotel in Hendersonville. Arnold Gingrich, editor of *Esquire*, armed him with a mantra to break his writer's block. Fitzgerald was to repeat, "I can't write stories of young love for the *Saturday Evening Post* because I can't write stories of young love for the *Saturday Evening Post* because . . . ," and so on. Strapped for funds and living on tinned meat and Uneeda biscuits, he wrote his "Crack-Up" articles instead, articles that in their exploration of his "dark night of the soul" amply demonstrated *why* "he couldn't go on writing stories of young love for *The Saturday Evening Post*" (qtd. in Potts, *The Price of Paradise*, 88–89).

The three "Crack-Up" articles ran in *Esquire* during February, March, and April 1936, and they elicited an extraordinary reaction. "I get letters from all over," Fitzgerald wrote Gingrich. Old friends counseled him to cheer up, and fans begged him to keep writing. But those in his immediate literary circle were generally appalled at Fitzgerald's account of his own emotional exhaustion and personal collapse. "Christ, man," John Dos Passos objected, "how do you find time in the middle of the general conflagration to worry about all that stuff?" Fitzgerald had become the "Maxie Baer" of writers, Ernest Hemingway wrote Perkins, associating him with the heavyweight fighter Hemingway thought had been cowardly in his bout with Joe Louis. Perkins considered the essays an "indecent invasion of [Fitzgerald's] privacy." Ober, his agent, feared that they would compromise his client's chances of securing a contract in Hollywood (Donaldson, "The Crisis," 171–73).

Subsequent critics have been divided as to the honesty of these essays. Glenway Wescott called them "wonderful" for their "candor; verbal courage; simplicity" (*Crack-Up*, 323–34) and Sergio Perosa admired Fitzgerald for examining himself with detachment and without pity or sentimentality. Milton Hindus, on the other hand, thought the author had not presented "enough close-ups of actual experience," and Alfred Kazin felt that "something is being persistently withheld, that the author is somehow offering us certain facts in exchange for the right to keep others to himself" (Potts, *The Price of Paradise*, 90; Donaldson, "The Crisis," 178). In fact, important things *are* withheld. The essays do not mention Zelda's illness and its effects. In addition, they bring up drinking only in order to rule it out as a cause of Fitzgerald's difficulties. This was not an intentional violation of the two rules he set for himself as an intellectual and a man of honor: "that *I do not tell myself lies that will be of value to myself*, and secondly, *I do not lie to myself*" (*Crack-Up*, 197). Fitzgerald was simply unable to admit to his alcoholism. Denial was part of the disease.

By the standards of Robert Lowell's *Life Studies* (1959) and the flurry of confessional novels, poems, and memoirs that followed that groundbreaking work, Fitzgerald's account of his breakdown seems positively reticent. A creative writing instructor at the turn of the twenty-first century, reading these essays in manuscript form, would probably scribble "More Specificity!" in the margins. For throughout the "Crack-Up" articles there is surprisingly little detail, and even less of the scene-and-picture that enlivens Fitzgerald's fiction. Only one character is involved: the distressingly enervated and somewhat cynical persona of F. Scott Fitzgerald, at the end of his rope. Other names, with the notable exception of Edmund Wilson, are conspicuously withheld.

Yet the "Crack-Up" articles clearly struck a nerve at the time of publication, and they continue to fascinate readers several generations later. Although vague in the lack of concrete detail, the essays still generate emotional power. The source of that power is that one is never in doubt, reading them, that they come from the heart, that they convey the very real depths of the author's depression. In one sense, the "tension between concealment and revelation" (Dolan, *Modern Lives*, 142), Fitzgerald's obvious reluctance to tell too much, is symptomatic of his troubles. He could hardly articulate what he could not admit to himself. Besides, if important matters are withheld, that is in part a consequence of the brevity of these essays: they occupy only sixteen pages in book form. Fitzgerald undoubtedly kept them short to satisfy the requirements of *Esquire* magazine, but he understood, too, the authority of the thing left out.

The essays gain further intensity from the clear division between "the cool, detached observer" whose voice dominates the narration and the desperately suffering figure whose story he is relating (*Afternoon*, 11). And of course it matters that the downfall under analysis involves one of the century's most accomplished writers. Furthermore, the chronicle of Fitzgerald's personal journey from boom to bust resonates in the wider culture as well. Particularly in "Handle with Care," the last of the three essays, he is also lamenting what has gone wrong in American society, as of 1936: materialism running roughshod over love, friendship, honor—all the lovely abstractions he once believed in.

Fitzgerald writes about his deepest feelings in the "Crack-Up" articles with the aid of almost no plot at all. Instead, he adopts the indirection of poetry and seeks to communicate how he felt through metaphor. It is extraordinary how often he compares himself in these essays: to other human beings, to animals, to inanimate objects. These comparisons are crucial to the artistic success of the whole, for they tell his unhappy tale without undue pointing or breast-beating.

Aging is the basic theme of "The Crack-Up" (February 1936), the first of the three essays. "Of course," it somberly begins, "all life is a process of breaking down." Then, however, Fitzgerald immediately segues back to the optimism of his youth, when he was capable of believing that "life was something you dominated if you were any good" (*My Lost City*, 139). As Morris Dickstein has observed, "this project of mastering life was very much in the American grain" ("Authority," 559). For a long time, Fitzgerald had clung to that sunny prospect, only reluctantly reducing his two "juvenile regrets"—not playing football in college, not getting overseas during the war—into "childish waking dreams," and he was still possessed by a romantic notion that with fame as the spur almost anything was possible (*My Lost City*, 139). But after hearing "a grave sentence" from a "great doctor" (in reference to his bouts of tuberculosis, probably) his outlook darkened. He stopped caring about others and went away to where he did not know many people. He found that he was "good-and-tired" and spent his time dozing or making lists. Suddenly he got better, and then "he cracked like an old plate," in the homely simile that structures this first essay and leads on to the next (*My Lost City*, 140–41).

In the paragraph after the cracked plate metaphor, Fitzgerald introduces a financial one: "I began to realize that for two years my life had been a drawing on resources that I did not possess, that I had been mortgaging myself physically and spiritually up to the hilt" (*My Lost City*, 141–42). This financial motif recurs in the second "Crack-Up" essay, and he also used it in a letter warning Scottie against reckless expenditure of her energy. "Our danger is imagining that we have resources—material and moral—which we haven't got," he wrote her on April 5, 1939. Every few years, he was forced to climb "uphill to recover from some bankruptcy." Scottie should understand exactly what bankruptcy meant: "drawing on resources which one does not possess" (*Letters*, 70).

In the paragraph after the one about mortgaging in "The Crack-Up," Fitzgerald reverted to language of the growing-up process with the comment that he "had weaned" himself away from all the things he used to love and was left with almost no fellow feeling for other people. He liked only doctors and girls short of puberty and boys eight and over and old men. There was a substantial list of those he could not stand the sight of: "Celts, English, Politicians, Strangers, Virginians, Negroes (light or dark), Hunting People, or retail clerks, and middlemen in general, all writers . . . and all the classes as classes and most of them as members of their class." With a measure of cynicism, Fitzgerald put a question to his readers: "All rather inhuman and undernourished, isn't it? Well, that, children, is the true sign of cracking up" (*My Lost City*, 142).

This first essay concludes with the only extended anecdote of the entire series. Fitzgerald recounts the attempt of an unnamed woman—Nora Flynn, almost certainly—to act as "Job's comforter" in ameliorating his distress. "Suppose this wasn't a crack in you," she says, adopting his metaphor, "suppose it was a crack in the Grand Canyon" (*My Lost City*, 143). She asks him, in effect, to stop feeling sorry for himself and start considering the wider world. To reinforce the message, she tells him of her private woes and how she had overcome them.

Fitzgerald feels the logic of what she says. He might even have fought free of his depression, he suggests, if he had been able to muster the vitality she possessed in such abundance. But vitality was a natural force that could not be passed on, not even if he waited "for a thousand hours with the tin cup of self-pity." There was no use in playing the beggar outside

Nora's door. All he could do was walk away, "holding himself very carefully like cracked crockery" (*My Lost City*, 144).

"Pasting It Together" (March 1936), the second "Crack-Up" essay, picks up the cracked-plate and bankruptcy metaphors, and adds several new ones designed to communicate the violent nature of his collapse. To begin with, Fitzgerald elaborates on the *condition* of the plate, which, despite its crack, still has to be kept in service. It will not be brought out for company. It will do only to "hold crackers late at night or to go into the ice box under left-overs." But late night brings on insomnia and sorrow and despair. At three o'clock in the morning, the hour of "the real dark night of the soul," he feels like "an unwilling witness of an execution," the disintegration or "shear[ing] away" of his own personality (*My Lost City*, 145–46).

In his crisis Fitzgerald is distressed by recollections of what he has twice lost in the past, and military images invade his thoughts. The first great crisis came at Princeton, where his departure in junior year (in Fitzgerald's not entirely forthcoming version, for medical reasons alone and not because of failing grades) had cost him the badges and medals he had rightfully earned and so ended his "career as a leader of men." The second involved the apparent loss of Zelda because of his dim financial prospects. While trying to emulate the rich, his horse had been "shot out from under" him.

This last martial expression is repeated as Fitzgerald summarizes the family resemblance among the periods of darkness in his life. Each had been the result of "an over-extension of the flank, a burning of the candle at both ends; a call upon physical resources that I did not command, like a man over-drawing at a bank": the triplet of metaphors substituting for what he could not or would not state explicitly. His most recent crack-up was more violent than the others, but in all three cases he felt as if he were "standing at twilight on a deserted range, with an empty rifle in my hands and the targets down" (*My Lost City*, 146–47)—only apparently armed, powerless to alter his fate.

The essay goes on to illustrate how Fitzgerald had been so unmanned. With the advent of motion pictures, he observes, the power of the written word had become subordinate to the "grosser power" of the image on the screen. The effect threatened to render him obsolete, just as "the chain stores have crippled the small merchant, an exterior force, unbeatable": an analogy that still applies forcefully at the start of a new century. In part, though, Fitzgerald was complicit in the "disintegration" of his personality since he had done so little to construct it himself. Instead, he had borrowed his intellectual conscience from Edmund Wilson (the only contributor named in the essay), his sense of the good life from Sap Donahoe (a friend going back to his days at Newman School), his artistic conscience from Ernest Hemingway, his concept of how to conduct his relations with other people from Gerald Murphy, and his political conscience from a "man much younger than myself," possibly V. F. Calverton. Because he was made up of parts of other people, there was no intrinsic self, no basis (as Fitzgerald put it) on which to organize his self-respect. In a closing comparison he reduced the soldier alone on the range at night to a still more pitiable figure: "It was strange to have no self—to be like a little boy left alone in a big house," knowing that he could do anything he wanted to, but finding there was nothing that he wanted to do (*Crack-Up*, 75–78; *My Lost City*, 148–49).

In the first two essays of the "Crack-Up" series, Fitzgerald appealed to his readers' compassion by ending with sentimental glimpses of himself in extremity: a beggar with a tin cup, a little boy left alone. He adopts a far more aggressively cynical tone in the final essay, "Handle with Care" (April 1936). In this profoundly bitter article, he excoriates American society and repeatedly diminishes himself by comparison to the least admirable people and things around him. The cracked plate, fashioned to arouse at least a modicum of pity, stays in the cupboard this time. Instead Fitzgerald writes of floundering in a "morass," of springing a "leak" through which his "enthusiasm and vitality" prematurely trickle away, of "self-immolation," of slaying "the empty shell" he has let himself become (*My Lost City*, 150–51).

In order to recover, Fitzgerald resolves that there will be no more "giving of [him]self." He will go off "the dispensing end of the relief roll forever." "The conjurer's hat [is] empty" (*My Lost City*, 150–51). In the foolishness of youth, as he wrote Scottie, he had imagined he was "a sort of magician with words" without any effort on his part. Later he came to realize that what seemed to be magic was really the result of unremitting effort (Epstein, "Fitzgerald's Third Act," 56). And there was only so much energy to go around. As with Dick Diver in *Tender is the Night*—a character who started out modeled on Gerald Murphy but later became closely identified with his creator—Fitzgerald felt drained of almost all vitality. Diver's charm, his compulsion to use his "fatal pleasingness," had worn him down: it led directly to his downfall. So in 1936, the same year that Dale Carnegie's immensely popular *How to Win Friends and Influence People* advocated success through glad-handing, Fitzgerald resolved to stop bestowing carnivals of affection on others and to save himself by becoming at last "a writer only" (Dickstein, "Fitzgerald's Second Act," 574).

"Handle with Care" also delivers a scathing attack on the rampant materialism of American culture. This attack becomes most vivid in Fitzgerald's sardonic description of how he plans to conduct himself in the future. He will no longer expend any of his time and energy on other people, unless he stands to profit by doing so. In order to get through unavoidable human encounters he will cultivate a false smile and develop a new voice. His practiced smile, Fitzgerald writes, will "combine the best qualities of a hotel manager, an experienced old social weasel, a headmaster on visitors' day," and so on through a catalogue of artificial smilers finishing with "all those from Washington to Beverly Hills who must exist by virtue of the contorted pan"—again, how up-to-date Fitzgerald's satire still seems. A lawyer is working with him on the voice, which will be designed to elicit the word "yes" from some but toward others will be notable for its "polite acerbity that makes [them] feel that far from being welcome they are not even tolerated" (*My Lost City*, 152–53).

The "Crack-Up" essays end with a series of demeaning self-characterizations expressed in similes or metaphors. In his youth Fitzgerald had aspired to be "an entire man"—athlete, scholar, artist, warrior, man of affairs, man of the world. Now, however, he has "cut . . . loose" that ambitious goal "with as little compulsion as a Negro lady cuts loose a rival on Saturday night." That early dream has been relegated to "the junk heap of the shoulder pads worn for one day on the Princeton freshman football field and the overseas cap never worn overseas" (*My Lost City*, 153). The most degrading metaphor comes at the very end. He no longer will allow himself to like anyone, Fitzgerald admits, and he has hung a sign, *Cave Canem*—beware of dog—above his door. "I will try to be a correct animal though, and if you throw me a bone with enough meat on it I may even lick your hand" (*My Lost City*, 154).

In his extremity, Fitzgerald compares himself to a dog who will alternately snarl or fawn, depending on how he is treated. It is not much of a role for a forty-year-old man to play, but he suggests that it is the only way he can adapt to a society of people who only pretend to honest emotions in their drive for self-aggrandizement. His mood of dejection, as he points out in the penultimate paragraph of "Handle with Care," parallels "the wave of despair" that swept the nation in the aftermath of the boom. In the days before boom turned to bust, Fitzgerald had been capable of a happiness so intense that he had to go off by himself to walk the ecstasy away. But that apparent happiness, he reflects, may have been no more than "a talent for self-delusion." Certainly it was an exception to what he has come to believe: "that the natural state of the sentient adult is a qualified unhappiness" (*My Lost City*, 153–54).

What chiefly makes Fitzgerald's writing last, Joseph Epstein has suggested, is his great theme of loss ("Fitzgerald's Third Act," 57). The worst loss of all, in his stories and novels, is the loss of illusion that overcomes Dexter Green at the end of "Winter Dreams" and that Jay Gatsby struggles against on the last day of his life. The "Crack-Up" essays, like nothing else he wrote, testify that Fitzgerald eventually cast his own private illusions aside and had to soldier on deprived of their emotional support. Gone, too, was most of the fund of energy that drove him to accomplish so much in the first fifteen years of his career and that he still desperately needed for his work. "Vitality shows in not only the ability to persist but the ability to start over," as he reminded himself in his notebooks (*Crack-Up*, 126). The theme of loss is pervasive throughout these essays that, despite their silences and evasions, take us to the core of a man in the throes of despondency.

Fitzgerald continued to work an autobiographical vein in the pieces for *Esquire*—some fact, some fiction, but in either case drawn from experience—that followed the account of his crack-up. In the summer of 1936, for example, he composed an "author" trilogy for the magazine: "Author's House," "Afternoon of an Author," and "An Author's Mother." Despite using the camouflage of fiction more than the "Crack-Up" essays had, this group of three cut close to the bone in revealing intimate details of Fitzgerald's life.

"Author's House" (July 1936) takes the form of a tour of the writer's home, from the damp unfinished cellar to the isolated cupola on top. One dark corner of the cellar, Fitzgerald as guide tells a visitor, conceals the crucial moment—three months before he was born—when his mother lost her other two children. "I think I started then to be a writer," he observes. Beneath a mound of dirt in another corner is buried his childhood self-love that enabled him to think that he "wasn't the son of [his] parents but a son of a king . . . who ruled the whole world." Outside the living room a group of children are playing football, reminding Fitzgerald of the time in prep school when he was accused of shying away from a tackle because of physical cowardice. It was not that way at all, he maintains in a probable distortion of the facts (*My Lost City*, 169–70). Another fiction develops as they progress upstairs. Fitzgerald invents a correspondence in which he has played a cruel hoax on an illiterate woman whose brother is in jail. The tale prompts him to regret that in his own writing he has necessarily meddled with other people's emotions, done "things he can never repair." The attic, pleasant enough for a short visit, is full of the school books and ballet programs and old magazines and maps that constitute "the library of a life." Finally they mount to the cupola where the wind whistles past.

He had lived there once in his youth, Fitzgerald says, probably referring to the summer of 1919 when he shut himself in the topmost room of his parents' row house in St. Paul to finish *This Side of Paradise*. He could not do that again, he confesses, even if he wanted to (*My Lost City*, 173–74).

The "emotional exhaustion" Fitzgerald refers to in the "Crack-Up" essays is poignantly demonstrated in "Afternoon of an Author" (August 1936). Unlike his previous autobiographical essays, Fitzgerald uses the third person here, and the article gains authority through such distancing. It purports to describe an actual day in the author's life. He wakes in his Baltimore apartment feeling better than he has in weeks, yet after breakfast lies down for fifteen minutes before starting work on a story that has "become so thin in the middle that it was about to blow away." He gives up this project, and after shaving he rests for five minutes "as a precaution" before getting dressed. He'd like to get away for a while, but lacks the time and energy to drive down the Shenandoah valley or ride the boat to Norfolk. Instead he goes downtown on the bus to see his barber. In the business section he suddenly sees "brightly dressed girls, all very beautiful," and the sight restores his spirits so that "he love[s] life terribly for a minute, not wanting to give it up at all" (*My Lost City*, 176–78).

After alighting from the bus, however, he must hold "carefully to all the railings" as he walks the block to the hotel barbershop. After his haircut and shampoo, he hears an orchestra playing across the way and is reminded of the review of his last book that declared that he was fond of night clubs and that he was "indefatigable." The mere word brings tears to his eyes. It was like the early days of his career, when despite laboring over every sentence Fitzgerald pretended to and was criticized for a "fatal facility." On this afternoon he is as easily fatigued as a man twice his forty years. He has some trouble mounting the steps of the bus that takes him home, then is revived by the sight of a couple of high school kids perched atop the Lafayette statue. As for himself, he "needed reforestation and . . . hoped the soil would stand one more growth." Back in his apartment, he drinks a glass of milk and decides to lie down for ten minutes before trying to get started on an idea for a new story (*My Lost City*, 179–80).

The slightest of the three "author" essays is "An Author's Mother" (September 1936). Presented in the guise of fiction, it chronicles the last day in the life of "Mrs. Johnston," a halting old lady patently modeled on Fitzgerald's mother. The piece was written after Mollie McQuillan Fitzgerald had fallen fatally ill and appeared in print shortly before her death. Mrs. Johnston, her fictional counterpart, is not particularly pleased that her son, Hamilton, has become an author. She had wanted him to become an army officer or go into business. Authors were regarded as "distinctly peculiar" (*My Lost City*, 181) in the Midwestern city she came from, and she thought the profession both "risky and eccentric." It would have been different if he were a popular author along the lines of Longfellow or Alice and Phoebe Cary, nineteenth-century sentimental poets she admires. Mrs. Johnston suffers a fall as she is leaving a bookstore where she has been unable to purchase a copy of the Carys' poems. Taken to a hospital, she rouses herself and in her delirium "announce[s] astonishingly" that Hamilton is the author of "The Poems of Alice and Phoebe Cary." As an obituary for Fitzgerald's own mother, this brief story is touching in its gentle account of her weakness and confusion. Yet there is more than a trace of resentment, too, in her lack of respect for her son as a serious man of letters (183–84).

In a number of stories published in *Esquire* during the next two years, Fitzgerald introduced material from his own life that he had ignored or barely touched on in the "Crack-Up" essays. "'I Didn't Get Over'" (October 1936), for example, combines his regret at not getting overseas in the war with his persistent sense of social insecurity. Fitzgerald used to keep lists of those who had snubbed him (*Crack-Up*, 72). Like his admirer John O'Hara, he was tremendously sensitive to real or apparent putdowns. The story itself, rather convoluted in form and dependent on a surprise ending, illustrates the sometimes deadly consequences of one such social snub (*Afternoon*, 169–76). "An Alcoholic Case" (February 1937) is based on the alcoholic binges that on several occasions placed Fitzgerald under the care of a trained nurse, and so comes to grips with the disease he had explicitly denied in "The Crack-Up" essays (*Crack-Up*, 70–71). The nurse in the story is taking care of a cartoonist whose indomitable will to die defeats her every attempt to make him better. She hates the idea of handling alcoholic cases. "It's just that you can't really help them and it's so discouraging" (*Short Stories*, 436–42).

"The Long Way Out" (September 1937) plays a variation on Zelda Fitzgerald's mental illness and hospitalization. The schizophrenic woman in the story has been promised a five-day trip with her husband away from the clinic. She joyfully prepares herself on the morning of their scheduled departure and is happily waiting when word comes to the doctors that her husband has been killed in an automobile accident. No one dares tell her what has happened; her husband has been delayed, they say, and will pick her up tomorrow. So she goes on each day for years, readying herself each morning for her holiday. After waiting so long, as she daily reassures herself, one more day hardly matters. Perhaps this story derives in part from Fitzgerald's feelings of guilt. Zelda often implored him in her letters to take her on trips away from the hospital. Occasionally he did so, as on a four-day journey to Charleston and Myrtle Beach in the same month that this story appeared in print. Almost always these trips had disastrous consequences for both of them (*Short Stories*, 443–47).

"Financing Finnegan" (January 1938), a fourth story dealing with material left out of the "Crack-Up" essays, addresses the subject of Fitzgerald's financial unreliability. The story is written with wry, self-deprecating humor. The tone is implicit in the very name of the protagonist, which is more suggestive of the stereotypical barroom Irishman than the distinguished-sounding "Fitzgerald." Like Fitzgerald, Finnegan borrows repeatedly from his agent and editor against the promise of work as yet undone. Like Fitzgerald, he signs over his life insurance to them. Like Fitzgerald, he has recently broken his shoulder during a dive from the high board. With so much invested in his cause, agent and editor become cheerleaders for Finnegan. The book he has promised may not have materialized, they acknowledge, but when it does it is bound to be wonderful. The problem is that they dispense so much to Finnegan that they become desperate for funds themselves. At the end of the story, the editor is reduced to putting the touch on another of his authors (*Short Stories*, 448–55).

Fitzgerald returns to the beginning of his literary career in the autobiographical "Early Success" (October 1937). Here he recalls the thrilling wind of success that sprang up with the letter from Scribner's accepting *This Side of Paradise*. That early-realized dream created the illusion that the gods were on his side, that life was a romantic matter. Yet from the beginning Fitzgerald understood that his time of ecstasy, like the "great gaudy spree" the nation was about to embark upon, could not last. All the stories that came into his head "had a touch of disaster in them." By 1937 he has taken on a protective shell to harden himself against the disappointments of his personal and professional life. But he will not dismiss from memory the intense excitement that had once enraptured him. There are still times, he concludes, when he can go back into the mind of the youth who had walked the streets with cardboard soles: "times when I creep up on him, surprise him on an autumn morning in New York or a spring night in Carolina when it is so quiet that you can hear a dog barking in the next county" (*My Lost City*, 190–91).

In the prose of this poetically evocative essay, the last important piece of nonfiction Fitzgerald published, he summoned all of his lyrical power to take us back into the realm of what has been sadly and irretrievably lost. Early success made him foolishly overconfident, even arrogant, and in that mood he capered and gamboled for the sheer pleasure of taunting his sober elders. In one sense, Fitzgerald must have rued that heedless exuberance, for it stamped him in the public mind as "larky" and unserious. Yet he will not repudiate that brief wonderful time when the young man with cardboard soles and the professional author in the making "were one person, when the fulfilled future and the wistful past were mingled in a single gorgeous moment—when life was literally a dream" (*My Lost City*, 191).

{ 9 }

THE CRISIS OF "THE CRACK-UP"

THE REACTION

F. Scott Fitzgerald's three "Crack-Up" articles that ran in *Esquire* for February, March, and April 1936 precipitated an extraordinary response from the magazine's readers. Letters came from old friends who wanted to cheer him up, from total strangers who recognized something of their own plight in Fitzgerald's account of emotional exhaustion, and most of all from other writers, among them James Boyd, John Dos Passos, Ernest Hemingway, Nancy Hoyt, John O'Hara, Marjorie Kinnan Rawlings, G. B. Stern, Julian Street, and Alexander Woollcott. As O'Hara put it in an April letter, "I suppose you get comparatively little mail these days that does not dwell at greater or less length on your *Esquire* pieces, and I guess few of the writers resist, as I am resisting, the temptation to go into their own troubles for purposes of contrast." O'Hara then revealed that he had recently been jilted by his girl and had picked up a dose of clap on the rebound (O'Hara, *Selected Letters*, 115).

The very nature of Fitzgerald's articles called for *some* response. Here a well-known writer was admitting in print that he had cracked like a plate and lost much of the vitality that made him successful. Furthermore, at the end of the second article, Fitzgerald openly appealed for reader reaction. His story might not be of general interest, yet if anyone wanted more, he announced, there was plenty left. But perhaps his readers had already had enough. If so, he hoped they'd let him know.

The correspondence that found its way to Fitzgerald varied enormously in tone. Much of it sympathetically proposed solutions to his dilemma. Some letter writers suggested God, some Alcoholics Anonymous, some a rendezvous. Others recounted their own troubles, delivered pep talks, tried to jolly him up. More than a few thought he should never have begun the series of autobiographical pieces at all. (Five more articles followed the three about the "Crack-Up" in *Esquire*, but the later pieces were not so painfully defeatist as the earlier ones.) "People have received this Esquire article ("An Author's Mother") with mingled feeling," he wrote Beatrice Dance in September 1936, "—not a few of them think it was a terrific mistake to have written any of them from Crack-Up. On the other hand, I get innumerable 'fan letters' and requests to republish them in the *Reader's Digest*, and several anthologist's requests, which I prudently refused" (*Letters*, 541–42). As he had acknowledged at the beginning of "Pasting It Together" (the second "Crack-Up" article), there were "always those to whom all self-revelation is contemptible, unless it ends with a noble thanks to the gods for the Unconquerable Soul" (*Crack-Up*, 75). There were also those who could not resist the opportunity to preach to Fitzgerald. "Please write me," he asked Max Perkins in February 1937, "you are about the only friend who does not see fit to incorporate a moral lesson, especially since the *Crack Up* stuff. Actually I hear from people in Sing Sing & Joliet all comforting & advising me" (Fitzgerald, *Dear Scott/Dear Max*, 235).

Certainly "The Crack-Up" essays conveyed a strong impression of personal depression. The *New Yorker*'s "Talk of the Town" dismissed them with its usual snide superiority. "F. Scott Fitzgerald has been telling, in *Esquire*, how sad he feels in middle life," the item began, and went on to refer to his "picturesque despondency" ("Notes and Comment," 11). The *San Francisco Chronicle* observed in similar vein that the "gentleman in question is being a little too sorry for himself" but acknowledged that one could "hardly help being interested in what he has to say," the more so since he seemed to strike a common chord: his essays went far "to explain the spiritual troubles of many another member of the almost-lost generation" ("Between the Lines").

Such friends as Margaret Turnbull and Marie Hamm agreed. "Your story is a mental snapshot of a rather universal experience," Mrs. Turnbull wrote after reading his first article. All of us end up "more or less defeated," but since so many shared this experience, Scott would discover "a chain of people, stretching around the world, to catch hold of [his] hands." One hand that reached out was that of Scott's first girl in St. Paul, Marie Hersey Hamm. "Cheer up, darling, life begins at forty!" she wrote early in October, responding both to the *Esquire* articles and to the account, in *Time*, of his disastrous fortieth birthday interview with Michel Mok for the *New York Post*. Mrs. Hamm granted that Fitzgerald had probably gone "on a more prolonged binge than the rest of us" and that therefore his "hang-over, awakening, or what have you" was that much more oppressive. But life, she insisted, was pretty swell, especially when you considered the alternative. Among their mutual friends, for instance, Joe Ordway was in a sanitarium and Theodore Schultze had died the week before. "When you're dead, you're dead, my pet, so why not enjoy it while you're here." Mostly, Fitzgerald refused to be cheered up by such correspondence. It was nice of Marie Hamm to try. "However, child," he told her, "life is more complicated than that" (*Letters*, 545).

Some people thought he demonstrated a lack of character by publishing the pieces in the first place. To Sara Murphy, for example, Fitzgerald seemed so wrapped up in himself as to be unable to sympathize with others. In a letter of April 3, 1936, she wrote, "I remember once your saying to me—in Montana [Switzerland] at Harry's Bar, you & Dotty [Parker] were talking about your disappointments, & you turned to me and said: I don't suppose you have ever known despair? I remember it so well as I was furious, & thought my god the man thinks no one knows despair who isn't a writer & can describe it. This is my feeling about your articles" ("As a Friend,'" 375–76).

John Dos Passos also proposed that Fitzgerald stop regarding his own navel. "We're living in one of the damnedest tragic moments in history—if you want to go to pieces I think it's absolutely O.K. but I think you ought to write a first-rate novel about it (and you probably will) instead of spilling it in little pieces for Arnold Gingrich [of *Esquire*]" (*Crack-Up*, 311). The important thing was that Fitzgerald should continue to do his work. "Katy & I . . . wish like hell you could find some happy way of getting that magnificent working apparatus of yours to work darkening paper; which is its business," as Dos Passos put it in another letter.

Even if he remained unhappy, Fitzgerald ought to turn that sorrow to literary account, Marjorie Kinnan Rawlings advised. "I suppose you know that nothing is wasted," she wrote him. "The hell you've been through isn't wasted. All you have to do, ever, is to forget everything and turn that terrible, clear white light you possess, on the minds and emotions of the people it stirs you to write about." Ernest Hemingway had offered much the same advice after reading *Tender Is the Night* and detecting traces of self-pity in the portrayal of Dick Diver. Forget your personal tragedy, he told Fitzgerald. "But when you get the damned hurt use it—don't cheat with it" (qtd. in Mizener, *The Far Side of Paradise*, 259–60).

Hemingway did not mean, however, that Fitzgerald should bleed all over the page. "The Crack-Up" articles struck him as a despicable whining in public. In "The Snows of Kilimanjaro," which appeared in the August 1936 *Esquire*, Hemingway dismissed Fitzgerald in print. "Poor Scott Fitzgerald" had been "wrecked," Hemingway wrote, by his worship of the rich. When Fitzgerald objected, Hemingway explained that since Scott had written himself off in "The Crack-Up" he figured it was open season on him (qtd. in *Letters*, 542).

Though he did not share Hemingway's vehemence, the gentlemanly Perkins also thought "The Crack-Up" articles embarrassing. Parading one's troubles in public simply wasn't done. The essays constituted an "indecent invasion of [Fitzgerald's] own privacy" (qtd. in Bruccoli, "The Perkins-Wilson Correspondence," 65). As an editor, therefore, Perkins faced a problem when Fitzgerald suggested on March 25, 1936, that his autobiographical magazine writing might be stitched together into a good and saleable book. Although Perkins had earlier discouraged this idea, Fitzgerald proposed that since "the interest in this *Esquire* series has been so big, . . . I thought you might reconsider the subject" (*Dear Scott/Dear Max*, 227). Perkins tactfully replied that he'd prefer "a reminiscent book— not autobiographical but reminiscent. . . . I do not think the Esquire pieces ought to be published alone. But as for an autobiographical book which would comprehend what is in them, I would be very much for it." It would need integration, however, and should not be a mere collection of articles (*Dear Scott/Dear Max*, 228).

Three months later, Gilbert Seldes echoed the point in a letter to Fitzgerald. Collections of scattered articles rarely made sense or money, Seldes observed, and he went on to make an argument for the book of reminiscence Perkins had favored: "More important, Scott, is that you seem more and more to me an essential figure in America and sooner or later you will have to say your complete say, not only in fiction, but in the facts about yourself and the part you played at the beginning and what you think of it now."

By the fall of 1936, Fitzgerald had abandoned any idea of collecting "The Crack-Up" articles. By that time both Perkins and Fitzgerald's agent, Harold Ober, had indicated that the articles were doing real damage to his reputation as a writer. "My Hollywood deal," he wrote Beatrice Dance in

September, "was seriously compromised by their general tone. It seems to have implied to some people that I was a complete moral and artistic bankrupt." Furthermore, he felt, the Mok interview might never have come about if he hadn't composed "those indiscreet *Esquire* articles" (*Letters*, 549). As a consequence he began disavowing them. They were not to be taken too seriously, he told Hamilton Basso. Later he withheld the articles from Sheilah Graham for some time before showing her the tear sheets with the admonition, "I shouldn't have written these" (qtd. in Graham and Frank, *Beloved Infidel*, 237).

When Edmund Wilson began assembling the volume of Fitzgerald's nonfiction and critical acclaim that emerged in 1945 as *The Crack-Up*, he encountered initial opposition from both Perkins and Ober. As early as February 1941 Wilson suggested to Perkins that "The Crack-Up" articles should be brought out in book form. "I hated it when it came out, just as you did," Wilson remarked, "but I have found several intelligent people that think highly of it. There was more truth and sincerity in it, I suppose, than we realized at the time. He wanted it published in a book himself, and after all I dare say it is a part of the real Fitzgerald record" (Wilson, *Letters*, 337–38). These were excellent reasons for Scribner's to publish such a book, but Perkins remained adamant.

Eventually Wilson took his project to New Directions, but not before he'd lobbied on its behalf with Fitzgerald's financial executor, John Biggs, to forestall objections from the family. He intended to call his book *The Crack-Up*, editor Wilson explained, not because he was enamored of the title but because "Glenway Wescott's appreciation is largely based on *The Crack-Up*, and . . . if you read *The Crack-Up* through, you realize that it is not a discreditable confession but an account of a kind of crisis that many men of Scott's generation have gone through, and that in the end he sees a way to live by application to his work." Wilson hoped that Biggs might be able to "counteract with [his] influence any influence that Ober and Max Perkins may have had on [Fitzgerald's daughter] Scottie," and that he might be able to allay her misgivings (Wilson, *Letters*, 348).

THE CIRCUMSTANCES

Fitzgerald wrote his three "gloom articles," as he referred to them in his *Ledger*, in the fall of 1935. He finished "The Crack-Up" itself in October 1935, "Pasting It Together" and "Handle with Care" in December. At the time he was suffering through an extremely low period in his life, during which he attempted to deaden with liquor and sex the awareness that

Zelda would never be wholly well, the realization that his earning power had drastically diminished while the bills mounted ever higher, and the sense that he'd let his life and his talent waste away. In 1935 and 1936, he observed, "all my products were dirges & elegies" (*Letters*, 107).

When Arnold Gingrich came calling in Baltimore one day in the spring of 1935, he found Fitzgerald in a "ratty old bathrobe" moaning about having to write another story of young love. He couldn't do them with enthusiasm any more, and the idea of having to produce one brought up his "cold gorge." "Well, why not write about that?" Gingrich suggested, then thought no more of the matter until, in the fall, the first of the three "Crack-Up" pieces turned up on his desk (Gingrich, "Publisher's Page," 12, 16).

Fitzgerald had spent the intervening summer in Asheville, North Carolina, carrying on a reckless affair with a married woman (Beatrice Dance) and consuming vast quantities of alcohol. Laura Guthrie (later Laura Hearne), who was his "secretary"—that is, his always-to-be-available companion, good listener, potential conquest, and occasional typist that summer—began by admiring and feeling sorry for her employer and ended in near disgust. In the exhaustive diary she kept of those days, Mrs. Guthrie set down her initial impression of Fitzgerald:

> He is completely alone because no persons are near to him, and he has no religion to comfort him. He makes me think of a lost soul, wandering in purgatory—sometimes hell. He tries so hard to drown it out with drinking and sex. Sometimes in the heights of these moments he forgets for a brief time—then it all comes back in overwhelming force. "Life is not happy," as he says. It isn't for him. He said it was a good thing he was not a rich man or he would have been dead before now (killing himself with indulgences!) but that the necessity of doing work had kept him going. Now he hopes that life will continue to be just endurable, which will only be if he keeps enough health to work.
>
> (GUTHRIE, MEMOIR, 73)

One can detect here the humble secretary parroting the thoughts of the great man, but by the end of the summer, after she had been exposed to every sort of indignity, including lying to cover up Fitzgerald's affair and witnessing his daily attempt to achieve oblivion through drink, Guthrie was only hoping to get rid of him. She finally managed to do so on Friday the 13th of September, when Scott, who had switched from beer and ale to gin a week earlier, broke down physically and allowed himself to be taken to the local hospital.

When she arrived at his hotel room that morning, Guthrie found empty glasses everywhere and Fitzgerald himself in terrible condition, with blood-shot eyes, drawn lips, skin raw from eczema, twitching leg muscles, and a distorted look about the face that made her realize he couldn't last much longer. "My nerves are going," he told her. "I'm about to break." He could not work at all. He wept, as he often had that summer. He pretended he was having a heart attack. Then, though it didn't seem fair that she should have to get him to the hospital, Guthrie helped her invalid pack up his dirty clothes and get dressed so that he could march through the lobby and check out as if he were on his way to the train. Upon depositing him at the hospital she "felt like a kid out of school," her responsibility over. "Nothing could ever happen to get me to put my head in this noose again," she noted in her diary. "At first I had thought that I could save him and help him to write steadily and really be his good angel, but I have decided that no one can be this" (Memoir, 138–43).

The collapse in Asheville was Fitzgerald's fourth breakdown from liquor in the space of about two years, he told Guthrie (Memoir, 148). Within a month he had dried out enough to write "The Crack-Up," but another year and more would elapse before his long spell of despondency and drunkenness came to an end. By mid-1937, he was able to confide some of the truth to his notebooks:

> What got me in the two years mess that reached its lowest point in the fall of 1936 [when he was again in Asheville under constant care by nurses, and attempted suicide twice] was the usual combination of circumstances. A prejudiced enemy might say it was all drink, a fond Mama might say it was a run of ill-luck, a banker might say it was not providing for the future in better days, a psychologist might say it was a nervous collapse—it was perhaps partly all these things—the effect was to prevent me from doing my work at the very age when presumably one is at the height of one's powers. My life looked like a hopeless mess there for a while and the point was I didn't *want* it to be better. I had completely ceased to give a good god-damn.
>
> (FITZGERALD, NOTE, N.D.)

THE ART

When *The Crack-Up* came out in 1945, a number of critics celebrated its honesty. Lionel Trilling hailed Fitzgerald's "heroic self-awareness" ("Fitzgerald," 182). Andrews Wanning detected "a desperate effort at self-disclosure" ("Fitzgerald and His Brethren," 545). In some ways, the essays *were* unusually candid. "The Crack-Up" accurately reflected Fitzgerald's tendency toward despondency, for example. "Please don't be depressed," Zelda had written him in 1931. "Nothing is sad about you except your sadness and the frayed places in your pink kimono and that you care so much about everything . . . O my love, I love you so—and I want you to be happy" (Fitzgerald, *Dear Scott, Dearest Zelda*, 109–10). But her husband was temperamentally unsuited to happiness. Hemingway's "instinct [was] toward megalomania," he commented in 1936, "and mine toward melancholy" (*Letters*, 543).

Still, Fitzgerald was far from totally forthcoming in these three articles for *Esquire*. As Milton Hindus commented, the essays lacked the kind of specific detail that lends conviction to the greatest confessional writing. The thing most conspicuously left out was, naturally, Fitzgerald's alcoholism: "naturally" because as both Glenway Wescott and Malcolm Cowley have observed, denying that one has a drinking problem constitutes one of the symptoms of the disease (*Crack-Up* 327–28; Cowley, introduction, xxi). It was obviously disingenuous of Fitzgerald to dismiss the issue in the first of his "Crack-Up" articles. There he referred to William Seabrook's book about alcoholism, which "tells, with some pride and a movie ending, of how he became a public charge." Seabrook's nervous system had collapsed, and so, admitted Fitzgerald, had his own, but not because of drink: "the present writer was not so entangled," he declared, "having at the time not tasted so much as a glass of beer for six months" (*Crack-Up*, 71).

Such denials did not convince everyone. John V. A. Weaver, another writer associated with the Jazz Age, found the first two *Esquire* articles disturbing since they described so exactly what had happened to him: "I can't drink *a drop*," he wrote Fitzgerald. "I can only sit impotent, day by day, and see a strange world careen by—a world in which I have no place." Weaver mailed his letter in February 1936, while George Martin (who did not know Fitzgerald) waited until after the publication of "An Alcoholic Case" in February 1937 to offer his assurance that he'd been in the same boat. "From the stuff you write in Esquire you seem to be having one hell of a time," Martin began. "If it's true . . . please know that I've lived all through it—will to die, dts, friends gone, money gone, job gone, self respect gone, guts gone . . . everything." He then suggested that Fitzgerald get hold of Peabody's *Common Sense of Drinking*.

This letter obviously struck a nerve, for in answering Fitzgerald advanced external reasons for his malady. Martin gently chided him in reply: "Certainly, as you say, the cause precedes the curse; but it is also true that the old ego breeds rationalizations like guinea pigs." Indeed, much of "The Crack-Up" reads like a rationalization of Fitzgerald's breakdown, and the three articles represent more an apologia than a confession. The blame for his crack-up, Fitzgerald implies, lies not within himself but elsewhere: the deficient genes he was bequeathed, the contemporary climate of materialism and insincerity, even the growth of motion pictures, which threatened to put fiction writers out of business.

By the middle of 1937, when he was drafting his autobiographical essay on "Early Success," Fitzgerald had matured enough to recognize this self-deception. There, in a passage later cut out of the essay, he compared himself unfavorably with his own father, a man who had failed without seeking scapegoats. This passage was intended to accompany the discussion of the relative importance of will and fate in determining success. "The man who arrives young," Fitzgerald wrote, "believes that he exercises his will because his star is shining. The man who only asserts himself at thirty has a balanced idea of what will power and fate have each contributed" (*Crack-Up*, 89). Then, in part of the typescript he later deleted, came the following, with Fitzgerald's lined-through corrections indicated in italics:

It is This [difference] comes out when the *various* storms *of professional life* strike your craft *that this comes out. My own father was a failure, once, in his own business, and once as a "high-salaried man"—What* success my father *success he had* had come fairly late in life and was brief in duration and never did I hear him blame his failure on anything but his own incompetence. *He* yet he might have since he was caught once in *the* a panic of '93 and once in the first rush to weed *passion for weeding out* older men out of business. *When* On the contrary when I went through several years of private misfortune and impeded production, I felt no loss of *confidence and* morale until one day a comparatively small blow *matter* gave me that idea my star had *miraculously* gone out. *and I mean gone out, not gone into eclipse.* For two years I sulked in bitter discouragement *and indifference before I could struggle out. I was so sure of it* so sure about it that I told everyone about it and even wrote about it with as little reticence as if I'd lost a leg in a railroad accident.

It is easy enough, generations later, to gloss Fitzgerald's reference to "several years of private misfortune"—these were the years of Zelda's final relapse into schizophrenia and his own immersion in drink. But what was the "comparatively small blow" that toppled him into the slough of despond? The dramatic logic of "The Crack-Up" articles demanded that

some immediate cause be located, and so in the first of his essays he indicated that it was a piece of unexpected good news from his doctor—a
reprieve from an earlier death sentence—that led him, paradoxically, to
crack like an old plate. Such an event may have happened, but no one has
documented it. Probably, Fitzgerald was dramatizing his own situation in
order to contrast the dreaded loss of vitality with the comparatively unimportant "small gift of life given back" (*Crack-Up*, 71–72). In the remaining
"Crack-Up" essays, he dropped all reference to this medical reprieve.

Obviously and understandably, Fitzgerald was telling less than the
whole truth about himself and his family. He was working, after all, in a
genre new to him. "Although presented as autobiography," Kenneth Eble
has commented, the articles "have the air of highly wrought and intensely
felt fiction" (Eble, *Fitzgerald*, 141). But that is not the case exactly, for how
often in Fitzgerald's short stories would one find references to the Bible, to
William Ernest Henley, to Wordsworth and Keats, to Lenin and Dickens
and Tolstoy, to Spinoza, to Descartes, to the Euganean Hills? And how often would Fitzgerald as a writer of fiction have allowed metaphor to substitute for action, as he does so often in "The Crack-Up" essays? Fitzgerald
compares himself to a cracked plate, a beggar carrying the "tin cup of self-
pity," a bankrupt who had overdrawn his account, a lecturer about to lose
his audience, an empty shell, a conjurer fresh out of tricks, a Negro lady
cutting out a rival, a Negro retainer pretending to jollity, and a dog who
will remain subservient if thrown a bone from time to time. Saying what
one is *like* provides an alternative to saying outright what one actually *is*.
Like the wealth of learned references, it was a form of evasion.

Fitzgerald was searching for a form, but he had not quite found it. Re-
reading "The Crack-Up" pieces, one is inclined to share the ambivalent
reaction of the woman who wrote Fitzgerald that she found it hard to
believe his articles really touched the depths of tragedy, yet they were "so
convincing as to leave little room for doubt that the author had at some
time *lived* those bitternesses and depressions" (Tyson, letter). The source
of this ambivalence, according to William Barrett, lay in the excessive art-
fulness of the essays. "The Crack-Up," he wrote,

is a frightening thing to read: rapid, brilliant, but also jerky and almost
metallically tense in tone, as if still vibrating with the receding hysteria of
the breakdown. No doubt Fitzgerald, writing for *Esquire* magazine, felt he
had to jazz up his material, but, even with allowance made for this, these
pieces leave the impression that the author is still seeing life much too
much in literary and dramatic terms. A man writing of his own human

defeat and failure ought to have passed beyond "literature" altogether, even to the point of risking a matter-of-factness that might appear prosy and plodding.

("FITZGERALD AND AMERICA," 349–50)

It is a dangerous business, this prescribing the correct technique for authors, but a more matter-of-fact approach would probably have given Fitzgerald's essays the authority and verisimilitude they lack. Apology masquerading as confession may well represent, in Alfred Kazin's words, "the best possible device for not revealing" the truth ("Fitzgerald: An American Confession," 341).

As it stands, "The Crack-Up" pieces tell their truths only between the lines. They are not about nervous exhaustion, emotional bankruptcy, or even an alcoholic breakdown. The subject of "The Crack-Up" is Fitzgerald's misanthropy and the self-hatred behind it. All these essays, but especially the first and last, deal with the author's attempted escape from people and, more particularly, his escape from that large group to whom he has felt obliged to give something of himself. He has given too much in the past. He will, he says, give no more.

When the writing touches on this subject, it achieves a vividness missing elsewhere. Upon hearing the "grave sentence" of his doctor, Fitzgerald writes in the first article, he "wanted to be absolutely alone" and so cut himself off "from ordinary cares." Instead, he sat around making lists. "It was not," he reveals, "an unhappy time." With his crack-up came the realization that "for a long time I had not liked people and things, but only followed the rickety old pretense of liking." In his casual relations—"with an editor, a tobacco seller, the child of a friend"—he had merely done what was expected. Even with love, he had been going through the motions. He had, in short, been guilty of emotional insincerity for some time, yet he does not publicly blame himself. Instead, he transfers his self disgust into distaste for most other human beings.

He still admires the looks of Midwestern Scandinavian blond women. He likes "doctors and girl children up to the age of about thirteen and well-brought-up boy children from about eight years old on." He likes old men and Katharine Hepburn's face on the screen and Miriam Hopkins's face and old friends if he only has to see them once a year. But almost everyone else he has come to detest, and he makes a list of them (Crack-Up, 72–73).

To escape politicians and retail clerks and hunting people and the rest, he withdrew into a period of "vacuous quiet" during which he was forced to think for himself. He then discovered, according to the second article, that he had never done this before. All his ideas had been borrowed from Edmund Wilson and from four other unnamed men, one of whom was surely Ernest Hemingway. Not only had he given too freely of himself to people he didn't care about, but he had submerged his mental development by passively adopting the ideas of others. There was no "I" any more, Fitzgerald concluded, no basis on which he could organize his self-respect (*Crack-Up*, 78–79).

The third article, "Handle with Care," moves from how to think to how to act. Unlike Descartes, Fitzgerald's motto had been, "I felt—therefore I was." He had, in fact, felt too much, and he decides that if he wishes to survive he must cease "any attempts to be a person—to be kind, just or generous." Instead, he rather cynically resolves to develop a false smile to win the favor of those who might be of use to him and otherwise to cultivate the habit of saying no in a voice that will make people never want to ask again (*Crack-Up*, 82–83).

In the last paragraph of this last "Crack-Up" article, Fitzgerald located the source of his malady in two telling comparisons. For too long he had concentrated on pleasing others, "and just as the laughing stoicism which has enabled the American negro to endure the intolerable conditions of his existence has cost him his sense of the truth—so in my case there is a price to pay." Now that he has determined to change, life will no longer be as pleasant as it once was. He will become a different sort of dog now, one who no longer likes "the postman, nor the grocer, nor the editor, nor the cousin's husband." He will only lick your hand now, Fitzgerald says, if you throw him a bone (*Crack-Up*, 84). This cynicism, like much cynicism, is directed against the self. In repudiating a past in which he has too often played the fawning servant or the lovable lap dog, Fitzgerald was implicitly condemning himself and preparing the way for a fresh start.

Despite these protestations, Fitzgerald never became really antisocial. But he did reorder his priorities so that doing his work and fulfilling his obligations came ahead of his drive to charm other people. During the Hollywood years he seems finally to have achieved a sense of self-respect, a term that Joan Didion has defined in a passage that uncannily echoes the theme of "The Crack-Up":

> To have that sense of one's intrinsic worth which constitutes self-respect is potentially to have everything: the ability to discriminate, to love and to remain indifferent. To lack it is to be locked within oneself, paradoxically incapable of either love or indifference. If we do not respect ourselves, we are on the one hand forced to despise those who have so few resources

as to consort with us, so little perception as to remain blind to our fatal weaknesses. On the other, we are peculiarly in thrall to everyone we see, curiously determined to live out—since our self-image is untenable—their false notions of us. We flatter ourselves by thinking this compulsion to please others an attractive trait. . . . *Of course* I will play Francesca to your Paolo, Helen Keller to anyone's Annie Sullivan: no expectation is too misplaced, no role too ludicrous. At the mercy of those we cannot but hold in contempt, we play roles doomed to failure before they are begun, each defeat generating fresh despair at the urgency of divining and meeting the next demand made upon us.

It is the phenomenon sometimes called "alienation from self." In its advanced stages, we no longer answer the telephone, because someone might want something; that we could *say no* without drowning in self-reproach is an idea alien to this game. Every encounter demands too much, tears the nerves, drains the will.

(147–48)

This "alienation from self" lies behind Fitzgerald's breakdown, and behind his announced misanthropy. The very process of putting words down on paper helped free him from that alienation. The insightful Perkins, who maintained that no one "would write those articles if they were really true," arrived at the conclusion "that in some deep way, when he wrote those articles, Scott must have been thinking that things would be different with him" (qtd. in Berg, *Max Perkins*, 282). Other readers agreed that the articles must surely have a purgative effect. He'd be willing to bet, Burton Rascoe observed after reading the first two essays, that Fitzgerald was "already feeling immensely better . . . self-confident and creative again." "You've been finding out a lot of things that have hurt like hell," Julian Street told Fitzgerald, "and at the end of it you'll be grown up . . . a bigger and better man and a bigger and better writer for it." In replying to Street on February 24, 1936, Fitzgerald acknowledged that since the intensity of despair had moderated somewhat, he could see that writing the articles "was a form of catharsis but at the time of writing them what I said seemed absolutely real." He could also see, he added defensively, that "an unfriendly critic might damn the series as the whining of a spoilt baby," but wasn't that true of most poetry? (*Letters*, 532–33).

It is true of Fitzgerald not only that his characters are modeled on himself but that he sometimes becomes his characters after the fact. Thus his retreat to Asheville, Tryon, and Hendersonville in North Carolina during the two years of his personal depression virtually repeated Dick

Diver's drifting among the small towns of upstate New York. Like Diver, too, Fitzgerald had to abandon his goal of becoming an "an entire man . . . with an opulent American touch, a sort of combination of J. P. Morgan, Topham Beauclerk and St. Francis of Assisi" (*Crack-Up*, 84). Now he will be "a writer only," he announces in the last of the "Crack-Up" articles, just as Dick Diver finally became only a doctor, no longer a scientist or entertainer or bon vivant. The difference is that Diver fades away, while Fitzgerald emerged from his fallen estate to live a useful and productive final four years.

Fitzgerald referred to the "Crack-Up" articles in his *Ledger* as "biography," not "autobiography." This apparent slip of the pen, as Robert Sklar has observed, revealed the "essential truth" that the Scott Fitzgerald of the essays was not the same as the man who wrote about him (*Fitzgerald*, 309). "I don't know whether those articles of mine in *Esquire*—the 'Crack-Up' series—represented a real nervous breakdown," Fitzgerald remarked in July 1939. "In retrospect it seems more of a spiritual 'change of life'—and a most unwilling one" (*Letters*, 309). "Transformation" might be an even better term than "change of life," for in "The Crack-Up" Fitzgerald sloughed off the skin of the Irish charmer and determined to let work instead of play dominate the time left to him. The articles hardly achieve a "heroic awareness." It took courage to say as much as he did, but Fitzgerald left a great deal only hinted at and blamed too many outside forces for his predicament to be adjudged a hero of self-revelation. Despite the false leads and evasions, however, Fitzgerald did uncover more of himself between the lines of these articles, and particularly of the last article, than anywhere else in his works. And in the end the process did him good. "The Crack-Up" may not measure up to the very best confessional writing, but it had something of the same therapeutic effect on the man who set it down on paper.

[10]

FITZGERALD'S POLITICAL DEVELOPMENT

THE IMAGE of the frivolous playboy clings to F. Scott Fitzgerald's reputation like a barnacle on a ship. He helped build the image himself, to be sure, but it's a false one. Most of his career Fitzgerald was a serious, hard-working, intelligent artist. Yet people persist in thinking of him as an artist in spite of himself, a bear of remarkable talent but lamentably little brain.

It follows that he has rarely been credited with having any political ideas at all. Fitzgerald knew "absolutely nothing" about politics "and was not interested in the slightest," one of his oldest friends observed in 1978 (Biggs, letter). At best he has been characterized as a dabbler in political questions, borrowing the thoughts of others and revealing considerable naiveté in the process (Mizener, letter).

No one was more responsible for creating this attitude than Edmund Wilson. Toward Wilson, two years his senior at Princeton and demonstrably his superior in breadth of knowledge, Fitzgerald adopted the role of the breathless novitiate receiving the mysteries. At times, though, Fitzgerald wearied of his position at the master's feet and resorted to poking fun at him. In the fall of 1928 Wilson spent a weekend with the Fitzgeralds at Ellerslie, their house outside Wilmington, and returned to New York with the astounding tale that Fitzgerald expected him to be named secretary of state in the next administration.

Over the weekend Fitzgerald asked Wilson to fill him in on current affairs. After Wilson expounded on the state of the world at some length, Fitzgerald said, "Well, I understand there is going to be an election soon, a change of administration. I suppose they're bound to make you Secretary of State." Upon hearing this story, T. S. Matthews, Wilson's colleague at the *New Republic* at the time, immediately said that Fitzgerald must have been pulling Wilson's leg. "Wilson was a sort of innocent about some people," Matthews concluded, "particularly about Fitzgerald."

Wilson was adamant, however. Thirty years later, in fact, Wilson still believed Fitzgerald meant what he said. In the spring of 1960 he wrote Matthews insisting that the latter had misunderstood the story. "It was in my radicalizing days," Wilson said, "and Scott thought that when the revolution came, I should inevitably be made Secretary of State." Wilson might have been disabused of his innocence about Fitzgerald, and Matthews undoubtedly would have felt his judgment confirmed, had they seen the following sarcastic entry in Fitzgerald's notebooks:

> To Mathews [sic]: I certainly do wish I could grow up like you fellows and write about all the wonderful things that are happening in the newspapers. But here I sit like a big fat fairy thinking that maybe if I really knew why . . . I would really know almost as much about the social revolution as those deep thinkers Mike Gold etc.
>
> (WILSON, *LETTERS*, 45, 596; MATTHEWS,
> "SOME RECOLLECTIONS," 13–14; FITZGERALD, NOTE)

Fitzgerald began as a political naif, but he was no longer innocent, no longer willing to be patronized, by the time he set down that remark in the middle or late 1930s.

His thinking about politics developed through three distinct phases. The first period, which might be called the stage of disillusionment, extended from his boyhood through the crash of 1929 and his return to the United States in 1931. In the second stage, and especially from 1932 to 1935, in Baltimore, he was moved by the Depression to study communism as a possible alternative to the capitalist system. Although he eventually declined to enlist in the communist cause, during the final period from 1937 to 1940, in Hollywood, he achieved his most mature understanding of political issues and his relationship to them.

THE GROWTH OF DOUBT: 1913–1931

In his youth, Scott Fitzgerald recalled, he "used to have awful rows on political subjects" with his father (*Apprentice*, 68). Edward Fitzgerald, as a staunch Republican, probably objected to his son's allegiance to the Democratic Party. Less than a month after matriculating at Princeton in the fall of 1913, Scott joined liberal Whig Hall instead of conservative Clio. Then in the spring of 1917, Fitzgerald discovered the embodiment of his political ideals in Henry Hyacinth Strater, of Louisville, leader of the democratic anti-club movement at Princeton and a pacifist disciple of Tolstoy and Edward Carpenter. Neither Fitzgerald nor Amory Blaine, the protagonist of *This Side of Paradise* (1920), totally succumbed to Strater's arguments (in the book he's called Burne Holiday), but certain seeds were planted. Edward Fitzgerald, the Southern gentleman, would not have cottoned to such views. And he would certainly have been disturbed by the advocacy of socialism with which his son brought his first novel to a close.

Given a ride by a goggled captain of industry, Amory launches into socialist dogma. Every child should have an equal start, there should be a fair trial of government ownership of all industries, wealth should be distributed more equally, and unless these desiderata came to pass, a revolution was likely. The "threat of the red flag," Amory asserts, "is certainly the inspiring force of all reform." He has no doubt that the Russian Revolution is "really a great experiment and well worth while" (253–54).

As a political statement, this is not very persuasive. Fitzgerald does not condemn the captain of industry, who turns out to be a reasonable, intelligent man and the father of one of Amory's friends killed in the war. Besides, Amory admits it's the first time in his life he's argued in favor of socialism and that he's doing so out of self-interest, "being very poor at present" (256, 245). His impecunious condition is particularly galling because Amory "detests" the poor and regards poverty as the "ugliest thing in the world. It's essentially cleaner," he thinks, "to be corrupt and rich than it is to be innocent and poor" (237).

Why did Fitzgerald end *This Side of Paradise* with this burst of somewhat insincere socialist rhetoric? For one thing, it gave the twenty-three-year-old author an opportunity to shock the older generation. Much of the novel, including the not-so-lurid petting scenes, aims at this objective. "The members of Fitzgerald's generation," Malcolm Cowley observed, "were not interested at the time in underlying social movements, any more than they were interested in local or international politics. What they felt in their hearts was that they had made an absolute break with the standards of the older generation . . . in those days the real gulf was between the young and the old" (Cowley, introduction, x–xi). The protest was personal and directed against received wisdom.

The other reason was artistic. Fitzgerald was trying to satisfy an objection his publishers had made against "The Romantic Egotist," the preliminary version of his novel. Scribner's felt that the story did not "work up to a conclusion;—neither the hero's career nor his character are shown to be brought to any stage which justifies an ending" (qtd. in West, *The Making*, 17). Sending Amory off to war wasn't conclusion enough. Killing him off wouldn't work either, although Fitzgerald tried that solution in an intermediate draft of the novel. Finally he decided to radicalize his protagonist. His editor, Maxwell Perkins, might object to the "length of the socialistic discussions in the last chapter," Fitzgerald wrote him upon mailing the manuscript to Scribner's in September 1919. But, he added, "I certainly think the hero gets somewhere" (Fitzgerald, *Dear Scott/Dear Max*, 20).

The political views Amory expresses, however unconvincingly, derived from George Bernard Shaw and H. G. Wells, especially Wells. But Fitzgerald was also influenced by currents of thought flowing through his own country. Among these was the conviction that American politics was absurd and that although plenty of things needed reforming, it would do no good to try to reform them. If the war had proved nothing else, it had proved that. Here is Fitzgerald's own statement on the question as of 1924:

> Something serious (which only professional evangelists, cheap novelists, and corrupt politicians profess to understand) is the matter with the world. It will be a strong heart that can fight its way upstream in these troubled waters and not be, like my generation, a bit cynical, a bit weary, and a bit sad: We have seen the war and its attendant ferocity, the hysteria both of the communists and, over here, of the "100% Americans," the cheating of the wounded veterans, the administration corruption, the prohibition scandal—what wonder if we are almost afraid to open the newspapers in the morning.
>
> ("WAIT TILL YOU HAVE CHILDREN," 193)

It was better to look the other way, safer to be *against* whatever had gone wrong than to be *for* any panacea that might make it right. The dominant attitude toward political subjects in Fitzgerald's fiction up to *The Great Gatsby* (1925) was one of cynicism—and the cleverer, the better.

The protagonists of Fitzgerald's first two novels both consider and reject careers in politics. Amory Blaine and Anthony Patch return from the war with vague dreams of entering the political arena, but are discouraged by the company they'd have to keep in "that incredible pigsty" of Congress (*Beautiful and Damned*, 56). "Why is it," Amory wonders, "that the pick of the young Englishmen from Oxford and Cambridge go into politics and in the U.S.A. we leave it to the muckers?—raised in the ward, educated in the assembly and sent to Congress, fat-paunched bundles of corruption" (*This Side of Paradise*, 152).

In his 1923 play, *The Vegetable*, Fitzgerald attempted to transform his disillusionment with the political process into humor. But the wit rarely rose above the sophomoric level of a Triangle club show at Princeton. A man named Fossile serves as chief justice of the Supreme Court. "Look at here," the postman turned president advises a character called Stutz-Mozart. "If you're one of those radical agitators my advice to you is to go right back where you came from." "I came from Hoboken," Stutz-Mozart replies (78, 102).

At the same time that Fitzgerald was working this shallow vein of political satire, he began to uncover more important and lasting discontents. One of these was an antiwar bias that later came to ally him with radical movements of the 1930s. Burne Holiday's pacifism had not quite convinced Amory Blaine, but John Dos Passos's *Three Soldiers* apparently converted Fitzgerald. In an extravagantly favorable 1921 review, Fitzgerald praised Dos Passos for laying bare the "filth and pain, cruelty and hysteria and panic" of that "whole gorgeous farce" of World War I (Fitzgerald, review, 121–24). In *The Beautiful and Damned* (1922) he made his own attack against the war: "In April war was declared with Germany. Wilson and his cabinet . . . let loose the carefully starved dogs of war, and the press began to whoop hysterically against the sinister morals, sinister philosophy, and sinister music produced by the Teutonic temperament" (306–7). Anthony Patch suspects that "the dim purpose of the war was to let the regular army officers—men with the mentality and aspirations of school-boys—have their own fling with some real slaughter" (320). One reviewer accused Fitzgerald of "flogging a dead horse" in satirizing the hypocrisies spawned by the war (Colum, review, 335). Perhaps that was true in 1922; it was much less true in the 1930s, when Fitzgerald stuck to his militantly antiwar position.

In his work leading up to *The Great Gatsby*, Fitzgerald was developing another line of thought that would make him sympathetic to the leftist movements ahead. This was his growing realization that although wealth might liberate the British aristocracy for lives of public service, in the United States the pursuit or possession of great amounts of money led to cruelty and wickedness. As Robert Sklar has observed, Fitzgerald's initial hopes for an admirable American aristocracy, perhaps encouraged by the elitism of Mencken, turned to condemnations of the plutocracy that came to pass (*Fitzgerald*, 86–87, 144, 166, 190–91). Anthony Patch is driven literally mad by the prospect of inheriting vast wealth. The tycoon himself grows more panicky, the more money he has to protect:

> Let two dozen workmen meet behind a barn and he bursts out in a cold sweat, casts aside eight centuries of justice and tries to get half a dozen bewildered foreigners sent to Leavenworth for 10 years. He stocks his cellar with liquor and then votes righteously for prohibition "for the good of the masses."
>
> ("WHAT KIND OF HUSBANDS," 190)

So Fitzgerald castigated the plutocrat in a 1924 article. In his fiction he had already created Braddock Washington of "The Diamond as Big as the Ritz"(1922), a man rich and arrogant enough to try to bribe God.

Next he was to get the despicably careless Buchanans of *The Great Gatsby* down on paper. "I would know Tom Buchanan if I met him on the street," Max Perkins wrote Fitzgerald, "and would avoid him" (*Dear Scott/Dear Max*, 83). Self-indulgent, cheaply sentimental, and totally insensitive to the rights of others, Buchanan represents the worst of his class. It is one measure of Fitzgerald's developing maturity of outlook that he assigned to Tom the racial and ethnic bias exhibited in earlier novels by such supposedly likable characters as Amory Blaine, Richard Caramel, and Maury Noble. Both Amory and Richard encounter what Fitzgerald calls "aliens": smelly, noisy foreigners with ugly faces and worse manners. Maury delivers a speech deploring the medical progress that has made it possible to keep too many inferior people alive (*This Side of Paradise*, 147; *Beautiful and Damned*, 74–75, 255). By assigning such racist notions to the brutish and insensitive Tom Buchanan, Fitzgerald began the process of casting aside his own prejudices, which culminated in his creation of the well-read Negro who causes Monroe Stahr, in *The Last Tycoon*, to rethink his function as moviemaker.

It is Tom's money, of course, that enables him to mistreat so many people with impunity. And it is his money, and the position it has purchased, that enables him first to marry Daisy and then to keep her. The novel thus personalizes Fitzgerald's embittered feelings about a culture in which the rich man gets the golden girl. His resentment did not lead directly to revolution, but he did see the problem as one of class conflict. peasant vs. plutocrat, or to describe his own case more accurately, middle class vs. upper class. As James F. Light points out, *Gatsby* can be read in terms of the way "in which the virtues and weaknesses of various social classes are played off against each other": Gatsby the nouveau riche, the Buchanans upper class, Nick Carraway upper middle class, the Wilsons working class (Light, "Political Conscience," 18).

Fitzgerald called himself a "Socialist in politics" as early as his first *Who's Who* entry in 1922 (Obituary), but it was a position easily undermined by his lack of confidence in the masses. Upton Sinclair's *The Brass Check*, he wrote Perkins in March 1922, persuaded him that in America "freedom [had] produced the greatest tyranny under the sun." He was still a socialist, he said, but feared that "things will grow worse and worse the more the people nominally rule. The strong are too strong for us and the weak too weak" (Fitzgerald, *Letters*, 154). Business was in the saddle, and riding mankind.

In 1924 Fitzgerald described himself as "a pessimist, [and] a communist (with Nietzschean overtones). . . . My enthusiasms at present include Stravinski, Otto Braun, Mencken, Conrad, Joyce, the early Gertrude Stein, Chaplin and all books about that period which lies between the V and XV centuries" (Baldwin, "Fitzgerald," 270). A more pervasive European influence came with Oswald Spengler's *Decline of the West*, a book that profoundly affected Fitzgerald's thinking after 1927. In an interview of that year he laid out the whole Spenglerian program. The West was desperate and on its last legs. The only hope lay in the birth of a modern hero. Otherwise, America was doomed. Then he returned to Otto Braun, the precociously literary German lad who died in the Argonne fighting. "Better that an entire division should have been wiped out," he said, "than that Otto Braun should have been killed" (Salpeter, "Fitzgerald, Spenglerian," 274–77). The individual—especially the artist—mattered too much to Fitzgerald for him to become a good party man.

Though he continued to take Spengler's apocalyptic views seriously, Fitzgerald was not at all sure that his own country was ready to fall. There was lots of talk about revolution in eastern cities, but when he and Zelda and Scottie repaired to Montgomery, Alabama, in the fall of 1931, he encountered no fears whatever on that score. "It seems foolish for an American to be afraid of any communistic revolution right now," Fitzgerald told a newspaper reporter there. He didn't think communism could catch hold in the United States (Keith, "Scott Fitzgerald," 285). It was an opinion he would modify in the years immediately ahead.

THE PINK PERIOD: 1932–1935

The week the Fitzgeralds moved into La Paix, the "soft shady place" on the Bayard Turnbull estate outside Baltimore, Scott ran an advertisement for a secretary. It was May 1932, and up to this time the Depression had made little impression on him. His own income had reached a peak of $37,599 during 1931 (Turnbull, *Fitzgerald*, 205). Fitzgerald was first surprised and then moved when dozens of women answered his ad, many of them obviously having known better days. Scottie Fitzgerald, then only ten years old, recalls one interview with a particularly attractive applicant. "Can you type?" she was asked. "No," she answered, "but I sure could learn." That sort of thing nearly broke her father's heart (Smith, interview).

This incident, along with the march of the Bonus Army on nearby Washington that summer (among the Fitzgerald papers at Princeton is a copy of the July 9, 1932, "B.E.F. News," which warned Bonus Expeditionary Force marchers against involvement with soapbox communists who might be government agents in disguise) brought the Depression home to Fitzgerald and undoubtedly stimulated his interest in politics. Spengler had made him a pessimist; now the tide of events threatened to make him a communist. The revolution might be coming to the United States, after all.

He resolved to learn what he could about Marxism. Not to do so was irresponsible, he said in a letter to the politically conservative Mrs. Turnbull about her son's education. The colleges should cover "all the current economic theories," he wrote, "if only that the boy should know where he stands and what he's fighting. When a United States Senator *after his election* has to look up the principles of Marxism by which one-sixth of the world is governed it shows he's a pretty inadequate defender of his own system" (*Letters*, 226). He did not propose to make the same mistake.

Zelda Fitzgerald's correspondence provides a useful guide to her husband's political preoccupations during this period. Her letters suggest that his original knowledge of Marxist principles came from M. Ilin's *New Russia's Primer*, an account of the Five Year Plan and the benefits of a planned economy written for schoolchildren from twelve to fourteen years old. He left the just-published book (a Book-of-the-Month Club selection) with Zelda when he went to Hollywood late in 1931, and she duly reported her judgment that "the U.S.A. comes in for an enormous bawling out [in the book] that is doubtless well deserved, but severe." Later, Zelda and Scottie "had a long bed-time talk about the Soviets and the Russian idea," and she gave Scottie the *Primer* to read. Politically Zelda went this far with Scott but no farther. She refused, for example, to follow his suggestion and draw her money out of the bank in Montgomery. "What good would it do if the economic system collapses anyway?" she asked. Nor did Scott need to worry about "social revolutionists" looting the house and making off with the chess set. She'd taken it herself (Fitzgerald, *Dear Scott, Dearest Zelda*, 135–36, 139).

After they settled in Baltimore in 1932, though, Fitzgerald developed "political worries" that were "almost neurosis." He read at least some of *Das Kapital*. He invited a local communist to come out to La Paix for sparring matches and Marxist discussions. He loaned out the house for party meetings (Turnbull, *Fitzgerald*, 214, 226–27; Piper, *Fitzgerald*, 175–76). Zelda adopted a tone of amused tolerance toward all this activity. "Scott reads Marx—I read the cosmological philosophers," she wrote John Peale Bishop in the summer. "The brightest moments of our day are when we get them mixed up" (qtd. in Mizener, *The Far Side of Paradise*, 234). His mother, she wrote Scott directly, "thinks we are both in the Russian secret service and prefer bombs to June strawberries for breakfast" (*Dear Scott, Dearest Zelda*, 152). Although touched by the sight of middle-aged men selling candy and apples on the sidewalks, Zelda was not a good candidate for conversion to communism.

The most overtly political act of Fitzgerald's most political year came on November 5, 1932, when he made a public appearance at an antiwar meeting sponsored by the Johns Hopkins University liberal club and the Baltimore district of the National Students League. As the printed flyer in his papers reveals, he was the second of three speakers, with his topic "How the War Came to Princeton." The final speaker was Joseph Cohen, a member of the national committee of the Students Congress Against War and a delegate to the International Students Conference in Amsterdam the previous summer. The Baltimore session, held at Homewood Friends meeting house, was to serve as a warm-up for the Students Congress Against War rally in Chicago on December 28 and 29. This organization was communist in makeup, an "international front organization."

In capturing Fitzgerald, the local group achieved something of a publicity coup. Although Cohen was the principal speaker, the news story announcing the meeting focused on Fitzgerald's part in the proceedings. "F. Scott Fitzgerald, author of . . . well known novels," the lead paragraph began, and later the story referred to him as "one of the leading contributors of short stories to the Saturday Evening Post." In a newspaper article after the event, however, Fitzgerald was not mentioned until the eleventh paragraph. He had begun his talk, the piece revealed, by self-consciously addressing the audience as "fellow cranks." He then recounted how he had "progressed from an enthusiastic first lieutenant" to his present antiwar convictions ("Baltimore Students"; "Hopkins Liberal Club"; "Mrs. Holloway").

Never comfortable on his feet, Fitzgerald was soon to complain of the "strain of making speeches at 'Leagues Against Imperialistic War'" (*Letters*, 417). He may also have suspected that he was being used. But that hardly altered his antiwar feelings and his distaste for jingoism. It was only as a joke, surely, that someone called him "Fitzboomski" during the Russo-Japanese war in 1933 (Fitzgerald, *Crack-Up*, 237). Two years later he wrote an original antiwar sketch for the Squibb-World Peaceways program on CBS radio. The short play depicts the backyard militancy of a youngster who is proud of his daddy fighting overseas. But then the boy is called inside from his play with "rocket pistols" and "incinerator bombs" to hear the terrible news that had come in the War Department envelope. Also appearing on the program were Senator Gerald P. Nye and the radical singer Paul Robeson (Script for CBS).

Fitzgerald's pacifist leanings coincided with the Communist Party line, and the speech in Baltimore suggests that during 1932 through 1935 he was considering joining the party. A number of reasons militated against his taking such a step, however. He distrusted the religious commitment demanded of political true believers. He thought the Communists were exploiting racial divisions within the culture. He could not shake off his loyalty to his class. He was disturbed by the social stigma that fell on him as an incipient communist. Most important of all, he came to realize that politics and art made uncomfortable bedfellows.

The Communists claim, he wrote Mrs. Turnbull in September 1932, that "no man not under a religious spell (in their case, Communism) can have a focal point from which to orientate their work," adding that he was "not philosopher enough" to think the question through. In time, however, he came to agree with Joseph Wood Krutch that no genuine writer could submit himself to a political religion. Besides, Fitzgerald concluded by late 1935 that he could not expect personal salvation through Marxism. He ended his second *Crack-Up* article with the observation that someone (he wasn't sure who) was "sound asleep—someone who could have helped [him] to keep [his] shop open. It wasn't Lenin, and it wasn't God" (*Letters*, 433; Krutch, qtd. in Aaron, *Writers on the Left*, 259; *Crack-Up* 79–80).

By that time, too, he had become disillusioned by Communist Party attempts to exacerbate tensions between the races. The party leadership's appeal to blacks, he thought, amounted to little more than a con game. Their "treatment of the Negro question finished me," he observed in August 1934 (*Letters*, 417). He could not understand how his friend and "intellectual conscience," Edmund Wilson, could have signed a manifesto supporting the 1932 Communist Party ticket of Foster and Ford, since putting Ford, a black man, on the ticket seemed to him the most transparent kind of opportunism.

As a child of the middle class brought up on the Horatio Alger myth of upward striving, Fitzgerald could not easily identify with the working class. What was required was a willingness to renounce the safe, bright, rational world of the bourgeoisie and enter the strange, dark, passional realm of the proletariat. Fitzgerald could manage only a sense of divided loyalties. He sympathized with the downtrodden yet could not feel himself their brother. As Fitzgerald told a newspaperman in the fall of 1935, he was "torn between a belief that he should lend his abilities and his pen to the [Marxist] cause in which he believed, and his friendship, love and association with delightful people whom he recognized as 'idlers' in the social sense of the word" ("Mr. Fain," "I Knew Scott").

By 1934, Fitzgerald's communist leanings had begun to alienate him from some of those delightful people. He tended to lose his temper in political arguments at social gatherings. During a tea party late in May he "got into a heavy political argument with a Hitlerite" (*Dear Scott, Dearest Zelda*, 200). In a note of apology the next day, Fitzgerald acknowledged that the argument was his fault. "Certain subjects simply do not belong to an afternoon tea," he admitted to his hostess, "and, while I still think Mrs. [ ]'s arguments were almost maddening enough to justify homicide, I appreciate that it was no role of mine to intrude my intensity of feeling upon a group who had expected a quiet tea party." "For two years," he wrote his cousin Ceci in August, "I've gone half haywire trying to reconcile my double allegiance to the class I am part of, and the Great Change I believe in" (*Letters*, 437–38, 417).

Fitzgerald's allegiance to that change must have been challenged by the reception of *Tender Is the Night* in the communist press. The "General Plan" he devised after moving to Baltimore in 1932 reconfigured the novel along Marxist lines, so that it depicted a world in which the old structures were collapsing. The novel also addressed the antiwar issue directly. No longer, the book argues, would hordes of young men go marching off to slaughter as in World War I. Now that everything was changing, only mercenaries and adventurers such as Tommy Barban were willing to risk their own blood for the old order. Barban outlines his position in an argument with the novelist Albert McKisco:

> "Why do you want to fight the Soviets?" McKisco said. "The greatest experiment ever made by humanity? And the Riff? It seems to me it would be more heroic to fight on the just side."
> "How do you find out which it is?" asked Barban dryly.
> "Why—usually everybody intelligent knows."
> "Are you a Communist?"
> "I'm a Socialist," said McKisco. "I sympathize with Russia."
> "Well, I'm a soldier," Barban answered pleasantly. "My business is to kill people. I fought against the Riff because I am a European, and I have fought the Communists because they want to take my property from me."
> "Of all the narrow-minded excuses," McKisco looked around to establish a derisive liaison with some one else, but without success.
>
> (35–36)

Fitzgerald's sympathies are hard to locate in this scene. McKisco's ideas, based on altruism instead of self-interest, seem morally sounder. But he is something of a coward and poseur, not a man to rely on in a tight spot. For all his narrow-mindedness, on the other hand, the belligerent Tommy is willing—even eager—to fight for what he believes in. Later in the novel, he helps a Russian aristocrat escape from the Soviets; the operation leaves three Red guards dead at the border. Fitzgerald makes it clear, however, that Tommy and the Prince Chillicheff he rescues belong to a dying class. The White Russian aristocrats no longer come to the Riviera every winter. Those who fled the revolution and stayed in France, such as the chauffeur who drives Rosemary Hoyt and her mother around, have become exiles serving in menial capacities.

The new American rich supplanted the Russians on the Riviera, with the Warrens from Chicago the novel's most conspicuous example. Fitzgerald emphasizes their corruption through sexual metaphor. Devereux Warren deflowers his daughter. Baby Warren, basically onanistic, tends toward frigidity. Nicole uses her beauty for sexual conquest. They are all selfish people whose money enables them to dominate and mistreat others. Consider how the Warrens exploit Doctor Diver. The book makes its point about the cruelty of the rich and about the decay of the world they inhabit, but it does so with too little explicit moralizing to please the left-wing reviewers.

Philip Rahv's review in the May 5, 1934 *Daily Worker* began with a conventional observation about Fitzgerald as chronicler of the Jazz Age. If he had read *The Great Gatsby* (as he almost surely had), Rahv was unwilling to recognize its attack on the rich. Instead, he insisted, during the 1920s Fitzgerald "was swept away by the waste and extravagance of the people he described, and he identified himself with them." In *Tender Is the Night* the author could not "escape realizing how near the collapse of his class" really was, but he was "still in love with his characters." Rahv then supplied a short paraphrase of the novel, which brought him to the inevitable conclusion that the book was a "fearful indictment of the moneyed aristocracy." Yet Fitzgerald had not sufficiently italicized and capitalized his indictment. Therefore many a reader would "let himself float on the novel's tender surface, without gauging the horror underneath" (Rahv, "You Can't Duck a Hurricane," 383–84). Here Rahv's sensitivity as literary critic gave way to a requirement of the party line: that a work of art must make its statement so obvious as to be available to the widest possible proletarian audience.

To the Marxist critic, merely writing about the rich was wrong. Novelists should write about the proletariat instead. Fitzgerald ought to transfer his interests to a new subject, one journal recommended, because embracing "some social movement, such as Communism" would invigorate his writing "with another cultural pattern instead of the Jazz Age" ("Representative Americans"). Alternatively, he should resist identifying himself with any political or economic group and write instead of the "total American scene." William Troy and John Chamberlain proposed that he "do a novel of the St. Paul, Minnesota of the Hills, the Tighes, the Pillsburys, the Heffelfingers— and [Populist] Governor Floyd B. Olson." Fitzgerald knew this St. Paul well, "with its curious links with the frontier, the American agrarian empire, and the more cosmopolitan East." If he tackled such a big subject, Chamberlain remarked, Fitzgerald could "present us, not really with the maxillary bone of the American mastodon, but with pretty nearly the whole skeleton. And with the whole skeleton before them, his critics would cease to murmur, 'Futile material'" (Chamberlain, "Books of the Times" review, 19).

It is hard to know what would have happened had Fitzgerald adopted the Troy-Chamberlain suggestion. He understood as well as anyone that the "world, as a rule, does not live on beaches and in country clubs." Yet he also realized he was not cut out to write a proletarian novel, inasmuch as he knew nothing of farms and factories. His friend Tom Boyd had been ruined as an author, Fitzgerald thought, by his attempt to become "one of the barnyard boys" who concentrated on the "Great Struggle the Great American Peasant has with the Soil" (*Letters*, 102, 484; Buttitta, *After the Good Gay Times*, 85).

If he had been able to do the job well, though, Fitzgerald would have been willing to write a proletarian novel. He responded to a newspaper inquiry that the book he'd most like to have written was Joseph Conrad's *Nostromo* because of its depiction of the central character. That kind of man had "always existed, whether as a Roman centurion or a modern top sergeant"—a man who knew how to motivate and lead the people. The type had often been portrayed in fiction, but usually superficially, Fitzgerald thought. In Kipling he became a kind of glorified servant, as well as a powerful preserver of the capitalistic system. "The literary attitude toward him has been that of an officer sitting at his club with a highball during drill. 'Well, I've got nothing to worry about. Sgt. O'Hara has the troop and—' this with a patronizing condescension—'I believe he knows just about as much about handling them as I do.'"

Conrad's contribution was to take Nostromo, this man of the people, and imagine him "with such a completeness that there is no use of anyone else wondering over him for some time. He is one of the most important types in our civilization. In particular he's always made a haunting and irresistible appeal to me. So," Fitzgerald concluded, "I would rather have dragged his soul from behind his astounding and inarticulate presence than written any other novel in the world" (Fitzgerald, "Confessions").

In making those comments Fitzgerald was thinking along political as well as artistic lines. He disapproved of the conventional treatment of the Nostromo type by Kipling and others, but he also disapproved of the lazy officer drinking at the club and denigrating the sergeant who was doing his work for him. The political implications in Conrad's portrait of this "man of the people" were clear enough. But more important to Fitzgerald was the artistic achievement of bringing to life on the page what had previously been a mere stereotype. In singling out this particular novel as the one he'd most like to have written, Fitzgerald was acknowledging how unsuited he felt to the task. The Nostromos of the world fascinated him, but capturing them in fiction was beyond his capabilities. He would not let political considerations dictate his subject matter.

By August 1934 a number of factors, including "disgust with the party leadership" and a conviction that he had "only health enough left for his literary work" prompted Fitzgerald to write his cousin Ceci that he was through with politics (*Letters*, 417). This comment may have been calculated in part to please her. In any event, it was not strictly true, for throughout 1934 Fitzgerald continued like many others to explore alternatives to the official party line. He was assisted in this exploration by two influential non-Stalinist Marxists, Jay Lovestone and V. F. Calverton.

As a result of the Stalin-Trotsky split, Lovestone and his group had been expelled from the party and had established their own "Communist Party, U.S.A. [Opposition]." Late in November 1934, Fitzgerald entertained this "Opposition Communist" in Baltimore and put him up for the night. He hadn't quite decided what he thought of Lovestone, Fitzgerald wrote Max Perkins (*Letters*, 256). And what did Lovestone think of him? Fitzgerald struck him as anything but the kind of superficial dabbler in left-wing politics who may have thought it "smart to be Marxist" and so joined the "Literary Playboys League for Social Consciousness." Fitzgerald, he felt sure, had not taken up politics as a form of entertainment. On the contrary, Lovestone regarded him as a man seriously interested in the issues of the day and in the Communist movement (Lovestone, interview).

As a result of that meeting Fitzgerald decided that he had something to say and wondered if *Workers Age*, the opposition publication Lovestone and Bertram Wolfe were bringing out, might not be the place to say it. "As I recall," Lovestone wrote him on January 4, 1935, "you had asked me to give you an estimate on what it would cost to run 20,000 words as a special literary supplement to the Age. . . . As to the other matter, I am afraid we will have to let this alone until our paper sort of finds its way as a weekly. Then we will seriously tackle your suggestion." What was the "other matter"? Fitzgerald had considered starting his own literary publication on the left, Lovestone said, but seemed naive about the financial costs involved. Nothing came of this idea, nor did Fitzgerald contribute to *Workers Age*. Lovestone doubted that the trade-union audience the magazine aimed at "would appreciate" Fitzgerald's commentary (Lovestone, letter; Lovestone, interview).

Fitzgerald's interest in writing articles, issuing a supplement, or starting his own magazine on the radical left stemmed from his desire to provide an alternative Marxist voice, not the usual echo. "Fitzgerald wanted an expression of *American* literary skill appropriate to the issues of the day, and not one dictated from Moscow" (Lovestone, interview). Dos Passos and Wilson wanted much the same thing. "Marxians who attempt to junk the American tradition . . . are just cutting themselves off from the continent," Dos Passos said in 1932. "Somebody's got to have the size to Marxianize the American tradition before you can sell the American worker on the social revolution. Or else Americanize Marx" (qtd. in Aaron, *Writers on the Left*, 191–92). In March 1934, aiming at just such a goal, Wilson joined the board of editors of V. F. Calverton's *Modern Monthly*.

Calverton (1900–1940) was a remarkable man. His career, as Daniel Aaron has observed, virtually represented a "one-man history of the American radical movement from 1920 to 1940." He began publishing his own magazine (originally called *Modern Quarterly*) when only twenty-three and printed in its pages the work of "almost every left-wing liberal and radical who had artistic aspirations." (He tried for, but did not get, a contribution from Fitzgerald.) He was interested in almost every topic under the sun and wrote about most of them, including sex, love and marriage, literature, philosophy, anthropology, sociology, psychology, religion, science and technology, and, of course, politics and economics. During his short life he wrote or edited seventeen books; traveled and lectured throughout the United States, Europe, and Canada; and maintained a large roster of friends, lovers, and correspondents. He kept a home base in his native Baltimore but after the mid-1920s also had a residence in Greenwich Village where he entertained artists and intellectuals of every stripe.

Calverton's tolerance for differing points of view inevitably led to trouble with the Communist Party. In 1933 *New Masses* printed a polemic accusing him of cryptofascism. This had the effect of driving Calverton and the *Modern Monthly* firmly into the anti-Stalinist camp, whence he rejected dogmatic Marxist authoritarianism and continued to publish all shades of thought on the radical left. Guiding the magazine along its eclectic way was the quest to "Americanize Marxism" (Gnizi; Fitzgerald to Calverton, 26 March 1935).

In April 1934 Calverton wrote Fitzgerald, inviting him to make a speech. He didn't make speeches, Fitzgerald replied, but he added that he'd been following Calverton's career "with deep interest" and hoped they might meet soon. There ensued a series of attempts by Calverton to arrange a weekend date in Baltimore. The two men did not meet until June 1, when Calverton came to dinner at Fitzgerald's 1307 Park Avenue address. "I don't know when I found a conversation as fine or as stirring as ours . . . or when I felt as free in talking to anyone as I did to you," Calverton wrote afterward, and Fitzgerald responded that he felt the same way. They met at least twice more during 1934. On one of those occasions, Calverton ended up massaging Fitzgerald's back (Fitzgerald to Calverton, April, May, and June 1934; Calverton to Fitzgerald, June and September 1934; Fitzgerald, *Ledger*, 189).

In October Fitzgerald read Calverton's book *The Passing of the Gods* and praised it in the warmest of terms. "I . . . never suspected anybody of such erudition," he wrote. "You are a modern Lecky and I congratulate you on the achievement. . . . The synthesis of anthropology, sociology and philosophy, salted with good eighteenth-century rationalism, seems like a triumph." Yet Fitzgerald expressed reservations about Calverton's basic theme. His book argued that religion originally developed as a psychological tool giving the masses, who lived in a constant state of economic insecurity, the illusion of power. Hence by bringing about relative economic stability, capitalism deprived religion of much of its appeal. Modern science, which enabled man to control his environment, then replaced the old necessity for religion. Fitzgerald was ready to agree about the death of religion. But he did not share Calverton's faith in science or his convictions about a Marxist future (Fitzgerald, *Correspondence*, 387; Graham and Frank, *Beloved Infidel*, 310).

Two years later Fitzgerald wrote Calverton about the latter's novel *The Man Inside*, a work of fiction that is really an essay advocating socialism. The book seemed cloudy to Fitzgerald, halfway between romance and realism, but it inspired him to comment on the messages implicit in his own fiction.

> To a great extent I have used the accepted technique of my time, feeling that what observations I have made need all the help that I can give the reader to carry on with them, and the more radical (I thought) my idea was, the more determinedly have I clothed it in sheep's wool and sugar-coated it, to change the metaphor.
>
> (CORRESPONDENCE, 460)

One way of sugar-coating was to disguise the message behind the distance of centuries. Thus the four "Philippe, Count of Darkness" stories Fitzgerald wrote in 1934 and early 1935 were set in ninth-century France, but were intended as comments on the present. At least one reader seemed to grasp what Fitzgerald was doing in these stories. In February 1940, before publication of the final Philippe episode, Neal Begley wrote Fitzgerald congratulating him on the historical stories, which he thought represented "one of the most interesting and reasonable ideas of the probable events surrounding the emergence of the poor dumb and oppressed peoples of western Europe from their serfdom and misery to a realization of what it means to have leadership and organization." In responding, Fitzgerald complained about the decision of the *Saturday Evening Post* to turn down his stories (they ran in *Red Book*) in favor of a series by Austin Chamberlain about medieval times. Chamberlain's stories were well enough written, he conceded, but they lacked "any interpretative point of view" and ignored both the "new data on the witch cult" and "the new Marxian interpretation" (Begley to Fitzgerald; Fitzgerald to Begley).

He knitted these two strands into "Gods of Darkness," the last of the Philippe stories and one of his most overtly political stories. Not yet sophisticated enough to think in terms of solidarity with the whole of mankind, Fitzgerald's ninth-century count elects to act on behalf of his county and his people, even at the risk of future damnation.

"Gods of Darkness" is hardly a revolutionary document, however. Whatever it may imply about the need for group solidarity, the story nonetheless focuses on the individual hero, Philippe. Occasionally Fitzgerald would deny his own individualism. "The value of the individual," he insisted to Zelda's psychiatrist in October 1933, "I place as low as any communist" (Fitzgerald to Rennie). Yet his fiction attested to his fascination with the charismatic figure who seemed able, for a time, to dominate life. Characteristically, the Communist he most admired was the romantic John Reed, Harvard man, actor, playwright, poet, journalist, and author of a famous book on the Russian Revolution, *Ten Days That Shook the World*. Reed died at thirty-three—"not too young for a man of action, yet not too old," Fitzgerald thought—"and he had lived by his convictions" (qtd. in Buttitta, *After the Good Gay Times*, 152–53).

Philippe and *The Last Tycoon*'s Monroe Stahr are heroic characters modeled on actual people: Ernest Hemingway and Irving Thalberg, respectively. In most of his earlier fiction, though, the protagonist bears a resemblance to Fitzgerald himself, and the unhappy fate that ordinarily befalls these protagonists reflects his obsession with failure. All of Fitzgerald's writing, the communist critic Isidor Schneider objected, fell into a pattern of failure, with the "sensitive and aspiring" losing out to "earthier, more brutish men." What troubled Schneider was the sense of hopelessness Fitzgerald's writing conveyed ("A Pattern of Failure," 23–24). Given such a temperament, he could hardly issue a call to revolution.

Still, when the Communist Party organized the first American Writers Congress in 1935, Fitzgerald was asked to "endorse the call" and attend the sessions in New York. This was significant, inasmuch as Alexander Trachtenberg, the party's cultural commissar, was determined to restrict invitations to this first congress (whose primary business was to create the League of American Writers) to reliable writers only, those "who have achieved some standing in their respective fields; who have clearly indicated their sympathy to the revolutionary cause; who do not need to be convinced of the decay of capitalism, of the inevitability of revolution" (Aaron, *Writers on the Left*, 282–85). On the first and third grounds, Fitzgerald qualified well enough. He was indeed a writer of some standing, and he believed that capitalism as a system was doomed. But he had not done much to indicate his sympathy for the revolution. Nor did he do so in 1935. Apparently, he never responded to the invitation to attend the congress.

His political conscience "had scarcely existed" for ten years, Fitzgerald observes in *The Crack-Up*, "save as an element of irony" in his writing. When he became again concerned with the system he should function under, it was "with a mixture of passion and fresh air" (79). But Fitzgerald did not actually become a member of the Communist Party, nor did he compromise his stature by indiscriminately espousing causes in his fiction. As Daniel Aaron concludes in *Writers on the Left*, the strongest writers of the 1930s "used politics and were not used by it." Aaron includes Dos Passos, Hemingway, Lewis, Dreiser, Steinbeck, and Wolfe among this company, but Fitzgerald belongs too. Most of his important writing from *Tender Is the Night* on shows the influence of his political convictions. But none of it was not art. None of it became mere propaganda.

FINAL REFLECTIONS: 1936–1940

In conversation and correspondence as well as in his published work, Fitzgerald showed the effects of his contact with communism during the last years of his life. He had learned that despite the Depression the United States would resist foreign ideas and icons. "You could paint Lenin's face inside every backhouse in Iowa and . . . might just manage to make him as important to the young as Santa Claus" (note on Lenin). Nonetheless he continued to insist that the revolution *could* happen here, sometimes in language designed more to frighten than persuade his audience. For example, he announced the demise of capitalism to Laura Guthrie, his secretary in Asheville during the summer of 1935, in tough-guy rhetoric: "Baby, in four years (later, another day, he said he'd meant twelve years) you'll have to have a bread card. No more sodas. No more world as we know it. A violent revolution is coming." But his behavior belied his convictions. Once when he and Laura went out together, their taxi was held up by a truck so jammed with passengers that no one could sit down. "Down with the proletariat," Fitzgerald yelled at them. "Give us capitalists room to pass. Fingers on the nose to you." Such incidents naturally made

Guthrie doubt his political sincerity. "He is a communist," she said, "or likes to justify himself by saying he is" (Guthrie, Memoir, 112, 128).

Fitzgerald's outrageous behavior toward the people on the truck probably resulted from embarrassment. He often felt ill at ease in proximity to the poor. When he was in Hollywood at the beginning of the Depression, he'd dressed up in evening clothes, silk hat and all, and was waiting in front of a theater for some movie actresses. The poor people passing by, he felt certain, would wonder what right he had to be dressed like that when they had nothing at all. "The only thing for me to do was to look arrogant," he told Guthrie. "So I did" (Guthrie, Memoir, 151–52). That was 1931. Six years later, he returned to Hollywood a humbler man. The place had changed too.

Hollywood had become politicized in the interim, and friends of Fitzgerald's tried to enlist him in the process. Dashiell Hammett, for example, asked him to join a group of Hollywood liberals organizing in 1938 to fight the California Republican machine and the motion-picture industry bosses (Hammett to Fitzgerald). Although he shared Hammett's sentiments, there is no evidence that Fitzgerald responded to this appeal. Mostly he remained on the sidelines, although he did send an occasional small check to the strike fund of the Hollywood unit of the Los Angeles Newspaper Guild or to "Spanish Intellectual Aid." He also attended the Anti-Nazi League dinner in 1937, where he flirted with Sheilah Graham. Later, after they became lovers, Scott and Sheilah went to Salka Viertel's house to listen to a man recently returned from the International Brigade in Spain. "I cannot understand how a rich man can be a liberal," Sheilah said at the time. Thereupon Scott set out to educate her politically and succeeded so well that at the time of the "vital Screenwriters election," the right vs. the left, she was ready to carry him to the polls to register his vote for the left (Graham, *College of One*, 48, 53, 150).

Politics was one of seven major subjects in the "College of One" curriculum Fitzgerald devised for Graham. For one assignment, she read sections of *Das Kapital* that he had annotated. In the chapter on "The Working Day" (read this "terrible chapter," Fitzgerald also advised his daughter, "and see if you are ever quite the same") Marx mentioned the "small thefts of the capitalists from the laborers' meals and recreation time" and the "petty pilfering of minutes." In the margin Fitzgerald noted that they "do this at M.G.M. in a big way; so the secretaries say." He also described as "grand prose" Marx's observation about the "unity of the ruling classes, landlords and capitalists, stock-exchange wolves and shopkeepers, protectionists and free traders, government and opposition, priests and free thinkers, young whores and old nuns, under the common cry, For the Salvation of Property, Religion, the Family and Society" (Graham and Frank, *Beloved Infidel* 264; Graham, *College of One*, 125–26; Fitzgerald, *Letters*, 102).

The *Communist Manifesto* was on Sheilah's reading list, and so was M. Ilin's *New Russia's Primer*, which Scott had urged Zelda to read back in 1931. His enthusiasm for this book had been tempered by time. "A beautiful, pathetic, trusting book," he called it, "old and young, rather haunting and inspiring like the things read and believed in youth. A sort of dawn comes up over the book all through—too often it illuminates old shapes that our cynicism has corrupted into nonsense." He'd read in the *New York Times*, Fitzgerald added, that Ilin had been sent to Siberia. He hoped it wasn't true (Graham, *College of One*, 123).

For Sheilah's benefit, Scott charted the key events in Soviet history from Brest-Litovsk in February 1918 to the junking of the Litvinov policy and the German pact of 1939 (*College of One*, 59–60). Spengler's *Decline of the West* was to provide the capstone of her education, but Fitzgerald died before they got that far. At the bottom of the last page of the syllabus, he laid out the recent course of history:

CIVILIZATION

(a) 19th Century. From Napoleon to the World War. "System of the Great Powers," standing armies, constitutions.

(b) 20th Century. Transition from constitutional to informal sway of individuals. Annihilation wars. Imperialism.

(c) ???

(*COLLEGE OF ONE*, 131).

What next? Fitzgerald did not know, but like Spengler he was not optimistic.

During his final years in Hollywood, Fitzgerald conducted another educational project, this one with his daughter. As his letters to Scottie attest, politics was one of the essential subjects in her curriculum, too. Scottie wondered all her life why her father should have been so insistent on sending her to the most exclusive rich girls' schools—first Miss Walker's and then Vassar—while he constantly inveighed against the plutocracy in his letters to her. Sometimes the tone ran to humor. Had Scottie met a boy from Groton? "They are very democratic there—they have to sleep in gold cubicles and wash at old platinum pumps. This toughens them up so they can pay the poor starvation wages without weakening" (*Letters*, 14).

Sometimes Fitzgerald played social historian for his daughter. The rich, he ranted, were "homeless people, ashamed of being American, unable to master the culture of another country; ashamed, usually, of their husbands, wives, grandparents, and unable to bring up descendants of whom they could be proud, even if they had the nerve to bear them, ashamed of each other yet leaning on each other's weakness, a menace to the social order in which they live." "If I come up and find you gone Park Avenue, you will have to explain me away as a Georgia cracker or a Chicago killer" (*Letters*, 101–2). When, despite these warnings, his daughter made friends—as it was inevitable that she should—with a boy from Park Avenue, Fitzgerald drafted (although he may not have sent) a letter compounded of vitriol and exasperation insisting that Scottie came from better blood than her rich beau:

> Jesus, we're the few remnants of the old American aristocracy that's man-aged to survive in communicable form—*we* have the vitality left. And you choose to mix it up with the cheap lower class settled on Park Avenue. You know the distinction—and in most of your relations you are wise enough to forget it—but when it comes to falling for a phoney your instincts should do a better job. All that's rude, tough (in the worse sense), crude and purseproud comes from vermin like the ____'s. Could you, by any stretch of the imagination, want to be one with the wall street brokers & their sucks, the wall street lawyers who'd fill a million kids full of lead for an extra nickle? Be yourself.
>
> (FITZGERALD TO FRANCES SCOTT FITZGERALD, N.D.)

The most doctrinaire socialist could hardly have expressed it more force-fully. The gospel of work he concurrently preached came from deeper roots, but it, too, meshed with Marxian doctrine. His generation had broken away from the restraints of the past, Fitzgerald told Scottie, but had "never found anything to take the place of the old virtues of work and courage." The greater of these was work, and he did not mean a "Bennington girl spending a month in slum work and passing the weekend at her father's mansion on Long Island" (*Letters*, 86, 89–90).

In a letter composed to reach his daughter on her first day at Vassar, Fitzgerald alerted her to expect a "strongly organized left-wing movement" at the college. "I do not particularly want you to think about politics," he went on, "but I do *not* want you to set yourself against this movement. I am known as a left-wing sympathizer and would be proud if you were." Conversely, he would be outraged if she "identified herself with Nazism or Red-baiting in any form." His motives were not entirely idealistic, Fitzgerald realized, for he thought it prudent for Scottie to know the left-wingers. Those radical girls, he told her, "may not look like much now but in your lifetime they are liable to be high in the councils of the nation" (*Letters*, 37–38).

In the same spirit he advised Scottie to keep on with her study of philosophy at least as far as Hegel, from whom "all Marxian thinking flows." He also suggested that she might want to go to the Soviet Union in the summer after her freshman year (she didn't) (*Letters*, 51–52, 56). Then, in the spring of her sophomore year, he advised her to think about joining the radicals: "You are in the midst of a communist dominated student movement at Vassar which you do nothing about. The movement will go both up and down in the next few years. You can join it or let it simmer but you have never even considered it outside of classroom work—except to say, perhaps, that your father is rather far to the left." He went on to say that it "would be foolish ever to make enemies of those girls. Silly and fanatical as they seem now some of them are going to be forces in the future" (*Correspondence*, 583).

Scottie must have answered that she felt unable to identify with the communist students, for when Fitzgerald next took up the subject, it was to gave her advice on how to get along with the "*Comrades.*" She should regard them as she might "a set of intensely fanatical Roman Catholics." It was better not to argue with them. "Communism has become an intensely dogmatic and almost mystical religion and whatever you say they have ways of twisting it into shapes which put you into some lower category of mankind ('Fascist,' 'Liberal,' 'Trotskyist') and disparage you both intellectually and personally in the process . . . think what you want, the less said the better" (*Letters*, 64–65). It sounds very much as if Fitzgerald was talking from his own experience.

In Budd Schulberg, a young man only a few years older than Scottie, Fitzgerald found a companion who could teach him both about Hollywood and politics. Budd had grown up in Hollywood, where his father was a producer. He himself had Marxist leanings and had spent the kind of summer in Russia between college terms at Dartmouth that Fitzgerald proposed to Scottie. The two men—twenty-four and forty-two years old—were teamed by producer Walter Wanger to write a script for a movie set at Dartmouth's Winter Carnival. They didn't finish that job but did have some long conversations. Expecting Fitzgerald to adopt a politically escapist attitude, young Schulberg was surprised to find him talking like a "confirmed leftist, anti-Stalinist but Marxist-oriented." He was struck, too, by the older writer's enthusiasm for knowledge. One day when Schulberg visited him, he found Fitzgerald reading Marx's "14th Brumaire" pamphlet with excitement. "Bunny [Edmund Wilson] is right," Fitzgerald said. "I don't know enough about revolutions" (Turnbull, *Fitzgerald*, 296–97; Schulberg, *Four Seasons* 100–101).

One quality that distinguished Fitzgerald from most novelists of the time, Schulberg felt, was "his intuitive grasp of American history and its shifting social classes." He wondered if Marx, Spengler, or Wilson had much to teach Fitzgerald on these topics. Yet Scott was the most willing learner imaginable. At the Hotel Warwick in New York, Fitzgerald committed one of the gaffes that testified to his social insecurity. A waiter with a German accent brought an order to their room. Fitzgerald was unconscionably rude: he signaled like Hitler, said "Heil," and routed the poor waiter from the premises. "You don't know that man," Schulberg protested. "He might be a refugee, who's come to the United States to escape from Hitler." Immediately contrite, Fitzgerald ran down the hall to apologize, probably terrifying the waiter in the process but eager to undo his wrong (Schulberg, interview).

Basically, Fitzgerald felt a measure of respect for the poor working stiff that contrasted with his scorn toward party functionaries. He characterized Earl Browder, then the American Communist Party leader, as a "know-nothing Kansan." He thought of a magazine title to designate a person who faddishly flirted with communism: "The Parlor Pink." He deplored the tendency of such talented Hollywood people as Dorothy Parker, John Howard Lawson, and Donald Ogden Stewart to compromise their writing through adherence to the party line (Schulberg, *Four Seasons* 105–6; Fitzgerald, note on Hollywood writers).

Stewart especially came in for disparaging comments in Fitzgerald's letters and notebooks. He exchanged letters with John O'Hara about their shared distaste for Stewart, a successful humorist, playwright, screenwriter, and friend of the super-rich who had, nonetheless, gone over to communism. "Don Stewart, who is full of shit," O'Hara wrote in April 1936, "has converted himself to radical thought, and goes to all the parties for the Scottsboro boys. . . . Don talked to me for an hour one afternoon about how he makes a much better radical than—well, than I. Because, he pointed out, he'd *had* Skull & Bones, he'd *had* the Whitney plantation, he'd *had* big Hollywood money" (O'Hara, *Selected Letters*, 116–17). This tack infuriated O'Hara, and it did not sit well with Fitzgerald either, who'd known Stewart since the summer of 1919. "If this seems toilet paper," he commented at the end of a long reply to O'Hara, "you can use it to wipe

Dr. Daniel Ogden Stewart's mouth when he finally gets the kick in the ass that he has been asking for so long." Elsewhere he referred to Stewart as a "wily old Kiss-puss" who'd had a "long pull at the mammalia of the Whitneys" (Fitzgerald to O'Hara; Fitzgerald, *Letters*, 551).

Manifestly, Fitzgerald was disturbed by the jarring contrast between Stewart's political beliefs and expensive lifestyle. It was one thing to profess communism and another to have your cake and eat it too, to make it with the aristocracy (as Fitzgerald never really had) and then swing left when that became politically fashionable.

Although Fitzgerald deplored the religious fervor and distrusted the motives of many radicals, his last unfinished novel was designed to be his most political one. In *The Last Tycoon*, he undertook to examine the current political climate from the standpoint of a "closet radical" (Ring, review, 412). He intended to focus the unfinished portion of the book on the conflicts between liberalism and conservatism, business and labor, and East Coast finance and West Coast production, then prevalent in the film capital. In the process, he would have moved away from his usual concentration on character to a concentration on events (Millgate, "Fitzgerald as Social Novelist").

Specifically, the plot was to involve a violent confrontation between Brady, the representative of the money men, and the individualistic Stahr, who attempted to run things his way despite pressures from the unions on the one hand, and the keepers of the purse strings on the other. Fitzgerald outlined a key dispute in his notes:

> We will go from there to what I hope will be a big scene in which Bradogue [Brady] asks the directors, writers, supervisors to accept a 50% cut which he says he is going to accept himself, using as his argument, to their surprise and rather to their confusion, the specious argument that by accepting this they will save those in the lower salary brackets—the secretaries from $12 a week up and the prop boys, etc., to whom the drastic cut would mean a terrible hardship. He gets over his idea for two reasons—one because the amorphous unions—though the name is not used—which are called into being among workers with common interest such as directors and writers are split by jealousies and factual disagreements, certain of them for example, have never even thought of themselves as workers and some are haunted by the old fashioned dream of communism and Bradogue is wise enough to use every stop on the organ including personal ties to increase these differences and to rule by dividing. In any case, he wins his point to the great disgust of those of the writers who are the more politically

advanced or the shrewdest and who detect in this a very definite manifes-
tation of a class war reaching Hollywood.

(QTD. IN BRUCCOLI, *THE LAST OF THE NOVELISTS*," 139–40)

The prospect of an impending class war is heightened, and the solidarity
among workers increased, when Brady goes back on his promise and
cuts the secretaries' salaries anyway. In constructing his novel, Fitzgerald
said, he "was analyzing the class interest of every one of the characters"
(Mizener, interview with Schulberg).

Stahr is outraged by Brady's deception. He himself tends to give the
benefit of the doubt to such tycoons of the past as "Gould, Vanderbilt,
Carnegie, Astor." But Fitzgerald made it clear in his notes that he planned
to differentiate Stahr from the robber barons who "merely gypped another
person's empire away from them." As a producer, Stahr is a builder, a maker.
He does not cheat others. There is nothing of the fascist about him, as
there definitely is about Brady. The latter "is the monopolist at his worst,"
Fitzgerald's note reads, while "Stahr, in spite of the inevitable conservatism
of the self-made man, is a paternalistic employer." As such an employer he
demands and expects absolute loyalty. In effect he operates as baron of a
feudal kingdom who treats his subjects with rare understanding.

When events overtake him, however, he is caught in the middle. "The
reds see him now as a conservative—Wall Street as a Red." Edmund Wilson,
as editor of the unfinished novel, characterized Stahr's dilemma thus:

> The split between the controllers of the movie industry, on the one hand,
> and the various groups of employees, on the other, is widening and leaving
> no place for real individualists of business like Stahr, whose successes are
> personal achievements and whose career has always been invested with
> a certain personal glamour. He has held himself directly responsible to
> everyone with whom he has worked: he has even wanted to beat up his
> enemies himself. In Hollywood he is "the last tycoon."

Stahr's day has passed. "You're doing a costume part and you don't
know it," the writer Wylie White tells him: "the brilliant capitalist of the
twenties" (Millgate, "Fitzgerald as Social Novelist" 32; Sklar, *Fitzgerald*,
130–31; Mizener, *Far Side*, 320).

To do him justice, Stahr realizes that the world is changing around him
and attempts to keep up with its transformations. He even hoped to make
a film about the new Russia, but "all the stories involved had the wrong
feel. He felt it could be told in terms of the American thirteen states, but

it kept coming out different, in new terms that opened unpleasant possibilities and problems." Stahr considered that he "was very fair to Russia," and he wanted to make "a sympathetic picture, but it kept turning into a headache" (Fitzgerald, *The Last Tycoon*, 60–61). His orientation is toward the past. The future confuses and annoys him. Impressed by a man's performance in a screen test, Stahr asks,

> "Can't we use him as the old Russian Prince in *Steppes*?"
> "He *is* an old Russian Prince," said the casting director, "but he's ashamed of it. He's a Red. And that's one part he says he wouldn't play."
> "It's the only part he could play," said Stahr.
>
> (57)

Stahr's closest contact with communism comes in the scene with the radical union organizer Brimmer, the last scene Fitzgerald wrote before his death. Artistically, Stahr's getting drunk and picking a fight with Brimmer does not square with his previously masterful behavior. Stahr does not know how to cope; he is beyond his depth on the subject of communism. He betrays his ignorance when asking Cecilia to arrange a meeting with an avowed communist by way of preparation for Brimmer. "'I don't think your father [Stahr's enemy, Brady] ought to know,' he said. 'Can we pretend the man is a Bulgarian musician or something?' 'Oh, they don't dress up anymore,' [Cecilia] said." To prepare for seeing Brimmer, Stahr runs off some films of the Russian Revolution and also, although they have nothing to do with communism, films with foreign-sounding titles like *The Cabinet of Doctor Caligari* and *Un chien andalou*. Then, since he is no reader, he gets the script department to work up a two-page "treatment" of the *Communist Manifesto* (117–18).

The story of the Brimmer-Stahr meeting is told through dialogue, with comments by Cecilia:

> He was a nice-looking man, this Brimmer—a little on the order of Spencer Tracy, but with a stronger face and a wider range of reactions written up in it. I couldn't help thinking as he and Stahr smiled and shook hands and squared off, that they were two of the most alert men I had ever seen.

It turns out that Brimmer's father was a Baptist minister; he reminds Cecilia not only of Spencer Tracy but also of a priest with his collar turned around and even of Superman. His heritage could not be more conspicuously American.

Brimmer gets the better of the verbal exchanges with Stahr, especially after the producer starts to drink. " 'The directors used to be my pals,' said Stahr proudly. It was like Edward the Seventh's boast that he had moved in the best society in Europe." Innocently, Stahr zeroes in on the issues of exploitation of labor and ownership of the means of production: "I never thought," he says, "that I had more brains than a writer has. But I always thought that his brains belonged to me—because I knew how to use them." Brimmer wants to leave, but Stahr bullies him into staying for table tennis and finally a fistfight, which the communist takes no pleasure in winning. "I always wanted to hit ten million dollars, but I didn't know it would be like this." Brimmer, in short, acts admirably, while Stahr visibly deteriorates. "He was pale—he was so transparent that you could almost watch the alcohol mingle with the poison of his exhaustion," Cecilia observes (*The Last Tycoon*, 119–27; Moyer, "A Child," 217–18; Light, "Political Conscience," 24).

Disappointment in love has supposedly driven Stahr to this diminished state, but this is not persuasively communicated in the manuscript as Fitzgerald left it. Stahr is beaten, at least in part, by forces he cannot grasp, forces stronger than he is. A scene not included in the published novel presents a second confrontation on the subject of communism, this time involving Stahr and Wylie White. Here Fitzgerald endows the producer with a communist past: "When I was sixteen, Wylie, during the war, I was an office monkey on the New York Call. I was there during the suppression and the raids and all us boys read the Communist Manifesto and swore by it." But Stahr soon became disillusioned. "I couldn't breathe with those people—nine-tenths of them ready to sell out for a nickel. More dirty politics than there is in a studio, and all covered up with holy talk, and not a laugh in a carload." Wylie agrees with him (and so would Fitzgerald have): "They're pretty awful but they're right" (Bruccoli, *"The Last of the Novelists,"* 68–71).

The Stahr-Brimmer scene is based on the actual encounter of MGM executive Harry Rapf with a Communist Party organizer, just as the Stahr-Kathleen scenes were fashioned after the Fitzgerald–Sheilah Graham relationship An author who liked to work close to reality, Fitzgerald also caught the atmosphere of fear pervading Hollywood during the 1930s. The panicky studios labored to destroy Upton Sinclair's EPIC movement and defeat his bid for the governorship, for example. They also railroaded their employees into contributing a day's pay to the campaign of the Republican candidate for governor (*The Last Tycoon*, 100; Light, "Political Conscience," 22; Hammett to Fitzgerald).

Political upheaval was very much in the air during Fitzgerald's Hollywood years. At the very beginning of *The Last Tycoon*, a young actress tells Cecilia Brady about her plan to escape to Yellowstone National Park with her mother when the revolution comes. The irreverent Cecilia thereupon conjures up a vision of "the actress and her mother being fed by kind Tory bears." Then she relates her own comes-the-revolution story about the director [King Vidor, in real life] who proposed to disappear into the crowd in an old suit. "But they'll look at your hands!" someone pointed out. "They'll know you haven't done manual work for years. And they'll ask for your union card." Discouraged, the director turned so gloomy that he could barely finish his dessert. To delay the day of reckoning, Stahr's studio decreed that typists were forbidden to eat together more than once a week. "At that time," the narrator observes, "the studios feared mob rule" (*The Last Tycoon*, 4–5, 22; Graham, *The Rest of the Story*, 174).

In *The Last Tycoon* Fitzgerald attempted to write both a novel of character and a political fable. Apart from the treatment of communism, the second intention is most apparent in the repeated references to American presidents, especially Andrew Jackson and Abraham Lincoln, whose rise from obscurity to eminence paralleled Stahr's success. In the manuscript as he left it, Fitzgerald had not succeeded in integrating this "presidential theme" into the story. As a result, the novel's treatment could be interpreted either as a way of representing "some kind of debasement of the national heritage" (Miller, *Fitzgerald: His Art*, 157–58) or as a technique for emphasizing Stahr's heroic stature (Bruccoli, *"The Last of the Novelists"*).

The political orientation of Fitzgerald's last book startled at least one critic who little expected to find it there. This was Maxwell Geismar, who qualified his approval of Fitzgerald's latter-day political awakening (as it seemed to him) with a scornful dismissal of his earlier work.

> The writer for whom the revolutionary roar of Europe in 1919 could barely stir the drawn curtains of the Ritz, nor the rioting mob outside Delmonico's mar the light *clat-clat* of afternoon tea—this prime story teller of a boom-town America now speaks of the Bonus Army, of labor troubles and early Fascists, and of the rich who since 1933 "could only be happy alone together."

The author had finally given up his partnership in "the firm of Maecenas, Morgan, & Fitzgerald," Geismar added, and it was about time. The critic was right in detecting the political maturity of *The Last Tycoon*, a novel that could hardly be more sensitive to class relations and the politico-economic structure of the Hollywood system. Had Geismar read more carefully, however, he would have found in even so early a story as the 1920 "May Day" (which the mob outside Delmonico's brings to mind) both a jaundiced view of the rich and an awareness of revolutionary currents in the culture. Fitzgerald knew a great deal more in 1940 than in 1920. He had read a great deal and absorbed ideas with enthusiasm. But at no time was he simply a political nincompoop or, in Geismar's belittling phrase, a pallid chronicler of the "American success story" (*The Last of the Provincials*, 345–46).

Despite his radical leanings, as a voter Fitzgerald remained a Jeffersonian democrat. He warned Sheilah Graham against Lord Charnwood's disparagement of Jefferson. That was the Tory Charnwood speaking, he said. "The great American line: Washington-Jefferson-Jackson-Lincoln would have been impossible without Jefferson, the French rationalist link" (Graham, *College of One*, 106). Fitzgerald did not get involved in the campaigns of the day, however, other than to cast his ballot for Franklin Delano Roosevelt and to encourage Scottie to do likewise (Frances Smith, interview, 3–4; Graham, *College of One*, 154). Otherwise he made fun of seeking office generally and of Republican candidates in particular. Wendell Willkie, who finally got the nomination to run against Roosevelt in 1940, struck him as doing an impersonation of Rhett Butler. "I had forgotten tomorrow was election eve," he wrote Bill Dozier in November 1940, "and I promised to sit up with some sick Republicans" (Fitzgerald, note on Willkie; Fitzgerald to Dozier).

Elections obviously stimulated Fitzgerald's sense of the ridiculous. The class structure, however, was not a joking matter to him. In one of his notes he compared himself to D. H. Lawrence: "Lawrence's great effort to synthesize animal and emotional—things he left out. Essential pre-Marxian. Just as I am essentially Marxian" (qtd. in Sklar, *Fitzgerald*, 325). The things Lawrence left out were those Fitzgerald could not have been more keenly aware of: economics and the struggle between the classes. "Most questions in life have an economic basis," he wrote Scottie in January 1939, "(at least according to us Marxians)" (*Letters*, 47).

The "essentially Marxian" Fitzgerald bore a particular animus against the successful businessman. According to Monroe Stahr, there could be "no such thing as a good man in big business." Rich capitalists got that way by exploiting others, just as Marx had taught. "Rockefeller Center: That it all came out of the chicaneries of a dead racketeer," a Fitzgerald note reads (Bruccoli, *"The Last of the Novelists,"* 135). And he regarded most of those who inherited fortunes as wastrels and overprivileged loafers. Hollywood writer Wylie White, who was depicted as having communist connections in the working drafts for *The Last Tycoon*, undoubtedly spoke for Fitzgerald when he slipped into an executive's speech a wisecrack about the "rugged individualism of Tommy Manville, Barbara Hutton, and Woolie Donahue"—all irresponsible and well-publicized heirs to fortunes (qtd. in Bruccoli, "Perkins-Wilson" 66).

Fitzgerald knew what it was to have money, even though he never had much of it for long. But he also knew what it was to be strapped for funds, particularly during the Hollywood years when his earning power diminished drastically while his family financial obligations continued to grow. Even then, however, he sympathized with those less well off than himself. During one of his least affluent periods, he decided he had to let his housekeeper go. When he discovered she was going to have a baby, "he continued her salary for a few weeks, though he was scraping the bottom of the barrel" (Ring, "Footnotes," 150). Still, as a child of the bourgeoisie, Fitzgerald was driven to seek identity with the plutocracy, not the proletariat.

Here, he realized, lay the source of his ambivalence about Scottie and her contacts with the rich. When he was accused (often by himself) of espousing revolutionary doctrine while following reactionary practice, Fitzgerald took solace in the reflection that Marx had done exactly the same thing. A curious fragment of a poem among Fitzgerald's papers raised the issue:

TO MY GRANDFATHER

To a . . . Grandfather
Old radical—you've posed enough
Your bitter iron is showing through
   the things you left us
Marx was not afraid
Of English crumpets with his tea . . .

In explaining his ambitions for Scottie, Fitzgerald elaborated on the point. His daughter would be coming out in Baltimore next October, he wrote in the spring of 1939 (Fitzgerald to Biggs). "That sounds odd from an old solitary like me with anti-bourgeois leanings," he admitted, "but remember Karl Marx made every attempt to marry his daughters into the British nobility."

PART IV

❖ REQUIEM ❖

{ 11 }

A DEATH IN HOLLYWOOD

FITZGERALD REMEMBERED

F SCOTT FITZGERALD spent the last three and a half years of his life in Hollywood, but he never really belonged there. His secretary, Frances Kroll Ring, recalls seeing him walking to Schwab's drug store on Sunset Boulevard, wearing a dark topcoat, a gray homburg, an indoor pallor, and looking for all the world as if he'd just got off the train.

Fitzgerald came west midway through 1937 to write for the movies and make enough money to keep his wife, Zelda, in the best sanitariums and his daughter, Scottie, in the best girls schools. He worked hard at learning the craft—"he didn't just take his $1,500 a week and run," as his young colleague Budd Schulberg put it—but Fitzgerald and Hollywood were the wrong mix. His scripts were not filmed, and he drank himself into trouble on the job.

By 1940 the big studio money had disappeared, yet Fitzgerald's future looked better than it had in years. He had the love and support of Sheilah Graham, the beautiful former showgirl in England who was making a success as a Hollywood columnist. His drinking had subsided, almost entirely. Best of all, he was at work on a novel, *The Last Tycoon*, that promised to convert his Hollywood experience into fiction. And fiction, of course, was what he was born to write. Although he had a lot of trouble sleeping, was easily distracted by noise, and was addicted to Raleighs and Coca-Cola, Fitzgerald was not at all unhappy when, late in November 1940, he took one of his walks to Schwab's for ice cream and suffered his first serious cardiac spasm. The attack was severe enough that he moved the one block from his third-floor apartment at 1403 North Laurel to Sheilah's ground floor apartment at 1443 North Hayworth. (Appearances counted for something in the Hollywood of 1940.) But he did not stay in bed, as his doctor had advised. Instead he continued to work on his Hollywood novel. On December 20 he managed to complete a difficult episode, and he and Sheilah celebrated by going to a press preview of *This Thing Called Love*, starring Rosalind Russell and Melvyn Douglas. When the film was over and Fitzgerald tried to stand up, he had to grab the arm rest for support. It was just like Schwab's, he told Sheilah; all at once everything started to go. Then he felt better, and since his doctor was supposed to come by the next day, they decided not to call him.

The accounts of the two people who saw Scott Fitzgerald alive on December 21, 1940, the Saturday before Christmas, tell us something about the capriciousness of memory. Scott slept well the night before, according to Sheilah; he slept fitfully, according to Frances Kroll Ring. The day was bright and sunny, Sheilah recalled; it was cool and overcast, Frances remembered. Scott was wearing slacks, slippers, and a sweater, Sheilah wrote; he was wearing tan slacks and a plaid jacket, Frances reported.

Frances stopped by late in the morning to drop off some typed manuscript pages and bring Fitzgerald his mail. Only Sheilah was with him when the fatal heart attack struck. She and Scott had lunched together, and then he settled down in her green armchair to read the *Princeton Alumni Weekly* while waiting for the doctor's visit. She gave him two Hershey bars for his raging sweet tooth. The last time their eyes met, he sheepishly looked up from making notes on the Princeton football team to lick the chocolate off his fingers. A few minutes later, he rose from the chair as if yanked by an invisible cord, grabbed at the mantelpiece, and crumpled to the floor. By the time the Pulmotor arrived, he was dead.

His body was laid out for viewing in the William Wordsworth room of a downtown Los Angeles mortuary. Few people bothered to come. One who did reported that not a line showed on his face and none of his hair was gray. He looked "like an A production in peace and security," except for the thin and terribly wrinkled hands. "The poor son of a bitch," Dorothy Parker is supposed to have said. The memorial service, held in Maryland, was attended by about thirty people. Zelda was absent for reasons of illness, Sheilah for reasons of propriety.

At the time of his death at forty-four, Fitzgerald's reputation was at its nadir. If people thought of him at all, it was as a back number, a Jazz Age writer time had passed by. Scribner's had six of his books in the warehouse, but hardly anyone was buying them. His last royalty check, in August 1940, was for the unlucky sum of $13.13 and represented sales of forty copies. Many of those copies he'd bought himself.

The Fitzgerald revival makes a remarkable chapter in the history of literary reputation. Begun in the 1940s under the stewardship of Max Perkins and Edmund Wilson, interest in Fitzgerald took a giant leap with the publication of Schulberg's novel, *The Disenchanted* (1950), whose alcoholic screenwriter hero was "70 per cent" modeled on Fitzgerald, and of Arthur Mizener's groundbreaking biography, *The Far Side of Paradise* (1951).

For many, the tragic story of Scott and Zelda—reckless, flaming youths who partied hard in the 1920s and crashed and burned in the 1930s—acquired the luster of a legend. Finally, though, Fitzgerald's writing has outlasted the legend. Today the books that were nearly unavailable fifty years ago are selling at a rate of 500,000 copies a year.

Scottie Fitzgerald Smith, the Fitzgeralds' only child, found herself in midlife both the beneficiary of her father's success and the uneasy caretaker of her parents' position in the literary and social history of the United States. "I am bewildered by what they have come to mean to so many people, both together and separately," she wrote me in November 1980. Some of it was wonderful, and some of it—the cultist worship of Scott and Zelda as fallen idols—was "not so good." Young people glamorized their collapse and even sought to emulate it. They wore Jazz Age clothes, drank too much, and swam through their days in a Fitzgeraldian haze. Terrible movies were made from his books. In the wake of the disastrous Robert Redford film of *The Great Gatsby*, bars called "Gatsby's" sprang up everywhere. In 1978 Scottie and I had a drink at one of these in Washington, D.C., where something very much like marijuana smoke issued from the air conditioning vents.

Turbulent as her parents' lives had been, Scottie never felt unloved. After Zelda's breakdown in 1930, Scott more or less assumed the role of both parents. Feeling the dual responsibility, he was excessively stern with Scottie. "What are you trying to do? Alienate her forever?" Sheilah asked him after reading one particularly carping letter he was about to send his daughter. Sometimes he embarrassed her when he was in his cups. Once, in a drunken rage, he sailed an inkwell by her ear. But he was not himself then, Scottie believed. Liquor made him into a different person entirely. She forgave him those lapses as she forgave the lectures he delivered through the U.S. mails.

Scottie is gone now—she died in 1986—and so is Sheilah, who passed away three years later. Among survivors, Honoria Murphy Donnelly's recollections stretch back furthest in time. The daughter of Sara and Gerald Murphy, whose own unhappy story has taken on the aura of romance,

Honoria was a little girl when Scott and Zelda came to visit her parents on the Riviera. She looked forward to those times, for Scott would sit down on the floor to talk to the children and ask them questions:

> "What is your favorite color?" he asked Honoria.
> She knew the answer to that one. "Red," she said. "It's red."
> "Why do you like red?" he wanted to know.
> She hadn't thought about it, but supposed it had something to do with flowers.

The more he had to drink, the more penetrating Scott's questions became. Honoria did not mind at all. He always seemed interested in her thoughts, and he really listened to what she had to say.

Honoria recalled Zelda in those days as beautiful, very blonde against her tan, in a pink dress with a peony at the shoulder. Then her memory fast-forwarded to tea with Scottie and Zelda twenty years later, in 1947. After many years of institutionalization, Zelda looked entirely different. She wore her hair in severe bangs, used no makeup, and had a perpetually troubled expression. Once she had been the gayest person alive, now she could barely make conversation. Sara said something about Ernest Hemingway, and Zelda looked blank. "Don't you remember Ernest?" Sara asked. "I don't think so," Zelda said. "I can't remember that person."

That was a poignant moment, but the Murphys had their own sorrows. Both of Honoria's brothers died in boyhood, Patrick after an extended siege with tuberculosis. When the end came for Patrick, it was Scott's letter that most comforted Sara Murphy. "The golden bowl is broken, indeed, but it was golden," he wrote her. "Nothing can ever take those boys away from you now."

The son of a Hollywood producer, Budd Schulberg was fresh out of Dartmouth in 1938 when he was assigned to team up with Fitzgerald for a script on his alma mater's winter carnival. On location at Dartmouth, Scott fell off the wagon hard, and producer Walter Wanger fired him. Other writers were called in, and *Winter Carnival* (1939), starring Ann Sheridan and Richard Carlson, was stitched together out of their efforts. The film is "pretty bad," Schulberg said, "so bad that it's almost good." It's still shown during the winter carnival for undergraduates to hoot at.

What Budd thought most striking about Fitzgerald was his enthusiasm for ideas. Together they debated into the night about politics and books, and Scott pumped Budd for inside information on Hollywood and the brilliant Irving Thalberg. Much of what Fitzgerald learned from Budd went into his depiction of Monroe Stahr in *The Last Tycoon*, published posthumously in 1941. Much of what Schulberg discovered about Scott went into his portrayal of Manley Halliday in *The Disenchanted*.

For years Schulberg kept a copy of *Tender Is the Night* in his study, and often he'd open it at random and start reading. "I love to read that book," he said. One reason was the beauty of the writing, but there was more to it than that. In *Tender*, he said, "Scott was able to take his own pain and suffering and transmute it into literature, and that's awfully hard to do." It required objectivity to deal with the emotion, and subjectivity to keep the feeling powerful. And it required courage, too.

Fitzgerald's spirit helped shape the career of yet another child of Hollywood, Sheilah's daughter Wendy Fairey. Born after Fitzgerald's death, she grew up in a fatherless household. "Our only father was the ghost of F. Scott Fitzgerald," she said, and this was especially true as her mother relived her relationship with Scott in *Beloved Infidel* (1958) and *College of One* (1966). For Wendy, the most important legacy Fitzgerald left were the books her mother read under his tutelage, her "College of One" library. As an awkward, intense teenager, she escaped into the pages of *Bleak House* and *Tom Jones*, *Sister Carrie* and *The Brothers Karamazov*. Eventually she took her doctorate in English literature and became a professor and dean: a career as different from her mother's gossip columning as could be imagined.

Fitzgerald's influence on American writing has been pervasive. Some writers have tended to identify with him. John Cheever, who volunteered to contribute the entry on Fitzgerald for *Atlantic Brief Lives*, praised and condemned him for precisely those qualities that were as much his own as his subject's. In Fitzgerald's fiction, Cheever pointed out, "there is a thrilling sense of knowing exactly where one is—the city, the street, the hotel, the decade and the time of the day." He did not write mere vignettes "but real stories with characters, invention, scenery and moral conviction." And yet he was personally subject to "appalling lapses in discipline," to "pranks, pratfalls and ghastly jokes." All of those observations apply to Cheever as well as to Fitzgerald.

For many excellent writers, *The Great Gatsby* serves as a kind of touchstone. Joan Didion has read the novel over and over again. "It's one of the three perfect books I go back to, along with [Ford Madox Ford's] *The Good Soldier* and [Joseph Conrad's] *Victory*. She first read *Gatsby* in high school, in Sacramento, California, but it didn't mean as much to her then as it did later. "I didn't know enough," she pointed out. "To really understand the book, you have to know about the east, about what it means to buck up against the east."

Allan Gurganus, author of 1989's best-selling *Oldest Living Confederate Widow Tells All*, undertook an exhausting tour of thirty-three cities to promote his novel. To make the trip less wearing, he promised himself a treat when he finally got back home: he sat down and read *The Great Gatsby* straight through. "It's one of the great American novels," Gurganus said, and it usefully reminded him that good writing has nothing to do with book signings and talk shows.

In one of her poems in *Westward* (1990), Amy Clampitt focused on the unprepossessing figure of Henry C. Gatz, Jay Gatsby's father, "An old man bundled into a long ulster / Who'd telegraphed and then taken the day coach / from somewhere in Minnesota," to attend his son's funeral, only to be "seduced out of his grief" by the splendor of his mansion. Herself a native Iowan, Clampitt was also moved by the passage in *Gatsby* about returning from the East at Christmastime to Chicago and then to Minneapolis–St. Paul, to "sleigh bells in the frosty dark and the shadows of holly wreaths thrown by lighted windows on the snow."

Tobias Wolff, who won the 1985 PEN/Faulkner award for *The Barracks Thief*, continues to read Fitzgerald "with astonishment and love." The astonishment derives not only from the beautifully sculpted prose but from Fitzgerald's uncanny ability to speak to readers across the generations. "He saw our American world—and I don't mean the historical country, but the contemporary United States, for what he wrote about has not gone away—with clearer eyes than any of his contemporaries."

In his fiction, Wolff believes, Fitzgerald portrayed "the entanglements of class, the situation of the outsider, the need for self-invention, and above all the great ruling paradox of American life: on the one hand the endless sense of possibility, on the other the lack of any stable identity or place where one belongs." Lacking that anchor, his characters sometimes drift into a romanticism that can become corrupt, as it did for Gatsby.

Their romantic quest has a powerful appeal, and when it ends in disillusionment or death—in Fitzgerald the diamond mountains blow up and love does not last—we are left to reflect on how and why the dream went wrong. The people and their stories we do not forget, for they are alive and real.

This essay, written for the Fitzgerald centenary in 1996, is based on the recollections of those who knew him—his daughter Scottie, Sheilah Graham, Frances Kroll Ring, Budd Schulberg, and Honoria Murphy Donnelly—and on correspondence and interviews with a number of important writers who share an appreciation for what Fitzgerald accomplished in his brief forty-four years.

{ Ernest Hemingway }

PART V

◈ GETTING STARTED ◈

{ 12 }

HEMINGWAY OF THE *STAR*

I F HEMINGWAY had stuck to his trade as a reporter, Philip Young judged, he "would have ranked among the best there ever were" (17). The reviewers of *Byline: Ernest Hemingway* (1970) did not go that far, but they generally admired Hemingway's articles in the Toronto *Star* papers, the *Daily Star* and the feature-oriented *Star Weekly*, for their liveliness and wit. These newspaper pieces, written from 1920 to 1923, were remarkably personal for a profession that prided itself on objectivity. In writing about what he saw and heard on his pan-Atlantic beat, Hemingway of the *Star* put his own personality and tastes, even his prejudices, into his articles. That was fine with his employers. They wanted color from him, and color was what he gave them.

When he first began contributing features to the *Daily Star* in the winter of 1920, young Hemingway had already benefited from an apprenticeship on one of the great American newspapers, the *Kansas City Star*. During seven months on the paper in 1917 and 1918, Hemingway absorbed the principles of the paper's style sheet, which advised reporters to write short sentences in vigorous English and to avoid extravagant adjectives. Hemingway the cub reporter, only weeks out of Oak Park High School, also discovered in Lionel Moise a newspaperman to emulate.

"Lionel Moise was a great re-write man," he later recalled in admiration.

He could carry four stories in his head and go to the telephone and take a fifth and then write all five at full speed to catch an edition. There would be something alive about each one. He was always the highest paid man on every paper he worked on. If any other man was getting more money he quit or had his pay raised.

He never spoke to the other reporters unless he had been drinking. He was tall and thin and had long arms and big hands. He was the fastest man on a typewriter I ever knew.

(HEMINGWAY COLLECTION, ITEM 553)

Hemingway celebrates the old-style reporter not just for his eccentricity and toughness but also for his skill. Moise was fast, he could carry five stories in his head and get them down on paper under pressure, and he could contribute something of his own to every story, something that made it come alive. That was what he was after, too.

Early in 1920 Hemingway began haunting the *Star* newsroom so ubiquitously that J. Herbert Cranston, editor of the *Star Weekly*, finally put him on a space-rate basis. That was a cheap arrangement for the paper, which only paid for what it wanted to print and not very much for that: half a cent to a penny a word for the features they ran beginning February 14, 1920. Within a month, however, Cranston raised Hemingway's psychic income by awarding him his first byline. The editor appreciated the young freelancer's gift for humor, or really for satire broad enough to appeal to the paper's middle-class readers. The *Star* ran fifteen pieces between February and May, when Hemingway went back to Chicago. Even at that distance, he continued to supply the *Star Weekly* with occasional features. Cranston liked his stuff, and so did John R. Bone, the *Star*'s managing editor. In February 1921 he wrote Hemingway suggesting a regular job.

Before replying Hemingway consulted his friend Gregory Clark, features editor of the paper, and got some bad advice. Clark told him to ask for ninety dollars a week (which would have made him the highest-paid reporter on the paper, including Clark) since the *Daily Star* wanted him "hard." "The chief wants men to jazz up the paper," Clark explained. "He hasn't any. He thinks of you" (28 February 1921). At the time Hemingway was earning forty dollars a week in Chicago as assistant editor of the *Cooperative Commonwealth*, a slick-paper monthly extolling the doubtful virtues of the Co-operative Society of America. In responding to Bone he inflated that salary somewhat. "At the present I am making $75.00 a week at agreeable, though rather dull work," he wrote the *Star*'s managing editor in March. "I would be glad to come with you at $85.00 a week and could report April 1" (2 March 1921).

That proposal elicited only silence, but Clark had another scheme in mind. The rumor was that Cranston would be hired away by the *Toronto Sunday World*. If Cranston left he'd take Clark with him, and Hemingway would be getting an offer too (13 April 1921). That shift did not materialize, however, and late in October, now a married man without any job at all—he'd quit the *Cooperative Commonwealth* when it became clear that the society it was supposed to promote, having fleeced its members, was going into bankruptcy—Hemingway began another letter to Bone. "You very kindly suggested . . . a position last February," he reminded the editor, "but at that time I was getting some valuable experience and a very satisfactory salary here . . . and in answering your letter named a salary figure which was more, I believe, than you wished to pay" (26 October 1921). Either that note, or some other communication to Toronto, struck fire. By Monday after Thanksgiving it was arranged that Hemingway should go to Paris as a roving correspondent for both Toronto papers, to be paid at regular space rates and expenses on most stories but at seventy-five dollars a week and expenses when covering specific assignments.

As Charles Fenton pointed out in his excellent book *The Apprenticeship of Ernest Hemingway*, the young writer was fortunate to go overseas under the sponsorship of the *Star*, which gave him virtually unlimited freedom in choosing material and expected in return "lively, entertaining dispatches, intimate and subjective." By contrast, the European bureau of one of the major American papers would have required much more routine factual reporting and permitted much less personal latitude (119). Given his head, Hemingway cultivated his satirical bent, writing pieces at the expense of phony would-be artists, thrill-seeking tourists, venal Frenchmen, and rude Germans.

Hemingway met the other foreign correspondents in Paris and made friends with a couple of them, notably Guy Hickok, but he clearly saw himself as different. He regarded serious writing, not journalism, as his real profession. And he was getting acquainted with leaders of the literary community in Paris, including Gertrude Stein and Ezra Pound. In an unpublished sketch that may have been originally intended for *A Moveable Feast*, Hemingway used the length of his unbarbered hair as a symbol of the difference.

As long as I did newspaper work and had to go to different parts of Europe on assignments it was necessary to have one presentable suit, go to the barbers, and have one pair of respectable shoes. These were a liability when I was trying to write because they made it possible to leave your own side of the river and go over to the right bank to see your friends there, go to the races and do all the things that were fun that you could not afford or that got you into trouble. I found out very quickly that the best way to avoid going over to the right bank and get involved in all the pleasant things that I could not afford and that left me with, at the least, gastric remorse was not to get a hair-cut. You could not go over to the right bank with your hair cut like one of those wonderful Japanese noblemen painters who were friends of Ezra's . . .

Sometimes I would run into foreign correspondents I knew when they were slumming in what they thought of as the Quarter and one would take me aside and talk to me seriously for my own good.

"You mustn't let yourself go, Hem. It's none of my business, of course. But you can't go native this way. For God's sake straighten out and get a proper haircut at least."

Then if I was ordered to some conference or to Germany or the Near East I would have to get a haircut and wear my one passable suit and my good English shoes and sooner or later I would meet the man who had straightened me out and he'd say,

"You're looking fit old boy. Dropped that bohemian nonsense I see. What are you up to tonight? There's a very good place, absolutely special, up beyond Taxim's."

People who interfered in your life always did it for your own good and I figured it out finally that what they wanted was for you to conform completely and never differ from some accepted surface standard and then dissipate the way traveling salesmen would at a convention.

(HEMINGWAY COLLECTION, ITEM 256)

This "goddamn newspaper stuff is gradually ruining me," Hemingway wrote Sherwood Anderson as early as March 1922. He planned to "cut it all loose pretty soon and work for about three months" (*Selected Letters*, 62–63). The *Star* had other plans for him. They had been promoting his articles vigorously, and they were attracting considerable readership. John Bone wanted Hemingway to understand that the overseas assignment was only temporary and that the paper would welcome him back at any time.

"If when you return you have a desire to live in Toronto," Bone wrote on February 20, 1922, "we shall be glad to find a place for you in the *Star* organization at a salary of $75.00 a week." Six months later Bone reminded

Hemingway that "if you were here, both you and we would now be making even greater progress" as to money and career (20 February 1922, 20 August 1922). Hemingway was disinclined to return, however. He was having a fine time traveling around Europe, cranking out feature material for the *Star* and crafting vignettes for himself. Greg Clark, back in Toronto, could see Bone's point, but he sided with Hemingway:

> It is the most natural thing in the world for Bone to want you home here. He admits you have talent. I admit it. You admit it. It's unanimous. Therefore, why not use that talent, them gifts, every day of the week . . . instead of being a desultory correspondent away abroad. That is the way he sees it. He is building up a great staff. But I agree with you.
>
> Why, at the age of twenty-four or five or whatever you are, should you pass up the most wonderful education in the world to come back here to the drab existence of even a star man on a second rate city paper?
>
> (21 NOVEMBER 1922)

So the *Star* had their low-cost correspondent in Europe for nearly all of 1922 and 1923, and they took advantage of it. They sent Hemingway to Genoa for the economic conference in April 1922, to the Near East for the Greco-Turkish fighting in October 1922, to Lausanne for the Near East peace talks in November and December 1922, to the occupied Ruhr in April and May 1923. They also tried repeatedly to persuade Hemingway to go to Russia, sending him credentials and nudges from both Bone and Clark. "Your reputation is big with us," Clark observed. "It will be bigger after Russia" (2 September 1922). For some reason—perhaps it was his wife, Hadley Hemingway, who had opposed Ernest's trip to the embattled Near East—this proposition fell through.

At the conferences, Hemingway widened his circle of influential acquaintances. He showed the fiction he was working on to Max Eastman and Lincoln Steffens, and at Lausanne sat at the feet of the irreverent William Bolitho Ryall, a South African who took his place alongside Moise in Hemingway's journalistic pantheon. Ryall's distrust of power and of those who wielded it only exacerbated Hemingway's debunking tendencies. Some of his most successful dispatches, in fact, offered intimate glimpses of the flaws in the physical and moral makeup of world leaders. Mussolini, Lloyd George, the Russian Tchitcherin—Hemingway's dispatches reduced them all to human size. But the *Star* refused to print his interview with the one European leader he most respected, Georges Clemenceau.

With Bill Bird of Consolidated Press, Hemingway went to interview Clemenceau at his seaside retreat in September 1922. The eleven-page account he sent the *Star* stressed the physical appearance of the French leader:

> A bulky man, thickened by age, wearing a brown tweed suit, a funny, felt cap, his face as brown as an Ojibway, his white moustache drooping, his white eye-brows bushy, looking the tiger his pictures show him, his eyes twinkling as he talked to his plump daughter-in-law he came plodding through the sand.

Clemenceau's eyes were remarkable. "They are the only things you can see while you are talking to him. They seem to get inside of your eyes somehow and fasten claws there. When he is talking all his brown, healthy, chinese mandarin's face seems to have nothing to do with them" (Hemingway Collection, Item 773b).

It was what Clemenceau said that made the interview unacceptable to the *Star*. At one point Hemingway suggested that Clemenceau might visit Canada, but at the word Canada "his face went tiger." "I will *not* come to Canada," he responded, "emphasizing the not like an insult." The Canadians had "rejected compulsory service and refused to help France," he said. Never would he set foot there. The article went on to discuss the failure of the Versailles Treaty and the possibility that Clemenceau might yet return to power in France, but inasmuch as the reference to Canada constituted the most interesting part of the interview, John Bone decided the paper should not use it at all, "although"—he told Hemingway to soften the blow—"I hate to pass up your excellent color to be found throughout the article."

In his letter of explanation, Bone was trying not to offend Hemingway but also to suggest where he had gone wrong. Bone did not bluntly insist, as Hemingway later maintained, that Clemenceau "can say these things, but he cannot say them in our paper" (Hemingway, "a.d. Southern" 25). Instead, he pointed out that the French leader was wrong about Canadian compulsory service, which was enacted and "in operation for a considerable period before the Armistice." Had Hemingway explained that point, perhaps the Tiger might have modified his statement. And if Clemenceau wanted to attack Canada, Bone went on, "all right, we can consider whether we will let him stir up bad feeling or not, but we should in no case allow him to do so in ignorance of facts which we ought to be in a position to give him" (25 September 1922)

Actually, Hemingway was not in a good position to feel indignant toward the *Star*. On September 25, 1922, the very day that Bone posted his letter about Clemenceau, the *Star*'s man in Europe entrained for Constantinople with a secret agreement to cable material to Frank Mason of International News Service on the side, a clear violation of his exclusive contract with the Toronto paper. Such double dealing "seared my Puritan soul," Hadley later remarked, and nobody felt entirely comfortable about the arrangement. Mason himself told Charles Fenton thirty years later that Hemingway contributed little of value to the wire service and that he'd put the young correspondent on the expense account out of the kindness of his heart (Baker, *A Life Story*, 97; Donaldson, *By Force of Will*, 38; Fenton, *Apprenticeship*, 171, 281). That seems doubtful, since Hemingway supplied enough copy to INS that it attracted the attention of John Bone back in Toronto.

The evidence suggests that Hemingway was sending the same Near East copy, or practically the same, both to the *Star* and to the wire service. That was true, for example, of one story on Kemal Pasha's single submarine in the Black Sea. The *Washington Times* of November 10, 1922, carried an article headed

Kemal's Lone Submarine Plays Pirate in Black Sea as British Hunt It

over the byline of "John Hadley, International News Service Staff Correspondent." On the same day, the *Toronto Daily Star* printed a Hemingway dispatch under the headline,

Destroyers Were on Lookout For Kemal's One Submarine

(STEPHENS, *HEMINGWAY'S NONFICTION*, 352)

Hemingway and Mason probably felt they could get away with minimally rewritten copy since INS had no outlets in Canada. But somehow Bone got wind of INS duplicating what he was paying for, and his query inspired Hemingway to a cock-and-bull explanation.

He'd run low on funds in Constantinople, Hemingway told Bone, and thus cabled his stuff marked "Receiver to Pay" to Frank Mason of the International News Service in Paris, with instructions to relay it to the *Star*'s London connection. Mason's office relayed it all right but also "proceeded to steal and re-write as much of it as they could get away with." He had placed more confidence in Mason's honesty than he should have done, Hemingway claimed, but he'd had it out with Mason now. "It was a personal matter and a question of ethics," he continued. Legally, Mason might have "a full right to re-write the dispatch considering the way it came to him, but ethically, as our ethics run in the profession over here, it was a very sorry business" (27 October 1922).

The ethics became still sorrier several weeks later, when Hemingway—on assignment in Lausanne for the *Star*—surreptitiously signed on to supply additional reports not only to Mason at INS but also to the Universal News Service. This time, Hemingway avoided duplication of copy. He sent spot news to the wire services and saved the features for the *Star*. But there weren't many of the latter. Robert O. Stephens's *Hemingway's Nonfiction* lists only two dispatches about Lausanne in the *Star*, neither before January, after the conference had ended. Covering the hard news at the conference amounted to a round-the-clock job. At that time, Hemingway later recalled, he "was running a twenty-four hour wire service for an afternoon and morning news service under two different names" ("Malady," 215).

Not much is known about Hemingway's arrangements with the Universal News Service, except that Charles Bertelli, then the bureau chief in Paris, remembered hiring Hemingway to fill in for him at Lausanne. The barrage of telegrams from Frank Mason to Hemingway suggests that he knew no more about Hemingway's arrangement with Universal than John Bone did about his agreement with INS. The young correspondent was apparently collecting expenses or salaries from as many as three different news organizations during the Near East peace talks in Lausanne.

The INS telegrams tell at least part of the story. Hemingway went on the wire service payroll on Wednesday, November 22, at a weekly rate of sixty dollars for salary and expenses. That was hardly enough to pay for hotel living in Switzerland (customarily, the *Star* paid him after he'd completed his assignments, and we don't know about Universal), and Hemingway was stretched pretty thin, financially as well as physically. On November 27, he missed a news break: "new york cables tell hadley we scooped curzons open door announcement—mason." Instead of promising to do better, Hemingway wired back, "Story Broke 2230 oclock. Twenty four hour service costly." Mason chose to misunderstand: "ernest story was surely worth tolls don't understand whether costly refers tolls or what regards." It wasn't the telegraph tolls Hemingway had in mind, and Mason took steps to keep his man in Lausanne functioning: "ernest increase for expenses thirty-five dollars weekly beginning wednesday twentyninth inclusive confirmed stop carbons of your file look good regards."

As it turned out, Hemingway's next check came at the rate of ninety dollars a week for salary and expenses instead of the agreed-upon ninety-five. That kind of penny-pinching, he thought, was characteristic of INS. Mason kept reminding Hemingway to save his receipts for telegrams and other expenses in order to justify his pay. Finally, when Hemingway asked for 800 Swiss francs on December 14, Mason drew the line:

> ernest our books show approximately 500 swiss francs will be due you Saturday but must have your receipts for continental telegrams and accounting for 250 originally advanced you before can make final settlement stop sending you our statement by mail express stop please rush your receipts and advise balance due us stop advise whether you working inclusive saturday and saturday night kindest regards you both.
>
> (14 DECEMBER 1922)

Hemingway shot back a response which capitalized on the possibilities for wit in the shorthand of cablese:

SUGGEST YOU UPSTICK BOOKS ASSWARDS

In a following letter he insisted that Mason's refusal to wire him the money had "smashed up" all his plans and caused him "a great deal of extra expense." He could only regard it as an unfriendly and insulting action. "There seems no possible way to regard your refusal to forward the money to me," Hemingway concluded, "except as a belief on your part that I was planning or trying to gyp you in some way" (14 and 15 December 1922). Actually, he was fully aware that he was engaged in dubious practices. As he confessed to Charles Fenton in 1951, the fact that he was working at the same time for INS, Universal, and the *Star* was, he believed, "covered by the statute of limitations."

Though the *Star* must have been disappointed by the paucity of Hemingway's Lausanne output, the paper nonetheless sent him off to the strife-ridden Ruhr for six weeks in the spring of 1923. Hemingway responded with some of his best articles, combining sensitivity to the political and economic pressures that led the French to occupy the area with characteristic attention to the human element: the effect the occupation had on the people he met and talked with. "I'm glad you liked the Franco-German articles," Ernest wrote his father in June. "They handle the show pretty well, at least make it an actual thing to people instead of simply a name on the map."

John Bone liked them, too, and ran six of Hemingway's articles on the front page of the *Daily Star* in Toronto. All were by-lined and copyrighted (a rarity); some were accompanied by house ads praising their reporter and his talents. "Hemingway has not only a genius for newspaper work, but for the short story as well," the *Star* proclaimed. "He is an extraordinarily gifted and picturesque writer. Besides his dispatches for the *Star*, he writes very little else, only two or three stories a year" (Fenton, *Apprenticeship*, 222–23).

In fact, his earnings in Switzerland and the Ruhr bought him enough time so that he spent the summer polishing his fiction and, toward the end, preparing for the return to Toronto and the birth of John Hadley Nicanor Hemingway. When the *Andania* docked in Montreal August 27, there was a message from Bone welcoming him "home" and adding, "We shall be glad to see you in Toronto as soon as possible." Greg Clark, on the contrary, suggested that Hemingway rest up a week or so before reporting to the *Star*. The paper "needs you bad," Clark pointed out, "and you will be in a position to tear into things here and write your name in the skies" (31 August 1923). Clark assumed that the paper would want to capitalize on its investment in Hemingway as the star foreign correspondent in residence, but he failed to reckon with the tactics of Harry C. Hindmarsh, the *Daily Star*'s assistant managing editor.

Hindmarsh, who was married to the daughter of the *Star*'s publisher, was determined to rid the paper of any potential prima donna. He immediately decided that Hemingway needed his ego punctured and gave his new staffer a series of piddling assignments. He was awakened in the middle of the night to cover one-alarm fires. "Go over to city hall," he was told, "and see what's going on." For two weeks after he went on the payroll on September 10, nothing that Hemingway wrote was deemed worthy of a byline in the *Daily Star*, a paper not at all stingy about bylines. Meanwhile, Hindmarsh was trying to convert his feature writer into an investigative reporter.

Hemingway was directed to cover two different stories involving possible attempts to swindle the public. He tackled one of them—the Sudbury coal hoax—with enthusiasm. Back in Chicago, he had been placed in the uncomfortable position of writing inaccurate news releases in order to absolve his employers in the Co-operative Society of America of charges of wrongdoing. The society was not bankrupt at all, Hemingway reported on the basis of false information: the wife of the founder was on her way to Chicago with up to $3,000,000 in securities on her person (Hemingway Collection, Items 576 and 722; Fenton, *Apprenticeship*, 96–99). The money never got there. Once bitten, twice shy.

On the basis of persistent rumors that coal had been discovered in the Sudbury basin in Ontario, British Colonial Coal Mines Ltd. had begun selling shares of stock from an office in Toronto. By the time Hemingway took over the story, the *Star* had collected a dossier on one of the principals in the company, Alfred F. A. Coyne. Coyne, who had been involved in stock fraud charges in western Canada, presented himself as a petroleum geologist affiliated with the University of Manitoba. His only connection with that university, the *Star*'s letter file reveals, was that he had once given a lecture to a geology club there, during which he made some extremely rash statements. "The only thing to do with Coyne," a university administrator advised, "is to cut off his head first and try him afterwards. If he were condemned to prison, he would in a week have the prison staff and all the inmates selling stock for some project of his" (Hemingway Collection, Item 682b).

Four days after he officially began work for the *Star* in Toronto, Hemingway produced a long and fascinating account involving two principals in British Colonial Coal Mines Ltd., both of whom insisted that Coyne was no longer associated in their enterprise. Hemingway's account began by creating a climate of suspicion: "Although the British Colonial Coal Mines, Limited appears in the telephone directory as being located in the Temple Building they are not listed on the alphabetical list of Temple Building tenants posted in the corridor of the building." Behind a door on the eleventh floor marked "National Finance Company," Hemingway found Stewart Hood, president of British Colonial, and J. W. Henderson, president of National Finance, the firm that sold shares in British Colonial. Involving himself in the story as he had done with his dispatches from Europe, Hemingway chipped away at the credibility of these men. Hood, for example, took him through the following charade:

> Another man in a brown suit, a hawk face, his hair parted on the side and a little inclined to hang dankly forward at the parting [this was Hood], commenced talking. He had a charming voice. He started right out speaking very slowly and convincingly and smiling quizzically. "There's something here I want to show you," he said. "Here are two pieces of coal. Look them over." He handed them to me. They looked identical. They might have come from the same coal pile.
>
> "Look them over," the soft soothing voice urged. "Examine them carefully."

I looked them over and examined them carefully. They looked like coal. The voice went on. The smile continued. There was the effect that it had all been said before. It was all so smooth, frank, reasonable and so straightforward.

"One of those pieces of coal," the voice continued, "is from Pennsylvania. The other," he paused, "is from Sudbury." He smiled at me. Then in a smooth voice, accenting the word *which*, "Which is which?"

Naturally I didn't know. But it was an even money shot so I picked. "This one came from Sudbury," I said.

"That piece of coal," the voice purred on, "came from Pennsylvania." Somehow I felt it had.

(HEMINGWAY COLLECTION, ITEM 682A)

As Hemingway explained in a 12:30 A.M. memorandum to Hindmarsh, he had written this copy "in detail with the atmosphere and verbatim correspondence in case we get proof they are crooks and you decide to do an exposure." He wanted to get the story down on paper while it was still fresh in his head. There were no notes. "In a thing like this British Colonial it is impossible to make notes when you get them started contradicting etc. as the pencil would shut them right up," Hemingway explained, adopting the stance of the expert (Item 682c).

Perhaps so, but the piece Hemingway submitted, though marvelously readable, was virtually unprintable. The *Star* did not run his copy. To do so would have invited a libel suit. What journalists used to call the Afghanistan Principle was at work here. It was relatively safe to label Mussolini the biggest bluff in Europe or to poke fun at Tchitcherin's gaudy military uniform, but dangerous to say an unkind word about the stock peddler working your home town.

The *Star* editors still hoped to get to the bottom of the Sudbury case. Was there coal up there or not? So Hemingway went north with the rascally Coyne (who continued to hold stock in British Colonial and had also begun his own drilling operation nearby) and filed two rather dull stories on September 25 to the effect that there certainly was anthraxolite in the Sudbury basin, but that drilling for coal remained a long shot.

Two days later Coyne sent Hemingway a ten-page typewritten report on the trip, which, he said, the *Star* was welcome to use "in part or whole." He only wanted to present his "contentions . . . frankly," Coyne said, and he was fully aware, as he disingenuously added, "that too rosy press reports in papers of the standing of the *Star* gives an opportunity for stock sellers to dupe the public." Some of the fellows who'd gone along on the trip north, he couldn't help adding in a postscript, had already put up money to keep the drilling going (Item 682b). Needless to say, the *Star* printed none of Coyne's self-interview and nothing more on the subject from Hemingway either. When he quit the *Star* and was on his way back to Europe, Hemingway listed two "Stories to Write": "The Story of the Sudbury Coal Co." and "The Son in Law," an obvious reference to Harry C. Hindmarsh (Hemingway Collection, Items 386, 720a).

His career as investigative reporter at an end, Hemingway was switched to cover any and all stories with a foreign flavor, from a Japanese earthquake to a delegation from Hungary seeking a loan. When the British statesman Lloyd George came to North America early in October, Hemingway was sent to New York to report on his arrival. This would have been a desirable assignment but for two things. First, Hemingway expected to have help from Mary Lowry and Bobby Reade in covering the story, but in the end he was asked to handle it by himself. It was a big job: he filed two stories for October 5 and no fewer than six for October 6. But he missed one solid news break, a speech by the deputy mayor of New York containing ugly remarks about Great Britain. Irate at being scooped, the *Star*'s publisher ordered Hemingway off the story, but he was already rushing home by then, since the second reason he did not covet the Lloyd George assignment was that Hadley was about to deliver. She had their baby early on the morning of October 10, when her husband was still on the train north. Both she and Ernest blamed Hindmarsh for sending him away at such a crucial time (Fenton, *Apprenticeship*, 289; Stephens, *Hemingway's Nonfiction*, 352–53; Baker, *A Life Story*, 116–17).

On October 11, Hindmarsh bawled Hemingway out at the office. He also continued to send him memoranda full of elementary advice on how to handle stories, as if to the rawest of cub reporters. "I notice the [rival] *Globe* managed to get a good interview with [Sir Henry] Thornton. I think we should have stayed with him until we got him, as a personal interview yields a lot of color in addition to subject matter." This to the paper's preeminent color man! Then again, "I notice that Sir Henry Thornton is coming to Toronto on November 5th. . . . It is highly important that we secure a good article from him this time and it would be advisable for you to start now to prepare the subject and frame questions to put to him" (Hemingway Collection, Item 773e; Hindmarsh, memorandum).

If the assistant managing editor had set out to make Hemingway miserable, he could hardly have succeeded more effectively. Matters came to a head a few days later in connection with Hemingway's interview of Count Aponyi, a Hungarian diplomat. Aponyi gave Hemingway some official documents to read, on condition that they be returned. Hemingway sent the documents to Hindmarsh asking him to place them in the office safe. Hindmarsh put them in the wastebasket instead, and later in the day they were burned. That, at least, is the story that Hemingway told Cranston in 1951, and it is supported in part by the fact that Hemingway's story on the diplomatic mission, headed "Hungarian Statesman Delighted with Loan" and printed in the October 15 paper, was the last he wrote for the *Daily Star* (Fenton, *Apprenticeship*, 256; Stephens, *Hemingway's Nonfiction*, 353). After that, he turned out copy for the *Star Weekly* supplement only, where he reported to Cranston and was relieved of the carping of Hindmarsh.

Before Hemingway came to Toronto, he pointed out in a letter to John Bone, all his dealings had been with Bone. Since he joined the staff they had been with Hindmarsh, who had proved himself "neither a just man, a wise man, nor a very honest man." He had made every effort to get along with Hindmarsh, but it was no good. "I was horrified while handling a big story," Hemingway explained,

> to be made the victim of an exhibition of wounded vanity from a man in a position of assistant managing editor on a newspaper of the caliber of the Star because he himself made a mistake. . . . For some reason Mr. Hindmarsh *says* that I think I know more about assignments he gives me than he does. I have given him no cause to think this and I cannot be accused of every[thing] that his inferiority complex suggests to him.

He realized that if it were a question of Hindmarsh or himself, he'd have to go, but, Hemingway concluded, it was "useless" for him "to continue to work on the *Star* under Mr. Hindmarsh" (Hemingway to Bone, undated).

Immediately after the birth of their son, he and Hadley began making plans to return to Europe. The situation at the office, Hadley wrote a friend, "is too horrible to describe or linger over and it will kill or scar my Tiny if we stay too long" (Baker, *A Life Story*, 117). Part of Hemingway's mind had already crossed the Atlantic. During the last months of 1923 he contributed features to the *Star Weekly* on bullfighting in Spain, hunting and fishing throughout the continent, Christmas in Paris, Christmas in Milan, nightlife in Constantinople. To seal the decision he sent Bone an official letter, resigning "from the local staff of the *Star*" (thus leaving open the possibility of further foreign assignments) effective January 1, 1924. They had come to Toronto planning to spend two years there, but the four months they actually stayed took five years off his life, Hemingway insisted. He held Hindmarsh, "a son of a bitch and a liar," largely to blame (Hemingway Collection, Item 274a; Fenton, *Apprenticeship*, 243, 261).

He'd never enjoyed himself so much, Hemingway told Cranston in 1951, as he did when working with him and Greg Clark and Jimmy Frise. He'd been sad to quit newspaper work, but "working under Hindmarsh was like being in the German army with a poor commander." After he became a famous fiction writer, Hemingway was asked to contribute to help organize a Newspaper Guild chapter at the *Star*. No union man himself, Hemingway first thought of sending a hundred dollars "to beat Hindmarsh," then raised the ante. "On second thought I'm making it $200. I welcome the opportunity to take a swing at that . . . Hindmarsh" (Fenton, *Apprenticeship*, 256–57).

You can find would-be novelists languishing in the newsrooms of every metropolitan daily in the country. Their work is not particularly onerous—they crank out news stories to a formula—but it takes time, and after a while the good intentions peter out and no fiction gets written. Might Hemingway have suffered such a fate in a more congenial working environment than that of the *Star*? Probably not. Harry Hindmarsh helped drive him out of the newspaper business, but he doesn't deserve the entire credit. Hemingway was different: he had more energy and ambition and talent than almost all of the newsroom yearners. From the beginning he knew he wanted to be a serious writer, and he put journalism and fiction in discrete categories. He also got plenty of good advice from other writers about the dangers of overexposure to the newspaper business. Significantly, in his own, mostly unpublished sketches about journalists, he tended to denigrate reporters and correspondents who did shoddy work and let their lives dwindle away.

As early as the Genoa conference in the spring of 1922, one of Hemingway's fellow correspondents sensed that he "really didn't give a damn" about the job except as "it provided some much needed funds and gave him an association with other writers." Both Max Beerbohm and William Bolitho Ryall cautioned him against the evils of tying oneself to commercial journalism (Fenton, *Apprenticeship*, 138, 158–59, 194; Baker, *A Life Story*, 89). Gertrude Stein was still more eloquent on the subject. "You ruined me as a journalist last winter," Hemingway wrote her in the same letter that announced his decision to quit the *Star* (*Selected Letters*, 101). In their talks Stein told him to get out of journalism before it used up the juice he needed for his fiction.

More specifically, Stein warned that the reliance of newspaper writing upon sticking to the facts might weaken one's inventive skills and that its insistence upon timeliness might lead one to rely upon a false sense of immediacy. Hemingway was acutely conscious of both problems, particularly the second. The difference between "good writing" and "reporting," he observed in a 1935 *Esquire* article, was that no one would remember the reporting.

> When you describe something that has happened that day the timeliness makes people see it in their own imaginations. A month later that element of time is gone and your account would be flat and they would not see it in their minds nor remember it. But if you make it up instead of describing it you can make it round and whole and solid and give it life.
>
> ("MONOLOGUE" 208–9)

On such grounds, Hemingway renounced journalism as a career. But his tenure on the *Star* was far from his final venture in the field. In the mid-1930s Arnold Gingrich at *Esquire* persuaded Hemingway to write a series of articles on any subject he fancied, including fishing and fiction and international affairs. After that, he wangled assignments from newspaper and magazine editors to take him to the Spanish Civil War, China, and World War II.

On four trips to Spain, he went as close as he could to the action in the company of Herbert Matthews of the *New York Times*. He thought Matthews a great correspondent: intelligent, courageous, and professional. They became friends as well as colleagues. But the *Times* man was an exception to the rule, for in several notes and manuscript fragments among Hemingway's papers, he disparaged other newsmen he encountered, especially war correspondents who wrote dispatches from their hotels instead of the front lines (Hemingway Collection, Items 411, 481).

In one of these comments, he analyzed Greg Clark of the *Star* with startling objectivity:

> I have not done Greg justice. Maybe I have hurt him. It would be cruel to hurt him but also difficult because he is not flat but round all around. He would be hard to hurt because he is well rounded. . . . He also loves to think. He thinks very well but never strains himself. He likes it about Canada too. What I dislike he dislikes too but it does not touch him. . . . You cannot dismiss him or classify him because he is always acting and you cannot tell how much of it is acting. He also acts inside himself. He is honestly interested in people. There is too much India rubber in him. I have never seen him angry. He has too much sense. If he has a weakness it is having too much sense.

Greg was his best friend on the paper, Hemingway wrote, but he did not really know him. He wished that he'd seen Greg drunk and that he'd seen him cry. Those, he thought, were "the tests on a man" (Item 24/a).

Here Hemingway was turning a writer's eye on his companion, beginning to plumb psychological depths of the sort that would not find their way into the afternoon's newspaper. He insisted always on the distinction between newspaper articles and his serious work. "If you have made your living as a newspaperman," he told Louis Henry Cohn, "learning your trade, writing against deadlines, writing to make stuff timely rather than permanent, no one has any right to dig this stuff up and use it against the stuff you have written . . . the best you can" (qtd. in White, *Byline*, 13).

Judgmental though he may have been about journalists and their trade, Hemingway nonetheless felt a measure of sympathy for burnt-out newspapermen who hung around the business too long. He made one of these newsmen, Morrow Alford, the protagonist of a sketch preserved among his voluminous papers at the John F. Kennedy library in Boston.

Alford does not fit the media stereotype of the reporter. He doesn't look or talk hard-boiled. He doesn't have an intent piercing look or carry a great sheaf of copy paper. He is not writing a play that will make him famous in the last reel. He doesn't even smoke cigarettes. In fact, Alford leads a dull everyday life. Every day he eats a roast beef sandwich and has a glass of milk for lunch. Every evening he takes the 5:45 home to his wife, his kids, and his garden. The city editor calls him Punk, and they both know that he's never going to amount to anything. "After fifteen years on the Gazette, Morrow Alford wished he had left the newspaper game in time, realized that it was too late, covered city politics for the day side, gardened in the evenings in the summer, studied seed catalogues in the winter and planned murder mystery stories that he started and never finished" (Hemingway Collection, Item 581).

Implicit in Hemingway's depiction of Punk Alford is the recognition that the "newspaper game" takes its toll on reporters. Elsewhere he made the point more explicitly. "In newspaper work," he observed in 1952, "you have to learn to forget every day what happened the day before." It was valuable experience "up to the point that it forcibly begins to destroy your memory. A writer must leave it before that point" (qtd. in Fenton, *Apprenticeship*, 161). In a typescript fragment, he compared "the real reporter" to a photographic plate:

When exposed to a murder, hanging, riot, great fire, eternal triangle or heavyweight box fight he automatically registers an impression that will be conveyed through his typewriter to the people who buy the paper. Great feature men are constructed like color photographing plates—humorous writers are cameras with a crooked, comically distorting lens. When a reporter ceases to register when exposed, he goes on the copy desk. There he edits the work of other men who haven't yet been exposed so many times as to cease to register

(ITEM 270.5)

Hemingway of the *Star* was a first-rate feature man, with a comic bent to brighten his color material. Unlike Punk Alford and many another reporter, he got out of newspaper work before too many exposures obliterated his memory and dulled his emotional capacity to react. It was a good thing for him, and for the rest of us.

PART VI

◈ THE CRAFTSMAN AT WORK ◈

{ 13 }

"A VERY SHORT STORY" AS THERAPY

ERNEST HEMINGWAY met Agnes von Kurowsky in the Red Cross hospital in Milan, where he had been taken to recuperate from his July 1918 wounding on the Austrian front. She was twenty-six, a Red Cross nurse, very attractive, and not without experience in affairs of the heart. He was barely nineteen, good-looking, charming in his eagerness to confront life, and innocent in the ways of courtship. Despite the difference in their ages, they fell in love. When he sailed for the States from Genoa in early January, it was understood that he would get a job, she would follow, and they would be married. That did not happen, however. Agnes soon transferred her affections to an Italian officer and wrote Ernest the bad news only two months after his departure from Italy.

When the letter arrived at Oak Park in mid-March 1919, young Hemingway was devastated. If, as he wrote his friend Howell Jenkins, he then attempted to cauterize her memory "with a course of booze and other women" (*Selected Letters*, 25), the therapy was not entirely successful. A residue of pain filled the hollow place that had housed his love for the Red Cross nurse and would not go away until he could write about it. "You'll lose it if you talk about it," Jake Barnes warned (*Sun Also Rises*, 249). And the obverse of the maxim was that you could get rid of it by talking—or writing—about it.

When Ernest Hemingway left his wife Hadley, it took him only two months to put the tale into fictional form in "A Canary for One." When

Agnes von Kurowsky rejected Ernest, it took him four years to write a story about it. At only two pages, it is aptly called "A Very Short Story" and it closely tracks what happened between Ernest and Agnes.

Actually, the story went through at least three versions: the pencil draft headed "Personal" or "Love" (Version A), chapter 10 of *in our time* (1924) (Version B), and "A Very Short Story" of *In Our Time* (1925) and the collected stories (Version C) (Hemingway Collection, Items 633, 94, 94a). Most of the changes Hemingway made between first draft and the finished story worked to render the account at once more impersonal and more bitter.

In the handwritten draft (Version A), the love affair is depicted tenderly, and little blame is directed at Agnes. In this version she is called "Ag," the narrator is unambiguously "I," and the two of them are often "we," as in the straightforward "We loved each other very much." Those six little words do not appear in either subsequent version, nor does the following account of letter writing inside the hospital: "Daytimes I slept and wrote letters for her to read downstairs when she got up. She used to send letters up to me by the charwoman."

Using the first person pronoun and the name "Ag," together with placing the story in Milan, conformed to the practice Hemingway often followed early in his career: beginning with names drawn from experience but later changing these as the experience became transformed from reportage into fiction. There were legal as well as artistic reasons for such changes. The female character remained "Ag" in chapter 10 of *in our time*, but became "Luz" in *In Our Time* upper case. That was the way it should stay, Hemingway instructed Max Perkins when *The First Forty-nine Stories* were in preparation in 1938: "Ag is libelous. Short for Agnes" (*Selected Letters*, 469). But Version A's accuracy in the matter of names may also have reflected Hemingway's desire to reconstruct the way it was when he fell in love with the Red Cross nurse who took care of him after his wounding. The subject was love, after all, and the tone is unmistakably romantic.

Version A was originally headed "Personal" and began "There were flocks of chimney swifts in the sky. The searchlights were out and they carried me . . ." Then this broke off, and was crossed out in favor of the new heading, "Love," and the remainder of the piece. Since chapter 10 of *in our time* (Version B) is also called "Love" in early typescripts, the presumption is strong that Version A functioned as a preliminary draft for the "chapter" published in 1924. Apparently Hemingway was trying during the interim to find the right way to approach the subject of lost love. In Version A he even penciled in one sexually suggestive passage: "I said, 'I love you, Ag,' and pulled her over hard against me. And she said, 'I know it, Kid,' and kissed me and got all the way up onto the bed." But this was deleted.

The most significant difference between Version A and the two that followed was that the first draft did not censure Agnes in its closing section, either overtly or through the sarcasm that pervades the later versions. Ag had not kept the faith, of course, but in Version A Hemingway provided her with an excuse for this failure. After the armistice, he wrote, "I went home to get a job so we could get married and Ag went up to Torre di Mosto (sic) to run some sort of a show. It was lonely there, and there was a battalion of Arditi quartered in the town. When the letter came saying ours had been only a kid affair I got awfully drunk. The major never married her, and I got a dose of clap from a girl in Chicago riding in a Yellow Taxi." The loneliness made her do it, and Ag got her due punishment when "the major" failed to marry her. These extenuating circumstances persist (and are even adumbrated on) in Versions B and C, but they are outweighed there by a sardonic resentment of Ag's faithlessness.

Each version begins with the wounded protagonist on the roof with Ag (or Luz) beside him on the bed, "cool and fresh in the hot night." In each version, too, the nurse "stayed on night duty for three months," and the patient, once he was moving about on crutches, took the temperatures of the other patients so that she would not have to "get up from the bed"—his bed. All three versions have the lovers praying together in the Duomo, along with the declaration that they wanted to get married. But the particulars of these scenes changed substantially from Version A to Versions B and C. Most of the revisions involve additions rather than deletions—the usual pattern, as Paul Smith established, of Hemingway's working method. The only important omissions are "We loved each other very much," the business about writing letters to each other during Ag's three months of night duty, and the confessional "I got awfully drunk." In the way of substitutions, Milan becomes Padova in Version B and is Anglicized to Padua in "A Very Short Story" itself, where Ag is changed to Luz.

More importantly, the "I" of Version A gives way to the seemingly more objective "he" in Versions B and C (in no case is the protagonist given a name). This objectivity is more apparent than real, as Scholes demonstrates in "Decoding Papa: 'A Very Short Story' as Word and Text." The story reads perfectly, Scholes points out, if the "he" of the text is transposed to "I" and makes no sense if the "she" is converted to the first person (116–17). In other words, the "I" voice continues to speak from behind the facade of the "he." Moreover, most of the other changes Hemingway made consist of addenda designed to sharpen awareness that the "he" of the story has been done wrong. The deck is stacked against Luz.

Version A contains only four paragraphs. Versions B and C—the story as printed in *in our time* and *In Our Time*—run to seven paragraphs and about twice as many words. The first three paragraphs of Version A are substantially transferred to subsequent versions, and the first paragraph itself (other than the change in pronouns and place name) remains fixed throughout. In paragraphs two and three, however, Hemingway made important additions. Paragraph two of Version A deals with Ag on night duty, her preparing him for his operation, a joke about "friend or enema," and his taking temperatures so she could stay in his bed. The same paragraph in Version C contains four additional sentences that strongly imply a sexual bond between the two. After the enema joke, Versions B and C add: "He went under the anaesthetic holding tight onto himself so he would not blab about anything during the silly, talky time." Not in front of the doctors and other nurses, that is, for as the other added sentences reveal, their affair was not a secret to his fellow patients. Versions B and C go on to state that "[t]here were only a few patients, and they all knew about it. They all liked Ag. As he walked back along the halls he thought of Ag in his bed." Presumably the thoughts were carnal. This was no casual nurse-patient infatuation, the story is insisting.

Paragraph three, about praying in the Duomo before he returns to the front and about their wanting to get married, is fleshed out by the addition of one clause and one full sentence. The clause places other people in the Duomo and hence tends to dispel the romantic aura of the two wartime lovers alone in the great cathedral. The sentence expands on their desire to get married. "They felt as though they were married, but they wanted every one to know about it, and to make it so they could not lose it." Once they were really married, they could tell the world: doctors, nurses, her Red Cross superiors, his parents, everyone. Marriage would validate their love and fix it in concrete. Again Hemingway's revisions stress the seriousness of their affair, but now he foreshadows the danger that what they have together might be lost.

Such foreshadowing is more appropriate in a short story of some length than in a brief sketch, and in the process of composition Hemingway was uncertain which of the two he was creating. The corrected proofs of *in our time* use the heading "Chapter 10," crossed out but restored by an authorial "Stet." Beneath that, another title, "A Short Story," is crossed out. So the piece appeared as yet another "chapter" (or sketch) among those collected in the 1924 *in our time*. The following year, however, Hemingway converted it from sketch to full status as "A Very Short Story" included among the longer ones of *In Our Time* and his collected stories. Hemingway must have decided that he'd broken off Version A too abruptly, for from the fourth paragraph on almost everything in "Chapter 10" and "A Very Short Story"—Versions B and C—is new.

The fourth paragraph takes up the love-letter motif, but in revision it is as if only Ag is writing them, hence giving him every reason to expect her undying love:

> Ag wrote him many letters that he never got until after the armistice. Fifteen came in a bunch and he sorted them by the dates and read them all straight through. They were about the hospital, and how much she loved him and how it was impossible to get along without him and how terrible it was missing him at night.

The fifth paragraph is concerned with their parting in Italy and the understanding they reached at that time. They "agreed he should go home," and she "would not come until he had a good job and could come to New York to meet her," but on this point Ernest and Agnes were in anything but agreement. "On the train from Padova to Milan they quarreled about her not being willing to come home at once. When they had to say good-bye in the station . . . they kissed good-bye, but were not finished with the quarrel. He felt sick about saying good-bye like that."

Still, the unnamed narrator—perhaps by this time we can call him Ernie, as Agnes did—was willing to accept this condition and any other she imposed. "It was understood he would not drink, and he did not want to see his friends or any one in the States." What was understood between them, in other words, was that he should give up all vices and entertainments, including friendship, and not get involved with anyone else. No such conditions were exacted of her.

The sixth paragraph, after presenting expository details about his going back to America and Ag's opening a hospital in Torre di Mosto (sic), proceeds to develop at length two topics barely touched on in Version A: Ag's seduction by the Italian major and the contents of her good-bye letter. In Versions B and C, it was not only lonely for Ag, but lonely "and rainy" as well:

> Living in the muddy, rainy town in the winter, the major of the battalion made love to Ag, and she had never known Italians before, and finally wrote a letter to the States that theirs had been only a boy and girl affair.

She was sorry, and she knew he would probably not be able to understand, but might someday forgive her, and be grateful to her, and she expected, absolutely unexpectedly, to be married in the spring. She loved him as always, but she realized now it was only a boy and girl love. She hoped he would have a great career, and believed in him absolutely. She knew it was for the best.

This long addition traces a curious emotional course. In the beginning it provides Agnes with still more valid excuses for her inconstancy. She had only succumbed after the rain and mud and the loneliness and the wiles of the Italian major conspired to diminish her resistance. This emphasizes the seriousness of the love between the narrator-protagonist and his nurse: she did not easily break the faith.

Once the paragraph switches to her final letter, however, the tone changes abruptly. The trigger to this change seems to be the phrase "boy and girl affair," later repeated as "boy and girl love." Following this phrase, the story launches into that long periodic sentence about how sorry she was and so on that ends with the sarcastic revelation that "she expected, absolutely unexpectedly, to be married in the spring." Here the full weight of her perfidy, built up previously by her love letters and the conditions she'd insisted on before they could be married, is compressed into the snide "expected, absolutely unexpectedly."

In the final paragraph, Version B omits mention of his getting drunk on receipt of the final letter but otherwise elaborates on the consequence of the breakup. The major "did not marry her in the spring," the story reads and rather nastily adds, "or any other time." Nor did the narrator demean himself by replying to the letter she wrote him about *her* being jilted by the major. He did not get drunk, either. Instead, he followed a foolish and costly course of male assertiveness. "A short time after he contracted gonorrhea [changed from "got a dose of the clap" in the typescript for "Chapter 10"] from a salesgirl from the Fair riding in a taxicab through Lincoln Park."

The few alterations from Version B to Version C are of minor significance. Some simply provide substitutions for actual people and place names. Milan becomes Padua, Torre di Mosto (sic) is changed to Pordonone (sic), "The Fair" converts to "a loop department store," and Ag becomes Luz. The most important revision inserts three words in the fourth paragraph. Fifteen of Luz's letters came in a bunch, Hemingway wrote, "to the front." Those words conjure up a picture of a harried soldier perusing letters from his loved one during a respite from combat. In fact, it was Agnes who went off to various "fronts" on duty with the Red Cross, while Hemingway was recovering in hospital, first from his wounds and then—after a very brief visit, not on duty, to the front—from jaundice. The attempt, obviously, is to arouse sympathy for the male narrator, and nearly all the revisions after Version A aim for a similar result. In effect, that is what is wrong with "A Very Short Story." The narrator is too good, too noble, too unfairly wronged. He is too close to Hemingway himself, or at least to that Hemingway who still bitterly resented his rejection by Agnes von Kurowsky.

Behind a pretense of objectivity, the two scant pages of "A Very Short Story" excoriate the faithless Agnes. Four years after his jilting, Hemingway was too close to his subject matter to achieve the requisite artistic distance. But he does seem to have dissipated his bitterness in the process. Twice again—in "Along with Youth," his abandoned 1925 beginning for a novel, and in *A Farewell to Arms* (1929)—he wrote about love between a wounded soldier and his nurse, and in both cases the romance remains and the rancor is gone. In "A Very Short Story," apparently, Hemingway did manage to get rid of it by writing about it.

{ 14 }

PREPARING FOR THE END OF
"A CANARY FOR ONE"

Old lady: And is that all of the story? Is there not to be what we called in my youth a wow at the end?
Ah, Madame, it is years since I added the wow to the end of the story.

—ERNEST HEMINGWAY, *DEATH IN THE AFTERNOON* (1932)

T HE TROUBLE with "A Canary for One," for many readers, is that it has a surprise ending, and while surprise endings may be all right for O. Henry, they seem all wrong for Ernest Hemingway. If he ever wrote such an ending, it is surely in this poignant tale of a broken marriage whose final one-sentence paragraph, "We were returning to Paris to set up separate residences," strikes with the force of a revelation. Yet if you reread the story immediately, as Julian Smith suggests ("Hemingway in the Wasteland," 355), you will begin to see the groundwork the author laid for this conclusion. Furthermore, by examining Hemingway's working manuscripts, it is possible to discover in detail what he did during textual revisions to cushion the shock.

There are three drafts of the story in the vast Hemingway collection at the John F. Kennedy Library. Each ends with the sentence about "separate residences," but Hemingway made substantial alterations elsewhere as he moved from a pencil manuscript to the final typescript, which corresponds almost exactly with "A Canary for One" as it appeared in *Scribner's Magazine* for April 1927, in *Men Without Women* later that year, and in his collected stories ever since.

Like "Cat in the Rain," "Hills Like White Elephants," and other Hemingway stories of love and marriage in disrepair, not much happens on the surface of "A Canary for One." Three passengers share a *lit salon* compartment during an overnight train journey on a *rapide* from the Riviera to

Paris. One, referred to throughout as the American lady, is an unaware, insensitive, overly cautious person who has succeeded in breaking off her daughter's engagement to a Swiss engineer of good family. She talks a great deal, especially as contrasted to her fellow travelers, the husband and wife, also American, who are about to separate.

The American lady thinks in absolutes. One of her settled convictions (twice insisted upon) is that "American men make the best husbands," and another is that "no foreigner can make an American girl a good husband." Acting on these axioms, she has destroyed her daughter's chance for happiness. The girl reacted badly; she would not eat or sleep after her mother took her away from her fiancé. By way of consolation, the American lady has bought her a canary, not because the girl likes canaries but because her mother has "always loved birds."

Through most of its five printed pages, the story focuses on the American lady and her daughter's frustrated romance. But eventually the impersonal narrative voice of the husband switches to the first person, intruding himself and his wife on the reader's consciousness, and in retrospect almost everything the American lady has said or done stands in ironic counterpoint to the other domestic tragedy that is taking place before her imperceptive eyes and ears.

The American lady is rather deaf, a clue to her general lack of awareness. When the train stops at Marseilles, she gets off to buy a *Daily Mail* and a half bottle of Evian water, and stays near the steps of the car because she is afraid she will not hear the "signals of departure." The journey abounds in such signals, none more deafening than the sound of silence. At no time in the story do the husband and wife address each other, a foreshadowing of their impending departure the one from the other that the American lady seems to notice not at all. Other signals are provided by the desolateness of the urban wasteland, the burning farmhouse, and the train wreck the *rapide* passes in the course of its journey to Paris. The American lady misses much of this. The careful reader, trying to be one of those on whom nothing is lost and mindful of Hemingway's injunction that in his work "there is much more there than will be read at any first reading" (qtd. in Plimpton, "Hemingway," 230), catches most of it, at least on second or third reading.

The single most important change Hemingway made in revision was to remove a large red herring from the roadbed. Both in the first (Hemingway Collection, Item 307) and second (Item 308) drafts, the narrator observes, following the American lady's chit-chat about the canary's morning song, that "[m]y wife and I are not characters in this story. It was just that the American lady was talking to my wife." That piece of deliberate misinformation he wisely eliminated from the final typescript (Item 309). Hemingway's task was not to mislead his audience but to guide it toward understanding without erecting obvious signposts. This he aimed to achieve in other ways: through the flatness of the narrator's voice; through manipulation of the color palette; through ironic emphasis on the gap between reality and the American lady's perception of the real; through suggestions about the unreliability and impermanence of human relation-ships; and finally though the story's penultimate paragraph.

Only in the first of these categories did Hemingway find his original draft satisfactory. In all three versions of the story the narrator relates his tale in a flat monotone. The opening paragraphs overuse the inert verb "to be" to an extraordinary extent. "A Canary for One" begins:

> The train passed very quickly a long, red stone house with a garden and four thick palm-trees with tables under them in the shade. On the other side was the sea. Then there was a cutting through red stone and clay, and the sea was only occasionally and far below against rocks.

The view from the compartment window is quite pleasant but it recedes rapidly, and the virtually ungrammatical "the sea was" suggests that the Mediterranean will cease to exist for the narrator once it passes from view. Contrasted with the blue Mediterranean is the stifling atmosphere of the train, again communicated through a series of "it was" and "there was" clauses:

> It was very hot in the train and it was very hot in the *lit salon* compart-ment. There was no breeze came through the open window. The Ameri-can lady pulled the window-blind down and there was no more sea, even occasionally. On the other side there was glass, then the corridor, then an open window, and outside the window were dusty trees and an oiled road and flat fields of grapes, with gray-stone hills behind them.

This beginning underscores what the narrator-husband will be doing throughout the trip. He listens, or fails to listen, to the chatter of the American lady. He speaks only three times: to make a feeble joke that the lady does not hear, to change a painful subject, and to say goodbye. Though the train is a *rapide*, the journey goes slowly for him in the over-heated compartment. He consults his watch or a timetable to discover how long the train will stop at Cannes (twelve minutes) and Marseilles (twenty-five minutes). He does not even read to pass the time. He merely sits, gazing first at the dusty roads and flat fields, later at the industrial detritus alongside the railroad tracks. The dullness of the narrator's prose and his selective perception of dreary land and cityscapes indicate that something is troubling him, a point further emphasized by two oddly unidiomatic phrases he uses. When the train stops in Avignon, he sees Negro soldiers on the platform. "Their faces were very black," he reports, "and they were too tall to stare." Too tall to stare? Why should they stare, unless possibly to stare back at the stranger on the train staring at them? He is the starer, seeking to shut off internal feelings through concentration on the world without.

The other curious passage has to do with breakfast. Though the American lady sleeps badly, she rises and goes to the restaurant car for breakfast the next morning. But to the narrator, "all that the train passed through looked as though it were before breakfast." The point is reinforced as the *rapide* reaches Paris: "Nothing had eaten any breakfast." Nothing? *Néant*? *Nada*? Since it would be awkward for them to go separately and there is no question of their going together, the narrator-husband and his wife have not had breakfast. Neither, it seems to him in his mood of negation, has anything or anyone other than the wholesome, middle-aged, and quite intolerable American lady.

Hemingway also uses chiaroscuro to communicate mood, with the sunlight outdoors opposed to the darker psychological mood of the narrator, a man who—like Robert Frost's persona in "Tree at My Window"—is more concerned with "inner weather" (Frost, *Poetry*, 251–52). This contrast is established early in the story. It is hot and sunny outside (the tables mentioned in the first paragraph are placed in the shade), but the narrator notes principally the coming of nightfall. As the train leaves Marseilles, he catches a glimpse of "the last of the sun on the water." "As it was getting dark," he sees the farmhouse burning, with the bedding spread in the field and people watching the house burn. "After it was dark the train was in Avignon." There he sees the black troops, dressed in brown uniforms, under command (as Hemingway wrote, for the first time, in Item 309) of "a short white sergeant."

This contrast between lights and darks, external brightness and internal darkness, is developed the following morning, when the sun shines cheerfully, and incongruously, into the compartment. (The narrator or his wife have presumably raised the blind and opened the window while the American lady had her breakfast.) The sunshine prompts the canary to chirp briefly but does not brighten the day for the narrator. Instead, as

Hemingway made clear through several additions to the final draft of his story, his vision is concentrated on a sterile world of muted colors. Here, italicized, are those additions:

> The train was now coming into Paris. The fortifications were levelled *but grass had not grown.* There were many cars standing on tracks—*brown* wooden restaurant-cars and *brown* wooden sleeping cars . . . and passing were the white walls and many windows of houses.
>
> Then the train was in *the dark of* the Gare de Lyons . . . and we were out on the *dim* longness of the platform.

In revising the story, Hemingway made a number of changes designed to lay stress on the American lady's unreliability. Missing in both the first and second draft, for example, is the husband's joke about wearing "braces" instead of "suspenders," inasmuch as the American lady has thought him and his wife, probably because of their reticence, to be English rather than American. She does not hear the joke. In her deafness she relies on reading lips, and the husband had not looked toward her. As usual, he "had looked out of the window."

Nor does the original draft include another piece of dialogue that calls attention to the American lady's deafness. The wife has begun to talk about her honeymoon in Vevey: "We had a very fine room and in the fall the country was lovely." To which the American lady responds, "Were you there in the fall?" Her tendency is to talk without listening, a point Hemingway calls attention to by altering the beginning of the American lady's discussion of her couturier in Paris. Item 307 reads, "My wife admired the dress the American lady was wearing." But this is out of character for the wife, and in later drafts it is the American lady who admires the wife's apparel and then rambles on without encouragement.

Actually, the wife initiates conversation but twice, once to ask pointedly, after hearing of the daughter's broken engagement, "Did she get over it?" and again to bring up the subject of her own honeymoon. This reminiscence about happier times and marital solidarity ("We" spent our honeymoon in Vevey. "We" stayed at the Trois Couronnes. "We" liked our room and enjoyed the good weather) seems to distress the husband. At any rate he interrupts to call attention to a train wreck involving three cars, of which the American lady—another touch missing in first draft—sees only the last car.

The wreck itself was the subject of an elaborate conceit in the original pencil manuscript:

Outside the window were three cars that had been in a wreck. They were splintered and opened up as boats are cross sectioned in a steam-ship advertisement showing the different decks or as houses are opened up by a bombardment.

In working toward final copy, Hemingway must have concluded that neither the holiday suggestions of the boat cruise nor the military connotations of the bombardment properly belonged in his story of marital separation. So the final draft reads, simply, "We were passing three cars that had been in a wreck. They were splintered open and the roofs sagged in."

With typical wrongheadedness, the American lady remarks of that part of the wreck she has seen that she had been afraid of just such a thing all night and congratulates herself on having "terrific presentiments." She will never travel on a *rapide* again, she says. "There must be other comfortable trains that don't go so fast." The adjectival qualification, "other comfortable," was omitted in the first draft and added later to flesh out the American lady's character. She is a woman who wants and expects life to be smooth and comfortable, as permanent as her own dress measurements or those of her daughter now that she is "grown up and there was not much chance of their changing" through pregnancy or other unsettling events.

She fails to realize that in taking her daughter away from the Swiss she was "simply madly in love" with she has repudiated a singularly eligible suitor. Hemingway makes two changes to emphasize his qualifications. The first is to describe the lovers taking long walks together, rather than the more adventurous alternative of going skiing (as they had in the first and second draft). The other is to provide the suitor, in Item 309, with the presumably methodical and trustworthy occupation of engineer. But letting her daughter marry any foreigner would have meant taking a risk, according to the American lady's prejudices, and she is wary of all risks. It is with relief that she "put[s] herself in charge" of the emissaries from Thomas Cook at the Gare de Lyons in Paris (originally, Hemingway wrote that she "was taken in charge of" by the men from Cook's).

But the world will not stand still for the American lady or anyone else, as Hemingway attempted to suggest through several additions to the first draft of his story. In telling the story of her daughter and the Swiss, for example, the American lady acquires a certain hesitancy in the third draft that was not in evidence earlier. These are the italicized additions:

"My daughter fell in love with a man in Vevey." *She stopped.* "They were simply madly in love." *She stopped again.* "I took her away, of course."

Then she goes on to explain her "of course":

"I couldn't have her marrying a foreigner." *She paused.* "Some one, a very good friend, told me once, 'No foreigner can make an American girl a good husband.'"

American men make the best husbands, she reiterates, just as the silent American husband in the compartment is playing the useful if soon-to-be-abandoned husbandly role of *"getting down the bags."*

Other important additions (again italicized) illustrate the narrator-husband's awareness that all customary arrangements and routines are subject to alteration. In the Gare de Lyons, he observes the train "that would go to Italy at five o'clock, *if that train still left at five,"* and the cars that would go to the suburbs that evening with "people in all the seats and on the roofs, *if that were the way it were still done."* The American lady, a great explainer, betrays a slight uncertainty through her pauses. The husband can no longer be certain of anything.

Aware of the hazard he ran with his ending, Hemingway tried five different versions of the passage that led up to it:

We found a porter with a truck and he piled on the baggage and we said goodbye to the American lady whose name had been found by the man from Cook's on a typewritten page in a sheaf of typewritten sheets he carried which he replaced in his pocket. We were returning to Paris to set up separate residences.

(ITEM 307)

The next attempt was:

The porter brought a truck and piled on the baggage and my wife said goodbye and I said goodbye to the American lady [the passage about the man from Cook's repeated]. We followed the baggage truck along beside the train. It was a long train. At the end was a fence and a man at the gate took the tickets of people coming to Paris. We ourselves were returning to Paris to set up separate residences.

(ITEM 308)

The most significant revision is the change from "we said goodbye to the American lady" to "my wife said goodbye and I said goodbye to the American lady." The husband and wife do not speak in unison; their status as a collective body of one is about to end. In addition, Item 308 adds several sentences to make the climax seem less abrupt.

Still not satisfied, however, in Item 309 Hemingway tried again, twice. First, he eliminated the intermediate sentences about following the baggage truck, the length of the train, and the man taking the tickets:

> The porter brought a truck and piled on the baggage and my wife said goodbye and I said goodbye to the American lady [passage about man from Cook's]. We were returning to Paris to set up separate residences.

Next he restored and rewrote the intermediate sentences, this time in handwriting, though the rest of the draft is typed:

> The porter brought a truck and piled on the baggage and my wife said goodbye and I said goodbye to the American lady [passage about the man from Cook's].
>
> We followed the porter with the truck down the long platform beside the train. At the gate a man took the tickets. We were returning to Paris to set up separate residences.

The husband and wife make the long walk together behind their luggage and pass through the gate toward separation. The extraneous comment about other "people coming to Paris" is crossed out in pencil, along with the repetitive mention of the length of the platform. Notably deleted from the Item 308 draft is the "fence" in front of which the ticket taker mans the gate. As Julian Smith has shown, "A Canary for One" is a story full of traps and cages: that of the canary itself, that of the daughter shut off from life by her domineering mother, that of the husband and wife in the hot compartment at the mercy of the mindless but painful talk of the American lady. The fence would surely reinforce this motif, but Hemingway must have concluded it was one touch he could do without.

He was not quite through tinkering with his conclusion, however. Somewhere, perhaps in galleys, the concluding sentence was given greater emphasis by being set apart as a paragraph all its own. Finally Hemingway added one word to connote the hard cold reality of the impending separation, The "long platform" of Item 309 is converted to the "long *cement* platform" of the printed story.

Considering its provenance, it is remarkable that Hemingway was able to write this story as soon as he did. "A Canary for One" almost exactly recreates the journey that he and his first wife, Hadley, took from Antibes in August 1926, on their way to establish separate residences in Paris (Baker, *A Life Story*, 177, 592–93). Ernest had broken off with Hadley, by all accounts a fine person and a loving wife and mother, in order to marry Pauline Pfeiffer. It was a decision that troubled him for the rest of his life. Much later, as in *A Moveable Feast*, he took to blaming others for permitting his first marriage to fail. But at the time of the separation he indulged in an orgy of self-disparagement. The separation was entirely his fault, he insisted in letters. He was a son of a bitch, and he felt miserable about the whole thing. Yet he put this story in the mail to *Scribner's Magazine* on October 25, 1926: it must have been written, and rewritten, within the two months following the actual separation. Perhaps sensing that he was too close to his material, Hemingway imposed a kind of distance by keeping the major characters anonymous (only the dressmakers have names) and by delaying until the last sentence the extent of the narrator's involvement in the proceedings.

Some may regard with skepticism Hemingway's repeated proclamations of self-disgust about the breakup, inasmuch as he was able so rapidly, in Carlos Baker's phrase, "to siphon off his sorrow" in the form of this story (177). But it is Hemingway the artist and not Hemingway the man who must stand judgment, and, on that basis, he emerges in "A Canary for One" as a masterly craftsman in command of difficult and sensitive subject matter.

What is more, he ended his story at the right time and in the right way. To reveal the separation earlier would have deprived the reader of the retroactive enjoyment that derives from the sense of discovery—discovery of the American lady's persistently obtuse remarks, of the emotional deadness of the husband's reactions to his surroundings, of the wife's patient listening and pointed questions. Hemingway did everything possible to lay a sound foundation for his "surprise ending."

{ 15 }

THE AVERTED GAZE IN
HEMINGWAY'S FICTION

I

Scopophilia runs dominant in modern dramatic arts. Marilyn Monroe's skirts go skyward in a gust of air-conditioning. Marlene Dietrich pulls on her stockings. Rita Hayworth strips off her gloves. The male audience observes, smiles, leers. Under such scrutiny the actress/woman is reduced to a sexual object. "The determining male gaze," as Laura Mulvey puts it, "projects its phantasy on to the female figure which is styled accordingly" ("Visual Pleasure," 808).

There is very little scopophilia in the work of Ernest Hemingway. Confrontational looks are common enough, as exemplified by the boxer Ad Francis's angrily locking eyes with Nick Adams in "The Battler" and by the hit man Max's challenging the counterman George for having the nerve to stare at him as he eats his ham and eggs with his gloves on in "The Killers." But the masculine gaze that represents sexual dominance rarely crops up. In fact *scopophobia* is more like it in Hemingway's stories about love and marriage. His characters look away, look down, look out the window, look at anything but the persons they are with.

The absence of a "determining [and degrading] male gaze" may seem odd to those who regard Hemingway as a macho writer and expect him to diminish his female characters into creatures existing solely for the use and entertainment of their male companions. But that view derives from

Hemingway's public persona, not from his writing. And it may seem odd, as well, because in technique Hemingway's stories closely resemble dramas in which scopophilia abounds. In most of his fiction dealing with relationships between men and women, there is little description and less narrative commentary. The plot unfolds by way of dialogue stripped of adverbial guidelines, just as in a play or film. When Hemingway's characters have something to say to one another, they go ahead and say it rather than saying it "coldly" or "angrily" or "cheerfully."

This reluctance to erect signposts was deliberate in Hemingway, who as a modernist aimed to write on the principle of the iceberg. "There is seven eighths of it underwater for every part that shows," he said. "Anything you know you can eliminate and it only strengthens your iceberg" (qtd. in Plimpton, "Hemingway," 84). To fathom the emotional undercurrents of a Hemingway story, one must seek below the surface. "The meaning of a work of fiction," as Thomas Flanagan observed in 1999, "is shaped as much by what is cut away from it as by what is kept, especially in the case of a writer [like Hemingway] who worked through counterpoints of silence and language" ("The Best He Could Do," 70).

In 1976 Nigel Cutting analyzed the ways in which Hemingway managed to convey what was going on under the surface in *The Sun Also Rises*. "Hemingway is deeply suspicious of language," he comments, citing as evidence a quotation from *Death in the Afternoon*: "All our words from loose using have lost their edge." Deep feelings are debased when expressed in words; direct statement inevitably obscures the emotion. "All people talk of it," Hemingway said of love, "but those who have had it are all marked by it and I would not wish to speak of it further since of all things it is the most ridiculous to talk of" ("Hemingway's Sub-Text," 192). Hemingway talks little of love in his writing, though it remains the central topic of many of his stories and novels.

Having eschewed the benefit of explicit language, how did Hemingway manage to carry us with him below the waterline? By means of *subtext*, Cutting argues, borrowing the term from Stanislavsky. As the Russian defined it, subtext constitutes "the inwardly felt expression of a human being in a part, which flows uninterruptedly beneath the words of the text, giving them life and a basis for being" (*Building a Character*, 113). Stanislavsky was talking about twentieth-century acting and its attempt to portray the subconscious, the deep psychological truth of a character. The task is difficult enough in drama, yet it is occasionally achieved through collaboration of actor, playwright, and director touched with genius: *Death of a Salesman* comes to mind. In addition to language, of course, the dramatic form offers wider opportunities for facial expression and body movement than are available to a writer of fiction. But subtext can still operate effectively in a story or novel, Cutting maintains, through "looks, gestures, silence, inaction, and observation."

Silence and near-silence function to reveal the emotional undercurrent of *The Sun Also Rises*. In most fiction, if a character is silent, we assume it is because he has nothing to say. In Hemingway the silence may derive from feelings too intense to be reduced to words. The final conversation between Brett Ashley and Jake Barnes provides a case in point. Jake has hurried to Madrid from San Sebastian after receiving Brett's telegram that she is "rather in trouble." It is an act of knight-errantry. He will protect and rescue the woman he loves, never mind his physical impairment or her continuing promiscuity, most recently with the young bullfighter Pedro Romero. Once he arrives in Madrid, however, Jake finds that there is nothing for him to do, even financially, to rescue Brett. What she requires of him is that he listen to her talk about her affair with Romero.

Without introducing the word *jealousy* (on Jake's part) or *obsession* (on Brett's), Hemingway uses dialogue to convey the depth of these emotions. Brett is not insensitive to Jake's feelings; she simply cannot stop herself from talking about the lover she sent away only the previous day on the grounds that she is "not going to be one of those bitches who ruins children." At first Jake is sympathetic. He takes Brett, trembling, into his arms. "Tell me about it," he says. "What was it about being in trouble?" he wants to know, harking back to her telegram, and she explains that she wasn't sure she'd be able to send Romero away: she didn't have a *sou* herself with which to leave him, and she couldn't take money from him (*Sun Also Rises*, 246). Jake's money, though, she could and would have taken to pay her hotel bill, had it been necessary. This was why she'd wired him.

Undoubtedly sensing Jake's discomfort, Brett repeatedly proposes that they drop the subject of Romero. Within two pages she says, "let's never talk about it," "Oh, let's not talk about it," "Don't let's ever talk about it," "But, oh, Jake, please let's never talk about it" (245–47). Each time, however, she goes back to the bullfighter: how he wanted her to grow her hair out to look more womanly, how he wanted to marry her, how well they got along, how generous and above all how young he was, nineteen to her thirty-four. "All right," Jake says when she first suggests not talking about it, and when she goes on he tries to discourage further talk by way of monosyllabic reactions: "No," "Yes," "Really?" "Good," "No," "Good," and "Dear Brett" (when she begins to cry). To her final suggestion that they not talk about it, he says nothing at all. Jake attempts to redirect the conversation to small talk about hotel bars and drinks and bartenders, but Brett circles back to Romero three more times, in each instance preceded by the phrase "You know." You know, he's only nineteen; you know, he was born in 1905; you know, he'd been with only two women in his life (248).

Jake greets these recurring revelations with silence and sarcasm before finally losing patience:

> "I thought you weren't going to ever talk about it."
> "How can I help it?"
> "You'll lose it if you talk about it."
>
> (249)

She's only talking "around" it, Brett insists, and allows that deciding not to be a bitch has made her feel rather good. "It's sort of what we have instead of God," she says, but Jake can't go along with that. "Some people have God quite a lot," he counters. Then he proceeds to drink the better part of five bottles of *rioja alta* at lunch to top off three pre-lunch martinis. Brett pleads with him, "Jake, don't get drunk," but in his emotional distress what is he supposed to do? (249–50).

As for Brett, when she first tells him about how it makes her feel "rather set up" to have sent Romero away, she is clearly fabricating the truth, a point illustrated by her unwillingness to look Jake in the eye. Early in the novel, when Jake and Brett take their taxi ride to Montparnasse together— a parallel to the final scene in Madrid and Jake's dismissive "Isn't it pretty to think so?" (251)—the narrator discourses at unusual length on "the way she had of looking that made you wonder whether she really saw out of her own eyes. They would look on and on after every one else's eyes in the world would have stopped looking." They talk about how impossible their situation is, Brett looking directly at Jake all the time. "Her eyes had different depths, sometimes they seemed perfectly flat. Now you could see all the way into them" (34).

Then the conversation turns bitter. Don't we pay for the things we do? Brett asks. What happened to me (the sexually debilitating injury) is supposed to be funny, Jake says. They sit like two strangers. And with that change of mood, Jake looks out the window at the Parc Montsouris, closed and dark, and Brett's extraordinary eyes that are described in such detail as to make them her single most defining feature "looked flat again" as she pointedly resists eye contact. "She wasn't looking at me," Jake reports. Brett "turned her head away" and "looked straight ahead" (34–35). Similarly, at the end of the novel, when she begins to cry and Jake holds her close to comfort her, again she looks away and—twice—will "not look up" at him (247).

In both instances Brett's averted gaze operates to suggest the sense of loss she feels (it also makes her a more sympathetic character). Nearly always in Hemingway's fiction, avoiding eye contact is associated with similar feelings. It is a device, a concealed stage direction, a form of subtext that Hemingway employs in those stories—his very best ones—when love has gone wrong or is going wrong.

II

"In Another Country" provides a rare example, for Hemingway, of a successful marriage, albeit one doomed to end too soon. At the hospital in Milan where the World War I wounded undergo physical therapy, Nick Adams meets an Italian major, once the greatest fencer in Italy, who now has "a little hand like a baby's" (*Complete Short Stories*, 207). Daily workouts with the machines, they are told, will restore the major's hand and Nick's leg to mint condition. The major comes every day for his therapy without believing a word that the doctors tell him and regarding the photographs of before-and-after healings with amused skepticism. He also instructs Nick in the intricacies of Italian grammar. Then one day he lashes out at his pupil. Nick is stupid, the major tells him, "look[ing] straight ahead at the wall" while the straps of the machine thump up and down on his deformed hand. When Nick goes back to the States, the major warns, he must not marry. Speaking "very angrily and bitterly" (an unusual adverbial stage direction), the major declares that if a man is "to lose everything, he should not place himself in a position to lose that." Why should he lose it? Nick asks. "He'll lose it," the major replies. The major does not look at Nick. He looks straight ahead as he talks, looks at the wall, and finally looks down at the machine as he jerks his hand free and commands an attendant to "turn this damned thing off."

The major's young wife has just died of pneumonia. He cannot resign himself, he tells Nick in apology for lashing out at him. "It is very difficult." Still he cannot bring himself to make eye contact. "He looked straight past me and out through the window." He starts to cry, and then he walks out the door in a soldierly posture, "with his head up looking at nothing." Three days later, when the major returns, some new photographs are on display of hands like his that had been fully restored. "The photographs did not make much difference to the major because he only looked out the window" (*Complete Short Stories*, 209–10).

The averted eyes of the Italian major, who has lost much in the war and still more at home, bespeak a sorrow almost beyond bearing. It is a situation very different from the dysfunctional marriage of Dr. and Mrs. Henry Adams, Nick's parents. The temptation is strong to regard the stories about them as autobiographical. Hemingway more than once declared that he "hated" his mother for emasculating his father. Stories such as "The Doctor and the Doctor's Wife" and "Now I Lay Me" make something of the same accusation in fictional form, as Mrs. Adams assumes the role of the domineering wife.

In "The Doctor and the Doctor's Wife," Dr. Adams undergoes two humiliating encounters. First he backs down from a fight with Dick Boulton, one of the Indians who have come to cut up some stray logs. Boulton is a big man who likes to get into fights. As he issues his challenge he "look[s] at the doctor" twice, and the doctor looks back at him only once before retreating, his back stiff with anger. He can hear Dick saying something in Ojibway and one of his companions laughing (*Complete Short Stories*, 74).

No comfort awaits Dr. Adams at the family's summer cottage. Mrs. Adams lies in a darkened room. Dr. Adams goes instead to his bedroom, where he busies himself pumping shells into his shotgun and pumping them out again. They talk from one room to the other without seeing each other. Dr. Adams admits he's had a row with Dick Boulton, and Mrs. Adams chastises him for losing his temper. She refuses to believe that Boulton picked the fight to get out of paying the money he owes the doctor. No one, she feels sure, would do anything like that (*Complete Short Stories*, 75). (Unlike Ernest's mother, Mrs. Adams is a Christian Scientist.)

When the doctor escapes to take a walk, he inadvertently lets the screen door slam, producing a gasp from his wife from behind the window with the blinds drawn. Dr. Adams finds Nick in the woods, reading with his back against a hemlock tree. As he "look[s] down at his son," he decides to assert himself to the extent of failing to tell the boy that his mother wants him to come home. Instead they head off together to hunt for black squirrels (*Complete Short Stories*, 76).

"Now I Lay Me" depicts another scene of husband-wife conflict, with no eye contact between the principals and Nick caught in the middle. Dr. Adams returns from hunting to discover that his wife—with Nick's help, according to a passage Hemingway excised from the story in final draft—has burned his valued collection of Indian artifacts. He "look[s] at the fire" and asks, "What's this?" His wife, who has come to the porch to greet him, explains that she's been cleaning out the basement. Dr. Adams does not look at her, and she goes back into the house. He looks at the fire instead, and sends Nick into the house twice, to fetch a rake and a news-paper where he can spread the charred remains of his treasures. The best arrowheads have gone to pieces (*Complete Short Stories*, 278).

"Soldier's Home" has a scene between a well-meaning but embarrass-ingly sentimental mother and her son, Krebs, who has returned from World War I with his illusions shattered. He has known French and Ger-man girls in the war, and he cannot bring himself to play the games of courtship American girls expect. "He liked the look of them much bet-ter than the French girls or the German girls. . . . But he would not go through all the talking" (*Complete Short Stories*, 113). Krebs also likes to look at his tomboy sister, Helen, and can talk to her about sports.

Serious talk, though, is what his mother demands of him. She con-fronts him about his future one morning at breakfast. Doesn't he have any plans for going to work? Doesn't he know that there can be no idle hands in God's kingdom? She has been praying for him all day long, she says. Hemingway conveys Krebs's reaction in a devastating single-sen-tence paragraph:

> "Krebs looked at the bacon fat hardening on his plate."
>
> (*COMPLETE SHORT STORIES*, 115)

The one-way dialogue proceeds, with the mother discoursing on the benefits of work and her son trying to end the discussion. "Is that all?" he asks, but she has a final trump card to play. "Don't you love your mother, dear boy?" "No" is all Krebs says. When she starts crying, Krebs first ex-plains that he doesn't love anybody and then takes it back. He was just angry and didn't really mean that he doesn't love her, he says. He even gets down on his knees while his mother prays for him. The emotional dishonesty of this charade troubles him. Later in the day he will go watch his sister play indoor baseball. Before long he will have to leave home (*Complete Short Stories*, 116).

Nick's father is not entirely exempt from criticism in these stories ei-ther. In "Indian Camp" Dr. Adams boasts of delivering a child by cae-sarean with a jackknife and without anesthetic. His elation turns sour, though, when it is discovered that the "proud father" has committed sui-cide while listening to the screams of the mother (*Complete Short Sto-ries*, 69). Further shortcomings of Dr. Adams are revealed in "Fathers and Sons." Nick is punished for lying when he disposes of his father's hand-me-down underwear he is supposed to be wearing and then claims he has lost it. The problem is that "Nick loved his father but hated the smell of him." Furious after his whipping, the boy sits with his shotgun loaded and cocked, "looking across at his father sitting on the screen porch reading the paper." He could blow him to hell, he thinks, but does nothing (*Complete Short Stories*, 375). In this story, too, Dr. Adams is satirized for his exaggerated strictures on sex. Mashing is a "heinous crime," he tells Nick, and masturbation "produce[s] blindness, insanity, and death" (371). The thing to do is to keep your hands off people.

These disparaging details are balanced by a countervailing sympathy for Dr. Adams. In looking back at his boyhood, Nick praises his father for teaching him about fishing and shooting—topics on which his father was "as sound as he was unsound on sex." More importantly, we are told that Dr. Adams has had excessive bad luck, not all of it his fault, and that he has "died in a trap that he had helped only a little to set." Nick hyperbolizes Dr. Adams's deep-set eyes that "saw much farther and much quicker than the human eye sees" (*Complete Short Stories*, 370). With his superhuman farsightedness Dr. Adams can pick out and describe objects across the lake that are only fuzzy patches to Nick. Unfortunately, Dr. Adams lacks the capacity to see what is happening closer to home. Although there is no explicit mention of his wife in the story, it is clear that she must have brought on some of the doctor's bad luck and must have been involved in springing the trap.

III

Given the unpromising nature of his parents' marriage, it is not surprising that Nick Adams and the other male characters fashioned more or less along the lines of Ernest Hemingway should have had such a difficult time making commitments to the women they love. This constitutes the underlying theme of five excellent stories written between 1924 (according to Paul Smith, the annus mirabilis for the composition of Hemingway stories) and 1927. All of them present troubled relationships, and all use the device of avoiding eye contact to imply what's going on.

"The End of Something"—to take the stories up chronologically according to the age of the characters—sketches the end of an adolescent love affair. Nick and Marjorie row from Hortons Bay to a beach where they will set their lines for trout and have an evening picnic together. They have made this journey before, but this time Nick has promised his friend Bill that he will break off his relationship with Marjorie. They pass a deserted old mill, now in ruins, foreshadowing the breakup. Marjorie, who does not know what is coming, is inclined to romanticize the mill.

It looks "like a castle," she says, a remark that Nick answers with silence. Next he criticizes her for improperly preparing a perch for bait. They work to set the lines, with Nick on shore and Marjorie in the boat. With that task completed, she pulls hard on the oars to bring the boat "way up the beach." That is not good enough for Nick: when she steps out, he pulls the boat still farther up the shore. "What's the matter?" she asks. "I don't know," Nick says, and goes off to collect driftwood for a fire. As long as there are jobs to be done he will put off the confrontation.

Marjorie stays busy as well, fetching a blanket and unpacking a basket for supper. They sit alongside each other, eating without talking and without looking at each other. Nick announces that there will be a moon, but when Marjorie, hoping for a change of mood, happily responds, "I know it," he picks a quarrel instead. "You know everything," he says. He's taught her everything, and that's the trouble. As they sit on the blanket watching the moon rise but not touching, Marjorie once again asks, "What's really the matter?" Forced to respond, Nick says, "It isn't fun any more," as he continues to look at the moon and not at Marjorie. He is afraid to look at her, Hemingway writes, and by the time he does, she has turned her back to him. "He looked at her back." She leaves, taking the boat back to Hortons Bay. Before long, lying face down on the blanket, he senses Bill coming up to the fire. Bill doesn't "touch him, either," and Nick sends him away so that he can be alone with his shame or sorrow (*Complete Short Stories*, 79–82).

Subsequent stories proceed from adolescent love to couples living together, getting married, and, in some cases, having a child. In "Cross-Country Snow," an aura of sadness invades the skiing trip of Nick and his friend George in the Swiss Alps. George is in college, and he must return to school. But it is marriage that threatens to keep the friends apart. Nick is married, his wife Helen is pregnant, they will go to the States for the birth. At an inn where they stop for a bottle of wine, the two men realize that they might never go skiing again. "It's hell, isn't it?" George asks, "look[ing] at the empty bottle and the empty glasses." "No. Not exactly," Nick responds. There is not much that lies ahead of them, but on this day, at least, they can enjoy the run home together (146–47).

"Hills Like White Elephants" also confronts the issue of an unwelcome child. In four beautifully crafted pages, "the American" attempts to persuade "the girl with him" to have an abortion (the word itself is never used). Hemingway paints in the setting as a way of establishing mood. The story takes place in a Spanish railroad station, where the man and woman are waiting for the express train from Barcelona to Madrid. On one side of the station, where they sit drinking beer and anise, there is no shade and no trees, but they can see long white hills in the distance. The hills, she remarks, remind her of white elephants, a phrase that instead of seeming charming to her companion, prompts him to bicker. The passage is reminiscent of Marjorie's description of the abandoned mill as a castle in "The End of Something." Like the husband in Frost's "West-Running Brook," Hemingway's male characters repudiate fanciful interpretations of nature by their female companions: "tak[ing] it off to lady-land," Frost calls it (*Poetry*, 258).

Midway through the story, the girl gets up and walks to the end of the platform, where she can see "fields of grain and trees along the banks of the Ebro" and the mountains beyond. On one side of the station, the two of them have been sitting looking at a fallow landscape; on the other side it is green and fertile. The contrasting landscapes reflect the choice that they must make, and the story is constructed around that setting and around the girl's unwillingness, until the very end, to even *look* at the man who is so persistently arguing that she should abort their child.

Much has been written about the dialogue of "Hills Like White Elephants," in which Hemingway effectively skewers the male for his insensitivity and lack of commitment. He repeatedly tells the girl that it's "really an awfully simple operation," "perfectly natural," "perfectly simple" (this last phrase is used four times). As he makes his case, she studiously avoids looking at him. To underline the point, on five separate occasions before she finally walks down to the end of the station to escape her companion's harangue, Hemingway calls specific attention to what she *is* looking at. She looks at the line of hills. She looks at the bead curtain separating them from the bar inside the station. She looks across at the hills again. She looks at the ground the table legs rest on. She looks at the bead curtain again.

When she returns from her walk that enables her to see the green fields on the other side of the platform, she attempts to make her case. They could get along, she tells him. But he doesn't want anyone else, he says, and he knows the operation is "perfectly simple." "You've got to realize," he tells her, and finally she is moved to embittered sarcasm. "I realize," she responds, and when that does not stop him, "Would you please please please please please please stop talking?"

At this stage he no longer fixes his persuasive gaze on her. "He did not say anything but looked at the bags against the wall of the station. There were labels on them from all the hotels where they had spent nights." What he wants is to continue a relationship in which, apparently without benefit of marriage, they can travel around Europe and sleep together. After her outburst he takes their bags across the platform where the train will soon come, and on his return stops in the bar for a drink on his own. He feels put upon. She won't listen to reason. He looks at the people in the bar, "all waiting reasonably for the train." When he goes outside to join the girl, she smiles at him. She feels fine, she says. There's nothing wrong with her. She will have her abortion, and afterward they will be no happier than the other couples they know who have done the same thing (*Complete Short Stories*, 211–14).

"Cat in the Rain" takes up a similar issue with characteristic subtlety and a similar indictment of the unresponsive male figure. "The American wife" and her husband, George, stop at a hotel in Italy (in Rapallo, though it is not named) on a rainy day. In the opening paragraph Hemingway uses the persistent rain—the "war monument . . . glistened in the rain. It was raining. The rain dripped from the palm trees. Water stood in pools on the gravel paths" (*Complete Short Stories*, 129) to establish an atmosphere of depression. On this soggy day George improves the time by reading in bed and cordially ignoring his wife. She looks out the window and sees a cat crouched under a table trying to avoid the raindrops. She goes downstairs to try to rescue the cat but is unsuccessful. When she returns, George is still on the bed. Did she get the cat? he asks, as he rests his eyes from reading. When she sits down on the bed with him, he ignores the overture and goes back to his book. She crosses to the mirror, looks at herself, and at last gets her husband's attention—gets him to look at her, anyway—by proposing to let her hair grow out. Wouldn't that be a good idea? she asks, at which point "George looked up and saw the back of her neck, clipped close like a boy's." He likes her hair the way it is, he tells her. He "hadn't looked away from her since she started to speak." She looks "pretty darn nice," he says.

He does not want anything to change, while she goes on to talk of the many things she wants but does not have: long hair she can brush out in front of a mirror and a kitty to purr in her lap and a dinner table with her own silverware and candles and new clothes. In short she wants a home, but, as she enumerates her desires, George goes back to his book and advises her to do the same. "Oh, shut up and get something to read," he says. She goes back to looking out the window instead. As the story ends, there is a knock at the door. The padrone of the hotel has sent up a "big tortoise-shell cat" for the signora. It is almost certainly not the poor kitty she saw trying to shelter from the rain, but at least, unlike her inert husband, the padrone has gone out of his way to please her (129–31).

Hemingway himself married young, at twenty-one, and at first he resisted the idea of fatherhood as incompatible with his career as a writer.

This information should not alter our evaluation of these stories. The characterization of the male figures in them may, however, suggest something about the burden of guilt the author carried around with him.

With "A Canary for One," the troubled marriage of Hemingway's early fiction plays out a final scene. The story employs what many have regarded as a surprise ending—"We were returning to Paris to set up separate residences"—although, in fact, Hemingway does a great deal to prepare for the presumed jolt of that disclosure. Unlike many of his stories, this one is told mostly by way of description. In meticulous detail the narrator describes the progress of an overnight train trip from the Riviera to Paris. He focuses on the country and cityscapes that the train passes: the sea, a dusty field, the smoke of Marseilles, finally in the morning near Paris the advertisements for aperitifs and the dark of the Gare de Lyons. Along the way the train also passes two omens of impending disaster: a burning farmhouse and the wreck of another train.

Description in "A Canary for One" has to accomplish much that Hemingway normally achieves through dialogue. Three characters are riding in the train compartment: the unnamed narrator, an American man; "the American lady," an older traveler of magnificent insensitivity; and the narrator's wife, who is not even mentioned until the story has run more than half its course. The American lady natters on about how she has had to break off her daughter's love affair with a Swiss on the grounds that she couldn't let her marry a foreigner and that Americans make the best husbands. The narrator's wife listens to the American lady and makes polite responses. The narrator speaks only twice, to call attention to the train wreck and to make a sarcastic remark directed at the American lady who has mistakenly taken him and his wife for an English couple. She does not hear the remark, for she is rather deaf and cannot read the narrator's lips. "I had not looked toward her," he says. "I had looked out of the window." He looks out of the window throughout the story. He does not look at his wife. They do not go to breakfast together in the morning.

The obtuse American lady, afraid of missing "signals of departure" and afraid of riding on fast trains and afraid of letting her daughter live her life, misses all of this. In effect she serves as a foil to reward those of Hemingway's readers who, in their relative acuity, may have noticed some of the clues that all is not right with the marriage of her traveling companions—most notably that they do not look at each other or exchange a single word throughout their trip (*Complete Short Stories*, 258–61).

IV

"The Short Happy Life of Francis Macomber," one of the two great Afri
can stories Hemingway published in 1936 ("The Snows of Kilimanjaro" is
the other), is a far more fully developed work of fiction than the stories
he wrote a decade earlier. At twenty-four pages in *The Complete Short
Stories of Ernest Hemingway*, "Macomber" is six times longer than any
of the stories published from 1924 through 1927. As before, Hemingway
examines a marriage that soon will collapse. In the African story, however, this theme is combined with a coming-of-age motif, and the subject
is less autobiographical, with the author introducing his characters from
the dispassionate perspective of a sociological commentator.

The principal characters are Francis Macomber himself; his wife, Margot; and Robert Wilson, the white hunter who is leading them on safari in
Africa. Francis Macomber is thirty-five, rich, well turned out, an accomplished player of racquet games, and a moral weakling who has ceded
the dominant role in their marriage to his wife. Margot Macomber is a
beautiful woman who has in the past asserted her authority over Francis
by cuckolding him and who will soon do so again. They remain in their
marriage, we are told, because he is too wealthy for her to leave him and
she is too beautiful for him to leave her. Robert Wilson is a highly professional hunter: disciplined, tough-minded, and well acquainted both with
the bush and with the sexual behavior of his wealthy clients.

The story has been much celebrated for its technical virtuosity, with respect both to Hemingway's handling of the time frame and his manipulation of points of view. "Macomber" begins in medias res, as the Macombers and Wilson are sitting under their dining tent about to have lunch and
"pretending that nothing had happened." Francis asks whether Wilson
would like lime juice or lemon squash—the usual drinks at lunch hour—
but Wilson responds that he'll have a gimlet instead (the lime juice, all
right, but laced with gin), and Margot adds that she'll have one too, since
she "need[s] something" (*Complete Short Stories*, 5). As the opening dialogue continues, it is clear that Macomber has little or no understanding
of how things should be done on safari. He must rely on Wilson to decide
how much money to distribute to the natives: money owing to them for
the morning's lion hunt during which, it is revealed midway down the
second page of the story, Francis had "shown himself, very publicly, to be
a coward" by running in terror from the charge of a wounded lion. After
this beginning the story flashes back to the previous night when Francis,

awakened by the deep roars and "coughing grunts" of the lion, had lain in bed afraid and with no one he dared tell about it, and to the morning's pursuit of the wounded lion and his eventual charge. As Francis fled, Wilson was left behind to kill the lion: events witnessed both by Margot and the gunbearers.

From that stage on, "Macomber" proceeds to the following night's emasculation of Francis when Margot abandons their tent to sleep with Wilson. Then comes the next day's buffalo hunt when Macomber loses his fear and redeems himself. The buffalo hunt mirrors the lion hunt, this time with a wounded buffalo secreting himself before making his charge. Given a second chance, Macomber bravely holds his ground and brings down the beast. But he does not live to enjoy his triumph over fear and his ascendancy to manhood, for "Mrs. Macomber, in the car, had shot at the buffalo . . . as it seemed about to gore Macomber and had hit her husband about two inches up and a little to one side of the base of his skull." Hemingway leaves the issue of Margot's intentions in doubt. On the one hand we are told that she "shot at the buffalo" when she killed Francis. On the other hand she has obviously been disturbed by her husband's sudden access of courage. As Wilson tells her afterwards, Francis "*would* have left you too" (28)

There are identifiable models for the main characters in "Macomber": for Robert Wilson, the white hunter Philip Percival, who led the Hemingways' safari to Africa in 1933; for the Macombers, Grant and Jane Mason, who became close friends of Ernest and Pauline Hemingway during the early 1930s. Jane Mason, especially, seems to have been the model for Margot. Michael Reynolds has documented the resemblance in his meticulously detailed biography of Hemingway. In the story, Margot Macomber is described as "an extremely handsome and well-kept woman of the beauty and social position which had . . . commanded five thousand dollars as the price of endorsing, with photographs, a beauty product which she had never used." Among the clippings in Hemingway's papers, Reynolds found an advertisement from *Ladies' Home Journal* with a stunning photograph of Jane Mason and her testimonial that she "could enthuse indefinitely" over the benefits of a particular face cream (*Hemingway: The 1930s*, 224). Ernest Hemingway and Jane Mason were probably lovers, but that was no longer true at the time he wrote "Macomber." And the Masons' marriage was not his own, so that Hemingway could imagine their story without the edgy involvement and implied self-criticism of, say, "Hills Like White Elephants."

Repeated shifting of the narrative point of view also helped distance the author from his characters in "The Short Happy Life of Francis Macomber." At times, as at the beginning, the story is told by a conventional omniscient narrator who observes and reports everything that is going on. But on occasion Hemingway goes inside the thoughts of his principal characters. Wilson, for example, reflects on the "simply enameled" cruelty of American wives. Francis lies alone with "the cold slimy hollow" of his fear. And in a tour de force Hemingway even reports the wounded lion's feelings when he is shot: "he felt the blow as it hit his lower ribs and ripped on through, blood sudden hot and frothy in his mouth, and he galloped toward the high grass where he could crouch and not be seen and make them bring the crashing thing close enough so he could make a rush and get the man that held it" (13).

These shifts of the narrative voice stand in sharp contrast to the love-and-marriage stories of 1924 through 1927, most strikingly so in comparison to "A Canary for One," which is told from the claustrophobic viewpoint of the husband, his observational capacities restricted to what he can see and hear in a narrowly confined railway compartment.

"Macomber" marks a change too in the *way* his characters look at, or refrain from looking at, each other. In his stories, Hemingway uses the verb "to look" with unusually high frequency. At a rough count, there are forty such occurrences in "Macomber." The looking functions somewhat differently than in the stories written a decade earlier. The characters look at one another, and the narrator describes what they see—or, in a curious variant, as one character looks at another, the narrator intervenes to comment on the appearance of the looker instead of the lookee. The passage about Margot and her endorsement of a beauty product is introduced that way: "Mrs. Macomber looked at Wilson quickly. She was an extremely handsome and well-kept woman." Only after Margot looks at both her husband and Wilson *again*, this time "as though she had never seen them before," does the focus shift from her appearance to a full-scale description of the two men. In this opening scene her gaze alternates between the two before she consciously looks away from Francis "and back to Wilson," and fixes him with a smile and some banter about his sunburned face as she makes up her mind to cuckold her husband with the hunter.

The decision does not make her happy. Still upset by what she has witnessed during the morning's hunt, she begins to cry and retires to her tent, leaving the two men in profound embarrassment. Wilson attempts to make light of Macomber's cowardice. "Forget the whole thing. Nothing to it anyway," he says, but the two avoid each other's eyes during this exchange. When Macomber's "personal boy" violates the tacit agreement to refrain from eye contact by "looking curiously at his master," Wilson snaps at him in Swahili. "The boy turned away with his face blank" (7).

Macomber and Wilson reach an accommodation for the rest of the safari. "I'm awfully sorry about that lion business," Macomber says, still without looking at Wilson, and he goes on to ask if anyone else need hear about it. This constitutes an insult to Wilson's standing as a professional hunter "We never talk about our clients," he tells Macomber, looking at him coldly with "his flat, blue, machine-gunner's eyes" (8)—a killer look that Wilson will use again at the end as he asserts his dominance over Margot. Wilson's appraising gaze is employed throughout to deepen characterization and advance the plot. At first he fails to assess Macomber's potential for being overcome by fear, although his client has provided him with clear indications of his terror. Wilson "look[s] at him quickly," for example, when Macomber asks if he should hold fire until the lion comes within a hundred yards (11). He "look[s] at him appraisingly" when Macomber suggests setting the grass on fire or sending "beaters" (unarmed natives) after the wounded lion. Later he "glances at Macomber" and sees him trembling (15). After Macomber runs, we are told, "two black men and a white man looked back at him in contempt" (17), but the entire incident might have been avoided, Wilson realizes, if he had had the prescience to order his client to wait while he, the professional hunter, finished off the lion.

Margot Macomber has also observed her husband's cowardly flight. On the drive back to camp afterward, she "had not looked at him nor he at her." When he takes her hand in his, "without looking at her," she removes her hand from his and reaches forward from the back seat to kiss Wilson, sitting in the front, on the mouth. "Then she sat down beside Macomber and looked away across the stream to where the lion lay. . . . No one . . . said anything more until they were back in camp." That night she leaves their tent to make love with Wilson, breaking her promise that there "wasn't going to be any of that" on safari (17–19).

Thereafter Wilson looks at the Macombers more carefully and accurately; his judgment becomes what the reader relies on. At breakfast, after the act of adultery, Wilson perceives at once that Macomber knows what has happened. "Looking at them both with his flat, cold eyes," he disavows responsibility. Why didn't Macomber keep his wife where she belonged? As they all venture out for the buffalo hunt in the car, Wilson "looked around at them," Macomber sitting grim and furious, his wife looking paradoxically younger, more innocent, and less professionally beautiful after the night before (21).

The adultery has another unexpected consequence. In his hatred for Wilson, Macomber loses the fear that has unmanned him. They race after the buffalo, then leap out of the car, and Macomber and Wilson, shooting skillfully, bring down the three bulls they have been pursuing. "In his life [Macomber] had never felt so good," but Margot attempts to spoil his triumph. Wasn't it wrong to chase "those big helpless things in motor cars?" she asks, and Wilson allows that it was not usually done. "Now she has something on you," Macomber remarks, prompting Wilson to look at them both and to wonder what the children should be called when a four-letter man marries a five-letter woman (23–24).

But there is work yet to be done on the hunt. The first buffalo bull they shot has gotten up and gone off into the bush. Just as on the previous day, they must face a wounded, fierce, hard to kill, and still dangerous animal. "Can we go after him now?" Macomber wants to know right away, and Wilson "looked at him appraisingly." Yesterday, he thinks, Macomber had been scared sick and today he's "a ruddy fire eater." Macomber says, in fact, that he doesn't think he'll ever be afraid of anything again. Margot, hearing this, "eyed [her husband] strangely" as he turns to Wilson and announces that he'd like to try another lion. Worst they can do is kill you, the two agree. Wilson is moved by watching Macomber conquer his fear. "Look at the beggar now," he thinks. And Margot also sees the change. From the far corner of the seat she "looked at the two of them," finding Wilson the same as before but her husband quite a different person.

The men talk about the feeling of happiness they share about the confrontation ahead, Wilson "looking in the other's face" as they bond. Margot says they're talking rot, but she is "very afraid of something." Macomber cheerfully suggests that it's time to go after the wounded buffalo. He takes the Springfield rifle and Wilson "his damned cannon" as they leave Margot with the Mannlicher in the car. "Macomber, looking back, saw his wife, with the rifle by her side, looking at him." They are, perhaps, making a final reassessment of each other, and that is the last time Francis Macomber sees his wife's beautiful face. "He waved to her and she did not wave back" (25–27).

In "The Snows of Kilimanjaro" we are on safari again, and brutal conversation again reveals a marriage coming apart. But in this second African story Hemingway narrows his point of view. Instead of serially invading the minds of various characters, he tells the story from the perspective of the principal male character throughout. This is a writer named Harry, married to a rich woman named Helen whose money has enabled him to slough off his dedication to his craft and idle away his talent. In Africa he has contracted gangrene, a physical rotting of his leg that parallels his moral rot. As he awaits the arrival of an airplane to take him to a hospital, the gangrene worsens. Near death, he is confined to a cot and can see only what comes within his constricted viewpoint. Memory widens the canvas, however. Hemingway's fictional writer thinks back on the years in Paris when he was poor and happy and working hard at learning his craft.

Harry's plight resembles that of Dick Diver in Fitzgerald's *Tender Is the Night* (1934), another man of promise undone by wealth. It also resembles Hemingway's own situation when he divorced Hadley Richardson to marry the well-to-do Pauline Pfeiffer and so purchase a great deal of time to pursue the fishing and hunting that he loved instead of doing the writing that he also loved—and that really mattered. In his extremity, Harry lashes out at his wife, although he realizes that there is no one but himself to blame for the stories and novels that he has not put down on paper and now never will. When he excoriates himself, it is as if Hemingway were speaking of what might happen to him: "Why should he blame this woman because she kept him well? He had destroyed his talent by not using it, by betrayals of himself and what he believed in, by drinking so much that he blunted the edge of his perceptions, by laziness, by sloth, and by snobbery, by pride and by prejudice, by hook and by crook.... It was strange, too, wasn't it, that when he fell in love with another woman, that woman should always have more money than the last one?" (*Complete Short Stories*, 45).

Almost everything Harry sees from his limited vantage point is associated with death. The story opens with vultures. He "looked out past the shade onto the glare of the plain [where] three of the big birds squatted obscenely, while in the sky a dozen more sailed." Helen tries to reassure him that he's not going to die, but Harry advises her to "ask those bastards." As he "looked over to where the huge, filthy birds sat," he sees a fourth one plane down to join the others (39–40). Then there is another "filthy animal," a hyena that crosses the open field every night when there is no longer enough light to shoot. As he glimpses "that bastard," it occurs to Harry that he is going to die. With the realization comes "a rush ... of an evil-smelling emptiness," the hyena slipping "lightly along the edge of it" (47).

Even his wife finally serves as a harbinger of death. There is no emphasis here on avoided eye contact. Harry makes a point of looking at his wife as he says terrible things to her. "I don't know why I'm doing it. It's trying to kill to keep yourself alive, I imagine" (43). In a reprise of the reversed-lens technique that Hemingway used to characterize Margot Macomber, as Helen "looked at him" Harry directs the camera to her instead, on "her well-known, well-loved face from *Spur* and *Town & Country*," except that those magazines "never showed [her] good breasts and . . . useful thighs and . . . caressing hands." Yet "as he looked and saw her well-known pleasant smile, he felt death come again" (49).

In the fevered imaginings of his last moments Harry is borne aloft on an airplane that has, presumably, arrived to take him away. "Looking down he saw a pink sifting cloud, moving over the ground, and in the air, like the first snow in a blizzard, that comes from nowhere, and he knew the locusts were coming up from the South." Then the plane banks east, and "all he could see, as wide as all the world, great, high, and unbelievably white in the sun, was the square top of Kilimanjaro," his final destination. In the tent the hyena's noise awakes Helen, and she sees that Harry has somehow worked his rotted leg out from under the mosquito net so that it hangs alongside the cot. He does not answer her call, and she cannot hear him breathing. The last sound, which she cannot hear for the beating of her heart, is the hyena's strange noise (56).

The habit of close observation was instilled in young Hemingway by his father. Dr. Clarence (Ed) Hemingway was a disciple of Louis Agassiz, the Swiss American scientist whose techniques of studying the natural world were in vogue at the turn of the twentieth century. Even before his own children were born, Ed Hemingway formed an Agassiz club in Oak Park, and he naturally continued that avocation with Ernest and his siblings. The Agassiz method involved taking children into the field to collect specimens of stones, fruits, flowers, and so on that they could take home for inspection. Ernest belonged to his father's Agassiz club from the ages of four to twelve, taking delight in what he was taught and, especially, in what he could learn on his own. At Oak Park high school also, his science courses adopted the Agassiz method of requiring students to look at nature closely and record their observations. In her essay on Hemingway's education as a naturalist, Susan Beegel noted that in his reports Ernest invariably used such words as "look," "notice," and "examine." "We *looked* at the laurel leaf and noticed that it had no stipules" ("Eye and Heart," 71). As a boy Hemingway was very good at this kind of work. With academic training he might well have gone on to a career as a naturalist.

But Hemingway did not go to college. He went instead to Kansas City, to Italy, to Toronto, to Paris, to Key West and Cuba and Ketchum. He put himself at risk in World War I, the Spanish Civil War, and World War II. He married four times and fathered three sons. A voluminous reader and accomplished autodidact, he received his education in the University of Experience. But he did not forget what his father and the Agassiz club taught him about close observation. Like all great writers, he became a world-class noticer, and not only of the natural world. Over time the noticing shifted from grasshoppers and trout to the human beings he knew and cared about. He looked at them as closely as he could. He looked, too, at what they were looking at, or away from, and in his stories he told us what he saw.

PART VII

◈ THE TWO GREAT NOVELS ◈

{ 16 }

HEMINGWAY'S MORALITY OF COMPENSATION

Books should be about the people you know, that you love and hate, not about the people you study up about. If you write them truly they will have all the economic implications a book can hold.

—ERNEST HEMINGWAY

I

While voyaging back to the United States in 1833, Ralph Waldo Emerson puzzled over a definition of morals. His thoughts, he admitted in his journal, were "dim and vague," but one might obtain "some idea of them ... who develops the doctrine in his own experience that nothing can be given or taken without an equivalent" (*Selections*, 14–15). In Emerson's sublime optimism, he weighted the scales of equivalence in favor of the taker. Only the half-blind, as he observes in his essay "The Tragic," had never beheld the House of Pain, which like the salt sea encroached on man in his felicity. But felicity was man's customary state, for he lived on the land, not at sea. If pain disturbed him, he could rest in the conviction that nature would proportion "her defence to the assault" and "that the intellect in its purity, and the moral sense in its purity, are not distinguished from each other, and both ravish us into a region whereinto these passionate clouds of sorrow cannot rise" (515–21).

On this issue, Emerson's Concord voice sounds in off-key opposition to that of Emily Dickinson in Amherst, who in poem 125, wrote of the primacy of pain in the equation of compensation:

> For each extatic instant
> We must an anguish pay

In keen and quivering ratio
To the extasy

For each beloved hour
Sharp pittances of years—
Bitter contested farthings—
And Coffers heaped with Tears!

(*POETRY*, 89–90)

For her, the transactions of life are costly; cosmic usurers demand payments of anguish, at unconscionable interest, for each momentary joy. But it is a debt that "*must*" be paid, however unfair the terms.

Ernest Hemingway, throughout his fiction but especially in *The Sun Also Rises*, sides with Dickinson in this hypothetical quarrel. The cost of ecstasy or happiness comes high, yet it must be met. Like the poet from Amherst, he expressed his view of compensation in the metaphor of finance—a metaphor that runs through the fabric of his first novel like a fine, essential thread.

The classical statement against Hemingway's lack of moral sensitivity in this book was made by James T. Farrell, who described the characters as "people who have not fully grown up" and their moral outlook as amounting "to the attitude that an action is good if it makes one feel good" (review, 56). That was not what Hemingway meant to convey. Lunching with a group of professors from the University of Hawaii in 1941, he advised against their students reading *A Farewell to Arms*. "That's an immoral book. Let them read *The Sun Also Rises*. It's very moral" (qtd. in Baker, *A Life Story*, 359).

Jake Barnes explicitly states the code of Hemingway's "very moral" novel. Lying awake at Pamplona, he reflects that in having Brett for a friend, he "had been getting something for nothing" and that sooner or later he would have to pay the bill:

I thought I had paid for everything. Not like the woman pays and pays. No idea of retributions or punishment. Just exchange of values. You gave up something and got something else. Or you worked for something. You paid some way for everything that was any good. I paid my way into enough things that I liked, so that I had a good time. Either you paid by learning about them, or by experience, or by taking chances, or by money. Enjoying living was learning to get your money's worth and knowing when

you had it. You could get your money's worth. The world was a good place
to buy in.

(SUN ALSO RISES, 152)

It is understandable that Jake, sexually crippled in the war, should think
that he has already paid for everything, and it is an index of his maturity,
as a man "fully grown up," that he comes to realize that he may still have
debts outstanding, to be paid, most often and most insistently, in francs
and pesetas and pounds and dollars.

Jake's musings on this topic are exemplified time and again in the profuse
monetary transactions of *The Sun Also Rises*. On the second page of the
novel, one discovers that Robert Cohn has squandered most of the $50,000
that his father, from "one of the richest Jewish families in New York," has
left him; on the last page of the book, that Jake has tipped the waiter (the
amount is unspecified) who has called a taxi for him and Brett in Madrid
(12, 250). Between the beginning and the end, Hemingway specifically
mentions sums of money, and what they have been able to purchase, a total
of thirty times. The money dispensed runs from a franc to a waiter, to the
fifty francs that Jake leaves for his *poule* at the dancings, to the two hundred
francs that Count Mippipopolous gives Jake's concierge, to the $10,000 the
count offers Brett for a weekend in her company. Mostly, though, the monetary amounts are small, and pay for the food, drink, travel, and entertainment that represent the good things in life available to Jake.

Hemingway reveals much more about his characters' financial condition and spending habits than about their appearance: the book would
be far more useful to the loan officer of a bank than, say, to the missing
person's bureau, which would have little more physical information to go
on, with respect to height, weight, hair, and eye color, than that Brett had
short hair and "was built with curves like the hull of a racing yacht" (30)
and that Robert Cohn, with his broken nose, looked as if "perhaps a horse
had stepped on his face" (12). When Hemingway cut 4,000 words out of
The Sun Also Rises but retained these ubiquitous references to the cost
of things, he must have kept them for some perceptible and important
artistic purpose.

II

In fact, he had several good reasons to note in scrupulous detail the exact
nature of financial transactions. Such a practice contributed to the veri-

similitude of the novel; it fitted nicely with Jake's—and his creator's—obsession with the proper way of doing things; and, mainly, it illustrated the moral conviction that you must pay for what you get, that you must earn in order to be able to buy, and that only then will it be possible, if you are careful, to get your money's worth.

In the early 1920s exchange rates in postwar Europe fluctuated wildly. Only the dollar remained stable, to the benefit of the expatriated artists, writers, dilettantes, and party goers who found they could live for next to nothing in Paris. Malcolm Cowley and his wife lived there the year of 1921 in modest comfort on a grant of $1,000: $12,000 by that year's rate (*Exile's Return*, 79–81). By the summer of 1924, when Jake Barnes and his companions left for the fiesta at Pamplona, the rate was still more favorable, almost nineteen francs to the dollar. And you could get breakfast coffee and a brioche for a franc or less at the cafés where Hemingway, expatriated with the rest, wrote when the weather turned cold (Baker, *Writer*, 18).

There were even better bargains elsewhere, and the Hemingways, somewhat strapped once Ernest decided to abandon journalism for serious fiction, found one of the best of them in the winter of 1924–25. They sublet their apartment in Paris and went to Schruns in the Austrian Vorarlberg, where food, lodging, snow, and skiing for the young writer, his wife, and their son came to but $28.50 a week (Baker, *A Life Story*, 174). Europe was overflowing with (mostly temporary) American expatriates, living on the cheap. Any novel about them and faithful to that time and that place was going to have to take cognizance of what it cost to live and eat and drink.

Hemingway regarded most of his fellow Americans on the left bank as poseurs pretending to be artists, "nearly all loafers expending the energy that an artist puts into his creative work in talking about what they are going to do and condemning the work of all artists who have gained any degree of recognition." The indignation of these words, in one of the first dispatches Hemingway sent the *Toronto Star Weekly* from Paris in 1922, is reinforced by the anecdote he includes about "a big, light-haired woman sitting at a table with three young men." She pays the bill, and the young men laugh whenever she does. "Three years ago she came to Paris with her husband from a little town in Connecticut, where they had lived and he had painted with increasing success for ten years. Last year he went back to America alone" (Baker, *Writer*, 5; Fenton, *Apprenticeship*, 124–25).

To a young writer like Hemingway, single-minded in dedication to his craft, the time-wasting of cafe habitués represented a great sin. It was work that counted, and talking about art was hardly a satisfactory substitute. In the posthumously published *A Moveable Feast* (1964), Hemingway laments accompanying the hypochondriacal Scott Fitzgerald on an unnecessarily drawn-out trip to Lyon. Nursing his travelling companion, he "missed not working and . . . felt the death loneliness that comes at the end of every day that is wasted in your life" (165–66). Observing the playboys and playgirls of Paris waste their lives on one long hazy binge, Hemingway as foreign correspondent felt much the same disgust that visits Jake after the revels at Pamplona, when he plunges deep into the waters off San Sebastian in an attempt to cleanse himself.

What distinguishes Jake Barnes from Mike Campbell and Brett, Lady Ashley, who make no pretenses toward artistic (or any other kind of) endeavor, and from Robert Cohn, a writer who is blocked throughout the novel, is that he works steadily at his regular job as a newspaperman. He is, presumably, unsupported by money from home and spends what he makes with conspicuous control. In addition, he is thoughtful and conscientious in his spending. Sharing a taxi with two fellow American reporters who also work regularly at their jobs but at least one of whom is burdened, as he is not, by "a wife and kids," Jake insists on paying the two-franc fare (*Sun Also Rises*, 45). He does the right thing, too, by Georgette, the streetwalker he picks up at the Napolitain. Not only does he buy her dinner as a preliminary to the sexual encounter she has bargained for, but upon deserting her for Brett, he leaves fifty francs with the patronne— compensation for her wasted evening—to be delivered to Georgette if she goes home alone. The patronne is supposed to hold the money for Jake if Georgette secures another male customer, but this being France, he will, Brett assures him, lose his fifty francs. "Oh, yes," Jake agrees, but he has at least behaved properly (31), and Jake, like his creator, was "always intensely interested in how to do a thing," from tying flies to fighting bulls to compensating prostitutes (Fenton, *Apprenticeship*, 150–51). Besides, he shares a double kinship with Georgette: she also is sick, a sexual cripple, and she pursues her trade openly and honestly.

The case is different with Lady Ashley, who acquires and casts off lovers nearly as casually as Georgette. There is a certain irony in Brett's telling Jake that it was wrong of him to bring Georgette to the dance "in restraint of trade" (30). Women like Brett—and even to a lesser degree, Cohn's companion, Frances Clyne—provide unfair competition to the streetwalkers of Paris.

After an unsatisfactory time with Brett, Jake Barnes returns to his room where he immediately goes over his bank statement: "It showed a balance of $2,432.60. I got out my checkbook and deducted four checks drawn since the first of the month, and discovered I had a balance of $1,832.60. I wrote this on the back of the statement" (38). This is make-work, an attempt to delay thinking about the love for Brett that he cannot consummate. But it is also characteristic of Jake's meticulousness about money. The surprising thing is that Jake should have spent as much as $600 in any given month, for he is a man who tries very hard to get his money's worth. He knows whom to write to secure good bullfight tickets, and he reserves the best rooms in the best hotels at the best price. In Bayonne, he helps Bill buy "a pretty good rod cheap, and two landing-nets," and checks with the tourist-office "to find what we ought to pay for a motor-car to Pamplona": 400 francs (96–97). At Burguete, he bargains to have the wine included in the twelve-pesetas-a-day hotel room he and Bill share, and they make certain at dinner that they do "not lose money on the wine" (115–16). He is annoyed when Cohn sends a wire of only three words for the price of ten ("I come Thursday"), and takes revenge by answering with an even shorter telegram ("Arriving to-night") (132–33). After the fiesta, when a driver tries to overcharge him for a ride from Bayonne to San Sebastian, Jake works the price down from fifty to thirty-five pesetas and then rejects that price, too, as "not worth it" (235). He is careful to fulfill his obligations but will not be taken advantage of.

Once, in church, regretting that he is such a rotten Catholic, Jake prays that he will "make a lot of money" (103), but here the verb is important, for he next begins thinking about how he might make the money. He does not pray or even hope to *have* a lot of money, or for it to descend upon him from heaven or through the deaths of relatives. Robert Cohn and Mike Campbell remind him, often and painfully, of what inherited money, or the promise of it, can do to undermine a man.

III

Though physically impotent and mentally tortured, Jake Barnes remains morally sound while Mike Campbell, Robert Cohn, and Brett Ashley, who are physically whole, have become morally decadent. As Carlos Baker observes, *The Sun Also Rises* has "a sturdy moral backbone," deriving much of its power from the contrast between the trio of Barnes, Gorton, and Romero, who constitute the "moral norm" of the book, and the morally aberrant trio of Ashley, Campbell, and Cohn (*Writer*, 82–83, 92). Money and its uses form the metaphor by which the moral responsibility of Jake, Bill, and Pedro is measured against the carelessness of Brett, Mike, and Robert. Financial soundness mirrors moral strength.

Bill Gorton is the most likable of the crew at the fiesta. Modeled upon the humorist Donald Ogden Stewart, Bill regales Jake with topical gags about Mencken, the Scopes trial, literary fashions, and middle class mores. An enthusiast, he finds every place he visits "wonderful" (75–76).The adjective becomes a private joke between Barnes and Gorton, for Bill knows as well as Jake that when things are really wonderful, it is neither necessary nor desirable to say so. Thus, hiking through the magnificent woods at Burguete, Bill remarks simply, "This is country" (122). The five days they share at Burguete stand in idyllic contrast to the sickness and drunkenness that characterize both Paris and Pamplona. It is not that Bill and Jake do not drink together on the fishing trip; they drink prodigious quantities of wine. But it is drinking for the pleasure they have earned, both through hard work (Gorton is a producing writer) and through the rigors of the outdoor life they choose to pursue on vacation. Furthermore, Bill knows when not to drink. After dinner at Madame Lecomte's and a long walk through Paris, Jake proposes a drink. "No," Bill says. "I don't need it" (83).

The first thing Jake says about Bill Gorton is that he is "very happy. He had made a lot of money on his last book, and was going to make a lot more" (76). He has paid for his fiesta, and like all who have earned "the good things," he is careful of the rights of others. In Vienna, he tells Jake, he had gone to an "enormous . . . prize-fight" in which a "wonderful nigger" knocked a local boy cold and aroused the anger of the crowd. People threw chairs into the ring, and not only was the victorious fighter deprived of payment (he had agreed not to knock out the local fighter) but his watch was stolen. "Not so good, Jake. Injustice everywhere," as Gorton remarks. Conscientious about money matters, he is disturbed by a world where fights are fixed and debts go unpaid. So, though drunk and on holiday, Bill lends the cheated fighter clothes and money and tries to help him collect what's owed to him (77).

Bill's comic determination to purchase stuffed animals foreshadows Jake's serious reflections on compensation. Passing a Paris taxidermist shop, Bill appeals to Jake to buy a stuffed dog: "Mean everything in the world to you after you bought it. Simple exchange of values. You give them money. They give you a stuffed dog" (78). His affinity for spending money on the ridiculous emerges again at Pamplona when he buys Mike eleven shoeshines in a row. "Bill's a yell of laughter," Mike says, but Jake, who has not had much to drink, "felt a little uncomfortable about all this shoe-shining" (177). Still, Bill's expenditures buy amusement for himself and others (including, of course, the reader), and these otherwise merely amusing incidents serve to illustrate the principle of exchange of values: to obtain stuffed dogs, shoeshines, or drinks, you must deliver payment.

I V

Robert Cohn, for whom Gorton conceives an immediate dislike, does not belong with the party at Pamplona. A romantic, he is unable at first to conceive that his weekend with Brett at San Sebastian meant nothing to her, but he forfeits any claim to sympathy by his stubborn and violent unwillingness to accept that obvious fact. Terribly insecure, he takes insult after insult from his companion, Frances, and from Mike without retaliation, though he is ready enough, anachronistically, to fight with his "best friend" Jake over what he construes as insults to Brett. A Jew in the company of Gentiles, he is a bore who takes himself and his illusions far too seriously. Unlike Jake, he has not learned about things. He does not know how to eat or drink or love. It is no wonder that Harold Loeb, recognizing himself in Hemingway's portrait of Cohn, "felt as if he had developed an ulcer" and—decades later—attempted to vindicate himself in his autobiography (Baker, *A Life Story*, 223).

Still, it would be possible to pity Cohn for his dominant malady of romantic egotism were it not for his callous and opportunistic use of money he has not earned. His allowance ($300 a month, from his mother) comfortably stakes him to his period of expatriation. He has written a novel which was "accepted by a fairly good publisher," but it is not, clearly, a very good novel, and now the well has run dry. In his idleness, he hangs around Jake's office, disturbing his work, and even proposes to pay Jake's way as his companion on a trip to South America, a continent he invests with an aura of romance (16–17).

How Hemingway felt about such proposals was to be made clear in *A Moveable Feast* when he reflects, in connection with the trip to Lyon with Fitzgerald, that he "had been a damned fool to accept an invitation for a trip that was to be paid for by someone else" (138). But biographical evidence is hardly necessary to make the point that Cohn, whose money comes to him through no effort of his own but fortuitously because of the accident of his birth, does not understand the proper way of spending it. The point is made implicitly by a number of incidents in *The Sun Also Rises*.

Having inherited a great deal of money, he has wasted nearly all of it on a little magazine, thereby gaining the prestige that came to him as its editor. He is consistently lucky in gambling, but that does him more harm than good. What comes too easily has a pernicious effect on him as a person. While he was in New York to see his publisher, for example, several women had been nice to him as a budding novelist.

> This changed him so that he was not so pleasant to have around. Also, playing for higher stakes than he could afford in some rather steep bridge games with his New York connections he had held cards and won several hundred dollars. It made him rather vain of his bridge game, and he talked several times of how a man could always make a living at bridge if he were ever forced to.
>
> (16–17)

Cohn wins a hundred-peseta bet with Gorton that Mike and Brett will not arrive as scheduled at Pamplona, but the bet costs him any possibility of friendship with Bill. Gorton wagers, in fact, only because Cohn's arrogance in parading inside knowledge of Brett's and Mike's habits makes him angry. Furthermore, when the wager has been agreed on, Cohn does Bill the indignity of asking Jake to remember it, and then—as if to make amends after he has won—pretends that it really does not matter (101, 104).

What most damns Cohn, however, is his habit of buying his way out of obligations to women. Frances Clyne, one of the bitchiest women in Hemingway's fiction, reveals this practice of Cohn's in a devastating scene. Flat broke and not so young or attractive as she once was, Frances is being packed off to England so that her paramour may see more of the world—and, he surely hopes, of Lady Ashley.

> "Robert's sending me. He's going to give me two hundred pounds [about a thousand dollars] and then I'm going to visit friends. Won't it be lovely? The friends don't know about it, yet."
>
> She turned to Cohn and smiled at him. He was not smiling now.
>
> "You were only going to give me a hundred pounds, weren't you, Robert? But I made him give me two hundred. You're really very generous. Aren't you, Robert?"

"I do not know," Jake thinks, "how people could say such terrible things to Robert Cohn." But Frances can say them and get away with it, because they are absolutely true. Cohn, in fact, has disposed of another girl, his "little secretary on the magazine," in just the same way, except cheaper (55–57). In buying his way out of entanglements, without expending anything of himself, Robert Cohn violates the morality of compensation.

Furthermore, there are suggestions in the book that Cohn is tight-fisted with his money. He has, apparently, tried to bargain with Frances. He directs Jake to buy him a double-tapered fishing line, but says he will pay later instead of now. After unleashing a stream of insults against Cohn ("Don't you know you're not wanted?"), Mike Campbell tells Bill Gorton, who is about to remove Cohn from the slaughter, to stick around. "Don't go," Mike said. "Robert Cohn's about to buy a drink" (147)—evidently, a rarity worth waiting for.

Mike, on the other hand, is more than willing to buy drinks on those rare occasions when he has the money to do it with. Brett is going to marry Mike Campbell, Jake tells Robert Cohn. "He's going to be rich as hell some day" (46). Cohn refuses to believe that Brett will marry Mike— and the matter remains in doubt at the end of the novel—but there is no question about Mike's potential wealth. He is trying, Brett says, to get his mother to pay for her divorce so they can be married. "Michael's people have loads of money" (60–70). But for the moment, he must make do on a skimpy allowance and is not even allowed to write checks. When he needs funds, he must "send a wire to the keeper" (88).

Mike is held under strict financial rein for the best of reasons: he is totally irresponsible about money. With his anticipated future wealth serving as a promissory note, he sponges off everyone in sight and simply does not pay his debts. After suffering a business collapse, he resorted to bankruptcy, an ungentlemanly if legal way of evading creditors. It is, as Brett realizes when she introduces him, one of the two most important and typical things about the man she intends to marry. The other is that he drinks too much: "This is Bill Gorton. This drunkard is Mike Campbell. Mr. Campbell is an undischarged bankrupt" (85).

Mike is no more conscientious about settling his debts to friends than to his former business "connections." Yet he possesses a charming self-deprecatory wit, and Bill Gorton, especially, is drawn to him. Bill likes Mike so much, in fact, that is very difficult for him to admit that Mike does not meet his obligations. One night in Pamplona, Mike, Bill, and Bill's girl, Edna, are thrown out of a bar by the police. "I don't know what happened," Bill says, "but some one had the police called to keep Mike out of the back room. There were some people that had known Mike at Cannes. What's the matter with Mike?" "Probably he owes them money," Jake says. "That's what people usually get bitter about" (192–93).

The next morning, Bill remembers the incident more clearly. "There was a fellow there that had helped pay Brett and Mike out of Cannes, once. He was damned nasty." The night before, Bill had emphatically defended his friend: "They can't say things like that about Mike." But in the light of dawn, he modifies the statement: "Nobody ought to have a right to say things about Mike. . . . They oughtn't to have any right. I wish to hell they didn't have any right" (208). Bill's loyalty to Mike eventually crumbles when, after the fiesta, another incident makes it clear *why* they have the right.

Jake, Bill, and Mike have hired a car together, and stop at "a very Ritz place" in Biarritz where they roll dice to see who will pay for the drinks. Mike loses three times in a row, but cannot pay for the third round:

> "I'm so sorry," Mike said. "I can't get it."
> "What's the matter?"
> "I've no money," Mike said. "I'm stony. I've just twenty francs. Here, take twenty francs."
> Bill's face sort of changed.
>
> (233)

He had had just enough money for the hotel in Pamplona, Mike explains, though it turns out that Brett has given him all of her cash to pay his bill. Mike is hence unable to help pay for their car, and his promise to send Jake what he owes is hardly reassuring.

Mike continually banters about his bankruptcy, as if making light of the obligations might somehow cause them to disappear. "I'm a tremendous bankrupt," he declares. "I owe money to everybody." He will not go into the ring after the running of the bulls because "it wouldn't be fair to my creditors." "One never gets anywhere by discussing finances," he comments, but he is unable to resist touching the wound by discussing his own (196, 204, 234). There is the story, for example, of the medals and Mike's tailor. Invited to "a whopping big dinner" in England where medals are to be worn, Mike prevails upon his tailor to supply him with some medals that had been left by another customer for cleaning. When the dinner fizzles out, he goes to a night club and passes the medals around. "Gave one to each girl. Form of souvenir. They thought I was hell's own shakes of a soldier. Gave away medals in a night club. Dashing fellow." The story delights his audience, but it had not seemed so funny to his tailor. If it was foolish to set too great store by military medals, as did the chap who left them with the tailor, it was quite wrong to wear medals that one had not earned. Mike fought in the war, and "must have some medals," but he does not know which ones and has never sent in for them. He is careless about them, quite as willing to don other people's ribbons as he is to spend other people's money (140–41).

Brett shares with Mike a carelessness of personal behavior that stems from a lifetime of having had things done for her. Her room in Madrid "was in that disorder produced only by those who have always had servants" (245). She makes appointments and does not keep them. She accepts the generosity of others as if it were her due. The Paris homosexuals who accompanied her to the dancings were undoubtedly paying her way. Count Mippipopolous finances her champagne binge. "Come on." she says at Pamplona. "Are these poisonous things paid for?" (149). In the bar of the Palace Hotel in Madrid, she asks Jake, "*Would* you buy a lady a drink?" (248). She has been given, she admits, "hell's own amount of credit" on her title (64). And, of course, she and Mike jointly ran up the bills they could not settle at Cannes. Moreover, she satisfies her demanding sexual appetites at the expense of others, effectively turning Robert into a steer, Mike into a swine, and Jake into a pimp. She is clearly not "très, très gentille," as Madame Duzinell, Jake's concierge, calls her after a bribe of 200 francs from the count (59–61).

On the other hand, Brett does adopt a strict code in connection with her sexual activity. She will not accept money for her favors. Thus she rejects the count's offer of "ten thousand dollars to go to Biarritz [or Cannes, or Monte Carlo] with him" (40–41). She pays Mike's way, not vice versa, out of the Hotel Montoya. Though Pedro Romero, the bullfighter, pays the hotel bill in Madrid, she will take nothing else from him. In sending Romero away against the urgings of the flesh, she has done the right thing at the cost of real personal anguish. She will be neither a whore nor "one of those bitches that ruins children" (247).

Furthermore, Brett's drunkenness and casual coupling can be at least partly excused by the unhappy circumstances of her past life. She lost one man she loved in the war and married another ("Ashley, chap she got the title from") who returned quite mad from serving as a sailor. "When he came home," Mike explains, "he wouldn't sleep in a bed. Always made Brett sleep on the floor. Finally, when he got really bad, he used to tell her he'd kill her. Always slept with a loaded service revolver. Brett used to take the shells out when he'd gone to sleep. She hasn't had an absolutely happy life" (207). Like Jake, she still suffers from war wounds. Like him, too, she articulates her awareness of the law of compensation. If she has put chaps through hell, she's paying for it all now. "Don't we pay for all the things we do, though?" (34).

Brett Ashley's case is more ambiguous than that of Robert Cohn or Mike Campbell. Morally, she is neither angel nor devil but somewhere, rather fascinatingly, in between. It is almost as if Hemingway himself were alternately attracted to and repelled by Brett. In Carlos Baker's biography there is a strong implication that Hemingway either had, or wanted to have, an affair with Duff Twysden, the prototype for Brett. In the fall of 1925, Duff sent Hemingway a note asking for a loan: "Ernest my dear, forgive me for this effort but can you possibly lend me some money? I am in a stinking fix but for once only temporary and can pay you back *for sure.* I want 3,000 francs but for Gods sake lend me as much as you can" (Baker, *A Life Story*, 196). In the novel, as if to protect Duff, Hemingway transfers her behavior to Mike Campbell: it is Mike and not Brett who repeatedly asks for loans.

V

Hemingway's insistence on the need to earn and pay for what you get is in no way a statement in support of materialism, for it is accompanied by evident disgust with the crooked and corrupting values of the commercial world. Eager to line their pockets, the merchants of Pamplona double prices during the fiesta (163). Away go the café's marble-topped tables and comfortable white wicker chairs, to be replaced by cast-iron tables and severe folding chairs. The place looks "like a battleship stripped for action." The warship's objective, of course, is to relieve peasants and tourists alike of their cash. At the start of the fiesta, the peasants confine their drinking to the outlying shops, where wine sells for a cheap thirty centimes a liter. "They had come in so recently from the plains and the hills that it was necessary that they make their shifting in values gradually. . . . Money still had a definite value in hours worked and bushels of grain sold. Late in the fiesta it would not matter what they paid, nor where they bought." When the peasants reach the stage of heedlessness (epitomized by the futile death of one of them during the running of the bulls), they lose all sense of the dignity of labor, of hours worked and bushels sold (156).

The cancer of commercialism also threatens to infect bullfighting. Pedro Romero is forced to face a dangerously bad bull, who cannot see well the lure of the cape, because the promoters have paid for the bull and "don't want to lose their money" (221). The crowd sends a volley of cushions, bread, and vegetables into the ring where Belmonte, ill and more cautious than he once had been, is performing his art. "Belmonte was very good. But because he got thirty thousand pesetas and people had stayed in line all night to buy tickets to see him, the crowd demanded that he should be more than very good." His greatness had been "discounted and sold in advance," and nothing he could do would satisfy those who watched him do it (217–19).

The hotel keeper Montoya, an *aficionado* who represents bullfighting's conscience, puts up all the good toreros at his hotel and keeps in his room framed photographs of the bullfighters he "really believed in." The pictures of the merely commercial bullfighters, though, are consigned first to a desk drawer and then to the waste basket. Montoya welcomes Jake, a fellow *aficionado*, and is grateful for his advice not to deliver to Romero his invitation from the American ambassador. "People take a boy like that," Montoya explains. "They don't know what he's worth. . . . They start this Grand Hotel business, and in one year they're through" (176). Montoya is disposed to forgive Jake his friends, but that tolerance dissolves when he sees "Pedro Romero with a big glass of cognac in his hand, sitting laughing between me [Jake] and a woman with bare shoulders, at a table full of drunks. He did not even nod" (180–81). When Jake and his companions check out, Montoya does "not come near" them (232).

Romero, however, remains immune to the disease of commercialism and the caution unto cowardice it is likely to breed. He wants and expects to make money as a bullfighter. When Brett reads in his hand that there are thousands of bulls in his future, "Good," he says, and in an aside to Jake in Spanish, "At a thousand duros apiece." He has not yet begun to compromise his bullfighting, as Belmonte has, by insisting on manageable bulls with smallish horns (189, 218). Hemingway invokes the metaphor of profit and loss in comparing Romero's afternoon of triumph to the jeers that had greeted Belmonte:

> Pedro Romero had the greatness. He loved bull-fighting, and I think he loved the bulls, and I think he loved Brett. Everything of which he could control the locality he did in front of her all that afternoon. . . . But he did not do it for her at any loss to himself. He gained by it all through the afternoon.
>
> (220)

His willingness to take chances—one of the ways, Jake has proposed, in which you could pay "for everything that was any good." gives the bullfight, his relationship with Brett, and the fiesta itself a kind of dignity.

It hardly matters that "the Biarritz crowd" does not appreciate what he has accomplished, either with his bad bull or his good one (222). Hemingway through his narrator Jake regards the rich English and American tourists from Biarritz, come for one day of the quaint fiesta at

Pamplona, with undisguised scorn. Those who buy false wares, like the secretly manipulated boxer toys hawked on the streets of Paris, deserve no more than they get.

The depth of this contempt can be measured against the sympathetic portrayal of Wilson-Harris, the Englishman who fishes and plays three-handed bridge with Jake and Bill at Burguete. When his companions must leave, Harris (as the Americans call him) insists on buying them a bottle of wine apiece. The atmosphere is one of warm camaraderie, punctuated by Harris's regret that Bill and Jake must leave. As they board the bus for Pamplona, Harris presses still another gift upon each of them: a dozen flies that he has tied himself. "They're not first-rate flies at all," he insists. "I only thought if you fished them some time it might remind you of what a good time we had." It has been a good time indeed, so that Jake first wishes Harris were coming along to Pamplona but then recalls that "You couldn't tell how English would mix with each other, anyway" (135). But you *can* tell: a man who spends his holiday trout fishing in the Pyrenees and behaves so generously would not have mixed at all well with the carousing crew at the fiesta.

Hemingway's major characters in the novel are all, with the exception of Romero, English and American, and each is easily distinguishable from the others. The foreigners, though, he tends to stereotype. Most of the Europeans in the book are French or Spanish, and these two nationalities are characterized almost solely on the basis of their attitude toward money. French standards of value are epitomized by Jake's concierge, who will not admit shabbily dressed friends of Jake to his quarters and who conveniently changes her mind about Brett—from "a species of woman" to "a lady . . . of very good family" on the strength of the count's largesse (39–40, 59). In *The Sun Also Rises*, Frenchmen always have their hands out, like the dining-car conductor who pockets ten francs but does nothing to earn them (91). In an interior monologue, Jake dissects the French national character after overtipping a waiter.

> Everything is on such a clear financial basis in France. It is the simplest country to live in. No one makes things complicated by becoming your friend for any obscure reason. If you want people to like you you have only to spend a little money. I spent a little money and the waiter liked me. He appreciated my valuable qualities.
>
> (237)

Repetition and the pun on "valuable qualities" underscore the irony.

Jake prefers Spain to France, just as he prefers bullfighting, a sport which cannot be fixed, to Viennese prize-fights and French and Belgian bicycle racing where the contestants "had raced among themselves so often that it did not make much difference who won. . . . The money could be arranged" (240). Spaniards, unlike Frenchmen, were likely to be friendly for no good financial reason at all. The Basques share a crowded bus with Bill and Jake, and they all share their wine, the Americans from bottles they have just bought, the Spanish from their wine-skins. When the bus stops at a *posada* in a small town, Bill and Jake each have an *aguardiente*, at twenty centimes apiece. "I gave the woman fifty centimes to make a tip, and she gave me back the copper piece, thinking I had misunderstood the price." Two of the Basques join them, and the cost of the drinks is split equally between them (109–12). On opening day of the fiesta at Pamplona, Spanish peasants in a wine-shop will not let Jake and his friends pay for wine and food. They will accept in return only "a rinse of the mouth from the new wine-bag" Jake has bought at the "lowest price," because the shopkeeper discovers he intends to drink out of it, not resell it in Bayonne (160–61). Spanish peasants, with their ethic of sharing, display a dignity and readiness for fellowship not to be thought of among the French.

The minor character who best exemplifies the morality of compensation is the Greek Count Mippipopolous. It is possible to consider him solely as the aging voluptuary that he appears, on the surface, to be. But to do so is to miss the point. It "means any amount to him" to buy fine champagne directly from Baron Mumm (63). All he wants out of wines, he says, is to enjoy them. When Brett objects to his ordering an expensive bottle of 1811 brandy, he responds in his customary demotic English.

> "Listen, my dear. I get more value for my money in old brandy than in any other antiquities."
> "Got many antiquities?"
> "I got a houseful."
>
> (68–69)

It is the same with food, and with women: the count can enjoy them properly because he has a sense of values acquired through long and painful experience (Rovit, *Hemingway*, 149–55). Count Mippipopolous has been involved in seven wars and four revolutions. In Abyssinia when he was twenty-one, two arrows went clean through his body: he shows Brett and Jake the scars. He is "one of us," as she says after this demonstration, because like them he has paid for the pleasures he now pursues (60). The temptation to judge the count by puritanical standards (Jake last sees him at Zelli's, surrounded by three girls he has just picked up) is tempered by an awareness that he has earned his pleasure, and that generosity and loyalty, as well as hedonism, form facets of his code.

VI

After delivering himself of his thoughts on the need to pay for the good things, Jake Barnes concludes rather cynically. "It seemed like a fine philosophy. In five years ... it will seem just as silly as all the other fine philosophies I've had" (152). Hemingway, however, did not abandon the code of compensation Jake enunciated, and continued to regard the rich—and the lure of easy money—as threats to artists in general and himself in particular. Money, he wrote John Dos Passos in 1929, had been the ruination of too many of their friends. Don Stewart had taken up with Jock Whitney, to say nothing of selling his soul to Hollywood for a $25,000 contract. John Peale Bishop's career had been spoiled by his wife's munificent income. The search for eternal youth had clearly sunk the Fitzgeralds (*Selected Letters*, 303). In *Green Hills of Africa* he cited money as the first way in which American writers could be destroyed. When they have made some money, he wrote, they "increase their standard of living and they are caught. They have to write to keep up their establishments, their wives, and so on, and they write slop" (23).

For his own part, as becomes clear in *A Moveable Feast*, Hemingway specifically blamed the demise of his first marriage on the predatory rich who followed Hadley, Bumby, and himself to the Vorarlberg:

> When you have two people who love each other, are happy and gay and really good work is being done by one or both of them, people are drawn to them. . . . Those who attract people . . . do not always learn about the good, the attractive, the charming, the soon-beloved, the generous, the understanding rich who have no bad qualities and who give each day the quality of a festival and who, when they have passed and taken the nourishment they needed, leave everything deader than the roots of any grass Attila's horses' hoofs have ever scoured.
>
> (188–92)

In the long story "The Snows of Kilimanjaro," Hemingway excoriated himself—in the guise of the writer-narrator Harry—for drinking and playing with the rich and letting his talent erode through idleness. The story, as Philip Young divined, was in part "a special and private . . . analysis of his past failures as a writer of prose fiction, as of 1936." He had not published a first-rate book since *A Farewell to Arms* seven years before, and like Harry, contemplated with despair all the stories he had not written (*Reconsideration*, 75–76).

The morality of compensation found expression not only in the fiction of the 1930s, but throughout Hemingway's work. In both *A Farewell to Arms* (1929) and *Across the River and Into the Trees* (1950) his protagonists are virtually obsessed with their obligations. After making his "separate peace" with the war, a totally justifiable escape, Frederic Henry feels "damned lonely" and tortures himself with recurring thoughts that he has deserted in a conventional way. Colonel Cantwell, facing certain death, carefully discharges his outstanding debts: he sends ducks to the waiter at the Gritti Palace Hotel, returns his girl's emeralds and her portrait, and makes her a gift of the shotguns that have served him so well. All of Hemingway's major protagonists share a sense of obligation—to a political ideal (Robert Jordan), to craft (Santiago as well as Romero), to wife and family (Harry Morgan). His heroes do not cast off commitments. They pay their bills in full, sometimes at the cost of their lives.

A teacher in the respectable suburb of Oak Park, Illinois, where Ernest Hemingway spent his youth, once wondered "how a boy brought up in Christian and Puritan nurture should know and write so well of the devil and the underworld" (Fenton, *Apprenticeship*, 2). He left Oak Park avid to experience, or at least witness, as much of life as he could. Yet as he explored the wider world, Hemingway carried with him an inheritance from the community where he grew up: a faith in the efficacy and staying power of certain moral values. Strong among these was the axiom that you had to earn your happiness, though the price might come high, with the corollary that easy money could ruin a man.

In his first novel, Hemingway imposed this standard on the expatriate world of the 1920s. At the end of *A Moveable Feast*, the last book he wrote, he looked back on his own years in Paris as an idyllic time when he worked hard and loved well and took nothing without making full payment. He expressed his nostalgia in the same metaphor that vibrates throughout *The Sun Also Rises*. "Paris was always worth it and you received return for whatever you brought to it. But this is how it was in the early days when we were very poor and very happy" (192).

HUMOR AS A MEASURE OF CHARACTER

I

Ernest Hemingway started out trying to be funny. On the evidence of his high school compositions, a classmate recalled, "one might have predicted that he would be a writer of humor" (Fenton, *Apprenticeship*, 12). In the *Trapeze*, the Oak Park and River Forest Township high school weekly paper, he made fun of himself, his sister, his friends, and the school itself. Some of these pieces were fashioned after the epistolary subliteracy of Ring Lardner's *You Know Me, Al* (1916).

"Well Sue as you are the editor this week I thot as how I would write and tell you about how successful I was with my editorials so you would be cheered up and feel how great a responsibility you have in swaying the public opinions." He had written "a hot editorial" on "Support the Swimming Team" and expected at least 500 people at the next meet, "and do you know how many guys there was there?" Only one, and he "never read no editorials" (Hemingway, "Ring").

Parody also figured in his contributions to the *Trapeze*. From the beginning, Hemingway understood how to take an elevated formal pattern—in this case, from Longfellow's "Psalm of Life"—and bring it crashing to earth.

> Lives of football men remind us,
> We can dive and kick and slug.

And departing leave behind us,
Hoof prints on another's mug.

("DEDICATED")

In his juvenile fiction, too, Ernest was working for laughs. One of his three published high school stories, "A Matter of Colour," does nothing but build up to a punch line delivered by and somewhat at the expense of a stolid Swede.

After brief tours with the Kansas City *Star* and the ambulance service on the Italian front during World War I, Hemingway came back to Chicago, landed a job writing booster copy for the *Cooperative Commonwealth*, and in his spare time experimented with humor. He fired off satirical rewrites of world news to *Vanity Fair*, which fired them right back. He also concocted mock advertising campaigns to entertain his friends. One involved bottling stockyard blood as "Bull Gore for Bigger Babies." Another ridiculed the "current Interchurch World campaign to sell Christianity in paid-for space" (Wright, "A Mid-Western Ad Man," 54) Together with Bill Horne and Y. K. Smith, he put together thirteen verses of the doggerel "Battle of Copenhagen," its humor aimed at ethnic groups.

Ten tribes of red Pawnees
Were sulking behind trees
at the Battle of Copenhagen.

Three thousand greasy Greeks
Arrayed in leathern breeks
And smelling strongly of leeks
at the Battle of Copenhagen.

A half a million Jews
Ran back to tell the news
of the Battle of Copenhagen.

Jokes at the expense of Jews were part of Hemingway's heritage. At school he was called Hemingstein, apparently because he was careful in money matters, and rather enjoyed the nickname.

When he caught on with the Toronto *Daily Star* and *Star Weekly*, first as a freelancer in 1920 and then as a regular feature writer and correspondent from early 1921 until the end of 1923, Hemingway found a commercial outlet for his brand of comedy. As *Star Weekly* editor J. Herbert

Cranston put it, "Hemingway . . . could write in good, plain Anglo-Saxon, and had a certain much prized gift of humor" (qtd. in Fenton, *Apprenticeship*, 72). His earliest pieces for the paper dealt with a shaky-kneed visit to a barber college for a free shave, a politician totally ignorant of the sport who appeared at prizefights to curry favor with the voters, and the disastrous consequences of believing the promotional copy issued by summer vacation resorts.

> Beautiful Lake Flyblow nestles like a plague spot in the heart of the great north woods. All around it rise the majestic hills. Above it towers the majestic sky. On every side of it is the majestic shore. The shore is lined with majestic dead fish—dead of loneliness.
>
> ("OUR CONFIDENTIAL")

Later, during nearly two years as a roving European correspondent based in Paris, Hemingway derided the empty life of do-nothing expatriates and refused to be impressed by the supposedly great men he encountered at conferences in Lausanne and Genoa. The watchword was "irreverence," the target all received wisdom. The attitude most commonly struck was that of the "wise guy," and as Delmore Schwartz pointed out, it was in this role that Hemingway first made an impression. "To be a wise guy," Schwartz wrote, "is to present an impudent, aggressive, knowing, and self-possessed face or 'front' to the world. The most obvious mark of the wise guy is his sense of humor which expresses his scorn and his sense of independence; he exercises it as one of the best ways of controlling a situation and of demonstrating his superiority to all situations" ("Fiction," 71).

The wise guy pose pervades "Condensing the Classics," an August 1921 venture into Shrinklit that reduced great novels and poems to a headline and a lead paragraph. Among the headlines were "Crazed Knight in Weird Tilt," "Big Cat in Flames," "Albatross Slayer Flays Prohibition," and "Slays His White Bride—Society Girl, Wed to African War-Hero, Found Strangled in Bed" (qtd. in Stephens, *Hemingway's Nonfiction*, 110–11). And this pose explains the irreverence with which Hemingway dismissed Benito Mussolini as the biggest bluff in Europe and the Russian foreign minister Tchitcherin as a homosexual dandy. Sometimes his journalistic humor was good-natured or high-spirited; more often it was satirical, with a target firmly in mind. As that satirical bent was translated into Hemingway's fiction, it became clear that no target was sacrosanct. His first fictional publication as a professional writer, the May 1922 two-page fable for the

Double Dealer called "A Divine Gesture," employed irony and dark humor in depicting the crucifixion of Jesus Christ.

When Hemingway left the newspaper business at the end of 1923, he had been turning out amusing copy for so long that he naturally tended to think of himself as a humorist. The wise guy strain of that humor led directly to *The Torrents of Spring*, the satiric novella he dashed off between drafts of *The Sun Also Rises* in November 1925. Like much of Hemingway's juvenilia, *Torrents* was a parody, in this case aimed at Sherwood Anderson and his novel *Dark Laughter*, which appeared earlier in the year. In that book, Anderson celebrated the wisdom and virtue of the unlettered primitive and indulged in a good deal of obtrusive philosophical musing. Anderson had earlier helped to introduce Hemingway to the literary world of Paris, but in *Torrents* the young writer relentlessly exposed the failings of his benefactor, while also making sport of expatriation, Literature with a capital L, Scott Fitzgerald, and Gertrude Stein.

Individual passages are very funny indeed. Scripps O'Neil, a Harvard graduate and would-be writer with two wives and minimal brain power, masquerades as the hero. He comes to a railway depot bearing the sign PETOSKEY in large letters. "Scripps read the sign again. Could this be Petoskey?" He comes across another sign advertising BROWN'S BEANERY THE BEST BY TEST. "Was this, after all, Brown's Beanery?" he wonders. He goes to a pump factory to get a job. "Could this really be a pump factory?" He walks up to a door with "a sign on it: KEEP OUT. THIS MEANS YOU. Can this mean me? Scripps wondered" (32, 35–36, 42). But the whole of *The Torrents of Spring* adds up to less than the sum of its sometimes hilarious parts. The characters are insignificant, the plot fantastic, the theme invisible. *Torrents* runs to about a hundred pages and could profitably have been cut to half that length.

Thirty years later, when his own work became the butt of various parodies, Hemingway renounced the genre. "Parodies," he told A. E. Hotchner, "are what you write when you are associate editor of the Harvard *Lampoon*. . . . The step up from writing parodies is writing on the wall above the urinal" (Hotchner, *Papa Hemingway*, 70). The epigraph to *The Torrents of Spring*, from Fielding, declares that "the only source of the true Ridiculous (as it appears to me) is affectation" (*Torrents*, 16). When Hemingway finished *Torrents* to resume work on *The Sun Also Rises* again, he remained keenly aware of the affected and the pretentious in all their forms but subordinated his wise guy satiric vein. In its place Hemingway achieved in *Sun* "a delicate balance of ridicule and affection" (Frankenburg, "Themes," 784–88) that contributes to character development and underscores the theme. The humor turns bitter as the novel progresses, but it does not start that way. And the bitterness is earned, not gratuitous.

II

Hemingway announced *The Sun Also Rises* with an inside joke. The two epigraphs—one from Gertrude Stein in conversation, the other from Ecclesiastes—are linked together rhetorically. "You are all a lost generation," Stein said, and in the Bible the preacher said, "One generation passeth away, and another generation cometh; but the earth abideth forever. . . . The sun also ariseth." But once one knows the provenance of Stein's remark, it becomes impossible to take it as seriously as the biblical passage.

In *A Moveable Feast*, written thirty years later, Hemingway told the story as he remembered it. Stein was having some trouble with her Ford, and the young mechanic who tried to repair it did not do a good job. Chastising him, the garage owner said, "You are all a génération perdue," and Stein appropriated his comment in talking to Hemingway. "That's what you all are," she told him, referring to the young people who served in the war. "You have no respect for anything. You drink yourselves to death. . . . You're all a lost generation, just exactly as the garage keeper said." When he wrote his first novel, Hemingway added, he "tried to balance Miss Stein's quotation from the garage keeper with one from Ecclesiastes," but he could not agree with her about the particular lostness of his generation: "all generations were lost by something and always had been and always would be" (*Moveable Feast*, 29–31).

It is not surprising that Hemingway, in *A Moveable Feast*, recalled the anecdote rather differently than he did on September 27, 1925, when he set it down as a foreword to the novel-in-progress he then intended to call *The Lost Generation*. The scene is the garage once again, but as it happens, the young mechanic who fixes Stein's car does an excellent job, and she asks the garage owner where he finds boys who work so well. She'd heard that one couldn't get them to work any more. He has no trouble with the young boys of 1925, the garageman says. He's taken and trained them himself. "It is the ones between twenty-two and thirty that are no good. C'est un génération perdu. No one wants them. They are no good. They were spoiled. The young ones, the new ones are all right again."

Two things vary in this earlier version of the "lost generation" story. First, Stein does not generalize from the garageman's remark. Second and more important, instead of denying the uniqueness of his generation, Hemingway insists upon it: "this generation that is lost has nothing to do with any Younger generation about whose outcome much literary speculation occurred in times past. This is not a question of what kind of mothers will flappers make or where is bobbed hair leading us [the sorts of subjects addressed by the Fitzgeralds in magazine articles at the time]. This is about something that is already finished. For whatever is going to happen to the generation of which I am a part has already happened." No matter what future entanglements or complications or promised salvations occur, "none of it will matter particularly to this generation because to them the things that are given to people to happen have already happened" (Hemingway Collection, Item 202c).

Hemingway's preface was subsequently cut, so that Stein's remark stands on the page without elaboration, unless you happen to read *A Moveable Feast* or Item 202c in the Hemingway Collection at the Kennedy library in Boston. But the private joke—that Stein's aphorism came originally from the lips of a French garage owner and that it is his voice, not that of the pontifical Stein, that is juxtaposed to the eternal Word—could not have escaped Hemingway's consciousness as he was working on *The Sun Also Rises*. The dual epigraphs suggest the complicated nature of the book's tone, an intricate mixture of humorous and serious elements, with the tone shifting according to which character is speaking.

The Sun Also Rises leans heavily on dialogue; the characters reveal themselves largely through what they do and say, with only occasional interpretive suggestions from the narrator. Most of the characters are capable of producing merriment in others, whether they intend to do so or not. What is remarkable is how different their kinds of humor are and how they are distinguished from one another in this way.

Hemingway had an excellent ear for talk, and much that is funny in *The Sun Also Rises* depends on that gift. Consider, for instance, the pidgin English of Count Mippipopolous, which features the rugged Anglo-Saxon verb "got," does not discriminate between tenses, and shows a knack for choosing almost the right word. "You got class all over you," he tells Brett. "You got the most class of anybody I ever seen." "Nice of you," she responds. "Mummy would be pleased" (65). This early discussion delineates Brett's wry manner and the count's serious attention to the best things in life: beautiful women and objects, excellent food and drink. Moreover, the discussion foreshadows certain questions that the novel eventually confronts. What constitutes "class" in human behavior? Do the count's hedonistic values suffice?

Belaboring the origins of humor is notoriously unrewarding. There used to be a course in comedy at Yale that the undergraduates critiqued as "English 63. Comedy. 63 dollars worth of books and not a laugh in the course." Still, it needs to be observed that Hemingway's humor in *The Sun Also Rises*, like that in the Count Mippipopolous–Lady Ashley exchange, usually depends on what the philosopher Paul Morreall calls "incongruity of presentation" (*Taking Laughter*, 69–84). "Hemingway's primary technique of humor," Sheldon Grebstein asserted in his fine treatment of the subject, "is that of incongruous juxtaposition," including the juxtaposition of "highbrow speech against the vulgate" (*Hemingway's Craft*, 172). Working with word play—verbal slips, puns, double entendre—James Hinkle located some sixty jokes embedded in the novel. But there is more to it than word play, for Hemingway plays with ideas as well, adopting an incongruous point of view, confusing categories, violating logical principles, and so forth. The precise technique varies from character to character, and some characters are a good deal funnier than others.

Jake Barnes tells the story of *The Sun Also Rises* so unobtrusively and convincingly that it never occurs to us to challenge his view of events, as for instance we tend to do with that of Frederic Henry in *A Farewell to Arms*. Jake deserves sympathy because of his wound, but he wins the reader's trust because of his capacity to assess human behavior with objectivity. Like the prototypical newspaperman, he has few illusions about anyone, including himself. So he adopts a posture of irony, one that moves from a good-natured sarcasm at the beginning of the novel to a biting, bitterly sardonic strain at the end.

In chapter 3 Jake picks up a streetwalker and takes her to dinner "because of a vague sentimental idea that it would be nice to eat with some one." But the girl objects to the place he takes her. "This is no great thing of a restaurant," she says. "No," Jake admits "Maybe you would rather go to Foyot's. Why don't you keep the cab and go on?" (24). He takes a cynical view of the political and journalistic professions as well.

At eleven o'clock I went over to the Quai d'Orsay in a taxi and went in and sat with about a dozen correspondents, while the foreign-office mouthpiece, a young Nouvelle Revue Française diplomat in horn-rimmed spectacles, talked and answered questions for half an hour. . . . Several people asked questions to hear themselves talk and there were a couple of questions asked by news service men who wanted to know the answers. There was no news.

(44)

His concierge has social pretensions and wants to make sure that all of Jake's guests measure up to her standards. If they do not, she sends them away. It gets to the point where one friend, "an extremely underfed-looking painter," writes Jake a letter asking for "a pass to get by the concierge" (60).

Where his war wound is concerned, Jake obviously does not think it funny himself, but he is capable of seeing the humor in the way others react to it. He is particularly amused by the "wonderful speech" of the Italian liaison colonel who came to see him in the Ospedale Maggiore in Milan:

"You, a foreigner, an Englishman" (any foreigner was an Englishman), "have given more than your life." What a speech! I would like to have it illuminated to hang in the office. He never laughed. He was putting himself in my place, I guess. "Che mala fortuna! Che mala fortuna!"

(39)

In conversation, the subject is taboo. He's "sick," Jake tells his *poule* (23). "Well, let's shut up about it," he tells Brett (34). When the count proposes that Jake and Brett get married, they collaborate on an evasive reply. "We want to lead our own lives," Jake says. "We have our careers," Brett chimes in (68).

Twice Bill Gorton hovers on the brink of the forbidden subject. Why, he wonders, did Brett go to San Sebastian with Cohn? "Why didn't she go off with some of her own people? Or you?—he slurred that over—or me? Why not me?" The next day, while they are fishing the Irati, Bill refers to the wound again in the course of satirizing the conventional stateside view of expatriation. According to this view, he tells Jake, expatriates like himself "don't work. One group claims women support you. Another group claims you're impotent."

"No," Jake responds forthrightly, "I just had an accident." But Bill shuns the topic. "Never mention that," he tells Jake. "That's the sort of thing . . . you ought to work up into a mystery. Like Henry's bicycle." The reference is to the improbable rumor that a childhood bicycle injury compromised the masculinity of Henry James. This passage caused a good deal of consternation at Scribner's before they allowed it to stand, stripped of the identifying surname. In context, it allows Jake and Bill to guide their conversation in a related but less personally sensitive direction.

The important thing to note is Jake's capacity to put himself in Bill's place. Bill had been doing splendidly but then, Jake thinks, "I was afraid he thought he had hurt me with that crack about being impotent." So Jake takes the cue from Henry's bicycle to launch into an inane discussion of whether it was on two wheels or three, on a horse or in an airplane, that the Master suffered his injury. This leads to joysticks, though, and eventually Bill can only clear the air by telling Jake how fond he is of him (120–21).

It is not talk about his injury that most distresses Jake, of course, but the way it impairs his relationship with Brett. At the fiesta the high spirits of the fishing trip dissipate as Brett transforms the men around her into steers or swine. Cohn adopts an annoying air of superiority, then an equally annoying pose of suffering. Mike Campbell rides him unmercifully in attacks that Jake despises himself for enjoying. Brett further compromises Jake's integrity by persuading him to take her to Pedro Romero. Eventually Jake's sardonic bent assumes a bitterness that inhibits rather than encourages laughter. "It seemed they were all such nice people," he reflects at mid-fiesta (150). On the last evening in Pamplona, after Brett has run off with Romero, Jake feels "low as hell" and drinks absinthe in an attempt to brighten his mood. "Well," Bill says, "it was a swell fiesta." "Yes," Jake answers, "something doing all the time" (226).

By the time he and Bill and Mike have parted, Jake Barnes is in the grip of a thoroughgoing cynicism. A few weeks earlier, he seemed to be enjoying the count's unabashed cultivation of material pleasures: "We dined at a restaurant in the Bois. It was a good dinner. Food had an excellent place in the count's values. So did wine. The count was in fine form during the meal. So was Brett. It was a good party" (68). During the fiesta, however, he learns how devastating it can be to stay on at a party with Brett. And he is reminded repeatedly by Cohn, by Campbell, and by Romero of his own incapacity to make love to the woman he loves. Food and drink and friendship are the pleasures left to him, but the first two have lost their savor, and it sometimes seems that all three must be purchased.

From that point to the end of the novel, Jake cannot enjoy human transactions. There is some healing benefit to be derived from diving into the ocean off San Sebastian, but at the hotel the corrupt bike riders are arranging who will win the following day and then the two wires from Lady Ashley arrive: "COULD YOU COME HOTEL MONTANA MADRID AM RATHER IN TROUBLE BRETT" (242). And Jake must answer the call.

In Madrid, things go badly. Jake is nervous about leaving his bags downstairs at the somewhat seedy Hotel Montana. Perhaps it is true that the "personages" of the establishment are "rigidly selected," but nonetheless he "would welcome the upbringal" of his bags. As for Brett, she keeps insisting that she doesn't want to talk about her time with Romero, but she cannot resist going on about it. Jake becomes increasingly mono-syllabic in response and then proceeds to get drunk. At the Palace Hotel bar downtown, they each have three martinis before lunch. Aside from Romero, there is nothing to talk about. "Isn't it a nice bar?" Brett asks. "They're all nice bars," Jake answers.

At the end they sit close to each other in the taxi and Brett says, "Oh, Jake, we could have had such a damned good time together." The mounted policeman ahead raises his baton and the taxi slows suddenly, pressing Brett against him. "Yes," Jake says, "Isn't it pretty to think so?" (245–51). Hemingway tried that closing line two other ways—"It's nice as hell to think so" and "Isn't it nice to think so"—before settling on "pretty" as the adjective that exactly communicates Jake's bitterness and despair (Baker, *Writer*, 155). Brett is going back to Mike, but for Jake there is no one, no hope, and no humor.

At certain places in the first draft of the novel, Hemingway inter-changed "I" with "Jake." The parallels between author and character are marked enough to suppose that for the most part Jake Barnes thinks and talks very much like Ernest Hemingway himself. Jake is a repository of the same ethnic and nationalistic prejudices, for instance, that often cropped up in Hemingway's juvenilia and journalism. Mrs. Braddocks, loud and rude, "was a Canadian and had all their easy social graces" (25). The German maître d'hôtel at Montoya's, nosy and knowing, is satisfac-torily put in his place by Bill Gorton (214–15). The French are grasping (237). Spanish peasants, on the other hand, generously share their food, wine, and companionship. The Basques who accompany Bill and Jake on the bus ride to Burguete offer them a drink from their big leather wine-bag. As Jake tips up the wineskin, one of the Basques imitates the sound of a klaxon motor horn so suddenly and surprisingly that Jake spills some of the wine. A few minutes later, he fools Jake with the klaxon again, and everyone laughs (109).

The most brutal ethnic humor in the book is directed at Robert Cohn. Harvey Stone and Jake are having a drink at the Select when Cohn comes up. "Hello, Robert," Stone says, "I was just telling Jake here that you're a moron" (50). Immediately thereafter Frances Clyne devastates Cohn at greater length, also in the presence of Jake: "friendly joking" compared "to what went on later" (56). What went on later, at its worst, came in the form of Mike Campbell's increasingly unfunny insults at Pamplona.

The primary source of information about Cohn and the group's attitude toward him is Jake as narrator. He artfully belittles Cohn throughout, but especially in the opening chapter. "Robert Cohn was once middleweight boxing champion of Princeton," the novel begins, and the depreciation follows at once: "Do not think that I am very much impressed by that as a boxing title, but it meant a lot to Cohn." As a "very shy and thoroughly nice boy," Cohn did not use his skill to knock down any of those who were snooty to him, as a Jew, at Princeton. In the gym itself, however, he was overmatched once and "got his nose permanently flattened. This . . . gave him a certain satisfaction of some strange sort, and it certainly improved his nose." Jake adds that he never met anyone in Cohn's class at Princeton who remembered him. Having disposed of Cohn's college career, Barnes continues his demeaning biographical account.

Cohn emerged from Princeton "with painful self-consciousness and the flattened nose, and was married by the first girl who was nice to him." Married by, not to. After siring three children in five years and losing most of the fifty thousand dollars his father left him, Cohn had just about made up his mind to leave his wife when she left him instead, running off "with a miniature-painter." A *miniature*-painter! Next, Cohn went to California and bought his way into the editorship of a literary magazine, but it became too expensive and he had to give it up. Meanwhile, he had "been taken in hand by a lady who hoped to rise with the magazine. She was very forceful, and Cohn never had a chance of not being taken in hand." This was Frances, who did not love Cohn but wanted to "get what there was to get while there was still something available" and then to marry him. She brought Cohn to Europe, where she had been educated, though he "would rather have been in America." Cohn managed to produce a novel that was "not really such a bad novel as the critics later called it," and for the first time began to think of himself as attractive to women and able to assert himself with them (12–13).

At this dangerous stage of his continuing adolescence, Robert Cohn meets Brett Ashley, with her curves like the hull of a racing yacht. Gazing at her, he "looked a great deal as his compatriot must have looked when he saw the promised land. Cohn, of course, was much younger. But he had that look of eager, deserving expectation" (29). The mode of discourse is obviously ridicule, and Cohn's subsequent behavior—romanticizing his affair with Brett, adopting an air of superiority toward Jake and Bill on that score, excessive barbering—well merits ridicule. Still, the opening salvo pretty much settles his hash.

To his credit, at one stage in Pamplona it appears that Cohn may be achieving a new maturity. He has foolishly proclaimed that he might be bored at the bullfights. Afterward, Bill and Mike kid him about that, and

Cohn is able to laugh at himself. "No. I wasn't bored. I wish you'd forgive me that." Bill forgives him, but not the rivalrous Mike. He continues baiting Cohn until even Brett tells him to "shove it along" (169–70). From then on, despite Cohn's outbreak of pugilistic violence, Mike supplants him as the villain of the piece. And Mike's descent can be accurately calibrated on the scale of his humor, which becomes decreasingly funny over time.

On first introduction, Mike Campbell seems an engaging ne'er-do-well. He is more than a little drunk on arrival in Paris and Brett accurately introduces him to Bill Gorton as "an undischarged bankrupt," but he is so excited about seeing Brett again and so eagerly anticipatory about the night ahead that these shortcomings appear unimportant. "I say, Brett," he thrice tells her, "you *are* a lovely piece." He also asks Jake and Bill twice, "Isn't she a lovely piece?" To taunt him, Bill asks Mike to go along to the prizefight, but he and Brett have something else in mind. "I'm sorry I can't go," Mike says, and Brett laughs (85–86).

When the group reassembles in Pamplona, Mike works his vein of humorous repetition once again. Brett suggests that he tell the story of the time his horse bolted down Piccadilly, but Mike refuses. "I'll not tell that story. It reflects discredit on me." Well, she suggests, tell them about the medals. "I'll not. That story reflects great discredit upon me." Brett could tell it, he supposes. "She tells all the stories that reflect discredit on me" (139). In the end, he tells the medal story himself, which does indeed place him in an unfavorable light.

Once started, Mike persists in self-deprecation. He went bankrupt two ways—"gradually and then suddenly." What brought it on were "Friends . . . —I had a lot of friends. False friends. Then I had creditors, too. Probably had more creditors than anybody in England" (136). Soon thereafter comes the one successful dinner at the fiesta, where both Bill and Mike were "very funny. . . . They were good together" (150). But Mike's bantering becomes progressively more strident as the drinking accelerates, Cohn continues to hang about in pursuit of his lady love, and Brett decides she must have Pedro Romero.

Mike ventilates his outrage in a vicious assault on Cohn. "Why do you follow Brett around like a poor bloody steer? Don't you know you're not wanted? I know when I'm not wanted. Why don't you know when you're not wanted? You came down to San Sebastian where you weren't wanted, and followed Brett around like a bloody steer." None of their friends at San Sebastian would invite him to come along, Mike tells Cohn. "You can't blame them hardly. Can you? I asked them to. They wouldn't do it. You can't blame them, now. Can you? Now answer me. Can you blame them? . . . I can't blame them, Can you blame them? Why do you follow Brett around?" (146–47). Here, the repetition abuses another human being, and there is nothing funny about it.

Mike's habit of disparaging himself also palls as his financial irresponsibility becomes increasingly manifest "Who cares if he is a damn bankrupt?" Bill remarks after they are ejected from a bar by people Mike owes money to (192). The answer, finally, is that everyone cares. Mike seeks to disarm criticism by accusing himself before others do so, but that does not always amuse. At the last meeting with Bill and Jake at Biarritz, when it turns out that Mike is broke and cannot pay for the drinks he's gambled for at poker dice, and that he's spent all of Brett's money as well, Mike again touches the wound, but less amusingly this time. Bill proposes another drink. "Damned good idea," Mike says. "One never gets anywhere by discussing finances." Since they've rented a car for the day, Mike suggests they "take a drive. It might do my credit good." They decide to drive down to Hendaye, although, Mike admits, he hasn't "any credit along the coast" (234). Under the circumstances, Mike's attempts at humor invite contempt. As Morreall points out, it can be "morally inappropriate to laugh about one's own situation, if by doing so we are detaching ourselves from our own moral responsibilities" (*Taking Laughter*, 112–13).

In less blameworthy fashion, Brett makes fun of her own drunkenness and promiscuity. The count advises her to drink the champagne slowly, and later she can get drunk. "Drunk? Drunk?" she replies (66). When Jakes brings his *poule* to the *bal musette*, Brett is amused by the supposed disrespect for her status as a pure woman. "It's an insult to all of us," she laughs. "It's in restraint of trade," she laughs again (30). Laughing at herself in this way serves, of course, to forestall any change in her style of life. In this sense it is fitting that in the end she plans to go back to Mike, who is "so damned nice" and "so awful" and so much her "sort of thing" (243).

III

As a character Bill Gorton is clearly modeled on the humorist Donald Ogden Stewart, who went to Pamplona in 1925 with the Hemingways, Harold Loeb, Bill Smith, Pat Guthrie, and Lady Duff Twysden. Stewart later characterized Hemingway's novel as almost reportorial in its fidelity to the events of the fiesta. He may have come to that judgment, which undervalues the book's artistry, largely as a consequence of recognizing so much of his own humor in Bill Gorton's material. In fact Don Stewart, like Bill Gorton, was almost constitutionally incapable of not amusing people. He "could turn a Sunday school picnic into a public holiday," Scott Fitzgerald said ("Reminiscences," 231–32).

It was very much in character, then, for Hemingway to make Bill Gorton–Don Stewart the source of humor in the two most high-spirited chapters of the novel. These are chapter 8, where Bill and Jake go out to dinner in Paris, and chapter 12, where they go fishing along the Irati. In the Paris chapter, Bill has only recently come to Europe and has just returned from a trip to Austria and Hungary. Gorton is described as "very happy." His last book had sold well. He's excited about the new crop of young light-heavyweights. He knows how to have a good time. He finds people and places wonderful. The States were wonderful, he tells Jake. New York was wonderful. Vienna was wonderful, he writes. "Then a card from Budapest: 'Jake, Budapest is wonderful.'" Jake greets Bill on his return to Paris: "Well," [Jake] said, "I hear you had a wonderful trip." "Wonderful," he said. "Budapest is absolutely wonderful" (75–76). A few days later, Jake and Bill meet an American family on the train to Pamplona, and the father asks if they're having a good trip. "Wonderful," Bill says (91).

This sort of nonsense is much funnier when spoken than on the page, as Jackson Benson has pointed out (*The Writer's Art*, 68–69). So is the marvelous stuffed dog discussion on the way to dinner. Jake and Bill walk by a taxidermist's and Bill asks, "Want to buy anything? Nice stuffed dog?"

> "Come on," I said. "You're pie-eyed."
>
> "Pretty nice stuffed dogs," Bill said. "Certainly brighten up your flat."
>
> "Come on."
>
> "Just one stuffed dog. I can take 'em or leave 'em alone. But listen, Jake. Just one stuffed dog."
>
> "Come on."
>
> "Mean everything in the world after you bought it. Simple exchange of values. You give them money. They give you a stuffed dog."
>
> "We'll get one on the way back."
>
> "All right. Have it your own way. Road to hell paved with unbought stuffed dogs. Not my fault."
>
> We went on.
>
> "How'd you feel that way about dogs so sudden?"
>
> "Always felt that way about dogs. Always been a great lover of stuffed animals."
>
> (78–79)

Then they go off on the subject of not being daunted, but Bill understands the humorous potential of the echo. "See that horse-cab?" he asks Jake. "Going to have that horse-cab stuffed for you for Christmas. Going to give all my friends stuffed animals." Brett comes along in a taxi—"Beautiful lady," said Bill. "Going to kidnap us" (79–80)—and they hit it off beautifully. It is too bad, Bill thinks, that she's engaged to Mike. Still, "What'll I send them? Think they'd like a couple of stuffed race-horses?" (81).

Liquor obviously helps to fuel Bill's comedy. "Don [crossed out] Bill was the best of the lot," Hemingway wrote in a discarded first draft, "and he was on a hilarious drunk and thought everybody else was and became angry if they were not" (Hemingway Collection, Item 202c). Alcohol not only encourages his tomfoolery, it also provides him with a potent source of the topical humor that runs through chapter 12: "Direct action . . . beats legislation," Bill remarks when Jake doctors their rum punches (116). Bill's voice so predominates in this Burguete section that in the first draft Hemingway tried switching to him as the first-person narrator (Svoboda, *Hemingway*, 42) before returning to Jake as narrator and straight man for Bill's repartee. Among other things, Bill makes fun of the clichés of literary criticism, Bible Belt morality, H. L. Mencken, and—especially—the Scopes trial and William Jennings Bryan's rhetoric in attacking the theory of evolution. Putting aside a hard-boiled egg and unwrapping a drumstick, Bill reverses the order "for Bryan's sake. As a tribute to the Great Commoner. First the chicken; then the egg."

"Wonder what day God created the chicken?"

"Oh," said Bill . . . "how should we know? We should not question. Our stay on earth is not for long. Let us rejoice and believe and give thanks."

"Let us not doubt, brother," he adds. "Let us not pry into the holy mysteries of the hen-coop with simian fingers." Instead, "Let us utilize the fowls of the air. Let us utilize the product of the vine. Will you utilize a little, brother?" (126).

Jake will, and so will Bill, and so will the genial Englishman named Wilson-Harris they play three-handed bridge with in the evening.

As almost every commentator on the novel has noticed, the interlude at Burguete stands in counterpoint to the sophisticated pretentiousness of Paris and the destructive passions of Pamplona. In the first draft, Hemingway let Jake and Bill confess how they felt about their lives on that fishing trip. No one can believe that he's happy, Bill remarks, but "honest to God," he is. Jake is too, he says, "ninety percent of the time," although they're both a little embarrassed to confess it (Item 202c). In fact, Jake and Bill are almost always in good spirits when together or with other male companions. Stewart himself blamed the trouble at Pamplona in 1925 on that old "devil sex." The previous year, when he, Ernest, Hadley, John Dos Passos, Bill Bird, and Bob McAlmon had gone to Pamplona for the bullfights, the trip had been a great success.

By and large, Bill Gorton directs his jibes at ideas and institutions, not human beings. In this way, he provides a model of behavior that—unlike the code of the intrepid Romero—others can emulate. "I did not care what it was all about," Jake reflects in one of his interior monologues. "All I wanted to know was how to live in it" (152). Gorton seems to have discovered how: without Jake's bitter sarcasm, without Mike and Brett's disingenuous self-deprecation, without Robert's self-pity, with the best will in the world.

Not everyone, it might be objected, is temperamentally suited to enjoy life as much as Gorton, just as very few could be expected to entertain one's companions as well as he. Yet in the very subject matter of his humor, Hemingway conveys an attitude toward existence available to all. It is easiest to understand, through negation, which attitudes are invalid. The religious preach brotherhood and arrange for special privileges. The do-gooding of the Prohibitionists does no good. The know-nothingism of the "creationists" is ridiculous, and so is the pedantic "Irony and Pity" catchphrase of the literati. On the positive side, at least one basic value emerges in the subtext of such ventures into comedy as the twelve shoeshines Bill buys Mike and his persistent sales pitch for stuffed dogs.

The shoeshine scene represents Bill's humor for once gone off the rails under the tensions of Pamplona. When bootblack after bootblack polishes Mike's shoes to a higher gloss, the repetition becomes more awkward than amusing. By contrast, even a taxidermist would be likely to find the stuffed dog passage funny. Whether successful in inducing laughter or not, both scenes have a bearing on the theme of compensation in the novel (Donaldson, "Hemingway's Morality"). Casually dropped into the stuffed dog dialogue is Bill's comment about the exchange of values. This seemingly unimportant observation underscores Hemingway's theme that the good things in life—not exclusively limited to hedonistic pleasure—have to be earned through effort and experience. It is for this reason, in part, that the shoeshine episode falls flat, since Bill's jest contradicts that message by demeaning the honest trade of the bootblacks.

In his autobiography, Donald Ogden Stewart chastised himself for having produced so much of the "crazy humor" characteristic of Bill Gorton and pervasive in such Stewart books of the period as *A Parody Outline of History* (1921), *Perfect Behavior* (a 1922 takeoff on Emily Post), *Aunt Polly's Story of Mankind* (1923), *Mr. and Mrs. Haddock Abroad* (1924), *The Crazy Fool* (1925), and *Mr. and Mrs. Haddock in Paris, France* (1926). As his political beliefs swung to the left, Stewart came to believe that he should have used his gift for humor less to amuse his readers than to alert them to the ills of American society. And he seems never to have recognized the accomplishment of his friend Hemingway—whom he thought an indifferent humorist—in incorporating certain strains of humor, including his own nonsensical and topical predilections, within the framework of a novel that has an ethical, if not a political, statement to make.

Hemingway's early humor consisted mostly of parodies and pieces that by mocking others tacitly asserted his superiority. Later in his career his humor became increasingly dark, as in the macabre "A Natural History of the Dead" (1932). In the course of writing another unpublished tale along similar grisly lines, Hemingway took issue with Henry Seidel Canby's claim that there was "no humor in American writing . . . no humor in the way we write nor in the things we write about. I always thought there was but perhaps it was not clear enough; it needed a label so that they [the critics] would know it was funny when they read it" (Hemingway Collection, Item 636). *The Sun Also Rises* does not carry such a label and does not need to. In this novel, Hemingway used humor brilliantly to assess character and underline theme without descending to parody or black comedy. The novel stands as proof that Hemingway was "above all a magnificent craftsman, and among his prime virtues was the ability to laugh" (Grebstein, *Hemingway's Craft*, 201).

{ 18 }

A FAREWELL TO ARMS
AS LOVE STORY

A FAREWELL TO ARMS has usually been read as a classic love story, the tragic tale of two lovers driven together by the war who give themselves to each other in a blissful bonding that might have lasted indefinitely had not death cruelly snatched one away. The events of the novel take on a "fully idyllic" cast as Frederic Henry recalls them, one eminent critic observed (Wilson, "Gauge," 242). Frederic and Catherine Barkley, according to another, represent counterparts "of Paolo and Francesca, of Lucy and Richard Feverel, of all great lovers" (Lovett, "Ernest Hemingway," 615). Yet to interpret Hemingway's novel in this way undervalues his accomplishment. *A Farewell to Arms* is far subtler and more complicated than the conventional romantic novel, and the story it tells is anything but straightforward.

In 1941 Hemingway told a group of University of Hawaii professors that their students should not be reading *A Farewell to Arms*. That's "an immoral book," he said. Let them read *The Sun Also Rises* instead, he suggested: that was "very moral" (Baker, *A Life Story*, 359). In the earlier novel, he had demonstrated the evils of wasting one's resources on dissipation and sex. By calling *Farewell* immoral by comparison, he was applying the same ethical standards, and—perhaps—implying that his professorial listeners had not detected Frederic Henry's complicity in the corruption that surrounds him.

Though Lieutenant Henry encounters in Europe a world he never made, he succumbs with suspicious ease to the temptations that the war's climate of moral ambiguity presents to him. Like the sudden expatriates in *The Sun Also Rises*, he drinks to excess and when in his cups blasphemes and whores like a trooper. After replacing the whores with Catherine Barkley, he impregnates her and returns to the front where, during the retreat, he loses his ambulances, shoots one Italian soldier in anger, and leads another to his death before diving into a river to save his own life. Then he escapes to Switzerland with Catherine, who dies bearing his child and to whom—until she lies dying in a Lausanne hospital—he gives very little of himself.

We learn of all these matters through the account of Frederic Henry himself, who in dealing with his own sins tries to smooth them away, just as he tried to brush the taste of harlotry away with toothpaste. But Hemingway makes it clear between the lines that we should take what Lieutenant Henry has to say with a grain of salt. The difficulty of grasping this point derives from the reader's tendency to identify with Frederic and to accept his version of the story. Moreover, he functions as a trustworthy enough guide to the *action*. But as Hemingway warned, even when he wrote a novel in the first person, he was not to be held accountable for "the opinions" of his narrators (qtd. in Scott, "In Defense," 309). And he was careful, in commenting specifically on *A Farewell to Arms*, to refer to his protagonist as "the invented character," thus distinguishing between author and narrator.

People are forever misspelling Frederic Henry's name, and no wonder: only once does Hemingway supply it in full, and those who know him best usually do not call him by any name at all. Only during their last meeting does his great friend and roommate Rinaldi address him as "Federico" and "Fred." These nicknames—like the "Rinin" Frederic uses for Rinaldi—suggest how close these two "war brothers" are, but they are not nearly as suggestive as the term of affection Rinaldi repeatedly uses in talking to Frederic: "baby."

In conversation, Frederic naturally refers to the priest as "father," but the priest does not call him "son" in return. Instead, during an early encounter (a scene that does not actually take place in the book) the priest called him "a boy." We discover this when Catherine, who is mad "only a little sometimes," directs Frederic through a charade designed to let her pretend that he is a reincarnation of the fiancé she lost in the "ghastly show" at the Somme. Do this, do that, touch me so, she directs him. Frederic does so, and she observes, in approval, that he is "a very good boy." That, he replies, is what the priest told him (*Farewell*, 31).

In the light of this curious scene, in which Frederic is instructed to call her "Catherine" and to say "I've come back to Catherine in the night" (30), it is the more remarkable that nowhere in the novel does she refer to him by his name. Her most frequent endearment is "darling," but on several occasions she too reverts to the use of "boy." Sending him off to the front, she cautions him to "be a good boy and be careful" (43). When he wants to make love before his operation, she calls him "such a silly boy" (102); when he sleeps with his arm around the pillow, he reminds her of "a little boy" (104). Nor are Catherine and the priest the only ones to regard Frederic Henry as a boy. The first nurse at Milan calls him "a sick boy" and he objects not to the noun but the adjective: "I'm not sick. I'm wounded" (85). The house doctor cautions him to be "a good boy" until Dr. Valentini can come (98). Valentini arrives and cheerfully tells him he is "a fine boy" (99). Rinaldi understands that Frederic must regard himself as "the fine good Anglo-Saxon boy" (168). "Poor baby," he comments when Frederic says he's in love (169); "poor boy," Count Greffi remarks when Frederic admits to his religious doubt (261).

Whether they use "baby" or "boy," the other characters in *A Farewell to Arms* perceive Frederic as young, inexperienced, and unaware. The officers in the mess conduct their priest-baiting ritual for his dubious benefit as greenhorn, and in the same fraternity-initiation spirit involve him in drinking contests and propel him in the direction of the bawdy-house.

The sense in which Frederic Henry most clearly qualifies for boyhood rather than manhood is illustrated at Stresa, after he and Catherine are reunited. Appearing unexpectedly, Frederic breaks up the vacation trip of Catherine and her friend Ferguson, who is bitter about that and angry at Frederic for getting Catherine with child. "Be nice" to Ferguson anyway, Catherine tells him; think "how much we have and she hasn't anything." "I don't think she wants what we have," Frederic says, moving her to comment that "you don't know much, darling, for such a wise boy" (257).

Indeed he does not, and his inability to put himself in Ferguson's place bespeaks a self-obsession characteristic of the young. A mere boy in many ways, Frederic suffers from a pervasive lack of awareness. He does not know why he enlisted in the Italian army, or what he is fighting for. He lacks any perceptible ambition or purpose in life. He wants to be good, but he heedlessly pursues pleasure. During the course of his experiences in love and war, he does to some degree develop understanding. Anyone exposed to such a series of shocks—the unreasonable wound, the bollixed-up retreat, the death of his lover—might be expected to acquire not only trauma but a certain working knowledge. The question at issue has to do with the extent of his education, with how far he has moved along the continuum from ignorant, self-centered youth to knowing, caring adulthood.

The contrast between sacred and profane love is established in the first scene of *A Farewell to Arms*. Frederic is drinking the afternoon away with a friend in the Villa Rossa, the officers' whorehouse, when the priest walks by. "My friend . . . pounded on the window to attract his attention. The priest looked up. He saw us and smiled. My friend motioned for him to come in. The priest shook his head and went on" (6). Later the priest provides his definition of love, which has nothing to do with the "passion and lust" Frederic has told him about. "When you love," the priest—with Hemingway—insists, "you wish to do things for. You wish to sacrifice for. You wish to serve" (72).

Henry learns from the priest that love amounts to more than sex, that—as Count Greffi later assures him—being in love is "a religious feeling" (263), that true lovers willingly serve and sacrifice. But actually living up to this gospel is very difficult. Neither Catherine nor Frederic manages to achieve the ideal love the priest describes, though they fail for strikingly different reasons.

The difference constitutes one of the ways in which Hemingway separates himself from his narrator. In a perfect love, both partners share equally, but manifestly Catherine is far more devoted to Frederic than he to her. When they first meet, Catherine is an emotional wreck because she had not given herself to the fiancé blown up at the Somme, and she sets out to correct that error with Frederic. She throws all of herself into the affair. She arranges to be transferred to the hospital in Milan and upon arrival immediately climbs into his bed, a practice she continues thereafter at some risk to her position as a nurse and with the eventual result of pregnancy. She willingly accompanies her lover up Lake Maggiore in a rainstorm on a dark night, never complains of her child-bearing discomfort, and even when dying thinks principally of him: "Poor darling" and "Don't worry, darling" (330–31).

Catherine's single goal has been to serve and protect Frederic. "I want what you want. . . . Just what you want" (106). She sees herself dead in the rain but feels sure she can keep him "safe. I know I can" (126). After his forced desertion from the army, she is eager to help him escape the military police. "I'll get you some place where they can't arrest you and then we'll have a lovely time" (252). In Switzerland she provides a world of physical sensation to keep him from obsessively thinking about the war.

Catherine makes these sacrifices for Frederic as part of her desire to obliterate herself. Several times she insists that she has submerged her personality into his. "There isn't any me any more," she says after they make love (106). And again, "there isn't any me. I'm you. Don't make up a separate me" (115). Shortly before he goes back to the front, she states that the two-way merger has been completed. "We really are the same one" (139). During these assertions, Frederic keeps his own counsel. Only once, near the end of the book, does he repeat her theory about their unity, and then he does so, paradoxically, in order to prevent her from trying to be more like him. Now large with child, Catherine proposes that he let his hair grow and that she cut hers so that then "we'd be just alike only one of us blonde and one of us dark"—a fetish Hemingway was to return to in several works, most notably the posthumously published *Garden of Eden*. Frederic resists the idea: he thinks his hair is long enough now and adds, "I wouldn't let you cut yours." But she persists. Wouldn't he like her hair short? "It might be nice short. Then we'd both be alike. Oh, darling, I want you so much I want to be you too." Frederic answers, "You are. We're the same one" (299), thereby avoiding any further talk about identical haircuts.

Significantly, Hemingway excised from an earlier draft of *A Farewell to Arms* a passage in which *Frederic* says that he felt a sense of identity with Catherine the moment they were reunited at the hospital in Milan. "We had come together as though we were two pieces of mercury that unite to make one. . . . We were one person." And in dialogue, *he* says, "Feel our heart. . . . It's the same" (Hemingway Collection, Item 64, 201–9). These sentiments are transferred to Catherine in the novel. When Frederic sees her, he says that he is in love with her, that he wants her. But when *she* says, "Feel our hearts beating," he only replies, "I don't care about our hearts. I want you" (92). It is Catherine who repeatedly asserts that they are but "one person." The effect of the change, as Hemingway certainly knew, was to transfer sympathy from Frederic to Catherine. He seeks physical satisfaction, while she is so romantically smitten as to lose herself in their love.

In her worshipful attitude toward Frederic, the best Catherine can hope for is that she might look like him by cutting her hair or act like him (another proposal of hers) by going to sleep at the same time. When the doctors sew her up after the caesarean, the scene in the operating room looks "like a drawing of the Inquisition" (325), and justly so, for she has committed the unpardonable sin of heresy. "You're my religion" (116), she tells Frederic, and she means it.

If Catherine fails to meet the priest's standard by loving not wisely but too well, with the prudential Frederic the case is quite the opposite. As the book progresses, he becomes more loving and less selfish, but only as compared to an initial policy toward Catherine that can best be defined as exploitative. During their first meetings in Gorizia, she poignantly reveals her vulnerability, but he treats her as he would any other potential conquest—as an opponent in a contest he intends to win. So he goes through the preliminary moves, saying "I love you" when he "did not love Catherine Barkley nor had any idea of loving her. This was a game, like bridge, in which you said things instead of playing cards" (30). In Milan, after his wounding, he has his reward for playing the game well, except that when she turns up at the hospital to be with him, he finds himself "crazy in love with her" although "God knows . . . he had not wanted to fall in love with any one" (91, 93).

The love he feels is almost entirely sexual, however, and derives from the pleasure she gives him, far superior to that dispensed by the girls at the Villa Rossa who "climbed all over you and put your cap on backward as a sign of affection between their trips upstairs with brother officers" (30). Since he is bedridden, she must come to him, a situation that symbolizes his role—then and later—as an accepter rather than provider of services.

During the fall and winter of 1918, presumably, their love reaches its most idyllic state. Waiting for Catherine's baby to arrive, they live in the mountains above Montreux, alone except for the landlord and his wife who were "very happy together too" (290–91), and as Frederic remembers it, "We had a fine life. We lived through the months of January and February and the winter was very fine and we were very happy" (306). But the flatness of the prose and the ominous touch about living through two winter months tend to undercut the explicit statement about their happiness, and even more contradictory is the novel's description of how they spent their time.

Happiness for Catherine consists of the opportunity to be alone, for the most extended period possible, with the man she worships. When they go to the racetrack in Milan with Mr. and Mrs. Meyers and others, she finds the company insupportable. "But, darling, I can't stand so many people," she says. "We don't see many," he objects, but she leads him off to watch the next race and have a drink together. Didn't he like it better when they were alone? Didn't being with the others make him feel lonely? Frederic agrees with monosyllabic curtness, and she capitulates, "Don't let me spoil your fun, darling. I'll go back whenever you want" (131–32).

In the mountains, where they know no one, the two lovers are very much alone. There is not much for them to do. They eat. They sleep. They read books and magazines bought in the town below. They buy a copy of "Hoyle" and play two-handed card games. They also play chess, and Frederic seems to prefer the game to making love.

> [Frederic:] "Now do you want to play chess?"
> [Catherine:] "I'd rather play with you."
> "No. Let's play chess."
> "And afterward we'll play?"
> "Yes."
> "All right."

> (300)

In short, they kill time, since her job ended with her pregnancy and his with his escape from the *carabinieri*.

In the way of "the winter sport" Frederic and Catherine take walks together, but neither of them knows how to ski. The doctor says she can't risk learning, but Frederic eagerly agrees to Mr. Guttingen's suggestion that his son teach him. Sensitive to his moods and increasingly aware of her matronly appearance, Catherine asks whether he wouldn't like "to go on a trip somewhere . . . and be with men and ski." Knowing that she would be devastated should he do so, Frederic refuses the suggestion. But he leaps at her proposal that he grow a beard. "All right," he says. "I'll grow one. It will give me something to do" (297–98). But growing a beard hardly amounts to "something to do," and in saying so he suggests how bored he must be. Two pages later he tells her again that he "won't ever go away . . . I'm no good when you're not there. I haven't any life at all any more" (300). The difference between them is clear-cut. Catherine has no life without him and desires none. Frederic has no life without her and regrets what he has left behind.

Short of idolizing her, Frederic could hardly have equaled the intensity of Catherine's love. But had he been more careful not to hurt her feelings, he would not have said that growing a beard would give him something to do or that he hadn't any life at all any more. The latter gaffe echoes his exquisitely inconsiderate remark at Stresa that "my life used to be full of everything. Now if you aren't with me I haven't a thing in the world" (256–57).

The most striking example of Frederic's insensitivity, however, occurs much earlier, when Catherine tells him she is nearly three months' pregnant. She brings up the subject reluctantly, afraid that the revelation will "worry" him or make him unhappy. She apologizes ("I took everything but it didn't make any difference"), offers him a drink to brighten his mood, and promises that she will see to all the details of finding a place for the baby to be born. But Frederic merely lies in bed without reassuring or even touching her. Finally she takes his hand, and this dialogue ensues:

> "You aren't angry are you, darling?"
> "No."
> "And you don't feel trapped."
> "Maybe a little. But not by you."
> "I didn't mean by me. You mustn't be stupid. I meant trapped at all."
> "You always feel trapped biologically."
> She went away a long way without stirring or removing her hand.
> "'Always' isn't a pretty word."

It certainly isn't, implying as it does that Frederic has had his share of affairs and gotten any number of girls pregnant and that they've always made him feel trapped. "But you see," Catherine points out, "I've never had a baby and I've never even loved any one. And I've tried to be the way you wanted and then you talk about 'always.'" He could cut off his tongue, Frederic says, yet he goes on to pick a quarrel as to whether she's "an authority" on the question of bravery and sends her away without the psychological comfort of lovemaking. She will visit him later in the night, but for the moment he prefers reading the old Boston papers with their stale news (139–41).

Another instance of Frederic's callousness follows shortly thereafter, on the night he must leave for the front. Having worked out the plan in advance, he takes Catherine to a hotel of assignation where one must pay in advance, the rooms are furnished in red plush with multiple mirrors, and she is made to feel like a whore. Throughout their time together, Frederic rarely displays honest, thoughtful concern for Catherine's feelings While she invariably thinks of him first, often he does not think of her at all.

All of this changes at the end as she lies dying of childbirth. Then Frederic wants to serve and sacrifice. As her pain intensifies, the doctor lets him administer the anesthetic, and though he is afraid of the numbers above two, he is glad of the chance to be of help. "It was very good of the doctor to let me do something," he reflects (317). Once her fatal hemorrhaging begins, he asks pleadingly, "Do you want me to do anything, Cat? Can I get you anything?" (331). But it is too late. There is nothing to be done.

Unlike Catherine, Frederic retains a belief in religion. Hence he prays for her in her extremity, and offers to call a priest to her bedside. Moreover, in another passage that Hemingway deleted from the novel, he thinks long and bitter thoughts about losing Catherine and the inadequacy of conventional religious consolation.

> They say the only way you can keep a thing is to lose it and this may be true but I do not admire it. The only thing I know is that if you love anything enough they take it away from you. This may all be done in infinite wisdom but whoever does is not my friend. I am afraid of god at night but I would have admired him more if he would have stopped the war or never have let it start. Maybe he did stop it but whoever stopped it did not do it prettily. And if it is the Lord that giveth and the Lord that taketh away I do not admire him for taking Catherine away.

> (HEMINGWAY COLLECTION, ITEM 64, 586–88)

This interior monologue stitches together the novel's joint themes of love and war, but Hemingway decided to leave it out, probably because to include it would arouse undue empathy with his narrator.

Ernest Hemingway believed in retribution, in rewards and punishments, in actions producing consequences. In correspondence he scornfully condemned those who behaved badly, caused trouble, and then gaily maintained that it was not their fault at all. Yet this is precisely the procedure Frederic follows near the end of *A Farewell to Arms*. He rails at a deterministic universe, virtually absolving himself of blame for Catherine's death. "The world" worked against the lovers. A vague "they" are responsible. "Now Catherine would die," he thinks. "That was what you did. You died. You did not know what it was about. You never had time to learn. They threw you in and told you the rules and the first time they caught you off base they killed you" (327). Adopting the rhetorician's device of the second person "you," Frederic tries to gain his audience's assent to this philosophy. But there is a logical inconsistency in the terrible game of life and death he constructs. Though he is at least an equal partner in going "off base," he survives and Catherine dies.

This philosophy also rings false in the light of two incidents Hemingway includes in the final chapter of the novel. In each of these. Frederic has an opportunity to alter the course of events for the better; in each, he responds by doing nothing constructive. The first incident involves a scavenging dog he observes nosing at a refuse can early on the morning of the day Catherine will die. "What do you want?" he asks the dog, and looks in the can, but "there was nothing on top but coffee-grounds, dust and some dead flowers." Frederic says, "There isn't anything, dog," to underscore the nihilism of the scene (315), but his efforts to help the dog have been halfhearted, inasmuch as he has not looked beneath the surface layer.

The other incident takes the form of a naturalistic death scene Frederic conjures up from his past.

> Once in camp I put a log on top of the fire and it was full of ants. As it commenced to burn, the ants swarmed out and went first toward the centre where the fire was; then turned back and ran toward the end. When there were enough on the end they fell off into the fire. Some got out, their bodies burnt and flattened, and went off not knowing where they were going. But most of them went toward the fire and then back toward the end and swarmed on the cool end and finally fell into the fire. I remember thinking at the time that it was the end of the world and a splendid chance to be a messiah and lift the log off the fire and throw it out where the ants could get off onto the ground. But I did not do anything but throw a tin cup of water on the log, so that I would have the cup empty to put whiskey in before I added water to it. I think the cup of water on the burning log only steamed the ants.
>
> (327–28)

In this passage, the narrator condemns himself while making nonsense of the deterministic world view he has been advocating. No omnipotent fate decrees the death of the ants. They die because a camper, who might have saved them, steams them instead while clearing his cup for a drink of whiskey, since he knows that water should be added to whiskey and not the other way around.

A number of readers have confessed to a certain uneasiness about Frederic Henry, among them Holden Caulfield, the young rationalizer of J. D. Salinger's *Catcher in the Rye*, who detected a certain "insincerity" in Hemingway's narrator (Wylder, *Hemingway's Heroes*, 67). And, as the critic E. M. Halliday observed, the philosophical reflections in the book seem tacked on. "One is likely to feel not so much that Frederic Henry thought these thoughts at the time, as that Frederic Henry—or Ernest Hemingway—thought them retrospectively, and is delivering short lectures with his eyes on the audience rather than on the story itself" ("Narrative Perspective," 211). But it is only the created character—not *either* Frederic Henry *or* Ernest Hemingway—who attempts under cover of determinism to evade responsibility years after his affair with Catherine Barkley. Worse yet, he does not love Catherine as she deserves. He takes without giving. He withholds. By depicting these shortcomings in Frederic and implicitly repudiating his philosophical justifications, Hemingway distances himself from his protagonist, one of those first-person narrators whose opinions are not to be trusted.

{ 19 }

FREDERIC'S ESCAPE AND THE
POSE OF PASSIVITY

SHERIDAN BAKER distinguishes between the early Hemingway hero, a passive young man somewhat given to self-pity, and the later, far more active and courageous hero (*Hemingway: An Introduction*, 2). Nick Adams is a boy things happen to; Robert Jordan, a man who makes them happen. This neat classification breaks down, however, when applied to the complicated narrator-protagonist of *A Farewell to Arms*. Frederic Henry consistently depicts himself as a passive victim inundated by the flow of events, which kills Catherine, one of the very good and gentle and brave who die young. But Frederic, who survives, belongs in another category altogether, and the determinism he evokes is hardly convincing.

It is the same in war as in love. At the beginning, Frederic tells us, he simply goes along. An American in Rome when World War I breaks out, he joins the Italian ambulance corps for no particular reason. He falls into the drinking and whoring routine of the other officers at Gorizia largely out of inertia. He follows and gives orders as required, but not out of patriotism or dedication to any cause. He suffers a series of disillusionments—his wound, the "war disgust" of his comrades, the overt pacifism of his men, the theatricality and incompetence of the Italian military generally, the moral chaos of the retreat from Caporetto, which climaxes in his plunge into the Tagliamento to avoid summary execution.

When he emerges from the river, Frederic is presumably reborn. But is he? Now he is on his own, and he must *act* to escape. Yet he has not sloughed off his old skin, and before completing his flight he will cover himself with the same cloak of passivity—as one whose activities are determined by forces beyond his control—that he donned when describing his relationship with Catherine, and for much the same reason. Rinaldi was right about Frederic. He is the quintessential "Anglo-Saxon . . . remorse boy" (*Farewell*, 168), so driven by guilt that he is unwilling, even when telling his story ten years after it happened, to accept responsibility for his actions. This view—implicit in the text of the novel as published—gains added authority through examination of passages Hemingway chose to delete in earlier drafts.

Consider Frederic's behavior after he escapes the murderous *caribinieri*, a section of the novel largely ignored by critics. While still being swept along by the swollen waters of the Tagliamento, he maps out a course of action. He considers taking off his boots but decides against it, because he would be "in a bad position" (226) should he land barefoot. He will need his boots, for he already knows where he is going—to Mestre—and that to get there he will have to hike to the main rail line between Venice and Trieste. Why must he reach Mestre? He does not tell us, but it comes out later in conversation with Catherine: because he has an old order of movement authorizing travel from Mestre to Milan, and he needs only to alter the date. In Milan, he expects to find Catherine at the hospital.

When he reaches shore safely, "Tenente" Henry begins "to think out" (227) what he should do next. He wrings out his clothes, and before putting his coat back on cuts off the cloth stars that identify him as an officer. The battle police (who were executing officers indiscriminately after the defeat at Caporetto) took his pistol, so he conceals his empty holster underneath the coat. Encountering an Italian machine-gun detachment, he limps to masquerade as one of the wounded and is not challenged. He crosses the flat Venetian plain to the rail line and jumps aboard a canvas-covered gondola car, avoiding one guard's notice and "contemptuously" staring down another, who concludes that he must have something to do with the train. He clambers inside the car, bumping his head on the guns within. He washes the blood away with rainwater because he does "not want to look conspicuous" when he gets off the train (227–30). He is on his way back to his lover, and he tries to think of nothing but their reunion and escape. "Probably have to go damned quickly. She would go. I knew she would go. When would we go? That was something to think about. It was getting dark. I lay and thought where we would go. There were many places" (233).

The next day in Milan, Frederic engages in three different conversations that confirm Switzerland as their destination. The first of these occurs when he goes to the wine shop in Milan for early morning coffee and bread. The owner realizes at once that Frederic is in trouble. He's seen him come "down the wall" from the train and noticed the bare spots on the sleeves where the stars have been cut away. But he is sympathetic and offers to put Frederic up, to arrange for false leave papers, and to help him get out of Italy. Nothing comes of this proposal, for the understandably cautious fugitive keeps insisting that he needs no assistance.

In an early draft, Frederic actually does contract for forged papers with the wine shop owner. This is the deleted passage

"I have no need for papers. I have papers. As for the stars, they never wear them at the front."

I thought a minute.

"I will be back."

"Only you must tell me now."

"A Tessera [identity card]," I said, "and leave papers."

"Write the name."

"Give me a pencil." I wrote a name on the edge of a newspapers. "Some one will call for them."

"Who?"

"I don't know. He will bring the photograph for the Tessera. You will know me by that."

"All right. That will be one hundred and fifty lire."

"Here is fifty."

"Do not worry Tenente."

"What do you say?"

"I say do not worry."

"I do not worry. I am not in trouble."

"You are not in trouble if you stay with me."

"I must go."

"Come back. Come again."

"I will see you."

"Come at any time."

"Don't forget I am your friend," he said when I went out. He was a strange enough man.

"Good," I said.

(HEMINGWAY COLLECTION, ITEM 64, 239)

Sheldon Norman Grebstein and Michael S. Reynolds both observed that when Hemingway cut this passage he tightened the plot of the novel (Grebstein, *Hemingway's Craft*, 211–12; Reynolds, *Hemingway's First War*, 35–36). With an identity card and leave papers, Frederic might have remained in Italy and avoided arrest for some time. Without them, he must leave the country very soon. But the deletion also functions in two other ways: to avoid a lapse in credibility and to flesh out the character of the protagonist. A man on the run, Frederic would be unlikely to trust the first stranger who accosts him after his escape/desertion. Furthermore, to go through the spy-story machinations outlined here—giving "a name," apparently not his own, sending an intermediary to pick up the counterfeit papers, paying only one-third down to encourage delivery, and maintaining despite this damning evidence that he has nothing to worry about—would war against Lieutenant Henry's nature. He already feels guilty, as we shall see. Active participation in illegal intrigue would only exacerbate that guilt.

Leaving the wine shop, Frederic skirts the train station to avoid the military police and goes to see the porter of the hospital and his wife. They tell him that Miss Barkley has gone to Stresa, on Lake Maggiore, with "the other lady English" (240). After extracting a promise that they tell no one he has been there, Frederic takes a cab to visit Simmons, an American singer trying to break into Italian opera.

Frederic Henry's plan is now taking shape. He has visited Lake Maggiore before—earlier he and Catherine had planned to vacation at Pallanza—and surely knows that the lake extends into Switzerland. So upon awakening Simmons, he wastes no time in coming to the point, He's in a jam, he tells the singer, and asks about "the procedure in going to Switzerland." He knows the Swiss will intern him, but wonder what that means in practical terms. "Nothing," Simmons reassures him. "It's very simple. You can go anywhere. I think you just have to report or something" (241).

Even with Simmons, Frederic is somewhat evasive. It's not yet "definite" that he's fleeing the police. He "think[s]" he's through with the war. But Simmons does not insist on the details and, like the wine shop owner, is more than willing to help. When Frederic asks him to go out and buy civilian clothes for his use, Simmons won't hear of it. Take anything of mine, he commands (Frederic may have decided to call on Simmons because they were of a size). In this way, the lieutenant is relieved of the danger of traveling around Italy in an officer's uniform with the stars cut off and his holster empty, without leave papers or proper orders. The way is clear for escape, and Frederic has to ascertain the means. Yes, he tells Simmons, he has his passport.

"Then get dressed, my dear fellow, and off to old Helvetia."

"It's not that simple. I have to go to Stresa first."

"Ideal, my dear fellow. You just row a boat across."

(242)

Once he reaches Stresa, Frederic continues to lay the groundwork for his flight. He takes a carriage to the hotel: it "was better," less attention-provoking, "to arrive in a carriage" than on foot. He looks up Emilio, the barman he fished with on an earlier visit, lies to him about his civilian clothes ("I'm on leave. Convalescing-leave"), discovers where Catherine and Miss Ferguson are staying, and chats with him about fishing (244–45). The following morning he persuades Emilio to leave the bar and take him out in the lake to troll. They catch no fish, but after two vermouths at the Isola dei Pescatori—the fisherman's island, not a tourist attraction like the Isola Bella they row past, and hence a safer stopping place—Frederic learns of Emilio's disaffection with the war (if called to serve, the barman says, he will not go) and admits that he himself had been a fool to enlist. Little else of consequence passes between them, but they have reached a tacit understanding. "Any time you want it," Emilio says after padlocking his boat, "I'll give you the key" (255–56).

Up to this point, Frederic has moved purposefully toward his goal. As a fugitive from military justice, he has repeatedly been forced to act, in both senses of the verb. He has calculated his chances and calculated well. He has located Catherine and knows where he can get a boat to take them to the neutral country down the lake. Yet with his lover he is all wide-eyed innocence and passivity: now he will "act" only in the theatrical sense. He understands precisely what must be done, but waits for her—and for Emilio—to tell him what that is. By adopting this pose, he appears far less calculating in her eyes. And by involving her and the barman, he tries to parcel out shares of his guilt.

After a long night of lovemaking, Catherine queries Frederic about his status:

"But won't they arrest you if they catch you out of uniform?"

"They'll probably shoot me."

"Then we'll not stay here. We'll get out of the country."

Frederic has, he confesses, "thought something of that," but he continues the charade, waiting for her to drag the scheme out of him.

"What would you do if they came to arrest you?"

"Shoot them."

"You see how silly you are. I won't let you go out of the hotel until we leave here."

"Where are we going to go?"

But Catherine will not cooperate. "Please don't be that way, darling," she says. "We'll go wherever you say. But please find some place to go right away." So Frederic reluctantly reveals his plan. "Switzerland is down the lake, we can go there" (250–51).

That midnight, as a rainstorm sweeps across Lake Maggiore, Emilio comes to announce that the military police will arrest Frederic in the morning, and the lieutenant once again plays the game of "tell me what to do." When the barman knocks on their door, Frederic takes him into the bathroom—so as not to waken Catherine, or alert her to his deviousness—and disingenuously asks, "What's the matter Emilio? Are you in trouble?" No, it is the Tenente who is in trouble, and this dialogue ensues:

"Why are they going to arrest me?"

"For something about the war."

"Do you know what?"

"No. But I know that they know you were here before as an officer and now you are here out of uniform. After this retreat they arrest everybody."

I thought a minute.

"What time do they come to arrest me?"

"In the morning. I don't know the time."

"*What do you say to do?*"

He put his hat in the washbowl. It was very wet and had been dripping on the floor.

"If you have nothing to fear an arrest is nothing. But it is always bad to be arrested—especially now."

"I don't want to be arrested."

"Then go to Switzerland."

"*How?*"

"In my boat."

"There is a storm," I said.

"The storm is over. It is rough but you will be all right."

"*When should we go?*"

"Right away. They might come to arrest you early in the morning"

(264–65; ITALICS ADDED)

"I thought a minute" exactly repeats the phrase Frederic used when—in the deleted passage—he undertook to purchase false leave papers. In both cases, it signals that he is about to embark on a deception. Here the deception consists of suggesting to Emilio, in the italicized questions, that the notion of crossing to Switzerland in the barman's boat has never occurred to him. This is patently untrue, but Frederic's purpose is not simply to fool Emilio. He is after bigger game: the raging tooth of conscience within.

Frederic Henry, in the version of the tale as he tells it, has every possible reason to bid a farewell to arms. As an officer with a foreign accent separated from his men, he faces almost certain death from the *carabinieri* unless he runs. Well before that climactic moment at the Tagliamento, however, Frederic introduces example after example of soldiers opting out of the war. Rinaldi, we learn, has few real wounds to treat early in the war, except for self-inflicted wounds. Frederic meets an Italian soldier with a hernia who has slipped his truss, and advises him to bloody his head as well to avoid being sent back to the front lines. The soldier does so, but the ruse does not work. When the lieutenant himself is wounded, the doctor dictates as he works: "with possible fracture of the skull. Incurred in the line of duty. That's what keeps you from being court-martialed for self-inflicted wounds" (59). At the hospital in Milan, Miss Van Campen accuses him of contracting jaundice to avoid return to active duty; in denying the charge Frederic admits that both he and Miss Van Campen have seen plenty of self-inflicted wounds (144). When he eventually rejoins his unit, things have gone so badly that even the major talks of desertion: "If I was away I do not believe I would come back" (165).

During the disastrous retreat from Caporetto, Frederic serves as a kind of moral policeman. He prevents his men from looting and goes so far as to shoot one of the two sergeants who hitch a ride with the ambulances but refuse to help when the vehicles are mired in mud. Bonello, who finishes off the wounded man (he's always wanted to kill a sergeant, he says), slips away himself the next day to surrender to the Austrians. In the confusion, Aymo is gunned down by "friendly fire" from Italian bullets. Frederic and the faithful Piani are left to plod along with the rest of the retreating soldiers, who chant "Andiamo a casa" and cast aside their weapons. "They think if they throw away their rifles they can't make them fight," Piani explains, but his lieutenant disapproves (219–20). Despite all the precedents for opting out of the war, Frederic sticks to his mission and his men up to the moment when he must either escape or be executed.

Furthermore, once he has escaped, nearly every civilian he meets either assists him in his flight or reinforces his conviction that the war is senseless and badly managed. The wine shop owner's offer of forged papers is only partly attributable to the profit motive. "Don't forget that I am your friend," he tells Frederic, in the text as well as in the deleted passage (239). Is he through with the war? Simmons inquires. "Good boy. I always knew you had sense" (241). Emilio the barman has served in Abyssinia and hates war. The wise Count Greffi thinks the war is, really, "stupid" (262). And Catherine, especially, reassures Frederic that he has done the right thing. Yet no amount of reassurance can shake him free of his nagging sense of guilt. Hemingway conveys the persistence of this debilitating emotion in two ways: through Lieutenant Henry's unsuccessful attempts to rationalize his desertion and through his equally unsuccessful attempts to shut the war out of his consciousness.

On the train to Mestre, Frederic calls up an analogy to justify his flight:

> You were out of it now. You had no more obligation. If they shot floorwalkers after a fire in a department store because they spoke with an accent they had always had, then certainly the floorwalkers would not be expected to return when the store opened again for business. They might seek other employment; if there was any other employment and the police did not get them.

The analogy seems curious until one reflects that Frederic had functioned during the retreat much as a floorwalker functions: to prevent thievery. Then he goes on, in internal monologue, to discuss "the outward forms" of soldiery. He would like to take the uniform off. He has removed the stars "for convenience," but it was "no point of honor." The abstract word "honor," rising to Frederic's mind at this moment, comes from the conscience which will not let him stop "thinking"—a code word, in this novel, for the functioning of the superego. He wishes the Italians "all the luck." Some good and brave and calm and sensible men were fighting for their cause. "But it was not my show any more and I wished this bloody train would get to Mestre and I would eat and stop thinking. I would have to stop" (232).

That he cannot stop is shown on the next train ride Hemingway describes, when Frederic is en route from Milan to Stresa in Simmons's civilian clothes. Presumably he should be happy: he will soon see Catherine. But he misses the sense of "being held" by his clothes in a uniform, and feels "as sad as the wet Lombard country" outside. He shares the compartment with some aviators:

They avoided looking at me and were very scornful of a civilian my age. I did not feel insulted. In the old days I would have insulted them and picked a fight. They got off at Gallarate and I was glad to be alone. . . . I was damned lonely, and was glad when the train got to Stresa.

(243)

"In the old days"—two days before—Frederic would not have stood for the scornful attitude of the aviators. Now he accepts their view of him as a slacker, a point emphasized in a sentence Hemingway cut from the novel as, perhaps, belaboring the obvious. "I did not feel indignant [vs. insulted]," he originally wrote. "I felt they were right" (Item 64, 477).

Ensconced at the bar of the Grand Hotel & des Isles Borromees, his nerves and stomach soothed by three cool, clean martinis, the same number of sandwiches, and olives, salted almonds, and potato chips, Frederic begins to feel "civilized," by which he means that he "did not think at all." But Emilio asks a question that starts the thought processes going again:

"Don't talk about the war," I said. The war was a long way away. Maybe there wasn't any war. There was no war here. Then I realized it was over for me. But I did not have the feeling that it was really over. I had the feeling of a boy who thinks of what is happening at a certain hour at the schoolhouse from which he has played truant.

(245)

The pattern is the same in the bar as on the train to Mestre. The fugitive insists to himself that he is through, that the war is over for him, that it isn't his show any longer, but then he cannot help touching the wound, striking a note of self-recrimination. Even when pleasantly fuzzy on gin, he is reminded of childhood truancies. Thus he also tells Count Greffi that he does not want to talk about the war, but soon brings up the subject himself. "What do you think of the war really?" he asks the ancient nobleman (260, 262).

Nurse Catherine Barkley provides the best medicine—sex—to enable Frederic to forget. As Stanley Cooperman comments, Frederic requires of Catherine not love "but medication and in this respect he is less the Byronic lover than patient." Cooperman also notes that "the hyena of passivity—always a nightmare for Hemingway—reduces Frederic Henry to a spiritual *castrado*" ("Death and *Cojones*," 183). That sex will work to prevent thoughts of the war is foreshadowed during the second meeting of Frederic and Catherine, when he initiates this exchange:

"Let's drop the war."

"It's very hard. There's no place to drop it."

"Let's drop it anyway."

"All right."

He then kisses her, is slapped, and the kiss and the slap succeed: at least "we've gotten away from the war," he observes (26). But they haven't, nor will they ever, despite the oblivion-inducing therapy she administers. Immediately after telling her that they will go to Switzerland, Frederic seeks and gets her reassurance:

> "I feel like a criminal. I've deserted from the army."
>
> "Darling, *please* be sensible. It's not deserting from the army. It's only the Italian army."
>
> I laughed. "You're a fine girl. Let's get back into bed. I feel fine in bed."
>
> A little while later Catherine said, "You don't feel like a criminal do you?"
>
> "No," I said. "Not when I'm with you."
>
> (251)

But they cannot make love all the time, and when Frederic returns from fishing and finds Catherine gone, he "lay down on the bed and tried to keep from thinking" without success until she came back and "it was all right again."

Safe in Switzerland, the two lovers ride a carriage to their hotel, where Hemingway introduces an ironic commentary on Frederic's problem. He is still groggy from the long night of rowing, and he neglects to tip the soldier who has brought them and their bags to Locarno. "You've forgotten the army," Catherine remarks, and for the moment she's right (284). But very soon, even during their first idyllic days at Montreux, the narcotic wears off. "We slept well and if I woke in the night I knew it was from only one cause," Frederic observes.

What was the cause? "The war seemed as far away as the football games of some one else's college. But I knew from the papers that they were still fighting in the mountains because the snow would not come" (291). When Catherine urges him to fall asleep simultaneously with her, he is unable to do so, instead lying "awake for quite a long time thinking about things" (301)—more specifically "about Rinaldi and the priest and lots of people I know" (298). He doesn't want to think about these comrades-in-arms or the war itself, he says. He's through with the war, he insists, yet he compulsively reads about it in the newspapers (Reynolds, *Hemingway's First War*, 101–3).

While convalescing in Milan after his wounding, Frederic read all the papers he could get his hands on, including even the Boston papers with their stale news of stateside training camps. After making his separate peace, however, he tries to repudiate the habit. Thus on the train to Stresa, he has the paper with him but does not read it; he is going to forget about the war. And the morning after he finds Catherine, he sticks to that resolve. "Was it so bad you don't even want to read about it?" she asks him. He promises to tell her about what happened if he can ever "get it straight" in his head (250). He never does tell her, yet that very afternoon while she is away he sits at the bar and reads the bad news in the paper. "The army had not stood at the Tagliamento. They were falling back to the Piave" (253).

At the Guttingens' cottage in the mountains, no papers are available, so he catches up on the news when they come down to Montreux. While Catherine is at the hairdresser, he drinks beer and eats pretzels and reads "about disaster"—the war was going badly everywhere—in "the *Corriere della Sera* and the English and American papers from Paris." The night they move to the hotel in Lausanne, he lies in bed drinking a whiskey and soda (liquor like sex makes him feel better temporarily) and reads the papers he has bought at the station. "It was March, 1918, and the German offensive had started in France" (308). During the three weeks they spend at the hotel, his days fall into a routine. In the morning he boxes at the gym, takes a shower, walks along the streets "smelling the spring in the air," stops at a cafe "to sit and watch the people and read the paper and drink a vermouth," and then meets Catherine at the hotel for lunch (310–11).

During the afternoon of her protracted labor, Frederic kills time reading the paper. Sent out to eat supper, he takes a seat across from an elderly man with an evening paper and, "not thinking at all," reads about "the break through on the British front." When the man across from him, annoyed that Frederic is reading the back of his paper, folds it over, he considers asking the waiter for one of his own but decides against it: "I could not concentrate" (329). He has been unable to forget the war; now Catherine's caesarean has given him something else to shut his mind to. "It was the only thing to do," the doctor assures him when she has hemorrhaged and died. "The operation proved—." But Frederic cuts him short. "I do not want to talk about it" (332).

Eventually Frederic Henry does bring himself to talk about his tragic love affair and about the horror of the war: ergo, *A Farewell to Arms*. But it is important to remember that we have the story *as he tells it to us*.

Maxwell Perkins, Hemingway's editor at Scribner's, thought like some others that the novel was insufficiently integrated. "The serious flaw in the book," he wrote Owen Wister on May 17, 1929, "is that the two great elements you named—one of which would make it a picture of war, and the other of which would make it a duo of love and passion—do not fully combine. It begins as one thing wholly, and ends up wholly as the other thing" (qtd. in Reynolds, *Hemingway's First War*, 76). But Perkins and Wister missed the point. The subject of the novel is not love and war, in whatever combination, but Frederic Henry.

Both Frederic Henry and Ernest Hemingway were Americans wounded on the Italian front, and both fell in love with nurses. Otherwise, they have not much in common. Frederic is certainly older than his creator, for one thing. Hemingway was only eighteen when he came to Italy, not as an officer in any army but as a Red Cross ambulance driver in the last summer of the war. Frederic, on the other hand, enlisted in the Italian army three years earlier, and before that had been studying architecture in Rome. Unlike the raw youth only a year out of Oak Park high school, he has been around enough to acquire a good deal of knowledge. He knows the geography of Italy very well indeed, as his movements after deserting testify. He even knows how the war should be fought: as Napoleon would have fought it, by waiting until the Austrians came down from the mountains and then whipping them.

Despite his background, however, the lieutenant does not conduct himself bravely or intelligently as a warrior. He is no Othello, nor even a Hemingway. After Frederic is wounded, Rinaldi tries to get him the medaglia d'argento. Hadn't he done anything heroic? Rinaldi wants to know. Didn't he carry anyone on his back? No, Frederic replies, he was "blown up while eating cheese" (63). It hardly matters. He has been wounded, he is an American, the offensive has been successful, and Rinaldi thinks they can get him the silver medal. Hemingway was in fact awarded the silver, but for better reasons. Unlike his narrator, young Hemingway *did* carry another soldier on his back while wounded.

During the retreat Lieutenant Henry is given his one chance to command, and he makes a botch of it. He orders his three ambulances onto side roads where they bog down permanently. He shoots the uncooperative sergeant to no particular effect. When they proceed on foot, the lieutenant leads the good soldier Aymo to a senseless death, and Bonello surrenders to save his skin knowing Frederic will not turn him in. In sum, the Tenente loses his ambulances and all his men but one, and it is, as he reflects, largely his own fault.

By exhibiting Frederic Henry's lack of competence as a leader, Hemingway aimed to achieve a certain distance from his narrator. That he was determined to maintain this separation is illustrated by his decision to delete reflective passages in which the narrator's thoughts too closely resemble his own. In one of these, Frederic in conversation with the priest asserts that he loves lots of things: "The night. The Day. Food. Drink. Girls. Italy. Pictures. Places. Swimming. Portofino. Paris. Spring. Summer. Fall. Winter. Heat. Cold. Smells. Sleep. Newspapers. Reading": all of which "sounds better in Italian" (Item 64, 168–70). It also sounds very much like the vigorous Hemingway, in love with all that life had to offer.

So does an excised digression on the subject of fear:

> (When I had first gone to the war it had all been like a picture or a story or a dream in which you know you can wake up when it gets too bad. . . . I had the believe [sic] in physical immortality which is given fortunate young men in order that they may think about other things and that is withdrawn without notice when they need it most. After its withdrawal I was not greatly worried because the spells of fear were always physical, always caused by an imminent danger, and always transitory. . . . I suppose the third stage, of being afraid at night, started about at this point . . .).
>
> (ITEM 664, 235–36)

This passage tells us a good deal about Hemingway and his obsession with fear and how to overcome it. This topic does not much concern Frederic Henry, however, and it was cut out of A Farewell to Arms.

On yet another discarded page of manuscript Hemingway typed a sentence that might stand as a motto for his novel: "The position of the survivor of a great calamity is seldom admirable" (qtd. in Reynolds, Hemingway's First War, 60). Indeed it is not, since no special glamour—rather the reverse—attaches to simply surviving. When one's lover is not so fortunate, one is liable like Frederic Henry to be troubled by guilt.

"There is generally nothing to which we are so sensitive," Karl Jaspers observed in his study of collective guilt in Germany during and after World War II, "as to any hint that we are considered guilty" (The Question, 107). Such sensitivity finds expression in more than one way. Most Germans, Jaspers discovered, reacted aggressively by challenging their accusers. When wall posters went up in German towns during the summer of 1945, with pictures from the concentration camps and the accusation, "You are the guilty!" consciences grew uneasy and people rebelled in protest. It was only human for the accused, whether justly or unjustly charged, to defend themselves. But when the accusation is not public but comes from within, the tendency may be, as with Frederic, to internalize the guilt, hug it to one's bosom, and retreat into inactivity.

Actually, Frederic twice faces accusations after his escape. The first takes the form of the aviators' silent scorn on the train to Stresa, and he mutely accepts their judgment. The other, more overt accuser is Catherine's friend Miss Ferguson, who lashes out at Frederic in Stresa. What is he doing in mufti? she wants to know. He's "sneaky," she tells him, "like a snake" for getting Catherine with child and then turning up unexpectedly to take her away. Catherine makes a joke of it ("We'll both sneak off"), but Frederic is not amused, probably because he is reminded of the dissimulation he has just gone through to avoid capture. So he remains quiet, and since no one else points a finger, he has no one to lash out against. Yet it is "only human" to defend oneself, even against one's own accusations. All of *A Farewell to Arms*, from this point of view, may be considered the narrator's *apologia pro vita sua*.

Throughout the book Frederic paints himself as a man more sinned against than sinning, as a passive victim of circumstances. Yet the portrait is not, finally, to the life, as Hemingway shows by daubing in occasional brush strokes of his own. One of these is the analogy between Frederic and (not the guileful snake but) the crafty fox. Walking one evening in the brisk mid-January cold of the mountains above Montreux, Frederic and Catherine twice see foxes in the woods. This is unusual, for foxes rarely show themselves. And when a fox sleeps, Frederic points out, he wraps his tail around him to keep warm. Then he adds:

"I always wanted to have a tail like that. Wouldn't it be fun if we had brushes like a fox?"

"It might be very difficult dressing."

"We'd have clothes made, or live in a country where it wouldn't make any difference."

"We live in a country where nothing makes any difference."

(303)

This peculiar exchange suggests a good deal about Hemingway's protagonist. Catherine has done all anyone could to protect him: she pulls his cloak around the two of them, makes a tent of her hair, administers the soporifics of sex and humor ("It's only the Italian army") to his hyperactive superego, urges him off to a neutral country where to her, at least, "nothing makes any difference." But it has not been enough, and Frederic still thinks conspiratorially of disguises and how to keep himself safe and warm. Like the wily fox in the woods, he pretends to an innocence he does not possess; the comparison itself constitutes a caveat against accepting as gospel Frederic Henry's presentation of himself. In the end, his pose of passivity cannot hide the guilt he feels, nor can he dissipate the guilt by playacting or by writing about it. Hemingway's narrator remains a principal agent of both his farewells: to war as to love.

PART VIII

◈ CENSORSHIP ◈

{ 20 }

CENSORING *A FAREWELL TO ARMS*

OST OF Ernest Hemingway's books were banned in one place or another, at one time or another (Haight, *Banned Books*, 89–90). *A Farewell to Arms* was banned in Boston, or, rather, the second installment of a six-part serial version of the novel running in *Scribner's Magazine* was banned there on June 20, 1929, by police chief Michael H. Crowley, who brought his wide expertise in such matters to bear and pronounced the book "salacious." Though his ruling barred distribution of the magazine by Boston booksellers and newsstands for the run of the serial over the next four months, it had little or no effect on the overall circulation figures of the magazine and undoubtedly served to stimulate sales of the book when it was published on September 27. But the police chief's action did help resolve an incipient dispute between Hemingway and his publishers in the latter's favor and to shape the final version of the novel. The most idiotic censorships can have unfortunate consequences.

Maxwell Perkins rarely laid a glove on Hemingway's prose, once the author had become a property that Scribner's (the book publishers) could both market and be proud of. But in the early years he and Hemingway were often at odds over the language of his books. Perkins was thrust into the position of mediator between his old-guard conservative publishers, as personified by the strait-laced figure of Charles Scribner, and a young writer who took it as his duty to set down the way people talked, even if that led him into the realm of obscenity. If it is true that Perkins was an "editor of genius," as his biographer A. Scott Berg calls him, it was in this capacity of middleman, quieting the outraged sensibilities of the old guard at the publishing house while soothing the outsized ego of young Hemingway.

"Do ask him for the absolute minimum of necessary changes, Max," Scott Fitzgerald implored their editor in connection with *The Sun Also Rises* (qtd. in Donaldson, "Wooing," 705–6). That was sound advice, for Hemingway resisted any change in his copy. Yet at the same time, Perkins worked for a man who "would no sooner allow profanity in one of his books than he would invite friends to use his parlor as a toilet." Faced with this dilemma, Perkins first persuaded Scribner's to publish *The Sun Also Rises*, dirty words and all ("We took it with misgivings," he reported after the editorial conference) on the grounds that the firm would suffer if knowledge of rejecting *Sun* got about among young writers (Berg, *Max Perkins*, 95–98). Then he started working on Hemingway to eliminate some of the objectionable verbiage. Out came the suggestion of *shitty*, in Bill Gorton's Irony and Pity jingle. Out came the bulls' *balls,* to be replaced by more acceptable *horns.* Out came the explicit reference to Henry *James's* bicycle.

It was some trick, this balancing act between author and publisher, and in the context it became clear that Perkins's own sensibilities often lay close to those of his employer. People were now attacking books on the grounds "of 'decency' which means *words*," he wrote Hemingway. "In view of this, I suggest that a particular adjunct of the bulls referred to a number of times . . . be not spelled out, but covered by a blank" (qtd. in Reynolds, *Hemingway's First War*, 4). Hemingway might write openly of the bulls' balls, but Perkins could not bring himself to set the word down on paper.

Three years later, editor and author were once more engaged in the similar kind of charade. On a February 1929 visit to Key West, Perkins read the script of *A Farewell to Arms* between fishing excursions on the Gulf Stream. He liked the novel a great deal, but recognized the problems it might pose. "BOOK VERY FINE BUT DIFFICULT IN SPOTS," he wired New York. Later, in a letter to Charles Scribner, he expanded on the point. "It is Hemingway's principle both in life and literature never to flinch from facts, and it is in that sense only, that the book is difficult. It isn't at all erotic, although love is represented as having a very large physical element" (Berg, *Max Perkins*, 141). Here Perkins began for the first time, in house, to sound like Hemingway's advocate; during their long days on the Gulf Stream, he must have succumbed to some of the writer's famous charm. A few weeks thereafter he offered Hemingway $16,000 for a serial of *Farewell* in *Scribner's Magazine*.

Along with the contract for the serial, however, came a catch. *Scribner's* was a family magazine. Schools used it for "collateral reading," and girls as well as boys attended those schools. Ernest would therefore understand, Max felt sure, that certain words "must be concealed by a white space" and that "several little passages" might have to be omitted later, though not in the first installment (Hemingway and Perkins, *Only Thing*, 92). In the glow of the $16,000, the highest price yet paid by *Scribner's* for a serialization, Hemingway agreed to understand, but he insisted on one caveat: "What I ask is that when omissions are made a blank or some sign of omission" appears to indicate the cut (*Only Thing*, 91).

Soon enough that proviso was ignored, to Hemingway's consternation. Early in March he read through the galleys of the second (June) installment and found that the magazine had made two significant cuts without consulting him and (in one case) without indicating the deletions by way of blank spaces or even dots. Blanks were used for the officers' "____house" and for "son of a ____" and even for a randy dog "in ____," but no such space was left in the crucial passage of omitted dialogue between Frederic and Catherine where he successfully persuades her to make love. "I'd rather return the money and call it all off than have arbitrary eliminations made without any mention of the fact they are being made," Hemingway angrily wrote Perkins. He especially objected to this omission because "the result in dialogue does not make sense—two consecutive sentences are left as . . . both spoken by the same person," an observation that should be kept in mind when debating the confusion of voices in "A Clean, Well-Lighted Place" (*Only Thing*, 95).

In smoothing things over, Perkins disingenuously maintained that the cut "was made for only the one reason of simplifying things and speeding them up. . . . There is, and was, and never will be, any idea of making any change without your approval; and I doubt if there will be any change except for a few blanks hereafter, anyhow" (*Only Thing*, 96). Besides, he promised, it would be different with the book. On April 16, Perkins wrote again to say that they were setting up *Farewell* for book publication and following the original copy exactly.

Or almost exactly, anyway. Still at issue was Hemingway's use of barracks language, including—so legend has it—three words so offensive to Perkins that he could not jot them down for Charles Scribner (Berg, *Max Perkins*, 142). The situation was complicated by the publication early in 1929 of Erich Maria Remarque's international bestseller *All Quiet on the Western Front*. Remarque freely used those words (or their German equivalents) most common among soldiers, including the ubiquitous "f" word. For him to do otherwise, Hemingway argued in a June 7 letter to Perkins, would only weaken his text. But he offered a way out, a way that the events in Boston two weeks later were to make available to his publishers: "If it [any given word] *cannot* be printed without the book being suppressed all right" (*Selected Letters*, 296–98).

As Paul S. Boyer observed in *Purity in Print*, "Massachusetts censorship came over on the *Mayflower*," and up to the mid-1920s it was a serious matter for a book to be banned in Boston. The suppression of undesirable books during the late nineteenth century and through the Progressive period was but one of the activities of the highly respected Watch and Ward Society. Supported by the city's Brahmins, the society also functioned as an "agency of reform and uplift, fighting prostitution, narcotics, gambling, and municipal corruption." From 1918 to 1925, the society ran its book censorship operation under the aegis of the "Boston Booksellers' Committee," a group made up of three booksellers and three Watch and Ward directors. They read current novels and determined which ones could and could not be sold by Massachusetts book dealers. From fifty to seventy-five books were banned in this way, usually without any objection or publicity whatever.

But the old-settler Protestant Watch and Ward Society gradually lost power to the Irish Catholic majority, and after 1926 the task of censoring books fell to the police. That was the beginning of the end, for police suppressions, including that of Theodore Dreiser's *An American Tragedy*, invited both legal action and national scorn. On April 16, 1929, two months before the *Farewell* ban, the city's literati held their annual banquet and frolic at Ford Hall, a gathering "By Undesirables—For Undesirables" presided over by Harvard historian Arthur M. Schlesinger as "Master of Rebelry" and celebrating such recently suppressed writers as H. G. Wells, Conrad Aiken, John Dos Passos, Sherwood Anderson, Sinclair Lewis, Dreiser, and Hemingway himself, for *The Sun Also Rises* (Boyer, *Purity in Print*, chapter 7). By the time the police clamped down on *Farewell*, the phrase "Banned in Boston" had become something of a joke.

The *Boston Evening Globe* paid little or no attention to the removal of *Scribner's Magazine* from the newsstands on June 20. The big censorship story of that week involved Edward J. Fitzhugh Jr. of Boise, Idaho, a Harvard senior, editor of the *Advocate*, and author of a prize-winning class hymn "sung in all solemnity" on the Sunday before commencement. Someone belatedly noticed that the first letters in the sixteen-line hymn, read as an acrostic, "spelled out four words which were in themselves obscene and profane and which slurred the high sentiments expressed in the hymn." For this crime, the authorities, who had after all selected Fitzhugh's hymn as the best submitted, summarily dismissed the senior on the day before graduation (*Boston Evening Globe*, 18 June 1929). That sort of nose-thumbing was not to be tolerated, and there were those who regarded Hemingway's novel as a similar attempt to shock the eminently respectable. "Naughty Ernest," Harry Hansen chided in his *New York World* column. And from across the Atlantic, some months later, J. B. Priestley tartly observed that "literature is not a matter of pleasing Aunt Susan. But we must also remember that it is equally not a matter of simply shocking Aunt Susan."

The *New York Times* gave the Boston ban page-two coverage and asked Scribner's to respond to the charge of salaciousness. Speaking for the firm, Alfred Dashiell declared its confidence in the integrity of the author and his work:

> The ban of the sale of the magazine in Boston is an evidence of the improper use of censorship which bases its objections upon certain passages without taking into account the effect and purpose of the story as a whole. "A Farewell to Arms" is in its effect distinctly moral. It is the story of a fine and faithful love born, it is true, of physical desire.
>
> If good can come from evil, if the fine can grow from the gross, how is a writer effectually to depict the progress of this evolution if he cannot describe the conditions from which the good evolved? If white is to be contrasted with black, thereby emphasizing its whiteness, the picture cannot be all white.
>
> ("BOSTON POLICE")

"Vive Dashiell!" Hemingway commented. "That was a statement to ring men's hearts" (Hemingway and Perkins, *Only Thing*, 112). Yet despite the eloquence of the "if good can come from evil" argument, the statement hardly qualified as a ringing defense of civil liberties. It objected only to "the improper use of censorship," not to censorship itself. It insisted not on the right to publication of the novel but on its underlying morality. The *New York Herald Tribune* took a more appropriate stance: "Many readers had doubtless missed Mr. Hemingway's powerful story," the paper commented editorially, "and they will be grateful to the [Boston police] chief for calling their attention to it" (qtd. in Boyer, *Purity in Print*, 195).

Scribner's had no legal recourse against the ban but was not unduly troubled by the action against the magazine. Probably Hemingway was more disturbed by word of the censorship than Perkins. For one thing,

Perkins suspected that the intervention might be commercially advantageous to the book. Personally, he hated the publicity, which "brought a frivolous and prejudicial attention to one aspect of a book which is deeply significant and beautiful," he wrote Hemingway, but he also realized that it might turn out to. be "greatly helpful" to sales. Besides, the trouble in Boston gave him a bargaining chip in his ongoing discussion with the author about his use of objectionable words.

"This incident affects the possibility of book suppression," Perkins noted in a letter written one week after the Boston ban. "There are things in the book that were never in another . . . since the 18th century anyway. . . . All right then! But I don't think we can print those three words, Ernest. I can't find *anyone* who thinks so. That supreme insult alone might turn a judge right around against us, and to the post office, it and the others, I think, would warrant (technically) action. It would be a dirty shame to have you associated in a way with people who write with an eye to tickle a cheap public" (Hemingway and Perkins, *Only Thing*, 106). Two weeks later he took up the cause again. There remained "considerable anxiety for fear of the federal authorities being stirred up. They seem to take curious activity of late, and if the post office should object, we would be in Dutch" (108).

There was some validity behind Perkins's assertions, expedient though they certainly were in dealing with his unruly author. Ever since the Tariff of 1842, United States Customs officials had been empowered to confiscate shipments of incoming books they regarded as obscene. Naturally the sensibilities of local customs inspectors varied widely. "A classic is a dirty book somebody is trying to get by me," one vigilant examiner commented in 1930, adding that in the preceding two years he had barred "272 different titles." Some cases were brought on appeal to the United States Customs Bureau, which in mid-1929 ruled against admitting the unexpurgatcd British edition of *All Quiet on the Western Front* (Little, Brown published a sanitized version for American readers). But customs censorship obviously threatened overseas books more than ones printed in the United States.

The United States Post Office was more to be feared, especially in the light of an April 1929 court decision against Mary Ware Dennett's pamphlet *The Sex Side of Life: An Explanation for Young People*. Mrs. Dennett told where the sex organs were and what they did, denied that masturbation was necessarily harmful, and celebrated the pleasures of sexual intercourse. The Post Office not only banned the pamphlet from the mails but brought court action against Mrs. Dennett for continuing to mail it under first-class seal. At the trial a Brooklyn clergyman took vigorous exception to the pamphlet's assertion that sexual intercourse was "the very greatest physical pleasure to be had in all human experience." Nursing a baby was far more pleasurable, he declared. Challenged on the point (how could he possibly know?), he said he knew this to be true because his wife had told him so (Boyer, *Purity in Print*, 208–9, 238–41).

In other words, the federal authorities had been busy censoring books in recent months, and Perkins made sure that Hemingway knew of his publisher's concern. The message got across. In a July 1929 letter to Fitzgerald, Hemingway wrote that "Max sounded scared. If they get scared now and lay off the book I'll be out of luck." He had not asked for an advance on the novel, but now he wished he had, since "it is more difficult to lay off a book if they have money tied up in it already." Then in a July 26 letter to Perkins, he capitulated entirely as to the three words in dispute. Scribner's could go ahead and blank out the word *balls* as spoken to Miss Van Campen, the word *shit* spoken by Piani before leaving Gorizia, and the word *cocksucker*, the "supreme insult" that Piani utters when Aymo is shot by the Italian rear guard and that Lieutenant Henry says when arrested by the battle police. "I understand about the words you cannot print—if you cannot print them—and I never expected you could print the one word (C-S) that you cannot and that lets me out" (*Only Thing*, 110). As it happens, yet another word (*fuck*) was almost certainly blanked out, along with several instances of *shit* (not one) on various pages, and Hemingway later substituted *scrotum* for *balls*, thus averting a blank space, but after the letter of July 26, it was clear that Perkins—and Scribner's—had won the dispute with Ernest Hemingway.

Of course it was not merely barracks talk that troubled Scribner's and was to trouble conservative readers and critics. The love affair between Frederic and Catherine, unsanctioned by the church ("All right then!"), probably aroused more sentiment against the book than its language and was unquestionably responsible for police chief Crowley's edict of suppression. Magazine readers cancelled their subscriptions rather than risk exposure to such "venereal fiction." Right-thinking commentators lamented that a writer obviously capable of higher things should choose to depict such "lustful indulgence" and, worse yet, depict it in a sympathetic light. Still others were critical of Frederic's "separate peace," since desertion by any name could not be condoned. A few inveighed against the author's outspoken use of obstetrical details, for "a lot of this biological and pathological data is neither necessary nor particularly relevant." And as Hemingway feared, many Italians were offended, possibly because they did not see his disclaimer in *Scribner's Magazine* that the novel was not autobiographical and no more intended as a criticism of Italy or Italians than *Two Gentlemen of Verona* (Stephens, *Hemingway: The Critical Reception*, 86–89; Scribner's Archive). There was something in *Farewell*, it seemed, to offend almost everyone.

Still, Perkins was right about the publicity generating book sales. *Farewell* was published late in September in a first printing of 31,050 copies, more than five times the first run of *The Sun Also Rises*, and by November it was on the best-seller lists. Much of the critical commentary was highly favorable, and several reviewers made a point of deploring the suppression of the magazine version in Boston. "Boston has banned the story, but the rest of the country seems to think it is pretty fine," as the *Tulsa Tribune* commented. For whatever reason, the Boston censors took no action against the book, though it was more explicit about Frederic and Catherine's lovemaking than the serial. The Post Office caused no trouble, either. *Farewell* was banned as a book only in Italy.

But this was not an unambiguous happy ending to the censoring of *Scribner's Magazine* by the Boston police chief. Financially, no one was really hurt. Nor were readers deprived of the pleasure of reading *A Farewell to Arms*, the book by virtue of which—according to Hemingway's friend Archibald MacLeish, who had no difficulty obtaining the magazine serial in western Massachusetts—Hemingway became "the great novelist of our time" (*Letters*, 230). But there are ways and ways that censorship, and beyond and beneath it the threat of censorship, can affect the final version of a work of art. For better or worse, Hemingway undoubtedly produced a somewhat different novel as a consequence of what happened in Boston and what he feared might happen elsewhere. Specifically, he backtracked on his conviction that fictional soldiers could only emerge as real on the page if they spoke and acted like real ones. Robert Herrick, in his diatribe against the novel entitled "What Is Dirt?" in November 1929, concluded that "no great loss to anybody would result" if *A Farewell to Arms* were to be suppressed (Herrick, 262). He could not have known that in a very real sense, Hemingway's novel already had been.

{ 21 }

PROTECTING THE TROOPS
FROM HEMINGWAY

AN EPISODE IN CENSORSHIP

I
N 1976, while looking through the Gertrude Stein papers at Yale's Beinecke library, I serendipitously ran across some United States Army
documents about an attempt to censor Hemingway's stories. How
that material found its way into the Stein papers remains a mystery; there
is no mention of her anywhere in the file. But here is the story, as recon-
structed from these military memoranda.

On May 16, 1945, Brigadier General Ernest J. Dawley, Commanding
General, Ground Force Reinforcement Command, European Theater of
Operations, wrote his superior, Lieutenant General John C. H. Lee, Commanding General, Communications Zone, European Theater, about the
trouble with Hemingway. Dawley had reason to expect a sympathetic audience for his complaint in Lee. "I am interested to know that you are anx-
ious to clean up some of the literature that is being made available to our
men," he began. "I should have known it would be so." Though he himself
was no "purist," Dawley went on, he did think that such literature had "an
extremely deleterious effect on our personnel" and tended to undermine
the efforts they were making toward, and I quote, "morality and morals."

To illustrate his point, he enclosed a sample, with "salacious passages . . .
marked," from the Armed Services Edition printing of Hemingway's *Selected Short Stories*. But Dawley did not so much as allow the name of
"the author in question," whom he had always regarded "as of extremely
questionable value from some of our better points of view," to appear in

his communication. He'd found copies of the offending book in the Special Services library at his headquarters, Dawley concluded, and had directed that "all of these volumes be withdrawn from circulation and sent in here for destruction."

If Dawley anticipated a letter of congratulation from Lee, it was not forthcoming. Instead Lee tossed Dawley's hot potato to Secretary General Staff "for comment and recommendation," and from there it was forwarded in turn to the Chaplain Section and to Special Services. The chaplain, Colonel L. Curtis Tiernan, substantially agreed with Dawley. The marked passages, he responded on May 21, 1945, were "rather an indication of the exceeding bad taste and lack of sense of moral standards than positive licencious [sic] and obscene matter." Still, books like Hemingway's were "detrimental to the culture and simple virtue of American civilization" and did not deserve to be published. He thought it "especially regrettable that agents of our Government should have reproduced and distributed such printed matter when there [was] such a wealth of good literature and profitable reading matter available."

Chaplain Tiernan, who was only a colonel, dodged the issue of whether army brigadier generals had the right to order the destruction of such unprofitable reading matter as Hemingway's stories. It remained for Oscar N. Solbert, himself a brigadier general and chief of Special Services, to call Dawley to account. In his six-point memorandum, Solbert drew upon established devices of argumentation; he appealed to the crowd, he appealed to authority, he appealed to the past, he even appealed to principle.

Point one: this book has been approved by committees. Solbert explained how the Armed Services Editions, paper-bound reprints of "current best sellers, popular classics, and other books of general interest," were chosen. These editions, printed for free distribution to American troops overseas or in hospital stateside, went through a several-stage screening process. First an advisory committee of representative publishers, critics, librarians, and booksellers prepared lists of approved books, which were then sent to Army Special Services and the Department of the Navy for concurrence. Next the selections were "subjected to final detailed scrutiny" by the book-reviewing section of a nonprofit corporation called Editions for the Armed Services, headed by Philip Van Doren Stern.

These Armed Services Editions—also called Council Books—undoubtedly advanced the reputations of the authors whose work was chosen. The edition of *The Great Gatsby* was a landmark event in the Fitzgerald revival, and scholars have written of the pleasure of reading Faulkner's fiction for the first time in these paperbacks. Apparently, all of the Armed

Services Edition titles were published in 1945. Two were by Hemingway: *To Have and Have Not* and *Selected Short Stories*. The stories were "The Short Happy Life of Francis Macomber," "The Snows of Kilimanjaro," "Indian Camp," "Mr. and Mrs. Elliot," "Cat in the Rain," "My Old Man," "The Undefeated," "Fifty Grand," "A Canary for One," "An Alpine Idyll," "Now I Lay Me," and "A Day's Wait." According to Audre Hanneman, every Armed Services title was issued in a printing of 57,000 copies. Matthew J. Bruccoli, however, states that 155,000 copies of *Gatsby* were printed (Hanneman, *Hemingway: A Comprehensive Bibliography*, 59, Bruccoli, *Fitzgerald: A Bibliography*, 66). In any event, a great many copies found their way into the hands of American service personnel.

Point two: Hemingway is popular, dammit, and important people like him. Hemingway was recently "chosen the outstanding American novelist by the leading literary critics of America including Dr. Henry S. Canby of the Book-of-the-Month Club, Clifton Fadiman, Carl Van Doren, Edmund Wilson, Malcolm Cowley and others in a poll conducted by *Life* magazine." His work was already included in many of the standard anthologies. And in addition, Solbert hyperbolically added, "month after month Hemingway's work has out-sold every other book in every book store in the United States, whether in New York, Atlanta, or [even] Boston," the very cradle of Comstockery.

Point three: it's unfair to judge the whole by its parts. If isolated passages were sufficient to condemn an author, "Chaucer, Shakespeare, Dickens, Whitman, and even the Bible would be so condemned." In fact, Solbert proposed an illuminating comparison of the Hemingway passages Dawley marked as salacious with, say, the first 25 lines of *Romeo and Juliet*, or lines 15–25, act 2, scene 2, of *King Lear*. At the same time, though, he accepted the dubious premise that books were to be judged—as a whole—by their "moral implications and conclusions."

Ergo, point four: Hemingway is really a very moral writer, which was demonstrated by the bad things that happen to people in his stories who live sordid, meaningless, and obscene lives. This was not true of genuine pornographic literature such as "'spicy' pulp magazines, trashy confessions, or privately printed postcards," Solbert pointed out, demonstrating his acquaintance with those genres. Besides, in *For Whom the Bell Tolls* Hemingway showed "his great social and moral purpose" by taking as his theme John Donne's famous "No man is an island . . ." sermon with its ringing conclusion that "any man's death diminishes me, for I am involved in mankind. And therefore never send to know for whom the bell tolls. It tolls for thee." Those of us "who are still fighting the war of mankind need more writing like this, not less," Solbert asserted, though—somewhat to the detriment of his argument—he introduced no inspiring quotations from Hemingway himself into evidence, only the appropriated one from Donne.

Point five: American soldiers know the score. They are no more ignorant of the facts of life than of the facts of death. They are "as fully capable and as fully justified" in reading Hemingway as the hundreds of thousands of civilians back home. In support Solbert cited a government pamphlet to the effect that "the fighting forces of the United States are not composed either of sybarites or of retarded adolescents."

Point six: don't destroy the books—or, in Army language, "it is recommended that the work of Ernest Hemingway remain available to soldiers in this theater. Council Books are expendable, but not destructible."

Solbert did an effective job of putting down Dawley, so that even if he does not emerge as an ideal defender of civil liberties—he didn't even mention the First Amendment—he's still the hero of this small story.

What were the passages that General Dawley found so salacious? Two are from "Macomber": the dialogue between Margot and Francis after she's had sex with Wilson, Francis's complaining that "there wasn't going to be any of that," and Wilson's bringing along a double-size cot to "accommodate any windfalls." Two are from "Snows": Helen getting drunk and taking lovers who bored her and Harry thinking he'd just as soon be in bed with Helen as anyone, "because she was richer" and would buy him anything he wanted. And four from the story Dawley found most offensive, "Mr. and Mrs. Elliot": trying to have a baby as "often as Mrs. Elliot could stand it"; Hubert staying "pure" before marriage and girls losing interest in him when they found out; Cornelia, on the other hand, delighted that he had kept himself "clean" for her, the "dear sweet boy"; their kissing for a long time in a way that Hubert had heard about; and once again the Elliots' trying "very hard to have a baby in the big hot bedroom on the big, hard bed." If this sort of thing turned General Dawley on, what would he have thought of Molly Bloom's soliloquy in *Ulysses* or the earth moving for Maria and Robert in *For Whom The Bell Tolls*, not to mention those French postcards?

However wrongheaded he may have been, and that was a lot, Dawley's reaction to Hemingway was by no means unique. His opinions were largely shared, for instance, by the prudish Dr. Clarence Edmonds Hemingway, who sent back the six copies of lowercase *in our time* that Ernest mailed him from Paris because he would not "tolerate such filth in his home," and who counseled his son, after reading the uppercase *In Our Time*, to do away with "the brutal" and "look for the joyous, uplifting, and optimistic and spiritual in character" (Flora, *Nick Adams*, 141, Baker,

A Life Story, 160). And there were a number of precedents for Dawley's act of censorship, including those of the Boston police who seized copies of *Scribner's* magazine containing installments of *A Farewell to Arms* and the Hitler youth who threw Hemingway's work into the bonfire, along with that of many others, on the infamous book-burning night of May 10, 1933 (Boyer, *Purity in Print*, 268).

Then, too, it is worth considering the unhappy situation Dawley found himself in. After he graduated from West Point in 1909, in the same class with Solbert and a year after Lee, for some years Dawley's career moved along more or less coterminously with those of the other two officers. All three served overseas during World War I. Dawley and Lee were awarded the Silver Star for gallantry in action in France, while Lee also received the Distinguished Service Medal. So did Solbert, who, although he was never a front-line officer, clearly possessed diplomatic talent. He served from 1917 to 1924 as military attaché to Denmark, Norway, and Great Britain, and in June 1924 as honorary aide-de-camp to the Prince of Wales during his visit to the United States. Then he left the service in 1925—though called back briefly as aide to the crown prince of Sweden during *his* visit to the States—to become a sales and advertising executive at Eastman Kodak, and he was not recommissioned until after Pearl Harbor.

Meanwhile, during the time between the wars, career officers Lee and Dawley held various posts and attended the usual command schools in the United States. Both were promoted to brigadier general (temporary) on October 1, 1940, but thereafter Lee's star began its ascendancy while Dawley's remained in eclipse. As early as May 1942 Lee was assigned to the European Theater of Operations, where he distinguished himself as the deputy commander for administration in charge of mounting the invasion in Normandy and as commander of the communications zone providing logistical support to Eisenhower's forces as they fought for the liberation of Europe. On the strength of his wartime accomplishments, he rose rapidly to major general in February 1942 and lieutenant general in February 1944. In due course he was decorated by Great Britain, France (four times), Belgium (twice), Luxembourg (three times), and Italy (three times), in addition to receiving the Oak Leaf Cluster to his Distinguished Service Medal, the U.S. Navy Distinguished Service Medal, the Bronze Star, and the Legion of Merit.

Dawley, on the other hand, suffered the worst fate a West Point officer could undergo. For two decades and more, he and his fellow officers waited for their opportunity. But when it finally arrived with the onset of World War II, he languished stateside in training missions while the action went on overseas. By the time he finally took charge of the Ground

Forces Reinforcement Command in Europe, on March 21, 1945, the fighting was almost over. VE Day came six weeks later, on May 8, 1945, and eight days after that Dawley sent his diatribe against Hemingway up to Lee. With only these bare facts as a guide, it is reckless but nonetheless tempting to speculate about Dawley's motives in doing so.

Once peace broke out, Dawley was faced with a challenge. As General Sir John Hackett points out in *The Profession of Arms*, command of a unit "is in many respects more difficult in peacetime than it is in war." In wartime there are fewer financial constraints, for example, and you "only have to be brave, competent, tireless and calm—but not all the time." During peacetime, however, a military leader has to concern himself "with soldiers' families, with welfare, with education, with barracks maintenance, with public occasions, with competitive sports, with a variety of inspections and with many other things which leave [him] untroubled on active service" (215–16). With no enemy left to conquer, Dawley's only chance to distinguish himself was by looking after his troops. In his West Point days, he had been taught that the officer who succeeds is "a leader of *character.*" Such a leader directs his organization to stand for something good and elevates his men "above their own self-interest to a higher purpose outside themselves"—or so it is set down in *The West Point Way of Leadership* (Donnithorpe, 164–65).

When, barely a week after VE Day, Dawley attempted to impose his private gag order on Hemingway's stories, he surely believed he was acting in accordance with the good of his troops, as part "of the efforts we are making toward morality and morals." As he saw it, he was simply protecting the troops from their own baser instincts. How were his men supposed to rise above their own self-interest to a higher purpose while reading of Margot Macomber's sleeping around, or Hubert and Cordelia Elliot's sweaty but futile attempts to make babies? Foolish and dangerous as his action may have been, it is still possible to feel a modicum of sympathy for poor General Dawley, slapped on the wrist by his old classmate, General Solbert, a man who spent most of the decades between the wars hobnobbing with royalty and making a pretty penny in the commercial world while Dawley and Lee and other career men sweated out their assignments in such garden spots as Fort Leavenworth and Camp Hood.

Though no court-martial was involved, one might even conjure up a picture of Dawley nervously manipulating a pair of ball bearings as he faced Solbert's devastating cross-examination by memorandum. Like Captain Queeg of the *Caine*, Dawley was on the job when no one much cared.

PART IX

◈ LITERATURE AND POLITICS ◈

[22]

THE LAST GREAT CAUSE

HEMINGWAY'S SPANISH CIVIL WAR WRITING

A LEFTWARD DRIFT

During the second half of the 1930s, almost all of Ernest Hemingway's writing followed a political agenda. In newspaper dispatches, magazine articles, a film, a play, his only public speech, a number of stories, and one of his greatest novels, he consistently—and sometimes passionately—wrote on behalf of the Spanish Republic.

Neither before nor after this time did Hemingway so devote himself to a political purpose. But this hardly means, as two of his biographers have argued, that he was "one of the least overtly political writers of his generation" and "basically bored by politics" (Kinnamon, "Hemingway and Politics," 149; Raeburn, "Hemingway on Stage," 14). Though Hemingway did not belong to any party, he was an interested observer of the politics of his time, and he often expressed himself on issues of the day, especially in his correspondence. In his excellent article "Hemingway and Politics," Keneth Kinnamon subdivides the author's political beliefs into three distinct positions. First, Hemingway disliked and distrusted all politicians, whatever their affiliation. Second, he resented governmental control over individuals. Third, and most important, "From the beginning to the end of his adult life, he had deep sympathies with the left, especially the revolutionary left" (159).

Not until the late 1930s did these sympathies demonstrate themselves in Hemingway's writing. He was too fiercely independent to be drawn into most liberal causes. In two angry letters of 1932, he engaged in an argument with Paul Romaine, a bookdealer who urged him to join "the Leftward drift" in writing. He wasn't about "to swallow communism as though it were an elder Boys Y.M.C.A. conference," Hemingway responded. Beyond that, he refused to outline his own political beliefs for Romaine, since he could be "jailed for their publication." But, he added, "if they are not much further left than yours which sound like a sentimental socialism I will move them further over." Still, he was damned if he'd "follow the fashions in politics, letters, religion etc. . . . There is no left or right in good writing. There is only good or bad writing" (*Selected Letters* 363, 365).

Various forces were at work, however, to persuade him to use his pen on behalf of causes beyond the boundaries of art. Like almost all sensate observers of the time, Hemingway was troubled by the poverty and misery of the Depression. "Country is all busted," he wrote Guy Hickok in October 1932. He had little confidence in the ability of Herbert Hoover ("The Syphilitic Baby"), Franklin Delano Roosevelt ("The Paralytic Demagogue"), or any other politician to remedy the apparent collapse of capitalism. Nor was he ready to accept communism as the answer. He described himself as an anarchist, one who believed that no unit larger than a village could be effectively governed. Still, it was all right with him if John Dos Passos decided to join the comrades, and he wrote admiringly of the "*wonderful* reporting" in *The American Jitters*, Edmund Wilson's 1932 portrayal of a nation in economic crisis (*Selected Letters*, 372–73, 375, 360).

The previous year, Hemingway had gone to Spain during the revolution that led to the second Spanish Republic. He had fallen in love with Spain—and with *toreo*—in the summer of 1923 and returned during bullfight season in most years since. In urging Howell Jenkins to join him at Pamplona for the 1925 fiesta of San Fermin, he expounded on the virtues of the country. There was "swell fishing" on the Irati, the fiesta itself offered "the godamdest wild time," the Spaniards had "any people in the world skinned," and the price was right. "Spain is the real old stuff," he declared, the best country of all now that the "post war fascisti" had ruined Italy (*Selected Letters*, 131). "If I could have made this enough of a book," he began the last chapter of *Death in the Afternoon* (1932), "it would have had everything in it," and he followed that with a lyrical evocation of the Spanish settings he'd visited. "The Prado, looking like some big American college building, with sprinklers watering the grass early in the bright Madrid summer morning; the bare white mud hills looking across toward Carabanchel; days on the train in August with the blinds pulled down on the side against the sun and the wind . . . ; the change when you leave the green country behind at Alsausa; . . . Burgos far across the plain and eating the cheese later up in the room" (270).

Feeling as he did about Spain, Hemingway naturally took an interest in its politics. These were much on his mind when he arrived in Spain in May 1931, only a month after the overthrow of the dictator Primo de Rivera and the departure of King Alphonso. In Madrid, he met the radical Spanish painter Luis Quintanilla, who quietly explained why a revolution was necessary, and the American newsmen Jay Allen and Elliot Paul, who felt the same way. "Been following politics closely," Hemingway wrote Dos Passos from Madrid late in June, and he proceeded to report on factional and regional complications. The Republicans were sure to win a landslide victory in the June 28 election but were themselves divided among "Red White and Black" configurations. Then, too, Spain's various regions had differing agendas. Andalusia was coming to a boil. Madrid loved the Republic. Catalonia was waiting to do business. The king was "permanently out," but Don Jaime the Pretender had entered the country incognito and made considerable headway in Navarre.

On Hemingway's voyage across the Atlantic he had talked with seven Spanish priests who were fearful of a Republican victory. The Catholic Church was aligned with the right, and there were reports that mobs had destroyed churches. The violence worked both ways, Hemingway reported. In Navarre, it was "no uncommon thing for a prelate to shoot down a good republican from the top of an autobus." Still, he saw no chance of a Marxian revolution. Spain was not Russia, and the local communists had "no money at all" (*Selected Letters*, 341–42).

Two years later, the Hemingways were in Cuba when the dictator Gerardo Machado was overthrown after a bloody insurrection. Ernest's sympathies lay with the Cuban people, and he was pleased that they had disposed of the "lousy tyrant" Machado (Baker, *A Life Story*, 245). En route to their African safari a few months later, he and Pauline stopped in Spain, where conditions under the second Spanish republic had turned sour. In a January 1934 article for *Esquire*, Hemingway outlined the situation. On the surface, the country seemed prosperous enough. More people were traveling and going to bullfights than before. More tax money was coming in than during the days of the monarchy, but the money was going into the pockets of "the innumerable functionaries of the republic," while the peasants remained as poor as ever. Politics in Spain remained "a lucrative profession," Hemingway cynically concluded ("The Friend of Spain," 147). "All the idealists now in power have their fingers in the pie." When they ran out of pie, there would be another revolution (*Selected Letters*, 398).

Presumably, the situation degenerated still further by October 1934, when Luis Quintanilla was sent to jail for conspiring against the government whose installation he had advocated three years before. Hemingway signed a petition on behalf of the artist that avoided all political issues, instead arguing for Quintanilla's release on the grounds that his work "redound[ed] greatly to the credit of the fatherland of Goya and Velasquez" (Baker, *A Life Story*, 267; letter to Zamora).

In that same year, Hemingway's work was published in Russia for the first time and immediately became popular. Between 1934 and 1939, his short stories, his three novels, and the play *The Fifth Column* all appeared in Russian translation. Asked to name their favorite foreign author in 1937, nine of fifteen Soviet writers chose Hemingway. In his eternally competitive way, Ernest was delighted to tell Maxwell Perkins that he was outselling Dreiser, Dos Passos, Sinclair Lewis, and "several other guys" in the Soviet Union (Baker, *A Life Story*, 277).

He also found a sensitive and intelligent Russian interpreter of his work in Ivan Kashkin, whose essay "Ernest Hemingway: The Tragedy of Craftsmanship" appeared in the May 1935 issue of *International Literature*. It was a pleasure, Hemingway wrote the Russian critic, "to have somebody know what you are writing about." But he disabused Kashkin of any notion that they shared the same political convictions. "Everyone tries to frighten you now by saying or writing that if one does not become a communist or have a Marxian viewpoint one will have no friends and will be alone. . . . I cannot become a communist now because I believe in only one thing: liberty. First I would look after myself and do my work. Then I would care for my family. Then I would help my neighbor. But the state I care nothing for. . . . I believe in the absolute minimum of government." His standards were Jeffersonian, not Marxian (Baker, *A Life Story*, 479–80).

Despite such disclaimers, the left continued to cultivate Hemingway. He was highly visible, widely respected, and, if not communist, at least aggressively antifascist as Hitler and Mussolini gained power in Europe. By the mid-1930s, it had become the policy of the Comintern (the Communist International) and its Popular Front to court all antifascists, especially if, like Hemingway, their name carried authority. His fame made him an inviting target for the Communist Party, both at home and abroad.

Still, it took a natural disaster to get Hemingway into the pages of the *New Masses*, the American Communist Party magazine. In the mid-1920s he was angered when the publication rejected two of his stories and ran a critical review of *The Sun Also Rises* by Dos Passos. It was nothing more than "a house organ" for parlor pinks, he told Ezra Pound. "FUCK the new masses and their revolution" (Baker, *A Life Story*, 473–74). Thereafter he had nothing to do with the *New Masses* until September 1935, when editor Joe North wired him for an article on the hurricane that wiped out the C.C.C. camps on Lower Matecumbe Key. The storm killed hundreds of World War I veterans who had been shipped to Florida after participating in the Bonus March on Washington.

Carefully preparing for the hurricane from his home at Key West, Hemingway moored the *Pilar* in the safest corner of the submarine base, brought the garden furniture and children's toys inside the house, and nailed down the shutters at all the windows. The full brunt of the storm missed Key West, striking at Islamorada and Upper and Lower Matecumbe Keys. When the winds subsided, Hemingway persuaded Bra Saunders and J. B. Sullivan to accompany him on an inspection tour of the devastation. In staccato prose, he wrote Max Perkins what they'd seen. "Between 700 and 1000 dead [an exaggeration: 458 veterans were killed]. . . . The foliage absolutely stripped as though by fire for forty miles and the land looking like the abandoned bed of a river. Not a building of any sort standing. Over thirty miles of railway washed and blown away. We were the first in to the camp five of the veterans who were working on the Highway construction. Out of 187 only 8 survived. Saw more dead than I'd seen in one place since the lower Piave in June of 1918" (Hemingway and Perkins, *Only Thing*, 226).

Hemingway placed the blame for the veterans' death squarely on Harry Hopkins and President Roosevelt. They "sent those poor bonus march guys down there to get rid of them all right all right." Then they'd had two full days to evacuate the vets from their flimsy quarters before the storm struck and done nothing. In his outrage, Hemingway tore off 2,800 words for the *New Masses*. North titled the piece "Who Murdered the Vets?" This only slightly misconstrued what Hemingway had to say. In the article itself, he posed his own rhetorical question: "And what's the punishment for manslaughter now?" As he'd written Perkins, "The veterans in those camps were practically murdered" (Baker, *A Life Story*, 481; Hemingway and Perkins, *Only Thing*, 226).

Privately Hemingway excoriated the editors of the *New Masses* as hypocrites who denigrated his work as "decadent" and lacking in class awareness then called on him for a contribution when they wanted the truth about the hurricane. But the literary left regarded "Who Murdered the Vets?" as an unmistakable sign that Hemingway had seen the light and was ready to join the crusade against capitalism. "That was a damn fine piece," Dos Passos wrote Hemingway after reading the article reprinted in the *Daily Worker*, the communist newspaper (Baker, *A Life Story*, 482). "Who Murdered the Vets?" was also translated into Russian for the December 1935 *International Literature*, where an editorial footnote welcomed it as "one of the most important documents of the development of revolutionary literature in America": especially important because Hemingway, "the most powerful American writer," had never previously "taken part in any sort of social action of writers and ha[d] consciously stood aside from the revolutionary movement" (Brown, *Soviet Attitudes*, 307).

Despite his awakened indignation about governmental mistreatment of the individual, and despite his hatred of the fascist regimes in Germany and Italy, Hemingway was not ready to join the revolution. In two articles for *Esquire* in the fall of 1935, he warned against American involvement in the war developing in Europe. "Not this August, nor this September. . . . Not next August, nor next September; that is still too soon. . . . But the year after or the year after that they fight." Europe always fought, and the thing to do was to stay out of it. "We were fools to be sucked in once on a European war and we should never be sucked in again" ("Notes on the Next War," 199, 206).

He cited several reasons, all bad, why the United States might be drawn into a European conflict: "through mistaken idealism, through propaganda, through the desire to back our creditors, or through the wish of anyone through war, notoriously the health of the state, to make a going concern out of a mismanaged one" (200). Now was the time to decide to stay out. "Now, before the propaganda starts." Above all, he maintained, "no one man nor group of men incapable of fighting or exempt from fighting should in any way be given the power . . . to put this country or any country into war" ("The Malady of Power," 220).

Hemingway followed these two "serious letters" for *Esquire* with "Wings Always Over Africa," a scarifying portrait of the miseries of the war Mussolini was waging against Ethiopia. The Italian dictator would do well, he wrote, to censor all reports from the African battlefields that described the activity of the carrion birds. These birds—especially the vultures and the marabou storks—would hit a wounded man as quickly as a dead one. Italian soldiers should be trained to roll over on their face if they were hit and could not keep moving. Otherwise the vultures and storks would shuffle over them and peck their faces away.

One might think that the Italians would have learned about the horror and futility of war from World War I, he pointed out. But the propaganda of Mussolini, "the cleverest opportunist in modern history," saw to it that this did not happen:

> No knowledge of the past war will help boys from the little steep-hilled towns of the Abruzzi where the snow comes early on the tops of the mountains, nor those who worked in garages, or machine shops, in Milano or Bologna or Firenze, or rode their bicycles in road races in the white dust-powdered roads of Lombardy, nor those who played football for their factory teams in Spezia or Torino, or mowed the high mountain meadows of the Dolomites and guided skiers in the winter, or would have been burning charcoal in the woods above Piombino, or maybe sweeping out a trattoria in Vicenza, or would have gone to North or South America in the old days. [In Africa] they will feel the deadly heat and know the shadeless land; they will have the diseases that never cure, that make the bones ache and a young man old and turn the bowels to water, and when there is a battle, finally, they will hear the whish of wings when the birds come down and I hope when they are hit someone will have told them to roll over.

Mussolini's own sons were pilots with no enemy planes to shoot them down, while poor men's sons from all over Italy were the foot soldiers. Hemingway wished them luck, and wished they knew who was "their enemy and why" ("Wings Always," 226–27).

Maxwell Perkins at Scribner's was mightily impressed by "Wings Always Over Africa," the antiwar pieces in *Esquire*, and the article about the veterans who died in the hurricane. There wasn't a man alive who could write as well as Hemingway about the turbulent times they were living through, Perkins wrote him on December 20, 1935, and he thought that the best of these articles ought to be preserved in more permanent form. That would be a way of showing "the proletarian boys, the Marxists . . . what could be done in the way of dealing with actual events and class conflicts that would make their stuff look silly" (Hemingway and Perkins, *Only Thing*, 230).

Four months later Perkins proposed including the "Wings" article, the hurricane one, and the best of the *Esquire* pieces in the book of stories he and Hemingway were considering bringing out in the fall of 1936. Readers who liked "journalism that transcends journalism" would prize these articles, Perkins pointed out, and he added, with a measure of calculation, they "would get a little of the radical vote too." Hemingway vigorously rejected the idea of "mixing in articles and stories," however. That would only give the left-wing New York critics a chance to dismiss them all as trash written for *Esquire*, that "Men's Clothing Trade magazine." Besides, he had no desire to be aligned with the "literary fashionable communist crowd" that Perkins apparently thought he should cultivate. They couldn't tell literature from shit, and he wasn't about to truckle to them (*Only Thing*, 242).

Still, when the *New Masses* asked him for a contribution to its twenty-fifth-anniversary issue later in the year, Hemingway sent a friendly wire explaining that he was "awfully sorry" but he was busy with a novel (*To Have and Have Not*) and couldn't write anything else. "Congratulations twenty-fifth anniversary will send you a good story for the fiftieth," he concluded. The magazine printed the telegram in its December 1, 1936, issue. By that time, the war in Spain was well underway.

In February 1936 Spanish voters elected by a narrow plurality a Popular Front coalition of anarchists, socialists, and communists loosely conjoined in support of the third Spanish Republic. With that election, the issue was joined between groups violently opposed to one another. On one side stood representatives of the old ruling order: bankers, landlords, the clergy, and the military—taken together, the Nationalists, sometimes called rebels, insurgents, or fascists. On the other side were ranged the peasants, the workers, and most of the writers and intellectuals—the Republicans, also known as Loyalists, or the government, or communists

Once in power, the Republicans started settling old scores with a brutal display of force. The Catholic Church, which supported and was supported by the establishment, became a target of opportunity. According to one estimate, some 60,000 people were killed during the first three months, "including twelve bishops, 283 nuns, 4,184 priests, and 2,365 monks" (Knightley, *The First Casualty*, 197). In July 1936, the Nationalists under Generalissimo Francisco Franco launched a rebellion that quickly made its way across the country to the gates of Madrid, committing a similar number of murders along the way. Jay Allen of the *Chicago Tribune* witnessed Nationalist troops rounding up 1,800 probable Republican sympathizers in the town of Badajoz, on the Portuguese border, and sending them to the bull ring to be machine-gunned (Knightley, *The First Casualty*, 201–2).

"No other war in recent times," Phillip Knightley said, "aroused such intense emotion, such deep commitment, such violent partisanship as the

Civil War in Spain" (*The First Casualty*, 192). Both sides were fighting for what they regarded as a holy cause: the Nationalists to resurrect a Christian Spain uncontaminated by communists and other unbelievers, the Republicans for the new age of a Marxist utopia. Behind and beneath the idealism lay the hard economic struggle of the rich against the poor. "In essence it was a class war," as George Orwell observed. "If it had been won, the cause of the common people everywhere would have been strengthened" (Knightley, *The First Casualty*, 192). Hemingway's sympathies, like Orwell's, rested with the common people and the Republic. Years later he was to write Edmund Wilson that the "believed in [the Spanish Republic] deeply long before it was an American Communist cause" (*Selected Letters*, 733).

It was something of a miracle that the war lasted nearly three years. Most military officers were supporters of the Nationalists, and their troops were well trained and well equipped. The Republicans—beset by factionalism and regional rivalries—had to scramble to assemble an effective fighting force, working with raw recruits and unskilled leaders. If it had not been for the International Brigades, made up of volunteers harking to the cause from Europe and North America, Madrid would undoubtedly have fallen to Franco in the autumn of 1936. But the Republicans managed to hold the capital then, and soon thereafter they launched offensives of their own.

Hemingway watched the civil war closely from his bases in Key West and Wyoming. "I hate to have missed this Spanish thing worse than anything in the world," he wrote Max Perkins on September 26, "but have to have this book [*To Have and Have Not*] finished first." On December 15, he expressed himself even more vehemently. "I've *got* to go to Spain," he told Perkins, but he had his book to finish, it was cold as hell in Madrid, and they'd be fighting for a long time (*Selected Letters*, 454–56).

Meanwhile, he was firming up his commitment to the Republican cause. Franco was "a good general but a son of a bitch of the first water," Hemingway declared, and he demonstrated his convictions by way of his pocketbook (*Selected Letters*, 455). He contributed $3,000 of his own money for the purchase of ambulances (an amount inflated in the press to $40,000) and paid passage for two volunteers to fight for the Loyalists.

His own passage to the Spanish Civil War came as a result of his celebrity. In his newspaper column, Walter Winchell ran an item that Hemingway was planning to go to Spain to write about the war. John N. Wheeler, the general manager of the North American Newspaper Alliance (NANA), thereupon proposed to Hemingway, in a letter of November 25, that he provide news coverage for them from Spain. NANA, he explained, was a news service affiliated with sixty leading newspapers in the United States and Canada, as well as others around the world. Hemingway soon closed a deal with Wheeler that made him the world's highest paid war correspondent. He was to receive $500 for each cabled dispatch and $1,000 for mailed articles of up to 1,200 words: nearly a dollar a word.

Before his departure at the end of February, Hemingway spent some time in New York, where he became involved in two films designed to promote the Spanish Republic. Helene van Dongen, companion of the Dutch communist filmmaker Joris Ivens, stitched together a film from newsreel material called *Spain in Flames*. The subtitles were written by Prudencio de Pereda, a young Spanish novelist, with contributions from Dos Passos, Archibald MacLeish, and Hemingway himself. Hemingway's commentary stressed the cruelty of the Spanish war, where indiscriminate bombing by Fascist planes killed women and children instead of soldiers. To accompany scenes of Madrid burning, he specifically noted that both Nazi Germany and Fascist Italy were helping the Nationalists shell the capital.

Dependent as it was on stale newsreel footage, *Spain in Flames* did not turn out to be especially effective propaganda. Ivens thereupon persuaded a number of sympathetic Americans to support another film that he would make in Spain itself, with live scenes from the front lines. A group called Contemporary Historians was formed to promote this endeavor. In addition to Ivens, the principals included MacLeish (who served as treasurer), Dos Passos, and Hemingway, along with the playwrights Lillian Hellman and Clifford Odets and the Broadway producer Herman Shumlin. A total of $18,000 was raised to finance the film, which was eventually called *The Spanish Earth*. The two largest contributions, $4,000 each, came from the North American Committee for Spain—a branch of an international committee formed in Paris by the Communist Party propaganda chief Willi Münzenberg—and from Ernest Hemingway. Before long, Hemingway and Ivens would be shooting the film in Spain, side by side in dangerous circumstances.

Hemingway's letters in early February to Harry Sylvester, a young Catholic novelist, and to his wife Pauline's devoutly Catholic family, set forth his reasons for going to Spain. To Sylvester he acknowledged that the Spanish war was a bad war, "and nobody is right," and he added his conviction that it was "a dirty outfit in Russia now." But the bulk of the letter amounted to an apologia for the Republican atrocities against the Church. While he was borrowing to finance ambulances for the Loyalist wounded, "the rebels have plenty of good Italian ambulances. But it's not very catholic or christian to kill the wounded in the hospital in Toledo with handgrenades or to bomb the working quarter of Madrid for no military reason except to kill poor people. . . . I know they've shot priests and bishops but why was the church . . . on the side of the oppressors instead of for the people . . . ?" (*Selected Letters*, 456).

Hemingway adopted a more defensive posture in his letter to the Pfeiffer family, introducing himself as "the leader of the Ingrates battalion on the wrong side of the Spanish war." Then he went on to explain his position in idealistic terms. For a long time, he pointed out, "me and my conscience both have known that I have to go to Spain." He'd staked the government to ambulances, but now it was time to see the war for himself. "The Reds may be as bad as they say but they are the people of the country versus the absentee landlords, the [M]oors, the [I]talians and the Germans. I know the Whites are rotten because I know them very well and I would like to have a look at the others to see how it lines up on a basis of humanity" (*Selected Letters*, 457–58).

In addition, he hoped his reporting from Spain might help to keep the United States out of the inevitable European war to follow. He expanded on the point as he boarded ship on February 27: "Everybody is trying to push us into the next war, the new style war, the kind of war they fought in Ethiopia and are fighting in Spain, the total war, where there is no such thing as a non-combatant, where everybody who lives across a line on the map is a target" (Watson, "Joris Ivens," 43). The horror of that kind of war hadn't been brought home clearly enough, and that was what he meant to do as an antiwar war correspondent.

LOVER

During two months in Spain in the spring of 1937—the first of four trips to the war-torn country he was to make over a period of twenty months—Hemingway converted from a presumably objective antiwar correspondent to a fervent supporter of the Republican cause. Much of the change in his attitude derived from what he saw and did there. But the people then closest to him had even more to do with it, particularly Martha Gellhorn, Joris Ivens, and Herbert Matthews.

Gellhorn and Hemingway met in the dankness of Key West's Sloppy Joe's one day in December 1936. The story, as Carlos Baker recorded it, was that Martha (called Marty), her mother, Edna, and her brother Alfred were traveling southeast from St. Louis and, finding Miami uninspiring, decided to head for the keys. Whether this was a chance encounter remains in some doubt, for the ambitious Martha had a knack for attracting the attention of the famous and powerful and may have presented herself at Hemingway's Key West hangout in order to get to know him. Only twenty-eight years old, she had already—before beginning her relationship with Hemingway—won the interest and support of Eleanor Roosevelt and served as H. G. Wells's protégé.

By any standard she was a remarkable young woman, who despite her youth had established a reputation as a rising journalist and fiction writer. She grew up in St. Louis, the daughter of a well-known doctor and his suffragist wife. After three years at Bryn Mawr, she left college for a job at the *New Republic*, went on from there to reporting for a newspaper in upstate New York, and landed in Paris in 1929, working successively for *Vogue*, the United Press, and the *St. Louis Post-Dispatch*. In 1933 she went to Capri to write *What Mad Pursuit*, a first novel about three young American women. The title came from John Keats, and the epigraph— "Nothing ever happens to the brave"—from Ernest Hemingway.

The following year she ended her marriage to Bertrand de Jouvenel, a titled French journalist who had in his day been one of Colette's young lovers, and came back to the States. Marquis Child, the Washington correspondent for the *Post-Dispatch*, got her an interview with Harry Hopkins, FDR's right-hand man. Gellhorn persuaded Hopkins to hire her as an investigator for the Federal Emergency Relief Administration (FERA), reporting back to Washington about the suffering of the nation's unemployed. Her reports were so moving that Hopkins made a point of introducing her to Eleanor Roosevelt, who was impressed by Gellhorn's writing, person, and dedication to the cause of the impoverished. Through Mrs. Roosevelt Martha met the president and, on another White House occasion, the famous British writer H.G. Wells, who was much taken with her. Wells contributed an admiring preface to *The Trouble I've Seen*, a fictionalized version of Gellhorn's FERA interviews that came out to excellent reviews in August 1936. "Who is this Martha Gellhorn?" Lewis Gannett asked. "Hemingway does not write more authentic American speech. Nor can Ernest Hemingway teach Martha Gellhorn anything about economy of language." Mrs. Roosevelt mentioned the book favorably three times in her syndicated "My Day" column. It was a wonder, she observed, that the youthful Gellhorn, coming from "more or less Junior League background, with a touch of exquisite Paris clothes and 'esprit' thrown in," should be able to write with such understanding about the travails of the Depression's downtrodden (Lynn, *Hemingway*, 464–66).

So it was on the wings of success that the energetic, talented, and ambitious Gellhorn sailed into Sloppy Joe's, where Hemingway was having a drink with owner Joe Russell. She had shoulder-length blonde hair, and was wearing a black cotton dress that showed off her lovely long legs— legs, Hemingway said, that started at her shoulders. When the two of them began talking, it reminded the bartender of beauty and the beast, for the unkempt Hemingway was wearing his usual grubby outfit of t-shirt and shorts tied with a rope. The conversation between them went on into the night, past the time when he was supposed to be home for a dinner party. Pauline sent Charles Thompson to fetch Ernest. Thompson returned without him, but with the disquieting news that Mrs. Hemingway's husband had been detained by an admirer, "a beautiful blonde in a black dress" (Mellow, *A Life Without Consequences*, 484).

What began that night continued for another fortnight, as Gellhorn extended her visit to Key West. She was working on a novel about French and German pacifists and he was putting the finishing touches on *To Have and Have Not*, but they made time for daily meetings. They went swimming together, and he showed her around the island. They talked about his books, about the Cuban revolution, about hurricanes, and above all about the civil war in Spain. He gave her his work in progress to read, and it left her "weak with envy and wonder" (Moorehead, *Gellhorn*, 104). Pauline was fully aware that Martha posed a danger to their marriage. "I suppose Ernest is busy again helping Miss Gellhorn with her writing," she once sarcastically remarked (Meyers, *Biography*, 300). Presumably to diminish the intensity of the relationship, she welcomed Martha to their home. Nothing worked. When Gellhorn left Key West, Hemingway pursued her as far as Miami, where they had a steak dinner, with boxer Tom Heeney serving as a beard, and then rode the train together as far as Jacksonville, whence she proceeded to St. Louis and he to New York. To correct a rumor that Ernest had fallen seriously ill, Pauline wired Arnold Gingrich with measured acerbity: "SECONDHAND REPORT ENTIRELY BASELESS ERNEST IN MIAMI ENROUTE TO NEW YORK IN SHALL WE SAY PERFECT HEALTH" (Baker, *A Life Story*, 299). Martha's thank-you letter soon arrived, telling Pauline that it was good of her "not to mind my becoming a fixture, like a kudu head, in your home" (Moorehead, *Gellhorn*, 105).

Hemingway's marriage was in disrepair even before Gellhorn appeared, as any close reader of "The Snows of Kilimanjaro" (in the August 1936 *Esquire*) might have intuited. Ernest felt he was living entirely too comfortable a life in Key West. "I could stay on here forever," he told the visiting writer Matthew Josephson, "but it's a soft life. Nothing's really happening to me here and I've got to get out" (Lynn, *Hemingway*, 485).

The war in Spain gave Hemingway a valid reason to make his departure, along with the opportunity to continue his relationship with Gellhorn. Both of them supported the Loyalist cause, she with an even stronger commitment than his. When Ernest told her about his contract with NANA to report on the war, Martha abandoned her pacifist novel and set about securing reportorial credentials of her own. "Please don't disappear," she wrote Ernest. "Are we or are we not members of the same union? Hemingstein, I am very very fond of you" (Moorehead, *Gellhorn*, 106). As coconspirators they plotted a reunion in Spain. "I have personally already gotten myself a beard and a pair of dark glasses," she reported in mid-February. "Please, please leave word in Paris."

Meanwhile, Hemingway refused Pauline's request to accompany him to Spain, on the grounds that it would be dangerous for her and distracting for him. Considering his secret plans with Gellhorn, he must have felt a pang of guilt when his wife's somewhat embittered farewell letter reached him in New York. "Would love to be with you instead of being here with nobody and the sea," Pauline wrote. "And all those telegrams about Spain and ambulances bring my situation of impending doom pretty near the front door. . . . So goodbye big-shot-in-the-pants, good luck and why not start keeping me informed?" (Lynn, *Hemingway*, 468).

Hemingway made the voyage across the Atlantic with the bullfighter Sidney Franklin and the poet and horseplayer Evan Shipman. Franklin, absolutely without politics but skilled in talking his way into favors and out of trouble, went along as general factotum. Shipman was en route to join the Abraham Lincoln Battalion and fight for the Spanish Republic. After spending ten days in Paris, Hemingway reached Madrid in the middle of March. Less than two weeks later, Martha Gellhorn joined him. It was not easy for her to get there.

First she had to wangle a letter of accreditation from Kyle Crichton, an editor at *Collier's*. She had no firm contract with the magazine, but the letter enabled her to secure a passport for Spain. Held up in Paris for a few days, waiting for papers from the French allowing her to cross the frontier, she looked in vain for other writers to travel with. Finally she set off alone, carrying a knapsack, a duffel bag full of canned food, and fifty dollars in her pocket. She reached Barcelona March 24, and Valencia two days later, where apparently by chance she ran into Franklin, who was gathering provisions. He offered her a ride to Madrid in a car loaded down with ham, coffee, butter, marmalade, and a hundred-kilo basket of oranges, lemons, and grapefruit. They reached the capital the evening of March 27.

Hemingway was proprietary about Gellhorn from the start. When she appeared at the basement restaurant on the Gran Via where the correspondents ate, Hemingway was surrounded by an admiring coterie of young soldiers. "I knew you'd get here, daughter, because I fixed it so you could," he announced. This was untrue, but Gellhorn accepted it as "one of the foibles of genius." Ernest had circumspectly booked adjoining rooms at the Hotel Florida for them, and on the first night he locked her in her room, presumably to protect her from the pimps and drunks roaming the hallways. Gellhorn was furious but decided to let it pass. Hemingway had much to teach her about war, she knew no Spanish, and as "just about the only blonde in the country," she thought it better to "belong to someone." Two weeks later, according to her account, they went to bed together for the first time (Moorehead, *Gellhorn*, 112–14).

The liaison was uncovered late one night when a rebel shell hit the hotel's water tank, forcing residents into the security of the basement. As John Dos Passos recalled the scene, men and women in various stages of undress scuttled from their rooms, among them Ernest and Martha. The French writer Antoine de Saint-Exupéry, magnificent in a blue velvet dressing gown, solemnly handed a grapefruit from his private store to all who passed his room, while Josephine Herbst took charge of providing coffee until the bombardment was over. They were all stopping at the Florida, home away from home for many foreigners and most correspondents in Madrid.

A sense of camaraderie bound them together, as well as a conviction that they were witnessing—and helping to shape—the course of history. Some became friends for life, with a particularly close bond springing up among Hemingway, Gellhorn, and Herbert Matthews of the *New York Times*. Six weeks after she arrived in Madrid, Gellhorn declared that she found "Spain superb," while Madrid "was heaven, far and away the best thing I have seen or lived through" (Moorehead, *Gellhorn*, 128). Years later, she tried to articulate what she meant. Being in Madrid under siege, in the spring of 1937, gave her a rare "fusion of body and soul," a feeling "of living one's life and believing with one's whole heart in the life around one" (154). She "just *knew* that Spain was the place to stop Fascism" (111). Hemingway shared her conviction and her sense of elation. "I think I can truly say . . . that the period of fighting when we thought the Republic could win the Spanish civil war was the happiest period of our lives," he wrote in 1940 (Bruccoli, *Mechanism of Fame*, 82). For both of them, as for Matthews and others, the civil war in Spain became a cause of tremendous importance: if it was won the next great war would not have to be fought.

More than anything else—more even than the excitement of their clandestine affair and the daily exposure to enemy bombardment—it was Hemingway and Gellhorn's devotion to this "last great cause" of the struggle against fascism that bound them together. "I think it was the only time in his life when he was not the most important thing there was," she commented years later, after their bitter divorce. "He really cared about the Republic and he cared about that war. I believe I never would've gotten hooked otherwise" (Mellow, *A Life Without Consequences*, 496).

Not everyone felt the way they did about the Republic. In one instance, a journalist dubious about the cause attempted to take advantage of Gellhorn's good nature. This was Frederick Voigt of the *Manchester Guardian*, who arrived in Madrid in April 1937 for a brief visit and began telling the other correspondents that a reign of terror gripped the city and that "thousands of bodies [were] being found." He'd not seen them himself, Voigt admitted, but would not back down from his assertion.

As it happened, Gellhorn was about to travel to Paris, and Voigt persuaded her to carry a sealed envelope with her to be mailed to his newspaper. It was merely a copy of an already censored dispatch he'd sent to the *Guardian*, he assured her; he asked her to mail it for him in case the original did not arrive. Hemingway, hearing about this request, immediately became suspicious. He took Voigt's envelope to the government censor in Madrid. It turned out to contain not a copy of an already censored dispatch but a new one that began: "There is a terror here in Madrid. Thousands of bodies . . ." (Knightley, *The First Casualty*, 198). Had Gellhorn been found with this document, she would have faced charges of smuggling uncensored material out of Spain. Only with difficulty did she persuade Hemingway not to start a fistfight with Voigt, who—fortunately for all parties—soon left town.

The siege of Madrid was at its fiercest in the early months of 1937. During the previous November the Fascist forces had reached the gates of the city, only to be turned back by the Republicans. Both sides then dug in to form a front line that ran through University City and the Casa del Campo. It was only two miles from the main shopping district, and more or less accessible to correspondents damn-fool enough to take the risk. "You took a tram halfway, walked the other half, and you were there," correspondent Virginia Cowles recalled (*Looking for Trouble*, 21).

During the six months after being stopped on the city's outskirts, the Nationalists—using German and Italian artillery—rained shells on downtown Madrid. Thousands were killed or wounded by the incessant shelling, but ordinary life went on pretty much as usual. People walked on one side of the street because shells usually fell on the other. Department stores emptied for a bombardment and filled up again when it was over. Madrileños went to see Greta Garbo in *Anna Karenina* and the Marx Brothers in *A Night at the Opera*. (Hemingway was convinced that the fascists timed their shelling to coincide with the time the movies let out). The siege drew the people together, Cowles believed. "Everyone was *camarada* and everyone was fighting the Fascists" (38).

Everyone was also hungry, for the usual supply routes were cut off. Queues formed daily, women and children waiting long hours for whatever beans, bread, and rice might be rationed to them. The professional foreign correspondents were only marginally better off at their basement restaurant on the Gran Via. Lunch usually consisted of salami and rice, followed by dinner of salami and beans. But if food was scarce, beer and whiskey were dispensed in abundance to an assemblage that in addition to the journalists included—in Dos Passos's somewhat jaundiced description—"young worldsaviours and . . . members of foreign radical delegations . . . , militiamen and internationals on sprees and a sprinkling of young ladies of the between the sheets brigade" (Dos Passos, *Journeys*, 372).

Hemingway drank his share of the liquor and managed with the aid of Sid Franklin to commandeer quantities of food in short supply. Josie Herbst recalled sitting in the lobby of the Florida as the heavenly odor of bacon and eggs wafted down from rooms 108 and 109 on the fourth floor. Hemingway also had seemingly unlimited access to transport, although gas was rationed and it was hard for most reporters to get a ride anywhere. His fellow correspondents knew that Hemingway was working on a film with Joris Ivens and needed a car and driver to shoot on location but still felt resentful about the privileges granted him—a resentment that tended to dissipate when they got to know him better.

Easily the most famous figure among those covering the Spanish war, Hemingway wore his prominence lightly. There was nothing pretentious about him. "He was a massive, ruddy-cheeked man who went around Madrid in a pair of filthy brown trousers and a torn blue shirt," as Cowles observed (*Looking for Trouble*, 31). The government censor Arturo Barea remembered him as "big and lumbering, with the look of a worried boy on his round face, diffident and yet consciously using his diffidence as an attraction, a good fellow to drink with, fond of dirty jokes 'pour epâter l'Espagnol,' questioning, skeptical and intelligent in his curiosity, skillfully stressing his political ignorance, easy and friendly, yet remote and somewhat sad" (Barea, "Not Spain," 208). Many nights Hemingway and Gellhorn held open bar in their rooms at the Florida for other correspondents, officers of the International Brigades on leave, and a motley crowd of tourists and tarts.

Hemingway proved useful to his fellow reporters when he discovered a battered apartment house on the outskirts of Madrid whose entire front had been ripped away by a bomb. He called the place "The Old Homestead," and it served as an excellent site from which to observe firefights from a safe distance. On an early April afternoon, he, Gellhorn, Cowles, Dos Passos, Matthews, and the British journalists Sefton (Tom) Delmer of the *Daily Express* and Henry Buckley of the *Daily Telegraph* watched as two Loyalist tanks tried—and failed—to take three houses where rebels were entrenched. War seemed banal at that remove, Cowles thought. Against the wide panorama of rolling hills, the tanks looked like children's toys. Hemingway, who had seen and studied other wars, observed with fascination. "It's the nastiest thing human beings can do to each other, but the most exciting," he said (Cowles, *Looking for Trouble*, 33–34).

To a considerable extent, of course, Hemingway operated under the same restrictions imposed on all correspondents. Everyone had to send dispatches from the Telefonica building directly across from the restaurant, and all dispatches had to clear censorship. Only two outside lines were available, and correspondents scrambled to get first access to them. But for the most part they were friendly competitors, members of the same guild. They lived through the repeated shelling together and adapted—at least two of them said so—by abandoning their sense of self. As she looked back on her time at the Hotel Florida, Josie Herbst could "see it only as a misty sort of unreality. . . . There was a disembodiment about my own entity, which didn't even bother me" (Herbst, *The Starched Blue Sky*, 137). Similarly, Hemingway observed that after two weeks in Madrid he "had an impersonal feeling of having no wife, no children, no house, no boat, nothing." All fear of death vanished. With the world in such a bad way, "to think about any personal future [seemed] very egoistic" (*Selected Letters*, 461).

COMRADE

Joris Ivens and Helene van Dongen turned up in Greenwich Village in March 1936 and set about charming everyone they met. Both Dutch by origin, they came to the United States directly from Moscow, where Ivens had learned his trade as a director of documentary films. Only thirty-eight, he had already produced two avant-garde films so well regarded that experts spoke of him as "the best new documentarist since Eisenstein" (Koch, *The Breaking Point*, 45).

He and his girlfriend were unusually attractive, and they had come to New York to make films advancing the communist cause. Within a month's time, Ivens touched base with John Dos Passos, and the two of them considered collaborating on a film attacking Hollywood. Dos Passos led Ivens to Archibald MacLeish, who admiringly described the Dutchman as "the great camera man of his time, an absolutely fearless man, a passionate and convinced Communist who was as mild as your grandmother, really quite a lovely guy" (*Reflections*, 112, 119). After the Spanish war broke out, Ivens abandoned the Hollywood project, along with a documentary about Harlem and another about deplorable health care for the poor in Detroit. Instead, he persuaded Dos Passos and MacLeish and others to send him to Spain. There he could shoot a documentary on-site, with fresh footage that would carry immediacy and power.

As Ivens's biographer makes clear, he was working during this time "in close consultation with party and Comintern functionaries" (Koch, *The Breaking Point*, 60). They saw an opportunity in Spain to win support for their goals, at least indirectly, by concentrating their propaganda not on the virtues of communism, but on the vices of fascism. The objective was to organize a Popular Front movement in western democracies against Hitler and Mussolini and against the Spanish Nationalists under Franco those dictators were supporting.

Ivens left for Spain in December 1936, shot a good deal of film involving the war's destruction and death, and came to Paris in February to show the results to the people—including the Communist Party propaganda czar Willi Münzenberg—who would let him know whether he "was making a film, or just newsreel shots." He planned to return to Spain early in March but reversed course and stayed in Paris. William Braasch Watson, an authoritative commentator on the subject, believed that Ivens remained in Paris in order to meet and indoctrinate Hemingway, who had been enlisted by MacLeish and others to write commentary for the film and who was on his way across the Atlantic. Ivens had not read much (if any) of Hemingway's work but understood that an internationally famous novelist could be of considerable benefit to the cause.

The two men met at the Deux Magots and immediately hit it off. As Ivens recalled in his memoirs, "Hemingway seemed to me that day like a simple and direct man, a kind of big boy scout who imposed himself by his physique and his manner of expressing himself. I knew he had been seriously wounded during the 1914–1918 war. . . . [He] knew Spain in peace, but not in war. In Paris he could see things from a distance, but I knew that once we were [in Spain] things would be different" (Meyers, *Biography*, 311). Hemingway seemed eager to be of help, and as they talked Ivens did his best to advance his political education. Ivens served, Carlos Baker said, as "Ernest's Political Commissar" (*A Life Story*, 307). Going one step further, Watson called Ivens Hemingway's secret "case officer," in the idiom of espionage the person designated "to develop an agent or an asset" (Watson, "Joris Ivens," 39).

Specifically, Ivens instructed Hemingway on the disastrous effects of the U.S. nonintervention policy in Spain. It was the heyday of isolationism in the United States, and most people—including Hemingway in his articles for *Esquire* at the end of 1936—were adamant in their conviction that the country should avoid any entanglement in foreign wars. Following the lead of England, the United States and many other countries signed a Non-Intervention Pact that effectively prevented dispensing aid to the Spanish Republic. It was to prove, as the diplomat Sumner Welles commented in 1944, the most disastrous "of all our blind isolationist policies." Italy and Germany ignored the pact, sending abundant artillery, airplanes, and troops to assist the insurgents. The western democracies sat on their hands, their arms embargo effectively working against the Republicans. Only Soviet Russia sold arms to the Loyalists, but this assistance—in Welles's words—amounted to "only a token compared to that obtained by Franco" (Matthews, *Education*, 93).

All of this was conveyed to Hemingway by Ivens, and in Spain he could see the results for himself in the form of shells launched by German and Italian guns and bombs dropped by their airplanes. Almost immediately he began campaigning in his dispatches for an end to nonintervention, a position diametrically opposed to the antiwar neutrality he'd been advocating back in the States. He lobbied for this change in policy throughout the war, and with even greater passion and frustration as the course of events swung against the Republicans.

During the first weeks of their time together in Madrid, Hemingway regularly accompanied Ivens and cameraman John Fernhout when they were filming. "Hemingway went everywhere with us," Ivens recalled, and he was a great help: carrying heavy cameras, taking orders willingly, speaking demotic Spanish to smooth their way, and suggesting how best to film actual battle scenes. Ivens was politically involved, and Hemingway was not, but they were both brave in the face of danger, strengthening the tie between them. As Ivens said in an interview with Watson, "if you are on the front line with a man, even for one day, you come to know who he is. We saw each other and we held each other in high regard" (Watson, "Joris Ivens," 49).

Hemingway benefited from the arrangement because Ivens had more or less carte blanche from the authorities to shoot film wherever he wanted. As part of the crew Hemingway could thus go much closer and oftener to the front than other correspondents. On these trips Ivens cemented their friendship and set himself the task of making Hemingway understand the antifascist cause.

In an obscure piece for an even more obscure journal, Hemingway wrote of the difficult conditions he and Ivens and Fernhout encountered while shooting battle scenes. "The first thing you remember is how cold it was; how early you got up in the morning; how you were always so tired you could go to sleep at any time; how hard it was to get gasoline; and how we were always hungry. It was also very muddy and we had a cowardly chauffeur." Then there were hot days, too, when they "ran with cameras, sweating, taking cover in the folds of the terrain on the bare hills," with dust in the nose and hair and eyes and the "great thirst for water, the real dry-mouth that only battle brings" (Hemingway, "The Heat"). To sustain himself Hemingway carried raw onions in his lumberman's jacket that neither Ivens nor Fernhout would eat, though they partook eagerly from the large, flat silver flask of whiskey he brought along.

The crew attached itself to the Twelfth International Brigade to film combat near Morata de Tajuna. Hemingway admired the officers of that brigade, who accepted him as a fellow soldier and as an artist. The convivial General Lukacs, the Hungarian commander, had written novels before the war. The chief medical officer, Werner Heilbrunn, a German Jew, looked "like a weary beggar-monk" as he tirelessly cared for the wounded and organized everything for the filmmakers. Gustav Regler, another refugee from Nazi Germany and a longtime antifascist, served as political commissar of the brigade, a task that he undertook with some reservations after witnessing the first purge trials in Moscow. These men more or less adopted Hemingway, who basked in the warmth of their comradeship. The brigade threw a farewell party for him on May Day, where Lukacs, late at night, played a tune on a pencil held against his teeth, "the music clear and delicate like a flute" (Hemingway, "The Heat").

Back in the States, Hemingway was crushed when he heard that Lukacs had been killed and Regler badly wounded by rebel artillery during a June 16 assault on Huesca and that Heilbrunn, grieving for the loss of Lukacs, had been shot dead by a Rebel plane as he drove alone toward the Pyrenees.

Hemingway cried when the news reached him, for he thought of the dead men as irreplaceable. "There is no man alive . . . who has not cried at a war if he was at it long enough," Hemingway wrote somewhat defensively (Bruccoli, *Mechanism of Fame*, 83). More philosophically, he reflected that "death is still very badly organized in war," an observation he would like to have been able to make "to Heilbrunn, who would grin, and to Lukacs, who would understand it very well" (Hemingway, "The Heat").

The International Brigades were badly needed in Spain, where the Loyalist army consisted largely of untrained and underequipped peasants under the command of inexperienced officers. The internationals were recruited in Europe and North America by the Communist Party, which organized transport to Spain and training. Altogether, about 40,000 came to fight for the Republic, the largest contingents including 10,000 French, 5,000 Germans and Austrians, 3,400 Italians, 2,800 Americans, and 2,000 British. Among them were party members, trade unionists, and left-wing intellectuals and artists who volunteered to stem the tide of fascism. "Our spirit," the English poet Louis MacNeice wrote, "would find its frontier on the Spanish front / Its body in a rag-tag army" (Moorehead, *Gellhorn*, 110).

Most of the Americans saw action in the Abraham Lincoln Battalion, part of the Fourteenth International Brigade. About a third of them were Jewish, and more than half had Communist Party affiliation. But they were less dedicated to Marxist doctrine than to antifascism, regarding the war in Spain as a crusade against Hitler, Mussolini, and Franco's Nationalist forces (who for their part saw the civil war as a crusade against the godless atheism of Marxism). Over a third of the Americans in the Lincoln Battalion lost their lives during the course of the war.

Each of the brigades fought under the command of a general officer appointed by the Communists. None of them were Russians (that would have given the game away), but most had undergone training in Russia. Each of the brigades was also assigned a political commissar, whose role was to stimulate and reinforce the soldiers' dedication to the cause and, if possible, to usher them into the party. John Gates, who served as commissar for the Lincoln Battalion, estimated that from 75 to 80 percent of the volunteers were members of the American Communist Party—the highest percentage in any of the International Brigades. Late in April, Ivens urged Hemingway to write an article "about the great and human function of the political commissar on the front," an endeavor sure to advance the Communist cause (Watson, "Joris Ivens," 51). Hemingway did not write such an article, although he did attempt to write a short story based on one such commissar, his friend Gustav Regler.

THE LAST GREAT CAUSE

Ivens saw it as his duty to bring Hemingway into the communist fold, or at least to make him sympathetic to its goals. When they were not shooting film, and sometimes being shot at, he introduced Hemingway to a number of the war's international participants, most of whom (like Ivens himself) were associated with the worldwide communist movement. The most important introduction was to Mikhail Koltsov, who was headquartered with other Russians at the Hotel Gaylord in Madrid. He brought the two men together, Ivens revealed in an interview with Watson, as part of his campaign to "develop" Hemingway as an asset to the party.

> Koltsov of Pravda and some of the Russians . . . were living in the Gaylord Hotel and I introduced Hemingway to them so that he would know some other communists. That gave him an edge and with it came more confidence . . . because other correspondents did not have this access. So through me he was able to get accurate, first-hand information. I didn't keep any secrets from him. "Yes, here are Russians," [Ivens admitted.] For many people the Gaylord Hotel was some kind of secret center. *I had a plan for Hemingway and I think I used the right tactics.* For this kind of man, I knew how far he could go and that he was not a traitor. *I didn't introduce Hemingway to the Russians when he first asked me. But after four weeks, I thought, now, he is ready to make that step, and it worked.*
>
> (WATSON, "JORIS IVENS," 50; ITALICS ADDED)

Indeed it did work. Ivens's tactics let Hemingway think of himself as an insider privileged to know more about what was going on in Spain than other correspondents. He learned, for example, that Russian communists were taking charge of the political and military structure of the Spanish Republic. But he also became convinced that this was necessary, and that only through the discipline (and sometimes the brutality) of the communists could the crusade against fascism succeed.

Regler used much the same technique to win Hemingway's confidence. As he wrote in his memoir, Regler thought it remarkably fortunate that "at just that time [the spring of 1937], when we were in urgent need of a sympathetic world-opinion to explain our defeats, Ernest Hemingway should have appeared as a war-correspondent on our front." In order to make Hemingway an ally, Regler provided him with "inside stories of operations and crises," as well as "secret material relating to the [Communist] Party" (qtd. in Sanderson, "'Like a Rock,'" 3–4). Like Ivens, he accompanied Hemingway on visits to the Gaylord Hotel for meetings with

Koltsov, who was in the best possible position to dispense information about communist control of the Republican war effort.

Koltsov, nominally a correspondent for *Pravda* and *Izvestia*, was in charge of Russian propaganda and reported directly to Stalin. He was "Stalin's man, Stalin's eyes and ears on the spot," Gellhorn said (Moorehead, *Gellhorn*, 126). Charming, witty, and urbane, with a touch of cynicism, Koltsov captured Hemingway's respect, just as he had that of André Malraux, André Gide, and Louis Aragon. He persuaded Hemingway that he wanted him to understand "how everything was run" so that when he came to write a book about the war he could "give a true account of it" (Koch, *The Breaking Point*, 56). Hemingway, who thought Koltsov "the most intelligent man" he had ever met, sat at his feet and took the indoctrination. "[Koltsov] knew I was not a communist and would never be one," he later commented. But he had seen men die for the cause in the field, and Koltsov knew that he "would not write anything . . . which could hurt the Republic" until the war was over (Mellow, *A Life Without Consequences*, 503).

In his newspaper and magazine reports, Hemingway avoided any mention of the clandestine intelligence Koltsov dispensed about Soviet manipulation behind the scenes or of atrocities committed by the Republicans. To reveal such machinations, he realized, would arouse anticommunist sentiments back in the States and effectively undermine any possibility of American intervention. So he stored that information away for his 1940 novel, *For Whom the Bell Tolls*. He was practicing what Ivens called "the law of half truths": "if you're in the domain of class struggle or a war of liberation and a particular truth is in the way of events, then you have to progress beyond that truth if you want to get anywhere" (Schoots, *Living Dangerously*, 127–28).

The film Ivens and Hemingway were making was *The Spanish Earth*, the title coming from MacLeish. Openly propagandistic, it was designed to evoke sympathy for the Spanish people, who were the victims of the war, or more particularly victims of the Nationalists and their fascist supporters, Hitler and Mussolini. In a plot outline, Ivens sketched out the story. In the village of Fuentiduena, a peasant youth works with others on an irrigation project. He joins the Loyalist forces to fight with his regiment in Madrid, returns to train other village boys, then goes back to the front. The film draws a parallel between the irrigation project bringing water to *The Spanish Earth* and the fight for the freedom of that earth. Initially Dos Passos was to have been involved in writing the commentary, with an overriding emphasis on the plight of the common people. By the spring of 1937, however, Dos Passos and the communists were mutually disillusioned with each other, and Hemingway—who wanted more scenes of actual battle—took over.

After forty-five days in Spain, Hemingway came back home, arriving May 18 on the *Normandie*. He planned to collect Pauline and the boys in Key West and head for Bimini for the summer, but he also had to write the commentary for *The Spanish Earth*, revise the episodic *To Have and Have Not* into a novel, and make a speech at Carnegie Hall. In late May Ivens, van Dongen, and Prudencio de Pereda were editing footage in New York, and Hemingway joined them there to write the script. "Don't write about what you see," Ivens advised him, "don't repeat the image." The trick was to "reinforce the image by writing about related things." Ivens also told him that his script would have to be cut; it was too long and too complicated. Hemingway balked at the criticism, then relented. "Now I see," he said, and wrote a tighter script that better fit text to film (Meyers, *Biography*, 312).

Meanwhile, Martha Gellhorn was using her connections to open doors for the film in progress. On May 28 she had lunch with Eleanor Roosevelt and secured an invitation for herself, Ernest, and Joris to show the final cut of *The Spanish Earth* at the White House. In her newspaper column the next day, Mrs. Roosevelt rather vaguely commented that Gellhorn had come back from Spain "with a deep conviction that the Spanish people are a glorious people and something is happening in Spain which may mean much to the rest of the world" (Lynn, *Hemingway*, 470).

On June 4, Hemingway made the only public speech of his life at the second congress of the League of American Writers, a Popular Front organization headed by his old friend Donald Ogden Stewart. Archibald MacLeish, a liberal but not a party member, chaired the opening program in Carnegie Hall. "Why they chose me I don't know," he said, "except that I was an editor of *Fortune*, so I was the other side. Also, I could produce Hemingway, who they particularly wanted, and nobody else could" (Donaldson, *MacLeish*, 264–65). Actually, though, Ivens was involved in choosing MacLeish *and* in excluding Dos Passos. As Gellhorn wrote Hemingway, Ivens had "a dandy meeting with our pals Archie and Doss [sic], and it must have been something. These communists are sinister folk and very very canny. The upshot is that [Archie] is president of the affair and Dos is the poison ivy" (qtd. in Koch, *The Breaking Point*, 222).

A capacity audience of 3,500 jammed a hot and smoky Carnegie Hall for the evening, and another thousand were turned away. Many came to see and hear Hemingway speak, and he was scheduled last on the program. First MacLeish read telegrams of support from Thomas Mann, C. Day Lewis, Upton Sinclair, and Albert Einstein. Stewart spoke next, reminding the audience how ineffectual it was to adopt the conventional liberal stance of seeing both sides of the question so well that it prevented you from acting on either. Earl Browder, secretary of the Communist Party of the United States, called the assembled writers to action against fascism, not necessarily as communists but under any political banner they chose. Then the "dark serious burning-eyed" Ivens (Folsom, *Days of Anger*, 9) showed a silent draft of *The Spanish Earth* and urged his listeners to join the battle for the Spanish Republic. "This picture," he said in his halting English, "[was] made on the same front where I think every honest writer ought to be." "Where were you in 1937?" posterity would ask of them. "Only talking at the New School?" (Schoots, *Living Dangerously*, 130).

About 10:30 P.M. it was finally Hemingway's turn at the rostrum. Sweaty and uncomfortable in his tweed jacket, and "well-inbibulated" for the occasion, he nervously raced through his brief talk, "A Writer in War Time." Writing and fascism were inherently incompatible, he began. A writer's problem was "always how to write truly and, having found what is true, to project it in such a way that it becomes a part of the experience of the person who reads it." But fascism was "a lie told by bullies," and "a writer who will not lie cannot live under fascism." He then characterized "the totalitarian fascist states" as murderers. He had seen "highly efficient" murdering done by German artillery during the shelling of Madrid. "Every time they are beaten in the field," he said of the enemy, "they salvage that strange thing they call their honor by murdering civilians."

Like Browder and Ivens before him, Hemingway called for the assembled writers to become active participants in the Spanish war. They must decide for themselves, he said, "whether the truth [was] worth some risk to come by." It would be easier "to spend their time disputing learnedly on points of doctrine. And there will always be new schisms and new falling-offs and marvelous exotic doctrines and romantic lost leaders for those who do not want to work at what they profess to believe in, but only to discuss and to maintain positions." But now—and for a long time to come during the "many years of undeclared wars" he anticipated—writers had the opportunity to learn about war for themselves (Hemingway, "Fascism").

It sounded as if Hemingway were trying to shame his listeners into action, yet when he abruptly finished and dashed into the wings, Carnegie

Hall erupted in applause. "It was magnificent," said Paul Romaine, the bookseller who five years before had urged Hemingway to become more political in his writing. Now Hemingway was clearly a companion, a comrade, in the fight against fascism. "How could this fight be lost, with Hemingway on our side?" (Baker, *A Life Story*, 364).

In a letter to Dos Passos, who was not in attendance, the novelist Dawn Powell took a more sardonic view. "About 10:30," she said, "all the foreign correspondents marched on, each one with his private blonde, led by Ernest and Miss Gellhorn, who had been through hell in Spain and came shivering on in a silver fox cape chin-up. . . . Ernest gave a good speech . . . and his sum total was that . . . writers ought to all go to war and get killed and if they didn't they were a big sissy" (Moorehead, *Gellhorn*, 130). Gellhorn herself spoke at the congress the following afternoon, sans the silver fox. In Spain, she declared, writers were judged not by their writing but by whether they were good soldiers.

Two weeks later Ivens cabled Hemingway that he had finished editing *The Spanish Earth*; only the soundtrack was lacking. Ernest flew to New York for final revisions and, in an eleventh-hour change of plans, to record the commentary in his own voice. Previously MacLeish had arranged for Orson Welles to do the narration, but upon hearing it Lillian Hellman and Frederic March thought that Welles's rich theatrical voice clashed with the spare, matter-of-fact script. Better that the author should do the job himself. Hemingway took some persuading—"I don't have the proper training in breathing," he objected—but eventually consented to speak the commentary. Despite his flat Midwestern voice, the result proved extraordinarily successful. "While recording," Ivens said, "Hemingway found the emotions that he had felt at the front [and that] no other voice would have been able to communicate" (Meyers, *Biography*, 314).

Hemingway's script for *The Spanish Earth*, which was published in an unauthorized version by a Cleveland high school student in the summer of 1938, does not pretend to objectivity. To accompany film of the bombardment of Madrid, Hemingway wrote, "Unable to enter the town, *the enemy* try to destroy it," adding that "Madrid, by its position, is a natural fortress and each day *the people* make its defenses more and more impregnable" (Hemingway, *Spanish Earth*, 41). The battle was thus joined between, on our side, "the people" and, on the other side, "the enemy" whose shells killed and maimed innocent civilians. The film took the optimistic position that the people would prevail, winning back possession of their land. As Republican troops are shown advancing, Hemingway's description says that "this is the movement that the rest of the war prepares for, when six men go forward into death to walk across a stretch of land and by their presence on it prove—this earth is ours. Six men were five. Then four were three, but these three stayed, dug in and held the ground. Along with all the other fours and threes and twos that started out as sixes. The bridge is ours. The road is saved" (qtd. in Cooper, *Politics*, 90).

This was strong stuff, and both Roosevelts were moved by it during the July 8 showing at the White House, their only reservation being that the filmmakers ought to add even "more propaganda" (*Selected Letters*, 460). Afterward, Harry Hopkins said he felt sure the Republicans would win. Hemingway replied that they might very well lose unless the arms embargo was ended and they got the weaponry they needed.

Four days later, Ivens and Hemingway showed *The Spanish Earth* in Frederic March's home for Hollywood's most prominent antifascists: six directors, seven actors, and six writers. The goal of the meeting was to raise money for ambulances in the field. "Now you have seen what it looks like," Hemingway said after the screening, adding that there were some things they could not get into the film. "The way the ground rocks and sways under your belly and against your forehead when the big bombs fall . . . the noises kids make when they are hit, [although] there is a sort of foretaste of that when the child sees the planes coming and yells, 'Aviacion!'" He spoke also of comrades killed in battle. "These men all knew what they were fighting for. . . . It is our fight as much as it is theirs." "I know that money is hard to make," he concluded, "but dying is not easy either." A thousand dollars would have an ambulance "rolling in action" in only four weeks.

F. Scott Fitzgerald, among those in attendance, wrote Max Perkins that Ernest spoke with a "nervous intensity" that had "something almost religious about it." Dorothy Parker was moved to tears. The group contributed seventeen thousand dollars, everyone making a donation except Errol Flynn, who was said to have "escaped through the bathroom window" (Baker, *A Life Story*, 316; Schoots, *Living Dangerously*, 131).

Ivens and Hemingway did not succeed, however, in arranging wide distribution for *The Spanish Earth*. None of the big distributors would take a chance on a documentary with so obvious a bias, and it was shown primarily to film societies and gatherings of viewers committed to the cause. Reviewers generally praised the film, the *New Republic* singling out "the carrying power in understatement" of Hemingway's commentary (Meyers, *Biography*, 316). It reached its widest audience through a four-page spread of stills in *Life* magazine under the heading "The War in Spain Makes a Movie with Captions by Ernest Hemingway" (Raeburn, "Hemingway on Stage," 9). Ivens was not mentioned.

In the spring of 1937, the friendship between Hemingway and Dos Passos dissolved under pressure of political differences aroused by the war in Spain. A 2005 book by Stephen Koch, *The Breaking Point: Hemingway, Dos Passos, and the Murder of Jose Robles*, presents a damning indictment of Hemingway in this dispute, "an unlovely portrait of the engagé artist as useful idiot" (Packer, "The Spanish Prisoner," 84). Koch undervalued his man, who may have been mistaken but was nobody's fool.

To retell the oft-told story, Dos Passos was a close friend of Jose Robles Pazos, the Spanish translator of his novels. In the summer of 1936, Robles left his professorship at Johns Hopkins to join the Loyalists as a colonel. A linguist who knew Russian as well as English and Spanish, Robles was arrested in December and not heard from again. Dos Passos came to Spain in March to find out what had happened to his friend. Soon after Dos Passos's arrival, Hemingway told him he had the word of Pepe Quintanilla, brother of the artist Luis Quintanilla and head of counterespionage for the Republic, that Robles would receive a fair trial. Nonetheless, Dos Passos was unable to get in touch with Robles or to learn where and under what charges he was incarcerated. Eventually it emerged that Quintanilla had lied, that Robles had been summarily executed. It fell to Hemingway to deliver this news to Dos Passos. Robles must have been "worthless," he told Dos Passos. If the Loyalists shot him, it was because he deserved it (Donaldson, "Dos and Hem," 176).

This terrible news, delivered with casual brutality, devastated Dos Passos. The execution of Robles struck him as disturbingly similar to the behavior of the Soviets during the Moscow purge trials. It seemed to him that Russian communism had appropriated the Republican cause for its own purposes, and that Robles had probably been killed because he "knew too much about the relations between the Spanish war ministry and the Kremlin" (Mellow, *A Life Without Consequences*, 507). Robles also had a brother who fought on the Franco side, rendering him suspect to a government that tended toward paranoia at the least hint of disloyalty or disaffection.

During lunch one day in Madrid with Hemingway, Virginia Cowles, and Josie Herbst, Pepe Quintanilla, familiarly known as the executioner of Madrid, cheerfully acknowledged that he was sometimes overzealous in rooting out enemies of the Republic. Shelling began just as lunch ended, and Hemingway kept insisting that he had to leave; "El Rubio" (the blonde Martha) was waiting for him, he had work to do. "Nonsense," Quintanilla kept saying, counting the shells as they struck in the street above. Ernest then began asking Quintanilla about his work. Sometimes, he must have made mistakes, hadn't he? "Yes," the executioner admitted, a very few mistakes, and very regrettable, and they had all died very well (Herbst, *The Starched Blue Sky*, 167–70). Hemingway filed the conversation away for his play, *The Fifth Column*, and (for the time being) accepted Quintanilla's position that lethal mistakes must sometimes be made in the pursuit of a greater good.

Dos Passos remained in Spain only briefly after hearing about Robles's death, but long enough to arouse in Ivens a wrath he freely communicated in letters to Hemingway. This correspondence makes it seem likely that Hemingway's callous attitude about Robles and Dos Passos derived in good part from Ivens. In Valencia, where the government was then headquartered, Dos Passos attempted to secure a death certificate that would enable Robles's widow to obtain a pension—a worthy and altruistic endeavor—but continued to ask difficult and embarrassing questions about why his friend had been eliminated. Ivens, also in Valencia at the time, wrote Hemingway that Dos Passos "is running here for the same cause as he did in Madrid. . . . Hope that Dos will see what a man and comrade has to do in this difficult and serious wartime" (qtd. in Schoots, *Living Dangerously*, 126).

Still in search of answers, Dos Passos traveled from Valencia to Barcelona, where he spoke with Andres Nin, leader of the Workers Party of Marxist Unification (POUM) and with George Orwell, who had fought with the POUM militia on the Aragon front. In May 1937 Barcelona was the site of bloody factional uprisings that threatened to tear the Loyalist movement asunder. The Stalinists regarded POUM as dangerously Trotskyite, many POUM members were jailed, and Nin himself was executed. Orwell had to flee the country to avoid arrest, as he wrote in his *Homage to Catalonia*. None of these arrests or executions troubled Ivens in the least. He saw them as necessary to successful prosecution of the war and confided to Hemingway on the clear assumption that he shared the same view. "I still get angry," he wrote Hemingway early in 1938. "when I think of the fact that Dos after being with us went into the POUM office in Barcelona—it [was] not only the worst political thing to do—but more: dirty disloyal to all of us." Thereafter Ivens referred to Dos Passos as an "enemy" and to Robles as "the friend-translator-fascist of Dos Passos" (Schoots, *Living Dangerously*, 127). Hemingway accepted these judgments. In wartime things were not always as they seemed. "If you want to have it simple . . . you can do one thing: take orders and obey them blindly" even if, in the process, you might well have to renounce friendship (Hemingway, "Three Prefaces," 11).

Ivens did not go back to Spain after finishing *The Spanish Earth*. This astounded Gellhorn, who with Hemingway was to return three more times. Ivens must not have been as committed to the cause as they thought, she concluded. In fact, he was acting under orders from the Comintern, which wanted him to make a film celebrating the rise of Chinese communism. To sponsor and help finance the film, Contemporary Historians segued into History Today, with a board including MacLeish and Broadway producer Herman Shumlin, but not Dos Passos.

Although bound for China himself, Ivens wrote two letters of introduction for Hemingway to communist friends of his in Europe: one to an undersecretary in the propaganda bureau in Valencia, the other to Paul Vaillant Couturier, who edited the newspaper of the French Communist Party. Hemingway "is a very good friend of ours," he told Couturier. "He has done and will do a great deal for our cause, the cause of Spain here in America and in England. . . . I am counting on you to help Ernest Hemingway if he needs anything. A letter for Diaz [José Diaz, head of the Spanish Communist Party] would [also] be good" (qtd. in Watson, "Joris Ivens," 53). Then, as he prepared to leave for China in January 1938, Ivens proposed an undercover arrangement to contribute to Hemingway's continuing political education. "If there is something you would like to talk over with one of our leading people [presumably, communist agents in the United States]," he wrote Ernest, Helene van Dongen would be glad to "fix the rendezvous for you." Destroy this letter, he told Hemingway, who did not (Koch, *The Breaking Point*, 250).

COLLEAGUE

Hemingway, like many American writers, got his start as a newspaperman. Having succeeded as an author after giving up journalism, he felt a measure of scorn for those who stayed in city rooms and never achieved their literary ambitions. Yet it was among newsmen, and particularly foreign correspondents, that he found a number of his friends and mentors.

As a young man Hemingway had a dream job working in Toronto for the *Daily Star* and its Sunday *Star Weekly*. He was headquartered in Paris, with all of Europe as his beat. In 1922 the *Star* sent Hemingway to cover two international meetings, the economic conference in Genoa and the peace conference in Lausanne. He acquired supporters at both conferences. In Genoa he met the superannuated muckraker Lincoln Steffens, who took an interest in Ernest's fiction. At Lausanne he encountered the impressive and sardonic William Bolitho Ryall, a South African reporting for the *Manchester Guardian*. Ryall was a man of opinions, which he dispensed over dinner to an admiring Hemingway. Those dinners, Carlos Baker said, "marked the real beginning of Ernest's education in international politics" (Baker, *A Life Story*, 102).

Ryall discoursed on "the malady of power," and took pleasure in debunking the great men of the day. Previously, Hemingway had been impressed by Benito Mussolini; after listening to Ryall, he started calling him "the biggest bluff in Europe." Newsmen like Ryall acquired authority by working close to the centers of power. He buttressed his disparagement of Mussolini, for example, by specific reference to what he had seen and heard in the actual presence of the Italian dictator. You had to be there, Hemingway learned. You had to be on the inside.

The lesson stayed with Hemingway when he went to Spain. There he formed a lasting friendship with another correspondent who matched him in bravery and in determination to see the truth for himself. This was Herbert L. Matthews of the *New York Times*, tall, gaunt, serious, and destined to become one of that paper's most distinguished foreign correspondents.

Matthews, like Ivens almost exactly Hemingway's age, was near the beginning of his forty-five-year career with the *Times*. He came to work for the paper after pursuing graduate work in Romance languages at Columbia. Matthews arrived in Madrid in November 1936, fresh from covering the Italian invasion of Ethiopia. By the time Hemingway arrived on the scene in March 1937, Matthews had become a dedicated partisan of the Republicans. This was characteristic of him as an "austere romantic" who, as *Times* editor Max Frankel put it, "yearn[ed] to give history a hand by directing society toward the good and the beautiful" (Frankel, *Times of My Life*, 191). Another *Times* editor, Turner Catledge, summed up Matthews as "an extremely sensitive man. I never saw him laugh; I did see him smile faintly, on occasion. He was a fearless man, ready to run any risk in pursuit of a story. He was also politically committed and concerned, given to deep emotional involvement in the stories he wrote" (Catledge, *My Life*, 265–66).

During the spring of 1937, when Hemingway was not on location with Ivens, he and Matthews often went foraging to the front together in search of stories. In Madrid, where conflicting reports from the propaganda bureaus of the combatants muddied the truth, Matthews learned once and for all the necessity of seeing for himself. His code, like that of

Ryall, resembled that of Dr. Johnson: "Trust as little as you can to report; examine all you can by your own senses."

Sometimes Marty Gellhorn accompanied the two correspondents as they ventured into dangerous territory. Matthews was in love with her, the Lincoln Battalion commander Milton Wolff decided (Moorehead, *Gellhorn*, 118). Usually the British correspondent Tom Delmer rode along too. On one occasion Delmer insisted that their car fly both the Union Jack and the Stars and Stripes to proclaim their neutrality, a precaution that backfired when rebel forces, assuming the flags meant staff officers were inside, concentrated their fire on the correspondents' vehicle.

As they faced jeopardy together, the bond between the *Times* man and the famous author grew stronger. In effect Matthews continued the indoctrination of Hemingway that Ivens and Regler had so effectively begun. He did not belong to the Communist Party—he belonged to no party—but Matthews vehemently espoused the Popular Front position that the Spanish Civil War offered the last best chance to stop the rise of fascism in Europe. "Those of us who championed the cause of the Republican government against the Franco Nationalists were right," he maintained. "It was, on balance, the cause of justice, legality, morality, decency" (Knightley, *The First Casualty*, 192).

Most other correspondents felt the same way. Their convictions did not always jibe with the official policies of the countries they came from or the news organizations they represented. But on the ground in Madrid and at the front, they were initiated into an informal fraternity pledged to support the Loyalists and by so doing help to stave off a wider war against fascism. No one felt this way more fervently than Matthews, who regarded his time in Spain—he was there for the entire duration of the war—as the high point of his life and career.

"I know," Matthews wrote in his 1946 *Education of a Correspondent*, "that nothing so wonderful will ever happen to me again as those two and a half years I spent in Spain. . . . There one learned that men could be brothers, that nations and frontiers, religions and races were but outer trappings, and that nothing counted, nothing was worth fighting for, but the ideal of liberty. . . . In those years we lived our best, and what has come after and what is to come can never carry us to those heights again. . . . We left our hearts there" (Matthews, *Education*, 67–68). And Hemingway was very much part of that experience. They were correspondents and comrades and colleagues. More than that, they were friends. Matthews thought Hemingway "great-hearted and childish, and perhaps a little mad," but wished there could be more like him. For Matthews, he represented "much that is brave and good and fine in a somewhat murky world" (Mellow, *A Life Without Consequences*, 496).

As the *Times* man in Spain, Matthews was one of the best-known correspondents reporting on the war. His editors at the paper were sometimes reluctant to print those of his dispatches—and of Hemingway's, which came to them as part of their participation in NANA—that seemed openly hostile to the Nationalist side. The powerful Catholic lobby in the United States tried to pressure the newspaper into recalling Matthews, whom they called "a rabid Red partisan" (Moorehead, *Gellhorn*, 124). And in the news room itself there were people who agreed with his critics. *Times* editorials backed the government's anti-intervention policy throughout the war, and the news side expected objectivity from its reporters in the field.

In order to cover the war with impartiality, the *Times* devised a policy that, while sensible in theory, proved a disaster in practice. The newspaper decided to print the news from both sides, with William P. Carney, a Catholic correspondent who felt strongly about Republican mistreatment of the clergy, assigned to Franco's forces, and Matthews to the Republicans. Their competing stories were to run to the same length and be given equal prominence. One problem was that Carney was not in Matthews's class as a correspondent, so that the *Times* often overplayed a bad story while cutting a good one. This unfortunate situation was made worse by the pro-Catholic orientation of the *Times* "bullpen," the cadre of senior editors who decided on how to handle incoming dispatches.

In particular, night managing editor Raymond H. McCaw decided that both Matthews and Hemingway were "too strongly prejudiced in favor of the Government side." Theoretically McCaw worked under the direction of managing editor Edwin L. (Jimmy) James, but in practice James ceded all decision making to McCaw when he left the office for the evening. As the former city editor Arthur Gelb described the procedure, McCaw "had final say about editing of stories, their space allotment and position, and, most importantly, which stories would appear on page one" (Gelb, *City Room*, 121). McCaw often cut Matthews's copy or buried it well inside the paper.

In March 1937, for example, a large Nationalist offensive towards Guadalajara was turned back by the Loyalists. Matthews went to the front and found that the routed troops were Italian. He interviewed Italian prisoners, saw the weapons they had left behind, witnessed dead Italians being buried, and filed a dispatch to the *Times*. This report established for the first time that Mussolini was sending not only armaments to aid the

Nationalists but an expeditionary force as well—a matter of considerable political and emotional importance. To emphasize the point, Matthews wrote that the troops "were Italian and nothing but Italian." McCaw on the night desk changed it to read that they "were Insurgent and nothing but Insurgent," and substituted "Insurgent" for "Italian" throughout, entirely obliterating what the correspondent reported. Not content with this intentional distortion of the facts, McCaw cabled Matthews, chiding him for the story. The only papers to emphasize that the attacking troops were Italian were those in Moscow, he maintained. (This was inaccurate, for Hemingway stressed the same point in his NANA dispatches). "We cannot print obvious propaganda for either side even under bylines," McCaw maintained (Matthews, *World in Revolution*, 25–28).

Matthews was naturally indignant about such treatment. Deeply concerned with the ethical obligations of the foreign correspondent, he believed that "an open, honest bias" was not only permissible but to be expected from chroniclers in the field, especially during wartime. With McCaw and the Catholic campaign against him in mind, he later set forth his convictions. "I always felt the falseness and hypocrisy of those who claimed to be unbiased and the foolish, if not rank stupidity of editors and readers who demand objectivity or impartiality [from war] correspondents" (Matthews, *World in Revolution*, 12). As human beings, these correspondents naturally had feelings and opinions that emerged in their reporting. "In condemning bias," Matthews asserted, "one rejects the only factors which really matter—honesty, understanding and thoroughness. A reader has a right to ask for all the facts; he has no right to ask that a journalist or historian agree with him" (qtd. in Knightley, *The First Casualty*, 195).

Raymond McCaw criticized Hemingway as well as Matthews and often consigned his NANA stories to the wastebasket. In June 1937, just as Hemingway and Jack Wheeler were preparing to sign a new contract, McCaw complained to the NANA editor about Hemingway's pro-Republican bias. Wheeler did not agree, arguing that Hemingway was simply trying to report what he saw and to give NANA the "straight, unbiased, colorful reporting" it wanted (Wheeler to Hemingway, 8 June 1937). Upon hearing about this discussion, Hemingway placed McCaw and the night desk at the *Times* near the top of his enemies' list.

Was McCaw right? Did Hemingway slant his reporting from Spain? Not ordinarily in the eye-witness accounts of battle that the intrepid correspondent sent back from the front. There Hemingway drew upon his considerable knowledge of tactics to describe in unusual detail what was going on and why. But the charge definitely had merit where the choice of material was concerned. In vividly describing the mutilation of civilians by fascist bombs, in repeatedly citing the involvement of the Italian and German dictatorships on the Nationalist side, and in adopting a false optimism about the chances of an eventual Republican victory, Hemingway tilted his copy to the left. Nor would he—or Matthews or Gellhorn—acknowledge in their dispatches the persecutions and summary executions that they knew the Republicans were carrying out or the control they knew that Soviet Russia was exercising over the government and military.

Gellhorn, who was damned if she would practice "all that objectivity shit" (Moorehead, *Gellhorn*, 125) the journalism schools taught, wrote an incendiary letter to the *Times* in defense of Matthews when he came under attack by the Catholics. With Hemingway, she shared Matthews's conviction that good reporters should write with their hearts as well as their minds and that in a war they had to take sides. If effect, all three of them were affiliated with the propaganda effort to bring the western democracies over to the Republican side. The battle was on for the hearts and minds of the American people, and although, yes, Hemingway and Matthews reported accurately on what they saw in the field, they chose an angle of vision that they hoped would win that battle for the Loyalists.

During 1936 and 1937, most Americans remained indifferent to the civil war in Spain. More than two-thirds of the public, the Gallup polls found, did not care which side won. But those who did care cared passionately. About 20 percent, disturbed by the intervention of Hitler and Mussolini, supported the Loyalists. Another 10 percent, motivated by hatred of communism, favored the insurgents. The two groups were divided by religious as well as ideological convictions, with the Roman Catholics supporting Franco and the Jews on the side of the government.

The news media generally stayed neutral, in effect adopting Washington's anti-intervention policy. A few publications, like *Time* magazine, opposed the Republicans from the start. *Time*'s coverage presented a highly favorable view of Francisco Franco, characterizing him as a soft-spoken, serious man of "soldierly simplicity," blessed with a winning sense of humor. The magazine's use of nomenclature also revealed its slant. Instead of referring to the government forces as Republicans or Loyalists, *Time* called them "Reds." Similarly, the opposition led by the "smiling Generalissimo Franco" was designated as "Whites," not rebels or insurgents. Readers were inevitably swayed by the terminology. "Reds" meant "communists," who were to be feared. "Whites" symbolized innocence and purity (Donaldson, *MacLeish*, 277–78).

After Hemingway's June 1937 star turn at the League of American Writers Congress in Carnegie Hall, he was invited to represent the United States at the Congress of the International Association of Antifascist Writers, held the following month in Madrid and Valencia. The congress brought together delegates from several European and Latin American countries, all dedicated to developing sympathy for Republican Spain. Hemingway could not be there: "regret finishing ivens film makes absolutely impossible attend madrid congress," he wired André Malraux in a telegram slimmed down to ten words (20 June 1937).

He was also busy revising *To Have and Have Not*. Cuts had to be made to avoid libeling Jane Mason and John Dos Passos in their thinly disguised fictional selves as Helene Bradley and Richard Gordon. In addition, Hemingway shuffled his previous drafts "to counterpoint the 'haves' (the very rich and the supercilious writers) and the 'have nots' (working poor and displaced vets)." Then he wrote eight new pages for an ending, culminating with Harry Morgan's dying words. "One man alone ain't got. No man alone now. . . . No matter how a man alone ain't got no bloody fucking chance."

"It had taken him a long time to get it out and it had taken him all of his life to learn it," Hemingway added in the book's final sentence (Reynolds, *Hemingway: 1930s*, 269–70).

This ending represented something new in Hemingway's fiction—a change from concentration on the courage in defeat of the isolated protagonist to a statement that men, and particularly working-class men, needed to band together against inimical economic and political forces. When *To Have and Have Not* came out in October, in an apparent shift of policy *Time* ran a cover story on Hemingway celebrating his newly awakened social consciousness, wrongly describing Harry Morgan as his "most thoroughly consistent, deeply understandable character," and pointing out that the author had gone back to war-torn Spain where, in the prime of life at thirty-nine, he chose "to be in the midst of death" ("All Stories," 84–85).

Before leaving, Ernest felt compelled to explain himself to Pauline's mother in Arkansas. In two weeks' time, his letter of August 2 said, he would be on his way "back to Spain where, if you get your politics from direct or indirect [Catholic doctrine], you know I am on the wrong side and should be destroyed with all the other Reds. After which Hitler and Mussolini can come in and take all the minerals they need to make a European war." In this letter he also dealt with Mrs. Pfeiffer's urging him to stay at home to spend more time with his sons. "Dear Mother I am sorry about going back to Spain and I think what you write about staying here and looking after the boys is very sound. But when I was there I promised them I would be back and while we cannot keep all our promises I do not see how not to keep that one. I would not be able to teach my boys much if I [broke that promise]" (*Selected Letters*, 460–61).

He did not mention Martha Gellhorn, or that they were both on their way back to Spain, discreetly traveling on separate ships and taking adjoining rooms at the Hotel Florida. The war had not gone well in their absence. Madrid had "a grim look" about it, two-thirds of the country lay in Nationalist hands, and Republican losses were steadily mounting. Still, Hemingway's room became a refuge for officers on leave from the International Brigades. "Among the American visitors, the outstanding one, and the one best loved by the Lincoln boys, was, with Matthews, Ernest Hemingway," Edwin Rolfe of the Abraham Lincoln Brigade said. "That such a man, with so pre-eminent a position in the world, was devoting all of his time and effort to the Loyalist cause did much to inspirit those other Americans who were holding the first-line trenches" (Bruccoli, *Mechanism of Fame*, 69).

Ernest and Martha entertained other visitors as well. Lillian Hellman came to dinner, contributing nothing to the evening except grumpiness and ill feeling. Mikhail Koltsov, a more entertaining guest, told a story about the poison he had been given to administer to Russians in case the Nationalists took Madrid. The Kremlin did not want it known that there were Russians in Spain.

As before, Hemingway and Gellhorn saw a great deal of Matthews, both professionally and socially. In late September, the three of them climbed rocky trails to observe the area around Belchite on the Aragon front, where a successful Loyalist offensive temporarily lifted the prevailing climate of gloom. Joined by Delmer, the correspondents went to see Brunete in early October, peering down from the heights at rebel troops occupying the city. On November 8, Gellhorn's twenty-ninth birthday, Matthews presented her with a large basket of flowers and somehow produced caviar, pâté, and other delicacies, while Hemingway supplied the champagne. The occasion was nearly ruined by Martha's having heard that "malicious gossip" about herself and Hemingway was circulating back in the States—gossip more hurtful because for the most part true (Moorehead, *Gellhorn*, 138).

Hemingway's single greatest combat adventure involved the capture of Teruel by the Republicans in December 1937. Franco planned to split the Republic in two, driving from the northwest down to the sea to cut off Valencia (then the government's headquarters) from Barcelona. Nationalist propagandists were claiming that their troops would reach the Mediterranean in a month's time. The Rebel stronghold Teruel, a well fortified mountain city, was to serve as the point of entry from which this salient would be launched. The Loyalist assault on the city, during a fierce blizzard, caught the Nationalists completely by surprise.

Only three correspondents—Hemingway and Matthews and Delmer—were there when Teruel fell to the Loyalists late on Monday, December 20. "On four occasions" during the previous ten days, Matthews recalled, "we drove, worked, and wrote for more than twenty-four hours . . . at a stretch. I have never in my life experienced such cold. We rarely got a square meal" (Meyers, *Biography*, 316). Harsh though the conditions were, Hemingway and Matthews agreed that the fall of Teruel "was the greatest day of our lives." Matthews referred to it as "the day we took Teruel," and if that was not entirely accurate, it was close enough (Matthews, *Education*, 7, 96). A great victory had been achieved, one that might change the course of the war, and they were there—not watching from a distance but walking into the city like conquering heroes. It was exhilarating.

Hemingway is supposed to have written three separate dispatches about the battle for Teruel. Only two have survived, and they rank with the best nonfiction pieces he ever created. He began the first dispatch, datelined Sunday, December 19, by stressing the triumph of the underdog. "In the biggest upset expert opinion has received since Max Schmeling knocked out Joe Louis, Government forces, while all the world awaited a Franco drive, launched a large-scale surprise offensive against Teruel Wednesday morning." After three days of fighting in a blinding snowstorm, they reached the outskirts of the city. Hemingway brought the weather and the battle to life in passages of description. On Friday, he and Matthews and Delmer watched the Loyalist troops—all Spanish, no internationals—advance "from a hillside above the town, crouching against boulders and hardly able to hold field glasses in a fifty-mile gale which picked up snow from the hillside and lashed it against our faces." He offered two more similes to communicate the conditions: it was "cold as a steel engraving and wild as a Wyoming blizzard on the Hurricane Mesa." Horses could not have stood it. Cars had their radiators frozen and cylinder blocks cracked. But men could and did fight through the storm. The lesson was that "you need infantry still to win battles and impregnable positions are only as impregnable as the will of those that hold them."

To send this dispatch, Hemingway had to drive to Valencia, where Constancia de la Mora, who had replaced Berea and Ilse Kulczar as director of censorship, approved it for cabling to NANA. "As this is filed and the result is not known," Hemingway concluded, "this correspondent is returning to Teruel by all-night driving with two frozen fingers and eight hours of nonconsecutive sleep in the last seventy-two" (Hemingway, "Dispatches," 61–63).

He arrived in time to participate in the taking of the city. The weather had moderated but not the intensity of the fighting. "At 11:20 this morning," Hemingway's report began, "we lay on top of a ridge with a line of Spanish infantry under heavy machine gun and rifle fire. It was so heavy that if you lifted your head out of the gravel you had dug your chin into . . . the machine guns on the next ridge beyond would lift the top of your head off. You knew this because you had seen it happen." Later they broke for the center of the advanced positions, "not a nice place to be either." The soldier Hemingway was lying next to was having trouble with his rifle, which jammed after every shot, and Hemingway showed him how to knock the bolt open with a rock. Then suddenly they heard cheering along the line as the fascists broke and ran "in a leaping plunging gait that is not panic but retreat." It went on like that all day, and by nighttime they were six kilometers beyond the site of the first attack.

At dusk Matthews and he were watching government planes swoop down to bomb enemy positions inside Teruel when two trucks full of dynamiters drove up, looking like a group of kids on their way to a football game. Under cover of machine gun and automatic rifle fire, they slipped quietly up to the edge of the town, hesitated a moment behind a wall, and "then came the red black flash and roar of the bombs and over the wall and into the town they went."

"How'd it be to follow them into the town?" Hemingway asked the colonel in charge.

"Excellent," the colonel said. "Marvelous project."

So, in "the pleasant autumn feeling dusk we walked the road down hill and into Teruel. . . . In town the population all embraced us, gave us wine, asked if we didn't know their brother, uncle, cousin in Barcelona, and it was very fine. We had never received the surrender of a town before and we were the only civilians in the place. I wonder who they thought we were. Tom Delmer looks like a bishop, Matthews like a Savanarola and me like, say, Wallace Beery three years back."

A burst of exultant sarcasm in Hemingway's concluding paragraph erased any doubts about where he stood. The New York papers just arrived in Madrid, Hemingway said at the end, were still talking about Franco giving the government five days to surrender before starting a final triumphant offensive. So "it seemed just a little incongruous . . . to be walking tonight into Teruel, that great Franco strongpoint, from which they were to drive to the sea in thirty days" (Hemingway, "Dispatches," 64–68).

Hemingway wrote this dispatch as a typescript rather than in cablese, and sent it by courier to Madrid with an explanation for John Wheeler at NANA: "UNCABLESED TODAY ACCOUNT COLOUR YOU ALSO BUYING STYLE" (Hemingway, "Dispatches" 64).

He rightly believed that he had done a real piece of writing in his dispatches from Teruel, especially the second one, and he didn't want editors tampering with his copy. He was accordingly furious when he discovered that NANA did not want to see his third report from Teruel and that the *New York Times* had not bothered to run either of the first two. Word reached him in Paris, where Pauline was awaiting him in an attempt to save their marriage, and provoked an angry cable to NANA headquarters in New York.

LEFT PARISWARD WHERE WIFE ILL AFTER HOLDOWN TERUEL ORDER. WAITED THREE MONTHS PROSTORY. FILED FIRST SUNDAY LONDON TEN HOURS BEFORE ANY COMPETITION. SARGINT [H. J. J. Sargint, head of NANA's London office] MADE WEDNESDAY MORNING HERALD. UNDERSTAND TIMES UNUSED. CONGRATULATE THEIR CATHOLIC NIGHT DESK. COVER BATTLE ENTER CITY WITH INFANTRY DRIVE DAY NIGHT SEVEN DAYS AHEAD FILING ALL THROWN AWAY. NICE WORK IF YOU CAN GET IT.

(HEMINGWAY, "DISPATCHES" 60)

NANA cabled back that the *Times* had slopped his dispatches because Matthews, its correspondent, was sending similar stories, and suggested that Hemingway come back to the United States. "TIMES USAGE MATTHEWS STORIES SEEMS REASON THEY UNPUBLISHED YOUR TERUEL ARTICLES STOP SUGGEST YOU UNTAKE FURTHER RISK SPAINWARD THIS TIME FAVOR YOUR RETURN REGARDS" (8 January 1938). Ernest was already planning to return, and he had his own ideas about where NANA might stick its regards and why the *Times* hadn't used his material.

His resentment was still festering when he wrote his first wife, Hadley, about it on January 31. He'd had the "most godwonderful housetohouse fighting story ready to put on wire" when NANA cabled him they didn't want any more. Then "the catholic night desk on the Times threw away all my stuff and cut my name out of Matthews dispatches and just last night in bed read in Time about how Matthews was the only newspaperman to actually be in Teruel. But first the Times retook the town for Franco on the strength of a [Nationalist headquarters] Salamanca communiqué. They refused to use my stuff so NANA would cable me to lay off" (*Selected Letters*, 462). In his fury Hemingway may have exaggerated the perfidy of the *Times*. He was probably right, though, in his implication that McCaw on the night desk decided not to run his dispatches, no matter how excellent or hard-won they were, because of their pro-Republican bias.

In fact, the *New York Times* played down the taking of Teruel in its issues of Tuesday and Wednesday, December 21 and 22. The Tuesday paper carried two accounts about the Loyalist offensive, both filed at a considerable distance from the action. The Associated Press story, from Hendaye, France, said that "three government columns *were reported* today to have captured the center of besieged Teruel" and that "a violent house-to-house battle *was reported* raging within Teruel." Obviously, these were not eyewitness reports. This dispatch characterized the campaign as the biggest government drive of the war but concluded with a reminder that its largest previous offensive, using 40,000 troops against Brunete, had failed to attain its objective. The second article in the *Times*, wired anonymously from San Sebastian, presented the insurgent side of the story. According to this account, their forces had recaptured several villages near besieged Teruel and "Generalissimo Francisco Franco's aviation gained a clear victory in the Teruel sector yesterday, shooting down ten planes." Nothing was said about the fall of the city ("Attackers Claim," "Rebels Say").

Wednesday's *Times*, under a "Teruel Captured, Madrid Announces" headline, used an AP story that led off with "the Spanish Government tonight announced the capture of Teruel, key city of the Insurgent salient, 135 miles east of Madrid" and ended with the validating information that "newspaper reporters in Madrid were invited to visit Teruel tomorrow." Once again the newsman filing the story, datelined Madrid, could furnish no information from the site, and apparently in the interests of objectivity, included a disclaimer from an Insurgent general saying "he had received no confirmation of Teruel's fall, but 'if so, it is only an episode in the struggle without importance'" ("Teruel Captured").

Not until Thursday, December 23, did Matthews's account of the taking of Teruel finally appear in the *Times*. Matthews's story concentrated solely on the Monday, December 20, fighting that ended with "your correspondent and two other journalists" strolling into the town. Sent "wireless to the New York Times" but "delayed," Matthews's dispatch did in fact duplicate much that Hemingway had written in his second, courier-sent dispatch from Teruel. Both stressed how dangerous the conditions were as the Loyalist troops struggled to traverse the last four miles into the city and how the correspondents were greeted as liberators by the men and women and children who had lived in their cellars during the six-day siege. But there were significant differences between the two reports as well. Matthews did not communicate the same sense of "being there" to his readers that Hemingway achieved in his dispatch, as in its under-fire opening scene and the brief conversation with the colonel about entering the city. On the other hand, Matthews gave his report greater structure, concentrating on the Loyalist assault on the insurgents' strongly fortified Mansueto Hill and providing an ongoing timeline for the battle that lasted all day and into the evening (Matthews, "Stronghold Reduced").

Unlike the Tuesday and Wednesday articles about Teruel, which both appeared on page sixteen, Matthews' eyewitness account began on page one, with a jump to page ten. The Times accompanied it with three other stories: two AP dispatches from Hendaye and another from Madrid. All of these represented the occupation of Teruel as an important Loyalist victory. "The fall of Teruel," according to the lead on the AP dispatch from Madrid, "was acclaimed here as marking the turn of the tide of the civil war for the government forces" ("Madrid Hails").

On the following day, however, the Times reversed course, running another page one story—"Rebel Artillery Rushed to Teruel"—to the effect that the battle was far from over. Sent "Wireless to the New York Times" from San Sebastian (a long way from Teruel) under the byline of William P. Carney, the story served as a corrective to Matthews's vivid on-the-scene dispatch. According to Carney, General Franco had visited the front, insurgent aviation was controlling the skies, and there were still 400 rebels holding out within Teruel. Carney's dispatch, dependent on insurgent data, reported 15,000 Loyalist casualties in the fighting, with 3,000 dead. An AP story from Teruel itself, quoting the government minister of defense, said that there were only 900 Loyalist casualties. Readers of the Times could choose whichever version of the truth best suited their prejudices ("Rebel Artillery"; "400 Rebels").

A week later, Carney inaccurately reported—again from a safe distance—that the Nationalists had recaptured Teruel, adding that the citizens joyfully welcomed Franco's troops with cheers and fascist salutes. The day the Times ran the story, Matthews and the photographer Robert Capa arrived in Teruel (Hemingway had gone to Paris to celebrate Christmas with his wife Pauline) and found it still in Republican hands. He duly filed a story to that effect, with eye-witness details to back it up.

This sort of "fair and balanced" handling by the *New York Times* infuriated Hemingway as well as Matthews. Matthews was "a wonderful guy," he thought, and they were colleagues rather than competitors. When he heard that Matthews's book, *Two Wars and More to Come*, was scheduled for January 1938 publication, Hemingway cabled a blurb from Paris for use in advertising. "Herbert L. Matthews," he wrote, "is the straightest the ablest and the bravest war correspondent writing today. He has seen the truth where it was very dangerous to see and in this book he brings that rarest commodity to you. In a world where faking is far more successful than the truth he stands like a gaunt lighthouse of honesty. And when the fakers are all dead Matthews will be read in the schools to find out what really happened" ("Ernest Hemingway Cables"). For Hemingway, Matthews, and most of the war correspondents in Spain, the principal "faker" was surely Carney, whose frequently false, pro-Franco dispatches sent at a safe distance from the front were designed to placate Catholic and other readers of the *New York Times* opposed to the Loyalists.

Aside from newspaper dispatches, Hemingway's major project for the fall of 1937 was to write *The Fifth Column*, his only play. *The Fifth Column* patently laid out the case for the Republican cause in Spain, and he was eager to see it published as soon as possible. In another cable from Paris early in January 1938 he urged the play's merits on Max Perkins. Following a query about sales of *To Have and Have Not* and a reference to the book of his collected stories Scribner's was interested in, Hemingway added, "ALSO MUST REMEMBER PLAY HIGHLY PUBLISH-ABLE PROBABLY BEST THING EYVE EVER WRITTEN WOULD BE POSSIBLE COMBINE IT WITH PRESENT THREE UNPUBLISHED STORIES ["The Capital of the World," "The Short Happy Life of Francis Macomber," and "The Snows of Kilimanjaro"] MAKE GOOD LENGTH BOOK COULD SETUP IMMEDIATELY" (Hemingway and Perkins, *Only Thing*, 252–53).

When Perkins had a chance to read the play, he shared his author's enthusiasm. *The Fifth Column* was "extraordinarily fine," he thought, and he'd been "mightily impressed" and "moved" by it. The play "confirm[ed] what *To Have* showed, that you have marched forward into new fields, and large ones" (*Only Thing*, 257). In July Hemingway had a new proposal for Perkins. Scribner's was planning to publish his collected stories in the fall. "Now what about the Fifth Column starting the whole thing off?" he suggested. Either that or bring out "The Fifth Column and the three new stories," saving the collection for later (*Selected Letters*, 470). Perkins opted for the first idea, and in October 1938 *The Fifth Column and the First Forty-nine Stories* appeared. Despite the play's placement at the beginning, most reviewers devoted their attention to the stories. What comments they made on the play were usually unfavorable.

Over time, Hemingway's opinion of his own play changed; eventually he labeled it "probably the most unsatisfactory thing I ever wrote" (*Byline*, 246). Much of his disillusionment stemmed from his unhappy experience of trying to get the play produced on Broadway—a project that took three years to develop, so long that by the time audiences actually saw *The Fifth Column* its propaganda value was drastically diminished. He realized, as he wrote Perkins, that he should have written it as a novel, but "there wasn't time while we were waiting for Teruel" (*Selected Letters*, 479).

In his seminal essay on *The Fifth Column*, John Raeburn described the play as "less egregiously propagandistic" than *The Spanish Earth* but nonetheless "intended to rally support for Republican Spain and to celebrate the unyielding commitment of those fighting for it" (Raeburn, "Hemingway on Stage," 7–8). Actually, Hemingway's play conveys an entirely different message than the documentary film he worked on the previous spring. Whereas *The Spanish Earth* celebrated the indigenous Spaniard peasants who rallied to the cause, *The Fifth Column* emphasized foreign contributions to the Loyalist war effort, which gains significance as the first battle in the international struggle against fascism. Philip Rawlings, the protagonist, praises the American volunteers with the Lincoln Battalion. It's an "awfully good battalion," he tells his companions; "it's done such things that it would break your damn heart if I tried to tell you about it" (Hemingway, *Fifth*, 56). Offstage, soldiers are heard singing anthems of the left such as "The Internationale" and "The Partizan." When they get to "Bandera Rossa," Rawlings declares that "the best people I ever knew died for that song" (85). The German communist Max, a sympathetic figure, spells out the reasons why he is fighting. "You do it so *no one* will ever be hungry. You do it so men will not have to fear ill health and old age; so they can live and work in dignity and not as slaves" (108).

Then there was the matter of the fifth column itself, and how to deal with it. The phrase originally referred to fascist sympathizers within besieged Madrid, conspiring to subvert the Loyalists. In the spring of 1937 the government created a counterespionage agency, the SIM, to combat these and other subversives. From the start, according to historian Hugh Thomas, "the SIM employed all the odious tortures of the NKVD" (the Soviet Union's secret espionage agency) and became "the bureaucratic instrument . . . through which the Communist Party murdered its enemies"

(Raeburn, "Hemingway on Stage," 13). In Hemingway's play, the Seguridad (his name for the SIM) is embodied in the character of Antonio, a figure modeled on Pepe Quintanilla, and the enemies Antonio ferrets out and executes are indeed fascists (except when mistakes were made). Under the rules of war, Hemingway asserted in his preface to *The Fifth Column and the First Forty-nine Stories*, fifth column operatives "deserved to be [shot] . . . and they expected to be" (Light, "Of Wasteful Deaths," 68). In actuality, the SIM did much of its deadliest work not against actual fascist spies but against factions on the left threatening the dominance of the Russian Stalinists in Spain. Hemingway knew about these activities but chose not to write about them. He did not want to complicate or compromise his message.

The Fifth Column is a didactic play, designed along Brechtian lines as a "fusion of instruction and entertainment" (Block and Shedd, *Masters of Modern Drama*, 841). Like most didactic works, it suffers from stereotyped and single-dimensional characterization. The theme of love vs. duty is played out through the figures of Philip Rawlings and Dorothy Bridges, neither of whom emerges as a fully developed character. Rawlings is a caricature of Hemingway himself, or rather—as Raeburn put it—"a caricature of a caricature, Hemingway's public personality of the 1930s touched up . . . and burnished with the luster of a righteous cause" ("Hemingway on Stage," 9). He drinks and gets into fights, walks like a gorilla, likes sandwiches made of bully beef and raw onions, and rarely takes baths. He is also an insider, privy to the "true gen," who can pronounce sound judgments on the fate of others.

As Michael Maiwald points out, *The Fifth Column* is constructed along the lines of a romantic triangle, with Rawlings torn between the idealistic Max and the long-legged blonde Dorothy Bridges. Bridges is a far from flattering version of Martha Gellhorn. Hemingway supplies her with Gellhorn's "curiously cultivated accent," her distaste for dirt and disorder, even her silver-fox cape. The Moorish tart Anita warns Rawlings against getting mixed up with Dorothy. "Listen, you don't want make mistake now with that big blonde," To which he replies, "You know, Anita, I'm afraid I do. . . . I want to make an absolutely colossal mistake" (Hemingway, *Fifth*, 66). Besides, Anita is unjust to Dorothy, he says. "Granted she's lazy and spoiled, and rather stupid, and enormously on the make. Still she's very beautiful, very friendly, and very charming and rather innocent—and quite brave" (68–69). Gellhorn could hardly have been pleased with this portrait or with the way her character is dismissed at the end when Rawlings, pleading a higher calling, announces that his time "is the

Party's time. . . . And where I go now I go alone, or with others who go there for the same reason I go." She cannot come along (131).

Why Hemingway "in the early blush of a romance" should have created such transparent representations of himself and his lover and why he should have had his alter ego spurn the lover in the name of duty pose interesting biographical questions. Perhaps, Raeburn suggested, by doing so Hemingway "projected and assuaged his guilt at his disloyalty to his wife Pauline" ("Hemingway on Stage," 8). Perhaps, too, he wanted somehow to reassure Pauline or himself that despite his affair with Martha he had not yet committed himself to her.

The Hemingways had been back in Key West barely a month before Ernest decided to return to Spain, armed with a six-week contract from NANA. The situation was worsening for the Loyalists. Franco's troops retook Teruel (truly) on February 21 and resumed their drive to the Mediterranean that sought to split the Republic in two. It was beginning to look as if the defeat of the Spanish Republic was inevitable, but as always Hemingway wanted to be where the action was and to advance the cause in any way he could. He and Martha Gellhorn rendezvoused in Miami on March 4 and agreed to meet in Spain as soon as possible. On March 15 Hemingway wrote Perkins that he couldn't sleep at night. "I feel like a bloody shit to be here in Key West when I should be in Aragon or in Madrid," he said (Watson, " 'Old Man,' " 152). The next day, the Rebels began bombing Barcelona, eighteen raids in forty-eight hours. Many bombs fell in the city's most crowded quarters, killing and injuring helpless civilians. Blood flowed into the gutters. Matthews, who was on the scene, reported that he had witnessed "things which Dante could not have imagined" (Moorehead, *Gellhorn*, 144).

It was in this climate of frustration and near-despair that Hemingway ran into Dos Passos in New York during a party at Gerald and Sara Murphy's penthouse apartment. The meeting was not auspicious. Archibald MacLeish detected "a terrible icy coldness" between the two men. "You think for a long time you have a friend," Dos Passos told Gerald Murphy, "and then you don't" (Koch, *The Breaking Point*, 251–52). Ten days later, Hemingway broke the friendship forever in a scathing letter from Paris. He had just finished reading Dos Passos's article in the February 1938 *Redbook*. The article, excerpted from his book *Journeys Between Wars*, described the lunch when the Fifteenth International Brigade was, presumably, converted into part of the "Spanish people's army." This was the very day, a year earlier, when Hemingway confronted Dos with the news of Robles's death. Robles was not mentioned in the article, or in Hemingway's letter, but their mutual and lasting animosity about that matter colored the terrible things he had to say.

Dos Passos's article does not so much criticize the Loyalist cause as make fun of the ceremonial aspects of the day—bands playing, generals making speeches, and so forth. But his worst offense, in Hemingway's judgment, came in his reference to "a Russian staffofficer who goes by the name of General Walter" (Dos Passos, *Journeys*, 376). This he regarded as an act of disloyalty, even treachery, inasmuch as it called attention to the Russian communist involvement in the war and would provide fodder for anti-Republican propagandists. Even worse, Dos Passos was wrong about Walter.

"A war is still being fought in Spain between the people whose side you used to be on and the fascists," Hemingway began. If Dos Passos with his "hatred of communism" felt justified "in attacking, for money, the people who are still fighting that war" he should at least try to get his facts right. Dos mentioned Walter's name and called him a Russian general, hence giving "the impression that it is a communist run war." But Walter was in fact a Pole, just as Lukacs was a Hungarian and Regler a German and so forth. "I'm sorry, Dos, but you didn't meet any Russian generals," Hemingway told him. (What Hemingway didn't say was that Walter, like most of the other European commanders of the International Brigades, had received extensive training and indoctrination in Soviet Russia).

Hemingway's letter went on to insult Dos Passos in a number of ways. Dos was guilty of pretending to knowledge he didn't have about what was going on in Spain. He had only been there for a short time during the war, and—Hemingway insisted—"you don't find out the truth in ten days or three weeks." For him to "try constantly to make out that the war the government is fighting against the fascist Italian Moorish invasion is a communist business imposed on the will of the people is sort of viciously pitiful." Here Ernest was attacking a conclusion that Dos Passos had not articulated, at least not in his *Redbook* article.

Hemingway ended his diatribe with a personal assault on Dos Passos's moral and ethical standards. Over the years of their friendship Ernest had loaned Dos money on several occasions, and now—rhetorically, at least—he called in those loans. "When people start in being crooked about money, they usually end up being crooked about everything," he wrote. Dos Passos might send him thirty dollars, or twenty or ten, when he had the chance, but Hemingway didn't really expect payment. What he expected was the same sort of traitorous attack on himself that Dos Passos was making on the Republican cause. "Good old friends," he wrote in a viciously sarcastic conclusion. "Always happy with the good old friends. Got them that will knife you in the back for a dime. Regular price two for a quarter. Two for a quarter, hell. Honest Jack Passos'll knife you three times in the back for fifteen cents and sing Giovanezza free" (*Selected Letters*, 463–64). "Giovanezza," they both knew, was the anthem of Mussolini's fascist supporters.

Instead of waiting for Dos Passos to knife him in the back, Hemingway launched a frontal barrage of his own: a piece for *Ken* magazine called "Treachery in Aragon" that disparaged an American writer—"a very good friend of mine," Hemingway called him—who had turned up in Madrid the previous year and been unwilling to believe that a Spanish friend of his (Robles) who had been shot as a traitor could possibly be guilty. This was simply an example of the typical liberal's "good-hearted naïveté," Hemingway maintained. He happened to know that the man was guilty, he added, and that he "had been shot . . . as a spy after a long and careful trial in which all the charges against him had been proven" (Hemingway, "Treachery"). Hemingway did not really *know* this at all. Undoubtedly it was what he had been told by Ivens and others, and he chose to believe it. An article by Herbert Solow in the *Partisan Review* called attention to Dos Passos's move away from communism and Hemingway's move toward it. "Substitution at Left Tackle: Hemingway for Dos Passos," it was called.

Hemingway arrived in Paris in late March, where a message from Matthews in Barcelona awaited him—a message making it clear that the two men were in effect working together as correspondents. Matthews telephoned the *New York Times* office in advance, advising them to give Hemingway a supply of typewriter paper and various envelopes, since "this town is out of them," to ask him to bring any accumulated mail for Matthews along with him, to show Hemingway a copy of his March 18 article on the bombing of Barcelona, and to tell him the "situation looks bad" (Matthews, telephone message). On March 20, the insurgents had begun their drive to the coast by striking at three points on a sixty-mile front. "The Loyalist lines," Matthews reported, "crumpled like paper" (*Education*, 118).

The end looked so near that Ernest, along with two other correspondents, alerted Claude Bowers, the American ambassador to Spain, of the need to prepare for evacuation of American medics and wounded should Franco's forces prevail. In addition, the government's supply of ambulances was again in short supply, so Hemingway, Vincent (Jimmy) Sheean, and Louis Fischer wired the League of American Writers in New York appealing for additional funds (*Writers Take Sides*, vii). The telegram arrived April 1, the same day Hemingway reached Barcelona with Sheean and young James Lardner, son of Ring Lardner, both of them representing the *New York Herald Tribune*.

Two days later, Hemingway and Matthews journeyed together to see the Republicans desperately trying to stave off Franco in fighting along the Ebro river north of Tortosa. Ernest filed dispatches three days in a row, April 3, 4, and 5, only to be greeted with a cable from NANA complaining once again that his reports were not being used by the *Times* because they were too similar to those of Matthews. "REQUEST THEY SEPARATE," NANA wired.

Hemingway replied angrily, as before blaming the problem on the editors at the *Times*. "TIMES SUGGESTION DUPLICATION MATTHEWS JESUIT MANOEUVRE AS COMPARISON OF DISPATCHES . . . WILL SHOW STOP IF TIMES WANTS MATTHEWS ME COVER DIFFERENT FRONTS REGARDLESS IMPORTANCE STORY WILL THEY FURNISH HIM WITH TRANSPORT CAR STOP BEEN SHARING COST STOP TWO THOUSAND DOLLARS IS UNPAID STOP" (Hemingway, "Dispatches," 75). In his next dispatch, Hemingway tried to make the worsening situation in Spain look better. In the north, he wrote, Franco's troops were advancing against token opposition, but "they were absolutely held up in their attempt to come down the Ebro . . . absolutely checked . . . for five days above Tortosa" (Hemingway, "Dispatches," 76–77). Hemingway was by that time "absolutely" wrapped up in the Republic's cause and what looked like it might be its last stand. He was supposed to write an introduction to Luis Quintanilla's drawings of battle scenes, but, he said, "this is Barcelona, and yesterday was Tortosa, and tomorrow will be Tortosa again, and it is very difficult to write an introduction when the only thing you can think about is holding the line of the Ebro" (Hemingway, "Three Prefaces," 9).

Early in May he went to Madrid for the first time in five months and was heartened by the city's continuing struggle to relieve the siege. In the meantime the Nationalists had reached the Mediterranean at Vinaroz, but, as he wrote Perkins, "there has been no collapse and we held solidly along the Ebro" (*Selected Letters*, 466). In a cable to Wheeler at NANA, he predicted that there was "a year of war clearly ahead where European diplomats are trying to say it will be over in a month" (Baker, *A Life Story*, 330). Hemingway was more nearly right than the diplomats.

When he got back to Key West after six weeks in Spain, Hemingway wrote Wheeler defending the objectivity of his reporting. "My stuff on

Spain has been consistently accurate," he insisted. "I gave full accounts of government disasters and criticized their weaknesses in [the] same measure I reported their success" (qtd. in Reynolds, *Hemingway: 1930s*, 288). But this was not and could not be true. He and Matthews and Gellhorn all gave their hearts to the cause, and it could not help showing it in what they wrote about the war. (In June 1938, Hemingway went so far as to dispense some blue-sky malarkey to New York reporters. Franco was short of troops, he told them, and beset by factional wrangling among the foreign components of his army. The Republicans were well-organized and stood a good chance of winning [Knightley, *The First Casualty*, 213].)

Wheeler remained somewhat bewildered about Hemingway's animus against the *New York Times* "beyond the Catholic matter you mentioned to me." He also wondered why—in covering the fighting along the Ebro—Hemingway had not left Matthews behind. Inasmuch as the *Times* did not furnish transport and Matthews did not drive, that would have enabled NANA, which *was* paying for Hemingway's transportation to the front, to have "exclusive material." In short, Wheeler said, "I don't understand why you took him with you" (14 June 1938). But Hemingway and Matthews were far more than competing journalists. They were road warriors linked by a common bravery and determination to see the war up close. They were friends. And they were on the same side.

Hemingway and Gellhorn came back to Spain one more time, in November. On a November 5 visit with other correspondents to observe the fighting near Tarragona, Hemingway saved all their lives. The Ebro was in flood, with its bridges down, so they hired a rowboat to cross to the east bank. The boat was being pulled along by a rope, which snapped, and the boat started drifting rapidly toward the rapids downstream. Hemingway took the oars and "by an extraordinary exhibition of strength . . . got [them] safely across. He was a good man in a pinch," Matthews decided (Lynn, *Hemingway*, 445–46). He described Hemingway's feat in a dispatch that the *Times* declined to print.

Ten days later, Ernest and Martha witnessed the farewell parade of the International Brigades in Barcelona. President Juan Negrín disbanded the brigades in the wan hope that Franco might do the same with the Italians and Germans fighting for the Nationalists. Also, the disbanding gave the troops a chance to get out of Spain before the end-of-the-war atrocities that were sure to follow. It was an admission of defeat, and they watched the troops in bitterness and despair. The men, Gellhorn thought, looked "very dirty and weary and young, and many of them had no country to go back to." Hemingway had nothing to say during the parade, silently tolerating the histrionics of the Spanish communist orator La Pasionaria (Dolores Ibarruri), who "always made him vomit always." "You can go proudly," she told the troops. "You are history. You are legend." That night, in their hotel room, he leaned against the wall and cried. "They can't do it!" he kept saying. "They can't do it!" It was the only time Gellhorn ever saw Hemingway cry. Their relationship was to end disastrously, with copious ill will on both sides. But at that moment, Gellhorn really loved him (Moorehead, *Gellhorn*, 153; Mellow, *A Life Without Consequences*, 514).

With the cause he cared about lost, Hemingway blamed the defeat on the unwillingness of the United States, England, and France to support the Loyalists, and on certain unspecified traitors within the Loyalist government. As he wrote Max Perkins in February 1939, there was only one thing to do in a war and that was to win it. "But in this one winning was made impossible by many circumstances outside the control of the military." Scornfully, he spoke of "the carnival of treachery and rottenness on both sides" (Baker, *A Life Story*, 334).

Matthews saw the war to its end the next spring and wrote Hemingway about it. It was just as well, he said, that "dear Scrooby" (a shortened version of "screwball," his and Gellhorn's nickname for Ernest) had not seen the final failed offensive along the Ebro, or the "heartbreaking" concentration camps set up for Republican troops. Matthews brought back several Spanish pistols that Loyalist officers had to throw away as they surrendered. He had given one to Eddie Rolfe of the Lincoln Battalion, now writing for the *Daily Worker*, and was keeping another as a souvenir for Ernest.

In that same letter of April 12, 1939, Matthews described his confrontation with the *Times* about the paper's handling of his (and Hemingway's) dispatches from Spain. For "one long dangerous moment," in a meeting with publisher Arthur Hays Sulzberger, it looked as if Matthews would have to quit. The publisher and the correspondent had forged close ties over the years—Sulzberger was godfather to Matthews's only son—and both of them wanted to avoid a parting of the ways. So Sulzberger asked Matthews to put his complaints in writing, Matthews did so, his report cleared the air, and the *Times* made its peace with its star correspondent. In the report, Matthews told Hemingway, "I couldn't accuse McCaw and Co. of dishonesty, because that couldn't be proved, but I did accuse them of bias." As for Matthews's own dispatches, "lots of people—including Sulzberger—accused me of giving the Loyalists too good a break and not making it clear that all was being lost. Maybe"

(12 April 1939). Maybe, to be sure, but how else could it be? They were partisans as well as reporters.

Twenty years later, looking over his clippings from the war inspired Matthews to write Hemingway. He still saw a lot of Luis Quintanilla in New York, Matthews said, and "so long as there are Spaniards like him," he'd be working "to see Franco & Co. go down the drain." The clippings confirmed his feeling that "Spain was the best thing" he'd done in his career, "and since said career is now drawing to a close, it [would] always remain the best" (17 February 1956).

In 1957, the year after he wrote Hemingway this letter, Matthews hiked his way alone into the Sierra Maestra in Cuba for an exclusive interview with the revolutionary Fidel Castro. At the time the propaganda arm of the Cuban government under dictator Fulgencio Batista was circulating a rumor that Castro had been killed. The account Matthews brought back established that Castro was very much alive—and that, in Matthews's judgment, Castro was not a communist and he and his followers promised to bring a new and better deal to Cuba. Matthews's story went around the world, transforming Castro from hotheaded communist rebel "into the youthful face of the future" (Alter).

The pattern in Cuba was not unlike that in Spain, Matthews believed. Batista's repressive regime beholden to landowners held power, and a revolutionary movement under Castro had sprung up to represent the working people. To his way of thinking, there could be no question which side merited support. And Hemingway, on the site at his home outside Havana, was on the same page as his friend, supporting the revolution against Batista as he had the one against Machado.

When Castro was on his way to the United States in April 1959, Hemingway sought an audience with him. Specifically, he wanted to warn Castro how to handle the American press. He should be wary of enemies at *Time* and the *Miami Herald*. He should have answers ready to questions about communism in Cuba, and about the executions that his government—like the one in Republican Spain—had resorted to as it took control. In July, when Castro appeared on the television show *This Is Your Life*, he was asked about those executions. "Let me tell you what Hemingway thinks about that," Castro replied, that "the military criminals who were executed by the revolutionary government received what they deserved" (Reynolds, *Final*, 332–33). Ernest's position, if Castro had it right, had not changed since the Spanish war when he justified the death of Robles and the activities of the SIM on similar grounds. A certain amount of collateral damage must be tolerated in the struggle for the greater good.

Hemingway lived long enough to realize that going back to live in Cuba, after the Bay of Pigs fiasco, was no longer a viable option. Matthews, however, did not let Cuba's close ties with Russian communism change his mind. Much to the consternation of his colleagues at the *New York Times*, Matthews continued to maintain that Castro's government was "free, honest and democratic" even after the Cuban missile crisis nearly started a war between the United States and the U.S.S.R. Editors at the *Times* didn't quite know how to deal with the famous veteran newsman. They couldn't muzzle him, but they devoutly wished he would pipe down.

NANA AND *KEN*

As the leading foreign journalist in Spain, much was expected of Hemingway, and whether or not his dispatches met those expectations is a matter of some dispute. In his biography, Carlos Baker called Hemingway's Spanish Civil War reports "not noticeably superior" to those he'd sent back to the Toronto *Star* in the early 1920s. He could, it was true, summarize grand strategy with uncommon force, evoke the terrain through descriptive passages, and create "arresting similes" and patches of dialogue. But these virtues, Baker felt, were matched by Hemingway's faults as a correspondent: "a curious monotony" in his stories of battles, a predilection to shock his readers, and the "note of triumphant boastfulness" he too often struck. Dos Passos had a keener eye for the telling detail, Baker wrote, and the dispatches of Matthews and Delmer outshone Hemingway's in their "meticulous exactitude and inclusiveness" (Baker, *A Life Story*, 329). The journalist Phillip Knightley was still more critical in *The First Casualty*, his authoritative study of war correspondence in the twentieth century. Hemingway's reporting was "abysmally bad," Knightley maintained, citing in particular "his total failure to report the Communist persecution, imprisonment, and summary execution of 'untrustworthy elements' on the Republican side." Knightley believed Hemingway failed his obligations as a reporter by salting away such material for use in *For Whom the Bell Tolls*. "For a novelist," he commented, "this was understandable. For a war correspondent, it was unforgivable" (212–14).

For the most part, these judgments have been echoed by other commentators, sometimes without demonstrable evidence that they have actually read Hemingway's reporting from Spain. An exception, certainly, is William Braasch Watson, the scholar responsible for assembling, introducing, and making accessible all thirty of the dispatches. In a judicious evaluation, Watson divided Hemingway's correspondence into several categories.

Some . . . were poorly done, trivial or incoherent or just plain perfunc-
tory. Some were done well enough, but they were so full of topographical
and place-name details that they were more appropriate for general staff
colleges than for newspaper audiences. Some provided superb examples
of his powers of observation, his responsiveness to human suffering and
human excellence alike. Some were masterpieces of characterization, of
analysis, of description, or of just plain factual reporting. A half dozen or
so of these dispatches can stand up to the best reporting from the Spanish
Civil War.

(HEMINGWAY, "DISPATCHES" 7)

Hemingway was not the best judge of his own writing and tended to
overvalue the work he had done most recently. Still, it is significant that
on several occasions from 1937 to 1939 he proposed to Max Perkins that
some or more of his dispatches from Spain should be collected in book
form along with stories, the speech at Carnegie Hall, and his piece "Who
Murdered the Vets?"

Any sensible estimate of the merit of Hemingway's Spanish Civil War
correspondence should take into account what his employer wanted him to
write. Jack Wheeler at NANA made it clear that he was not looking for
"meticulous exactitude and inclusiveness" from Hemingway. He was looking for "color and drama and the personal adventures of the celebrated
writer": material that NANA's syndicated members could find nowhere
else. In a "promotion box" sent to its papers, NANA proclaimed that Hemingway would provide "both from the bombed towns and the bombed
trenches the human side of the war, not just an account of the game being
played by general staffs with pins and a map" (Cooper, *Politics*, 82–83).

His assignment was to present the war in Spain up close and personal,
and he did his best to fulfill it, often placing himself in harm's way. When
he wrote, for example, that "for two days, this correspondent [his usual
way of referring to himself in the dispatches] has been doing the most
dangerous thing you can do in a war. That is, keep close behind an unsta-
bilized line where the enemy is attacking with mechanized forces," it was
not so much a show of bravado or "triumphant boastfulness" as part of the
job he signed on to do (Cooper, *Politics*, 89). In the fall of 1938, Edmund
Wilson disparaged Hemingway's newspaper dispatches for "always divert-
ing attention to his own narrow escapes from danger," whereupon Ernest
reminded Wilson that "if you are paid to get shot at and write about it you
are supposed to mention the shooting" (Hemingway, "Dispatches," 157,

159). It was part of his job. As Matthews put it, "a war correspondent who avoids danger had better be doing other things" (Matthews, *World*, 22).

Another criticism of Hemingway's reporting from Spain—that it amounted to propaganda for the Republican side—had more justification. In three ways particularly, his dispatches sought to advance the government's cause. First, he crafted his accounts of the shelling of Madrid to evoke the deepest possible feelings of horror and of sympathy for the victims. Second, the undue optimism of his battlefield reports ignored Loyalist defeats and exaggerated the importance of its victories. And third, he repeatedly called attention to the participation of Italians and Germans on Franco's side in an effort to persuade the Western democracies to end their policy of nonintervention.

The shelling of Madrid began in earnest on April 11, 1937. It was a Sunday, and the shells exploded when the streets were full of crowds. Hemingway filed his vivid and grisly report later in the day. The shells "killed an old woman returning home from market, dropping her in a huddled heap of black clothing, with one leg suddenly detached whirling against the wall of an adjoining house." A car "stopped suddenly and swerved after the bright flash and roar, and the driver lurched out, his scalp hanging down over his eyes, to sit on the sidewalk with his hand against his face, the blood making a smooth sheen down over his chin." The Telefonica building was struck three times that day, and—Hemingway commented—that was legitimate enough, since it was a communication center, "but the shelling that traverses the streets seeking the Sunday promenaders was not military" ("Dispatches," 27). For twenty days in a row, the shelling continued, and in his dispatch of April 30 Hemingway cited the government figures on casualties: 312 killed . . . and more than 3,000 wounded (37).

Twice, in descriptions of close calls in the field, Hemingway harked back to the continual shelling of the city. Late in April he wrote about riding in an armored car with machine gun bullets pinging off its side. The bursts of fire were "very unimpressive," he said, when compared with the thirty-two shells that fell within 200 yards of his hotel the night before ("Dispatches," 57). Similarly, when high explosive shells were launched at the Ford flying the American and British flags that he and Matthews and Delmer were using, he commented that "being sniped at with six-inch stuff is a compliment journalists rarely receive, but it was actually a relief to hear shells strike the earth and burst with an honest mud-throwing thump being fired at a definite objective after the feeling one gets about the indiscriminate shelling in the stony streets of Madrid." It was nothing less than murder, he thought, and he wanted his readers to share his outrage.

Gellhorn and Matthews felt the same way. In an article for *Collier's* entitled "Only the Shells Whine," Gellhorn painted a word picture of one child's terrible death. "A small piece of twisted steel, hot and very sharp, sprays off from the shells; it takes the little boy in the throat. The old woman stands there, holding the hand of the dead child, looking at him stupidly, not saying anything, and the men run out toward her to carry the child" (qtd. in Moorehead, *Gellhorn*, 122). Years later, Matthews celebrated the grace and dignity with which the Madrileños suffered through the bombardment. "In the centuries to come," he wrote, "Madrid will be to Spain what London and her high bravery during the German 'blitz' will be to England" (Matthews, *Education*, 94).

Most of Hemingway's reporting during the war dealt with military engagements, and he adopted a stance of exuberant optimism about the outcome of the war that proved—and much of the time he knew it—to be unwarranted. In his fourth and fifth dispatches, late in March 1937, he described government victories in the battle of Guadalajara. Dispatch four focused on the defeat of Italian troops sent by Mussolini to aid Franco. Inspecting the battlefield a few days later, Hemingway saw three dead Italians who looked less like soldiers than "curiously broken toys. One doll had lost its feet and lay with no expression on its waxy stubbled face. Another doll had lost half of its head. The third doll was simply broken as a bar of chocolate breaks in your pocket." After so miniaturizing the enemy, he concluded his dispatch with the estimate that the fortunes of the war had turned "when the supposedly invincible Italian mechanized columns were defeated on the Guadalajara front" ("Dispatches," 19–20). In dispatch five, about another rout of the Italians, Hemingway stated "flatly that the battle of Brihuega will take its place in military history with the other decisive battles of the world" (22). It has not, but Hemingway's account of the forced retreat of the Italians and his on-the-scene proof that organized Italian troops were fighting for the Nationalists were of considerable propaganda value to the Loyalist cause.

Before leaving Spain early in May 1937, with the Nationalists then attacking Bilbao, Hemingway boldly forecast that no matter what happened in the short term the Loyalists would eventually win. "This correspondent believes that if the Fascists take Bilbao, the war will last two years, with the Government still winning. If Franco fails to take Bilbao, the Government should win the war by next spring" ("Dispatches," 38). In December, after the Loyalists captured Teruel, he speculated that this battle might prove to be "the decisive one of this war" (62). And even after it became clear in the spring of 1938 that the superior Nationalist army, abetted by support from other fascist regimes, would prevail, Hemingway refused to acknowledge that fact in his dispatches. "After a week along the Ebro and Segre Rivers and a month on the front," he wrote on April 29, 1938, "your correspondent has been unable to see a conclusion to the Spanish war" (87).

Hemingway, who had a good understanding of military tactics and strategy, surely knew that the future was dark. Under the circumstances, he must have felt that a false optimism was mandatory. If there was a single goal that as a Loyalist partisan he was aiming for, it was to persuade the United States to abandon the nonintervention policy and lift the arms embargo that played into Franco's hands. And that would only happen if the United States and the other democracies believed that their assistance might help the Loyalists win. Certainly they would be unlikely to support a lost cause.

As early as his second dispatch from Spain, Hemingway documented the participation of Italian and German forces in the war. According to a "most reliable source," he wrote on March 15, 1937, there were already 88,000 Italian and 16,000 to 20,000 German troops fighting with Franco, and every day in Salamanca trucks arrived from Portugal carrying German materiel ("Dispatches," 14–15). Subsequent reports noted that German-made artillery was shelling Madrid, that Savoia-Marchetti and Heinkel bombers, accompanied by Messerschmidt pursuit planes, were bombing Tortosa, and so forth. These dispatches were implicit cries for help. Italy and Germany were aiding Franco's Nationalists in a fascist alliance, and if they were to be defeated the antifascist countries had to provide aid to the Spanish Republic.

Only on one occasion did Hemingway make that appeal explicit, in a brief and eloquent piece written on May Day 1938. This was not published by NANA and, Watson speculates, may not even have been sent to them. Hemingway told Jack Wheeler a month later, probably with the May Day account in mind, that he had decided against "a summing-up story as people might think it was propaganda no matter how true." The piece itself does indeed read like propaganda, and as such belonged on the editorial page rather than in the news columns. In it Hemingway combined his customary unjustified optimism with an overt call for armaments.

"There was war in Spain on last May Day, there was war in Spain on this May Day, and there will be war in Spain on next May Day," he began. The Republic was divided between those at the front—"young, brave, determined and already forged in two years of fighting into a skillful army," with morale "solid and unshaken" in the face of the fascist advance—and those in the rear—"politicians without faith, generals without ability." As the front came closer to the rear (as the Loyalists lost ground, in other words) it had a purifying effect, and "in the purification of that merging is Spain's hope of ultimate victory." This sounded very much like whistling past the graveyard, finding the best opportunity for victory in the discouraging fact of the Loyalist retreat.

"But meantime," Hemingway concluded, the Spanish Republic "must have planes and guns. Anyone who thinks the war is over in Spain is a fool or a coward. A great fighting people who are for the first time being led by generals who are of the people, who are not fools, nor traitors, will not be defeated that easily. But she must have planes and guns; and she must have them at once" ("Dispatches," 87–88).

Actually Hemingway was a good deal less hopeful about the war's outcome in the spring of 1938 than his dispatches indicated. The situation of James Lardner offers a case in point. The youth, a son of writer Ring Lardner, rode down to Barcelona on the same train as Hemingway and Vincent (Jimmy) Sheean. Lardner was backing up Sheean as a correspondent for the *New York Herald Tribune* but became restless in that role and decided to join the International Brigades. Hemingway cabled a brief story about it on April 25, in which he depicted the "dark serious scholarly" twenty-four-year-old as an idealistic supporter of the Spanish Republic. "I believe absolutely in the justice of the Spanish Loyalist cause," Lardner is quoted as saying in explanation of his enlistment. "From what I've seen in the last two weeks at the front, I know all they need to win is the right to buy artillery, planes and war material, and I want to back up my beliefs by joining the Brigade" ("Dispatches," 84–85).

Although he did not say so for NANA, Hemingway did everything he could to discourage Lardner from enlisting. Agreeing with Sheean that Lardner's enlistment so late in the war made no sense, Ernest tried to talk him out of it. In their conversation at the Majestic Hotel in Barcelona, he and Lardner kept going over the same question: where and how could he be "most useful" in the Spanish war? Hemingway's answer was that Lardner should go to Madrid and stay there "until it falls and after it falls stay on and then come out and write the truth about what happened." Lardner, who had no registered political beliefs, could do this task without being jailed and would not have to write any propaganda. "All you have to do," Hemingway told him, "is write the truth and be there where you can write it. . . . If no honest man is in Madrid to write about what really happens if it ever falls it will be one of the tragedies of history" (Sheean, *Not Peace*, 248; Hemingway, "The Writer").

Lardner listened, but Hemingway's remarks sounded "far-fetched" and like "defeatist talk" to him. The next day he joined the International Brigades. In some frustration, Ernest wrote Jack Wheeler, a friend of the lad's mother, that Lardner ranked at the top of "all the pigheaded kids and gloomy superior little snots" he'd ever encountered. But at least, he added, he was undergoing artillery training "with the intention of his being shifted to anti-aircraft and not being sent to the front" ("Dispatches" 121). Wheeler could tell Ellis Lardner that her son was in no more immediate danger than if he had to walk across the street a few times a day in traffic.

In making this assurance, Hemingway did not reckon with James Lardner's persistence. Lardner managed to get himself transferred to the Fifteenth International Brigade's infantry and was soon serving in the fierce fighting along the Ebro. He was slightly wounded late in July, and after a period of recovery came back to the front in less than a month. On September 4 he wrote his mother that he'd passed up an opportunity to go to Barcelona. "The Fascists are making heavy attacks on our sector and I want to stay until it is over," he explained. "To leave now would be equivalent to deliberately running away." On September 19, he told her that his company had recently taken a position on an exposed hill "almost enclosed by the Fascist lines." They arrived at night, and four of them spent seven hours digging with pick and shovel in stony ground to make a trench. Soon after daybreak it was deep enough to sit in with their heads below the surface, and they climbed in just as the mortars began to land. The mortars exploded around them all day. "I was never so well paid for hard labor," he said, "as by that feeling of comparative safety" (Nelson and Hendricks, *Madrid 1937*, 413).

Three days later, on September 22—the last day the Fifteenth Brigade was in the lines and a day after Negrín announced that all international volunteers would be withdrawn from the field—James Lardner was killed. Hemingway wrote a requiem to him the following year. "Well, he joined the Brigades and soldiered well and everybody liked him and he was a fine kid and he ran into a fascist patrol, or onto a fascist post by mistake . . . and he was killed. His joining the Brigade was a fine example and he was a brave and cheerful soldier, if not a particularly skillful soldier, and he is dead" (Hemingway, "The Writer"). He left it to others, to Jimmy Sheean and Jack Wheeler and assuredly Lardner's mother, to say that his death was a terrible waste.

Hemingway was never compensated for his brief dispatch about Lardner, he complained to NANA. It was only a minor instance in the ongoing dispute between the news service and its celebrity correspondent in

Spain. The famous writer signed a contract that would pay him $500 for each cabled story and $1,000 for mailed stories, where he could work his literary magic without having to resort to the shorthand of cablese. These were extraordinary terms at the time, when most reporters were being paid fifteen to twenty-five dollars an article (Hemingway, "Dispatches," 6, 91). Predictably, NANA's editors tried to rein in Hemingway to hold down expenses. From the beginning to the end of their two-year connection, the famous writer and the syndicate supplying copy to sixty leading newspapers were at financial loggerheads.

As early as March 20, after receiving but three cabled dispatches from its new man in Spain, H. J. J. Sargint, NANA's European editor based in London, forwarded a message from New York calculated to slow him down. "WIRE HEMINGWAY CONGRATULATIONS HIS FIRST STORIES BUT ADVISE WE UNWANT DAILY RUNNING NARRATIVE HIS EXPERIENCES AS PREFER HE MAKE THOROUGH SURVEY BEFORE WRITING CONSIDERED APPRAISAL SITUATION" ("Dispatches," 18). If not exactly a rebuke, the message could hardly have pleased Hemingway, but he did respond with his "considered appraisal" (an accurate one) that in order to win the war Franco would have to cut the lines of communication between Valencia and Barcelona by driving to the Mediterranean.

Two weeks later New York weighed in again with what Watson called "a stinging rebuke." "NOTIFY HEMINGWAY IMMEDIATELY LIMIT ONE STORY WEEKLY UNLESS OTHERWISE REQUESTED" ("Dispatches," 26). In case Hemingway wasn't listening, NANA repeated its message four days later. "ADVISE HEMINGWAY WANT MAXIMUM ONE WIRE STORY WEEKLY ONLY OF WORTHWHILE MATERIAL. WE WILL REQUEST IF ANYTHING SPECIAL" (29). The cable specified but "one wire story" a week but said nothing about mailed pieces. So Hemingway sat down and wrote one of his best dispatches, about visiting the badly wounded American volunteer Robert J. Raven in a Madrid hospital, and put it in the mail. NANA accepted this article, and another mailed at the $1,000 rate, but refused to publish a third. This one, sent May 9, presented Hemingway's sanguine assessment of the strategic situation in Spain and may have been rejected as much because of its apparent bias as because of its exorbitant cost. In the article, Hemingway wrote that the Italians lost more killed and wounded at Brihuega than in the entire Ethiopian campaign. "The simple truth," he added, "is that these Italian troops cannot or will not fight in Spain . . . [and their] infantry could not compare with the rawest of the new Spanish troops." He also described Madrid as "an impregnable fortress" (40–41).

The next day another cable arrived from Sargint. "NEW YORK CABLE ME ASK YOU UNSEND ADDITIONAL STORIES. WHEN NEW YORK INFORMED YOUR IMPENDING DEPARTURE EXSPAIN IT EXPRESSED WISH HAVE ONE CABLE STORY IF FACTS WARRANTED... EYE MAILING TO NEW YORK YOUR STORY RECEIVED TODAY. PLEASE DO NOT SEND THE OTHER TWO" ("Dispatches," 39).

What seems clear from all these cables is that Wheeler and Hemingway had made a deal that Hemingway was eager to exploit and NANA was reluctant to fulfill. The wonder is that the two parties were able to continue working together, yet in late June Wheeler sent Hemingway a letter of agreement for his next trip from Spain, along with a handwritten note: "If there is ever a general European war, we would like to make a deal with you as our correspondent" (8 June 1937).

The crucial capture of Teruel occurred during Hemingway's fall tour of duty, and occasioned a flurry of accusations against the *New York Times* "Catholic Night Desk" from both Hemingway and Matthews. Then, in the spring of 1938, Hemingway and NANA went to the mat again about money. Hemingway turned out more reporting from the front in early April 1938 than during any other period during the Spanish war. This was too expensive for NANA in New York. On April 19, they instructed Sargint to "WIRE HEMINGWAY PLEASE RESTRICT CABLES TO VITALLY IMPORTANT DEVELOPMENTS UNTIL FURTHER NOTICE" ("Dispatches," 83). Early in May, a misunderstanding arose about how many of the stories Hemingway developed at considerable risk to himself NANA would be willing to publish. Eventually Wheeler sent a check for $1,000 (later upped to $1,250) to dispose of the matter. By way of explaining NANA's actions, Wheeler told Ernest that there had been "loud cries for economy" at the annual meeting of NANA, and that he (at least in part because of his agreement with Hemingway) was the target at which they were aimed (31 May 1938). Despite disagreements about money, the two men remained on good terms. As late as 1956, with the Suez crisis heating up, Wheeler asked Hemingway if he was interested in "attending" any resulting war and writing articles about it for the North American Newspaper Alliance (13 September 1956).

By the spring of 1938 Hemingway was covering the Spanish War not only for NANA but also for a new, short-lived magazine called *Ken*. He'd signed a contract with *Ken* the previous summer after discussions with David Smart and Arnold Gingrich. Gingrich, the editor of *Esquire*, and Smart, publisher of that magazine, jointly conceived the idea for *Ken*. It was to be a rival to *Look* and *Life*, *Collier's* and the *Saturday Evening Post*, differentiated by its political purpose: "the first mass-circulation, public-opinion-forming magazine in history on the liberal side—'one step left of center,'" as publisher David Smart put it (Seldes, *Witness*, 328). Its mission, as Gingrich expressed it in a telegram to Hemingway, was to spread the gospel of antifascism: "WILL BE NEITHER COSMO NOR CHICAGO TRIBUNE BUT WILL BE BIG LEAGUE POPULARIZATION OF MILITANT ANTIFASCISM HITHERTO CONFINED INTELLECTUAL MAGAZINES SMALL CIRCULATION" (10 January 1938). "What's needed," Gingrich explained in a letter, "is not another little magazine in between the New Masses and the New Republic, but a big popular commercially successful magazine, big enough to exert a real influence" (6 February 1938).

What they wanted from Hemingway, besides the selling power of his name, was precisely the kind of opinion articles he could not write for NANA. In a telegram of January 9, 1938, Gingrich spelled out his requirements for *Ken*'s first issue. "HAVE URGENT EXTREME NEED EDITORIAL GIVING VIVID PROJECTION TO AVERAGE AMERICAN READER WHAT FASCISM WILL MEAN IF ALLOWED DEVELOP OVER HERE." The piece, he added, should be strongly worded like Ernest's "Notes on the Next War" for *Esquire* or his speech to the Writers' Congress. "HAVE EVERY ASSURANCE ENORMOUS SUCCESS KEN AFTER LONG PUBLIC ANTICIPATION AND MANY MONTHS BUILDUP YOUR PARTICIPATION KEN HAS RECEIVED WIDEST PUBLICITY GREAT CHANCE ACQUIRE HUGE AUDIENCE HEAR WHAT YOU REALLY BELIEVE IN AND WONDERFUL OPPORTUNITY WARN THEM OUT THEIR APATHY."

Hemingway shared *Ken*'s objectives and welcomed the opportunity to express his views with greater latitude than newspaper correspondents were allowed. He agreed to write for *Ken* for the paltry fee of $200 per contribution and to serve (at least honorifically) as one of four joint editors of the magazine.

As the time approached for the first issue, due out on April 7, 1938, Hemingway began to have second thoughts about his affiliation. These arose because of the disillusionment experienced by friends of his who had quit or been fired during the magazine's formative months. One of these was Jay Allen, whose connection with Ernest went back to Spain in the early 1930s. Allen was hired to serve as *Ken*'s news editor, but he and Gingrich fell into disagreements about the magazine's makeup and content, and the embittered Allen left. Next George Seldes, who had been covering the Spanish war from Madrid with Hemingway, attempted to fill Allen's role, but he too jumped ship.

Gingrich maintained that these departures resulted from editorial disagreements and issues of competence. "ALLEN DRIFTED TOWARD WEAK IMITATION TIME AND NEWSWEEK WITHOUT ACTUALLY ACHIEVING EVEN THAT," he wired Hemingway (30 January 1938). Allen and Seldes, however, told Hemingway that the trouble lay with *Ken* abandoning its political principles. As Seldes described the situation in a telegram to Hemingway, "UNPRINTED TYPEWRITTEN PROSPECTUS KEN DEFINITELY LEFTWING ANTIFASCIST. ADVERTISING AGENCIES THREATENED BOYCOTT. PRINTED PROSPECTUS ANTICOMMUNIST. REDBAITING PRONOUNCEMENTS FOLLOWING. ANTIRED POEMS CARTOONS ATTACKING MURDEROUS RUSSIA BOUGHT. ADVERTISERS DEMANDING REACTIONARY ANTILABOR POLICY SMART SURRENDERING KEN COMPLETELY PHONY" (23 February 1938).

Gingrich had been telling him that *Ken* would "SCINTILLATE AND SHINE FORTH AS AN ALMOST LONE CANDLE OF ENLIGHTENMENT IN THIS NAUGHTY, CHILD BOMBING, KLAN RIDDEN, BLACK LEGION TRAMPLED WORLD" (31 January 1938). But Allen and Seldes made Hemingway wonder; committed as he was to the Loyalist cause in Spain, he did not want to be affiliated with an anticommunist publication. After hearing from Seldes, he wired Gingrich asking for an explanation of the "new setup": he couldn't write for *Ken* intelligently without knowing who he was working with (30 January 1938). In a letter of February 6, 1938, Gingrich attempted to clear the air. Circumstances altered cases, he argued, and it did not follow that "if *Ken* praises, as it should, the communists in Spain, that it must equally laud the communists in [the United States]. Because *Ken* is avowedly anti-totalitarian it is against a seizure of this government by a dictatorship of either the left or the right. To that extent, *Ken* must be anti-communist to be consistent." Meanwhile, Gingrich went on, Ernest could feel sure that if there was "any confusion in the public mind about *Ken* it will be on the side of considering it a communist sheet, a Bolshevik magazine."

Hemingway was not entirely convinced by this argument, especially after he heard that *Ken*'s first issue contained "two cartoon cracks at Communism, as protective coloring" (Baker, *A Life Story*, 331). That sort of redbaiting, Hemingway thought, marked the magazine's editor as either a fool or a knave. But he decided to write articles for *Ken* anyway, on the grounds that they might do some good in the war against fascism. In addition, he may well have been swayed by the 1,000 shares of *Esquire* stock (at sixteen dollars a share) that Gingrich and Smart sent him early in March.

Hemingway would not, however, allow himself to be listed as an editor, nominal or otherwise. "SORRY CAN'T BE EDITOR IF NOT EDITING," he telegraphed Gingrich (14 March 1938). He also demanded that the magazine print a boxed notice accompanying his article in its first issue. It read: "Ernest Hemingway has been in Spain since KEN was first projected. Although contracted and announced as an editor he has taken no part in the formation of its policies. If he sees eye to eye with us on KEN we would like to have him as an editor. If not, he will remain as a contributor until he is fired or quits" (Hanneman, *Hemingway: A Comprehensive Bibliography*, 157). On this basis Hemingway contributed to the first thirteen issues of the biweekly magazine during the spring and summer of 1938, and to one more, on January 13, 1939. Soon thereafter *Ken* went under.

His initial contribution, headlined "The Time Now, the Place Spain," repeated two themes prominent in his NANA dispatches. First, the Italian troops fighting for Franco lacked drive and motivation and could be defeated. In fact, the Spanish troops on the ground would defeat them, and "do it gladly, if only they can be allowed to buy planes, artillery and munitions." This constituted his second and overriding point: that only by ending the arms embargo could fascism be stopped in Spain. Why not beat them now, in Spain, before Hitler and Mussolini started the larger war that was otherwise sure to come? The only way to stop that war—and "brother, when it starts, we will be put in it"—was to "beat Italy, always beatable, and to beat her in Spain, and to beat her now. Otherwise you will have to fight tougher people than the Italians, and don't let anybody ever tell you that you won't."

Gingrich was pleased with this article and the next one. "THESE SHORT PUNCHES," he wired Hemingway, "HAVE DONE MORE GOOD LOYALIST CAUSE THAN VOLUMES ORDINARY REPORTING" (18 April 1938). Even better was his fourth contribution, "The Old Man at the Bridge." This was Hemingway's best piece of writing during the Spanish war and was later printed, without any changes from its appearance in *Ken*, in Hemingway's collected stories. Remarkably, Hemingway turned it out in only a few hours' time, and cabled it to *Ken* at deadline. The story depicts a poignant victim of the war: an old man driven from his home by artillery, resting tired and alone near the pontoon bridge at Amposta, more worried about the animals he had to leave behind than himself.

Hemingway's next article, called "The Cardinal Picks a Winner," generated a tremendous amount of trouble for *Ken*. In it he attacked Patrick

Cardinal Hayes and a number of leading Spanish Catholic leaders for supporting the fascists. The article was structured around two photographs and a news clipping about a press conference. The first photograph showed the bodies of dead children lying neatly in a row. They were among the 118 children, 245 women, and 512 men killed in the bombing of Barcelona on St. Patrick's Day, Hemingway said in his lead. Next he moved to the clipping about Cardinal Hayes's press conference March 24. The cardinal said that he was praying for a Franco victory because the Loyalists were controlled by radicals and communists. Asked about the recent bombing of Barcelona, Hayes said "he didn't know the facts, but *didn't believe* that Franco would do such a thing."

"Now somebody dropped the bombs that killed those 118 children," Hemingway commented in a paragraph dripping with sarcasm. "The Cardinal says he is sure it wasn't Franco. So that is okay with me. It wasn't Franco. Franco wouldn't do anything like that. We have it on the Cardinal's authority."

Finally Hemingway dealt with the second photograph. It showed Nationalist military officers and Catholic dignitaries standing in front of the cathedral at Santiago de Compostella. The officers are saluting, the salute of the old regular Spanish army. But the priests—among them the bishop of Lugo, the archbishop of Santiago, the canon of Santiago, and the bishop of Madrid—raise their right arms directly in front of them. "Is that the fascist salute they are giving?" Hemingway asked. "Is that the salute of the Nazis and the Italian fascists?" Then, once more resorting to irony, he declared that "if they are giving the fascist salute I *refuse to believe* it. Maybe the photograph is faked."

In a final paragraph Hemingway used repetition to underline his point:

> Maybe there isn't any moral to these pictures. But the children of Barcelona are dead as you can see from the picture and millions of other people will die before it is their time because of the policy of might makes right that strange outstretched arm salute stands for. So I *don't believe* the people shown in the photograph can really be making it. I would rather prefer to think that the photograph was faked.

This sort of irony may have escaped some of *Ken's* subscribers, but it surely aroused the ire of the Catholic community in the United States. Most American Catholics, like Cardinal Hayes, devoutly wanted Franco's forces to win the Spanish war. The Republicans in Spain, after all, had been guilty of destroying churches and murdering priests.

In the middle of June Gingrich wrote Hemingway a frantic letter asking him to keep religion out of his articles about Spain. The Catholics had made "enormous progress" on a campaign to get both *Ken* and its parent publication, *Esquire*, banned from the mails. They were also working to undermine the company financially in three different ways. By boycott threats they were scaring news dealers out of selling the magazines, hence knocking circulation for a loop. Through an organized letter and postcard campaign they were scaring advertisers into canceling their ads: *Ken* had lost nearly all of its ads and *Esquire* was down more than 50 percent. And finally, they were knocking the stock down in the face of a rising market by putting blocks of it on sale "at less than the lowest bids." Hemingway, tongue-in-cheek, wrote Gingrich to let him know when that happened, so he could buy shares of the stock at cut-rate prices and make some money (letter to Gingrich, summer 1938).

He wasn't "spooked" or in a panic, Gingrich told Hemingway, but added that "we will have to avoid any open or overt offense to [the Catholics] for a while if we are to survive." Accordingly he instructed Ernest to ignore the Catholic angle in anything he wrote about Spain: "take the treachery angle or the tactical angle or the economic or any goddamn angle except the direct religious one" (Gingrich to Hemingway, mid-June 1938). Without saying so, Gingrich was probably incensed about the way Hemingway's Cardinal Hayes piece stirred up the trouble.

Personally, Hemingway felt deeply conflicted about his own Catholicism. The only way he could run his life decently was to accept the discipline of the Church, he wrote Pauline's mother in August. But he was so troubled by the Catholics in Spain siding with the enemy that he couldn't even bring himself to pray. It seemed "crooked" to have anything to do with a religion that supported fascism. He was embittered by "reading in the Sunday Visitor about the atrocities of the Reds, the wickedness of the Spanish 'Communist' Government, and the humaneness of General Franco ... that sort of lying kills things inside of you" (Baker, *A Life Story*, 333; *Selected Letters*, 476).

In any event, Hemingway followed his editor's proposal and laid the "Catholic angle" to rest in his articles. (He did send a July 1938 telegram to Bishop Francis J. McConnell and Dr. Walter B. Cannon, adding his name to the sponsors of the "American Relief Ship for Spain" scheduled for a fall sailing.) For *Ken*, however, he wrote about "Treachery in Aragon," which gave him an opportunity for a swipe at Dos Passos. He attacked alleged fascists in the American State Department doing their "level, crooked ... best" to lose the Spanish war. He denounced British diplomats in general and Neville Chamberlain in particular for betraying the cause. He called on President Roosevelt to take the lead in repudiating the nonintervention policy on the Spanish war (Baker, *A Life Story*, 331). As late as September 8, 1938, he was harping on the same theme. "It is still not too late," Hemingway wrote, "to lift the arms embargo and allow the legal Spanish government to buy arms to defend itself against German and Italian invasion" (Hemingway, "False News," 18).

Hemingway's contractual writing on the Spanish Civil War ended with his final articles for *Ken*. But he also wrote two other propaganda pieces upon being solicited to do so by two communist publications. In July 1938, M. J. Olgin, the American correspondent for *Pravda*, wired him asking for an article of 1,000 to 1,500 words on the "Barbarism of Fascist Interventionists in Spain" for the August 1 issue of the Russian newspaper. Hemingway wired right back with "regards to [Mikhail] Koltsov," who had served as his urbane and somewhat cynical guide to the Soviet involvement in the war, and dropped everything to meet the deadline. The *Pravda* invitation, as Will Watson pointed out, gave Hemingway an opportunity to "vent his anger openly and without pulling punches" (Hemingway, "'Humanity,'" 115). None were pulled in his article, which appeared on page 4 of the Soviet newspaper, alongside contributions from Koltsov, Upton Sinclair, Chou En-lai, and Mao Tse-tung.

In this article, as in several of those for *Ken*, Hemingway made the conflict in Spain sound less like a civil war than one of the Spanish people against a foreign invasion. "During the last fifteen months," his diatribe began, "I saw murder done in Spain by the Fascist invaders." The murdering came from the indiscriminate shelling and bombing of innocent civilians. He had lived through the artillery attacks on Madrid, timed—he once again said—to catch the Sunday crowds just as the cinema let out. He had seen the devastation of the bombing of Lerida and Barcelona and Alicante. "There is no bitterness when the Fascists try to kill you," he added, because they had a right to. "But you have anger and hatred when you see them do murder. And you see them do it almost every day." So "you hate the Italian and German murderers who do this as you hate no other people."

In his conclusion Hemingway argued that the fascist invaders made a terrible mistake in killing civilian noncombatants, "for the brothers and the fathers of the victims will never forgive and never forget. The crimes committed by Fascism will raise the world against it" ("'Humanity,'" 116, 118).

Hemingway's other propaganda piece was written at the very end of the war, for the February 14, 1939, "Lincoln Brigade Number" of the American Communist Party magazine, the *New Masses*. "On the American Dead in

Spain," a prose poem of about 600 words (cut down from 3,000), was written as a memorial for the volunteers who gave their lives to the cause. "Our dead are a part of the earth of Spain now and the earth of Spain can never die," he wrote. "Each winter it will seem to die and each spring it will come alive again. Our dead will live with it forever." They will live, too, "in the hearts and the minds of the Spanish peasants, of the Spanish workers, of all the good simple honest people who believed in and fought for the Spanish republic." And these people would not accept defeat.

> The fascists may spread over the land, blasting their way with weight of metal brought from other countries. They may advance aided by traitors and by cowards. They may destroy cities and villages and try to hold the people in slavery. But . . . the Spanish people will rise again as they have always risen before against slavery.

In an editorial note, the *New Masses* editors hailed this article as "one of the finest tributes yet paid to the boys who won't be coming back" and praised its expression of "faith in the ultimate victory of the Spanish people—and of all folk battling for liberty." They called it "a bugle call to action. No pasarán!" (2). To back up his rhetorical contribution, Hemingway donated the typescript of the piece and the manuscript of *The Spanish Earth* to be auctioned off for the rehabilitation fund of the Abraham Lincoln Brigade.

It was difficult to write about the American dead, he told his Russian translator Ivan Kashkin. There was really not much to say about the dead except that they were dead. But he had lost many friends in the war, and what he wanted to do now was "to write understandably about both deserters and heroes, cowards and brave men, traitors and men who are not capable of being traitors." He had learned "a lot about all such people" during the war in Spain (*Selected Letters*, 480). Much of what he learned came to light in the four stories about the war he wrote late in 1938 and, most notably, in *For Whom the Bell Tolls*.

CIVIL WAR STORIES AND
FOR WHOM THE BELL TOLLS

"Christ it is fine to write again and not to have to write pieces," Hemingway told Arnold Gingrich in October 1938 (*Selected Letters*, 472). He was relieved not to be obliged to turn out, every two weeks, another editorial call to arms in *Ken*. Instead, he mailed Gingrich the typescript of "Night

Before Battle" for publication in *Esquire*. This story, like "The Denunciation" and "The Butterfly and the Tank," was set in Chicote's, the Madrid bar that, before the war, had been a favorite watering place for the Spanish aristocrats who sided with Franco's Nationalists. Chicote's thus became an ideal place for exploration of the themes of betrayal and loyalty, subjects much on Hemingway's mind as the Spanish Republic slid toward defeat.

In "The Denunciation," a waiter in Chicote's recognizes a customer as a Rebel spy and decides that he must turn him in with a telephone call to the secret police. In "The Butterfly and the Tank," based on an actual incident Hemingway mentioned briefly in *The Fifth Column*, a drunk at the bar begins squirting others with a flit gun full of eau de cologne. In a violent ending, disgusted soldiers at the bar beat up the drunk and then shoot him.

"Night Before Battle" and "Under the Ridge" express Hemingway's disillusionment about the conduct of the war. Both stories are narrated by a character (called Edwin Henry in "Under the Ridge") who has been making propaganda films for the Loyalists, and both are set in the spring of 1937, when Hemingway was doing just that with Joris Ivens. But by the time he wrote the stories, late in 1938, much of Hemingway's initial idealism has evaporated. Adopting a somewhat cynical stance, the stories dramatize the effects of political and military incompetence in the Loyalist leadership.

In "Night Before Battle," a tank commander named Al Wagner is drinking at Chicote's before taking part in an offensive scheduled for the following day. He knows the attack will fail. Although his tank might "photograph well," he and the narrator both know it is ill equipped for battle. Moreover, the attack has been poorly conceived by Largo Caballero, a prime minister so puffed up by publicity that "he thinks he's Clausewitz." Al expects to be killed, and although he is angry about it as "wasteful," he will obey his orders (Hemingway, *Fifth*, 170).

"Under the Ridge," the best of these stories, introduces another sympathetic character who, like Al, understands the futility of what he has been ordered to do but who, unlike the tank commander, decides to walk away from the battle. Again an attack has been ordered, but the International Brigade designated to carry it out is so short on artillery that there is no chance of success. As the narrator watches, a tall middle-aged Frenchman, with a blanket rolled over his shoulder, comes "walking alone down out of the war." The narrator could understand, he says, "how a man might suddenly, seeing clearly the stupidity of dying in an unsuccessful attack, ... walk away from it as the Frenchman had done. He could walk out of it not from cowardice, but simply from seeing too clearly." Watching the Frenchman striding out of the attack with great dignity, the narrator "understood him as a man." But he also understood that as a soldier, the Frenchman would be tracked down and killed by the Soviet battle police, who are described as "hunting dogs."

"The nearest any man came to victory that day was probably the Frenchman who came, with his head held high, walking out of the battle," the final paragraph reads. "But his victory only lasted until he had walked halfway down the ridge. We saw him lying stretched out there on the slope of the ridge, still wearing his blanket." In war, the narrator dryly observes, "it is necessary to have discipline" (*Fifth*, 205, 209–10, 215).

The disillusionment evident in these stories marked a midpoint in the process by which Hemingway transformed himself from a propagandizing journalist with a cause, as in *The Spanish Earth* and *The Fifth Column*, "into a political novelist of the first magnitude"(Raeburn, "Hemingway on Stage," 16). The stories were far more autobiographical and political than most of his fiction. As Allen Josephs persuasively argues, they served collectively to purge Hemingway of the bitterness he felt about the defeat of the Spanish Republic (*For Whom*, 38).

Once he'd gotten them out of his system, he settled down to work on *For Whom the Bell Tolls*. He began writing the novel March 1, 1939, and three weeks later found that he "had 15,000 words done, [and] that it was very exciting" (*Selected Letters*, 482). Hemingway vowed to stay with the book until it was finished, and he did so. At the same time, however, he did not abandon those companions who had fought for the Republic. Many of these men were imprisoned after the war, and Hemingway interrupted his work on the novel long enough to make several public appeals on their behalf.

"All those who went from here to Spain to fight are home now. That is they are all home except the men who are stranded in Ellis Island, or in Franco's prison corrals, or those who made their permanent homes in Spain in plots of ground six feet long" (qtd. in Bruccoli, *Mechanism of Fame*, 72), Hemingway wrote in a foreword to Joseph North's *Men in the Ranks*, published in 1939 by the Friends of the Abraham Lincoln Brigade. Those interned at Ellis Island had gone to Spain to join the International Brigades from the United States, only to be stopped and interned on their return because they were not U.S. citizens. In a fundraising letter for the American Committee for Protection of Foreign Born, Hemingway pointed out that these heroic veterans were "being cast into disrepute by an avalanche of legal technicalities" and that they would face "imprisonment and possible death" if deported to "Germany or Italy or Greece or Yugoslavia" (Bruccoli, *Mechanism of Fame*, 74).

At least the men at Ellis Island managed to escape the concentration camps that were set up in France—"Franco's corrals"—to confine the soldiers of the International Brigades. If the internationals had fallen into Nationalist hands in Spain, they would probably have been summarily executed, as regularly happened to those taken prisoner during the war. As foreigners interfering in Spanish "domestic affairs," they were shown no mercy. Yet even after crossing the border to France, as many as 7,000 internationals were captured and "interned in barbed-wire concentration camps . . . with little food, water, or clothing, and no shelter or medicine" (Sanderson, "'Like a Rock,'" 7–8). Hemingway cosigned a letter seeking the release of the writers among these men for the League of American Writers in 1939 (Bruccoli, *Mechanism of Fame*, 75).

The following spring, with the Nazis about to take Paris, he was incensed to read Archibald MacLeish's comments linking him among the writers and intellectuals—the "Irresponsibles," MacLeish called them— who had failed to provide the United States with the conviction "that fascism is evil and that a free society of free men is worth fighting for." Specifically, he argued that novels like *A Farewell to Arms* and Dos Passos's *Three Soldiers* had virtually unmanned the nation through their condemnation of the empty rhetoric used to justify World War I. Furiously, Hemingway launched an ad hominem broadside against MacLeish in the June 24, 1940, issue of *Time* magazine. Archie must have a guilty conscience for having skipped the war in Spain, he wrote. "If MacLeish had been at Guadalajara, Jarama, Madrid, Teruel, first and second battles of the Ebro, he might feel better." As for himself, "having fought fascism in every way that I know how in the places where you could really fight it," he had no remorse whatever, neither literary nor political (Donaldson, *MacLeish*, 334–36).

As an illustration of his ongoing commitment to the cause, Hemingway lobbied for the soldier and author Gustav Regler. The friendship between the two men, initially forged on the battlefield in Spain, deepened in January 1938 when the German, wounded in battle, came to the United States as a propagandist and organizer for the Republican cause. Ernest invited Regler and his wife, Mieke, to his house in Key West, where they stayed several weeks. In March, when Regler went to Washington, D.C., to raise funds for the Republic, Hemingway came along to introduce him and—in order to attract the interest and sympathy of American audiences—lifted Regler's shirt and invited people to place their fists in the cavities of Regler's wounds.

Back in Spain later in the year, Regler crossed the border to France as the war was winding down. He volunteered for the French army, but within hours was arrested and taken first to a concentration camp in Paris and then to the atrocious camp at Le Vernet, where inmates were confined in unlit, cold, and rat-infested quarters. He was there for seven months, from fall 1939 to spring 1940, when he was released to put the finishing touches on his novel *The Great Crusade*.

Hemingway eagerly agreed to write a preface for the English translation of Regler's novel. He journeyed down to Mayito Menocal's sugar and rice plantation to do the job, temporarily setting aside work on the final chapters of *For Whom the Bell Tolls*. In the preface Hemingway had very little to say about *The Great Crusade* itself. Instead he praised the officers and men of the Twelfth International Brigade and lobbied for allowing the Reglers to settle in the United States. As a refugee Regler deserved a place to live and work, he pointed out, and could hardly expect to find one in his homeland. Surely America was "a big enough country to receive the Reglers who fought in Germany and in Spain; who are against all Nazis and their allies; who would honor America as much by living in it as we would aid them by granting them the right to asylum we have always accorded to those who have fought in their own land against tyranny and been defeated" (Bruccoli, *Mechanism of Fame*, 83). In due course the Reglers did come to the States, and then moved to Mexico.

Also in 1940, word reached Hemingway that Hans Kahle, another German who commanded Loyalist troops in Spain, was being held in a Canadian prison camp. Hemingway met Kahle in March 1937, when the general conducted the correspondent on a tour of the battle of Guadalajara, and saw him in action the following year, leading Republican troops during the battle along the Ebro. He admired Kahle for his generalship and for his capacity to remain cheerful when things went wrong in the field. "I am very sorry to hear you are in a prison camp," Hemingway wrote Kahle upon hearing of his internment. "Don't those Canadians know that you are one of the most valuable living warriors against Fascism?" He also sent Kahle a check—"hope you can cash it"—and offered to do whatever else he could to help him (Bruccoli, *Mechanism of Fame*, 98–100).

When Regler's *Great Crusade* came out in September 1940, a Comintern report—citing the review in the Sunday *New York Times*—criticized the book as "anti-Soviet" in character and doubly dangerous because the

preface by Hemingway would attract readers. The novel reflected the disillusionment that Regler, formerly "a dogmatic Communist," felt after the
end of the Spanish Civil War. In a June 1940 note in his diary, Regler went
so far as to link the Stalin and Hitler regimes as totalitarian enemies of the
people: "what cold criminals are these Russians and these Nazis. They're
always right and we die of our 'idealistic' passion." Within a year, he would
publicly announce his defection from the Communist Party (Sanderson,
"'Like a Rock,'" 12).

The Great Crusade sold only a few thousand copies. A few weeks later,
For Whom the Bell Tolls was published, its best-seller status guaranteed
as a Book-of-the-Month Club selection. The two novels were alike, however, in displeasing the Soviets: so much so in Hemingway's case that For
Whom the Bell Tolls was not translated into Russian, and neither was
anything else he wrote in the next fifteen years.

Hemingway was perfectly aware that his book would annoy the communists. In December 1939 he cautioned Max Perkins not to talk to Alvah
Bessie or any of the "ideology boys" about his novel in progress, which
aimed to present a balanced view of what went on during the Spanish Civil
War. "Those poor unfortunate bastards [the absolutely dedicated commu-
nists] need all the ideology they can get and I would not want to deprive
anyone of [it] any more than would make cracks about religion to a nun."
Bessie had written a good fine straight book about the war for Scribner's
called Men in Battle (1939), Hemingway added, but "what was wrong with
his [International Brigade] outfit was too much ideology and not enough
military training, discipline or materiel" (Selected Letters, 498–99).

Bessie did not see that letter, of course, but Hemingway was right to
anticipate his censure. As Bessie wrote in The Heart of Spain, published in
1951 by the Veterans of the Abraham Lincoln Brigade,

> Hemingway's talent and the personal support he rendered to many phases
> of the loyalist cause were shockingly betrayed in his work "For Whom the
> Bell Tolls," in which the Spanish people were cruelly misrepresented and
> leaders of the International Brigade maliciously slandered. The novel in its
> total impact presented an unforgivable distortion of the meaning of the
> struggle in Spain. Under the name and prestige of Hemingway, important
> aid was given to humanity's worst enemies.
>
> (QTD. IN BRUCCOLI, MECHANISM OF FAME, XXIII–XXIV)

Retrospectively, it is difficult to accept Bessie's judgment that Hemingway betrayed the cause in For Whom the Bell Tolls. Soon after he began

writing his novel in earnest, Hemingway realized that it would be substantially better than his Spanish Civil War stories: "rounded" where the stories were "flat," "invented" where the stories were "recalled" (Josephs, *For Whom*, 38). He poured into the book everything he had learned in Spain. It might well have been subtitled "The Education of Robert Jordan," as the author's protagonist moves through various stages of disillusioning knowledge without, quite, abandoning his faith in the Spanish Republic.

In a number of superficial ways Hemingway distances himself from Jordan, a college professor who volunteers to serve in Spain and becomes an expert on explosives. Jordan is ordered by the admirable General Golz to blow up a bridge in support of a planned Loyalist offensive. To accomplish the task, he must infiltrate himself into and win the confidence of a band of guerilla fighters who have been striking at the enemy from a secret camp in mountainous terrain. The group is led by Pablo, who sees at once that its location will be revealed if the bridge is blown and sets about trying to undermine Jordan's mission. When his treachery is revealed, the *partisans* turn over leadership of the band to Pablo's wife, Pilar. A commanding figure, Pilar is also instrumental in promoting the love affair between Jordan and the girl Maria, a victim of atrocities who has seen her parents killed and then been raped by the Nationalists. In the few days they have together, Jordan falls deeply in love with Maria. Eventually he does manage to destroy the bridge, but by that time word of the Loyalist offensive has been leaked to the Nationalists and it is doomed to fail. At the end, the wounded Jordan—knowing he will be killed—mans a machine gun to delay the advance of the Nationalist troops and give Maria and the others who have survived the day's battle time to escape.

The plot proceeds slowly, for much of the novel takes place in Jordan's reflections, which clearly echo those of his creator. Like many volunteers, Jordan believed completely in the Loyalist cause when he first joined the International Brigades in Spain. It was like joining a religious order. "It gave you a part in something that you could believe in wholly and completely and in which you felt an absolute brotherhood with the others who were engaged in it," he recalls. "It was something you had never known before but that you had experienced now and you gave such importance to it and the reasons for it that your own death seemed of complete unimportance" (*Bell*, 235). This "puritanical, religious communism" he associates with Velazquez 63, the Madrid palace that served as the International Brigade headquarters in the capital.

Velazquez 63 is contrasted in the novel with Gaylord's hotel (the buildings, like a few of the characters, are undisguised with fictional names).

After his initial exposures to battle, Jordan comes to Gaylord's, the hotel the Russians had taken over, and discovers certain unpleasant facts that subvert the purity of the cause he had been zealously fighting for. "Gaylord's was the place where you met famous peasant and worker Spanish commanders who had sprung to arms from the people at the start of the war without any previous military training and found that many of them spoke Russian," Jordan recalls. That had been "the first big disillusion," but he refused to let it make him cynical, for the propaganda buildup was at least partly true (*Bell*, 228–29). The Spanish generals were in fact peasants or workers who had been active in the 1934 revolution and had to flee the country when it failed. In Russia they had been trained in military tactics and communist doctrine so they would be ready to lead the fight the next time around.

Still, this information was carefully withheld from the public, along with the fact that commanders like Lister and Campesino and Modesto were "told many of the moves they should make by their Russian military advisers. They were like students flying a machine with dual controls which the pilot could take over whenever they made a mistake" (*Bell*, 234). During a revolution in Spain you could not admit that outsiders were in control. "If a thing was right fundamentally the lying was not supposed to matter," Jordan thinks, but there was a lot of lying to get used to. Jordan hated the lying at first and then came to like it. "It was part of being an insider but it was a very corrupting business" (*Bell*, 229).

Jordan's political education at Gaylord's obviously paralleled that of Hemingway himself, extending to the portrayal of Mikhail Koltsov (called Karkov in the novel) as his principal instructor. "Wearing black riding boots, gray breeches, and a gray tunic, with tiny hands and feet, puffily fragile of face and body, with a spitting way of talking through his bad teeth, [Karkov] looked comic when Robert Jordan first saw him. But he had more brains and more inner dignity and outer insolence and humor than any man he had ever known" (*Bell*, 231).

Karkov's humor extends to making fun of the excesses of his own side's propaganda. He recites for Jordan's benefit his favorite Republican communiqué, from the Córdoba front: in translation, "our glorious troops continue to advance without losing a foot of ground." Jordan is disgusted by the high-flown rhetoric but disturbed as well by Karkov's cynicism and his own acceptance of it. "You could remember the men you knew who died in the fighting around Pozoblanco; but it was a joke at Gaylord's." Jordan realizes that his original idealism has eroded. "You corrupt very easily, he thought. But was it corruption or was it merely that you lost the naïveté that you started with? . . . Who else kept that first chastity of mind about their work that young doctors, young priests, and young soldiers usually started with?" (*Bell*, 238–39).

For Whom the Bell Tolls deals harshly with the empty catchphrases of Republican propagandists—particularly as circulated by La Pasionaria, the "leftist saint" Dolores Ibarruri, a communist from the Basque provinces. In the book, her histrionic sloganeering proves of little value to El Sordo's band, which is trapped on a hilltop and faces systematic destruction by fascist aircraft (identified as of Italian and German origin). The callow Joaquín counsels the other soldiers to remember that "Pasionaria says it is better to die on your feet than to live on your knees." He continues to repeat the phrase to himself until the bombs begin to fall, when he shifts suddenly to "Hail Mary, full of grace, the Lord is with thee" (*Bell*, 309, 321). Neither mantra can save him or any of the others.

The novel makes it clear that during the Spanish Civil War both sides were engaged in wholesale lying and a great deal of false rhetoric. Hemingway had learned, as George Orwell observed, "that no event is ever correctly reported in a newspaper, but in Spain, for the first time, I saw newspaper reports which did not bear any relation to the facts, not even the relationship which is implied in an ordinary lie" (qtd. in Knightley, *The First Casualty*, 191).

"The facts" were often very hard to swallow. *For Whom the Bell Tolls* vividly portrays treachery and incompetence within the Loyalist ranks, for example. The principal villain, identified in the novel by his real name, was André Marty, the paranoid French Stalinist who led the International Brigades. "Only Stalin himself had a more suspicious nature than André Marty," according to the Spanish Civil War historian Hugh Thomas (*The Spanish Civil War*, 458). From his position of power, Marty simply eliminated anyone who aroused his suspicions. When, in the spring of 1937, Gustav Regler told Hemingway that Marty had brutally executed two shell-shocked Brigade volunteers, Hemingway exclaimed "Swine!" and spat on the ground (Sanderson, "'Like a Rock,'" 3). Later, he heard still other tales of Marty's unwarranted cruelty from Evan Shipman: information he would not use during the war itself, filed away for the novel to come.

In *For Whom the Bell Tolls*, the hopelessly suspicious Marty refuses to believe the intelligence Robert Jordan provides and so allows the Loyalists to launch an offensive doomed to end in disaster. A corporal working at Marty's headquarters spells out the indictment against him. Marty is "crazy as a bedbug," he says, with "a mania for shooting people." Moreover, he doesn't kill fascists, as his troops do. Instead he does away with "Trotsky-ites. Divigationers. Any type of rare beasts" (*Bell*, 418). Here Hemingway condemns the very practices he had apparently accepted as necessary to the cause in *The Fifth Column*, written only two years earlier.

In addition to excoriating the Frenchman Marty for his paranoia, Hemingway (through the thoughts of Robert Jordan) accuses the Spanish of a temperamental predilection for treachery. As he tries to win the confidence of the guerilla band, Jordan knows that eventually they will turn against him as a foreigner. "They turned on you often but they always turned on every one. They turned on themselves, too. If you had three together, two would unite against one, and then the two would start to betray each other" (*Bell*, 135). This could lead to disaster when they were competing for positions of leadership. "Muck all the insane, egotistical, treacherous swine that have always governed Spain and ruled her armies," Jordan thinks. "Muck everybody but the people and then be damned careful what they turn into when they have power" (*Bell*, 370).

Hemingway's novel also characterizes the Republican leadership as incompetent in its conduct of the war. Irony abounds, for example, in the excellent General Golz's account of the "complicated" and "beautiful" battle plan he is supposed to execute, a "masterpiece" designed by a professor in Madrid. Golz is not given adequate resources with which to carry it out. He must "put in" for artillery, knowing he will not be get what he asks for. But that is the least of it, he tells Jordan. "You know how these people are. . . . Always there is something. Always some one will interfere" (*Bell*, 5). In scenes like these, *For Whom the Bell Tolls* approaches that "cruel misrepresentation" of the Spanish that Bessie complained of.

But what most outraged Bessie and other doctrinaire communists was the novel's depiction of the massacre of the fascists in Pablo's hometown. Pilar tells the story in thirty extraordinarily vivid and powerful pages early in the book. First Pablo and his Republican followers execute the *guardia civil*. Next they form a gauntlet of workers and peasants armed with flails and sickles that the town's fascist officials and sympathizers are forced to run. At the end, they are flung over the cliff to their death. At first, the townspeople are somewhat reluctant to strike at their neighbors, but drunkenness and a camaraderie in brutality overcome their scruples. Some of the victims die badly, some bravely. Some are actual enemies of the common people, some are not. Pilar, who has seen more than her share of good and bad, can hardly bear to watch as the hapless Don Guill-ermo—a humble merchant, and only a fascist by virtue of his own snob-bery—is viciously beaten and killed.

There were of course atrocities on both sides, particularly at the start of the war. And Hemingway to some extent balances the books through the character of Maria. Her parents were shot by the fascists, declaring "Viva la República" as they died, and then she was raped. But these terrible events—deeply moving as Maria recalls them—are recounted in but four pages near the end of the book, and without the vividness of Pablo's wholesale massacre.

Many of those who supported the Loyalist cause during the war were shocked by Hemingway's emphasis on an atrocity committed by their fellow fighters. He must have abandoned his principles, they felt. But the killings in Pablo's hometown—a village that resembles Ronda, with its precipitous chasm—perform a crucial role in adumbrating the novel's underlying theme. "No man is an *Iland*, intire of it selfe . . . any mans *death* diminishes *me*, because I am involved in *Mankinde*": so the epigraph from John Donne spells it out, and it is a truth that Robert Jordan repeatedly reflects upon.

As he scouts the enemy soldiers occupying an abandoned sawmill to guard the bridge he must blow up, Jordan thinks of them as basically his fellows. "I have watched them all day and they are the same men that we are," he observes. They were not fascists, but poor men enlisted into the war against the Republicans. In the end, he knows, they must be eliminated if his mission is to succeed, but he does "not like to think of the killing" (*Bell*, 192–93). Later in the novel, after the *partisans* have had to kill a cavalryman to avoid detection, Jordan goes through the soldier's pockets, only to discover a letter from his sister proud of him for "liberat[ing] Spain from the domination of the Marxist hordes" and another from his fiancée that is "quietly, formally, and hysterically hysterical with concern for his safety" (*Bell*, 303). The dead boy was only twenty-one, son of a blacksmith from Tafalla in Navarra. He liked the people of Navarra better than those from any other part of Spain, Jordan thinks. He might well have seen this lad running through the streets of Pamplona during the *feria*.

This prompts Jordan to consider how many of the twenty men he has killed during the war were "real fascists." Only two that he was sure of, he decides, and he took no pleasure in disposing of them. More killing will come during and after the blowing of the bridge, and he does not look forward to that either. But it is a sacrifice he will make on behalf of a cause greater than himself or those he must destroy: an end to tyrannical fascist rule. To the extent that it condemns killing, *For Whom the Bell Tolls* fulfills something of the mission Hemingway declared upon first coming to Spain in March 1936: that he intended to function as an antiwar war correspondent. Yet despite clearly deploring the wasteful deaths that war inevitably led to, the novel takes pains to justify this particular war.

Even among members of the guerilla band, Jordan realizes, only Pilar and the admirable old man Anselmo shared his belief in the Spanish Republic. And *belief* was very much at issue, for the Republicans needed a secular faith to replace the religion they have left behind. As Pilar says, "I believe firmly in the Republic, and I have faith. I believe in it with fervor as those who have religious faith believe in the mysteries" (*Bell*, 90). With the Catholic Church on the side of the Nationalists, Anselmo observes that he misses God, having been brought up in religion, but that now he must be responsible to himself alone. Like Jordan, he has no taste for killing. If it were left to him, he would "not kill even a Bishop" or "a proprietor of any kind." Instead, he would put them to work as the common people work in the fields or the forests "all the rest of their lives" (*Bell*, 41). That way, the fascists would learn what it meant to be among those they oppress.

Jordan himself maintains a similar faith in the Republic, despite all that he has witnessed of Soviet control of the war, Spanish incompetence and treachery, and phony propaganda. He noticed everything, and listened carefully; nobody owned his mind, and in due course, he thinks, he would form his judgments. But for the time being, he "was serving in a war and he gave absolute loyalty" to the effort (*Bell*, 136). The important thing was to win the war. "He fought now in this war because it had started in a country that he loved and he believed in the Republic and that if it were destroyed life would be unbearable for all those people who believed in it." Though he was not a communist himself, he would remain under communist discipline—the best discipline, the soundest and sanest—for the duration of the war (*Bell*, 163). "Remember this," he tells himself, "that as long as we hold them here we keep the fascists tied up. They can't attack any other country until they finish with us." As he lay awaiting his certain death, Jordan has no regrets. He has fought for a year for what he believes in. "If we win here," he thinks, "we will win everywhere" (*Bell*, 467).

Robert Jordan's hopes for the future were not to be realized. The Republicans lost the war, and before long the fascist governments in Germany and Italy widened the struggle into a World War. The Loyalists who lived to see this happen were bound to be disillusioned, Ernest Hemingway included. But like Jordan himself, he did not abandon his conviction that the lost cause had been worth the effort. *For Whom the Bell Tolls*—despite its honest depiction of nearly everything wrong with the conduct of the war—does not waver in its idealistic portrayal of those who were willing to sacrifice everything, their lives included, for the battle against fascism.

For the twenty years left to him after finishing this novel, Hemingway held firmly to the antifascism that drove him to support the Spanish Republic. In March 1942, a few months after Pearl Harbor, he visited Gustav Regler in Mexico, where—as the communist dissident Regler confided to his diary—Hemingway "talked much political nonsense." All Nazis "must be castrated," he said (he insisted on the same point in his introduction to the 1942 *Men at War*). And since only the communists offered a viable "organization" to win the war, he advised Regler to rejoin the Party (Sanderson, "'Like a Rock,'" 12–13). Invited to the tenth reunion of the Abraham Lincoln Brigade in 1947, Hemingway sent his regrets along with a tape to be read at the banquet. It made him proud, he said, to be "in the company of premature anti-Fascists": those who would be demonized during the Red scare following World War II (Hemingway, tape). The following year, he wrote Charles Scribner that he felt loyalty to a number of people and institutions: "to Scribners and to Max [Perkins]...to the Spanish Republic, the 4th U.S. Infantry Division and the 22nd Infantry Regiment [the units he'd been with during the Battle of the Hürtgenwald]." But he felt even more deeply "about he 12th International Brigade and my children and Mary" (*Selected Letters*, 638).

The months Hemingway spent in Spain during 1937 and 1938 did more than give him the experience and inside knowledge that he needed to write *For Whom the Bell Tolls*. They taught him, too, that there were some things worth fighting for: an end to fascism, and his friends and colleagues at the front and under siege at home and abroad. "All of us who *lived* the Spanish Civil War felt deeply emotional about it," his friend Herbert Matthews wrote more than thirty years later (Matthews, *World*, 11). Books about the war might provide the historical facts, Martha Gellhorn commented, but they could not capture "the emotion, the commitment, the feeling that we were all in it together, the certainty that we were *right*"(Knightley, *The First Casualty*, 215): comrades bound together in the last great cause of their time.

PART X

◈ LAST THINGS ◈

{ 23 }

HEMINGWAY AND SUICIDE

D EATH WAS Hemingway's great subject, and his great obsession. He wrote about it in his earliest stories and in his last ones. Of his seven completed novels, five end with the death of a male protagonist, and a sixth with the death of the heroine. Only in *The Sun Also Rises*, with its dying fall of an ending, do the characters survive to live and drink and fornicate another day. Yet that novel's moral center is located not in the cafes of Paris and Pamplona but in the bullring where Pedro Romero confronts animals bred to kill and be killed with what Hemingway famously called "grace under pressure." This confrontation—the drama, the ritual, the inevitable death—was also the subject of *Death in the Afternoon*, his 1929 book on bullfighting in Spain that remains, according to aficionados, the single best work in English on the subject. When the *torero* failed to kill properly, the bull was dispatched with the short knife, or *puntilla*. Women loved to see the *puntilla* do its work, Hemingway wrote. It was "exactly like turning off an electric light bulb" ("Soul").

There was a trace of the macabre in that remark, and more than a trace in "A Natural History of the Dead"—where he reported in matter-of-fact detail the color change among unburied Caucasian corpses from white to yellow to yellow-green to black, as well as their tendency to swell up in the heat, in his diatribe against the Italian war against Ethiopia, where, he warned, the East African carrion birds would strike a wounded man as quickly as a dead one and tear his flesh from his bones as if he were a zebra or any other prey—and in the grisly "An Alpine Idyll," in which an Austrian peasant hangs a lantern from the jaw of his wife's frozen corpse all one winter. An artist had to look at death squarely and without flinching, Hemingway believed.

But it was not only the demands of craft that drove him to concentrate his gaze on death, a creature he variously personified as "a beautiful harlot" and "the oldest whore in Havana" (qtd. in Baker, *A Life Story*, 432)—women worth knowing but expensive to go upstairs with. He had something to prove and was forever testing himself against danger. He climbed into the bullring during the amateurs, faced murderous animals in Africa, attended every war of his time. He put himself at risk and suffered the consequences. Hemingway was frequently and grievously hurt in an astounding series of blows to the head and arms and legs.

In 1928 he yanked on what he thought was a commode chain and brought a Paris skylight crashing down on his head, causing a concussion and nine stitches above the right eye. In the spring of 1930 it took six stitches to sew up his right index finger, cut to the bone when he was working on a punching bag. In the summer of that year still more stitches were required to close a facial wound suffered when he was thrown from his horse; that fall he also broke his right arm in an auto accident. In 1935 he shot himself in both legs while trying to kill a shark. A London auto accident in 1944 hospitalized him with a severe concussion and forty-seven stitches. In 1950 he fell on the deck of his boat, the *Pilar*, and struck his head on a metal clamp, producing a three-stitch cut. In 1954 he barely survived two African plane crashes in two days. Among his injuries were a bad concussion; a ruptured liver, spleen, and kidney; temporary loss of vision in the left eye; loss of hearing in the left ear; a crushed vertebra; a sprained right arm and shoulder; a sprained left leg; paralysis of the sphincter; and first-degree burns on his face, arms, and head. A month later his legs, abdomen, chest, lips, left hand, and right forearm were burned as he tried to fight a brushfire. A less hardy man might not have lived to kill himself.

The above summary, of course, leaves out the worst wound of all, at Fossalta di Piave on the Austrian front, July 8, 1918. Not quite nineteen and a year out of high school, Hemingway joined the American Red Cross in Italy and was shipped to the Austrian front to drive ambulances. He was passing out chocolate and cigarettes to the Italian troops when a mortar canister landed in his forward trench, immediately killing several others and lodging more than two hundred mortar fragments in his feet and legs. As he dragged another wounded man to the command post, a heavy-machinegun bullet ripped through his right knee. Part of him "died then," he wrote, and as he lay among the wounded and dying, he contemplated suicide. For years after that wounding he could not sleep at all at night without a light. Yet his physical wounds seem to have stimulated his courtship of danger. He made himself brave, so much so that during World War II he struck General Buck Lanham, a veteran combat soldier, as the calmest man under fire he had ever seen. Hemingway achieved his victory by an act of will and by constantly confronting his trauma. The popular theory that he "was destroyed by a wound (mental, physical, moral, psychiatric)," he wrote Carlos Baker in 1953, was "shit." When he went back to Fossalta after World War I, he defecated on the spot where he'd been hit.

"'*Fraid a nothing*," Hemingway proclaimed at age three, but that was childish braggadocio. His fiction provides another story, particularly the autobiographical tales about Nick Adams, like Hemingway himself a boy born, bred, and hurt in the Middle West and badly wounded in the war. Particularly significant is the discarded beginning of "Indian Camp," the first Nick Adams story in Hemingway's first full-scale book, *In Our Time*. Nick at nine or ten years old has been taken camping by his father, a doctor, and by his Uncle George. The two men go fishing at night, leaving Nick alone in the tent. If there's an emergency, he's to fire three shots with the rifle to summon them back. Lying in the dark, Nick begins to think about a hymn he'd heard in church, "Some day the silver cord will break." While they were singing the hymn he realized for the first time that he himself would have to die, and now—alone in the stillness of the night—he suddenly becomes very afraid of dying and fires the three shots. When his father and uncle return as promised, Nick makes up a yarn about a fox or a wolf fooling around the tent. Uncle George is upset about this obvious fib, which has interrupted his fishing, but Dr. Adams shows more understanding. "I know he's an awful coward," he says, "but we're all yellow at that age" (*Nick Adams Stories*, 14).

Hemingway chose to cut this opening, probably because it makes explicit what is otherwise conveyed implicitly in the course of this and other stories about Nick Adams: that unlike later protagonists he is a boy and then a youth things happen to, and that he does his cautious best to avoid trouble. (That in writing about Nick the author was thinking of his own boyhood seems clear: in the manuscripts Nick is sometimes called Ernest or Wemedge, one of Ernest's nicknames.) Deleting this opening satisfied Hemingway's famous dictum about the dignity of fiction, like icebergs, depending on keeping seven-eighths of its base beneath the surface, but it also deprived the ending of some of its force.

As the story proceeds, Dr. Adams is called in the wee hours of the morning, to leave his tent and go to the Indian camp at the end of the lake. There he performs a caesarean delivery without anesthetic on an Indian woman who has been in labor for two days. She screams in pain but, Dr. Adams explains to Nick, he does not hear the screams because they are not important. Nick hears them, though, and refuses to look as his father goes about his work. Also listening is the woman's husband in the upper bunk. The other Indian men have left the camp to get away from the sound of the screaming, but the husband has cut his foot with an axe and cannot leave the bunk. When the operation, a success, is finally over, Dr. Adams basks in the glory of his accomplishment, but his postoperative exhilaration is brief. "Ought to have a look at the proud father," he says expansively. "They're usually the worst sufferers in these little affairs." When he pulls the blanket back, he sees—and so does Nick—that the woman's husband has cut his throat from ear to ear.

In the rowboat afterwards, Nick asks his father the kinds of questions about dying, and suicide, that have been troubling him.

> "Why did he kill himself, Daddy?"
> "I don't know, Nick. He couldn't stand things, I guess."
> "Do many men kill themselves, Daddy?"
> "Not very many, Nick."
> "Do many women?"
> "Hardly ever."
> "Don't they ever?"
> "Oh, yes. They do sometimes." . . .
> "Is dying hard, Daddy?"
> "No, I think it's pretty easy, Nick. It all depends."
>
> (*COMPLETE SHORT STORIES*, 69–70)

Five years after this story was written, Ernest Hemingway's father, a doctor with special training in delivering babies, took his own life.

Dr. Clarence Edmonds Hemingway, a Puritanical man with an abiding interest in the outdoors and an unsatisfied wanderlust, married Grace Hall, a musically talented woman who abandoned a possible career as a concert singer in favor of husband and family. Ernest was their second child, and in his childhood was more or less twinned with his one-year-older sister, Marcelline. Grace Hemingway dressed them alike until it was time for school, in girls' costumes during the winter months at Oak Park, Illinois, and in boys' outfits up in Michigan during the summer. And she held back Marcelline so that she and Ernest would be in the same class at school. Brother and sister read the same books, too, among them, Marcelline recalled in her memoir, Stevenson's little-known "The Suicide Club" (Donaldson, *By Force of Will*, 285).

Like many another romantic youth, Ernest was fascinated with suicide. It was the subject of "Judgment of Manitou," his very first published fiction in high school (Hemingway, *Apprenticeship*, 96–97). This story, like "Indian Camp," takes place in the north woods, where the Indian Pierre, thinking that his white partner Dick Haywood has stolen his wallet, sets a trap for him. Discovering that Haywood is innocent, Pierre sets off to rescue him, but it is too late. The timber wolves have left their tracks in the bloody snow, and two ravens are at work on the "shapeless something" of Haywood's corpse, caught in the trap. Pierre, in a state of shock, stumbles into a bear trap himself, an accident he understands as a judgment on him. As the story ends, he reaches for his rifle to kill himself and save the wolves the trouble. In a high school notebook, Ernest sketched out yet another tale along these lines: "Mancelona. Rainy night. Tough looking lumberjack. Young Indian girl. Kills self and girl" (Donaldson, *Cambridge Companion*, 285). Suicide also figured in one of young Hemingway's best pieces of reporting for the school newspaper, the *Trapeze*. The hero of the story was a schoolmate who bravely dived into the Oak Park pond and pulled a would-be suicide to safety.

In these adolescent accounts of self-destruction, Hemingway was writing about other people, real or imagined. But for the last forty years of his life, he himself was victimized by severe attacks of depression—black ass, he called it—and repeatedly talked and wrote about the prospect of taking his own life. One such spell struck him on the eve of his wedding to Hadley Richardson in 1921. Two years later, in Canada for the birth of their son and involved in a feud with his managing editor, he wrote Gertrude Stein that he understood how a man could get so caught up in the tangled web of obligations as to commit suicide. He and Hadley lived in Paris for most of the early twenties, and there he made savage sport of sidewalk cafe dilettantes who were constantly attempting suicide but never quite succeeding. A Chinese boy managed to kill himself, a Norwegian boy killed himself, a model killed herself making "almost unbearable trouble for the concierge"; yet the "people one knows" could be found at the cafe every afternoon, salvaged by "sweet oil, the white of eggs, mustard and water soapsuds and stomach pumps" ("Montparnasse").

When Ernest broke off his marriage in 1926 to marry Pauline Pfeiffer, he and Pauline agreed at Hadley's insistence to stay apart for one hundred days as a step preliminary to divorce. During this period the black ass descended, and Hemingway contemplated suicide seriously enough to worry his friends. About the best way to do the job, he confided to his notebook, "would be to go off a liner at night." That did not seem a nasty death, and it was easy for him "to take almost any sort of jump" (qtd. in Baker, *A Life Story*, 167). In this case, his depression was undoubtedly exacerbated by guilt. Hadley Hemingway was by all reports a wonderful woman, and the divorce was, as he acknowledged, entirely his fault. It was as if the least he could do, by way of justification, was to kill himself, or at least threaten to. This period of suicidal gloom ended when he and Pauline were reunited. What you had to do was last through the hell, he said, because then life would be worth living again.

The subject of suicide became more than something to talk or write about in December 1928, when his father shot himself with a Smith and Wesson revolver in his Oak Park home. Dr. Hemingway, who was suffering from diabetes, had made some disastrous investments in the Florida land boom, but Ernest always believed that the principal reason for his father's suicide was his emasculation by his wife. "We are the generation whose fathers shot themselves," he observed in an unpublished note. "It is a very American thing to do and it is done, usually, when they lose their money, although their wives are almost always a contributing cause" (Hemingway Collection, item 816). Much as he was disposed to blame his mother—and in later years he declared often and with vigor that he hated her—Ernest could not condone what his father had done. "My father was a coward," he wrote in a cancelled passage for *Green Hills of Africa* (1935). "He shot himself without necessity" (qtd. in Baker, *A Life Story*, 609). Hemingway and Buck Lanham used to talk about suicide during some of the fighting of World War II. If pushed to extremities, they agreed, people should have the right to decide whether to live or die. Nonetheless, Lanham concluded that Ernest "had not one goddamned bit of respect for his father." He could probably have accepted Dr. Hemingway's murdering his wife, Lanham speculated, but killing himself to escape her was simply an act of cowardice. "It wasn't suicide *qua* suicide that got to Ernest, but suicide in the sense of a guy running out on a fight" (Lanham to Baker).

Generalizing from his own experience, Sigmund Freud called the death of a father the most important event in a man's life. And the *suicide* of a father was obviously a still more traumatic experience. It also established a dangerous precedent, for in killing himself Dr. Hemingway had in effect given his son tacit permission to do the same. In death as in life, Ernest's father failed to provide him with a suitable example to follow, and in his letters and fiction the son repeatedly sought to distance himself from those who committed suicide without adequate cause.

In *To Have and Have Not*, his near-proletarian novel of 1937, Hemingway wrote scornfully of people who shot themselves or took an overdose or "made the long drop from the apartment . . . window" or "took it quietly in two-car garages with the motor running" (237–38) because of financial reverses. In that book, too, he ridiculed the decision of Henry Carpenter, an unemployed thirty-six-year-old homosexual with a master's degree from Harvard, to do away with himself because his income had been reduced to $200 a month. "The money on which it was not worth while for him to live," Hemingway pointed out by way of a moral, "was one hundred and seventy dollars more a month than the fisherman Albert Tracy had been supporting his family on at the time of his death [not by suicide] three days before" (233).

For some time Hemingway considered writing a novel directly based on his father's "killing himself and why." He did not do so, he explained, because his mother was still alive. But in his bestselling *For Whom the Bell Tolls* (1940), his protagonist manifestly repudiates that suicide. As Ernest wrote Hadley the previous year, the important thing was not to let discouragement tempt you into taking the easy way out, as both her father and his had done. So Hemingway's fictional Robert Jordan, an American in Spain to fight for the Loyalist cause, steels himself against self-destruction though wounded and in terrible pain. Jordan, a professor of Spanish, hardly qualifies as a close counterpart of the author, but his father and grandfather closely resemble Hemingway's. Jordan's grandfather, like Anson T. Hemingway, was a Civil War veteran who had distinguished himself under fire. And Jordan's father, like Dr. Hemingway, shot himself with a Smith and Wesson pistol because he was a coward and could not stand up to his wife's bullying. Perhaps, Jordan thinks as he lies wounded, his grandfather had used up the family supply of courage. As the fascist troops approach and the pain becomes excruciating, Jordan must fight off his father's example to keep from killing himself. "Oh, let them come," he said. "I don't want to do that business that my father did" (*Bell*, 469).

The father-suicide theme struck home when the poet John Berryman heard the news of Hemingway's death. Berryman broke down in tears. "The poor son-of-a-bitch blew his fucking head off," he told his friend Robert Fitzgerald, although at the time the way Hemingway killed himself—shotgun to head, tripping both barrels—had not yet been revealed. Berryman did not know Hemingway, but he felt an inevitable kinship with him, inasmuch as both of them had fathers who took their own lives,

Berryman's with a shotgun. "Save us from shotguns & fathers' suicides," he wrote in one of his dream songs.

> It all depends on who you're the father *of*
> If you want to kill yourself—
> A bad example, murder of yourself.

Eleven years later, Berryman took his own life (Haffenden, *Life*, 287–88).

In subsequent years Hemingway continued to reflect on suicide in conversation and correspondence. Two letters he wrote Lillian Ross in 1950 underscore his ambivalence on the subject. In the first he comments sardonically on the apparent suicide of Thomas Heggen, author of the critically and financially successful *Mister Roberts*. "You'd think he might buy himself all the women in the world; or go to China; or take a good room in the Ritz in Paris and be the Proust of the people. No, he kills himself. Pretty soon we will probably have little children hanging themselves because they are not yet President" (27 April 1950). The second and contrasting letter, written when he was "bad low," tells of his taking "a long deep dive out in the Gulf Stream. . . . It was awfully nice down there and I was tempted to stay there. But you have to set a good example to your children and etc" (August 1950).

In the end Ernest Hemingway could neither escape his father's fate nor succeed in setting a proper example for his three sons. Shortly after dawn on July 2, 1961, he stole downstairs in his Ketchum, Idaho house, loaded his shotgun, pressed it against his forehead, and tripped both barrels. The one question that any supposed "expert on Hemingway" is invariably asked is, Why? The quick answer is: for any number of reasons. Let us consider another famous event by way of analogy. On December 23, 1888, Vincent van Gogh sliced off half of his left ear, took it to a brothel, and gave it to a prostitute named Rachel. In attempting to comprehend his motives, biographers and critics have produced no fewer than fourteen explanations. There's the analogy to the bullfight, where an ear is awarded to the successful *torero*, and jealousy of his brother Theo, various Freudian readings, and even a Christian interpretation in which van Gogh is construed as symbolically repeating the scene at Calvary by "giving the mother surrogate, Rachel, a dead segment of his body" (Runyan, "Why Did Van Gogh," 41). The explanations vary as to credibility, and none is entirely convincing. But the point is that several of them may have a measure of validity. Why did van Gogh maim himself? Why did Hemingway kill himself? Some things are overdetermined.

In a fictional rendering of Hemingway's suicide, Joyce Carol Oates vividly evokes a number of the problems besetting him. In Hemingway's last days as she reimagines them, he cannot shake off his inheritance—the weak father unmanned by the hateful mother—and even seems to be repeating the pattern in his own marriage. He wakes in the night as if in the old body of the father he had scorned as a boy. Looking in the mirror at the Mayo Clinic, he beholds his father's face: the terribly creased forehead, the vacant eyes, the clenched jaw. Perhaps, he reflects, his father had taken the coward's way out. Yet it was no joke when he told others that his father had killed himself to avoid torture, and he is determined to do the same to escape his own oppressor wife, or simply "the woman," as Oates calls her in her stream-of-consciousness account ("Papa at Ketchum," 110, 117, 119). Oates's Hemingway is a sick man, disgusted with himself and everyone around him: reasons enough to end it. And then, too, he suffers from depression.

Hard as Hemingway tried to disavow the manner of his father's death, he could hardly slough off his genetic inheritance. It has now been established that Dr. Hemingway was subject to bouts of depression, though at the time of his death every effort was made to cover them up. Melancholia ran in the family. Ernest's only brother and one of his four sisters also committed suicide. As Archibald MacLeish said of Ernest in the mid-1920s, "I've never seen a man go through the floor of despair as he did" (qtd. in Hynan, "Portrait"). The severity and the frequency of these periods of depression increased with age, and by the late 1950s were joined by traces of paranoia. During his final years Hemingway was convinced that the authorities—the FBI, the IRS, the Immigration and Naturalization Service—were out to get him and that close friends were trying to kill him by arranging automobile or airplane accidents.

He was never the same physically after the two disastrous plane crashes in Africa. "I should have stayed in that second kite at Butiaba," he said. He had high blood pressure, and his liver was badly damaged by years of drinking to excess. Like his father before him, he showed signs of incipient diabetes. His once powerful frame grew frail. Michael Bessie, who saw him in April 1961, thought he looked like "a wounded animal who should be allowed to go off and die as he chose." Later a series of remedial procedures at the Mayo Clinic, including electroshock therapy, failed to restore his vigor or brighten his outlook—though he was artful enough to secure his release by persuading the doctors that he was no longer suicidal. From the clinic he scrawled a last note to General Lanham. "Buck, stop sweating me out. Sweat only flying weather and the common cold" (Donaldson, *Force of Will*, 305).

Worst of all, he could no longer write. "Mornings when work does not come are long mornings," Oates has him think ("Papa at Ketchum," 102, 117). Work was the final justification, the ultimate reason to live, and up to the end he sat at his desk waiting patiently through the morning, up to one P.M., for the words that would not come. Richmond Lattimore suggests how it may have been for "Old Hemingway" who killed himself in his sixty-second year:

> lost youth lost art and mumbled till he knew
> he mumbled, and so drew the trigger: like one
> of his own brave decrepit fighters dancing
> his final grace of now uncertain art
> too close against the horns, which speared him home.

{ 24 }

HEMINGWAY AND FAME

GENERATIONS AFTER his death Ernest Hemingway remains a famous American writer. Even those who have never read a word he wrote are aware of his presence in the world of celebrity—a rugged macho figure called Papa with a signature white beard. The outpouring of recognition and praise that followed his suicide on the morning of July 2, 1961, nearly obliterated the boundaries of space and time. His passing was memorialized by the Kremlin and the White House, in the Vatican and the bullrings of Spain. "It is almost," the *Louisville Courier-Journal* observed, "as though the Twentieth Century itself has come to a sudden, violent, and premature end" (Raeburn, *Fame Became of Him*, 168).

Manifestly, Hemingway represented something more—or less—than a writer of stories and novels. He had become a legendary figure and seems fated to remain one. Critics and college professors lament this state of affairs. They fear that the spurious anecdotes and half-baked biographies and Key West contests for Hemingway look-alikes draw attention away from his work, so that the great unwashed public will not take his artistic accomplishment seriously. This is a danger, all right, the same danger that faced that other most celebrated of American writers, Mark Twain. Twain wore a white suit and a wide mustache, took his comedy act on the road, and otherwise made himself so conspicuous as to be widely considered a mere entertainer.

Like most middle-class American boys at the turn of the twentieth century, Hemingway was brought up on the improbable tales of Horatio Alger, in which worthy, healthy-minded, hard-working lads rapidly ascended the ladder of success. Such rewards lay within reach of any youth willing to apply himself, Alger taught. Success was the goal, and in American culture success amounted to rising above the station you were born into or, to put it more baldly, doing better than your father had. If your father was a butcher, you should own the meat market. If he sold shoes, you should manufacture them.

But to outdo one's forebears, generation after generation, was simply impossible. Only in a society of consistently rising expectations, like that of late-nineteenth-century America, could such a doctrine have taken hold, and only in a society as determined to cling to its progressive past could it have continued to exert its power in the following century. In France, by way of contrast, the fundamental dignity of remaining in one's native station found expression in the derogatory terms assigned to those who strained to rise higher. Consider how such terms as "parvenu" and "nouveau riche" conflict with the American "self-made man" (Cawelti, *Apostles*, 2).

Money, of course, constituted the standard by which success could most easily be measured. But as Richard M. Huber makes clear in *The American Idea of Success*, you had to *make* the money; it was not enough to inherit it or have it descend from the skies. Moreover, others had to take notice. Particularly in the other-directed United States, recognition became an essential ingredient in the stewpot of success. (No wonder, then, that the culture descended to ostentatious displays of wealth, or in the parlance of Marx and Veblen, to commodity fetishism and conspicuous consumption.) So important was this external recognition by others—fame, to give it a title—that for writers or artists it could take the place of money, or very nearly so.

Hemingway's case is interesting in this respect. As an apprentice writer living in Paris in the mid-1920s, he vigorously repudiated what he regarded as his friend F. Scott Fitzgerald's obsession with how much he was paid for his stories. Yet later in his life, Hemingway himself demanded compensation for his magazine work that was at least slightly higher than anyone else got. His attitude toward money changed as his career wore on. So did his attitude toward fame, and it was fame that drove him.

In his 1967 book *Making It*, Norman Podhoretz presented a confessional and, to many, shocking disquisition on his own pursuit of recognition. From his first appearances with articles in *Commentary*, Podhoretz admitted, what he wanted was "to see my name in print, to be praised, and above all to attract attention." Many who started out writing for newspapers and magazines have felt the same. Getting paid was important, but bylines were even better. When his mentor Lionel Trilling asked Podhoretz what kind of success he sought—money, fame, professional eminence, social position—he replied immediately that it was fame he was after. He aimed to be a famous critic and expected that everything else would follow from that. Any intelligent person, he wrote, could walk into a room and tell the generals from the lieutenants, and the lieutenants from the privates—and he wanted to be a general (96, 146, 335).

Making It caused something of an uproar in literary circles, not so much because its author wrote about his ambitions as because he did so with such unabashed frankness. This exposed a nagging contradiction in the American ideal of success. On the one hand you had to get ahead, and on the other you were not supposed to try too hard to do so. But Podhoretz tried hard and told all, offending those academic overseers who with William James considered "the exclusive worship of the bitch goddess SUCCESS our national disease," who were inclined like Podhoretz's professors at Columbia to equate *successful* with *corrupt*, who felt that unseemly ambition had replaced lust as the "dirty little secret" festering in the American soul. Envy flourished in this environment, and excessive public acclaim for one's work was taken as evidence of pandering after the bitch goddess (*Making It*, xi–xvii, 61, 265). In such a climate it was best to keep a low profile. Win the election, but don't let the campaigning show. By all means publish, but don't advertise.

This reticence about public renown owes something to the paradox at the heart of the Protestant ethic. Capitalism demands that we struggle against one another in a sometimes brutal contest of individual wills. But religious morality dictates that we treat one another with compassion and generosity. Hence many who achieve substantial gains are tormented by guilt—a malady relieved to a degree by the gospel of wealth's rationale that we must first get in order to give.

In addition, the egalitarian strain in American culture exerts a powerful restraint against excessive acclaim. Our political heroes manage to do great things while looking and acting very much like the rest of us: honest George, humble Abe, rough-riding Teddy, to name three of the four iconic figures chiseled into Mount Rushmore. (Theodore Roosevelt was *the* politician most admired during Hemingway's boyhood in Oak Park.) So, too, we ask our artists to minimize rather than insist upon their difference from common folk. Walt Whitman, sensitive to this democratic anomaly, proclaimed his involvement in humankind while at the same time trumpeting his individuality:

> I celebrate myself, and sing myself,
> And what I assume you shall assume,
> For every atom belonging to me as good belongs to you.
>
> (*COMPLETE POETRY*, 27)

Whitman wrote as if to obliterate all distinctions among persons. As Leo Braudy commented in *The Frenzy of Renown*, "No other country so enforces the character-wrenching need to be assertive but polite, prideful but humble, unique but familiar, the great star and the kid next door" (11).

Generally fame has had better press than money as a yardstick of success. Fame harms no one else, the argument goes, whereas money is often acquired through ill treatment of others. Besides, money results from materialism, while fame comes from accomplishment (Podhoretz, *Making It*, 245). Yet it is also clear that fame has often had "a baroquely warping effect" on the lives of those engaged in its pursuit (Braudy, *Frenzy*, 12). This debilitating effect mostly derives from the devaluation of fame by its exploitation in the mass media. Often, if not universally, famous people dwindle into celebrities under the klieg lights of publicity. What they achieve is more or less forgotten as their personal lives undergo intense scrutiny and they are reduced to stereotypes.

"Two centuries ago," Daniel J. Boorstin lamented in his 1962 diatribe against celebrity, "when a great man appeared, people looked for God's purpose in him; today we look for his press agent." Fame and greatness were never precisely synonymous, he acknowledged, but with the proliferation of the mass media into every corner of modern life and the development of image makers, the distance between the hero (who had achieved something of importance) and the celebrity (defined by Boorstin as "a person who is known for his well-knownness") widened enormously. "The hero created himself, the celebrity is created by the media," he sadly concluded (*The Image*, 45–61).

Even those who began as genuine heroes were degraded into celebrities through the media's relentless exploration of their private lives. A major case in point for Boorstin was Charles Lindbergh, the Lone Eagle who boldly flew solo across the Atlantic in 1927. Lindbergh's act of individual courage and daring established him as a hero to be admired. It also subjected his most personal thoughts and actions to public examination. The media left no corner of his life unexposed, leading finally to deadly consequences when the much-publicized first child of his marriage to Anne Morrow was kidnapped and killed.

Braudy draws lines of comparison between Lindbergh and Hemingway as Midwestern lads, approximate contemporaries, and self-made men who gained international fame through mastery of a professional craft. In Braudy's judgment, fame both gives and takes away. "In part it celebrates uniqueness, and in part it requires that uniqueness be exemplary and re-producible" (*Frenzy*, 5). The "reproducible" could take shape as an object, like Franklin D. Roosevelt's jauntily displayed cigarette holder, or a gesture, like Winston Churchill's V for Victory, or a physical signature, like Hemingway's beard—but every repetition worked to devalue the original. We pursue fame to escape drab anonymity, but upon reaching that objective we find ourselves trapped and depreciated by the gaze others fix upon us.

That was what happened to Lindbergh, Braudy pointed out. Initially eager for admiration, he later found it impossible to withdraw from public attention. He could conquer distance in flight but could not outrace the celebrity his fame engendered. Ernest Hemingway, Braudy suggested, "could almost be considered Lindbergh's wiser older brother," but only almost, for he was eventually to emerge as "the prime case of someone caught between his genius and its publicity." Toward the end of his life, the image of Papa Hemingway outdoors, fishing or hunting or attending wars and bullfights, came to supplant that of the dedicated artist at his desk. He existed less as a great storyteller and prose stylist than as a rugged, no-nonsense fellow with a prodigious appetite for eating and drinking, brawling and defying death. This image—Papa with beard and shotgun, say—became so deeply imprinted that the person behind it disappeared into the shadows. Members of some Native American tribes resist being photographed, on the theory that some part of themselves will vanish with each snap of the shutter. From the middle of the twentieth century on, this policy has come to seem more sensible than superstitious (Braudy, *Frenzy*, 22–27, 544–47).

❖ ❖ ❖

In his book on Hemingway's fame, John Raeburn emphasized two basic points. First, Hemingway was the most celebrated of all American writers. During his lifetime, both slick magazines aimed at the college-educated and pulp-paper publications designed for the hoi polloi kept their readers informed about Hemingway's exploits, while syndicated columnists like Leonard Lyons and Earl Wilson reported on his travels and opinions. Then, within eight years after his death, seven biographies appeared. Scanning through this outpouring of prose, much of it inaccurate and badly written, Raeburn concluded that it was Hemingway's *personality* that generated most of the interest. The media concentrated on him as a sportsman or a warrior, not as a writer, for there wasn't much glamour in darkening paper with words.

Raeburn's second and somewhat judgmental point is that what happened was Hemingway's own fault. "Far from being either the unwitting or unwilling recipient of this personal attention as he liked to intimate he was, [Hemingway] was the architect of his public reputation" (*Fame Became of Him*, 2, 6–7). Even during his youth in Paris, when he was very little known across the Atlantic, he radiated a kind of charisma that inspired people to talk about him. But in the 1920s, Hemingway was far less openly engaged in the building of a reputation and far more insistent upon absolute fidelity to his work than he would be later in his career. One useful way of illustrating the difference is to compare two profiles of him in the *New Yorker*: Dorothy Parker's "The Artist's Reward" of November 30, 1929, and Lillian Ross's "How Do You Like It Now, Gentlemen?" of May 13, 1950.

Parker was obviously smitten with Hemingway, whom she met through their mutual friends Gerald and Sara Murphy. Her three-page profile presented an adoring portrait of the author, who had just published his second novel, *A Farewell to Arms*. She raved both about Hemingway's person and his achievement. "He certainly *is* attractive," she assured her readers, "even better than his photographs." Not only that, but to her mind he ranked—at but thirty years of age—as "far and away the first American artist." A great many falsehoods had been circulated about him, Parker pointed out. "Probably of no other living man has so much tripe been penned and spoken." She humorously recounted some of the wild rumors about his toughness and athleticism, concluding with a passage reminiscent of Gatsby. "About all that remains to be said is that he is the Lost Dauphin, that he was shot as a German spy, and that he is actually a woman, masquerading in man's clothes" (28).

Having warned against apocryphal tales, Parker proceeded to contribute a few of her own. In his youth, she wrote, Hemingway left home to become a prizefighter. Then he served in the Italian army during World War I, suffering seven major wounds, acquiring an aluminum kneecap, and receiving unspecified "medals." Such accounts were either outright inventions, like the one about boxing, or distortions of the truth, like the inflated version of his wartime service in a Red Cross ambulance unit. This was sloppy reporting, but Parker did not have much to work with, for Hemingway was loath to provide facts about himself—"I can find out nothing about his education," she sadly observed—and at the same time willing to encourage yarns about his prowess in the ring or on the battlefield. Parker simply put down what he saw fit to tell her or others about himself, including the legend that his art derived from "the kind of poverty you don't believe—the kind of which actual hunger is the attendant." Now, though, she added, he did his writing "mostly in bed," like a latterday Proust (28–29).

Parker's descriptions of Hemingway were more reliable when she relied on her own powers of observation. She commented, for instance, on his abundance of energy and "capacity for enjoyment so vast . . . that he can take you to a bicycle-race, and make it raise your hair." She acknowledged his sensitivity to criticism, citing a few examples of wrong-headed commentary that greeted his early work. She detected beneath his manly exterior "an immense, ill-advised, and indiscriminate tenderness." And in calling attention to his bravery and unwillingness to compromise, she printed for the first time his definition of "guts" as "grace under pressure": a phrase that was to become famous as part of his public legend. Throughout she insisted on Hemingway's integrity as a dedicated writer. "He works like hell, and through it," she observed. As evidence she asserted that he rewrote the ending of A Farewell to Arms seventy times; in fact, more than thirty variant endings eventually came to light among his working drafts. The Hemingway who emerged from her pastiche of half-truths, inaccuracies, and admiring asides was well on his way to becoming a public figure, someone "people want to hear things about." But her 1929 profile never lost sight of the fact that it was his art that made him worth writing about (30–31).

With Lillian Ross's far longer and very different piece twenty-one years later, Hemingway's situation had changed considerably. By 1950 he had become a star, and Ross kept him on center stage throughout. She set out "to describe as precisely as possible how Hemingway, who had the nerve to be like nobody else on earth, looked and sounded when he was in action, talking, between work periods—to give a picture of the man as he was, in his uniqueness and with his vitality and his enormous spirit of fun intact" (189). The trouble was that in her reportorial account Hemingway sounded like a boor to others and egocentric about himself. She liked Hemingway immensely, Ross maintained, yet for many readers her profile remains the most damaging document about him ever published.

She caught the author off guard, during a two-day trip to New York immediately after finishing the manuscript of *Across the River and Into the Trees*. With that project behind him—and it had been ten years between novels—Hemingway was very much on holiday and proud of the new book he was bringing with him for delivery to Scribner's. Ross met the author and wife Mary at the airport, where he was maintaining a viselike grip on a wiry little fellow who had been his seatmate on the flight from Cuba. This chap had been coerced into reading the manuscript en route. "He read book all way up on plane," Hemingway said in a patois stripped of articles. "He liked book, I think." "Whew!" said the seatmate (195).

"Whew!" pretty well summed up the frenetic activities of the next two days, which included visits to Abercrombie and Fitch and the Metropolitan Museum of Art; meetings with Marlene Dietrich, Charles Scribner, and son Patrick; and an enormous amount of drinking. Readers of Hemingway are sometimes incredulous about the quantities of liquor his characters consume, but on the basis of Ross's profile it seems clear that his fiction did not exaggerate from the life. Liberated from the grind of completing his book and subject to what he called "the irresponsibility that comes in after the terrible responsibility of writing," Hemingway commenced his drinking with double bourbons at the airport cocktail lounge. At his hotel room, two champagne buckets were pressed into use to keep the wine cold for consumption at all hours, including breakfast time. During the tour of the Metropolitan, he took long pulls from a silver flask. It's as daunting as Jake Barnes's tremendous consumption at the end of *The Sun Also Rises* or that of Colonel Cantwell in *Across the River*.

In the most memorable passages in Ross's portrait, Hemingway compared his own writing to that of great figures from the past, employing metaphors from the world of sport. A novelist was like a starting pitcher with no relievers in the bullpen, he declared. "Novelist has to go the full nine, even if it kills him." During his Paris years, he said, he had perfected his pitching by reading such French masters as "Mr. Flaubert, who always threw them perfectly straight, hard, high and inside . . . Mr. Baudelaire, that I learned my knuckle ball from, and Mr. Rimbaud, who never threw a fast ball in his life." In a burst of braggadocio, he used boxing instead of baseball to lay claim to his place in the company of great fiction writers. "I started out very quiet and I beat Mr. Turgenev. Then I trained hard and I beat Mr. de Maupassant. I've fought two draws with Mr. Stendhal, and I think I had an edge in the last one. But nobody's going to get me in any ring with Mr. Tolstoy unless I'm crazy or I keep getting better." When he signed a contract with Scribner's, he announced himself ready to take on the present-day competition. "Never ran as no genius, but I'll defend the title again against all the good new ones" (196, 202, 208–9, 212).

In 1929 Parker called Hemingway "the first American artist." In 1950 it was Hemingway who proclaimed his supremacy. Instead of insisting on the dignity of his craft, Ross's hard-drinking bearded Papa called the roll of the great, placing himself at the forefront. The admirably dedicated young man reluctant to talk about his past had seemingly deteriorated into something of a buffoon, whose talk and actions smacked of grandiosity. He may well have been poking fun at himself, but it is hard to detect self-parody in the absence of any commentary to that effect from Ross, who kept to a posture of strict objectivity throughout.

What seems clear, retrospectively, is that Hemingway was determined to distance himself from the conventional image of the artist as aesthete. He was no innocent victim of the press. He knew why Ross was at his elbow and the kind of reporting she did. (A few years earlier, she had interviewed him for her profile on his friend Sidney Franklin, the bullfighter from Brooklyn.) If possible, Hemingway wanted it both ways: he wanted to be recognized for his mastery of fiction and at the same time as a rugged manly fellow. So he emerged from the 1950 profile not merely, like Whitman, as "one of the roughs" but as the roughest of all, a man who wrestled bears, spoke pidgin English, and by the way wrote some of the most enduring stories and novels of his time.

The sensitive tough guy has become a cliché, and Hemingway was cast in that part at least as early as 1933, when a William Steig cartoon in *Vanity Fair* depicted him with a rose in his hairy tattooed fist. It was the fist and not the rose—he had no tattoos—that he chose to emphasize in his public appearances and comments. When Malcolm Cowley sent him the draft of his "Portrait of Mister Papa," which appeared in *Life* magazine the year before Ross's profile, Hemingway asked for but one alteration. Cowley had written that in high school Hemingway "was a literary boy, not a sports boy." This was true enough, but Hemingway wanted the passage cut, and so it was (Raeburn, *Fame Became of Him*, 132). He understood and fostered his public role, but it led to at least two dangers: first, that he would become so stereotyped as to be uncastable in other roles and, second, that he would be so integrated into the part as to give up any distinct identity of his own. In Ross's article, he appeared to be falling victim to both dangers.

As Braudy accurately observed, Hemingway "seemed to carry the burden of early success fairly well" (*Frenzy*, 543). He had the good fortune not to be overwhelmed by popular or critical attention at the beginning of his career. In 1924 he wrote Ezra Pound from Spain about the recognition accorded young bullfighters, the "ovations, Alcoholism, being pointed out on the street, general respect and the other things Literary guys have to wait until they are 89 years old to get" (*Selected Letters*, 119). He did not have to wait that long, however. His expatriate pamphlets *Three Stories and Ten Poems* (1923) and *in our time* (1924) caught the canny eye of Edmund Wilson, whose review in the *Dial* struck Hemingway as "cool and clear minded and decent and impersonal and sympathetic" and best of all, concentrated on the work itself and not its creator. "Christ how I hate this terrible personal stuff," he added (*Selected Letters*, 129). Not until he was thirty and the controversial *A Farewell to Arms* came out to a mingled chorus of praise and outrage for its straightforward language and frank depiction of a love affair out of wedlock did he begin to generate *New Yorker* articles and other public explorations of his personality.

Thereafter, working in collaboration with the mass media, Hemingway shaped his own public image. Much of this was accomplished in his nonfiction of the 1930s, which included *Death in the Afternoon* (bullfights); *Green Hills of Africa* (safari); a series of articles for *Esquire* on sports, politics, and art; and correspondence from Spain during the Spanish Civil War. As Raeburn remarked, whether the subject was bullfighting, game fishing, or the battle for Madrid, in these publications Hemingway was actually writing about himself. Taken together, the nonfiction constituted "sketches toward an autobiography"—the autobiography of the personality he chose to present to the public (*Fame Became of Him*, 15).

That personality, in Raeburn's analysis, consisted of no fewer than nine roles: the sportsman, the "tough and virile" man, the exposer of sham, the arbiter of taste, the world traveler, the bon vivant, the insider, the stoic veteran, and the heroic artist (39–43). The image that stuck was reduced to that of the tough guy who also happened, incredibly, to be a literary genius, the man of action eager to test his courage against great beasts and the weapons of war merged with the artist who shaped a brilliant new prose style. By the end of World War II, during which he served as war correspondent and uncommissioned leader of his own band of irregulars, that persona had taken a strong hold on the American consciousness. And of course it was the first half of the combination—the sportsman-warrior rather than the heroic artist—whose activities were most widely reported upon and talked about. Over time Hemingway became a celebrity rather than a writer, and if he was not only willing but complicit in the formation of that celebrity's image, he eventually found that carrying that persona around with him could be psychologically and even physically troubling.

In 1952 a young scholar named Philip Young brought out *Ernest Hemingway*, a book Hemingway tried to stop before publication and disparaged afterward. While his volume was ostensibly a critical study of the fiction, Young relied upon the Freudian concept of "repetition compulsion" to explain the extraordinary pattern of wounds suffered by both the author and his fictional protagonists. As Young saw it, this pattern had its origin in Hemingway's serious wounding in Italy during World War I. His traumatic reaction to that wound led not only to nightmares but to a compulsion to relive the terrible experience. This theory, he proposed, explained the psychological makeup of Hemingway's heroes and provided a rationale for his own repeated confrontations with danger and the many mutilating wounds—to arms and legs and head—that he suffered as a consequence. If this was not biography, and Young insisted that it was not, it certainly represented an invasion of the author's privacy. Young's book made him out to be "crazy," Hemingway complained, and though he railed against critics taking such liberties during his lifetime, he had long before opened the gates to intruders and was hardly in a position to close them (Raeburn, *Fame Became of Him*, 139–41).

Hemingway's most widely reported brush with death occurred in January 1954, when he and his wife Mary, on safari in Africa, survived two plane crashes in two days. When wreckage of the first crash was sighted, word went out that he had been killed, so that Hemingway had the pleasure of reading his own obituaries. "My luck, she is still good," he told interviewers afterward, but in fact the crashes took a severe toll. The second one left him with a "full-scale concussion" and such other injuries as "a ruptured liver, spleen, and kidney, temporary loss of vision in the left eye, loss of hearing in the left ear, a crushed vertebra, a sprained right arm and shoulder, a sprained left leg, paralysis of he sphincter, and first degree burns on his face, arms, and head" (Baker, *A Life Story*, 522). Carlos Baker, his official biographer, believed that these were the worst injuries of the many he underwent and that he never really recovered from them.

In the aftermath of the accidents, the process of recuperation called for rest and quiet, but these were difficult for a celebrated man like Hemingway to find. Weeks later he was driving through the Italian Alps with companion (and unofficial biographer) A. E. Hotchner when the cost of his international fame was vividly brought home to him. They stopped to buy a bottle of scotch in the town of Cuneo, and Hemingway was recognized in the liquor store. Soon a crowd surrounded him, demanding that he autograph his books (the local bookstore was next door). Then the crowd turned into a mob, effectively preventing the writer from making his way back to the car. A small detachment of soldiers was required to liberate him from the crush. Badly shaken, Hemingway shaved off his beard the next day in hopes of avoiding further violent displays of affection from strangers (Hotchner, *Papa Hemingway*, 115–16).

A few months later, he was back in the news as winner of the 1954 Nobel Prize for literature. Still in poor health and unable to attend the ceremonies, he sent a statement about the loneliness of the writer and how he "should always try for something that has never been done or that others have tried and failed." With luck, success might follow, but only if the writer was willing, like Santiago in *The Old Man and the Sea*, to be "driven far out past where he can go, out to where no one can help him." "A writer," he concluded, "should write what he has to say and not speak it" (qtd. in Baker, *A Life Story*, 528–29). By urging upon his worldwide audience the lonely and courageous and difficult task confronting the writer, he was calling up once again the image of the artist as hero.

Lillian Ross, in an apologia written after Hemingway's death in 1961, judged him to have been just such an artist. At work, she wrote, "he was heroically and uncorruptedly and uncompromisingly occupied day after day with writing as hard as he could." And when he wasn't at work, he lived his life to the full and generously made "his private experience public, so that everybody else could also have a wonderful time." This observation served to show Hemingway's "gin-crazed Indian" of her profile in a more flattering light and was probably intended to make amends, but it oversimplified the motives behind his public image (Ross, "Portrait of Hemingway," 191; Hotchner, *Papa Hemingway*, 117). Hemingway's presentation of himself may have owed something to a desire to entertain others, but he may also have adopted that image to gain approval and attention, to prevent raids on his psyche, to prove himself against the most demanding tests, or for all those reasons. As Baker and all subsequent biographers have discovered, he was an extremely complex human being whose behavior could rarely be ascribed to any one single cause.

There were those who argued after Hemingway's suicide that he had long before lost his touch, that he peaked early and went downhill from 1930 on. His celebrity kept people from noticing the decline, Dwight Macdonald said in a retrospective article that satirized his public image. In the end he realized that he could no longer defend the title, "the position is outflanked the lion can't be stopped the sword won't go into the bull's neck the great fish is breaking the line and it is the fifteenth round and the champion looks bad" (qtd. in Raeburn, *Fame Became of Him*, 171). Most would agree that Hemingway did in fact write his greatest fiction in the 1920s, although he produced important and valuable books for thirty years thereafter and left behind still other manuscripts that well deserved their posthumous publication. Like many other American authors, he had to deal with the problem of encore. How was he supposed to surpass the wonderful stories written during the Paris years and the two great novels, *The Sun Also Rises* and *A Farewell to Arms*?

His celebrity exacerbated the difficulty, as the general public concentrated its gaze on the exploits of his private life and only occasionally could be roused to acknowledge—as by the entire issue of *Life* containing *The Old Man and the Sea* and the awarding of the Nobel Prize in Sweden—that the Papa Hemingway they knew was an artist as well. As Braudy pointed out, "the media-soaked years after World War Two spawned a whole tribe of artistic suicides, many of whom had discovered how hard it was to retain their personal integrity, when interest in their work played a weak second to fascination with their private lives and whether they would be able to repeat their past performances." In addition to Hemingway, he cited Sylvia Plath and Anne Sexton, Ross Lockridge Jr. and Thomas Heggen. Suicide offered all of these American writers a "final act of cohesion . . . in a world where the false and the true [were] hard to tell apart," Braudy wrote, but Hemingway was more famous than the others, and hence more subject to "a fragmentation of self and public image" (*Frenzy*, 28). But if "the frenzy of renown" helped to spur Hemingway's demise, it has not proved fatal to his literary reputation. The stories and novels of Hemingway, the consummate craftsman, have managed to outlive the curse of celebrity.

BIBLIOGRAPHY

Aaron, Daniel. *Writers on the Left*. New York: Oxford University Press, 1977.

"All Stories End." *Time*, 18 October 1937, 79–85.

Alter, Jonathan. "Taking Sides." Review of *The Man Who Invented Fidel*, by Anthony DePalma. *New York Times Book Review*, 23 April 2006.

American Writers Congress. Letter to F. Scott Fitzgerald. 21 March 1935. Fitzgerald Papers. Princeton University Library.

Baker, Carlos. *Ernest Hemingway: A Life Story*. New York: Scribner's, 1969.

——, ed. *Ernest Hemingway: Selected Letters, 1917–1961*. New York: Scribner's, 1981.

——. *Hemingway: The Writer as Artist*. Princeton, N.J.: Princeton University Press, 1963.

Baker, Sheridan. *Ernest Hemingway: An Introduction and Interpretation*. New York: Holt, Rinehart and Winston, 1967.

Baldwin, Charles C. "F. Scott Fitzgerald." In *The Men Who Make Our Novels*. New York: Dodd, Mead, 1924. Reprint, in *F. Scott Fitzgerald in His Own Time: A Miscellany*, ed. Matthew J. Bruccoli and Jackson R. Bryer, 267–70. Kent, Ohio: Kent State University Press, 1971.

"Baltimore Students Meeting Against WAR!" Fitzgerald Papers. Princeton University Library.

Barea, Arturo. "Not Spain But Hemingway." In *The Literary Reputation of Hemingway in Europe*, ed. Roger Asselineau, 197–210. New York: New York University Press, 1965.

Barrett, William. "Fitzgerald and America." *Partisan Review* 18 (May–June 1951): 345–53.

Basso, Hamilton. Letter to Edmund Wilson. 14 October 1944. Fitzgerald Papers. Princeton University Library.

Baxter, Charles. *Burning Down the House: Essays on Fiction*. St. Paul, Minn.: Graywolf, 1997.

Beegel, Susan F. "Eye and Heart: Hemingway's Education as a Naturalist." In *A Historical Guide to Ernest Hemingway*, ed. Linda Wagner-Martin, 53–92. New York: Oxford University Press, 2000.

Begley, Neal. Letter to F. Scott Fitzgerald. 29 February 1940. Fitzgerald Papers. Princeton University Library.

Benchley, Robert C. "Books and Other Things." *New York Morning World*, 21 April 1920. Reprint, in *F. Scott Fitzgerald: The Critical Reception*, ed. Jackson R. Bryer, 14–15. New York: Burt Franklin, 1978.

Benson, Jackson J. *Hemingway: The Writer's Art of Self-Defense*. Minneapolis: University of Minnesota Press, 1969.

Berg, Scott. *Max Perkins: Editor of Genius*. New York: Dutton, 1978.

Berman, Jeffrey. "*Tender Is the Night*: Fitzgerald's *A Psychology for Psychiatrists*." *Literature and Psychology* 29, no. 1–2 (1979): 34–48.

Berman, Ronald. *The Great Gatsby and Modern Times*. Urbana: University of Illinois Press, 1994.

"Between the Lines." *San Francisco Chronicle*, 20 March 1936.

Biggs, John. Letter to Scott Donaldson. 10 July 1978. Personal collection.

Biographical sketches of Generals Ernest J. Dawley, John C. H. Lee, and Oscar N. Solbert. Department of the Army Center of Military History. Washington, D.C.

Block, Haskell M., and Robert G. Shedd, eds. *Masters of Modern Drama*. New York: Random House, 1962.

Bone, John. Letters to Ernest Hemingway. 20 February 1922, 20 August 1922, 25 September 1922, 18 August 1923. Hemingway Collection. John F. Kennedy Library.

Boorstin, Daniel J. *The Image*. New York: Atheneum, 1962.

Booth, Wayne C. *The Rhetoric of Fiction*. Chicago: University of Chicago Press, 1961.

"Boston Police Bar Scribner's Magazine." *New York Times*, 21 June 1929.

Boyer, Paul S. *Purity in Print: The Vice-Society Movement and Book Censorship in America*. New York: Scribner's, 1968.

Braudy, Leo. *The Frenzy of Renown: Fame and Its History*. New York: Oxford University Press, 1986.

Brown, Deming. *Soviet Attitudes Toward American Writing*. Princeton, N.J.: Princeton University Press, 1962.

Bruccoli, Matthew J. *The Composition of "Tender Is the Night": A Study of the Manuscripts*. Pittsburgh, Penn.: University of Pittsburgh Press, 1963.

——. *F. Scott Fitzgerald: A Bibliography*. Pittsburgh, Penn.: University of Pittsburgh Press, 1972.

——. *Hemingway and the Mechanism of Fame*. Columbia: University of South Carolina Press, 2006.

——. *"The Last of the Novelists": F. Scott Fitzgerald and The Last Tycoon*. Carbondale: Southern Illinois University Press, 1977.

——. "The Perkins-Wilson Correspondence." *Fitzgerald/Hemingway Annual 1978*, 63–66. Detroit: Gale Research, 1979.

——. *Some Sort of Epic Grandeur: The Life of F. Scott Fitzgerald*. New York: Harcourt Brace Jovanovich, 1981.

Bruccoli, Matthew J., and Jackson R. Bryer, eds. *F. Scott Fitzgerald in His Own Time: A Miscellany*. Kent, Ohio: Kent State University Press, 1971.

Bryer, Jackson R., ed. *F. Scott Fitzgerald: The Critical Reception*. New York: Burt Franklin, 1978.

Bryer, Jackson R., and John Kuehl. Introduction to *The Basil and Josephine Stories*, by F. Scott Fitzgerald, vii–xvi. New York: Scribner's, 1973.

Butcher, Fanny. "New Fitzgerald Book Brilliant; Fails as Novel." *Chicago Tribune*, 14 April 1934. Reprint, in *F. Scott Fitzgerald: The Critical Reception*, ed. Jackson R. Bryer, 298–99. New York: Burt Franklin, 1978.

Buttitta, Tony. *After the Good Gay Times*. New York: Viking, 1974.

Calverton, V. F. Letters to F. Scott Fitzgerald. 3 June 1934, 29 September 1934. Fitzgerald Papers. Princeton University Library.

Carney, William P. "Rebel Artillery Rushed to Teruel." *New York Times*, 24 December 1937.

Castle, Henry A. *History of St. Paul and Vicinity*. Chicago: Lewis, 1912.

Catalog of the Ernest Hemingway Collection at the John F. Kennedy Library. Boston: G. K. Hall, 1982.

Catledge, Turner. *My Life and The Times*. New York: Harper & Row, 1971.

Cawelti, John G. *Apostles of the Self-Made Man*. Chicago: University of Chicago Press, 1965.

Chamberlain, John. "Books of the Times" (review of *Taps at Reveille*). *New York Times*, 27 March 1935.

——. "Books of the Times." *New York Times*, 13 and 16 April 1934. Reprint, in *F. Scott Fitzgerald: The Critical Reception*, ed. Jackson R. Bryer, 294–96, 311–12. New York: Burt Franklin, 1978.

Clark, Gregory. Letters to Ernest Hemingway. 28 February 1921, 2 September 1922, 31 August 1923. Hemingway Collection. John F. Kennedy Library.

Colum, Mary M. Review of *The Beautiful and Damned*, by F. Scott Fitzgerald. *The Freeman*, 26 April 1922. Reprint, in *F. Scott Fitzgerald in His Own Time: A Miscellany*, ed. Matthew J. Bruccoli and Jackson R. Bryer, 334–36. Kent, Ohio: Kent State University Press, 1971.

Cooper, Stephen. *The Politics of Ernest Hemingway*. Ann Arbor, Mich.: UMI, 1987.

Cooperman, Stanley. "Death and *Cojones*: Hemingway's *A Farewell to Arms*." In *World War I and the American Novel*, 181–90. Baltimore, Md.: Johns Hopkins University Press, 1967.

Cortada, James W., ed. *Historical Dictionary of the Spanish Civil War, 1936–1939*. Westport, Conn.: Greenwood, 1982.

Cowles, Virginia. *Looking for Trouble*. New York: Harper, 1941.

Cowley, Malcolm. *Exile's Return*. New York: Viking, 1951.

——. Introduction and Note to *Tender Is the Night*, by F. Scott Fitzgerald, ix–xviii, 349–56. New York: Scribner's, 1951.

——. Introduction to *The Stories of F. Scott Fitzgerald*, vii–xxv. New York: Scribner's, 1951.

Cullum, George W. *Biographical Register of the Officers and Graduates of the U.S. Military Academy*. Supplement, vol. 8, 1930–1940, and supplement, vol. 9, 1940–1950.

Cutting, Nigel. "Hemingway's Sub Text in *The Sun Also Rises*." M.A. Thesis, College of William and Mary, 1976.

Dawley, Ernest J., John C. H. Lee, Oscar N. Solbert, and L. Curtis Tiernan. United States Army correspondence. 16 May 1945–24 May 1945. Filed among papers of Gertrude Stein, Beinecke Library, Yale University.

Dessner, Lawrence Jay. "Photography and *The Great Gatsby*." In *Critical Essays on "The Great Gatsby*," ed. Scott Donaldson, 175–86. Boston: G. K. Hall, 1984.

Dickinson, Emily. *The Poems of Emily Dickinson*. Vol. 1. Ed. Thomas H. Johnson. Cambridge, Mass.: Harvard University Press, 1958.

Dickstein, Morris. "The Authority of Failure." *American Scholar* 69 (Spring 2000): 69–81.

———. "Fitzgerald's Second Act." *South Atlantic Quarterly* 90 (Summer 1991): 555–78.

Didion, Joan. *Slouching Towards Bethlehem*. New York: Simon and Schuster, 1979.

Dolan, Marc. *Modern Lives: A Cultural Re-Reading of "The Lost Generation."* West Lafayette, Ind.: Purdue University Press, 1996.

Donaldson, Scott. *Archibald MacLeish: An American Life*. Boston: Houghton Mifflin, 1992.

———. *By Force of Will: The Life and Art of Ernest Hemingway*. New York: Viking, 1977.

———, ed. *Cambridge Companion to Hemingway*. New York Cambridge University Press, 1996.

———. "The Crisis of Fitzgerald's 'Crack-Up.'" *Twentieth-Century Literature* 26 (Summer 1980): 171–88.

———. "Dos and Hem." *Centennial Review* 29 (Spring 1985): 163–85.

———. *Fool for Love: F. Scott Fitzgerald*. New York: Congdon and Weed, 1983.

———. "Hemingway's Morality of Compensation." *American Literature* 43 (November 1971): 499–520.

———. *Hemingway vs. Fitzgerald: The Rise and Fall of a Literary Friendship*. Woodstock, N.Y.: Overlook, 1999.

———. "The Political Development of F. Scott Fitzgerald." In *Prospects*, vol. 6, ed. Jack Salzman, 313–35. New York: Burt Franklin, 1981.

———. "The Wooing of Ernest Hemingway." *American Literature* 53 (January 1982): 691–710.

Donnithorpe, Col. Larry R. (Ret.). *The West Point Way of Leadership*. New York: Doubleday, 1993.

Dos Passos, John. *Journeys Between Wars*. New York: Harcourt, 1938.

———. Letter to F. Scott Fitzgerald. 1934 (?). Fitzgerald Papers. Princeton University Library.

Eble, Kenneth. *F. Scott Fitzgerald*. Boston: Twayne, 1977.

Emerson, Ralph Waldo. *Selections from Ralph Waldo Emerson*. Ed. Stephen Whicher. Boston: Houghton Mifflin, 1957.

———. "The Tragic." *Dial* 4 (April 1844): 515–21.

Epstein, Joseph. "F. Scott Fitzgerald's Third Act." *Commentary* 98 (November 1994): 52–57.

Farrell, James T. Review of *The Sun Also Rises*. *New York Times*, 1 August 1943. Reprint, in *Studies in "The Sun Also Rises,"* ed. William White, 53–57. Columbus, Ohio: Merrill, 1969.

Fenton, Charles A. *The Apprenticeship of Ernest Hemingway*. New York: Farrar, Straus and Young, 1954.

Fitzgerald, F. Scott. *Afternoon of an Author*. Ed. Arthur Mizener. New York: Scribner's, 1958.

———. *The Apprentice Fiction of F. Scott Fitzgerald, 1909–1917*. Ed. John Kuehl. New Brunswick, N.J.: Rutgers University Press, 1965.

———. *As Ever, Scott Fitz: Letters Between F. Scott Fitzgerald and His Agent Harold Ober, 1919–1940*. Ed. Matthew J. Bruccoli. Philadelphia: Lippincott, 1972.

———. *The Basil and Josephine Stories*. Ed. Jackson R. Bryer and John Kuehl. New York: Scribner's, 1973.

——. *The Beautiful and Damned*. New York: Scribner's, 1922.

——. "The Bowl." *Saturday Evening Post*, 21 January 1928. Reprint, in *The Short Stories of F. Scott Fitzgerald*, ed. Matthew J. Bruccoli, 256–77. New York: Scribner's, 1989.

——. "Confessions." In scrapbook 3. Fitzgerald Papers. Princeton University Library.

——. *Correspondence of F. Scott Fitzgerald*. Ed. Matthew J. Bruccoli and Margaret M. Duggan. New York: Random House, 1980.

——. *The Crack-Up*. Ed. Edmund Wilson. New York: New Directions, 1956.

——. "The Cruise of the Rolling Junk." *Motor* 41 (February 1924): 24–25, 58, 62, 64, 66.

——. *Dear Scott, Dearest Zelda: The Love Letters of F. Scott and Zelda Fitzgerald*. Ed. Jackson R. Bryer and Cathy W. Barks. New York: St. Martin's, 2002.

——. *Dear Scott/Dear Max: The Fitzgerald-Perkins Correspondence*. Ed. John Kuehl and Jackson R. Bryer. New York: Scribner's, 1971.

——. "The Death of My Father." *Princeton University Library Chronicle* 12 (Summer 1951): 187–89.

——. "A Debt of Honor." In *The Apprentice Fiction of F. Scott Fitzgerald 1909–1917*, ed. John Kuehl, 36–38. New Brunswick, N.J.: Rutgers University Press, 1965.

——. "Early Success." Typescript. Fitzgerald Papers. Princeton University Library.

——. *Flappers and Philosophers*. New York: Scribner's, 1959.

——. Foreword to *Colonial and Historic Homes of Maryland*. Baltimore, Md.: Etchcrafters Art Guild, 1939.

—— *F. Scott Fitzgerald: A Life in Letters*. Ed. Matthew J. Bruccoli. New York. Scribner's, 1994.

——. *F. Scott Fitzgerald's Ledger: A Facsimile*. Intro. Matthew J. Bruccoli. Washington: NCR/Microcard Editions, 1972.

——. *F. Scott Fitzgerald's St. Paul Plays, 1911–1914*. Ed. Alan Margolies. Princeton, N.J.: Princeton University Library, 1978.

——. *The Great Gatsby*. Ed. Matthew J. Bruccoli. New York: Cambridge University Press, 1991.

——. "Gretchen's Forty Winks." In *All the Sad Young Men*, ed. James L. W. West III, 166–85. New York: Cambridge University Press, 2007.

——. "The Ice Palace." In *The Short Stories of F. Scott Fitzgerald*, ed. Matthew J. Bruccoli, 48–69. New York: Scribner's, 1989.

——. "The Last of the Belles." *The Short Stories of F. Scott Fitzgerald*, ed. Matthew J. Bruccoli, 449–63. New York: Scribner's, 1989.

——. *The Last Tycoon*. New York: Scribner's, 1941.

——. *The Letters of F. Scott Fitzgerald*. Ed. Andrew Turnbull. New York: Scribner's, 1963. Letter to Neal Begley, 26 March 1940. Fitzgerald Papers. Princeton University Library.

——. Letter to John Biggs. Spring 1939. Fitzgerald Papers. Princeton University Library.

——. Letters to V. F. Calverton. 23 April 1934, 16 May 1934, 5 June 1934, 17 October 1934, 4 November 1934, 26 March 1935. New York Public Library.

——. Letter to William Dozier. 5 November 1940. Fitzgerald Papers. Princeton University Library.

——. Letter to Frances Scott Fitzgerald. Fragment, n.d. and unsent (?). Fitzgerald Papers. Princeton University Library.

——. Letter to John O'Hara. 25 July 1936. Fitzgerald Papers. Princeton University Library.

——. Letter to Dr. Thomas Rennie. 6 October 1933. Fitzgerald Papers. Princeton University Library.

——. *A Life in Letters*. Ed. Matthew J. Bruccoli. New York: Scribner's, 1994.

——. *My Lost City: Personal Essays, 1920–1940*. Ed. James L. W. West III. New York: Cambridge University Press, 2005.

——. Note. N.d. F. Scott Fitzgerald Papers. Princeton University Library.

——. *The Notebooks of F. Scott Fitzgerald*. Ed. Matthew J. Bruccoli. New York: Harcourt, 1978.

——. Note on Hollywood writers. N.d. Fitzgerald Papers. Princeton University Library.

——. Note on Lenin. N.d. Fitzgerald Papers. Princeton University Library.

——. Note on Willkie. N.d. Fitzgerald Papers. Princeton University Library.

——. *The Price Was High: The Last Uncollected Stories of F. Scott Fitzgerald*. Ed. Matthew J. Bruccoli. New York: Harcourt, 1979.

——. "Reminiscences of Donald Stewart." *St. Paul Daily News*, 11 December 1921. Reprint, in *F. Scott Fitzgerald in His Own Time: A Miscellany*, ed. Matthew J. Bruccoli and Jackson R. Bryer, 231–32. Kent, Ohio: Kent State University Press, 1971.

——. Review of *Three Soldiers*, by John Dos Passos. *St. Paul Daily News*, 25 September 1921. Reprint, in *F. Scott Fitzgerald in His Own Time: A Miscellany*, ed. Matthew J. Bruccoli and Jackson R. Bryer, 121–24. Kent, Ohio: Kent State University Press, 1971.

——. Script for CBS radio. Squibb-World Peaceways. Broadcast 3 October 1935. Fitzgerald Papers. Princeton University Library.

——. "'The Sensible Thing.'" *All the Sad Young Men*. Ed. James L. W. West III, 151–65. New York: Cambridge University Press, 2007.

——. *The Short Stories of F. Scott Fitzgerald*. Ed. Matthew J. Bruccoli. New York: Scribner's, 1989.

——. *Six Tales of the Jazz Age and Other Stories*. New York: Scribner's, 1960.

——. *Tales of the Jazz Age*. 1922. Ed. James L. W. West III. New York: Cambridge University Press, 2002.

——. *Tender Is the Night*. New York: Scribner's, 1934.

——. *Tender Is the Night*. Ed. Malcolm Cowley. New York: Scribner's, 1951.

——. *This Side of Paradise*. Ed. James L. W. West III. New York: Cambridge University Press, 1995.

——. "To My Grandfather." Poem fragment. Fitzgerald Papers. Princeton University Library.

——. *Trimalchio: An Early Version of The Great Gatsby*. Ed. James L. W. West III. New York: Cambridge University Press, 1971.

——. "Two Wrongs." In *The Short Stories of F. Scott Fitzgerald*, ed. Matthew J. Bruccoli, 513–30. New York: Scribner's, 1989.

——. *The Vegetable*. New York: Scribner's, 1923.

——. "Wait till You Have Children of Your Own." *Woman's Home Companion* 51 (July 1924). Reprint, in *F. Scott Fitzgerald in His Own Time: A Miscellany*, ed. Matthew J. Bruccoli and Jackson R. Bryer, 192–201. Kent, Ohio: Kent State University Press, 1971.

Fitzgerald, Zelda. *Save Me the Waltz*. 1932. Carbondale: Southern Illinois University Press, 1967.

Flanagan, Thomas. "The Best He Could Do." *New York Review of Books* 46 (21 October 1999): 64–67, 70–72.

Flandrau, Grace. *Being Respectable*. New York: Harcourt Brace, 1923.

Flora, Joseph M. *Hemingway's Nick Adams Stories*. Baton Rouge: Louisiana State University Press, 1982.

Folsom, Franklin. *Days of Anger, Days of Hope: A Memoir of the League of American Writers*. Niwot: University Press of Colorado, 1994.

Frankel, Max. *The Times of My Life*. New York: Random House, 1999.

Frankenburg, Lloyd. "Themes and Characters in Hemingway's Latest Period." *Southern Review* 7 (Spring 1942): 776–88.

Frost, Robert. *The Poetry of Robert Frost*. Ed. Edward Connery Lathem. New York: Holt, Rinehart and Winston, 1975.

Gelb, Arthur. *City Room*. New York: Putnam, 2003.

Geismar, Maxwell. *The Last of the Provincials*. Boston: Houghton Mifflin, 1943

Gingrich, Arnold. Letters to Ernest Hemingway. 6 February 1938, mid-June 1938. Hemingway Collection. John F. Kennedy Library.

———. "Publisher's Page." *Esquire* 62 (December 1964): 12, 16.

———. Telegrams to Ernest Hemingway. 9 January 1938, 30 January 1938, 31 January 1938, 18 April 1938. Hemingway Collection. John F. Kennedy Library.

Gnizi, Haim. "V. F. Calverton, Independent Radical." Ph.d. diss., City University of New York, 1968.

Graham, Sheilah. *College of One*. New York: Viking, 1967.

———. *The Rest of the Story*. New York: Coward-McCann, 1964.

Graham, Sheilah, and Gerold Frank. *Beloved Infidel*. New York: Henry Holt, 1958.

Grebstein, Sheldon Norman. *Hemingway's Craft*. Carbondale: Southern Illinois University Press, 1973

Grenberg, Bruce L. "Fitzgerald's 'Figured Curtain': Personality and History in *Tender Is the Night*." *Fitzgerald/Hemingway Annual* 10 (1978): 105–36.

Guthrie, Laura. Memoir. Summer 1935. Fitzgerald Papers. Princeton University Library.

Hackett, General Sir John. *The Profession of Arms*. New York: Macmillan, 1983.

Hackl, Lloyd C. *"Still Home to Me": F. Scott Fitzgerald and St. Paul, Minnesota*. Cambridge, Minn.: Adventure Publications, 1996.

Haffenden, John. *The Life of John Berryman*. Boston: Routledge, 1982.

Haight, Anne Lynn. *Banned Books*. New York: Bowker, 1970.

Halliday, E. M. "Hemingway's Narrative Perspective." *Sewanee Review* 60 (Spring 1952): 202–18.

Hamm, Mrs. William (Marie Hersey). Letter to F. Scott Fitzgerald. 5 October 1936. Fitzgerald Papers. Princeton University Library.

Hammett, Dashiell. Letter to F. Scott Fitzgerald. 11 May 1938. Fitzgerald Papers. Princeton University Library.

Hanneman, Audre. *Ernest Hemingway: A Comprehensive Bibliography*. Princeton, N.J.: Princeton University Press, 1967.

Hansen, Harry. "The First Reader." *New York World*, 27 September 1929. Scribner's Archive. Princeton University Library.

Hemingway, Ernest. *Across the River and Into the Trees*. New York: Scribner's, 1951.

———. "a.d. Southern Style." *Esquire* 5 (May 1935): 25, 156.

———. "The Battle of Copenhagen." In *Ernest Hemingway: 88 Poems*, ed. Nicholas Gerogiannis, 22–24. New York: Harcourt Brace Jovanovich, 1979.

———. *By-Line: Ernest Hemingway*. Ed. William White. New York: Penguin, 1970.

———. "The Cardinal Picks a Winner." *Ken* 1 (5 May 1938): 38–39.

———. *The Complete Short Stories of Ernest Hemingway*. New York: Scribner's, 1987.

———. "Our Confidential Vacation Guide." In *Hemingway: The Wild Years*, ed. Gene Z. Hanrahan, 38–41. New York: Dell, 1962.

——. *Death in the Afternoon.* 1932. Intro. William F. Buckley Jr. Norwalk, Conn.: Easton Press, 1990.

——. "Dedicated to F.W." *Oak Park Trapeze* 16 (February 1917): 3.

——. "A Divine Gesture." *Double Dealer* 3 (May 1922): 267–68.

——. *88 Poems.* Ed. Nicholas Gerogiannis. New York: Harcourt Brace Jovanovich, 1979.

——. "Ernest Hemingway Cables from Paris." *New York Times Book Review,* 30 January 1938.

——. *Ernest Hemingway's Apprenticeship: Oak Park, 1916–1917.* Ed. Matthew J. Bruccoli. Washington: NCR Microcard, 1971.

——. "False News to the President." *Ken* 2 (8 September 1938): 17–18.

——. *A Farewell to Arms.* 1926. New York: Scribner's, 2003.

——. "Fascism Is a Lie." *New Masses* 23 (22 June 1937): 4.

——. *The Fifth Column and Four Stories of the Spanish Civil War.* New York: Bantam, 1970.

——. *For Whom the Bell Tolls.* 1940. New York: Scribner's, 2003.

——. "The Friend of Spain: A Spanish Letter." In *Byline: Ernest Hemingway,* ed. William White, 145–52. Harmondsworth: Penguin, 1970.

——. *Green Hills of Africa.* New York: Scribner's, 1935.

——. "The Heat and the Cold." *Verve* 1 (Spring 1938): 46.

——. "Hemingway's Spanish Civil War Dispatches." Intro. William Braasch Watson. *Hemingway Review* 7 (Spring 1988): 4–92.

——. "'Humanity Will Not Forgive This!': The *Pravda* Article." Intro. William Braasch Watson. *Hemingway Review* 7 (Spring 1938): 114–18.

——. Hemingway Collection. John F. Kennedy Library.

——. Letter to Carlos Baker. 1953. Baker Papers, Princeton University Library.

——. Letters to John Bone. 2 March 1921, 25 October 1921, 27 October 1922, undated, letter of resignation n.d. Hemingway Collection. John F. Kennedy Library.

——. Letter to Charles Fenton. 31 August 1951. Privately held.

——. Letter to F. Scott Fitzgerald. July 1929. Fitzgerald Papers. Princeton University Library.

——. Letter to Arnold Gingrich. Summer 1938. Privately held.

——. Letter to Dr. C. E. Hemingway. 20 June 1923. Hemingway Collection. John F. Kennedy Library.

——. Letter and telegram to Frank Mason. 14 December 1922, 15 December 1922. Hemingway Collection. John F. Kennedy Library.

——. Letters to Lillian Ross. 27 April 1950, August 1950. Hemingway Collection. John F. Kennedy Library.

——. Letter (petition) to President Niceto Alcala Zamora. November 1934. Hemingway Collection. John F. Kennedy Library.

——. "The Malady of Power." In *Byline: Ernest Hemingway,* ed. William White, 213–20. Harmondsworth: Penguin, 1970.

——. "Monologue to the Maestro." In *Byline: Ernest Hemingway,* ed. William White, 206–13. Harmondsworth: Penguin, 1970.

——. "Montparnasse." In *88 Poems,* ed. Nicholas Gerogiannis, 50. New York: Harcourt Brace Jovanovich, 1979.

——. *A Moveable Feast.* New York: Scribner's, 1964.

——. *The Nick Adams Stories.* New York: Scribner's, 1972.

——. "Notes on the Next War: A Serious Topical Letter." In *Byline: Ernest Hemingway,* ed. William White, 199–206. Harmondsworth: Penguin, 1970.

——. "On the American Dead in Spain." *New Masses* 30 (14 February 1938): 3.

——. Preface to Gustav Regler, *The Great Crusade*. 1940. Reprint, in *Hemingway and the Mechanism of Fame*, by Matthew Bruccoli, 81–82. Columbia: University of South Carolina Press, 2006.

——. Public letter to American Committee for Protection of Foreign Born. 1939. Reprint, in *Hemingway and the Mechanism of Fame*, by Matthew Bruccoli, 74. Columbia: University of South Carolina Press, 2006.

——. "Ring Lardner, Jr., Discourses on Editorials." *Oak Park Trapeze* 16 (February 1917): 3.

——. *Selected Letters, 1917–1961*. Ed. Carlos Baker. New York: Scribner's, 1981.

——. "The Soul of Spain." In *88 Poems*, ed. Nicholas Gerogiannis, 73. New York: Harcourt Brace Jovanovich, 1979.

——. *The Spanish Earth*. Intro. Jasper Wood. Cleveland: J. B. Savage, 1938.

——. *The Sun Also Rises*. 1926. New York: Scribner's, 2006.

——. Tape cassette to Abraham Lincoln Brigade. Winter 1947. Distributed with *Remembering Spain*, ed. Cary Nelson. Urbana: University of Illinois Press, 1994.

——. Telegram in *New Masses* 21 (1 December 1936): 21.

——. Telegrams to Arnold Gingrich. 30 January 1938, 14 March 1938. Privately held.

——. Telegram to André Malraux. 20 June 1937. Hemingway Collection. John F. Kennedy Library.

—— Telegram to Bishop Francis J. McConnell and Dr. Walter B. Cannon. 11 July 1938. On display at "Facing Fascism: New York and the Spanish Civil War" exhibition, March 23–August 12, 2007, Museum of the City of New York.

——. Telegram to M. J. Olgin. Late July 1938. Hemingway Collection. John F. Kennedy Library.

——. "Three Prefaces." In *All the Brave*, by Luis Quintanilla, 7–11. New York: Modern Age, 1939.

——. "The Time Now, the Place Spain." *Ken* 1 (7 April 1938): 36–37.

——. *To Have and Have Not*. New York: Scribner's, 1937.

——. *The Torrents of Spring*. New York: Scribner's, 1926.

——. "Treachery in Aragon." *Ken* 1 (30 June 1938): 26.

——. "Wings Always Over Africa: An Ornithological Letter." In *Byline: Ernest Hemingway*, ed. William White, 221–27. Harmondsworth: Penguin, 1970.

——. "The Writer as a Writer." *Direction* 2 (May–June 1939): 3.

Hemingway, Ernest, and Maxwell Perkins. *The Only Thing That Counts: The Ernest Hemingway/Maxwell Perkins Correspondence, 1925–1947*. Ed. Matthew J. Bruccoli. New York: Scribner's, 1996.

Herbst, Josephine. *The Starched Blue Sky of Spain*. New York: HarperCollins, 1991.

Herrick, Robert. "What Is Dirt?" *Bookman* 70 (November 1929): 258–62.

Higgins, Brian, and Hershel Parker. "Sober Second Thoughts: Fitzgerald's 'Final Version' of *Tender Is the Night*." In *Proof 4*, ed. Joseph Katz, 129–52. Columbia, S.C.: Faust, 1975.

Hindmarsh, Harry C. Memoranda to Ernest Hemingway. N.d. Hemingway Collection. John F. Kennedy Library.

Hinkle, James. "What's Funny in *The Sun Also Rises*." *Proceedings of the First National Conference of the Hemingway Society*, 62–71. Traverse City, Mich., 1983.

Hobson, John A., and Thorstein Veblen. *Veblen and the Theory of the Leisure Class*. London: Routledge, 1994.

"Hopkins Liberal Club to Sponsor Anti-War Meeting." Fitzgerald Papers. Princeton University Library.

Hotchner, A. E. *Papa Hemingway: A Personal Memoir*. New York: Random House, 1966.

Huber, Richard M. *The American Idea of Success*. New York: McGraw-Hill, 1971.

Hynan, Patrick, ed. "Hemingway—a Portrait in Sound." CBC radio: 1970.

Irish, Carol. "The Myth of Success in Fitzgerald's Boyhood." *Studies in American Fiction* 1 (1983): 176–87.

Ivens, Joris. *The Camera and I*. New York: International, 1969.

Jackson, M. W. *Fallen Sparrows: The International Brigades in the Spanish Civil War*. Philadelphia: American Philosophical Society, 1994.

James, Henry. *Hawthorne*. New York: Macmillan, 1887.

——. *The Portrait of a Lady*. Intro. Fred B. Millett. New York: Modern Library, 1951.

Jaspers, Karl. *The Question of German Guilt*. Trans. E. B. Ashton. New York: Capricorn, 1947.

Josephs, Allen. *For Whom the Bell Tolls: Ernest Hemingway's Undiscovered Country*. New York: Twayne, 1994.

Kazin, Alfred. "Fitzgerald: An American Confession." *Quarterly Review of Literature* 2 (1945): 341–46.

Keith, Walling. "Scott Fitzgeralds to Spend Winter Here Writing Books." *Montgomery Advertiser*, 8 October 1931. Reprint, in *F. Scott Fitzgerald in His Own Time: A Miscellany*, ed. Matthew J. Bruccoli and Jackson R. Bryer, 284–86. Kent, Ohio: Kent State University Press, 1971.

Kennedy, William F. "Are Our Novelists Hostile to the American Economic System?" *Dalhousie Review* 35 (Spring 1955): 32–44.

Kinnamon, Keneth. "Hemingway and Politics." In *Cambridge Companion to Hemingway*, ed. Scott Donaldson, 149–69. New York: Cambridge University Press, 1996.

Knightley, Philip. *The First Casualty*. New York: Harcourt Brace Jovanovich, 1975.

Koblas, John J. *F. Scott Fitzgerald in Minnesota: His Homes and Haunts*. St. Paul: Minnesota Historical Society Press, 1978.

Koch, Stephen. *The Breaking Point: Hemingway, Dos Passos, and the Murder of Jose Robles*. New York: Counterpoint, 2005.

Lanham, C. T. Letter to Carlos Baker. 7 December 1966. Baker papers. Princeton University Library.

Lattimore, Richmond. "Old Hemingway." In *The Stride of Time*, 50–51. Ann Arbor: University of Michigan Press, 1966.

League of American Writers. *Writers Take Sides*. New York: League of American Writers, 1938.

Lehan, Richard D. *F. Scott Fitzgerald and the Craft of Fiction*. Carbondale: Southern Illinois University Press, 1966.

Light, James F. "Political Conscience in the Novels of F. Scott Fitzgerald." *Ball State University Forum* 4 (Spring 1963): 13–25.

Light, Martin. "Of Wasteful Deaths: Hemingway's Stories About the Spanish Civil War." In *The Short Stories of Ernest Hemingway: Critical Essays*, ed. Jackson J. Benson, 64–77. Durham, N.C.: Duke University Press, 1975.

Lhamon, W. T., Jr. "The Essential Houses of *The Great Gatsby*." In *Critical Essays on F. Scott Fitzgerald's The Great Gatsby*, ed. Scott Donaldson, 166–75. Boston: G. K. Hall, 1984.

Lodge, David. *The Art of Fiction*. New York: Penguin, 1992.

Loeb, Harold. *The Way It Was*. New York: Criterion, 1959.

Lovestone, Jay. Interview by author. 28 December 1978.

——. Letter to F. Scott Fitzgerald. 4 January 1935. Fitzgerald Papers. Princeton University Library.

Lovett, Robert Morss. "Ernest Hemingway." *English Journal* 21 (October 1932): 609–17.

Lynn, Kenneth. *Hemingway*. New York: Simon and Schuster, 1987.

MacLeish, Archibald. *Letters of Archibald MacLeish, 1907 to 1982*. Ed. R. H. Winnick. Boston: Houghton Mifflin, 1983.

——. *Reflections*. Ed. Bernard A. Drabeck and Helen E. Ellis. Amherst: University of Massachusetts Press, 1986.

Maiwald, Michael. "Foreign Bodies: Documenting Expatriate Involvement In 'Night Before Battle" and 'Under the Ridge." Paper presented at twelfth International Hemingway Conference. Ronda, Spain, 28 June 2006.

Martin, George. Letters to F. Scott Fitzgerald. 20 January 1937, February (?) 1937. Fitzgerald Papers. Princeton University Library.

Martin, Jay. "Biography and Humanity." *Humanitas-Commnunitas: Occasional Papers on Humanities and Public Affairs* 3 (Winter 1999): 5–62.

Marx, Karl. *Early Writings*. Ed. T. B. Bottomore. New York: McGraw-Hill, 1964.

Mason, Frank. Letters and telegrams to Ernest Hemingway. 24 November 1922, 25 November 1922, 27 November 1922, 29 November 1922, 4 December 1922, 14 December 1922, 15 December 1922. Hemingway Collection. John F. Kennedy Library.

Matthews, Herbert L. *The Education of a Correspondent*. New York: Harcourt, Brace, 1946.

——. *Half of Spain Died*. New York: Scribner's, 1973.

——. Letters to Ernest Hemingway. 12 April 1939, 17 February 1956. Hemingway Collection. John F. Kennedy Library.

——. "Stronghold Reduced." *New York Times*, 23 December 1937.

——. Telephone message. 26 March 1938. Hemingway Collection. John F. Kennedy Library.

——. *A World in Revolution*. New York: Scribner's, 1971.

Matthews, T. S. "Some Recollections of T. S. Matthews." 1959. Oral History Research Office. Columbia University Library.

May, Henry F. *The End of American Innocence*. New York: Knopf, 1959.

Mayfield, Sara. *Exiles from Paradise: Zelda and Scott Fitzgerald*. New York: Delacorte, 1971.

Mellow, James R. *Hemingway: A Life Without Consequences*. Boston: Houghton Mifflin, 1992.

Mencken, H. L. "Books More or Less Amusing." *Smart Set* 62 (August 1920): 140. Reprint, in *F. Scott Fitzgerald: The Critical Reception*, ed. Jackson R. Bryer, 28. New York: Burt Franklin, 1978.

Meyers, Jeffrey. *Hemingway: A Biography*. New York: Harper & Row, 1985.

——, ed. *Hemingway: The Critical Reception*. London: Routledge, 1982.

Milford, Nancy. *Zelda*. New York: Harper & Row, 1970.

Miller, James E. *Scott Fitzgerald: His Art and His Technique*. New York: New York University Press, 1974.

Millgate, Michael. "Scott Fitzgerald as Social Novelist: Statement and Technique in *The Last Tycoon*." *English Studies* 43 (February 1962): 29–34.

Mizener, Arthur. *The Far Side of Paradise: A Biography of F. Scott Fitzgerald.* 1951. New York: Random House, 1959.

——. Interview of Budd Schulberg. 7 August 1947.

——. Letter to Scott Donaldson. 12 August 1978. Personal collection.

Moorehead, Caroline. *Gellhorn: A Twentieth-Century Life.* New York: Holt, 2003.

Morreall, Paul. *Taking Laughter Seriously.* Albany: State University of New York Press, 1983.

Moyer, Kermit. "A Child of the Last Days: The Historicism of F. Scott Fitzgerald." Unpublished essay.

"Mr. Fain." "I Knew Scott Fitzgerald." Fitzgerald Papers. Princeton University Library.

"Mrs. Holloway Would Force Teachers' Oath to Save Nation." Fitzgerald Papers. Princeton University Library.

Mulvey, Laura. "Visual Pleasure and Narrative Cinema." In *Film Theory and Criticism: Introductory Readings*, ed. Gerald Mast and Marshall Cohen, 802–16. New York: Oxford University Press, 1985.

Murphy, Sara. "'As a Friend You Have Never Failed Me': The Fitzgerald-Murphy Correspondence." *Journal of Modern Literature* 5 (September 1976): 375–76.

Nason, Thelma. "Afternoon (and Evening) of an Author." *Johns Hopkins Magazine* (February 1970): 2–15.

Nelson, Cary, and Jefferson Hendricks. *Madrid 1937: Letters of the Abraham Lincoln Brigade.* New York: Routledge, 1996.

New York Times. "Attackers Claim Center of Teruel." *New York Times*, 21 December 1937.

——. "400 Rebels Still Hold Out." *New York Times*, 24 December 1937.

——. "Isolated Bands Resisting." *New York Times*, 23 December 1937.

——. "Madrid Hails Teruel Fall." *New York Times*, 23 December 1937.

——. "Rebels Say Teruel Is Safe." *New York Times*, 21 December 1937.

——. "Teruel Captured, Madrid Announces." *New York Times*, 22 December 1937.

——. "Victors at Teruel Drive to the West." *New York Times*, 23 December 1937.

North American Newspaper Alliance. Telegram to Ernest Hemingway. 8 June 1938. Hemingway Collection. John F. Kennedy Library.

"Notes and Comment (The Talk of the Town)." *New Yorker* 12 (14 March 1935): 11.

Oates, Joyce Carol. "Papa at Ketchum, 1961." *Salmagundi* 155–56 (Summer–Fall 2007): 99–130.

Obituary: F. Scott Fitzgerald. Associated Press, 22 December 1940.

O'Hara, John. *Selected Letters of John O'Hara.* Ed. Matthew J. Bruccoli. New York: Random House, 1978.

Olgin, M. J. Telegram to Ernest Hemingway. 23 July 1938. Hemingway Collection. John F. Kennedy Library.

Orwell, George. *Homage to Catalonia.* New York: Harcourt, Brace, 1952.

Packer, George. "The Spanish Prisoner." *New Yorker* 31 October 2005, 82–87.

Parker, Dorothy. "The Artist's Reward." *New Yorker*, 30 November 1929, 28–31.

Parker, Hershel. *Flawed Texts and Verbal Icons.* Evanston, Ill.: Northwestern University Press, 1984.

Parker, Stephen Jay. "Hemingway's Revival in the Soviet Union, 1955–1962." In *The Literary Reputation of Hemingway in Europe*, ed. Roger Assselineau, 177–95. New York: New York University Press, 1965.

Parr, Susan Resneck. "Individual Responsibility in *The Great Gatsby*." *Virginia Quarterly Review* 57 (Autumn 1981): 662–80.

Payne, Stanley G. *The Spanish Civil War, the Soviet Union, and Communism.* New Haven, Conn.: Yale University Press, 2004.

Piper, Henry Dan. *F. Scott Fitzgerald: A Critical Portrait.* New York: Holt, Rinehart & Winston, 1965.

Plimpton, George. "Ernest Hemingway." *Paris Review* 18 (Spring 1958): 60–89.

Podhoretz, Norman. *Making It.* New York: Random House, 1967.

Posnock, Ross. "'A New World, Material Without Being Real': Fitzgerald's Critique of Capitalism in *The Great Gatsby.*" In *Critical Essays on F. Scott Fitzgerald's "The Great Gatsby,"* ed. Scott Donaldson, 201–13. Boston: G. K. Hall.

Potts, Stephen W. *The Price of Paradise: The Magazine Career of F. Scott Fitzgerald.* San Bernardino, Calif.: Borgo, 1993.

Priestley, J. B. Review of *A Farewell to Arms. Now and Then* 34 (Winter 1929): 11–12. Reprint, in *Hemingway: The Critical Reception,* ed. Jeffrey Meyers, 136–37. London: Routledge, 1982.

Raeburn, John. *Fame Became of Him: Hemingway as Public Writer.* Bloomington: Indiana University Press, 1984.

——. "Hemingway on Stage: *The Fifth Column,* Politics, and Biography." *Hemingway Review* 18 (Fall 1968): 5–16.

Rahv, Philip. "You Can't Duck a Hurricane Under a Beach Umbrella." *Daily Worker,* 5 May 1934. Reprint, in *F. Scott Fitzgerald in His Own Time: A Miscellany,* ed. Matthew J. Bruccoli and Jackson R. Bryer, 303–04. Kent, Ohio: Kent State University Press, 1971.

Rascoe, Burton. Letter to F. Scott Fitzgerald. 10 February 1936. Fitzgerald Papers. Princeton University Library.

Rawlings, Marjorie Kinnan. Letter to F. Scott Fitzgerald. n.d. Fitzgerald Papers. Princeton University Library.

Regler, Gustav. *The Owl of Minerva.* New York: Farrar, Straus and Cudahy, 1960.

"Representative Americans #1: F. Scott Fitzgerald." Manuscript for first issue of *The Nationalist.* Fitzgerald Papers. Princeton University Library.

Review of *Tender Is the Night. Journal of Nervous and Mental Diseases* 82 (July 1935): 115–17.

Reynolds, Michael. *Hemingway: The 1930s.* New York: Norton, 1997.

——. *Hemingway's First War: The Making of "A Farewell to Arms."* Princeton, N.J.: Princeton University Press, 1976.

——. *Hemingway: The Final Years.* New York: Norton, 1999.

——. "Words Killed, Wounded, Missing in Action." *Hemingway Notes* 6 (Spring 1981): 4.

Ring, Frances Kroll. "Footnotes on Fitzgerald." *Esquire* 52 (December 1959): 149–50.

——. Review of *"The Last of the Novelists,"* by Matthew J. Bruccoli. *Fitzgerald/Hemingway Annual 1978,* 412. Detroit: Gale Research, 1979.

Ross, Lillian. "Portrait of Hemingway." In *Reporting,* 194–222. New York: Simon and Schuster, 1964.

Roulston, Robert. "Dick Diver's Plunge Into the Roman Void: The Setting of *Tender Is the Night.*" *South Atlantic Quarterly* 77 (Winter 1978): 85–97.

Rovit, Earl. *Ernest Hemingway.* New York: Twayne, 1963.

Runyan, William McKinley. "Why Did Van Gogh Cut Off His Ear?" In *Life Histories and Psychobiography,* 38–50. New York: Oxford University Press, 1984.

Salpeter, Harry. "Fitzgerald, Spenglerian." *New York World,* 3 April 1927. Reprint, in *F. Scott Fitzgerald in His Own Time: A Miscellany,* ed. Mattthew J. Bruccoli and Jackson R. Bryer, 274–77. Kent, Ohio: Kent State University Press, 1971.

Sanderson, Rena. "'Like a Rock': Hemingway's Politics Through the Eyes of Regler." Paper presented at twelfth International Hemingway Conference. Ronda, Spain, 27 June 2006.

Schneider, Isidor. "A Pattern of Failure." *New Masses* 57 (4 December 1945): 23–24.

Scholes, Robert. "Decoding Papa 'A Very Short Story' as Word and Text." In *Semiotics and Interpretation*, 110–26. New Haven, Conn.: Yale University Press, 1981.

Schoots, Hans. *Living Dangerously: A Biography of Joris Ivens*. Amsterdam: Amsterdam University Press, 2000.

Schulberg, Budd. *The Four Seasons of Success*. Garden City, N.Y.: Doubleday, 1972.

——. Interview by author. 27 December 1978.

Schwartz, Delmore. "The Fiction of Ernest Hemingway." *Perspectives U.S.A.* 13 (Autumn 1955): 70–88.

Scott, Arthur L. "In Defense of Robert Cohn." *College English* 18 (March 1957): 309–14.

Scribner's Archive. Princeton University Library.

Seldes, Gilbert. Letter to F. Scott Fitzgerald. 26 June 1936. Fitzgerald Papers. Princeton University Library.

——. Telegram to Ernest Hemingway. 23 February 1938. Hemingway Collection. John F. Kennedy Library.

——. "True to Type: Scott Fitzgerald Writes Superb Tragic Novel." *New York Evening Journal*, 12 April 1934. Reprint, in *F. Scott Fitzgerald: The Critical Reception*, ed. Jackson R. Bryer, 292–93. New York: Burt Franklin, 1978.

——. *Witness to a Century*. New York: Ballantine, 1987.

Sheean, Vincent. *Not Peace but a Sword*. New York: Doubleday, 1939.

Shulman, Jeffrey. "Hemingway's Observations on the Spanish Civil War: Unpublished State Department Reports." *Hemingway Review* 7 (Spring 1988): 147–51.

Sklar, Robert. *F. Scott Fitzgerald: The Last Laocoön*. New York: Oxford University Press, 1967.

Smith, Frances Fitzgerald. Personal Interview. 21 May 1978.

Smith, Julian, "'A Canary for One': Hemingway in the Wasteland." *Studies in Short Fiction* 5 (1968): 355–61.

Smith, Paul. "1924: Hemingway's Luggage and the Miraculous Year." In *Cambridge Companion to Hemingway*, ed. Scott Donaldson, 36–54. New York: Cambridge University Press, 1996.

——. *A Reader's Guide to the Short Stories of Ernest Hemingway*. Boston: G. K. Hall, 1989.

Solow, Herbert. "Substitution at Left Tackle: Hemingway for Dos Passos." *Partisan Review* 4 (April 1938): 62–64.

Spindler, Michael. *American Literature and Social Change: William Dean Howells to Arthur Miller*. Bloomington: Indiana University Press, 1983.

Stanislavsky, Konstantin. *Building a Character*. Trans. Elizabeth R. Hapgood. New York: Theatre Arts, 1950.

St. Paul Academy (S.P.A.). F. Scott Fitzgerald Archive.

Steinberg, A. H. "Hardness, Light, and Psychiatry in *Tender Is the Night*." *Literature and Psychology* 3 (February 1953): 3–8.

Stephens, Robert O., ed. *Ernest Hemingway: The Critical Reception*. New York: Burt Franklin, 1977.

——. *Hemingway's Nonfiction: The Public Voice*. Chapel Hill: University of North Carolina Press, 1968.

Stern, Milton R. "Introduction." In *Critical Essays on "Tender Is the Night,"* ed. Stern, 25–30. Boston: G. K. Hall, 1986.

Stewart. Donald Ogden. *By a Stroke of Luck.* London: Paddington, 1975.

Street, Julian. Letter to F. Scott Fitzgerald. 12 February 1936. Fitzgerald Papers. Princeton University Library.

Svoboda, Frederic Joseph. *Hemingway and "The Sun Also Rises."* Lawrence: University of Kansas Press, 1983.

Terry, Laura. "Albert McKisco's Role in Dick Diver's 'Intricate Destiny.'" M.A. thesis, College of William and Mary, 1987.

Thomas, Hugh. *The Spanish Civil War.* New York: Harper, 1961.

Trachtenberg, Alan. "The Journey Back: Myth and History in *Tender Is the Night.*" In *Experiences in the Novel: Selected Papers from the English Institute,* ed. Roy Harvey Pearce, 138–52. New York: Columbia University Press, 1968.

Trilling, Lionel. "F. Scott Fitzgerald." *Nation* 161 (25 August 1945): 182–84.

Turnbull, Andrew. *Scott Fitzgerald.* New York: Scribner's, 1962.

Turnbull, Mrs. Bayard (Margaret). Letter to F. Scott Fitzgerald. 12 February 1936. Fitzgerald Papers. Princeton University Library.

Twain, Mark. *Life on the Mississippi.* 1883. New York: Harper and Row, 1951.

Tyson, Mrs. E. H. Letter to F. Scott Fitzgerald. n.d. Fitzgerald Papers. Princeton University Library.

Wanning, Andrews. "Fitzgerald and His Brethren." *Partisan Review* 12 (Fall 1945): 545–51.

Watson, William Braasch. "Joris Ivens and the Communists: Bringing Hemingway Into the Spanish Civil War." In *Blowing the Bridge: Essays on Hemingway and "For Whom the Bell Tolls,"* ed. Rena Sanderson, 37–57. New York: Greenwood, 1992.

——. "'Old Man at the Bridge': The Making of a Short Story." *Hemingway Review* 7 (Spring 1988): 152–65.

Way, Brian. *F. Scott Fitzgerald and the Art of Social Fiction.* New York: St. Martin's, 1980.

Weaver, John V. A. Letter to F. Scott Fitzgerald. 17 February 1936. Fitzgerald Papers. Princeton University Library.

Wescott. Glenway. "The Moral of F. Scott Fitzgerald." In F. Scott Fitzgerald, *The Crack-Up,* ed. Edmund Wilson, 323–27. New York: New Directions, 1956.

West, James L. W. III. *The Making of "This Side of Paradise."* Philadelphia: University of Pennsylvania Press, 1983.

Wexelblatt, Robert. "F. Scott Fitzgerald and D. H. Lawrence: Bicycles and Incest." *American Literature* 59 (October 1987): 378–88.

Wheeler, John N. Letters to Ernest Hemingway. 8 June 1937. 31 May 1938. 14 June 1938. 13 September 1956. Hemingway Collection. John F. Kennedy Library.

White, William, ed. *Byline: Ernest Hemingway.* Harmondsworth: Penguin,1970.

Whitman, Walt. *Complete Poetry and Collected Prose.* Ed. Justin Kaplan. New York: Library of America, 1982.

Wilson, Edmund. "Hemingway: Gauge of Morale." In *Ernest Hemingway: The Man and His Work,* ed. John K. M. McCaffery, 214–42. Cleveland: World, 1950.

——. "Imaginary Conversations II: Mr. Van Wyck Brooks and Mr. Scott Fitzgerald." *New Republic* 38 (30 April 1924): 249–54.

——. *Letters on Literature and Politics, 1912–1972.* Ed. Elena Wilson. New York: Farrar, Straus & Giroux, 1977.

——. Letter to John Biggs. 3 June 1943. Fitzgerald Papers. Princeton University Library.

——. "The Literary Spotlight—VI: F. Scott Fitzgerald." *Bookman* 55 (March 1922): 20–25.

——. "A Weekend at Ellerslie." In *The Shores of Light*, 373–83. New York: Farrar, Straus & Young, 1952.

"With College Men." *New York Times Review of Books*, 9 May 1920:240. Reprint, in *F. Scott Fitzgerald: The Critical Reception*, ed. Jackson R. Bryer, 21. New York: Burt Franklin, 1978.

Woodward, Jeffrey Harris. *F. Scott Fitzgerald: The Artist as Public Figure, 1920–1940*. Ann Arbor, Mich.: University Microfilms, 1973.

Wright, Donald M. "A Mid-Western Ad Man Remembers." *Advertising and Selling* 28 (25 March 1937): 54.

Wycherly, H. Alan. "F the Lecturer." *Fitzgerald Notes* 24 (Winter 1964): 1–3.

Wylder, Delbert E. *Hemingway's Heroes*. Albuquerque: University of New Mexico Press, 1969.

Young, Philip. *Ernest Hemingway: A Reconsideration*. University Park: Pennsylvania State University Press, 1966.

——. Foreword to *Byline: Ernest Hemingway*, ed. William White. Harmondsworth: Penguin, 1970.

INDEX